T0140076

Self-Aware Computing Systems

Samuel Kounev · Jeffrey O. Kephart
Aleksandar Milenkoski · Xiaoyun Zhu
Editors

Self-Aware
Computing Systems

 Springer

Editors
Samuel Kounev
University of Würzburg
Würzburg
Germany

Jeffrey O. Kephart
Thomas J. Watson Research Center
Hawthorne, NY
USA

Aleksandar Milenkoski
University of Würzburg
Würzburg
Germany

Xiaoyun Zhu
VMWare Inc.
Santa Clara, CA
USA

and

Futurewei Technologies, Inc.
Santa Clara, CA
USA

ISBN 978-3-319-83744-4   ISBN 978-3-319-47474-8   (eBook)
DOI 10.1007/978-3-319-47474-8

Printed on acid-free paper

This Springer imprint is published by Springer Nature
The registered company is Springer International Publishing AG
The registered company address is: Gewerbestrasse 11, 6330 Cham, Switzerland

Preface

Background

During the past several years, many different research communities have explored the aspects of self-awareness in computing systems, each from their own perspective. To the artificial intelligence community, the natural unit of self-awareness is the software agent; to those who study the autonomic computing, it is the autonomic element. One can identify at least a dozen other research communities for which the *self-awareness* of a computing system is a central issue. However, the underlying commonalities in these notions of self-awareness are often obscured by the differences in the nomenclature and the lack of precise definitions.

Recently, there have been efforts to put a spotlight on the topic of self-awareness in the computing systems and treat it as a worthwhile object of study in its own right. Examples include the SElf-awarE Computing (SEEC)[1] project at MIT and University of Chicago, the ASCENS[2] and EPiCS[3] FP7 EU Projects, and the FOCAS FET Coordination Action.[4] There have also been efforts to assemble the researchers with a common interest in self-adaptive systems and to publish compendia of works on the topic—a notable example being the SEAMS Dagstuhl seminars and workshop series. However, such collections have tended to group contributions either by community or by theme, leaving the reader without a single clear unifying definition of self-aware computing that applies broadly across multiple domains.

In an effort to establish a clear definition and understanding of self-aware computing, we organized a Dagstuhl seminar[5] entitled "Model-driven Algorithms and Architectures for Self-Aware Computing Systems," which was held in the week

---

[1] http://hdl.handle.net/1721.1/67020.

[2] http://www.ascens-ist.eu/.

[3] http://cordis.europa.eu/project/rcn/95042_en.html.

[4] http://www.focas.eu/.

[5] http://www.dagstuhl.de/15041.

of January 18–23, 2015. The seminar brought together researchers from several different communities to discuss the past and future trends in self-aware computing and encourage the active collaborations and cross-fertilization among related research efforts. Special attention was paid to achieve the diversity along several dimensions, including the field of study, age, and gender, with stronger-than-usual participation from industry. Over 40 participants presented brief perspectives on self-awareness from their respective fields, interleaved with long periods of discussion aimed at developing a cross-disciplinary understanding of self-awareness. A key outcome from one such discussion was a consensus definition of the term "self-aware computing system" that was both broad enough to cover the interdisciplinary research landscape and precise enough to distinguish the aspects of those disciplines that are relevant to self-awareness from those that are not. Roughly speaking, we say that computing systems are self-aware if they possess the capability to learn and exploit the models of themselves and the environment in which they are situated so as to act in accordance with the high-level goals.

Seeking to capitalize on the considerable positive energy and momentum created by the seminar, many of the participants agreed to contribute to a book on self-aware computing systems. Rather than following the usual formula of organizing the seminar presentations into a book, we decided to write the book completely from scratch and to organize the writing effort in such a way that the chapters would be well-integrated and cross-referenced, and based upon the collaborative efforts and perspectives of authors from multiple disciplines.

Given this ambition and approach, writing this book proved to be an enormous undertaking, and one that overachieved on our desire to foster fruitful and ongoing collaborations among researchers who might never have worked together had they not met at Dagstuhl. Discussions regarding the purpose and structure of this book began during the seminar and continued online for several weeks afterward. Once we reached a tentative agreement about which chapters should be written, and by whom, the authors of each chapter convened numerous times, working individually and collectively across many institutions (both academic and industrial) and time zones to write the initial drafts. About six months after the Dagstuhl seminar, a checkpoint workshop was held at the International Conference on Autonomic Computing 2015 in Grenoble to review the progress of the book and to make some midcourse corrections regarding the content and organization. Some additional authors were recruited to fill the perceived gaps in content and expertise. During the ensuing months, drafts of each chapter were circulated and reviewed to ensure the quality and coherency across chapters (i.e., adequate cross-referencing).

This book is the result of those efforts. Here, professionals, researchers, lecturers, and students will find formal and informal definitions and taxonomies of self-aware computing systems, explanations of how self-aware computing relates to many existing subfields of computer science and software engineering, descriptions of architectures and algorithms for self-aware systems, benefits and pitfalls of self-awareness, reviews of many of the latest relevant research efforts across a wide array of disciplines, and a set of open research challenges. Our hope is that this book will help establish the self-aware computing as a worthy subject of study in its own right, and inspire the research and development on self-aware computing systems for years to come.

Content

The chapters of this book are organized into five parts: Introduction, System Architectures, Methods and Algorithms, Applications and Case Studies, and Outlook—each of which is now described in further detail.

The four chapters of Part I constitute an introduction that defines *self-aware computing systems* from multiple perspectives and establishes a formal definition, a taxonomy, and a set of reference scenarios that help to unify the remaining chapters of this book. First, in Chap. 1, we propose a formal definition of self-aware computing systems expressed in terms of models, learning, and reasoning. This definition represents a carefully considered consensus among experts from multiple diverse fields who were brought together for the Dagstuhl seminar. Not only does it serve as a motif for the other chapters of this book, but also we hope that the research community will find in this definition a useful and unifying distillation of ideas that contribute to the notion of self-aware computing as a field of study in its own right. The formal definition of self-aware computing systems is supplemented by some positioning of self-aware computing relative to other fields. Chapter 2 elaborates this theme further, relating in greater detail how self-aware computing systems have been described in a dozen fields of study, including control theory, artificial intelligence, autonomic computing, organic computing, and cloud computing. Examining the similarities and the contrasts among these multiple perspectives on self-awareness not only improves one's understanding of the formal definition, but also helps to justify the need for one in the first place. Chapter 3 supplements the formal definition of self-aware computing systems with a theoretical framework that serves as a taxonomy for self-aware computing systems— another motif that recurs frequently throughout the remainder of this book. Finally, Chap. 4 introduces a set of reference scenarios that illustrate how self-aware computing systems differ from their non-self-aware counterparts. The scenarios, which are used and built upon in subsequent chapters of this book, have been chosen to cover a broad range of application areas and to span to the fullest possible extent the taxonomy established in Chap. 3. The simplest, least complex point on this scale is a self-aware sorting algorithm, which nonetheless affords some interesting explorations of self-awareness at design time and run time. The self-aware data center scenario allows us to explore multiple interacting self-aware components representing multiple interests, and several medium- to large-scale cyber-physical systems' scenarios (including smart homes, smart grids, and smart transportation systems) allow us to explore the issues of cooperation, competition, and heterogeneity.

Part II of this book consists of four chapters that explore the architectures for self-aware computing systems. First, Chap. 5 introduces generic concepts and notations that allow one to describe and compare a wide range of self-aware system architectures in terms of elements and relationships among those elements. Based upon UML (Unified Modeling Language), these architectural concepts follow explicitly from the self-aware computing definition and taxonomy introduced in Part I of this book. Moreover, the smart home reference scenario introduced in Chap. 4 serves as a running illustration of how the notation can be used to describe the architecture of a self-aware system. Subsequent chapters in Part II build upon the foundation laid in Chap. 5. Specifically, Chap. 6 delves into architectures for individual (isolated) self-aware systems, while Chap. 7 treats architectures for collectives in which multiple self-aware systems interact with one another. Both of these chapters explore several points in the self-aware systems taxonomy established in Chap. 3. In Chap. 6, special consideration is given to pre-reflective, reflective, and meta-reflective self-aware system architectures, while in Chap. 7, the major emphasis is placed upon the various types of relationships and organisational patterns that may exist among the interacting self-aware systems that make up the collective, as well as the relationship between the individual and collective self-awareness. The final chapter of Part II, Chap. 8, reviews the present state of reference architectures, architectural frameworks, and languages for self-aware systems and compares them with the ideas presented in the previous chapters of Part II. It also lays out a set of open challenges for self-aware system architectures.

Part III contains seven chapters that focus on the methods and algorithms for self-aware computing systems. The first three chapters treat issues pertaining to system design, such as modeling, synthesis, and verification. First, Chap. 9 discusses the nature, origin, scope, and purpose of self-modeling and its critical role in supporting system self-awareness. An interesting insight is that while models of a system may certainly be imbedded within that system at design time, a system can be much more flexible and adaptive if it possesses the capability to create and modify models of itself at run time—and endowing systems with the ability to learn both the structure and the parameters of such models is an interesting design challenge in itself. Chapter 10 offers a set of strategies for retrofitting self-awareness into legacy non-self-aware systems, and Chap. 11 discusses the synthesis and verification of self-aware computing systems. The next two chapters of Part III discuss a key run-time issue: adaptation. Chapter 12 explores how adaptation arises from an interplay among learning, reasoning, and acting in individual self-aware systems, while Chap. 13 explores how collective interactions among adaptive self-aware entities may lead to disastrous or beneficial emergent behaviors, and offers a number of possible diagnoses and remedies for undesirable behavior. The final two chapters of Part III discuss a variety of approaches for characterizing and measuring the self-awareness. Chapter 14 defines the metrics and benchmarks for the self-aware computing systems, while Chap. 15 discusses the problem of assessing self-awareness from a more general and philosophical perspective.

Part IV contains ten chapters on the applications and case studies in various domains, and the degree to which self-aware computing approaches have been adopted within those domains. The first seven chapters focus on the aspects of self-awareness in the context of cloud computing. Chapters 16 and 17 discuss using and learning models to support the performance management in data centers, while Chap. 18 treats online workload forecasting, which can be viewed as learning models of the environment in which the performance management system is situated. Chapter 19 reviews the state of virtual machine (VM) management in data centers, which (as also explained in the data center reference scenario section of Chap. 4) falls short of self-awareness for several reasons. One reason is that VM management systems tend to address lower-level metrics rather than adopting the application perspective—a shortcoming that is addressed in Chap. 20, which explores self-awareness of cloud applications. This is followed by two chapters that explore the self-awareness and security in cloud-based systems. Chapter 21 explores the software architectures for self-protection, while Chap. 22 discusses the benchmarks for intrusion detection systems. The final three chapters of Part IV extend the applications and use cases beyond the domain of data centers. Chapter 23 discusses the self-aware networks. Chapter 24 discusses the cyber-physical systems, with a special emphasis on run-time architectural models that may well apply broadly, beyond this specific application domain. Both Chaps. 21 and 24 can serve as practical complements to the more general and theoretical treatment of architecture in Part II. In the final chapter of Part IV, Chap. 25, we expand our horizons quite literally by discussing the vital role that self-aware computing plays in the control of autonomous spacecraft.

The final section of this book, Part V, consists of a single chapter on open challenges and future research directions for self-aware computing systems.

Intended Readership

This book is intended to serve two audiences. First, it may be used as a handbook for professionals and researchers who work in the areas related to self-aware computing. Second, it may be used as an advanced textbook for lecturers and students of postgraduate courses on any of the many subjects that relate to self-aware computing, such as advanced software engineering, autonomic computing, self-adaptive systems, data center resource management, and any of the other fields mentioned in Chap. 2. The reader is assumed to be generally acquainted with the principles and practices of computer science or software and systems engineering, but no specific expertise in any subfield of computer science is required. For the most part, each chapter is self-contained, and plenty of references are provided for those who wish to pursue the topic more deeply.

Würzburg, Germany   Samuel Kounev
Hawthorne, NY, USA   Jeffrey O. Kephart
Würzburg, Germany   Aleksandar Milenkoski
Santa Clara, CA, USA   Xiaoyun Zhu
January 2017

Contents

Part I Introduction

1 The Notion of Self-aware Computing......................... 3
Samuel Kounev, Peter Lewis, Kirstie L. Bellman, Nelly Bencomo,
Javier Camara, Ada Diaconescu, Lukas Esterle, Kurt Geihs,
Holger Giese, Sebastian Götz, Paola Inverardi, Jeffrey O. Kephart
and Andrea Zisman

**2 Self-aware Computing Systems: Related Concepts
and Research Areas** 17
Javier Cámara, Kirstie L. Bellman, Jeffrey O. Kephart, Marco Autili,
Nelly Bencomo, Ada Diaconescu, Holger Giese, Sebastian Götz,
Paola Inverardi, Samuel Kounev and Massimo Tivoli

**3 Towards a Framework for the Levels and Aspects
of Self-aware Computing Systems** 51
Peter Lewis, Kirstie L. Bellman, Christopher Landauer, Lukas Esterle,
Kyrre Glette, Ada Diaconescu and Holger Giese

4 Reference Scenarios for Self-aware Computing 87
Jeffrey O. Kephart, Martina Maggio, Ada Diaconescu, Holger Giese,
Henry Hoffmann, Samuel Kounev, Anne Koziolek, Peter Lewis,
Anders Robertsson and Simon Spinner

Part II System Architectures

5 Architectural Concepts for Self-aware Computing Systems....... 109
Holger Giese, Thomas Vogel, Ada Diaconescu, Sebastian Götz
and Samuel Kounev

**6 Generic Architectures for Individual Self-aware
Computing Systems**..................................... 149
Holger Giese, Thomas Vogel, Ada Diaconescu, Sebastian Götz
and Kirstie L. Bellman

7 Architectures for Collective Self-aware Computing Systems 191
Ada Diaconescu, Kirstie L. Bellman, Lukas Esterle, Holger Giese,
Sebastian Götz, Peter Lewis and Andrea Zisman

8 State of the Art in Architectures for Self-aware Computing
Systems.. 237
Holger Giese, Thomas Vogel, Ada Diaconescu, Sebastian Götz,
Nelly Bencomo, Kurt Geihs, Samuel Kounev and Kirstie L. Bellman

Part III   Methods and Algorithms

9 Self-modeling and Self-awareness........................... 279
Kirstie L. Bellman, Christopher Landauer, Phyllis Nelson,
Nelly Bencomo, Sebastian Götz, Peter Lewis and Lukas Esterle

10 Transition Strategies for Increasing Self-awareness in Existing
Types of Computing Systems 305
Marco Autili, Kirstie L. Bellman, Ada Diaconescu, Lukas Esterle,
Massimo Tivoli and Andrea Zisman

11 Synthesis and Verification of Self-aware Computing Systems 337
Radu Calinescu, Marco Autili, Javier Cámara, Antinisca Di Marco,
Simos Gerasimou, Paola Inverardi, Alexander Perucci, Nils Jansen,
Joost-Pieter Katoen, Marta Kwiatkowska, Ole J. Mengshoel,
Romina Spalazzese and Massimo Tivoli

12 Self-adaptation for Individual Self-aware Computing Systems 375
Martina Maggio, Tarek Abdelzaher, Lukas Esterle, Holger Giese,
Jeffrey O. Kephart, Ole J. Mengshoel, Alessandro V. Papadopoulos,
Anders Robertsson and Katinka Wolter

13 Self-adaptation in Collective Self-aware Computing Systems...... 401
Jeffrey O. Kephart, Ada Diaconescu, Holger Giese,
Anders Robertsson, Tarek Abdelzaher, Peter Lewis, Antonio Filieri,
Lukas Esterle and Sylvain Frey

14 Metrics and Benchmarks for Self-aware Computing Systems 437
Nikolas Herbst, Steffen Becker, Samuel Kounev, Heiko Koziolek,
Martina Maggio, Aleksandar Milenkoski and Evgenia Smirni

15 Assessing Self-awareness................................. 465
Lukas Esterle, Kirstie L. Bellman, Steffen Becker, Anne Koziolek,
Christopher Landauer and Peter Lewis

Part IV Applications and Case Studies

16 **Run-Time Models for Online Performance and Resource
    Management in Data Centers**. 485
    Simon Spinner, Antonio Filieri, Samuel Kounev, Martina Maggio
    and Anders Robertsson

17 **Online Learning of Run-Time Models for Performance
    and Resource Management in Data Centers**. 507
    Jürgen Walter, Antinisca Di Marco, Simon Spinner, Paola Inverardi
    and Samuel Kounev

18 **Online Workload Forecasting**. 529
    Nikolas Herbst, Ayman Amin, Artur Andrzejak, Lars Grunske,
    Samuel Kounev, Ole J. Mengshoel and Priya Sundararajan

19 **State of Practice of Non-self-aware Virtual Machine
    Management in Cloud Data Centers**. 555
    Lydia Y. Chen, Robert Birke and Evgenia Smirni

20 **Self-awareness of Cloud Applications**. 575
    Alex Iosup, Xiaoyun Zhu, Arif Merchant, Eva Kalyvianaki,
    Martina Maggio, Simon Spinner, Tarek Abdelzaher, Ole Mengshoel
    and Sara Bouchenak

21 **Software Architectures for Self-protection in IaaS Clouds**. 611
    K.R. Jayaram, Aleksandar Milenkoski and Samuel Kounev

22 **Benchmarking Intrusion Detection Systems with Adaptive
    Provisioning of Virtualized Resources**. 633
    Aleksandar Milenkoski, K.R. Jayaram and Samuel Kounev

23 **Self-aware Networks: The Cognitive Packet Network
    and Its Performance**. 659
    Erol Gelenbe

24 **Leveraging Design and Runtime Architecture Models
    to Support Self-awareness**. 669
    Philippe Lalanda, Stéphanie Chollet and Catherine Hamon

25 **Spacecraft Autonomous Reaction Capabilities, Control
    Approaches, and Self-aware Computing**. 687
    Klaus Schilling, Jürgen Walter and Samuel Kounev

Part V Outlook

**26 Self-aware Computing Systems: Open Challenges
and Future Research Directions** 709
Robert Birke, Javier Cámara, Lydia Y. Chen, Lukas Esterle,
Kurt Geihs, Erol Gelenbe, Holger Giese, Anders Robertsson
and Xiaoyun Zhu

Contributors

Tarek Abdelzaher Computer Science Department, University of Illinois at Urbana-Champaign, Urbana, IL, USA

Ayman Amin Swinburne University of Technology, Melbourne, Australia

Artur Andrzejak Heidelberg University, Heidelberg, Germany

Marco Autili University of L'Aquila, L'Aquila, Italy

Steffen Becker Technical University Chemnitz, Chemnitz, Germany; Aerospace Corporation, El Segundo, CA, USA

Kirstie L. Bellman Aerospace Integration Science Center, The Aerospace Corporation, Los Angeles, CA, USA; Topcy House Consulting, Thousand Oaks, CA, USA; Technische Universität Chemnitz, Chemnitz, Germany

Nelly Bencomo Aston Institute for Systems Analytics, Aston University, Birmingham, UK

Robert Birke IBM Research Zurich, Zürich, Switzerland

Sara Bouchenak INSA Lyon, Lyon, France

Radu Calinescu University of York, York, UK

Javier Camara Carnegie Mellon University, Pittsburgh, PA, USA

Lydia Y. Chen IBM Research Zurich, Zürich, Switzerland

Stéphanie Chollet Grenoble University LCIS, Valence, France

Javier Cámara Carnegie Mellon University, Pittsburgh, PA, USA

Ada Diaconescu Equipe S3, Departement INFRES, Telécom ParisTech, Paris, France; Telecom ParisTech, CNRS LTCI, Paris Saclay University, Paris, France

Lukas Esterle Department of CS, Vienna University of Technology, Vienna, Austria; Alpen-Adria-Universität Klagenfurt, Klagenfurt, Austria; Technische Universität Wien, Vienna, Austria

Antonio Filieri Department of Computing, Imperial College London, London, UK

Sylvain Frey Computing and Communications Department, Lancaster University, Lancaster, UK

Kurt Geihs University of Kassel, Kassel, Germany

Erol Gelenbe Department of Electrical and Electronic Engineering, Imperial College, London, UK

Simos Gerasimou University of York, York, UK

Holger Giese Hasso Plattner Institute for Software Systems Engineering at the University of Potsdam, Potsdam, Germany

Kyrre Glette University of Oslo, Oslo, Norway

Lars Grunske Humboldt-Universität zu Berlin, Berlin, Germany

Sebastian Götz University of Technology Dresden, Dresden, Germany

Catherine Hamon Orange Labs, Meylan, France

Nikolas Herbst University of Würzburg, Würzburg, Germany

Henry Hoffmann Department of Computer Science, University of Chicago, Chicago, IL, USA

Paola Inverardi University of L'Aquila, L'Aquila, Italy; University of L'Aquila, Coppito (AQ), Italy

Alex Iosup Delft University of Technology, Delft, The Netherlands

Nils Jansen University of Texas at Austin, Austin, TX, USA

K.R. Jayaram IBM Thomas J. Watson Research Center, New York City, NY, USA

Eva Kalyvianaki Imperial College of London, London, UK

Joost-Pieter Katoen RWTH Aachen University, Aachen, Germany

Jeffrey O. Kephart IBM Thomas J. Watson Research Center, Yorktown Heights, NY, USA

Samuel Kounev Department of Computer Science, University of Würzburg, Würzburg, Germany

Anne Koziolek Institute for Program Structures and Data Organization, Karlsruhe Institute of Technology, Karlsruhe, Germany

Heiko Koziolek ABB Ladenburg, Ladenburg, Germany

Marta Kwiatkowska University of Oxford, Oxford, UK

Philippe Lalanda Grenoble University LIG, Grenoble, France

Christopher Landauer Aerospace Integration Science Center, The Aerospace Corporation, Los Angeles, CA, USA; Topcy House Consulting, Thousand Oaks, CA, USA; Aerospace Corporation, El Segundo, CA, USA

Peter Lewis Aston Lab for Intelligent Collectives Engineering (ALICE), School of Engineering and Applied Science, Aston University, Birmingham, UK

Martina Maggio Department of Automatic Control, Lund University, Lund, Sweden

Antinisca Di Marco University of L'Aquila, L'Aquila, Italy

Ole Mengshoel CMU Silicon Valley at the NASA Ames Research Center, Moffett Field, PA, USA

Ole J. Mengshoel Department of Electrical and Computer Engineering, Carnegie Mellon University, Pittsburgh, CA, USA

Arif Merchant Google, Inc., Menlo Park, CA, USA

Aleksandar Milenkoski University of Wurzburg, Würzburg, Germany

Phyllis Nelson California State Polytechnic University, Pomona, CA, USA

Alessandro V. Papadopoulos Department of Automatic Control, Lund University, Lund, Sweden

Alexander Perucci University of L'Aquila, L'Aquila, Italy

Anders Robertsson Department of Automatic Control LTH, Lund University, Lund, Sweden

Klaus Schilling Department of Computer Science, University of Würzburg, Würzburg, Germany

Evgenia Smirni College of William and Mary, Williamsburg, VA, USA

Romina Spalazzese Malmö University, Malmö, Sweden

Simon Spinner Department of Computer Science, University of Würzburg, Würzburg, Germany

Priya Sundararajan Carnegie Mellon University, Pittsburgh, CA, USA

Massimo Tivoli University of L'Aquila, L'Aquila, Italy

Thomas Vogel Hasso Plattner Institute for Software Systems Engineering at the University of Potsdam, Potsdam, Germany

Jürgen Walter Department of Computer Science, University of Würzburg, Würzburg, Germany

Katinka Wolter Institute of Computer Science, Freie Universität Berlin, Berlin, Germany

Xiaoyun Zhu Futurewei Technologies, Santa Clara, CA, USA

Andrea Zisman The Open University, Milton Keynes, UK

Part I
Introduction

Chapter 1
The Notion of Self-aware Computing

Samuel Kounev, Peter Lewis, Kirstie L. Bellman, Nelly Bencomo, Javier Camara, Ada Diaconescu, Lukas Esterle, Kurt Geihs, Holger Giese, Sebastian Götz, Paola Inverardi, Jeffrey O. Kephart and Andrea Zisman

Abstract We define the notion of "self-aware computing" and the relationship of this term to related terms such as autonomic computing, self-management, and similar. The need for a new definition, driven by trends that are only partially addressed by existing areas of research, is motivated. The semantics of the provided definition are discussed in detail examining the selected wording and explaining its meaning to avoid misleading interpretations. This chapter also provides an overview of the existing usage of the term self-aware computing, respectively self-awareness, in related past projects and initiatives.

S. Kounev (✉)
Universität Würzburg, Am Hubland, 97074 Würzburg, Germany
e-mail: skounev@acm.org

P. Lewis · N. Bencomo
Aston University, Birmingham B4 7ET, UK
e-mail: p.lewis@aston.ac.uk

N. Bencomo
e-mail: nelly@acm.org

K.L. Bellman
The Aerospace Corporation, Los Angeles, CA, USA
e-mail: Kirstie.L.Bellman@aero.org

J. Camara
Carnegie Mellon University, Pittsburgh, PA 15213, USA
e-mail: jcmoreno@cs.cmu.edu

A. Diaconescu
Telecom Paris Tech, 75013 Paris, France
e-mail: ada.diaconescu@telecom-paristech.fr

L. Esterle
Department of CS, Vienna University of Technology, Vienna, Austria
e-mail: lukas.esterle@tuwien.ac.at

K. Geihs
University of Kassel, 34121 Kassel, Germany
e-mail: geihs@uni-kassel.de

© Springer International Publishing AG 2017
S. Kounev et al. (eds.), *Self-Aware Computing Systems*,
DOI 10.1007/978-3-319-47474-8_1

1.1   Introduction

There have been a number of research projects and initiatives in computer science and engineering that have explicitly engaged with the notion of self-awareness in computing. Some examples include the SElf-awarE Computing (SEEC) project at MIT and University of Chicago, the ASCENS and EPiCS FP7 EU Projects, the FOCAS FET Coordination Action, and the SEAMS Dagstuhl Seminars and workshop series. Relevant work can be found in several different areas and communities including autonomic computing, machine learning and artificial intelligence, multiagent systems, self-organizing and self-adaptive systems, situation- and context-aware systems, reflective computing, model-predictive control, as well as work from the models@run-time community. Recent reviews of relevant work [21, 29, 32] have grouped contributions either by community or by thematically and have found that the terms themselves often lack precise definitions.

This book adopts the notion of *self-aware computing* as defined by the Dagstuhl Seminar 15041 "Model-driven Algorithms and Architectures for Self-Aware Computing Systems"[1] held on January 18–23, 2015. The seminar brought together researchers from the respective communities to discuss the past and future trends in self-aware computing and encourage active collaborations and cross-fertilization between related research efforts. An important first step in this direction was the formulation of a new definition of the term "self-aware computing system" integrating the different ways in which this term is used in the interdisciplinary research landscape. In this chapter, we introduce this new broader notion of "self-aware computing" and provide an overview of previous projects and initiatives that have explicitly used this term in the past. By providing a common language, we aim to foster interaction and collaboration between the respective research communities, raising the awareness about related research efforts and synergies that can be exploited to advance the state of the art.

---

[1]http://www.dagstuhl.de/15041.

H. Giese
Hasso-Plattner-Institut, 14482 Potsdam, Germany
e-mail: Holger.Giese@hpi.de

S. Götz
University of Technology Dresden, Dresden, Germany
e-mail: sebastian.goetz@acm.org

P. Inverardi
University of L'Aquila, 67100 L'Aquila, Italy
e-mail: paola.inverardi@univaq.it

J.O. Kephart
Thomas J. Watson Research Center, Yorktown Heights, NY, USA
e-mail: kephart@us.ibm.com

A. Zisman
The Open University, Milton Keynes, UK
e-mail: andrea.zisman@open.ac.uk

1.2   Definition of Self-aware Computing

Definition 1.1 Self-aware computing systems are computing systems that:

1. *learn models* capturing *knowledge* about themselves and their environment (such as their structure, design, state, possible actions, and runtime behavior) on an ongoing basis and
2. *reason* using the models (e.g., predict, analyze, consider, and plan) enabling them to *act* based on their knowledge and reasoning (e.g., explore, explain, report, suggest, self-adapt, or impact their environment)

in accordance with *higher-level goals*, which may also be subject to change.

It is assumed that a self-aware system is built by an entity with some higher-level goals in mind. This entity may be a human (e.g., a developer) or a set of humans (e.g., a developer team), but it does not necessarily have to be. The entity that built the system may also be another computing system, at a higher level, that generates a new system for a given purpose (e.g., in the form of executable code or models).

The major distinctive characteristics of a self-aware computing system are as follows: (i) it must have the capability to learn models on an *ongoing basis*, capturing knowledge relevant to the purpose for which it is built, and (ii) it must be able to use the models to reason about this knowledge and act accordingly. Both the learning and reasoning parts are driven by the system's goals, which may be established by the entity that built the system, by the end user of the system, or by a combination of the two. The goals are referred to as *higher-level* goals to emphasize that they are at a higher level of abstraction than the system itself and they are not under its direct control. Note that the system itself may generate its own goals (at lower levels) as part of its learning and model-based reasoning processes.

It is assumed that the learned models capture knowledge about the system and its environment. We note that for some systems, the boundary between what is considered "knowledge about the system itself" and what is considered "knowledge about the environment" is somewhat blurred. Therefore, we do not require a strict separation of the learned models with respect to whether they capture knowledge about the self or knowledge about the environment in which the self operates. However, it is expected that both the amount and scope of the acquired knowledge should be driven by the higher-level goals and what information could possibly be of use to achieving them.

The term "model" is used here in a general sense and refers to any abstraction of the system and its environment that captures some knowledge and may be used for reasoning with respect to the system goals. In his general model theory, Stachowiak [33] identifies the following three features as essential for models: (i) *mapping*: a model is always a model of some *original* (which can be a model itself), (ii) *reduction*: a model always *abstracts* from the original by reflecting only a subset of its attributes, and (iii) *pragmatic*: a model only replaces the original for a certain *purpose*. We note that "purpose" in this context is understood as potential purpose or a general utility, allowing for exploratory behavior. Usually, we further distinguish *descriptive* models, which capture the originals as they are, from *prescriptive* models, which describe envisioned futures (planned originals). Descriptive models, in our context, describe a given system aspect that may be relevant with respect to the system's higher-level goals. We further distinguish *predictive models* that support more complex reasoning such as predicting the system behavior under given conditions or predicting the impact of a considered possible adaptation action. We note that the descriptive, prescriptive, and predictive model categories are not strictly mutually exclusive as both descriptive and prescriptive models can also be used for predictive analysis and therefore can be predictive models as well.

Some examples of different types of models capturing various aspects that may be relevant in a given scenario include:

- a descriptive model capturing the system's resource landscape and software architecture and their performance-relevant parameters,
- a descriptive model describing the system's possible adaptation actions (degrees of freedom at runtime),
- a prescriptive model describing how to act in a given situation (e.g., after a component failure),
- a descriptive model describing the system's goals and policies (e.g., service-level agreements),
- a predictive statistical regression model capturing the influence of user workloads on the system resource consumption and energy efficiency,
- a predictive stochastic model allowing to predict the system performance for a given user workload and resource allocation, and
- a control theory model used to guide the system behavior.

We stress that the term "learn" does imply that some information based on which models are derived is obtained at system runtime, while also additional static information built into the system at design time can be employed as well. Typically, a combination of both would be expected; for example, a system may be built with integrated skeleton models whose parameters are estimated using monitoring data collected at runtime. The model learning is expected to happen on an *ongoing basis* during operation, meaning that models should be continuously refined and calibrated in order to better fulfill the purpose for which they are used.

Taken together, the learning and reasoning are expected to enable model-based analysis at runtime that goes beyond applying simple rules or heuristics explicitly programmed at system design time. Depending on the considered type of system and its respective goals, different types of model-based reasoning may be relevant. For example, in the context of an IT system that has been designed to guarantee certain performance requirements, the following types of reasoning may be relevant:

- predict the load of an IT system (e.g., number of users or requests sent per unit of time) in a future time horizon,
- predict the system performance (e.g., response time) for a given workload and resource allocation (e.g., number of servers),
- predict the expected impact of a given system adaptation action (e.g., adding or removing system resources) on the end-to-end system performance,
- determine how much resources need to be added to ensure that performance requirements are satisfied under an increasing system workload, and
- estimate the system's energy consumption at runtime and compare it to other system configurations (e.g., with respect to voltage and frequency) in order to select an optimal configuration.

An example of reasoning in the context of a cyber-physical system for traffic management may be to analyze the traffic situation in order to provide a recommendation which routes to take for a given target destination. Another example, in the context of medical implants, is a system that monitors concentrations of substances in the body to determine if release of medication is needed in case these substances are not at the right level. Further, a system monitors signals in the body (those before an epileptic attack) in order to issue a warning signal/alarm in case patterns are identified that match the pattern of an attack.

To clarify our intentions, we compare the terms *learning*, *reasoning*, and *acting*, employed in our definition, with the weaker alternative terms *observing* and *reacting*. While *observing* is a critical prerequisite for learning, *learning* clearly goes beyond only observing by accumulating knowledge about the subject of observation over time and manifesting this knowledge in reflective models. Also, *reacting* can be the result of *reasoning* and *acting*; however, a system that only reacts, but does not reason, does not have the capability to consider the current situation and its options before it takes any action. Therefore, according to our definition, a self-aware computing system is expected not only to observe and react, but also to learn, reason, and act.

By stressing the role of model learning and model-based reasoning, driven by higher-level goals, we distinguish the term self-aware computing from related terms such as autonomic computing or self-adaptive systems. Although, in most cases, it would be expected that the system uses the learned models to reason and *self-adapt* to changes in the environment, we note that self-adaptation (often referred to as *self-expression* in this context) is not strictly required. In this way, we accommodate cases where all adaptation actions must be supervised and authorized by an entity outside the system, such as the entity that built the system or a human system user. For example, in mission-critical cognitive computing applications, systems may provide recommendations on how to act; however, the final decision on what specific action to take is often made by a human operator.

1.3   Previous Initiatives in Self-aware Computing

As mentioned earlier, there have been a number of research projects and initiatives that have explicitly engaged with the notion of *self-awareness* in computing. Here, we provide an overview of some of the most significant efforts, perspectives, and key contributions. In the next chapter, we discuss previous work in self-aware computing in more detail, contextualizing the perspectives taken in this book.

1.3.1   Self-awareness in Artificial Intelligence

Self-awareness has long been of interest in the artificial intelligence (AI) community. In particular, studies have focused on higher levels of self-awareness such as *meta-self-awareness*: a system's awareness of its own self-awareness. This concept overlaps significantly with meta-cognition, defined by Metcalfe and Shimamura [22] as *knowing about knowing*. Integration of AI technologies into the systems that, as a result of the integration, exhibit self-awareness of this meta-cognitive form has been on DARPA's research agenda for some time [27]. Indeed, architectural issues in building such integrated systems which then exhibit self-awareness were the subject of a DARPA workshop [4] in 2004.

One example of the consideration of self-awareness in the artificial intelligence community is the algorithm selection problem, where a system can reason about its own reasoning; that is, it possesses meta-cognition and can select an appropriate reasoning method according to its situation [8]. In autonomous robotics, it has been argued that self-awareness is not only beneficial, but also essential for safety and robot ethics [29].

Furthermore, self-awareness is not only a property that can be observed at an individual level, but also something that can arise in a collective intelligence context. For example, a group of robots with simple behavioral rules and local interactions may arrive at an emergent awareness of the properties of the group, including its history and interactions with the world, though this awareness is distributed across the individual units [23].

1.3.2   Engineering Self-aware Systems

While meta-cognition or meta-self-awareness is concerned with higher reasoning abilities and is of particular interest in artificial intelligence, efforts exist at a more fundamental level to engineer systems that explicitly consider knowledge about themselves. Agarwal et al. [1, 2] put forward a case for a paradigm shift in system design practice. The idea here is to move from a procedural design methodology wherein the behavior of the computing system is preprogrammed or considered beforehand (i.e., at design time), toward a self-aware system where this is not required and the system adapts to its context at runtime. One aim is to avoid or reduce the need to consider the availability of resources and various other constraints beforehand, instead intelligently trading-off available resources for performance at runtime.

For example, the programming effort required to build a system to satisfy carefully considered specifications could be reduced if there are resources at hand for the system to use in an automated manner in order to optimize its own behavior, such that it achieves a goal given the current constraints. A self-aware computer is thus given a goal, and it automatically works to achieve the goal, for example with the minimal amount of energy or other resources. In order to facilitate the engineering of such systems, Hoffman et al. have developed a general and extensible framework for self-aware computing [14], which integrates both control theory and machine learning methods.

Self-awareness has also been proposed as a way to tackle the increasing complexity and dynamics associated with modern service-based IT systems. Huber et al. [19] proposes that self-aware software services, which have built-in models of their own architecture and dynamic aspects of the system's interactions with its environment, can improve the utilization of resources, while continuing to satisfy quality-of-service requirements. Further, Kounev et al. [18] highlight self-reflection, self-prediction, and self-adaptation as key characteristics of self-aware service-based systems and propose that methodologies for the systematic engineering of self-aware systems are needed.

Importantly, for a system to be self-aware, it is not required to be highly complex; indeed, the scalability of the concept means that self-awareness has also been considered in much simpler systems. An example of this is the so-called *cognitive radio devices* [11], which monitor and control their own capabilities and also communicate with other radio devices to monitor theirs. This enables them to improve the efficiency of communication by negotiating changes in parameter settings [34]. We will explore a wide range of self-awareness concepts in the following chapter, where both minimal examples such as this and more "full-stack" self-aware systems will be compared.

In order to design self-aware systems, various enabling technologies have been proposed in the form of application heartbeats [13, 31], for establishing a standard way of setting application goals and evaluating the performance of the system while trying to achieve the goals and the use of heuristic and machine learning techniques for adaptation and decision making on the part of the system. An example of the latter is the use of reinforcement learning in order to optimize a scheduling policy for system components to gain access to the critical section within applications [10].

1.3.3   Self-awareness in Pervasive Computing

The pervasive computing community is also interested in self-awareness, due to the typically mobile characteristics of agents, whose context continuously changes. As such, they need to synthesize knowledge based on their own state and environment, in order to adapt to changes. Often, monitoring and adaptation are studied in the context of human–computer interaction, since the interest is on how such systems self-adapt in order to be useful to humans in different situations (e.g., "going for a run"). Ye et al. [35] discuss issues and challenges involved in assimilating sensor data from a myriad of sources in order for pervasive computing systems to identify situations that human users may be in. They show a shift in techniques over time from *logic-based* ones toward those that are *learning-based*, as the sensor data have become more complex, erroneous, and uncertain, with sensors becoming ever more pervasive. The learning of mappings between sensor data and the situation, given the current model building techniques, poses challenges such as the lack of training data, which can lead to low performing models. This has been tackled by considering unsupervised learning [5, 12] and Web mining [28], allowing for extracting commonsense knowledge. Another line of research within pervasive computing concerns constructing simulation models of contexts, for applications to be tested in [15].

1.3.4 Systems with Decentralized Self-awareness

Self-awareness research is not limited to an entity or system in itself being able to monitor and reason about itself, but also describes emergent phenomena [23] in collective systems. In natural systems such as ant colonies and the immune system, the awareness of the global state is distributed across the elementary units that make up the system (e.g., ants and their trails) and is statistical in nature. This helps the system stay robust at the global level in the face of disturbances. In essence, the system as a whole is aware enough of itself to understand when the globally stable state gets disturbed and engages the elementary units to collect information locally, which builds up in a statistical fashion, helping the elementary units use this statistical information to get the system back into the globally stable state. Mitchell proposed [23] that such systems can provide guidelines for designing artificial intelligence systems with decentralized architectures, for example robotic swarms, which exhibit apparent self-awareness.

One example of where such a system has been developed is within the SWARM-BOTS project [24]. One of the objectives of the SWARM-BOTS project was the design and implementation of a novel mobile robot, called an *s-bot*. While s-bots' individual capabilities within an environment are physically limited (much like individual insects in the natural world), through local communication they are able to *self-assemble* [9] into larger structures, known as *swarm-bots*, which are capable of achieving goals not reachable by individual s-bots. Examples of such goals might include navigation over challenging terrain or the transportation of large objects; in all cases, these tasks cannot be solved without the coordinated movements of individual *s-bots*.

In this context, it is important to consider the relationship between the individual systems' self-awareness, the self-awareness of neighboring systems, and the self-awareness of the collective as a whole. Zambonelli et al. [36] discuss some of the issues involved here, considering the aspects of self-awareness relating to the ability of the components to recognize situations and changes in situations (both internal and external) in a collective system. This self-awareness is then used to drive self-expression, including adaptation to the new situation. Importantly, this self-expression also occurs at the level of the collective.

Other research challenges within the area of self-assembly, or *structural self-organization*, include better understanding of how system structures, rather than individual behaviors, can be adapted over time with respect to the system's distributed sense of *self-concept* [17].

1.3.5   Computational Self-awareness

Lewis et al. [20] propose that human self-awareness can serve as a source of inspiration for a new notion of *computational self-awareness* and associated *self-expression*, behavior based on self-awareness. These comprise various capabilities, encapsulated as different "levels" of self-awareness, based on cognitive psychologist Ulric Neisser's [25] broad set of levels of human self-awareness. The intention is to explicitly account for a full spectrum of existing and future systems, including simple systems which sense and learn about themselves, as well as what might typically be considered highly advanced artificial intelligence. The levels of computational self-awareness provide one axis on which to compare *how* self-aware a computing system is. Lewis et al. argue that increased self-awareness (in terms of the levels) can improve a system's ability to manage complex trade-offs in changing conditions.

They introduce a general framework for the description of the self-awareness properties of computing systems, which includes a reference architecture and a series of derived architectural patterns. These can be used by engineers to determine whether, how, and to what extent to build self-awareness capabilities into a system. The framework proposed by Lewis et al. has been used to consider the self-awareness properties of such diverse systems as distributed smart cameras [30], heterogeneous reconfigurable multi-core systems [3], and fault tolerance in avionic systems [26].

Lewis et al.'s notion of *computational self-awareness* [20] intentionally includes many existing and prior systems, which have not been previously described as self-aware. Nevertheless, these systems use capabilities, which fulfill some self-awareness aspect, often due to their benefit in a complex environment.

1.4   A Concept of a Self-aware Learning and Reasoning Loop

In autonomic computing, the system behavior is typically represented as a control loop. To structure the principle of operation exhibited by autonomic managers, [16] defined a reference architecture based on a control loop, typically referred to as the

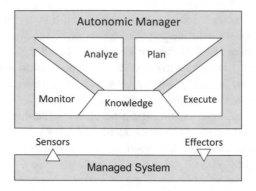

Fig. 1.1 MAPE-K autonomic control loop [16]

MAPE-K loop. This reference architecture has the advantage that it offers a clear way to identify and classify areas of particular focus, and thus, it is used by many researchers to communicate the architectural concepts of autonomic systems.

In the following, we contrast the MAPE-K loop used in autonomic computing to the concept of self-aware computing as defined above. To this end, we first briefly describe the MAPE-K loop. The acronym MAPE-K reflects the five main constituent phases of autonomic loops, i.e., MONITOR, ANALYZE, PLAN, EXECUTE, and KNOWLEDGE, as depicted in Fig. 1.1. Basically, the MONITOR phase collects information from the sensors provided by the managed artifacts and its context. The ANALYZE phase uses the data of the MONITOR phase to assess the situation and determine any anomalies or problems. The PLAN phase generates an adaptation plan to solve a detected problem. The EXECUTE phase finally applies the generated adaptation plan on the actual system. A cross-cutting aspect shared among all phases of the loop is the KNOWLEDGE about the system and its context, capturing aspects such as the software architecture, execution environment, and hardware infrastructure on which the system is running.

The software engineering community uses a similar feedback loop concept, distinguishing the four phases COLLECT, ANALYZE, DECIDE, and ACT [7]. Conceptually, the behavior of these phases is similar to the phases in the MAPE-K loop; however, this concept does not explicitly consider the KNOWLEDGE part. More details about the use of feedback loops in self-adaptive systems, such as the use of multiple, multi-level, positive, or negative feedback loops, are given by [6].

Although the notion of self-aware computing, as defined in this book, has some common aspects with the concept of a feedback loop, such as MAPE-K, there are some important differences. While the MONITOR and ANALYZE phases of MAPE-K imply that information is gathered and analyzed continually at runtime, this does not necessarily imply that the acquired information is abstracted and used to learn models on an ongoing basis during operation. Similarly, while taken together, the ANALYZE and PLAN phases can be compared to the model-based learning and reasoning processes in self-aware computing, the latter requires that the type of analysis

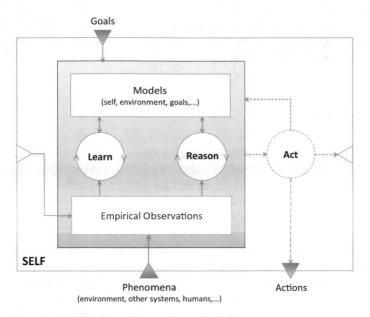

Fig. 1.2 Self-aware learning and reasoning loop: LRA-M loop

conducted at runtime based on the learned models goes beyond applying simple rules or heuristics explicitly programmed at system design time. Finally, the EXE-CUTE phase in MAPE-K implies that the system self-adapts at runtime. In contrast, as mentioned earlier, self-adaptation (or self-expression) is not strictly required in self-aware computing. A self-aware computing system may provide recommendations on how to act; however, the final decision on what specific action to take may be left to a human operator, for example, as typical for many cognitive computing applications.

Figure 1.2 illustrates our concept of a model-based learning and reasoning loop (LRA-M loop) capturing the main activities in a self-aware computing system. The figure shows the *self* and its interfaces to the environment in which it is operating. The activities within the self are driven by its goals and its observations collected as empirical data about relevant aspects of the system and its environment, its users, and so on. The empirical data are used as a basis for the ongoing LEARNING process, as part of which observations are abstracted into models capturing potentially relevant aspects of the system and its environment (such as their structure, design, state, possible actions, and runtime behavior). The learned models form the system's knowledge base (corresponding to the KNOWLEDGE part in the MAPE-K loop), which provides the basis for the system's REASONING process. The reasoning process may trigger ACTIONS affecting both the behavior of the system itself (self-adaptation) and possibly impacting the environment. The actions may also affect the system's learning and reasoning activities themselves, for example, by focusing the learning process on selected aspects or observations. We note here that although we explicitly distinguish the learning process from the reasoning process, it is not strictly required that in a self-aware computing system, these processes are separated, since in many cases the two activities may be interwoven.

1.5   Conclusion

The two major distinctive characteristics of a self-aware computing system are as follows: (i) it must have the capability to learn models on an *ongoing basis*, capturing knowledge relevant to the purpose for which it is built, and (ii) it must be able to use the models to reason about this knowledge and act accordingly. The term "model" refers to any abstraction of the system and its environment that captures some knowledge and may be used for reasoning with respect to the system's goals. Both the learning and reasoning parts are driven by the system's goals, which may be established by the entity that built the system, by the end user of the system, or by a combination of the two. Taken together, the learning and reasoning are expected to enable model-based analysis at runtime that goes beyond applying simple rules or heuristics explicitly programmed at system design time. As discussed in this introductory chapter, the notion of "self-aware computing" is strongly related to existing notions such as autonomic computing, self-management, and similar. The novelty of the term is that it explicitly stresses model learning and reasoning as ongoing processes built into a system's design. Thus, the role of models capturing static and dynamic knowledge about the system, as well as the use of model-driven algorithms and architectures as a basis for reasoning, is central to the vision of self-aware computing systems.

References

1. Anant Agarwal and Bill Harrod. Organic computing. Technical Report White paper, MIT and DARPA, 2006.
2. Anant Agarwal, Jason Miller, Jonathan Eastep, David Wentziaff, and Harshad Kasture. Self-aware computing. Technical Report AFRL-RI-RS-TR-2009-161, MIT, 2009.
3. Andreas Agne, Markus Happe, Achim Lsch, Christian Plessl, and Marco Platzner. Self-awareness as a model for designing and operating heterogeneous multicores. *ACM Trans. on Reconfigurable Technology and Systems (TRETS)*, 7(2):13:11–13:18, 2014.
4. Eyal Amir, M. L. Anderson, and Vinay K. Chaudhri. Report on darpa workshop on self-aware computer systems. Technical Report UIUCDCS-R-2007-2810, UIUC Comp. Sci., 2007.
5. Oliver Brdiczka, James L. Crowley, and Patrick Reignier. Learning situation models in a smart home. *IEEE Trans. Sys. Man Cyber. Part B*, 39:56–63, 2009.
6. Yuriy Brun, Giovanna Marzo Serugendo, Cristina Gacek, Holger Giese, Holger Kienle, Marin Litoiu, Hausi Müller, Mauro Pezzè, and Mary Shaw. Engineering self-adaptive systems through feedback loops. In Betty H. Cheng, Rogério Lemos, Holger Giese, Paola Inverardi, and Jeff Magee, editors, *Software Engineering for Self-Adaptive Systems*, pages 48–70. Springer-Verlag, Berlin, Heidelberg, 2009.
7. Betty H. C. Cheng, Rogério Lemos, Holger Giese, Paola Inverardi, Jeff Magee, Jesper Andersson, Basil Becker, Nelly Bencomo, Yuriy Brun, Bojan Cukic, Giovanna Marzo Serugendo,

Schahram Dustdar, Anthony Finkelstein, Cristina Gacek, Kurt Geihs, Vincenzo Grassi, Gabor Karsai, HolgerM. Kienle, Jeff Kramer, Marin Litoiu, Sam Malek, Raffaela Mirandola, Hau-siA. Müller, Sooyong Park, Mary Shaw, Matthias Tichy, Massimo Tivoli, Danny Weyns, and Jon Whittle. Software Engineering for Self-Adaptive Systems: A Research Roadmap. In Betty H. C. Cheng, Rogério Lemos, Holger Giese, Paola Inverardi, and Jeff Magee, editors, *Software Engineering for Self-Adaptive Systems*, volume 5525 of *Lecture Notes in Computer Science*, pages 1–26. Springer Berlin Heidelberg, 2009.

8. M.T. Cox. Metacognition in computation: A selected research review. *Art. Int.*, 169(2):104–141, 2005.
9. Marco Dorigo, Vito Trianni, Erol Şahin, Roderich Groß, Thomas H. Labella, Gianluca Baldassarre, Stefano Nolfi, Jean-Louis Deneubourg, Francesco Mondada, Dario Floreano, and Luca M. Gambardella. Evolving self-organizing behaviors for a swarm-bot. *Autonomous Robots*, 17:223–245, 2004.
10. J. Eastep, D. Wingate, M.D. Santambrogio, and A. Agarwal. Smartlocks: lock acquisition scheduling for self-aware synchronization. In *Proceeding of the 7th international conference on Autonomic computing*, pages 215–224. ACM, 2010.
11. B.A. Fette. *Cognitive radio technology*. Academic Press, 2009.
12. Raffay Hamid, Siddhartha Maddi, Amos Johnson, Aaron Bobick, Irfan Essa, and Charles Isbell. A novel sequence representation for unsupervised analysis of human activities. *Artificial Intelligence*, 173(14):1221 – 1244, 2009.
13. H. Hoffmann, J. Eastep, M.D. Santambrogio, J.E. Miller, and A. Agarwal. Application heart beats for software performance and health. In *ACM SIGPLAN Notices*, volume 45, pages 347–348. ACM, 2010.
14. Henry Hoffmann, Martina Maggio, Marco D. Santambrogio, Alberto Leva, and Anant Agarwal. Seec: A general and extensible framework for self-aware computing. Technical Report MIT-CSAIL-TR-2011-046, MIT CSAIL, 2011.
15. M.C. Huebscher and J.A. McCann. Simulation model for self-adaptive applications in pervasive computing. In *Proceedings of the Database and Expert Systems Applications, 15th International Workshop*, pages 694–698. IEEE Computer Society, 2004.
16. Jeffrey O. Kephart and David M. Chess. The vision of autonomic computing. *Computer*, 36(1):41–50, 2003.
17. Serge Kernbach. From robot swarm to artificial organisms: Self-organization of structures, adaptivity and self-development. In Paul Levi and Serge Kernbach, editors, *Symbiotic Multi-Robot Organisms*, volume 7. Springer, 2010.
18. Samuel Kounev, Nikolaus Huber, Fabian Brosig, and Xiaoyun Zhu. *A Model-Based Approach to Designing Self-Aware IT Systems and Infrastructures*. IEEE Computer, 49(7):53–61, July 2016, IEEE.
19. Nikolaus Huber, Fabian Brosig, Simon Spinner, Samuel Kounev, and Manuel Bähr. *Model-Based Self-Aware Performance and Resource Management Using the Descartes Modeling Language*. IEEE Transactions on Software Engineering (TSE), PP(99), 2017, IEEE Computer Society.
20. Peter R. Lewis, Arjun Chandra, Funmilade Faniyi, Kyrre Glette, Tao Chen, Rami Bahsoon, Jim Torresen, and Xin Yao. Architectural aspects of self-aware and self-expressive computing systems. *IEEE Computer*, 2015.
21. Peter R. Lewis, Arjun Chandra, Shaun Parsons, Edward Robinson, Kyrre Glette, Rami Bahsoon, Jim Torresen, and Xin Yao. A survey of self-awareness and its application in computing systems. In *Proc. Int. Conference on Self-Adaptive and Self-Organizing Systems Workshops (SASOW)*, pages 102–107, Ann Arbor, MI, USA, 2011. IEEE Computer Society.
22. Janet Metcalfe and Arthur P. Shimamura, editors. *Metacognition: Knowing about knowing*. MIT Press, Cambridge, MA, USA, 1994.
23. Melanie Mitchell. Self-awareness and control in decentralized systems (Tech Report SS-05-04). In *AAAI Spring Symposium on Metacognition in Computation*, Menlo Park, 2005. AIII Press.

24. Francesco Mondada, Giovanni C. Pettinaro, Andre Guignard, Ivo W. Kwee, Dario Floreano, Jean-Louis Deneubourg, Stefano Nolfi, Luca Maria Gambardella, and Marco Dorigo. Swarmbot: A new distributed robotic concept. *Autonomous Robots*, 17:193–221, 2004.
25. Ulric Neisser. The roots of self-knowledge: Perceiving self, it, and thou. *Annals of the New York Academy of Sciences*, 818:19–33, 1997.
26. Tatiana Djaba Nya, Stephan C. Stilkerich, and Cristian Seimers. Self-aware and self-expressive driven fault tolerance for embedded systems. In *IEEE Symposium on Intelligent Embedded Systems (IES)*, pages 27–33. IEEE, 2014.
27. L.D. Paulson. DARPA creating self-aware computing. *Computer*, 36(3):24, 2003.
28. Mike Perkowitz, Matthai Philipose, Kenneth Fishkin, and Donald J. Patterson. Mining models of human activities from the web. In *Proceedings of the 13th international conference on World Wide Web*, pages 573–582, 2004.
29. Jeremy Pitt, editor. *The Computer After Me: Awareness and Self-awareness in Autonomic Systems*. Imperial College Press, 2014.
30. Bernhard Rinner, Lukas Esterle, Jennifer Simonjan, Georg Nebehay, Roman Pflugfelder, Peter R. Lewis, and Gustavo Fernndez Domnguez. Self-aware and self-expressive camera networks. *IEEE Computer*, 2015.
31. M.D. Santambrogio, H. Hoffmann, J. Eastep, and A. Agarwal. Enabling technologies for self-aware adaptive systems. In *Adaptive Hardware and Systems (AHS), 2010 NASA/ESA Conference on*, pages 149–156. IEEE, 2010.
32. J. Schaumeier, J. Pitt, and G. Cabri. A tripartite analytic framework for characterising awareness and self-awareness in autonomic systems research. In *Self-Adaptive and Self-Organizing Systems Workshops (SASOW), 2012 Sixth IEEE Conference on*, pages 157–162, 2012.
33. Herbert Stachowiak. *Allgemeine Modelltheorie*. Springer, Wien, 1973.
34. J. Wang, D. Brady, K. Baclawski, M. Kokar, and L. Lechowicz. The use of ontologies for the self-awareness of the communication nodes. In *Proceedings of the Software Defined Radio Technical Conference SDR*, volume 3, 2003.
35. Juan Ye, Simon Dobson, and Susan McKeever. Situation identification techniques in pervasive computing: A review. *Pervasive and Mobile Computing*, In Press., 2011.
36. F. Zambonelli, N. Bicocchi, G. Cabri, L. Leonardi, and M. Puviani. On self-adaptation, self-expression, and self-awareness in autonomic service component ensembles. In *Self-Adaptive and Self-Organizing Systems Workshops (SASOW), 2011 Fifth IEEE Conference on*, pages 108–113, 2011.

Chapter 2
Self-aware Computing Systems: Related Concepts and Research Areas

Javier Cámara, Kirstie L. Bellman, Jeffrey O. Kephart, Marco Autili, Nelly Bencomo, Ada Diaconescu, Holger Giese, Sebastian Götz, Paola Inverardi, Samuel Kounev and Massimo Tivoli

Abstract Self-aware computing systems exhibit a number of characteristics (e.g., autonomy, social ability, and proactivity) which have already been studied

J. Cámara (✉)
Carnegie Mellon University, Pittsburgh, PA 15213, USA
e-mail: jcmoreno@cs.cmu.edu

K.L. Bellman
The Aerospace Corporation, Los Angeles, CA, USA
e-mail: Kirstie.L.Bellman@aero.org

J.O. Kephart
Thomas J. Watson Research Center, Yorktown Heights, NY, USA
e-mail: kephart@us.ibm.com

M. Autili · P. Inverardi · M. Tivoli
University of L'Aquila, 67100 L'Aquila, Italy
e-mail: marco.autili@univaq.it

P. Inverardi
e-mail: paola.inverardi@univaq.it

M. Tivoli
e-mail: massimo.tivoli@univaq.it

N. Bencomo
Aston University, Birmingham B4 7ET, UK
e-mail: nelly@acm.org

A. Diaconescu
Telecom Paris Tech, 75013 Paris, France
e-mail: ada.diaconescu@telecom-paristech.fr

H. Giese
Hasso-Plattner-Institut, 14482 Potsdam, Germany
e-mail: Holger.Giese@hpi.de

S. Götz
University of Technology Dresden, Dresden, Germany
e-mail: sebastian.goetz@acm.org

S. Kounev
Universität Würzburg, Am Hubland, 97074 Würzburg, Germany
e-mail: skounev@acm.org

© Springer International Publishing AG 2017
S. Kounev et al. (eds.), *Self-Aware Computing Systems*,
DOI 10.1007/978-3-319-47474-8_2

in different research areas, such as artificial intelligence, organic computing, or autonomic and self-adaptive systems. This chapter provides an overview of strongly related concepts and areas of study from the perspective of self-aware computing systems.

2.1 Introduction

The notion of self-aware computing encompasses different aspects which have already been the subject of study in different research areas of computer science. In fact, systems that feature one or several desirable characteristics in a self-aware computing system, such as being able to learn models about itself and its environment, reasoning, planning, or providing explanations, are already a reality. The construction of such systems has been made possible thanks to the research efforts carried out in areas such as artificial intelligence, autonomic computing, self-adaptive and self-organizing systems, or cognitive computing. As it happens, many of these disciplines will foreseeably be strongly intertwined with research in the area of self-aware computing, making it stand on the proverbial *shoulders of giants*.

This chapter presents an overview of concepts and research areas strongly related to self-aware computing. Every section presents a different area of research and explores its relation to self-aware computing systems. Note that there are disciplines that cannot be considered as fully within the scope of computer science (e.g., cybernetics) in which engineers employ ideas that are well aligned with the areas for which we provide an overview in this chapter. However, those areas are not discussed in this chapter due to space limitations.

This chapter starts with an overview of different related forms of control in Sect. 2.2. Next, Sect. 2.3 lays down the foundation for the rest of the chapter by presenting an overview of one of the existing perspectives on artificial intelligence that resonates most closely with self-aware computing systems.

After the introduction of the basics, Sect. 2.4 presents an overview of autonomic computing, which enables the construction of systems able to manage themselves in accordance with a set of high-level objectives specified by administrators or system users. Section 2.5 describes organic computing, which deals with the study of systems that dynamically adapt to changing conditions and exhibit a number of self-* properties, as well as context awareness. Next, Sect. 2.6 introduces service-based systems and cloud computing, including concepts such as location-transparent computation and autonomous services as agents. Section 2.7 provides an overview of self-organizing systems, which are able to organize themselves according to the laws of the environment within which they execute. Then, Sect. 2.8 introduces self-adaptive systems, which are strongly related to autonomic systems and able to adjust their own behavior in response to its perception of the environment and the system.

Section 2.9 introduces reflective computing and the notion of *computational reflection* as the system's ability to reason about its own resources, capabilities, and limitations in the context of its current operational environment. Next, Sect. 2.10

introduces *models at run-time*, that is, abstract self-representations of a system focused on a given aspect that may include its structure, behavior, or goals. This section also explores the relation between models at run-time and the concept of computational reflection presented in Sect. 2.9. Section 2.11 presents situation-aware and context-aware systems, in which the emphasis is made on building human–machine systems that observe, evaluate, and act within diverse situations that include a comprehensive set of factors that correspond to people, location, and events, as well as other environmental factors. Section 2.12 presents symbiotic cognitive computing, which are multi-agent systems that comprise both human and software agents that collectively perform cognitive tasks such as decision-making better than human or software agents can by themselves. Then, Sect. 2.13 covers auto-tuning, which deals with the automation of performance tuning, mostly for scientific applications.

After presenting an overview of different related areas and concepts, Sect. 2.14 provides a constructive definition of self-aware computing system that makes some considerations concerning the different factors influencing feasibility, capabilities, and ultimately determine under which conditions it is possible to actually develop a self-aware computing system, and how.

2.2 Control

In control theory, several advanced forms of control and adaptive control have been developed that involve learning, reasoning, and acting as well as models employed online as outlined for self-aware computing systems as introduced in Chap. 1. To compare self-aware computing systems with adaptive control architectures applied to software, we look at first into *model reference adaptive controllers* (*MRACs*) and *model identification adaptive controllers* (*MIACs*) in the following.

In case of *model reference adaptive controllers* (*MRACs*) [33, 37], a reference model defining desired closed-loop performance is employed to steer the adaptation. Consequently, the scheme is comparable to a prediction model of what is wanted that is used to steer the adaptation of the controller. However, as we have a prediction model of the plant only but not of the controller there is no process like learning involved, as the reference model is given at design time. The reference model is more a form of a given (high level) goal that is employed to steer the adjustments.

The *model identification adaptive controller* (*MIAC*) [37] scheme performs some form of system identification while the system is running, which can be compared to learning a model and then reasoning about the learned model to determine how to adjust the controller. However, we learn only a model only of the plant and not of the controller and therefore, if the plant is the context, we have context awareness only, and if the plant is a part of the system, we have self-awareness. As both cases are required for self-awareness according to Chap. 1, employing the MIAC scheme only leads to a self-aware computing system if the software and the environment are somehow subject to system identification.

Model-predictive control (MPC) [72] uses a model of the plant and a finite horizon for the predictions of the future output. The predicted outputs are employed to compute optimal set points (steady-state optimization). The optimal set points are then employed to calculate required control inputs to achieve the set points. When self-aware computing systems are compared with model-predictive control, architectures using a predictive model to plan the impact of future control actions such that the given criteria are optimized (according to goals) can be mapped to the reasoning and action. MPC can also be combined with system identification (cf. [40]) similar to MIAC as thus also a learning component is possible. However, MPC employing system identification learns a model only of the plant and not of the controller and therefore, if the plant is the context, we have context awareness only, and if the plant is a part of the system, we have self-awareness. As a link in the case of MIAC, both cases are required for self-awareness according to Chap. 1, employing the MPC with system identification scheme only leads to a self-aware computing system if the software and the environment are somehow subject to system identification.

Overall we can conclude that if the software and the environment are somehow subject to system identification, the system identification in control theory is comparable to the learning of self-aware computing systems. Also the MPC scheme of control theory can be seen as a special case of reasoning and acting (adapting) of self-aware computing systems. Finally, reference models in the MRAC scheme of control theory are a special case of static goals as considered by self-aware computing systems. Consequently, it can be argued that also self-aware computing systems in case they adapt the software behavior like less advanced forms of self-adaptive systems can likely largely benefit from the achievements of control theory. However, as also for the less advanced forms of self-adaptive systems principles and solutions of control can only be applied to software systems in restricted cases and the transfer of applicable control theory results to self-aware computing systems is still in its infancy.

2.3 Artificial Intelligence

There are many different perspectives on artificial intelligence, but the one that resonates most closely with self-aware systems is that adopted by Russell and Norvig in their book "Artificial Intelligence: A Modern Approach" [69], according to which artificial intelligence is fundamentally about designing and building rational agents. Wooldridge and Jennings [85] further define an agent as a *software-based computer system that enjoys the following properties*:

1. *autonomy*: agents operate without the direct intervention of humans or others and have some kind of control over their actions and internal state;
2. *social ability*: agents interact with other agents (and possibly humans) via some kind of agent-communication language;

3. *reactivity*: agents perceive their environment and respond in a timely fashion to changes that occur in it; and
4. *proactiveness*: agents do not simply act in response to their environment, and they are able to exhibit goal-directed behavior by taking initiative.

By emphasizing social ability as an essential property of agents, Wooldridge and Jennings suggest that agents typically exist in environments in which other agents are present, and that they interact with one another via some sort of agent-communication language, thereby forming multi-agent systems.

Self-aware computing systems as defined in this chapter possess the characteristics of autonomy, social ability, reactivity, and proactivity and can therefore be understood as types of agents or multi-agent systems that achieve these characteristics via the specific approach of learning models and using those models to determine how best to satisfy their goals.

2.3.1   Overview of Agents and Multi-agent Systems

A software agent can be defined, very generally, as a software entity that can accomplish tasks on behalf of its user, by acting within its environment [60]. In [69], agents are also referred to as *rational entities*, meaning that they would take the best possible action, considering available information and capabilities, to approach their objectives: "For each percept sequence, a rational agent should select an action that is expected to maximize its performance measure, given evidence provided by the percept sequence and whatever built-in knowledge the agent has."

A wide variety of agent types, with more specific abilities and characteristics, has been defined within this vast area to address the particularities of different domains, based on different approaches. An extensive review of all agent types would be well beyond the scope of this chapter. We merely aim to highlight here the most relevant types that would help us compare multi-agent systems with self-aware computing.

We consider several dimensions of comparison, whereby agents can be either *deliberative* or *reactive*; *mobile* or *static*; and feature various combinations of key characteristics, such as *autonomy*, *learning*, and *social interaction*. In the context of self-aware computing, we are mainly concerned with aspects of autonomy, reasoning, learning, and social abilities. Hence, we will focus on discussing these next.

A *deliberative agent* is the "one that possesses an explicitly represented, symbolic model of the world, and in which decisions (e.g., about what actions to perform) are made via symbolic reasoning" [85]. Conversely, *reactive agents* reach their objectives by implementing a stimulus-response (or reflex) behavior, merely reacting to changes in their environment with corresponding actions. Hence, they do *not* posses symbolic representations or reasoning capabilities [15].

Russel and Norvig [69] refine this agent typology further, defining *goal-oriented* and *utility-based* agents. These correspond to deliberative agents that pursue goals in a binary manner—either achieving the goal or not achieving it—or in a more modulated manner—where goal achievement can be equated to various degrees of utility. Russel and Norvig also refine reflex-based agents into basic and *model-based reflex agents*, which are reactive agents with or without internal state, respectively.

An agent's *autonomy* refers to its capability to operate without requiring human intervention, in order to achieve its objectives, or goals, on behalf of its user. In the context of deliberative agents, *proactiveness* is also considered as a key agent feature, related to its autonomy. It implies that the agent will be "taking the initiative" for reaching its goals, rather than simply reacting passively to its environment [85]. Of course, deliberative agents can also react to environmental changes.

An agent's *learning* ability allows it to adapt its behavior—e.g., via changes in its knowledge and reasoning, or in its reflexes—based on interactions with its environment, in order to increase its performance over time. Finally, an agent's *social ability* refers to its capability to interact with other agents, via some well-defined communication language.

A *multi-agent system (MAS)* consists of multiple agents that are engaged in some sort of interaction in order to accomplish one or several tasks, or goals. MAS is typically employed to address complicated computing problems via a divide-and-conquer technique—i.e., dividing the problem among a set of (specialized) agents, which interact to compose partial results into a global solution. In the case of deliberative agents, this implies that knowledge representation, acquisition, and reasoning processes are also distributed among the agents.

2.3.2 Comparison with Self-aware Computing

Since the concept of *agent* has been used rather broadly across various applications and domains, it has become an umbrella term for a wide variety of computing entities that feature highly different capabilities and characteristics. Therefore, it is quite difficult to provide an exact comparison of multi-agent systems with self-aware computing systems, not at least since these later can also feature different kinds and levels of self-awareness (Chap. 3). Considering these reasons, we only attempt here to provide a general comparison, highlighting the main differences in focus between the two concepts.

The concept of a *self-aware computing system* (as defined in Chap. 1) is mostly compatible with that of a *deliberative agent*, which features autonomy, learning, and social abilities—i.e., a "smart agent" in [60]. Indeed, like deliberative agents, self-aware computing systems can possess models of the world that are explicitly represented and on which they can reason in order to achieve higher-level goals (representing the user). In addition to an agent's world models, self-aware systems must also possess models of themselves and must reason on these to perform actions—e.g., self-adaptation to ensure system autonomy in a changing environment; explaining and reporting their current states (and their probable causes) to users, or to other systems; or suggesting means of rectifying undesirable or suboptimal states. Consequently, the learning capabilities of self-aware systems must apply to both models representing their environments and themselves. Here, self-aware systems focus on the particular problem of agent autonomy, within a changing environment and/or in the presence of internal faults, rather than on problem-solving in general, as is the case for multi-agent systems.

Like social agents, self-aware computing systems may also interact with other systems, either by direct communication or by indirect influence within a shared environment. The systems that such a self-aware system interacts with may feature various levels of self-awareness, or may be non self aware. In case of direct communications, a self-aware system's interactions can be equated to agent communications (and hence represent social skills). A specific feature of self-aware computing systems consists in the extent to which they can be, or become, self-aware of the other systems that they interact with—e.g., acquiring and maintaining models of them. This can also be the case in some agent-oriented approaches, like with game theoretical agents, yet here the agents' awareness of each other is typically provided at design time, then potentially refined during run-time. Another interesting feature here consists in the lack of assumptions on the other systems' self-aware capabilities (i.e., heterogeneity of self-awareness levels across a collective of systems). Again, this can be the case in some multi-agent systems—such as some game theoretical cases—yet the agent's self-awareness levels are typically predefined, depending on their roles.

2.4   Autonomic Computing

The autonomic computing initiative [35] was spurred by a concern that rapid growth in the complexity of IT systems would outstrip the ability of IT administrators to cope with that complexity. The proposed solution was for the system to take upon itself a large portion of the management burden. Just as the autonomic nervous system governs our pulse, our respiration, and the dilation of our pupils, freeing our conscious brain to attend to higher-level cognitive functions, the goal of autonomic computing is to create computing systems that manage themselves in accordance with high-level objectives from administrators or system users. While initially conceived as a paradigm for the future of IT management, over the course of time the principles, objectives, and techniques of autonomic computing have come to be applied more broadly, extending to physical systems such as data centers (and data center robots), the Internet of things, and smart homes.

An early paper that outlined the vision and research challenges of autonomic computing [41] laid out an architecture in which autonomic behavior was exhibited at two levels. Autonomic elements (such as databases, Web servers, or physical servers) were envisioned to use a combination of monitoring, analysis, planning, and execution driven by knowledge (often referred to as the *MAPE-K architecture* or *MAPE-K loop*) to accomplish their own individual goals.[1] System-level auto-nomic behavior was to be driven by system-level goals and accomplished through well-designed interactions among multiple interacting autonomic elements whose individual goals might be designed to support the desired system-level behavior. The vision did not specify how the goals of autonomic elements might be derived from system-level goals, nor did it specify how to design the interactions among the autonomic elements; these were cited as difficult and important research challenges.

Comparing the definition and vision of autonomic computing systems to that of self-aware computing reveals several similarities and a few distinctions. Employing Knowledge to support the Monitoring, Analysis, Planning, and Execution functions matches very closely the second clause of the self-aware computing definition, which states that self-aware systems "reason using ... models ... enabling them to act." Con-tained within the Knowledge component of an autonomic element are one or more models that the Analysis component can use to anticipate the likely consequence of an action or a plan (a sequence of actions) that it is contemplating. The objective of the Planning component is to move the autonomic element (or perhaps the autonomic system in general) from its current state (as assessed by the Monitoring component) to a state that it is deemed more desirable according to the high-level goals, which are also held within the Knowledge component. One common approach to using models and high-level goals to drive the behavior of autonomic elements and sys-tems is utility functions. The state space is described in terms of attributes that the administrator deems important (e.g., response time and power consumption), a utility value is ascribed to each possible state, and the system selects an action that would (according to models) lead to a state with the highest achievable utility value, given the current resource of other constraints. Finally, regardless of the means by which analysis and planning are accomplished, the autonomic element Executes the action or plan deemed most desirable by the Planning component, the state of the auto-nomic element (or the autonomic system) evolves (either in reaction to the action(s) or an external change such as an increase in workload), and the MAPE-K process continues. The execution step is the one point at which the autonomic computing definition may differ from the *reasoning* clause of the self-aware computing defini-tion. Autonomic computing *requires* execution, while self-aware computing *permits* execution but does not require it. Nonetheless, in practice the field of autonomic computing embraces work in which the system recommends an action, but allows a human to judge whether or not to take it, viewing this as an important and necessary evolutionary step toward full-fledged autonomic computing, not just as a matter of making incremental technological progress, but also as a means for building user trust.

---

[1] In actuality, MAPE-K was not strictly an architecture (it was more of a statement about required functionality than it was a statement about how those functions were to be woven together) nor was it necessarily a loop, as the various components might typically be operating in parallel at all times and not running in a strict order.

The first clause of the self-aware computing definition concerns learning. Learning has always been viewed as an important aspect of autonomic computing, and a preferred means by which models are created, but autonomic computing does not strictly require that an element or a system learn to be regarded as autonomic.

To summarize, while autonomic computing was initially proposed as an IT management solution, the current understanding of the term is much broader, and it overlaps strongly with the definition of self-aware computing systems. The main differences are that autonomic systems are not strictly required to learn, and self-aware systems are not strictly required to act.

2.5 Organic Computing

An organic computing (OC) system is "a technical system which adapts dynamically to the current conditions of its environment. It will be self-organizing, self-configuring, self-healing, self-protecting, self-explaining, and context-aware" [58].

From its inception, OC started with a strong industry pull (including Daimler-Crysler, Siemens, and Bosch) because of the shared belief across several industries that we can no longer adequately design very large-scale, complex systems; complex systems need to help us by designing parts of themselves and by managing parts of themselves.

As part of this was the strong recognition by OC that complex systems have emergence. That is, they have unplanned and unexpected side effects and emergent properties at different levels because of the interactions among large numbers of components under different operational conditions. The OC attitude is "How can we take advantage of the fact that complex systems have emergence?" How can systems use emergence as a source of controlled variation? How can we shape emergence to go in desired directions?

Hence, from its inception, OC emphasized the importance of having systems that could not only observe and adapt to the changing and demanding external world, but also could observe and adapt their own goals, plans, resources, and behaviors as necessary to correctly map to new contexts and requirements. Moreover, in OC approaches, one will take advantage of this self-awareness to adapt to not only changing conditions and requirements, but even to new, emergent properties in the system and its environment.

Although OC has different approaches to meeting the challenges of creating self-adaptive and self-aware systems, the observer/controller architecture is an especially important contribution to mention here because of its clear relationship and similarity to several of the architectures in this book (see more in Chaps. 6 and 8). An early description of the observer/controller architecture is depicted in Fig. 2.1.

A key emphasis in OC is that complex systems need to have self-control and self-adaptation abilities while always retaining important human-in-the-loop capabilities so that humans can suitably monitor and control when necessary the results of interacting and relatively autonomous computing systems. Hence, the observer/controller

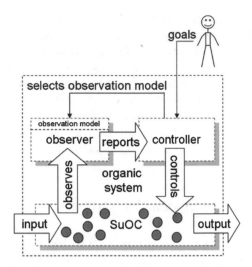

Fig. 2.1 Early observer/controller architecture

architecture is comprised of two top-level concepts: the organic system and a human user, where the organic system adheres to the basic input/compute/output principle of computing. The human user is seen as imposing goals and constraints at times on the organic system, while reviewing the system status based on the OC system's self-reporting capabilities and whatever special human interfaces to system instrumentation have been added.

The organic system is further decomposed into three major components: the system under observation and control (SuOC), the observer, and the controller. All human interaction is relayed by the controller. Notably, the input/compute/output principle is realized by the SuOC. Observer and controller impose a feedback loop onto the SuOC, where the first observes the SuOC and reports to the controller, which in turn controls the SuOC.

An important characteristic of the SuOC in organic computing is that it is comprised of agents, i.e., autonomous entities. In other words, the SuOC is already a set of self-organizing systems. The observer and controller enhance this system to achieve controlled self-organization.

As can be seen by this very brief description, there can be multiple observer–controller layers in a given system. Furthermore, different kinds of self-awareness capabilities, as discussed in the rest of this book, can contribute at many points in this architecture; they will certainly occur in the observational and reasoning capabilities of the *observer*, as well as potentially in the adaptive behaviors directed by the *controller*.

2.6 Service-Based Systems and Cloud Computing

In this section, we first introduce some basic concepts related to service-oriented computing, followed by an overview of the area of cloud computing, emphasizing concepts relevant to self-aware computing systems, such as location-transparent computation and the notion of autonomous services as agents.

2.6.1 Service-Based Systems

Service-oriented computing (SOC) and service-oriented architecture (SOA) are now largely accepted as well-founded reference paradigm and reference architecture for Internet computing [62]. Under SOC, networked devices and their hosted applications are abstracted as autonomous loosely coupled services that, while playing the roles of service providers, consumers (aka clients), and registries, they also interact by following the service-oriented interaction pattern (see Fig. 2.2).

According to this pattern, a service has to define an interface publishable on the Internet, researchable, and callable independently from a particular language or platform. In order to obtain these requirements, a SOA application has to define roles (not all required) as shown in Fig. 2.2.

- *Service Consumer*: the entity that uses the service; it can be an application module or another service;
- *Service Provider*: the entity that provides the service and exposes the interface;
- *Service Contract*: defines the format for the request of a service and the related response;
- *Service Registry*: Directory on the Internet that contains the services.

Despite the remarkable progress of the SOC paradigm and supporting technologies in the last ten years, substantial challenges have been set through the evolution of the Internet. Over the years, the Internet has become the most important networking infrastructure, enabling all to create, contribute, share, use, and integrate information and extract knowledge. As a result, the Internet is changing at a fast pace and is called to evolve into the Future Internet, i.e., a federation of self-aware services

Fig. 2.2 Service-oriented interaction pattern

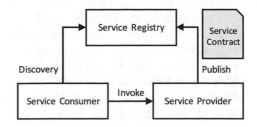

and networks that provide built-in and integrated capabilities such as service support, contextualization, mobility, security, reliability, robustness, and self-* abilities of communication resources and services [28, 38].

In this wide spectrum, a SBS can be meaningfully seen as a composition of service providers and consumers that interact by providing/requiring functionalities to/from each other. A SBS is often opportunistically built for the purpose of achieving a given goal. The goal typically expresses functional and non-functional high-level requirements that the resulting composition has to fulfill. The former class captures the qualitative behavior of a SBS, its functional specification. The latter defines the SBS's quantitative attributes such as performance, reliability, and security.

From a software engineering perspective, goal changes are always done to meet the new requirements; e.g., users and involved business organizations may change their functional needs and non-functional preferences. Moreover, it can be that the services currently involved in the composition no longer perform as expected. On the practical side, the source of this type of run-time changes can be, e.g., changing conditions of the network through which services communicate, degrading computational resources of the execution environments where services are deployed, upgrading the version of the middleware on top of which services run, and remote service substitution.

The knowledge that service consumers have depend on the contract (often expressed by means of service behavioral models) exposed by the service providers they want to interact with (interface only, interface plus interaction protocol, interface plus interaction protocol plus non-functional attributes, etc.). As a consequence, also the kind of reasoning that enables a SBS to act based on its knowledge depends on the kind of models and notations used to describe service contracts.

Last but not least, since a SBS can be seen as a composition of services, the way the system can act to enable self-awareness is constrained by the structure and behavior of the adopted composition means. In particular, two forms of composition to build SBSs can be distinguished, one centralized, i.e., service orchestration, and one distributed, i.e., service choreography [5].

2.6.2 Cloud Computing

Cloud computing refers to the on-demand delivery of IT resources and applications via the Internet, possibly with a pay-as-you-go pricing. By referring to the NIST definition of cloud computing [53], "cloud computing is a model for enabling ubiquitous, convenient, on-demand network access to a shared pool of configurable computing resources (e.g., networks, servers, storage, applications, and services) that can be rapidly provisioned and released with minimal management effort or service-provider interaction." In other words, cloud computing is essentially about moving services, computation, and data off-site to a location-transparent entity. Cloud computing distinguishes three service models, as described below:

- *Software as a Service (SaaS)*: WAN-enabled application services (e.g., Google Apps, Salesforce.com, and WebEx). The capability provided to the consumer is to use the providers' applications running on a cloud infrastructure. The applications are accessible from various client devices through either a client interface, such as a Web browser (e.g., Web-based email), or a program interface.
- *Platform as a Service (PaaS)*: Foundational elements to develop new applications (e.g., Coghead and Google Application Engine). The capability provided to the consumer is to deploy onto the cloud infrastructure consumer-created or acquired applications created using programming languages, libraries, services, and tools supported by the provider.
- *Infrastructure as a Service (IaaS)*: Providing computational and storage infrastructure in a centralized, location-transparent service (e.g., Amazon). The capability provided to the consumer is to provision processing, storage, networks, and other fundamental computing resources, where the consumer is able to deploy and run arbitrary software, which can include operating systems and applications.

Some of the main characteristics of cloud computing are concerned with (i) elasticity, in which it requires on-demand capabilities of resources; (ii) broad network access, in which access to the cloud can be done using any computer-based device; (c) resource pooling, in which data can be used and added in the cloud at any time; (d) measured services, in which consumers only pay for the resources they use from the cloud; (e) energy efficiency, in which the energy consumption of cloud data centers are optimized; and (f) virtualization, in which the infrastructure is divided and seen as separated logic components.

The above characteristics of cloud computing require a degree of self-awareness of the technology. For example, it is necessary for the system to be aware of the need of new resources and to be able to free the not-used resources at a certain moment of time. However, it is not possible to say that cloud computing technologies have the necessary level of self-awareness, as per the definition given in Chap. 1.

2.6.3 Comparison with Self-aware Computing

Since the vision of Weiser [81] was published almost 25 years ago, pervasive systems have almost become reality. Computers have become ubiquitous and are available in areas nobody would have expected them 20 years ago such as cars, parks, or even pot plants at home. Nevertheless, these computers are often far from being self-aware. In many cases, these computers act as simple sensors merely storing the sensed environment on a local memory or transmit it to a central server. The two main points in the self-aware computing definition are often not fulfilled. Pervasive systems only in some cases *learn* about their environment but they only rarely reason about this knowledge.

Nevertheless, there are novel areas of research within the pervasive computing community, such as the *smart environment* community. Here the devices try to learn behavioral patterns about the user in order to anticipate certain actions, requirements, or desires of the user. This anticipation is often founded on predefined rules and only allows very limited flexibility with respect to defining new goals for the individual device or the entire system. Furthermore, the interplay between the individual devices and the impact of their actions on each other is often hardwired within the individual devices. This limits the capabilities to include new devices during run-time without explicit setup of the system. While implementing individual autonomous computing agents within the different devices and using a service-based approach introduce higher flexibility and robustness to the pervasive system, the higher, system-wide goals are still not considered when actions of the individual devices are performed.

2.7 Self-organizing Systems

As their name suggests, *self-organizing systems* are systems that are able to organize themselves adaptively and without external control. *Organization* is at the core of this definition and generally comprises the relations, interconnections, conditionality or dependencies between the system's components, or variables. Hence, organization relates heavily to the system's *structure*, defining its main components and their interrelations.

In the remainder of this section, we first present a general overview of self-organizing systems, followed by a discussion of cross-pollination opportunities with self-aware computing.

2.7.1 Overview of Self-organizing Systems

From a general perspective, if a system (or general "machine" [4]) is viewed as a set of states S, with a set of inputs I and a function f that maps $I \times S$ into S—i.e., determining the system's future state based on the current state and inputs—then the system's organization represents the manner in which its variables are interrelated via the mapping function f. A self-organizing system here implies that the system is able to change its own mapping function. This raises some controversies around the system's boundary definition, since it implies the extension of the initial system with a controller that monitors and updates its organization [4].

However, most often, self-organization is understood as a dynamic adaptive and autonomous process that results from the inherent behavior of each system component and of the "laws" of the environment within which they execute [4, 20]; and which results in a progressive increase in system structure [84]. Examples of natural self-organization include the spontaneous assembly of protons, neutrons, and electrons into atoms; of different atoms into organic molecules; and the evolution of living organisms adapted to their environments. Examples in artificial systems include the adaptive formation of ad hoc mobile networks, of robot swarms, and of component- and service-based software system assemblies. Ashby prefers referring to this type of self-organization as the "spontaneous generation of organization."

This is also the typical understanding of self-organization in the computing systems domain, notably in research communities such as the self-adaptive and self-organizing (SASO) systems—as reflected for instance in the proceeding series of the International Conference on SASO Systems.[2] Here, self-organization is interesting because of the advantageous properties that it features in general (e.g., resilience and adaptability to a wide range of environmental changes; robustness in the face of internal failures; and scalability with the number of components and adaptation frequency). In the SASO community, self-organization is also seen as a bottom–up alternative to achieving self-adaptation, which was originally designed as top–down.

The main challenge here is: How to design self-organizing systems that also meet desirable goals? Indeed, in natural systems, most instances of self-organization have no other obvious purpose than their own existence and survival within their environment. In more "interesting" cases (from a goal-oriented system perspective), different organisms self-organize into more-or-less temporary formations in order to achieve via collective action a common goal that none of them could have achieved individually (e.g., swarms, flocks, herds, teams, and societies). Yet, when building artificial systems, determining which component behaviors and interaction laws will lead to the self-organization of systems that meet the designer's goals within targeted environments is a difficult task, subject to active research. These challenges differ from those highlighted by self-aware computing, where the research focus is placed on the system's knowledge acquisition and the way in which usage of this knowledge can serve the system's achievement of goals.

2.7.2 Cross-pollination Opportunities with Self-aware Computing

In self-organizing systems, any knowledge available is decentralized and distributed across the participating system components, or agents. An exception may occur if global knowledge were encoded within the environment shared by the system's components. This aspect will be interesting to study within the context of decentralized (or self-organized) self-aware systems.

Conversely, it will be interesting to explore how self-awareness could help a system's components self-organize in order to achieve a shared goal. Here, the hard-coded elementary behaviors and "laws" of the environment that fuel self-organization could be adapted dynamically by the system components, as they become aware of their shared goals (e.g., already the case in social organizations). Also, components that become aware of their own characteristics (e.g., range of behaviors and properties they can exhibit), of the characteristics of other components, and of the key theoretical principles of self-organization (still to be produced by the corresponding research

---

[2]SASO history in 2016: http://saso2016.informatik.uni-augsburg.de/history.html.

fields) may be better able to select the components with which they connect in order to have a better chance of achieving their goals.

2.8 Self-adaptive Systems

In the self-adaptive software community, self-* properties are organized into levels where *self-adaptiveness* is at the top (or general level), while self-awareness is considered only a primitive level like context awareness and the typical autonomic computing like self-* properties such as self-configuring, self-healing, self-optimizing, or self-protecting are considered major level properties in between the other two levels (cf. [70]). Furthermore, in the self-adaptive software community most approaches emphasis an architectural perspective (cf. [70]) where besides the control of parameters changes of the architecture may matter.

In the rest of this section, we first present a general overview of self-adaptive systems, followed by a discussion of anticipatory self-adaptive systems, which are those that exhibit a specific set of characteristics which are strongly related to self-aware computing systems, such as the ability to predict, or self-adapt proactively.

2.8.1 Overview of Basic Self-adaptive Systems

Like in autonomic computing for self-adaptive systems, control loops are often considered one of the core objects of the design efforts [16, 74] and it is advocated that in order to achieve real self-management capabilities besides a direct layer for change management also a goal management is required (cf. reference architecture [44]). However, besides some specific approaches that emphasize architectural models or goals in contrast to the notion for self-aware computing systems of Definition 1.1 for the basic efforts for self-adaptive systems hold that neither the learning of models nor the capability to reason based on this models to realize the adaptation loop has been emphasized so far.

In a series of Dagstuhl seminars, the community has identified mainly modeling dimensions, requirements, engineering through feedback loops, assurances, the design space, processes, decentralized control, and practical run-time verification and validation as the main issues that have to be addressed (see two research road maps [18, 21]. However, again neither the employed knowledge nor the capability to reason based on this knowledge as advocated by the notion for self-aware computing systems of Definition 1.1 plays a prominent role.

The notion for self-aware computing systems of Definition 1.1 is overlapping with the notion of self-adaptive software as it also covers systems where no self-adaptation happens. As advocated in [31], the limitation to only fully automatic adaptation is probably too limited and instead, it would be better to also consider related manual activities such as change management and their coordination with automated adaptation steps. Therefore, to include also mixed forms where people supervise the adaptation or the self-awareness helps with manual adaptation in the notion for self-aware computing systems of Definition 1.1 seems somehow beneficial to better cover the real needs and the real design options.

For the subset of self-aware computing systems that realize some self-adaptation behavior, however, we can conclude that they describe a subset of the self-adaptive software, where in addition to the existence of the feedback loop we also learn models capturing knowledge and reason about these models allowing them to act according to internal and external conditions in accordance with higher-level goals. While several suggestions go in a similar direction as Definition 1.1 (cf. [44]), the community will likely benefit from the suggested notion for self-aware computing systems of Definition 1.1 that clearly separate lower-level solutions without explicit knowledge capturing and reasoning from approaches that have these capabilities based on learning models and reasoning based on the models.

2.8.2 Anticipatory Self-adaptive Systems

What distinguishes a *self-adaptive system* from any other system is its ability to adjust its behavior in response to its perception of the environment and the system itself [18]. Self-adaptive systems typically operate employing a knowledge base that can incorporate an explicit representation of the system's structure, goals, and assumptions about its environment. However, there is an ample variation in the level of detail in which the different elements of this knowledge base are described, as well as in the reasoning capabilities that different approaches exhibit [70].

The characteristics of early proposals to self-adaptation [32, 44] tend to be far from the traits of self-aware computing systems listed in Definition 1.1. These approaches tend to be reactive and adapt in response to the changes without anticipating future changes or reasoning about the long-term outcome of adaptation (e.g., a system may adapt to a transient change, only to adapt again and go back to its original configuration moments later). Moreover, these proposals tend to be rather limited in terms of learning capabilities. In contrast, recent approaches to self-adaptation [17, 19, 34] are better aligned with the description of self-aware computing system given in Chap. 1. The general trend among these proposals is a paradigm shift from reactive to proactive adaption, incorporating the ability to learn, predict, and systematically exploit knowledge to improve the operation of the system.

These approaches fit well into the category of *anticipatory self-adaptive system*, defined as "able to anticipate to the extent possible, its needs and behaviors and those of its context, and able to manage itself proactively" [63]. Based on this definition, we can identify the main criteria that anticipatory self-adaptive systems should ideally satisfy:

1. *Predictive*. The system can likely determine *ahead of time* if a condition that requires adaptation will take place. Predictions can be exploited to avoid unnec-

essary adaptations or improve the overall choice of adaptation (e.g., by factoring in information about future resource availability or workload and other environment conditions into the decision-making process [19, 55]). Predictions can also help to enforce safety properties when reachability of a potential safety violation from the current state of the system is detected [48].

2. *Proactive.* The system can enact adaptation before a deviation from its functionality or qualities takes place. A representative proactive approach to self-adaptation in cyber-security is Moving Target Defense (MTD) [86]. MTD assumes that a system that remains static with the same configuration over long periods of time gives potential attackers time for reconnaissance and exploitation of system weaknesses. Hence, the idea behind MTD is adapting to change the configuration of the system periodically, thus reducing the chance of an attacker of finding and exploiting a weakness. Another example of proactivity is latency-aware proactive self-adaptation (PLA) [55], which anticipates changes in environment conditions and triggers adaptations with enough lead time to deal with them in a timely fashion, based on information about the execution time required to complete adaptations and achieve their effects in the controlled system (i.e., their latency). In the area of service-based systems, PROSA [34] is an approach that carries out tests at run-time to detect potential problems before they happen in real transactions, triggering adaptations when tests fail.

3. *Learning.* The system can generate and incorporate new knowledge (typically derived from observations of the system and its environment at run-time), and use it to improve subsequent adaptions. Simple forms of learning can also be found in reactive approaches. To select adaptations, Rainbow [32] employs information about the actual outcome of past adaptations to derive probabilities that represent the likelihood of possible outcomes of future adaptations. Proactive approaches can employ more sophisticated learning techniques to leverage its prediction capabilities (e.g., employing Bayesian learning to estimate the future behavior of the environment [17, 27]).

Table 2.1 categorizes some anticipatory approaches to self-adaptation. It is worth noticing that although a proactive self-adaptive system can benefit significantly from predictions, proactive approaches are not necessarily predictive. One example is MTD. In the simplest form of MTD, the system's configuration is changed proactively with a fixed frequency, without any reasoning involving a model of the envi-

Table 2.1 Anticipatory self-adaptation approaches

Approach	Learning	Predictive	Proactive
KAMI [27]	✓	✓	✓
QoSMOS [17]	✓	✓	✓
Cheng et al. [19]		✓	✓
PLA [55]		✓	✓
Li et al. [48]		✓	✓
PROSA [34]			✓
MTD [86]			✓

ronment or predictions about its future behavior. Moreover, we can observe that in terms of learning, anticipatory self-adaptive approaches are still far from the ideal of self-aware computing systems. In particular, learning capabilities are employed only in approaches that involve relatively simple adaptations (e.g., parameter optimization [17, 27]), but not combined with adaptations that entail complex changes to a system's architecture.

2.9 Reflective Computing

In 1987, Maes [51] defined and implemented "computational reflection" as "the process of reasoning about and/or acting upon oneself." Computational reflection is an engineered system's ability to reason about its own resources, capabilities, and limitations in the context of its current operational environment. Reflection capabilities can range from simple, straightforward adjustments of another program's parameters or behaviors (e.g., altering the step size on a numerical process or the application of rules governing which models are used at different stages in a design process) to sophisticated analyses of the system's own reasoning, planning, and decision processes (e.g., noticing when one's approach to a problem is not working and revising a plan).

Reflection processes must include more than the sensing of data, monitoring of an event, or perception of a pattern; they must also have some type of capability to reason about this information and to act upon this reasoning. However, although reflection is more than monitoring, it does not imply that the system is "conscious." Many animals demonstrate self-awareness; not only do they sense their environment, but they are also able to reason about their capabilities within that environment. For example, when a startled lizard scurries into a crevice, rarely does it try to fit into a hole that is too small for its body. If it is injured or tired, it changes the distance that it attempts to run or leap. This adaptive behavior reveals the ability of the animal system to somehow take into account the current constraints of the environment and its own body within that environment [9, 10].

In order to bring out the ways in which the self-awareness processes and architectures enhance and further develop reflective architectures, we will quickly overview one approach to implementing computational reflection and the building of reflection processes in a robotic-car example (also see Chap. 9 for additional discussion of self-modeling issues in this test bed).

The Wrappings' approach uses both explicit meta-knowledge and recursively applied algorithms to recruit and configure resources dynamically to "problems posed" to the system by users, external systems, or the system's own internal processing. The problem manager (PM) algorithms use the Wrappings to choreograph seven major functions: discover, select, assemble, integrate, adapt, explain, and evaluate. "Discover" programs (or as called in the Wrappings, "resources") identify new resources that can be inserted into the system for a problem. "Selection" resources decide which resource(s) should be applied to this problem in this context.

"Assembly" is syntactic integration and these resources help set up selected resources so that they can pass information or share services. "Integration" is semantic, including constraints on when and why resources should be assembled. "Adaptation" resources help to adjust or set up a resource for different operational conditions. "Explanation" resources are more than a simple event history because they provide information on why and what was not selected. "Evaluate" includes the impact or effectiveness of the given use of this resource in the current problem. The meta-knowledge for a Wrapping is always for the USE of a resource within a particular context and for a specific posed problem. It includes assumptions and constraints, the required services and input, the resulting services and output, and the best practices for using this resource in this situation.

The Wrappings' "problem-posing" has many benefits, including separating problems from solution methods and keeping an explicit, analyzable trace of what problems were used to evoke and configure resources. Because all of the resources are wrapped, even the resources that support the Wrappings' processing, the system is computationally reflective—it can reason about the use of all of its resources [12].

Wrappings [45, 46] provide an implementation strategy for computational reflection that provides control over the level of self-awareness available in the system and the levels of self-awareness to be used at any given time. The mechanism that allows this flexibility is the Problem-Posing Programming Paradigm, which strictly and completely separates the information service requests (the problems) from the information service providers (the resources) and reconnects problems in context with resources using explicit interpretable rules collected into Wrappings' Knowledge Bases. Moreover, the processes that perform the connection (called PMs, or problem managers) are also resources and are also Wrapped, so they can be swapped out as easily as any other resources. We emphasize that the designers have control over the level of detail of decomposition of the processes in the system, and of the rules by which resources are used for particular problems. There is no inherent limit on that level of detail (some implementations go down to the individual hardware instruction, but most go to the typical software component/module level). More detail on the implementation architecture is given in Chap. 8.

The flexibility of the Wrappings' approach provides multiple entry points for the reflective processes. A reflective resource has the general form: Given a goal, purpose, or function, a reflective process uses the sources of information to do some action, decision or to create data that is used by other processes. The goal or function for that reflective process could be built in during design time or assigned dynamically to that reflective process by other programs. It may be in continual use or it may be recruited or evoked only when certain resources are active or conditions exist. The sources of information can be, e.g., data sets, sensor output, or monitors. The reasoning process for reflection can be done with an algorithm, decision process, rulebase, cognitive model, or planner. The resulting actions are myriad, but include sending messages, setting program or context parameters, recruiting new components, initiating new processes, or instigating a replan or undo process.

Although the Wrappings' approach and reflective architectures approach briefly outlined here have proven its value for resource management and dynamic integration among large numbers of resources, the original approach was in practice limited to largely the management and adaptation of single large distributed systems. Although, the benefits of reflection were clear for interactions among systems (e.g., the self-knowledge could be made available to other systems for coordination [11] and external viewpoints by other systems could help a system identify its own problems or state and learn better [8, 47], in fact, the new work in self-aware systems as seen in this volume will help greatly by expanding new ideas for how collections of self-aware systems could interact and organize.

2.10 Models@run.time and Reflection

A model at run-time (models@run.time) [14] is defined as an abstract self-representation of a system that is focused on a given aspect of the running system. Such aspects include its structure, behavior, and goals. The run-time model exists in tandem with the given system during the actual execution time of that system. As in the case of traditional model-driven engineering (MDE) [30], a self-representation of the system in the form of run-time models can also be used as the basis for software synthesis, but in this case the generation can be done at run-time [57, 82].

Before describing the role of models@run.time in the area of self-aware computing, it is useful to briefly introduce the relationship between models@run.time and reflection (the topic reflection is more extensively covered in Sect. 2.9) and other aspects. Computational reflection focuses on the representations of an underlying system that are both self-representations and causally connected [14]. The causally connected representations of aspects of the system are constantly mirroring the running system and its current state and behavior. Causal connection implies that if the system changes, the self-representations of the system (i.e., the models) should also change, and vice versa.

Even if closely related, models@run.time and reflection are not the same. Reflection deals with models that are linked to the computation model and therefore tend to be focused on the solution space and in many cases at a rather low level of abstraction. The research area models@run.time deals with models that are defined at a much higher level of abstraction. Further, run-time models more frequently relate to the problem space. Examples of applications using run-time models are self-adaptation [57] or generation of mediators to support interoperability [12].

Traditionally, the structure of a run-time model has been conceived at design time (e.g., architecture models [57]). However, they can also be learned at run-time. In [12], the authors show how using learning methods the required knowledge of the context and environment can be captured and distilled to be formulated and made explicitly available as a run-time model and therefore support reasoning. Another example of techniques to be used to learn run-time models are shown in [87].

Models@run.time are at the core of self-aware systems. They are relevant to support self-awareness as defined in Chap. 1. (i) The run-time models correspond to the learned models which capture knowledge about the system itself and their environment. Specifically, the run-time models support learning to capture the needed knowledge about the system itself (e.g., its own goals and requirements [71, 82]) or its perception of the environment [77, 87]. (ii) The run-time models when consulted should provide up-to-date information about the system and therefore support reasoning (e.g., predict, analyze, and plan) enabling the system to act based on their knowledge. As the run-time model is causally connected, actions taken based on the reasoning can be made at the model level rather than at the system level [56].

We argue that the definition of self-awareness requires a self-representation (i.e., run-time model) of the subject of awareness. For example, if the system is aware of its own architecture the system would need a representation of its architecture (a architecture run-time model). Other examples are awareness of its own requirements or any other aspect about itself. If the object of the awareness is part of the environment of the system (i.e., it is outside the system), it should be considered a self-representation as well as the representation includes the perspective of the system. Two different systems will usually have different representations (or models) of their perception of the same object of awareness.

2.11   Situation-Aware Systems and Context Awareness

Situation awareness (SA) is an ongoing body of research with many conferences, workshops, and papers which develops theory and applications in building human–machine systems that observe, evaluate, and act within diverse situations. Here we are using the term "situation" in the technical sense [6, 23, 50] where a situation includes at least the elements of the situation, e.g., objects, events, people, systems, and environmental factors, and their current states, e.g., locations and actions.

Fracker [29] described SA as the combining of new information with existing information for the purpose of developing a "composite picture of the situation along with the projections of future status and subsequent decisions as to appropriate courses of action to take." Dominguez et al. [23] added to this view an emphasis on the "continuous extraction of environmental information" with the explicit feedback loop that would use the developed perceptions and understanding to direct the next collection of data.

Credited with seminal work in this field, Endsley [24] argues that "it is important to distinguish the term situation awareness, as a state of knowledge, from the processes used to achieve that state. These processes, which may vary widely among individuals and contexts, will be referred to as situational assessment or the process of achieving, acquiring, or maintaining SA." Thus, in brief, situation awareness is viewed as "a state of knowledge," and situational assessment as "the processes" used to achieve that knowledge. Endsley's model illustrates three stages or steps of SA formation: perception, comprehension, and projection. Perception is considered Level 1 of a SA system. "The first step in achieving SA is to perceive the status, attributes, and dynamics of the relevant elements in the environment. Thus, Level 1 SA, the most basic level of SA, involves the processes of monitoring, cue detection, and simple recognition, which lead to an awareness of multiple situational elements (objects, events, people, systems, and environmental factors) and their current states (locations, conditions, modes, and actions)."

By this framework, Level 2 in a SA is comprehension and is a synthesis of the Level 1 SA elements through the "processes of pattern recognition, interpretation, and evaluation. Level 2 SA requires integrating this information to understand how it will impact upon the individual's goals and objectives. This includes developing a comprehensive picture of the world, or of that portion of the world of concern to the individual." The highest level of SA, Level 3, is "projection" or the ability to predict the future actions of elements in the environment. "Level 3 SA is achieved through knowledge of the status and dynamics of the elements and comprehension of the situation (Levels 1 and 2 SA), and then extrapolating this information forward in time to determine how it will affect future states of the operational environment" [24]. With SA, one does not guarantee successful decision-making, but does provide some of the necessary inputs, it is argued, for successful decision-making with cue recognition, situation assessment, and prediction. As in self-aware systems, goals play a key role in SA. Both multiple goals, the fact of competing goals, and goal prioritization are emphasized in SA. However, it appears that for most SA systems these goals are "given" to it and predesigned, whereas in self-awareness (as shown in Chap. 3) although there are certainly goals given to a self-aware system, it is also expected that the self-aware system will alter and adapt even high-level goals and possibly generate low-level goals.

Many researchers have discussed the limitations of the current SA approaches, noting especially that the most widely cited models of SA lack support from the cognitive sciences (Banbury and Tremblay, [6]) and that there is also important mathematical and logical work to be done in defining these terms computationally (M. Kokar, [59]). In terms of self-awareness processes, we would say that SA has not yet incorporated the same sophistication (e.g., in learning, model-building) to its internal models that it applies to its external models of the situation. That is, as clearly seen from SA research, although SA certainly includes cognitive processes such as "mental models," attention, and decision-making, there has historically in SA been less of an emphasis on any reflection processes or self-models as used in this volume. Although models are emphasized for use by the cognitive/intelligent processes for situation awareness, these models are not explicit models of the system itself, its reasoning and learning capabilities, or its limitations, but rather focus on the objects and the situations to be perceived. It appears from Endsley and other SA-leading researchers that they are making some assumptions about what is useful in terms of their class of problems. While in self-aware systems, we are recognizing the need for both short-term and longer-term processes, it appears that SA is focused more on immediate and fast responses, proceeding from pattern recognition of key factors in the environment—"The speed of operations in activities such as sports, driving, flying, and air traffic control practically prohibits such conscious deliberation in the majority of cases, but rather reserves it for the exceptions." From Endsley [26], it would appear that SA views some of the cognitive processes that build models as largely "backward focused," forming reasons for past events, while situation awareness is typically forward looking, projecting what is likely to happen in order to inform effective decision processes. In self-awareness, we see the benefits for learning, understanding, and model-building processes as leading to more adaptive behavior in the long-term certainly, and even leading to better behavior at run-time in accordance with the real-time requirements.

Related to SA is the area of research called "sensemaking." Klein, Moon, and Hoffman [43] distinguish between situation awareness and sensemaking as follows: "Situation awareness" is about the knowledge state that is achieved—either knowledge of current data elements, or inferences drawn from these data, or predictions that can be made using these inferences (Endsley, [24]). In contrast, sensemaking is about the process of achieving these kinds of outcomes, the strategies, and the barriers encountered (p. 71). Hence, sensemaking is viewed more as "a motivated, continuous effort to understand connections (which can be among people, places, and events) in order to anticipate their trajectories and act effectively" (Klein et al. [43], p. 71) rather than the state of knowledge underlying situation awareness. Although Endsley [26] points out that sensemaking is actually considering a subset of the processes used to maintain situation awareness, as noted above it is unclear how such longer-term processes such as understanding, self-awareness and self-aware models, and "sensemaking" fit into the current concepts of SA.

There has been an emphasis on SA on comparing the models of experts and novices, noting how the available data in a complex environment can overwhelm the novice's ability to efficiently process those data (Endsley, [25]) and how "experts" in contrast often have very efficient ways to notice and integrate a large amount of data. Interestingly, although this result is in line with the experience in early Artificial Intelligence with building "expert systems," the focus of many SA studies appeared to be on cues in the environment to activate these mental models rather than internal knowledge bases or rulesets that could become the basis for self-models [73].

In the future, it will be interesting for the field of self-awareness to pull from SA some very interesting research that they have been developing on how teams of situationally aware human and robotic agents best work together. Team SA is defined as "the degree to which every team member possesses the SA required for his or her responsibilities" (Endsley [26], p. 39). The success or failure of a team depends on the success or failure of each of its team members. If any one of the team members has poor SA, it can lead to a critical error in performance that can undermine the success of the entire team. By this definition, each team member needs to have a high level of SA on those factors that are relevant for his or her job. It is not sufficient for one member of the team to be aware of critical information if the team member who needs that information is not aware.

Shared situation awareness can be defined as "the degree to which team members possess the same SA on shared SA requirements" (Endsley and Jones [25], p. 47). As implied by this definition, there are information requirements that are relevant to multiple team members. A major part of teamwork involves the area where these SA requirements overlap—the shared SA requirements that exist as a function of the essential interdependency of the team members. In a poorly functioning team, two or more members may have different assessments on these shared SA requirements and thus behave in an uncoordinated or even counter-productive fashion. Yet in a smoothly functioning team, each team member shares a common understanding of what is happening on those SA elements that are common.

2.12   Symbiotic Cognitive Computing

Symbiotic cognitive systems (SCS) [42] are multi-agent systems comprising both human and software agents that collectively perform cognitive tasks such as decision-making better than humans or software agents can by themselves. A driving principle of symbiotic cognitive systems is that humans and intelligent agents each have their respective cognitive strengths and weaknesses. The goal is not to surpass humans at challenging intellectual tasks such as chess or Jeopardy!, but rather to create agents that both support and rely upon humans in accomplishing cognitive tasks. This philosophy traces its lineage back to the vision espoused by Licklider in his essay on Man-Computer Symbiosis [49] and is today experiencing a revival among researchers in academia and industry who are pursuing aspects of the symbiotic cognitive systems research agenda from a variety of perspectives. One realm in which the principles and technologies of SCS are being applied is robotics, exemplified in the work of Rosenthal, Veloso and colleagues at Carnegie Mellon University on the Co-Bot [66, 68]. One also finds aspects of symbiotic cognitive computing in cognitive assistants such as Apple's Siri and IPsoft's Amelia (designed for help desks and related applications), and in the cognitive boardroom being developed by IBM Research [42], in which a multi-agent system interacts with humans via speech and gesture to provide seamless access to information and support for high-stakes decision-making.

One aspect of the challenge of creating SCS is that of developing algorithms (and the agents in which they are embodied) that are at least as competent as humans at the cognitive task for which they are designed. This task is made somewhat easier by focussing efforts on those aspects of cognition for which human biases, irrationality, and other deficiencies are well documented [3, 39, 78], and for which machines seem inherently better suited. A second general class of challenges for symbiotic systems is related to making human–agent interactions as seamless as possible. These include:

- Developing multi-modal forms of interaction that combine speech, gesture, touch, facial expression, and perhaps other manifestations of emotion [75];
- Learning mental models of other agents and humans, including their intent, to form a basis for adapting behavior so as to improve the speed and likelihood of accomplishing a task that the collective is trying to solve [68, 79]; and
- Storing, maintaining, and retrieving mental models of the environment, the task, and the other agents and human participants in the task to provide a shared context that can be used for communication among humans and agents [52, 67].

Kephart [42] discussed correspondences between autonomic computing systems and symbiotic computing systems, including the need for a means by which humans can effectively communicate objectives to the system and the fact that the natural architecture for both is a multi-agent system, and hence, issues of inter-agent communication and interaction are very important. Moreover, self-management in all of its usual forms (self-optimization, self-healing, self-configuration, etc.) is essential for cognitive applications and the cognitive services from which they are built. A key difference is that, in SCS, humans are not just regarded as providers of high-level goals, but are expected to collaborate deeply with symbiotic cognitive systems, interacting with them constantly.

Given the strong overlap between autonomic computing systems and self-aware systems (detailed in Sect. 2.4), there is also a strong relationship between SCS and self-aware computing systems. A three-way comparison among AC, SCS, and self-aware systems is instructive. Like self-aware computing systems, but unlike autonomic computing systems, SCS do not require that agents take action. The reason that some software agents within an SCS may be self-aware without being autonomic is that they are not expected to perform all cognitive tasks by themselves, but instead to work collaboratively with humans. As a result, they may propose actions to humans, who can then use their judgment to decide whether or not to follow the agent's recommendations. Another connection between SCS systems and self-aware computing systems is that, while it is not a strict requirement, SCS are expected to learn models of intent and likely behavior by other participants (including both software agents and humans). In the case of SCS, there is a slight twist—the models may be used not just to manage resources wisely according to fixed goals, but the goal itself (the intent of the human users of the system) may not be revealed fully at the outset, so behavior models may be used to predict future goals and actions—thereby enabling the system to configure itself appropriately in anticipation of what it may be asked to do.

2.13 Auto-tuning

Auto-tuning covers techniques from high-performance computing (HPC), which automate the process of performance tuning for scientific applications (e.g., weather forecasts and genome expression analysis). Various approaches have been developed throughout the past decades [13, 54, 61, 64, 65, 76, 80, 83].

The motivation for auto-tuning in HPC is the problem that the frequency of new hardware increases, but the required time to manually tune high-performance code for this new hardware remains unchanged. Hence, approaches to automate the performance tuning for new hardware are needed.

The common way of performance tuning in HPC relies on source code transformations. Thus, the goal of auto-tuning approaches is to find those source code transformations, which improve performance. A basic prerequisite of most auto-tuning approaches is the existence of a kernel library. Such a library contains kernel (i.e., core) algorithms, which are used by scientific applications. Auto-tuning is applied to those kernel libraries instead of the applications themselves. This adheres to the standard principles in HPC, where manually optimized kernel libraries are commonly used. The application of auto-tuning enhances these libraries with code transformations, which adjust the libraries' algorithms to the given hardware architecture.

In general, there is a distinction between static and dynamic approaches, depending on when decision-making takes place. This is either at compilation time, denoting static auto-tuning, or at run-time, denoting dynamic auto-tuning.

Auto-tuning approaches are closely related to self-adaptive systems (SAS) in that they realize feedback loops. For example, the CADA loop [22] is realized in the following way: (1) Information about the available hardware is *collected*; (2) this information is *analyzed* with respect to its effect on the kernel algorithms; (3) a *decision* selecting code transformations improving (or optimizing) the performance of the kernel algorithms is made; and (4) the code transformations are applied (*act*).

Thus, auto-tuning can be seen as a special kind of SAS, which operates on source code level with a restricted focus on scientific applications (i.e., HPC). Notably, approaches of the SAS community usually realize the feedback loop on higher levels of abstraction. Commonly, the elements of variation are components, features, or classes, whereas auto-tuning works on source code statements. Auto-tuning approaches mainly apply techniques known from compiler optimization like loop unrolling to identify code variants that optimally utilize the underlying hardware (e.g., by not exceeding the number of available registers or available memory).

2.14 Constructive Definition

According to our definition, self-aware systems are complex systems that while in operation might need to access and analyze pieces of information about themselves and about the execution environment. In large part, this information is made available/created and managed during the various phases of development, e.g., design, architectural structure, code structure, execution machine structure, and deployment information. Thus, it is recognized nowadays that developing self-* systems requires some activities that traditionally occur at development time to be moved to run-time [2, 7, 36]. Activities here refer to the usual development process activities extended with execution monitoring activities. Responsibilities for these activities shift from developers to the system itself, the self-part, causing the traditional boundary between development time and run-time to blur. If a system needs to adapt in order to better respond to an increased and unexpected load of service requests, it might decide to change its configuration, e.g., by substituting one of its components by a more efficient one. In practice, this means being able to detect the situation by monitoring and analyzing the execution environment and its own behavior and also to carry on reconfiguration activities at run-time in a correct and time-efficient way.

The discriminating factor for deciding whether an activity has to be performed at development time or at run-time is cost. Cost can be explained in terms of resources needed to take responsibility of the activity and its achievement. Resources can be software and hardware capabilities ultimately resulting in time or memory costs that need to be affordable with respect to the system goal and operational requirements.

Service-oriented and cloud computing paradigms permit reconsidering offline activities in a new perspective making it possible for a self-aware system to rely on heavy loaded system infrastructure for self-* system attributes, thus in practice mitigating the traditional cost-driven dichotomy between compile time and run-time.

This consideration leads us to consider also a constructive definition of self-aware computing systems that stresses the fact that the question is not only whether it is possible to make a system or portions of the system self-aware, but also whether it is economically reasonable/sustainable. This requires to focus on the amount of resources, software and hardware, that may be needed in order to support the self-awareness degrees of a system. The cost factor thus becomes the self-enabling factor that may influence design and architectural choices, and coding and execution choices as well as monitoring and analysis system capabilities, and may ultimately determine whether in the given conditions it is actually possible to develop, and how, a self-aware system. This also impacts the complexity of the techniques used to achieve self-awareness that may be more or less advanced depending on whether they are economically justified and sustainable.

So the extent to which a self-aware computing system is able to learn knowledge about itself and/or its environment and reason and adapt to internal and external changes is heavily dependent on development choices (design, architecture, programming languages, coding techniques), and deployment constraints (deployment infrastructure and resource availability). This requires quantitative reasoning capabilities at the process definition level as suggested in [2]. Depending on the system lifetime, these development choices may also be rediscussed; what could have been too costly at a certain stage of maturity of the system and of the technology may become convenient and affordable at a later stage of maturity. This suggests the architecture of the system to be flexible enough to easily accommodate evolutions of system with respect to its self-aware degrees.

2.15 Summary

The area of self-aware computing systems is still incipient, but promising concerning the construction of systems that are required to learn models on an ongoing basis and use them to reason about aspects related to the purpose for which the systems themselves were built.

Self-aware computing systems pose new opportunities and challenges for the research and engineering communities, some of which are related to prior experience in different disciplines.

This chapter has reviewed different concepts and research areas strongly related to self-aware computing. Different sections have explored topics such as AI, autonomic computing, self-organizing systems, or cognitive computing, among others, as well as their relation to self-aware computing systems and potential opportunities for cross-pollination. Moreover, the landscape outlined in this chapter provided the basis for a constructive definition of self-aware computing system, as well as for some considerations concerning the different factors that influence the feasibility and the capabilities of a self-aware computing system. These considerations serve as a starting point to investigate important questions related to the conditions under which it is possible to actually develop a self-aware computing system, and in what way.

Acknowledgements The authors thank Lukas Esterle, Kurt Geihs, Philippe Lalanda, Peter Lewis, and Andrea Zisman for the useful feedback provided during the elaboration of this chapter.

References

1. *31st International Conference on Software Engineering, ICSE 2009.* IEEE, 2009.
2. Jesper Andersson, Luciano Baresi, Nelly Bencomo, Rogério de Lemos, Alessandra Gorla, Paola Inverardi, and Thomas Vogel. Software engineering processes for self-adaptive systems. In *Software Engineering for Self-Adaptive Systems II - International Seminar, Dagstuhl Castle, Germany, October 24-29, 2010 Revised Selected and Invited Papers*, pages 51–75, 2010.
3. Dan Ariely. *Predictably irrational the hidden forces that shape our decisions.* Harper Collins, New York, 2010.
4. W. Ross Ashby. Principles of the self-organizing system. In *Principles of SelfOrganization: Transactions of the University of Illinois Symposium.*
5. M. Autili, P. Inverardi, and M. Tivoli. Automated synthesis of service choreographies. *Software, IEEE*, 32(1):50–57, Jan 2015.
6. S. Banbury and S. Tremblay. *A cognitive approach to situation awareness: Theory and application.* Aldershot, UK: Ashgate Publishing, 2004.
7. Luciano Baresi and Carlo Ghezzi. The disappearing boundary between development-time and run-time. In *Proceedings of the Workshop on Future of Software Engineering Research, FoSER 2010, at the 18th ACM SIGSOFT International Symposium on Foundations of Software Engineering, 2010*, pages 17–22, 2010.
8. K.L. Bellman and C. Landauer. A web of reflection processes may help to de-conflict and integrate simultaneous self-optimization. In *SAOS 2014: The 2nd International Workshop on Self-optimisation in Organic and Autonomic Computing Systems.*
9. K.L. Bellman and C. Landauer. Towards an integration science. *Journal of Mathematical Analysis and Applications*, 249(1):3–31, 2000.
10. K.L. Bellman, C. Landauer, and P.R. Nelson. Developing mechanisms for determining "good enough" in sort systems. In *Second IEEE Workshop on Self-Organizing Real Time Systems, 2011.*
11. K.L. Bellman, C. Landauer, and P.R. Nelson. chapter System Engineering for Organic Computing: The Challenge of Shared Design and Control between OC Systems and their Human Engineers, pages 25–80. Understanding Complex Systems Series. Springer, 2008.
12. Nelly Bencomo, Amel Bennaceur, Paul Grace, Gordon S. Blair, and Valérie Issarny. The role of models@run.time in supporting on-the-fly interoperability. *Computing*, 95(3):167–190, 2013.
13. Jeff Bilmes, Krste Asanovicy, Chee-Whye Chinz, and Jim Demmel. Optimizing matrix multiply using PHiPAC: a portable, high-performance, ANSI C coding methodology. In *Proceedings of the 11th International Conference on Super Computing*, pages 340–347. ACM, 1997.
14. G. Blair, N. Bencomo, and R.B. France. Models@ run.time. *Computer*, 42(10):22–27, Oct 2009.
15. Rodney A. Brooks. *Cambrian Intelligence: The Early History of the New AI.* MIT Press, Cambridge, MA, USA, 1999.

16. Yuriy Brun, Giovanna Di Marzo Serugendo, Cristina Gacek, Holger Giese, Holger Kienle, Marin Litoiu, Hausi Müller, Mauro Pezzè, and Mary Shaw. Engineering Self-Adaptive Systems through Feedback Loops. In *Software Engineering for Self-Adaptive Systems*, 2009.

17. Radu Calinescu, Lars Grunske, Marta Z. Kwiatkowska, Raffaela Mirandola, and Giordano Tamburrelli. Dynamic qos management and optimization in service-based systems. *IEEE Trans. Software Eng.*, 37(3):387–409, 2011.

18. Betty H.C. Cheng et al. Software Engineering for Self-Adaptive Systems: A Research Roadmap. In *Software Engineering for Self-Adaptive Systems*. Springer, 2009.

19. Shang-Wen Cheng, VaheV. Poladian, David Garlan, and Bradley Schmerl. Improving architecture-based self-adaptation through resource prediction. In *Software Engineering for Self-Adaptive Systems*. Springer, 2009.

20. Michel Cotsaftis. *From System Complexity to Emergent Properties*, chapter What Makes a System Complex? - An Approach to Self Organization and Emergence, pages 49–99. Springer, 2009.

21. Rogério de Lemos et al. Software Engineering for Self-Adaptive Systems: A second Research Roadmap. In *Software Engineering for Self-Adaptive Systems II*. Springer, 2013.

22. Simon Dobson, Spyros Denazis, Antonio Fernández, Dominique Gaïti, Erol Gelenbe, Fabio Massacci, Paddy Nixon, Fabrice Saffre, Nikita Schmidt, and Franco Zambonelli. A survey of autonomic communications. *ACM Transactions on Autonomous and Adaptive Systems*, 1(2):223–259, 2006.

23. Vidulich M. Vogel E. Dominguez, C. and G. McMillan. *Situation awareness: Papers and annotated bibliography*. Armstrong Laboratory, Human System Center, ref. AL/CF-TR-1994-0085, 1994.

24. M.R. Endsley. Toward a theory of situation awareness in dynamic systems. *Human Factors*, 37(1):32–64, 1995.

25. M.R. Endsley. *The role of situation awareness in naturalistic decision making*. 1997.

26. M.R. Endsley. *Situation awareness: Progress and directions*. 2004.

27. Ilenia Epifani, Carlo Ghezzi, Raffaela Mirandola, and Giordano Tamburrelli. Model evolution by run-time parameter adaptation. In *31st International Conference on Software Engineering, ICSE 2009* [1], pages 111–121.

28. European Commission. Digital Agenda for Europe - Future Internet Research and Experimentation (FIRE) initiative, 2015.

29. M.L. Fracker. Measures of situation awareness: Review and future directions (report no. al-tr-1991-0128), 1991b. Wright-Patterson Air Force Base, OH: Armstrong Laboratories.

30. Robert B. France and Bernhard Rumpe. Model-driven development of complex software: A research roadmap. In *International Conference on Software Engineering, ISCE 2007, Workshop on the Future of Software Engineering, FOSE 2007, May 23-25, 2007, Minneapolis, MN, USA*, pages 37–54, 2007.

31. Cristina Gacek, Holger Giese, and Ethan Hadar. Friends or Foes? – A Conceptual Analysis of Self-Adaptation and IT Change Management. In *Proc. of the ICSE Workshop on Software Engineering for Adaptive and Self-Managing Systems (SEAMS 2008)*, pages 121–128. ACM, May 2008.

32. David Garlan, Shang-Wen Cheng, An-Cheng Huang, Bradley R. Schmerl, and Peter Steenkiste. Rainbow: Architecture-based self-adaptation with reusable infrastructure. *IEEE Computer*, 37(10):46–54, 2004.

33. Chang-chieh Hang and P. Parks. Comparative studies of model reference adaptive control systems. *IEEE Transactions on Automatic Control*, 18(5):419–428, October 1973.

34. Julia Hielscher, Raman Kazhamiakin, Andreas Metzger, and Marco Pistore. A framework for proactive self-adaptation of service-based applications based on online testing. In *Towards a Service-Based Internet*. Springer, 2008.

35. Paul Horn. Autonomic Computing: IBM's Perspective on the State of Information Technology. Technical report, 2001.

36. Paola Inverardi and Massimo Tivoli. The future of software: Adaptation and dependability. In *Software Engineering, International Summer Schools, ISSSE 2006-2008, Salerno, Italy, Revised Tutorial Lectures*, pages 1–31, 2008.

37. Rolf Isermann, Karl-Heinz Lachmann, and Drago Matko. *Adaptive Control Systems*. Prentice Hall International series in systems and control engineering. Prentice Hall, New York, 1992. ISBN 0-13-005414-3.
38. Valerie Issarny, Nikolaos Georgantas, Sara Hachem, Apostolos Zarras, Panos Vassiliadist, Marco Autili, MarcoAurlio Gerosa, and AmiraBen Hamida. Service-oriented middleware for the future internet: state of the art and research directions. *Journal of Internet Services and Applications*, 2(1):23–45, 2011.
39. Daniel Kahneman. *Thinking, fast and slow*. Farrar, Straus and Giroux, New York, 2011.
40. Gorazd Karer and Igor Skrjanc, 2012.
41. Jeffrey O. Kephart and David M. Chess. The vision of autonomic computing. *Computer*, 36(1):41–50, 2003.
42. Jeffrey O. Kephart and Jonathan Lenchner. A symbiotic cognitive computing perspective on autonomic computing. In *2015 IEEE International Conference on Autonomic Computing*, pages 109–114. IEEE Computer Society, 2015.
43. Moon B Klein, G. and R.R. Hoffman. Making sense of sensemaking 1: Alternative perspectives. *IEEE Intelligent Systems*, 21(4):70–73, 2006.
44. Jeff Kramer and Jeff Magee. Self-Managed Systems: an Architectural Challenge. In *FOSE '07: 2007 Future of Software Engineering*, 2007.
45. C. Landauer. Infrastructure for studying infrastructure. In *ESOS 2013: Workshop on Embedded Self-Organizing Systems*.
46. C. Landauer and K.L. Bellman. Generic programming, partial evaluation, and a new programming paradigm.
47. C. Landauer and K.L. Bellman. Self-modeling systems.
48. Wenchao Li, Dorsa Sadigh, S.Shankar Sastry, and SanjitA. Seshia. Synthesis for human-in-the-loop control systems. In *Tools and Algorithms for the Construction and Analysis of Systems*. Springer, 2014.
49. J. C. R. Licklider. Man-machine symbiosis. *IRE Transactions on Human Factors in Electronics*, HFE-1:4–11, March 1960.
50. Mieczyslaw Kokar M. and M. R. Endsley. Situation awareness and cognitive modeling. *IEEE Intelligent Systems*, 27(3):91–96, 2012.
51. P. Maes and D. Nardi (eds.). *Meta-Level Architectures and Reflection*. 1986.
52. Matthew Marge and Alexander I. Rudnicky. Towards evaluating recovery strategies for situated grounding problems in human-robot dialogue. In *IEEE International Symposium on Robot and Human Interactive Communication, IEEE RO-MAN 2013*, pages 340–341. IEEE, 2013.
53. Peter M. Mell and Timothy Grance. Sp 800-145. the nist definition of cloud computing. Technical report, Gaithersburg, MD, United States, 2011.
54. A. Morajko, P. Caymes-Scutari, T. Margalef, and E. Luque. MATE: Monitoring, analysis and tuning environment for parallel/distributed applications. *Concurrency and Computation: Practice and Experience*, 19(11):1517–1531, 2007.
55. Gabriel A. Moreno, Javier Cámara, David Garlan, and Bradley R. Schmerl. Proactive self-adaptation under uncertainty: a probabilistic model checking approach. In *Proceedings of the 2015 10th Joint Meeting on Foundations of Software Engineering, ESEC/FSE 2015*, pages 1–12, 2015.
56. Brice Morin, Olivier Barais, Grégory Nain, and Jean-Marc Jézéquel. Taming dynamically adaptive systems using models and aspects. In *31st International Conference on Software Engineering, ICSE 2009*[1], pages 122–132.
57. Brice Morin, Franck Fleurey, Nelly Bencomo, Jean-Marc Jézéquel, Arnor Solberg, Vegard Dehlen, and Gordon S. Blair. An aspect-oriented and model-driven approach for managing dynamic variability. In *Model Driven Engineering Languages and Systems, 11th International Conference, MoDELS 2008*, pages 782–796, 2008.
58. Christian Müller-Schloer, Hartmut Schmeck, and Theo Ungerer, editors. *Organic Computing - A Paradigm Shift for Complex Systems*. Springer, 2011.
59. B.E. Ulicny M.M. Kokar and J.J. Moskal. *Ontological structures for higher levels of distributed fusion*. 2012.

60. Hyacinth S. Nwana. Software agents: an overview. *Knowledge Eng. Review*, 11(3):205–244, 1996.
61. Jakob Ostergaard. Discrete optimization of the sparse QR factorization. http://unthought.net/OptimQR/OptimQR/report.html, Oct 1998.
62. Mike P. Papazoglou, Paolo Traverso, Schahram Dustdar, and Frank Leymann. Service-oriented computing: State of the art and research challenges. *IEEE Computer*, 40(11), 2007.
63. Manish Parashar and Salim Hariri. Autonomic computing: An overview. In *Unconventional Programming Paradigms*. Springer, 2005.
64. Markus Püschel, José M. F. Moura, Jeremy Johnson, David Padua, Manuela Veloso, Bryan Singer, Jianxin Xiong, Franz Franchetti, Aca Gacic, Yevgen Voronenko, Kang Chen, Robert W. Johnson, and Nicholas Rizzolo. SPIRAL: Code generation for DSP transforms. *Proceedings of the IEEE, special issue on "Program Generation, Optimization, and Adaptation"*, 93(2):232–275, 2005.
65. R. Ribler, J. Vetter, H. Simitci, Huseyin Simitci, and Daniel A. Reed. Autopilot: Adaptive control of distributed applications. In *Proceedings of the 7th IEEE Symposium on High-Performance Distributed Computing*, pages 172–179, 1998.
66. Stephanie Rosenthal, Joydeep Biswas, and Manuela M. Veloso. An effective personal mobile robot agent through symbiotic human-robot interaction. In Wiebe van der Hoek, Gal A. Kaminka, Yves Lespérance, Michael Luck, and Sandip Sen, editors, *9th International Conference on Autonomous Agents and Multiagent Systems (AAMAS 2010)*, pages 915–922. IFAA-MAS, 2010.
67. Stephanie Rosenthal, Sarjoun Skaff, Manuela M. Veloso, Dan Bohus, and Eric Horvitz. Execution memory for grounding and coordination. In Hideaki Kuzuoka, Vanessa Evers, Michita Imai, and Jodi Forlizzi, editors, *ACM/IEEE International Conference on Human-Robot Interaction, HRI 2013*, pages 213–214. IEEE/ACM, 2013.
68. Stephanie Rosenthal, Manuela M. Veloso, and Anind K. Dey. Task behavior and interaction planning for a mobile service robot that occasionally requires help. In *Automated Action Planning for Autonomous Mobile Robots, Papers from the 2011 AAAI Workshop*, volume WS-11-09 of *AAAI Workshops*. AAAI, 2011.
69. Stuart J. Russell and Peter Norvig. *Artificial Intelligence - A Modern Approach (3. internat. ed.)*. Pearson Education, 2010.
70. Mazeiar Salehie and Ladan Tahvildari. Self-adaptive software: Landscape and research challenges. *ACM Trans. Auton. Adapt. Syst.*, 4(2):1–42, 2009.
71. Peter Sawyer, Nelly Bencomo, Jon Whittle, Emmanuel Letier, and Anthony Finkelstein. Requirements-aware systems: A research agenda for RE for self-adaptive systems. In *RE 2010, 18th IEEE International Requirements Engineering Conference*, pages 95–103, 2010.
72. Dale E. Seborg, Duncan A. Mellichamp, Thomas F. Edgar, and Francis J. Doyle, 2011.
73. MacMillan J. Entin E.E. Serfaty, D. and E.B. Entin. *The decision-making expertise of battle commanders*. 1997.
74. Mary Shaw. Beyond objects: A software design paradigm based on process control. *ACM SIGSOFT Software Engineering Notes*, 20(1):27–38, 1995.
75. Stefanie Tellex, Pratiksha Thaker, Joshua Mason Joseph, and Nicholas Roy. Learning perceptually grounded word meanings from unaligned parallel data. *Machine Learning*, 94(2):151–167, 2014.
76. A. Tiwari and J.K. Hollingsworth. Online adaptive code generation and tuning. In *Proceedings of 2011 International Symposium on Parallel Distributed Processing (IPDPS)*, pages 879–892, 2011.
77. Romina Torres, Nelly Bencomo, and Hernán Astudillo. Market-awareness in service-based systems. In *Sixth IEEE International Conference on Self-Adaptive and Self-Organizing Systems Workshops, SASOW 2012*, pages 169–174, 2012.
78. Amos Tversky and Daniel Kahneman. Judgment under Uncertainty: Heuristics and Biases. *Science*, 185(4157):1124–1131, September 1974.
79. Laura Pfeifer Vardoulakis, Lazlo Ring, Barbara Barry, Candace L. Sidner, and Timothy W. Bickmore. Designing relational agents as long term social companions for older adults. In

Intelligent Virtual Agents - 12th International Conference, IVA 2012, volume 7502 of *LNCS*, pages 289–302. Springer, 2012.

80. Michael J. Voss and Rudolf Eigemann. High-level adaptive program optimization with adapt. In *Proceedings of the eighth ACM SIGPLAN symposium on principles and practices of parallel programming*, PPoPP '01, pages 93–102. ACM, 2001.

81. Mark Weiser. The computer for the 21st century. *Scientific American*, 265(3):94–104, September 1991.

82. Kristopher Welsh, Pete Sawyer, and Nelly Bencomo. Towards requirements aware systems: Run-time resolution of design-time assumptions. In *26th IEEE/ACM International Conference on Automated Software Engineering (ASE 2011)*, pages 560–563, 2011.

83. R. Clinton Whaley, Antoine Petitet, and Jack Dongarra. Automated empirical optimizations of software and the ATLAS project. *Parallel Computing*, 27(1–2):3–35, 2001.

84. Tom Wolf and Tom Holvoet. *Engineering Self-Organising Systems: Methodologies and Applications*, chapter Emergence Versus Self-Organisation: Different Concepts but Promising When Combined, pages 1–15. Springer, 2005.

85. Michael Wooldridge and Nicholas R. Jennings. Intelligent agents: theory and practice. *Knowledge Eng. Review*, 10(2):115–152, 1995.

86. Jun Xu, Pinyao Guo, Mingyi Zhao, Robert F. Erbacher, Minghui Zhu, and Peng Liu. Comparing different moving target defense techniques. In *Proceedings of the First ACM Workshop on Moving Target Defense*, MTD '14, pages 97–107. ACM, 2014.

87. Eric Yuan, Naeem Esfahani, and Sam Malek. Automated mining of software component interactions for self-adaptation. In *Proceedings of the 9th International Symposium on Software Engineering for Adaptive and Self-Managing Systems*, SEAMS 2014, pages 27–36. ACM.

Chapter 3
Towards a Framework for the Levels and Aspects of Self-aware Computing Systems

Peter Lewis, Kirstie L. Bellman, Christopher Landauer, Lukas Esterle, Kyrre Glette, Ada Diaconescu and Holger Giese

Abstract Increased self-awareness in computing systems can be beneficial in several respects, including a greater capacity to adapt, to build potential for future adaptation in unknown environments, and to explain their behaviour to humans and other systems. When attempting to endow computing systems with a form of self-awareness, it is important to have a clear understanding of what that form looks like. This chapter therefore first introduces the general concept of self-awareness and its various facets. Second, we provide an overview of the range of efforts to interpret the concept of self-awareness in computing. Third, we provide a structured conceptual

P. Lewis (✉)
Aston Lab for Intelligent Collectives Engineering (ALICE),
Aston University, Birmingham, UK
e-mail: p.lewis@aston.ac.uk

K.L. Bellman · C. Landauer
Aerospace Integration Science Center,
The Aerospace Corporation, Los Angeles, CA, USA
e-mail: Kirstie.L.Bellman@aero.org

C. Landauer
e-mail: topcycal@gmail.com

L. Esterle
Vienna University of Technology, Vienna, Austria
e-mail: lukas.esterle@tuwien.ac.at

K. Glette
University of Oslo, Oslo, Norway
e-mail: kyrrehg@ifi.uio.no

A. Diaconescu
Equipe S3, Departement INFRES, Telécom ParisTech,
46 rue Barrault, 75013 Paris, France
e-mail: ada.diaconescu@telecom-paristech.fr

H. Giese
Hasso Plattner Institute for Software Systems Engineering
at the University of Potsdam, Prof.-Dr.-Helmert-Str. 2-3, 14482 Potsdam, Germany
e-mail: holger.giese@hpi.de

© Springer International Publishing AG 2017
S. Kounev et al. (eds.), *Self-Aware Computing Systems*,
DOI 10.1007/978-3-319-47474-8_3

framework that organizes this variety of different forms of self-awareness. This provides a broad set of concepts and a language that can be used to describe and reason about self-aware computing systems.

3.1 Introduction

In this book, we are aiming to implement the self-awareness capabilities, that is to say, capabilities resembling and inspired by human self-awareness, in computing systems. This chapter, and indeed this book as a whole, is based on the idea that increased self-awareness in computing systems *can* be beneficial in several respects. These benefits are centred around systems' increased capacity to adapt, build potential for future adaptation in unknown environments, and explain their behaviour. Such capacity is derived from their ability to learn about themselves, including aspects such as their state, their goals and progress towards them, their behaviour and interactions with other systems, their environment, their perspective, and their evolution over time.

But increased self-awareness will also come at a cost, whether it be in terms of more processing power, increased storage, or the need for further data gathering and communication. In designing self-aware systems, *we* must have the concepts and tools readily available to be able to reason about the benefits and costs increased self-awareness will bring in its various forms. And in realising self-aware computing systems, *the systems themselves* will also require concepts and tools to enable them to perform meta-reasoning about the benefits and costs of their own self-awareness.

The ability of self-aware computing systems to reflect on their their own self-awareness properties and behaviour, termed *meta-self-awareness*, leads to the ability to model and reason about changing trade-offs during the system's lifetime. Meta-self-awareness enables advanced adaptation and explanatory behaviour at multiple levels within a system, including why it has spent resources on self-awareness related activities.

An important distinction to make from the outset is that in the process of doing this, we are not aiming to explain human self-awareness or consciousness. There are those (e.g., [57]) who build intelligent systems with the primary aim of developing a better understanding of human minds and human self-awareness. Instead, we aim to learn and gain inspiration from self-awareness in order to build better computational systems, following the tradition of a range of efforts in computer science that have sought inspiration elsewhere, such as bio-inspired computing, socially inspired computing, and economics-inspired computing. In order to be clear, and in line with a previous work [34], we refer to the forms of self-awareness implemented in a computing system as *computational self-awareness*.

As highlighted by many (e.g., as reviewed Lewis et al. [35]), self-awareness is *not* a binary property; it makes little sense to characterize a system (biological or computational) as either being self-aware or not. Indeed, the term self-awareness encompasses a broad range of related processes and capabilities, which include various types of explicit self-knowledge, an understanding of the subjectivity and

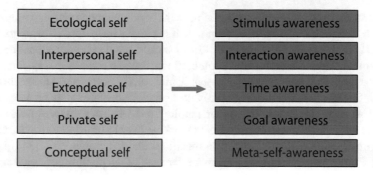

Fig. 3.1 Lewis et al.'s [34] levels of computational self-awareness (*right*) describe various different aspects of self-knowledge and are derived from those by Neisser [44] (*left*). These are discussed in Sects. 3.2.1.4 and 3.2.2.2

context of that knowledge, and processes for its acquisition. Some of these aspects concern situated knowledge acquisition processes (e.g., subjectively context-aware learning, reasoning, and acting), while others are related to the architecture of these learning processes, and how they reflect on and are influenced by each other. In much of the self-awareness literature, particularly in psychology (e.g., [42]), these varieties of self-awareness are characterized as *levels of self-awareness*. Recent work on self-aware computing [34] has borrowed from this, developing the notion of levels of computational self-awareness. Lewis et al.'s levels of computational self-awareness are illustrated in Fig. 3.1.

Our aims in this chapter are as follows. First, we review these treatments of self-awareness and computational self-awareness in the existing literature. Second, we extend initial characterisations of different levels and aspects of computational self-awareness, in order to provide a broad set of concepts and language that can be used to describe and reason about self-aware computing systems. Third, we organize these concepts into a coherent framework that provides a set of related considerations for designers of computing systems who are interested in incorporating self-awareness concepts into their systems. Fourth and finally, we position the definition of self-aware computing systems proposed in Chap. 1 in the context of existing work in self-aware computing. The framework developed in this chapter is then explored in a variety of contexts, throughout the rest of the book.

3.1.1   Why Consider Types of Self-awareness in Computing Systems?

As described above, in this chapter, our aim is to characterize various levels of self-awareness as they might pertain to current and future computing systems. However, first we motivate the need to do this.

As a starting point, since we are claiming that endowing computing systems with increased self-awareness can have benefits, it is clearly important to begin to at least sketch, if not define, what we mean by this. It should stand as obvious that one should not begin implementing a form of computational self-awareness in a system, unless one has a clear understanding of what that form looks like. Based on the multifarious nature of self-awareness briefly discussed above, and elaborated on later in this chapter, we argue that an explicit understanding of the sort of self-awareness targeted is necessary. Indeed, as outlined in recent work on how to translate self-awareness to the engineering domain and apply it in specific scenarios, Lewis et al. [34] highlight the importance of beginning with an understanding of the plethora of different forms self-awareness may take, and the wide range of methods and approaches that can be used to implement self-awareness to different extents, as needed. Chen et al.'s handbook [12] for engineering self-aware computing systems in particular describes a structured process for determining and evaluating the inclusion (or not) of various levels of self-awareness in a system's architecture, and approaches to realising them.

Pragmatically, this is important since as part of the engineering design process, one would want to understand the role and benefits of different levels and aspects of self-awareness, along with different approaches and mechanisms for realising them, before implementing. This supports the ability to choose the most effective methods and the desired level of self-awareness for a given application, its context, and requirements.

We expect that in working with self-aware computing systems, one will often be in situations where there are a number of agents or components within the system that possess self-awareness capabilities, and potentially of different types. Understanding different approaches and levels of self-awareness, and how they interact, will help developers to institute the appropriate communication mechanisms, supporting interfaces and desirable policies among these different entities, for a given purpose. By considering forms of computational self-awareness at an abstract level, our aim is that generic interfaces and communication mechanisms between levels of self-awareness may be specified. If this is achieved, then self-awareness capabilities may be able to be provided in reusable "context-free" ways, to enable the development and evolution of arbitrarily complex architectures appropriate to varying applications.

In this chapter, we organize this plethora of different approaches into a structured conceptual framework, based around *levels of self-awareness*. In doing so, we aim to eventually create a foundation for strategies that consider forms of self-awareness included and excluded by our definition in Chap. 1. This will support the engineering process by enabling the automation of design decisions relating to self-awareness, thereby not only supporting the efforts of engineers, but also of systems themselves, that reason about their own self-awareness.

Our aim is therefore to make progress towards understanding how different application and environmental requirements map to the need to implement different levels of self-awareness (or not), in different ways. Such an understanding should incorporate explicit knowledge of the trade-offs implicit in implementing higher levels of self-awareness including meta-self-awareness. This type of self-knowledge, and techniques by which a system can acquire it itself, will then enable strategies by which transitions between levels of self-awareness in evolving systems may occur.

We would also like to make clear to the reader that in laying out the conceptual framework that we do in this chapter, we are not claiming to provide a definitive characterisation; indeed, we believe it cannot be so, and this framework is one more step along the road to mapping out important considerations in self-aware computing. Therefore, we aim at developing a conceptualisation of relevant and important aspects, and in doing so provide a tool by which engineers and systems may structure their thoughts, considerations, arguments, and decisions. We target the provision of a range of concepts, with an eye to helping the researchers adopt the notions most suitable to their needs and bring out the issues they need to consider as they pertain to self-awareness concerns. As suggested above, we fully expect many systems to ignore some of the aspects presented here, but to do so based on a sound understanding that the costs outweigh the potential benefit in that case. To interpret the framework as a comprehensive list of requirements would be incorrect. Instead, engineers may use the concepts presented to orient themselves, and to ask questions about what the benefits of different kinds of self-awareness would be, and what the costs are of implementing them.

3.1.2 Summary of This Chapter

In summary, this chapter:

- Introduces and briefly discusses the general concept of self-awareness and its various aspects, thereby providing context for the explorations in the rest of the book.
- Briefly surveys the state of the art in interpreting the concept of self-awareness in computing, putting this book in its wider context.
- Discusses the similarities and differences in the computational self-awareness approaches taken so far, with a particular focus on the scope of the approach, with respect to notions of self-awareness.
- Presents a conceptual framework for describing and comparing various levels and aspects of self-awareness, which may be desirable or present in computing systems, including their potential benefits and costs.

3.2 Fundamentals, Inspiration, and Interpretations in Computing

In this book, we are interested in taking inspiration from self-awareness across natural systems, in order to design the future computing systems that are better able to learn, reason, and ultimately adapt and explain themselves. Some of the mechanisms used to achieve the self-awareness in computing systems will also be inspired by naturally occurring ones; others will not. We expect the benefits of self-awareness in computing systems will be most apparent when systems inhabit a world characterized by unfolding situations, particularly when changes are unforeseen at design time. In this section, we first ask the fundamental question: *what is self-awareness?* In other words, what inspiration can we gain, by looking at self-awareness in biological and social systems? Second, we expand on Chap. 2, describing the efforts in computer science and engineering that have directly and explicitly attempted to translate the concepts from self-awareness in natural systems to the computing domain.

3.2.1 What Is Self-awareness?

Self-awareness is a concept long studied in philosophy, and personal and social psychology. One recent example is a work by Morin [42], which defines self-awareness as *"the capacity to become the object of one's own attention."* Many modern theories of human self-awareness stem from work of psychologists since the 1960s, and trace their roots back to notions proposed at the closing of the nineteenth century. Smith [6] and Tawney [58] wrote on the self, but perhaps the most influential was James's [27] distinction between the *me self* and the *I self*. James's *me self* describes the parts of a person that are objects within the world. By contrast, the *I self* is to James not the objects experienced, but the *experiencer*. The *me self* is now often referred to in psychology literature as the *explicit* or *objective* self, or as the *self-as-object*. Conversely, the *implicit* or *subjective* self, sometimes also referred to as the *self-as-subject*, is the self which is the subject of experiences. While we will present a more comprehensive review of work that explores self-awareness in a computational context later in this section, it is helpful to highlight a few links here as motivation, as we introduce the foundational concepts. For example, as argued by some who have considered computational forms of self-awareness (e.g., Lewis et al. [34]), both self-as-subject and self-as-object are important concepts to include in a consideration of how computing systems may be made more self-aware.

3.2.1.1 Reflective Self-awareness

We have found that many researchers who are unfamiliar with the notion of self-awareness find that the *explicit* self, or self-as-object lends itself to a reasonably intuitive interpretation in a computational setting. This form of self-awareness is concerned with things that "belong" to the system itself, objects that comprise the *me self*. These can be learnt about and modeled, becoming concepts in the system's knowledge. This process is often referred to as *reflection*, and when language is used as the modeling tool, reflection can also be referred to as *self-reference* [45]. The aspects of the self in explicit reflective self-awareness are things that can therefore be recognized, monitored, modeled, and reasoned about, including in relation to other objects in the world.

In addition to self-as-object, we may also consider an individual that is aware of its own thinking and experiencing of the world, i.e., its *self-as-subject*. This is also a form of reflection, in which a system has the capability to monitor and conceptualize its own (mental) processes. For example, I may be aware of how much I have been thinking about my parents recently, or in a computational setting, a system may be aware of the algorithm being used to perform a particular interaction with the world. In this way, aspects such as the algorithm's efficiency, memory usage, or time-to-completion can be modeled, and the algorithm be replaced with an alternative version, if required.

This form of self-awareness is powerful, since it permits recursion: the processes of which the system is aware may be its own self-awareness processes. This is the form of self-awareness discussed in much of the literature on meta-reasoning or meta-cognition, which overlap significantly with, and rely on the notion of meta-self-awareness introduced in this chapter.

3.2.1.2   Pre-reflective Self-awareness

The notion of self-as-subject also draws attention to the idea that a system making observations and taking actions in its environment can be thought of as the subject of those experiences and that, despite any similarity to other systems, those experiences are unique to that system. Observations (through sensors, for example) are necessarily from that system's own point of view, and as such are not only influenced, but determined by factors such as their sensing apparatus, their situation within the world, and their own state. This explicit acknowledgement of the perspective from which (self-)knowledge exists is a core theme running through self-awareness literature, highlighted for example by Metzinger [39], and by Newen and Vogeley [46], and acknowledges a *pre-reflective* component in self-awareness.

The assumption that subjectivity is associated with a system's experience of its world underlies the elicitation of reflections of both self-as-subject and self-as-object. We might call this subjectively known self the *self-as-experienced*. In practical terms, this provides one of the key differences between context-aware systems (e.g., [10, 15]) and self-aware systems. The former typically assumes a ground-truth-based environmental context, which holds as true for all entities. Systems can learn more or less complete and accurate models of the context, which are then used to inform things such as actions. In a self-aware system, by contrast, it is explicitly acknowledged that systems will have different experiences of a shared environment (which includes themselves), since they observe things from different perspectives, using different apparatus.

This form of self-awareness is not reflection but is *pre-reflective*. It underlies an individual's ability to develop a reflective self-awareness, in either self-as-object or self-as-subject form. Indeed, the presence of this implicit subjectivity does not require that any reflection takes place afterwards: self-awareness may simply stop at this *pre-reflective* stage.

3.2.1.3 Notions of Self and Collectivity

While self-awareness is most commonly and perhaps most intuitively thought of as a property of a single "mind", self-awareness can also be a property of a collective system. What, in any case, is the self that possesses the self-awareness?

In recent years, we have come to develop an understanding of the role of collectivity and emergence in complex systems. Rather than require the existence of a CPU-like entity within the brain, interactions between many distributed components can give rise to a range of complex mind-like entities, which have no single central physical presence. Mitchell [41] provides some excellent examples of apparent self-awareness in collective systems, highlighting the absence of a single controlling mind-like thing in each case. In addition to the human brain, she explores the human immune system and ant colonies, where self-awareness appears at the level of the collective, even though this property may not be present at the level of the individual components.

Mitchell describes this form of *collective self-awareness* as one in which information about the global state of the system is distributed throughout the components, and builds up statistically, in a bottom-up manner, through interactions. Despite its distributed nature, this information feeds back to enable the control of the system's lower level components. The right information ends up where it needs to be, and the system achieves a form of parallelized self-awareness, implemented across decentralized hardware. Furthermore, when viewed from the outside, the entire system appears to have a sense of its own state that is both "coherent and useful" [41].

When we talk of self-aware computing systems, we may therefore be referring to several different types of self. Firstly, it should by now be clear that self-awareness may be a property of an autonomous agent, which is capable of obtaining and representing knowledge concerning itself and its experiences. Indeed, much of the literature on autonomous and intelligent agents is concerned with techniques for agent learning, knowledge acquisition and representation, and architectures to support these capabilities. Secondly, according to this notion of collective self-awareness, self-awareness may be present at the level of a collective system. The boundary of a self-aware entity, indeed the "self", is therefore not limited to encapsulating a single agent with a central knowledge-gathering and decision-making process.

3.2.1.4 Notions of Levels of Self-awareness

In Sect. 3.2.1, we established a distinction in *levels of self-awareness* between pre-reflective and reflective self-awarenesses, and within reflective self-awareness, between reflections on the self-as-subject and self-as-object. Morin [42] dives further into a stratified explanation of self-awareness, reviewing various sets of more fine-grained levels of self-awareness in the psychology literature.

Of these, Neisser's [44] have received the most attention to date in computational treatments of self-awareness. His five levels range from basic awareness of environmental stimuli through awareness of interactions and time, up to awareness of one's own thoughts and one's own self as a concept. Unusually, among the sets of levels presented in psychology, Neisser's model also includes "lower-level" aspects of implicit self-awareness.

Rochat takes a developmental angle on the question of levels of self-awareness, asking how self-awareness competences develop in human children. His experiments take inspiration from and extend the well-known classical "test" for self-awareness, the *mirror test* [19]. While the mirror test is flawed as a method for establishing the presence of some supposed binary notion of self-awareness [21],[1] Rochat makes good use of observations of the behaviour of children in front of a mirror, to draw more general conclusions.

Newen and Vogeley [46] argue that sets of levels such as those discussed so far, while helpful, are based upon a more fundamental set of self-awareness forms. They draw attention to different levels of complexity associated with human self-awareness or self-consciousness, derived from developmental and linguistic psychology. They argue that there are at least five of these levels, describing increasingly complex forms of first-person representations, from nonconceptual representations, through conceptual, sentential, meta, and iterative meta-representations.

While there are important differences in both emphasis and content in different sets of self-awareness levels, there are also key themes. Acknowledging this, Morin [42] attempts an integration of these and other sets of levels, into broad themes reflective of the overarching levels presented earlier. Morin labels these *consciousness, self-awareness* and *meta-self-awareness*.

3.2.1.5 Agency, Ownership and Models of a Minimal Self

It is hopefully clear by now that when considering the self-awareness properties of an individual, rather than thinking of self-awareness as a binary property that can be present or not, there is a wide range of notions to consider. It is then reasonable to ask what is the minimal requirement for self-awareness?

Examples of such explorations include Gallagher's [18] *minimal self* and Dennetts *narrative self*. These highlight that even in systems without agency, we can begin to consider the self-awareness question.

In practice, for the design of self-aware computing systems, either strong single-entity-based or emergent approaches to providing a unity and consistency of self

---

[1]As discussed earlier, the binary notion of self-awareness is in any case a mischaracterisation. Further, Haikonen [21] showed that very little sophistication can enable a computational system to "pass the test".

could be beneficial, though we believe that at this early stage in research into self-aware computing, it is important not to limit subsequent thinking to either one.

A synthesising role for self-awareness able to integrate implicit and explicit sources of (self-)knowledge now comes into play. In general, a system may (a) intend to take actions and fail to realize them, (b) intend to take actions and realize them, or (c) not intend to take actions, and involuntarily take them. Self-awareness levels that include models of causality (i.e., forms of interaction awareness) should account for these different cases, as the distinctions between them will be as relevant for computers as they are for humans.

3.2.2 Interpretations and Applications

While self-awareness has been studied extensively in natural systems, including in psychology, philosophy, and sociology, it has also more recently been explicitly considered in computational systems. Lewis et al. [35] provided an early survey on self-awareness and its application in computing systems. Recent books [37, 51, 62] also provide excellent overviews of a range of work incorporating the self-awareness concepts into computer science and engineering, and a recent special issue of *Computer* [59] highlights the state of the art in various self-awareness-related efforts.

In this book, Chap. 2 gave an introduction to the broad range of efforts in computing which relate to self-awareness. In this section, however, we expand on Chap. 2, focussing on efforts in computer science and engineering which directly and explicitly attempt to translate concepts from self-awareness in natural systems to computing. This is not a full survey; however, we aim to provide an overview of how some of the key areas where self-awareness has been explicitly interpreted and applied in computer science and engineering.

3.2.2.1 Self-awareness and Meta-cognition

Some of the earliest literature that began to explicitly address self-awareness in computing, emerged around 2004. A DARPA workshop on "Self-Aware Computer Systems" [4] drew together contributions from a range of researchers, many of whom provided position papers proposing key challenges to move beyond the initial stages of understanding about what self-aware computing might come to mean.

Other works to follow soon after would consider those aspects of self-awareness that form part of a *meta-cognitive loop* [5], where the key challenges are associated with knowledge representation and logical reasoning to provide self-awareness. Schubert [56], in expectation that self-awareness will "push the AI envelope", proposes requirements for both knowledge representation and reasoning to support explicit self-awareness. Meanwhile, Cox [14] highlights that such a feedback loop is inherent to self-awareness, arguing that being aware of oneself is not merely about possessing information. He argues that self-awareness includes the ability to use that information in order to generate goals that may in turn lead to the information being modified. Both Schubert [56] and Cox [13] argue that a key expected benefit of self-awareness is the possibility of resultant self-explanation, the ability of a system to draw on its self-awareness in order to explain or justify itself to an external entity such as a human. It is easy to see how in the face of ever more complex *black box* AI, e.g., as provided by many machine learning techniques, comprehensibility would be facilitated by this approach.

Providing helpful intuition, Cox also suggests [14] that meta-cognition is similar to the algorithm selection problem, wherein the task is to choose the most efficient algorithm from a set of possibilities. This notion of an ability to select one's own method of collection and processing of information, according to goals which may themselves be modified by the individual, has much in common with the conceptual self described by Neisser and discussed in Sect. 3.2.1.4. Cox further considers the differences between cognition and meta-cognition and argues, in line with Maes [38], that a meta-cognitive system is one whose domain is itself. Such a meta-cognitive system can therefore reason about its knowledge, beliefs, and own reasoning process, as opposed to merely *using* knowledge about itself.

3.2.2.2 Computational Self-awareness

Lewis et al. [34] and Faniyi et al. [17] provide an attempt at characterising the self-awareness in computational systems, in a framework inspired by and translated from psychology. They propose the notion of *computational self-awareness*, arguing that human self-awareness can serve as a source of inspiration for equivalent concepts in computing. They describe a taxonomy of forms of computational self-awareness, based on (i) notions of *public* versus *private* self-awareness, (ii) *levels of computational self-awareness*, and (iii) collectivity in and emergence of self-awareness. Their levels of computational self-awareness [17, 34] are inspired by Neisser's levels for humans, introduced in Sect. 3.2.1.4 above, but translated appropriately for describing the capabilities of computer systems. By translating the concepts such as this to the computing domain, it is argued that designers are then able to adopt a common language in considering the various self-awareness capabilities that their systems may or may not possess. While "full-stack" computational self-awareness may often be beneficial, with several processes responsible for one or more levels of self-awareness, there are also cases where a more minimal approach is appropriate.

In a recent book, Lewis et al. [37] present their framework for computational self-awareness more fully. The book further describes a set of derived architectural patterns and a collection of engineering case studies, where explicit consideration of the patterns has been beneficial.

Several engineering efforts have built on Lewis et al.'s [34] conceptual framework and reference architecture for computational self-awareness, including notably as part of the EU-funded EPiCS Project.[2] In one line of work, self-awareness has been used to improve user experience in interactive music systems [49]. As demonstrated through case studies in rhythm [47], chord progression [48], and the sharing of solos around a music group [11], self-awareness enables musical devices to provide varying degrees of control to the user, based on their behaviour and preferences at run-time.

Meanwhile, a work on heterogeneous multi-core nodes [3] illustrates how self-awareness can support the dynamic vertical function migration between the hardware and software at run-time. At the network level, an FPGA-based self-aware network node architecture [28] supports the autonomous configuration of dynamic network protocol stacks, reducing the communication overhead in terms of sent packets, when compared to static stacks. Incorporating the self-awareness in smart camera networks [16, 36] has facilitated the move from static design-time network calibration to run-time management of the network, enabling adaptation to changing and unforeseen deployment conditions. These systems share the characteristics of being large, decentralized, dynamic, uncertain, and heterogeneous and have benefited from the explicit consideration of self-awareness properties and additional online learning compared to "classic" designs.

3.2.2.3 Reflective Architectures

While many of the examples discussed in the self-aware computing literature include algorithms inspired by the biological systems (e.g., evolutionary algorithms, reinforcement learning, neural networks), approaches to implementing architectures for reflection have also been based on inspiration from biology. Indeed, such systems have many characteristics that support their rich reflective processing [7, 9, 42, 50]. The multilayered architectures of biological systems and the biological style of using both opposing processes and the combination of global and local processing for control lead to two main results in terms of reflection: First, there are a variety of direct and indirect sources of information and control available for reflection and adaptation. Second, these direct and indirect control points can be used as "entry points" for monitoring (instrumentation) and reasoning about the data collected and adjusting effects (reflective processes). Bellman, Landauer and colleagues have explored this over several years (e.g., [9, 32, 33]).

The *Wrappings* approach is one way to implement computational reflection and self-modeling systems. In continuous development since 1988, the Wrappings approach grew out of work in conceptual design environments for space systems which had hundreds of models and computational components [8].

---

[2]http://www.epics-project.eu/.

3.2.2.4   Self-awareness in Computer Engineering

While meta-cognition, supported by meta-self-awareness, is concerned with higher order reasoning abilities and of particular interest to the artificial intelligence community, at a more practical level, efforts exist to engineer systems which explicitly consider knowledge about themselves. Project Angstrom [1, 2] is one such effort, where Agarwal and others propose a new way of approaching the system design. The core idea is to move from a procedural design methodology wherein the behaviour of the computing system is pre-programmed or considered at design time, towards a self-aware system where the system adapts to its context at run time. As a result, many decisions can be delayed from design time at the expense of providing the system with the possibility of taking these decisions during run-time. For example, this avoids the need to consider what resources will be available to the system once it is operational. Instead, the system discovers resources and makes decisions about how to allocate them during its operation.

The intention is that this will lead to reduced programming effort, since if a system can automatically discover how to meet its goals at run-time, based on what it finds available, then designers are no longer required to determine how to satisfy resource constraints themselves. In describing this vision, Agarwal [2] proposes five properties that self-aware computers should possess:

- Introspective: they can observe and optimize their own behaviour,
- Adaptive: they can adapt to changing needs of applications running on them,
- Self-healing: they can take corrective action if faults appear whilst monitoring resources,
- Goal-oriented: they attempt to meet user application goals,
- Approximate: they can automatically choose the level of precision needed for a task to be accomplished.

More recently, Hoffman [23], Santambrogio [54], and others have extended Agarwal's work, developing systems that, based on an Observe-Decide-Act (ODA) loop, seek to automatically adapt to meet high-level goals online. The monitoring aspects of self-awareness are facilitated by technology called *application heartbeats* [24]. The aim is to define a general method for monitoring the behaviour of an application against high-level goals. Typically, machine learning techniques are then used to adapt, in order to continue satisfying the goals [25, 40].

3.2.2.5   Self-awareness in Complex IT Systems

With a focus on the engineering of IT systems and services, Kounev [31] proposes self-awareness as an extension to the autonomic computing architecture, in which systems possess built-in self-models. Such models include aspects such as the system's own architecture, and its interactions with its environment, enabling these things to be reasoned about at run-time. Kounev et al. further argue [30] that self-reflection (awareness of hardware and software infrastructure, execution environment, and operational goals), self-prediction (the ability to predict the effects of environmental changes and of actions) and self-adaptation are key characteristics of self-aware systems. Self-awareness itself is then considered from a fundamentally pragmatic perspective, as concerning the nature of (self-)models required for more effective predictive and adaptive behaviour. In taking this approach in software and systems engineering, it is argued that quality of service requirements can be met despite changes in the environment. A challenge is highlighted around the need for systematic engineering methodologies for self-aware systems.

3.2.2.6 Self-awareness in Collective Systems

Zambonelli et al. [63] consider the self-awareness properties of collective systems they term *ensembles*. An example of such an ensemble is a robot swarm. In their work, Zambonelli et al. consider self-awareness to be the ability to recognize the situations of their current operational context that require self-adaptive actions. Hence, self-awareness is here closely tied to knowledge supporting the need for resulting actions. In particular, they envisage the utility of self-awareness to be targeted towards radical run-time modification of structure, at both the individual and ensemble level. In order to reason about this, they highlight that self-awareness is not only concerned with what is currently happening (in terms of oneself and the state of the world), but also what could happen. This includes what the individual or collective could become by adapting, how the world could change, or how these things may affect each other. Hence, the notions of *time awareness*, as will be discussed in Sect. 3.3.2, are important, motivating the development of models that have a predictive or anticipatory power, and those that capture causality in complex collective systems.

This line of research was pursued in the EU-funded ASCENS[3] project, primarily through the application of formal methods to reason about the knowledge encapsulated in ensemble-based systems. In particular, the *general ensemble model (GEM)*, is proposed [26], as a common integrated system model for describing components and their interactions in mathematical terms. A recent book [62] discusses progress made during the ASCENS project.

Lewis et al. [34] also explicitly discuss systems with collective self-awareness. Building on Mitchell [41], they describe components *"within a collective that interact with each other locally as part of a bigger system"*, which *"might not individually possess knowledge about the system as a whole. Although global knowledge is distributed, each system within the collective can work with other systems, giving rise to the collective itself obtaining a sense of its own state and thus being self-aware at one or more of the five self-awareness levels."*

---

[3]http://ascens-ist.eu/.

3.2.2.7 Systems with Minimal Self-awareness

One example of where self-awareness has been applied in a small somewhat simple system is in *cognitive radio*, where devices control their own capabilities and communicate with other devices to monitor theirs. This enables them to improve the efficiency of communication by negotiating changes in parameter settings [60]. Another area where a comparatively simple self-awareness loop is used to great practical effect, is in cognitive packet networks (CPNs) [52]. Here, nodes on a network are able to monitor the effect of choosing different routes through the network, enabling them learn during run-time to adapt the route between a source and a destination on an ongoing basis. The approach is able to naturally deal with changing quality of service requirements of different nodes and has been demonstrated to be highly resilient to denial of service attacks [20].

3.2.2.8 Self-awareness in Robotics

In robotics, research is also concerned with replicating forms of self-awareness that *appear to be human*, such as the robot, *Nico* [22], which learns about its own body, deliberately attempting to mimic an infant. Meanwhile at the collective level, Schmickl et al. [55] showed that a group of robots with simple behavioural rules and local interactions may achieve collective awareness of a global state, distributed across the individual units.

Winfield has highlighted a crucial role for self-awareness in future robotics. He proposes [61] that many robots operating in the world should possess internal self-models, arguing that such models are essential for safe and ethical robot behaviour. The key idea is that by constructing and evaluating a model of the robot and its surroundings, unsafe and unethical outcomes can be avoided. A consequence evaluator predicts the future events through the use of self-models, and as a result moderates the actual robot controller.

3.2.2.9 Self-awareness Elsewhere and in Future Systems

In this section, we have provided an overview of the major research efforts over the last decade or so, in self-aware computing. However, there are many other areas of computer science and engineering research, where self-awareness is mentioned. Two notable ones are autonomic computing [29] and organic computing [43]. Both of these visions have spawned rich literatures, and self-awareness is frequently mentioned as a desirable property. However, in neither case has the notion been further developed. Similarly, in the self-adaptive software community, the so-called self-* properties are organized in levels where *self-adaptiveness* is emphasized as being the most general level, and self-awareness and context-awareness are considered only as primitive levels [53]. Here too, concepts of self-awareness have not been explicitly explored.

Finally, it is clear that there are many computer systems available today, and dating way back before the previous decade, that exhibit the sorts of self-awareness capabilities that we describe in this chapter. These systems, along with autonomic and organic ones, also have the potential to offer crucial insights into the computational self-awareness. In the vast majority of cases, however, there has simply not yet been any explicit engagement with self-awareness concepts. In the report on the 2004 DARPA workshop on self-aware computing, Amir et al. noted [4] that there were even then already systems in existence that exhibited what they called "features of self-aware computer systems." On the evidence presented in this and the previous chapters, we agree. It is our hope that by providing a principled and clear conceptual framework for the description of different self-awareness types, it will become easier for others to engage in discussing and reasoning about the self-awareness properties of their own systems, and how they might be extended.

3.3 A Conceptual Framework

In this section, we present an inclusive conceptual framework for describing computational self-awareness. Taking inspiration from the varieties of self-awareness present in human and animal systems, we outline a structured set of technical concepts, which describe the types of capabilities that self-aware computing systems might possess, and how they might be present in such systems. As such, capabilities described using our framework might form building blocks for self-aware system architectures, which will be elaborated on in Chaps. 6 and 7. We also provide axes on which computational self-awareness may vary, and may indeed be quantitatively or qualitatively compared, in anticipation of Chap. 15, where this topic is revisited.

The framework described here is inspired by, and builds on, the conceptual framework presented by Lewis et al. [34]. In building on that prior work, we highlight two important differences. First, this framework takes a more inclusive and extensible approach, where levels of self-awareness are not directly mapped to psychological levels (as was done with Neisser's levels by Lewis et al.), and thus may be adapted to suit a particular application context. Second, we include an explicit treatment of the concepts of pre-reflective, reflective and meta-reflective self-awareness processes, and how they relate to one another. In this section, we do not however yet discuss techniques or approaches to realising the concepts introduced, except by means of illustrative example. Therefore, our framework aims to serve as a sort of space of possible conceptual requirements of a computationally self-aware system.

Our proposed framework is based on the following high-level concepts:

- Levels of self-awareness,
- Aspects of reflective self-awareness, and
- The domain of self-awareness.

These are elaborated upon below, and can together be used to characterize the form of self-awareness processes that a system might possess. In general, self-aware computing systems will possess many such processes, which interact, for example in reflective relationships, and by acting on one another. We distinguish three over-arching levels of self-awareness: *pre-reflective*, *reflective*, and *meta-reflective*. We then characterize various aspects of reflective models, which may be present in a self-aware system. These include time, interactions, identity, goals, etc. The *domain* of self-awareness includes the *span* of self-awareness (that is the subject of the self-awareness, i.e., who is self-aware in this case), as well as the *scope* of self-awareness (the objects of the systems sensing and reflection).

3.3.1 Overarching Levels of Self-awareness

As discussed in Sect. 3.1, an important concept in self-awareness is the existence of different levels of self-awareness. These range from basic subjective awareness of stimuli, from both the system itself and its environment, through an awareness of how knowledge can represent concepts such as social interaction, causality, and time, up to an awareness of one's own thoughts. Advanced organisms engage in meta-self-awareness [42], an awareness that they themselves are self-aware. Meta-self-awareness may also take many forms, including awareness of self-awareness processes, awareness of reflective knowledge, and iterative meta-reflection on meta-self-aware processes and meta-representational knowledge [46]. Computational self-aware systems will also similarly vary a great deal in their complexity, and levels of computational self-awareness are also needed to express this variety.

Taking a coarse grained view, we can distinguish three overarching levels of self-awareness: pre-reflective self-awareness, reflective self-awareness, and meta-reflective self-awareness. These are elaborated upon below.

3.3.1.1 Pre-reflective Self-awareness

Pre-reflective self-awareness is the subjective awareness a system has from its sensory input - its ability to perceive and make observations. This includes environmental stimuli, internal stimuli from the system itself, the sensing of carrying out an action, receiving signals from the outside world, etc. This level aligns with Lewis et al.'s [34] *stimulus awareness*, based on Neissers ecological self, and describes the presence of subjective knowledge being obtained by the system before (or perhaps without) any reflective modeling of this knowledge takes place.

At this level, the system has no knowledge of historical data, and no models of interaction or causality. In terms of actions possible by a system with only pre-reflective self-awareness, these are limited to stimulus-action rules, since any reasoning (if one can still call it that) is limited to that based on perception, rather than any pre-existing internal models (since none exist). As such the system is able to adapt only to immediate observations. Indeed, at this level, the system has no conceptualisation of its experiences, it merely senses for itself, and possibly acts.

Pre-reflective self-awareness describes the minimal form of computational self-awareness. While in computing systems, it describes nothing beyond a typical system able to interact with its environment, it is a prerequisite for all later forms of self-awareness. A system cannot learn a reflective model, conceptualize its experiences, reason, and act based on them, if there is no experience present in the first place, represented in the system. From a pragmatic point of view, the inclusion of pre-reflective self-awareness in our taxonomy of computational self-awareness, invokes an important question: for a given application, is pre-reflective self-awareness sufficient to achieve the desired behavior? Or, are reflective models (and possibly more) also needed? Thus, the explicit consideration of pre-reflective self-awareness enables the engineers to justify the use of more advanced forms of self-awareness for their systems.

Pre-reflective self-awareness is however more than simply *data*: it is data that has been sensed, that has come from somewhere according to the ability of the system to obtain it (e.g., through physical sensors). Therefore, this level of self-awareness also implicitly includes the notion of subjectivity. Two different systems with different sensors are in different locations would sense the same phenomenon differently, and thus end up with *different data*. In formalising any notion of pre-reflective self-awareness, it is crucial to include the subjective source of the data itself. In turn, this means that this "meta"-data, if we should indeed call it that, can be used in the reflective processes, elsewhere in the system. Ultimately, this may lead to radically different outcomes in terms of knowledge or action.

3.3.1.2   Reflective Self-awareness

Reflective self-awareness is the process of producing a conceptualisation (i.e., a model) of a one's knowledge and experiences. In the first instance, the reflective model will be of a pre-reflective self-aware experience, i.e., a reflective model of a sensory input, observation etc., as described in Sect. 3.3.1.1. In other words, as the system goes through life, experiencing its environment through its sensors, reflective self-awareness processes build models of the empirical and subjective data gathered by these sensors, as well as (potentially) models of the subjectivity with which they were obtained. We call the specific observation (or pre-reflective representation of a phenomenon) captured by the modeling process the *object* of the reflective self-awareness process.

As with human self-awareness, such models or conceptualisations can also capture various different aspects of an experience (of an object). For example, a reflective self-awareness process may build a model that conceptualizes an experience over time. Alternatively, it may build a model that conceptualizes the causality present in an experience, for example, based on modeling how the experienced environment responded to an action. In general, there are many such *aspects* to reflective self-awareness; these will be discussed in Sect. 3.3.2. In our framework, we may therefore describe a reflective self-awareness process according to its *aspect(s)* and *object*.

3.3.1.3   Meta-Self-Awareness

Meta-reflective self-awareness, or meta-self-awareness is essentially reflective self-awareness where the object of the reflection is a reflective self-awareness process. Hence, we may describe the meta-reflective processes in the same ways that we describe the reflective processes (since they are a subset of them). It is important to note, however, that there are at least two high level classes of object that a meta-reflective process could be concerned with: the underlying *process* that forms the object of the meta-reflection (e.g., a learning process), and/or the *output* of the underlying process, (i.e., the models produced by the process being reflected upon). In practice, both are likely to be valuable, and indeed integrating reflection upon both process and output will provide the necessary knowledge to be able to reason about how the two relate to each other. As an example, a meta-reflective process could model the behavior (e.g., memory usage) of another learning process, while also judging the fidelity of its learnt models. Thus, the meta-reflective process has the ability to reason about when it might be advantageous to switch to a different learning method that better balances this trade-off. In general, there are many types of processes that could be learnt and reasoned about, such as reasoning processes, decision processes, problem-solving approaches, and other meta-reflective processes.

There is a strong link between this level and the meta-cognition or meta-reasoning literature discussed in Sect. 3.2.2.1. Indeed, our distinction above echoes Cox's [14] and Maes's [38] arguments that the difference between cognition and meta-cognition is that a meta-cognitive system is one whose domain is itself. Hence, a meta-cognitive system can reason about its knowledge, beliefs, and reasoning processes, as opposed to merely using knowledge about itself as sensed.

In practical terms, our experience with meta-reflection has so far focussed these types of meta-self-awareness processes on resource management, trade-off management, and integration in complex systems. However, while meta-reflection is certainly useful in these regards, we expect there to be additional areas where meta-reflection can help. Examples might include in building higher-order models of causality, or in reflecting on the self-awareness of others in a social system, or on the emergent collective self-awareness of a group of which the individual is a part. However, there will be many additional challenges when we move beyond our current emphasis on resource and trade-off management, and system integration. One challenge is that part of the reason for meta-self-awareness is to gain a perspective on the overall goals for the whole system (much like the role of a central nervous system). One new type of role for this meta-self-awareness would be to decide what type of decision processes should be in control when there are several alternatives possible, or indeed simultaneously running in the system. This type of meta-self-aware reasoning would have to deal with the role of attention in addition to run-time trade-offs. This brings up more new challenges in terms of what actions and what types of information will be needed for such processes and also how to become increasingly liberated from a particular domain and set of experiences to something that begins to look more like general intelligence. This of course greatly changes the nature of the self-models and the models of the situation.

For the avoidance of doubt, it is worth emphasising that given that the object of a meta-reflective process is a reflective process, and meta-reflective processes are themselves reflective processes, then this permits the iterative meta-reflection. This layering permits arbitrarily complex internal reasoning about the behavior of different self-awareness processes with respect to their aspects, goals, expectations, conceptualisation, etc., and also with respect to the systems continuing pre-reflective perceptions (i.e., empirical data taken from observations in the world).

3.3.2 Aspects of Reflective and Meta-reflective Self-awareness

We have so far introduced three overarching levels of self-awareness: pre-reflective, reflective and meta-reflective self-awareness. We further discussed that (meta-) reflective processes, those that build conceptual models of their objects, might capture different *aspects* of the object, or the experience of the object, in their modeling. In this section, we discuss *some* of these aspects of *reflective* self-awareness processes, and how they may combine and build upon each other to form complex self-aware behavior.

In much of the psychological literature, the aspects discussed here are often described as part of a more fine-grained set of *levels* of self-awareness. In this chapter, we have restricted the term "levels" to refer to capabilities and processes that build upon each other, for example as discussed in Sect. 3.3.1. As this section highlights, reflective self-awareness processes in a system can and typically will comprise a rich variety of learning, reasoning and acting behaviors, each of which models or focuses on a particular aspect of self-awareness. We now proceed to describe those aspects of reflective self-awareness that we at present identify as important to self-aware computing systems.

3.3.2.1   Identity Awareness

Identity awareness in a reflective process concerns the modeling of experiences such that they contribute towards a conceptualisation of a coherent identity, possibly over time. This describes the ability to recognize and model the identity of entities, such as other systems, objects in the world, and humans. Without identity awareness, experiences form isolated stimuli, as part of a noisy "soup" of an environment. Identities as modeled may be unique, such as the identities of specific other systems with which to interact (e.g., through unique IDs, such as MAC addresses or DOIs), or simply by affixing one's own label to an encountered object to track it over time (e.g., the third client I saw join the network). Alternatively, identities may be modeled at the level of roles (e.g., a web server, a small robot in my environment). Ultimately, the level of expressiveness and uniqueness required of identities in a reflective model will depend on the application requirements and context. Finally, identity awareness also extends to oneself. Neisser's highest level of self-awareness, the self-concept [44], concerns the conceptualisation of the whole self as a unified entity within the world. An awareness of the identity of oneself (or one of its many identities) is a prerequisite for self-concept. Extending this notion of self-identity to the external sphere, identity awareness also includes the concepts such as one's own role(s) within a wider system.

3.3.2.2   State Awareness

State awareness builds upon the knowledge captured in any and all other aspects of self-awareness, by providing the ability to model and recognize the identity of states of oneself, the world or other entities within it. For example, a system may have a variety of knowledge present in its various conceptual models, associated with various other aspects. With the addition of state awareness, the system would then be able to use this knowledge to characterize the state of the world. Examples might include "winter," "in low power mode," or "waiting for a reply," although there is no requirement for states to have intuitive names or meanings outside of the individual itself. Indeed, unsupervised learning presents a promising technique for the realisation of state awareness, since experiences might be clustered to identify particular emergent states.

3.3.2.3   Time Awareness

Time awareness describes the aspect of reflective models that are concerned with historical knowledge, or knowledge of potential future phenomena. In its simplest form, this may include knowledge of past or potential future basic stimuli. Temporal aspects of models may of course be expressed in a wide range of ways, from precise associations (e.g., timestamping) to ordinal relationship information (e.g., x happened before y). When combined with other conceptual aspects, awareness of the temporal nature of these may be also be modeled. Examples of these may include historic interactions, future states or previous identities.

3.3.2.4   Interaction Awareness

In *interaction awareness*, run-time models are used to take into account patterns of interactions between entities. There are various sub-aspects here, which build on each other. Most obviously, the system must be able to recognize that some actions form part of interactions, such that they are in some way causally connected. An example of this includes message passing, such as is used in a communications protocol, where one message may be a response to another, rather than an isolated action. There may be, in simple interaction awareness, simply a model of the flow of actions over time (e.g., action b typically occurs after action a), or there may be additional semantics associated with the actions or the combination of them (e.g., actions b is a response and action a is a query).

As a prerequisite to the above form of interaction awareness, there must be some form of identity awareness, at least insofar that the system can identify messages, as apart from the general noise in the environment. It may also be important to be able to identify individuals as those engaged in an interaction, if not in terms of their unique identity, then perhaps in terms of role.

Interaction awareness can also build upon state awareness, since models may encapsulate knowledge of causality such as "when action a is taken in state s, this leads to state t." Markovian approaches may be effective choices for modeling state-based interaction awareness.

Finally, the interactions need not be external. Causality of internal processes may also be modeled in meta-reflective processes. For example, a system might model the behavior of one of its own decision-making processes, when other parts of the system are either operational or not. In the former case, the system may learn a model of how decision-making degrades (due to more stringent resource constraints), when load elsewhere is high. Such models of internal causality may then be used to provide adaptive internal re-architecting, or perhaps more effective scheduling of tasks.

3.3.2.5   Behavior Awareness

In *behavior awareness*, run-time models represent the internal behavior of the system or behavior of external entities. Behavior here is taken to mean an action, or more normally a group of actions, taken by an individual. Models of behavior may, at the simplest end of the spectrum, comprise a representation of an observed action. More useful forms of behavior awareness, however, will link these representations together, over time, and with awareness of states. For behavior awareness to be particularly meaningful, it would usually be coupled with some identity awareness, i.e., knowledge of the identities of individuals or roles carrying out the behavior, or subject to it. Behavior awareness can apply also to oneself, by modeling either ones externally facing behavior in the world or one's own internally facing behavior. Behavior awareness can be applied in a meta-reflective context, where models are built that describe self-awareness processes in terms of their behavior.

3.3.2.6   Appearance Awareness

In human self-awareness, one's *public self*, the image an individual presents to the world, is often considered important. This may also be true of computational systems, for example where the environment or individuals within it might respond differently depending on the appearance of the individual to which they are responding. Thus, *appearance awareness* is concerned with how the individual appears, or may appear, to others in the environment. At one end of the spectrum, this might simply concern an awareness of physical properties (i.e., a robot may be aware of its height, or if it is dirty). At the other end, a system may learn models of how it presents itself, including its own knowledge and self-awareness. In this way, appearance awareness is linked to notions such as self-explanation, acknowledging that a system's explanation or justification for its actions form part of the way it presents itself, and may go on to have subsequent implications for how the environment responds to it. The reflective processes that deal with the aspect of appearance awareness are able to explicitly learn and reason about these factors.

3.3.2.7   Goal Awareness

Goal awareness, in a general sense, includes the ability to conceptualize the internal factors that drive the behavior, such as a system's goals, objectives, and constraints. In some cases, goals will be explicitly available and formally specified. Note that this is not the same as a goal being *implicitly* present in the system, due to the advance decisions of designers. Goal awareness implies the presence of goal knowledge at run-time, in such a way that it may be reasoned about at run-time. Further, this presence of explicit goal knowledge at run-time permits the acknowledgement of and adaptation to changes in goals, either internally generated, or due to external forces (e.g., a user's changing needs).

Not all goals will be expressed in this way. In some cases, goals will be implicit in the environment or need to be derived from higher-level more abstract goals (e.g., the goal to replenish energy may be derived from a higher-level goal to survive). In other cases, goals will take the form of motivations: impulses and drives that are not tied to formally specified objectives or goal states. In these cases, goals may be less obvious, and only intentions or even actions will be observable. Thus, learning will need to be employed to model those goals implicitly in the architecture of the system.

Note that the goal awareness may apply to oneself or to others. In the latter case, a system may possess a model of another system's goals, or those of a human or organisation. Further, the goal awareness may be combined with other aspects, such as time awareness, where models of how goals change over time might be one benefit.

3.3.2.8   Belief Awareness

Belief awareness is concerned with, in general, things believed to be true by a system and differs from expectation awareness since beliefs do not, in general, need to capture the notion of time. In this way, belief awareness provides a generic mechanism for reflecting on other aspects of self-awareness, in both oneself and in others, with degrees of uncertainty. In simpler cases, belief awareness models will capture the knowledge that the system itself believes something in terms of one of the afore-mentioned aspects to be the case (e.g., I believe that I have an expectation that an apple will fall when thrown into the air). This may appear superfluous; however, the added benefit here is that belief awareness provides a *generic mechanism* for arbitrary meta-reflection on one's own awareness. A belief awareness process may be added to reflect on any other process, to express knowledge of the level of belief associated with the model. In terms of arbitrary reflective architectures, processes that are concerned only with belief awareness allow us to add models of uncertainty, as well as sources of knowledge and uncertainty, in arbitrary arrangements.

Belief awareness also applies in the public sphere, since awareness of others' beliefs may also be modeled. This provides the necessary machinery for iterative meta-representational self-awareness, for example cases such as system x believing that system y believes system z to be aware of system x's origin.

3.3.2.9 Expectation Awareness

Expectation awareness combines belief awareness and time awareness, to form models that express what the system or others believe about how the world will unfold over time. This includes, for example, awareness of how the laws of physics act on objects over time. For example, the idea that "when I throw an apple in the air in front of me, I expect that I will see it come down" can be modeled as a belief over the state of an observation of an object over time. A further example is that of knowledge of social conventions (e.g., when a person greets me, he expects me to respond with a greeting within a short time window). In this way, expectations in fact can form part of a requirements model (requirements awareness might be seen as a sub-aspect of expectation awareness), where the expectations are those of a user, client machine, or interaction partner in a collective system.

At the meta level, this may be used to model the requirements or expectations over other aspects. A system may, for example, be watching two individuals engaged in a conversation. In this case, a model may capture the expectations over the sequence of messages being passed in the interaction (see interaction awareness, above): there may be a model that the response b is *expected after* query a. Subsequent reasoning may concern the implications of this expectation being broken and appropriate actions that may be triggered.

3.3.2.10 Applicability and Extensibility

In the above characterisation, we have presented the aspects of reflective self-awareness that we anticipate will be most relevant to self-aware computing systems. However, as in psychology, we expect that various different set of aspects will be used, as appropriate for the particular context or system design process. Therefore, the above list should *not* be considered our proposal for a complete list, but instead as a starting point for further consideration as to the aspects captured in reflective and meta-reflective self-awareness.

3.3.3   Domain of Self-awareness

In this section, we are concerned with two important questions when considering a self-aware computing system: *what is it that is self-aware*, and *of what is it aware?* By now it should be clear that in a given self-aware computing system, there are various entities that are involved, or potentially involved, in a particular aspect of self-awareness that is present. These entities exist at various levels of abstraction and aggregation, and include the system that *is aware*, the parts of that system that are involved in providing the awareness, and the things it is *aware of*. Without limiting this collection of entities, we refer to them together as the *domain* of self-awareness. In this section, we define various concepts, chief among them are the *span* and *scope* of self-awareness, that comprise the domain. These provide a helpful basis for discussions that rely on these notions, in the rest of the book.

3.3.3.1   Scope of Self-awareness

In *reflective self-awareness*, we are primarily concerned with a relationship between the *subject* of the awareness, that is, the entity doing the reflecting, and the *object* of the awareness, that is, the entity being reflected upon. A self-aware system will be aware of a broad range of objects over its lifetime. These include, for example, externally sensed things, the system's sensing apparatus, internal reflective processes, a sense of self-concept, and indeed these things at different points in time, and in other individuals. Collectively, we call the objects of self-awareness that system's *scope of self-awareness*. The scope comprises all the entities observed, or able to be observed, by the system.

3.3.3.2   Span of Self-awareness

In general terms, we refer to the extent of the entity that has the awareness, the entity at which the knowledge is available, as the *span* of self-awareness. We must refine the concept of span somewhat; however, since it is not sufficient to base the definition of span on the notion of an entity that is *doing the reflecting*. This is too ambiguous to be particularly helpful. In general, reflecting on a particular entity will be carried out by one *or more* reflective self-awareness processes within a system, and candidates for being the *span* in this case could be any one of these processes, all of them combined, or the system of which they are part. Coming back to the discussion of what constitutes *a self* (as begun in Sect. 3.2.1), we may accept that all of these interpretations are potentially valid answers to the question: *what is doing the reflecting?*

3.3.3.3   Complexities in Span and Scope

As an example, consider a system that processes sensor data and passes messages to other neighbouring systems. In the system, a number of self-awareness processes reflect on different aspects of what the system's sensors observe. One process that captures a time-awareness aspect may, through its learning, become aware of a pattern in what is being observed, corresponding, albeit noisily, to the time of day. A second self-awareness process does not reflect on time aspects of the observation, but instead provides some interaction awareness. This process develops a model of potential cause and effect, as it becomes aware of a certain type of incoming messages triggering a shift in sensor readings. A third self-awareness process observes outgoing and incoming messages, reflects on the correlations between these, and becomes aware that the type of incoming messages noticed by the second process is received shortly after the system sends a reset signal to its neighbouring systems. It observes that the reset signal is generated once per hour. Finally, a meta-self-awareness process reflects on the knowledge obtained by the second and third self-awareness processes, and is therefore able to develop an awareness that hourly reset messages precede a change in sensor readings.

There are now two *different and coexisting* models that explain the shifts in sensor readings observed by the system. The first, provided by the first self-awareness process, correlates shifts with regular time intervals. The second, provided by the meta-self-awareness process, through its reflection on the knowledge acquired by the second and third processes, associates the timing of the shifts with the system's own reset messages.

It is reasonable to ask at this stage, what is the system aware of, in terms of how its environment changes, and its effect on those changes?

This small example serves to illustrate that the span of reflective self-awareness, the *entity doing the reflecting*, is both several things at once, and specific to the particular reflective self-awareness aspect, and role of that self-awareness process within the wider system.

3.3.3.4   Hierarchical Reflection View of Span and Scope

If we take a view of self-awareness, only as it arises from hierarchical subject-object views of reflection, then we can consider that there might be several different *spans* at work here, each with their own different (but overlapping) *scope*:

- A span comprising reflective process 1, which has the system's observations through its sensors, some aspects of the entities observed, and the time of day, as its scope.
- A span comprising reflective process 2, which similarly has the system's observations through its sensors, some (partially different) aspects of the entities observed, and incoming messages as its scope.
- A span comprising reflective process 3, which has the observation of system's incoming and outgoing messages as its scope.

If we, however, consider a span comprising the meta-self-aware process, then the scope includes the models and learning contained within processes 2 and 3. However, in doing so, the span must be expanded to also include those processes, since without them being part of the *entity doing the reflecting*, there would be no possibility for the sensor observations or messages to be part of the scope of the meta-self-aware process—and they clearly are. Hence, our fourth option is a span comprising self-awareness processes 2 and 3 and the meta-self-aware process.

In this case, we see an overlap between both the span and the scope of the same self-awareness phenomenon. Even in this simple example, as the self-awareness processes are broken down into individual reflective processes, the system, as defined here by the span, is aware of (as defined by its scope) part of its own self-awareness. This is in addition to its awareness of the external things being observed by the sensors.

3.3.3.5 Collectivity in Span and Scope

The one potential span missing from the above discussion, which is perhaps more intuitive, is to consider the system-as-a-whole (as comprising the three reflective, one meta-reflective process and pre-reflective observing apparatus) as a single span. It would follow that the associated scope of such a span consists of everything that is known to it.

Since in the example system there is no single reflective process that has a whole-system view, we must instead return to the notion of collectivity in self-awareness, as first discussed in Sect. 3.2.1.3. The unity of the system in the example, which provides us with the intuition of such a system-as-a-whole span, arises from considering the system as a "well-defined" entity within its broader environment. This is in much the same way that we often consider a human, a dog, a smart phone, or a daffodil as a single system, even though there is no omniscient component within them. Of course, this does not come without the requirement for someone, another observer perhaps, to do the "well defining".

One way of reasoning about such a well-defined entity is based on behavior. In our example system, and coming back to the fact that there are now two different and coexisting models describing what is occurring, we can of course allow for either or both to trigger observable behaviors. In such a case, we may observe a behavior that suggests that the system has a coherent view integrating both models, even though none is present. Is the "system-as-a-whole" then aware of both models? From this external behaviorist observer, it is the case, and this is clearly sufficient for behavior to be generated based on both hypotheses.

This *collective span* can indeed be a highly useful concept, when concerned with the actions driven by self-awareness. It requires us to accept that a span may not be bound only by the presence of subject-object relations in a reflective hierarchy, but can be enabled through collectivity. In this case, this collectivity arose from a unity of behavior, as observed. A final point to make on the unity of behavior and its reliance on being observed is that there is no requirement for the observer to be an entity apart from the system itself. Indeed, most humans have a sense of their own self, which according to this discussion is of the collective type. This arises from that person's own self-awareness and not (directly at least) the awareness of others.

3.3.3.6   Types of Self-awareness Objects and Scopes

We have indicated above that a system's span, which is the subject of self-awareness, is aware, according to some descriptions based on its levels and aspects, of a variety of objects, collectively termed the system's scope. The systems reflective processes (part of the span) produce various conceptualisations, or models, of internal and/or external entities (part of the scope), which in turn may feature pre-reflective, reflective, or meta-reflective self-awareness.

In general, the object of a reflective self-awareness process is the answer to the question what is the thing the system is paying attention to? A reflective process produces a conceptualisation (i.e., a model) of any pre-reflective or reflective self-awareness. Let us first consider the initial case, where the object is a sensed experience, i.e., an observation. As with model characteristics, the list of possible object types cannot be exhaustive and will to a large degree be domain dependent. However, we provide here a suggested list of important types of objects.

Let us therefore take a look at some of the main *types of objects* that a system can be aware of. From these, we can also define corresponding *scope types*. The list of possible object types cannot be exhaustive, and will, to a large degree, be domain-specific. However, we provide here a suggested list of important types of objects.

Generally, we consider that a system and its environment consist of various entities (or resources) and that the system can be (self-)aware of the existence and various characteristics of these entities. Such characteristics would notably include:

- Property characteristics: include both the parameters that define an entity's characteristics or state, and the actual values of those parameters at different times. Also this includes potential states and their characteristics;
- Observability capabilities: specify the measures that can be taken from an entity, given the available sensing apparatus. These may additionally provide a more detailed description, including recommended observation frequencies, expected resource overheads, and accuracy of measurements;
- Action capabilities: specify the actions that are being or can be performed on an entity; these may additionally provide a more detailed description, including the expected effects within various contexts, quality parameters, and necessary resources;
- Interconnections among objects: represent any kind of relation between objects of any of the types listed above, including links among computing entities (e.g., system architecture); dependencies between state characteristics; and conflicts among action capabilities. At higher levels of abstraction, this may include groups, organizations, or sets of and relations between objects.

We may, as such, derive several types of a system's self-awareness scopes. An *action scope* includes all entities that the system may act upon. These will typically include not only internal entities, but also external entities (if we consider communications with other systems as some sort of actions). We may also find useful the notion of *influence scope* to refer to entities upon which the system may only act indirectly (e.g., via direct communication or indirect effects via a shared environment). The *self-awareness scope* includes all "entities" the system can observe, either directly (e.g., through sensors) or indirectly (e.g., through acquired knowledge obtained from elsewhere). The entities in the scope may include both internal and external entities.

Crucially for all but the simplest of self-aware systems, the entities that are the objects of reflection can themselves be self-awareness processes, including their own acquired knowledge. These observed processes may operate over different scopes and at different resolutions and self-awareness levels, than the reflecting process. We may now use the terminology of the domain of self-awareness to establish that when the scope of self-awareness includes (at least partially) the span of self-awareness, we have meta-self-awareness. Namely, by virtue of its role and connectivity within the concert of self-awareness processes, the subject of a reflective self-aware process is a meta-self-awareness process. In general, we envisage that self-aware systems will have many such meta-self-awareness processes, operating over different objects and with respect to different aspects (goals, interactions, time, etc.). Furthermore, it is likely that reflecting on these further still, meta-meta-self-awareness processes will provide the system with knowledge about the role and impact of operating such an array of self-awareness processes. There are many architectural alternatives for structuring reflection relationships in a self-aware system, as will be explored in Part II of this book. At one extreme however, we may consider a particular type of overarching meta-self-awareness process, able to reflect on the entire system and its self-awareness, providing the system with a complete self-concept.

3.3.3.7 Overlapping Spans and Scopes

In summary, we refer to the subject(s) of reflective self-awareness as the span, comprising all entities that contribute to the formation of self-awareness, and to the object(s) of self-awareness as the scope, comprising all the entities observed by the subject's self-awareness. We refer to the domain of self-awareness as the combination of subjects (span) and objects (scope).

Finally, in practice in many self-aware systems, we find and expect that the span and scope will not be distinct from each other. As in the above example, there may be substantial overlap, through meta-self-awareness. For a fully meta-self-aware system, where every reflective process was itself reflected upon by the system, then the scope necessarily includes the span.

3.3.4 Putting It All Together

In summary, we have in this section sketched a conceptual framework for describing and comparing qualitative aspects of self-awareness in computing systems. Our framework is based on three tenets:

- Levels of self-awareness,
- Aspects of reflective self-awareness,
- The domain of self-awareness.

Using the intersection of all three tenets, we may produce descriptions of the specific self-awareness of a system. For example, we might construct a sentence as follows: Peter (span) is aware of Ada's (scope) goal (aspect) to reduce the power usage (object). Further, Ada (span) is aware of her own reasoning (meta-self-awareness) about what to do (act) about it.

3.4 Self-awareness and Goals

The notion of domain can also be associated with goal definitions. Typically, the goal domain of a self-aware computing system would be included in its self-awareness domain. Exceptions would represent cases where the system achieved its goal without being aware of it and without making use of any of its reflective self-awareness capabilities for this purpose.

A goal's span identifies the entity or entities that are responsible for achieving the goal, from the perspective of the entity that requested the goal. For instance, if a system is required, by an external entity, to achieve a goal, then that system represents the goals span. If a collective of systems is required to achieve a goal, then the entire collective of systems represents the goal's span.

We can also relate a span and scope to the goals of a self-aware computing system where the span refers to the group of entities that is responsible for achieving the goals, while the scope is the group of entities the goal refers to in its specification of what has to be achieved.

Usually, we would expect that if self-awareness is employed to realize a goal the span of the self-awareness must be a subset of the span of the goal (as otherwise the self-awareness would include entities that do not share the related goal and therefore will also not contribute to it) and that the scope of the self-awareness must include the scope of the goal (as otherwise the span is not able to judge whether the goal has been achieved for the scope of the goal).

A goal's scope represents the set of resources over which the constraints defined by the goal should be attained. The goal's achievement can then be evaluated by taking measures from the resources in the goal's scope.

As indicated above, if a system is aware of a goal that it must achieve, then the goal's domain will impact the systems self-awareness domain which is necessary for achieving the goal.

Of course, the considerations discussed here do not apply to cases where the system reaches a goal without being aware of that goal (i.e., lack of goal awareness).

Let us now take a closer look at way in which a goals scope impacts the different types of objects in the targeted systems self-awareness scope, provided that the system is goal-aware. Here, the targeted system is the goals span.

Firstly, the systems self-awareness scope must include the resources (including potentially other systems) upon which the system can act to achieve its goal. These are part of the system's action-awareness scope.

Secondly, the systems' self-awareness scope must include the aspects of the environment (or context) that are relevant to the reasoning process involved in achieving the goal. These aspects are part of the systems context-awareness scope. For instance, the system must be aware of the outside temperature in order to decide whether or not to open the window shutters for achieving an inside temperature.

Thirdly, in some cases, it may be helpful if the system's self-awareness scope included the resources upon which the system could not act directly but could influence by indirect means. These would be part of the system's interaction awareness. For instance, if the smart home aimed to achieve a power prosumption goal—e.g., not consume more than the local production—then the smart home might try to ask a local producer to produce more (rather than asking its own devices to consume less).

3.5   Challenges

In this chapter, we began by reviewing what is understood by self-awareness, both as it pertains to humans, and to computers. We provided a brief overview of relevant work in psychology and computing, on the topic of self-awareness. The main contribution of this chapter is a new conceptual framework for computational self-awareness, extending a characterisation by Lewis et al. [34], in order to (i) provide inclusion and extensibility, (ii) distinguish between reflective levels of self-awareness and aspects of reflective modeling, and (iii) introduce the notion of the domain of self-awareness, in terms of span and scope. In doing so, we provided the language to engage with a broad set of concepts that can be used to describe and reason about self-aware computing systems. The characterisations presented here are concerned with how they might pertain to both current and future computing systems.

There are many challenges that need to be tackled in further developing the notion and practicalities of self-aware computing.

Firstly, the formalisation of the framework sketched in this chapter would provide engineers with the ability to make use of more rigorously processes for the production of self-aware computing systems. Further, such a formalisation could be used by self-aware systems themselves, in order to better reason about their own self-awareness capabilities in a principled and comprehensible way.

Secondly, though we have described a wide range of capabilities, which rely heavily on learning, modeling, instrumentation, and more, we have not here touched on methods or techniques for implementing such capabilities. Some of these are addressed in the later chapters in this book, but there is as yet no fundamental understanding of the linkage between algorithms and self-awareness levels, or if new algorithms are needed in some cases. Such a linkage would again prove valuable to designers of self-aware systems.

Thirdly, how might we structure self-awareness processes with respect to each other, such that the right sort of learning and reasoning is operating on the right internal and external objects (including self-awareness processes themselves)? In other words, what should architectures for self-aware systems look like? Further, how might and should such structures change over time, as the needs of the system change, or more is learnt about the system, its environment, and about what is needed to be learnt?

Finally, there is no assumption that at any given moment, all forms of self-awareness are being used for the same problem or context. Systems may engage multiple parallel self-awareness processes in related or unrelated tasks. How should we organize and manage this? Both architectures and meta-management processes must acknowledge that attention is a limited resource, reflective of the limited computational power, memory, and time for running self-awareness processes on real systems. Another way of phrasing this challenge is to consider how a system itself should decide how to engage and disengage different self-awareness processes dynamically, as relevant or beneficial, given its experience of a changing world.

Acknowledgements Peter Lewis acknowledges the teams of the EPiCS and AWARENESS EU projects, for their contributions to many discussions in the development of the notion of computational self-awareness.

References

1. Anant Agarwal and Bill Harrod. Organic computing. Technical Report White paper, MIT and DARPA, 2006.
2. Anant Agarwal, Jason Miller, Jonathan Eastep, David Wentzlaff, and Harshad Kasture. Self-aware computing. Technical Report AFRL-RI-RS-TR-2009-161, MIT, 2009.
3. Andreas Agne, Markus Happe, Achim Lsch, Christian Plessl, and Marco Platzner. Self-awareness as a model for designing and operating heterogeneous multicores. *ACM Trans. on Reconfigurable Technology and Systems (TRETS)*, 7(2), 2014.
4. Eyal Amir, M. L. Anderson, and Vinay K. Chaudhri. Report on darpa workshop on self-aware computer systems. Technical Report UIUCDCS-R-2007-2810, UIUC Comp. Sci., 2007.
5. Michael L. Anderson and Don R. Perlis. Logic, self-awareness and self-improvement: The metacognitive loop and the problem of brittleness. *Journal of Logic and Computation*, 15(1):21–40, 2005.
6. Smith Baker. The identification of the self. *Psyc. Rev.*, 4(3):272–284, 1897.
7. K. L. Bellman and D. O. Walter. Biological processing. *American Journal of Physiology*, 246, 1984.

8. Kirstie. L. Bellman, April Gillam, and Christopher Landauer. Challenges for conceptual design environments: the VEHICLES experience. *Revue Internationale de CFAO et dInfographie*, 8(2):185–217, 1993.
9. Kirstie. L. Bellman, Christopher Landauer, and Phyllis R. Nelson. *Systems engineering for organic computing: The challenge of shared design and control between OC systems and their human engineers*, chapter 3. Understanding Complex Systems Series. Springer, 2008.
10. Cristiana Bolchini, Carlo A. Curino, Elisa Quintarelli, Fabio A. Schreiber, and Letizia Tanca. A data-oriented survey of context models. *SIGMOD Rec.*, 36(4):19–26, 2007.
11. Arjun Chandra, Kristian Nymoen, Arve Volsund, Alexander Refsum Jensenius, Kyrre Glette, and Jim Torrcsen. Enabling participants to play rhythmic solos within a group via auctions. In *Proc. Int. Symp. on Computer Music Modeling and Retrieval (CMMR)*, page 674689, 2012.
12. Tao Chen, Funmilade Faniyi, Rami Bahsoon, Peter R. Lewis, Xin Yao, Leandro L. Minku, and Lukas Esterle. The handbook of engineering self-aware and self-expressive systems. Technical report, EPiCS EU FP7 project consortium, 2014.
13. Michale T. Cox. Metareasoning, monitoring, and self-explanation. In Michael T. Cox and A. Raja, editors, *Metareasoning: Thinking about thinking*, pages 131–149. MIT Press, Cambridge, MA, USA, 2011.
14. M.T. Cox. Metacognition in computation: A selected research review. *Artificial Intelligence*, 169(2):104–141, 2005.
15. Anind K. Dey. Understanding and using context. *Personal Ubiquitous Computing*, 5(1):4–7, 2001.
16. Lukas Esterle, Peter R. Lewis, Xin Yao, and Bernhard Rinner. Socio-economic vision graph generation and handover in distributed smart camera networks. *ACM Transactions on Sensor Networks*, 10(2):20:1–20:24, January 2014.
17. Funmilade Faniyi, Peter R. Lewis, Rami Bahsoon, and Xin Xao. Architecting self-aware software systems. In *Proc. IEEE/IFIP Conf. on Software Architecture (WICSA)*, pages 91–94. IEEE, April 2014.
18. Shaun Gallagher. Philosophical conceptions of the self: implications for cognitive science. *Trends in Cognitive Sciences*, 4(1), 2000.
19. Gordon G Gallup. Chimpanzees: self-recognition. *Science*, 1970.
20. E. Gelenbe and G. Loukas. A self-aware approach to denial of service defence. *Computer Networks*, 51:1299–1314, 2007.
21. Pentti OA Haikonen. Reflections of consciousness: The mirror test. In *Proceedings of the 2007 AAAI Fall Symposium on Consciousness and Artificial Intelligence*, pages 67–71, 2007.
22. Justin W. Hart and Brian Scassellati. *Robotic Self-Modeling*, chapter 14. Imperial College Press/World Scientific Book, 2014.
23. H. Hoffmann, J. Eastep, M.D. Santambrogio, J.E. Miller, and A. Agarwal. Application heartbeats for software performance and health. In *ACM SIGPLAN Notices*, volume 45, pages 347–348. ACM, 2010.
24. Henry Hoffmann, Jim Holt, George Kurian, Eric Lau, Martina Maggio, Jason E. Miller, Sabrina M. Neuman, Mahmut Sinangil, Yildiz Sinangil, Anant Agarwal, Anantha P. Chandrakasan, and Srinivas Devadas. Self-aware computing in the Angstrom processor. In *Proceedings of the 49th Annual Design Automation Conference*, DAC '12, pages 259–264, New York, NY, USA, 2012. ACM.
25. Henry Hoffmann, Stelios Sidiroglou, Michael Carbin, Sasa Misailovic, Anant Agarwal, and Martin Rinard. Dynamic knobs for responsive power-aware computing. In *Proceedings of the Sixteenth International Conference on Architectural Support for Programming Languages and Operating Systems*, ASPLOS XVI, pages 199–212, New York, NY, USA, 2011. ACM.
26. Matthias Hölzl and Martin Wirsing. Towards a system model for ensembles. In *Formal Modeling: Actors, Open Systems, Biological Systems*, pages 241–261. Springer, 2011.
27. William James. *The principles of psychology*. Henry Holt & Co., 1890.
28. Ariane Keller, Daniel Borkmann, Stephan Neuhaus, and Markus Happe. Self-awareness in computer networks. *Int. Journal of Reconfigurable Computing (IJRC)*, 2014.

29. Jeffrey O. Kephart and David M. Chess. The Vision of Autonomic Computing. *IEEE Computer*, 36(1):41–50, 2003.
30. Samuel Kounev. Engineering of Self-Aware IT Systems and Services: State-of-the-Art and Research Challenges. In *Proceedings of the 8th European Performance Engineering Workshop (EPEW'11), Borrowdale, The English Lake District, October 12–13*, 2011. (Keynote Talk).
31. Samuel Kounev. Self-Aware Software and Systems Engineering: A Vision and Research Roadmap. In *GI Softwaretechnik-Trends, 31(4), November 2011, ISSN 0720-8928*, Karlsruhe, Germany, 2011.
32. Christopher Landauer and Kirstie L. Bellman. Knowledge-based integration infrastruc ture for complex systems. *International Journal of Intelligent Control and Systems*, 1(1):133–153, 1996.
33. Christopher Landauer and Kirstie L. Bellman. Self-modeling systems. In H. S. R. Laddaga, editor, *Self-Adaptive Software*, Lecture Notes in Computer Sci ence, pages 238–256. Springer, 2002.
34. Peter R. Lewis, Arjun Chandra, Funmilade Faniyi, Kyrre Glette, Tao Chen, Rami Bahsoon, Jim Torresen, and Xin Yao. Architectural aspects of self-aware and self-expressive systems: From psychology to engineering. *Computer*, 48(8), August 2015.
35. Peter R. Lewis, Arjun Chandra, Shaun Parsons, Edward Robinson, Kyrre Glette, Rami Bahsoon, Jim Torresen, and Xin Yao. A Survey of Self-Awareness and Its Application in Computing Systems. In *Proceedings of the International Conference on Self-Adaptive and Self-Organizing Systems Workshops (SASOW)*, pages 102–107, Ann Arbor, MI, USA, October 2011. IEEE Computer Society.
36. Peter R. Lewis, Lukas Esterle, Arjun Chandra, Bernhard Rinner, Jim Torresen, and Xin Yao. Static, dynamic, and adaptive heterogeneity in distributed smart camera networks. *ACM Trans. Auton. Adapt. Syst.*, 10(2):8:1–8:30, 2015.
37. Peter R. Lewis, Marco Platzner, Bernhard Rinner, Jim Torresen, and Xin Yao, editors. *Self-Aware Computing Systems: An Engineering Approach*. Springer, 2016.
38. P. Maes. Introspection in knowledge representation. *Advances in Artificial Intelligence II*, pages 249–262, 1987.
39. T. Metzinger. *Being no one*. MIT Press, Cambridge, MA, USA, 2003.
40. Sasa Misailovic, Stelios Sidiroglou, Henry Hoffmann, and Martin Rinard. Quality of ser-vice profiling. In *Proceedings of the 32nd ACM/IEEE International Conference on Software Engineering-Volume 1*, pages 25–34. ACM, 2010.
41. Melanie Mitchell. Self-awareness and control in decentralized systems (Tech Report SS-05-04). In *AAAI Spring Symposium on Metacognition in Computation*, Menlo Park, 2005. AIII Press.
42. Alain Morin. Levels of consciousness and self-awareness: A comparison and integration of various neurocognitive views. *Consciousness and Cognition*, 15(2):358–71, 2006.
43. Christian Müller-Schloer, Hartmut Schmeck, and Theo Ungerer. *Organic computing: a para-digm shift for complex systems*. Springer, 2011.
44. Ulric Neisser. The Roots of Self-Knowledge: Perceiving Self, It, and Thou. *Annals of the NY AoS.*, 818:19–33, 1997.
45. Albert Newen. The logic of indexical thoughts and the metaphysics of the self. In In W. Künne, A. Newen, and M. Anduschus, editors, *Direct reference, indexicality and propositional attitudes*, pages 105–131. CSLI publications, Stanford, USA, 1997.
46. Albert Newen and Kai Vogeley. Self-representation: Searching for a neural signature of self-consciousness. *Consciousness and Cognition*, 12:529–543, 2003.
47. Kristian Nymoen, Arjun Chandra, Kyrre Glette, and Jim Torresen. Decentralized harmonic synchronization in mobile music systems. In *Proceedings of the International Conference on Awareness Science and Technology (ICAST)*, 2014.
48. Kristian Nymoen, Arjun Chandra, Kyrre Glette, Jim Torresen, Arve Voldsund, and Alexan-der Refsum Jensenius. Pheromusic: Navigating a musical space for active music experiences. In *Proc. Int. Computer Music Conference (ICMC) joint with the Sound and Music Computing Conference*, page 17151718, 2014.

49. Kristian Nymoen, Arjun Chandra, and Jim Torresen. *Self-Awareness in Active Music Systems*, chapter 14.
50. L. I. Perlovsky and R. Kozma, editors. *Neurodynamics of Cognition and Consciousness*. Springer, Berlin, 2007.
51. Jeremy Pitt, editor. *The Computer After Me: Awareness and Self-awareness in Autonomic Systems*. Imperial College Press, 2014.
52. Georgia Sakellari. The cognitive packet network: A survey. *The Computer Journal*, 53, 2010.
53. Mazeiar Salehie and Ladan Tahvildari. Self-adaptive software: Landscape and research challenges. *ACM Trans. Auton. Adapt. Syst.*, 4(2):1–42, 2009.
54. M.D. Santambrogio, H. Hoffmann, J. Eastep, and A. Agarwal. Enabling technologies for self-aware adaptive systems. In *Adaptive Hardware and Systems (AHS), 2010 NASA/ESA Conference on*, pages 149–156. IEEE, 2010.
55. Thomas Schmickl, Ronald Thenius, Christoph Moslinger, Jon Timmis, Andy Tyrrell, Mark Read, James Hilder, Jose Halloy, Alexandre Campo, Cesare Stefanini, et al. CoCoRo–The Self-Aware Underwater Swarm. In *Proceedings of the International Conference on Self-Adaptive and Self-Organizing Systems Workshops (SASOW)*, pages 120–126, Ann Arbor, MI, USA, October 2011. IEEE Computer Society.
56. Lenhart Schubert. Some knowledge representation and reasoning requirements for self-awareness. 2005.
57. Aaron Sloman. Prospects for ai as a general science of intelligence. In *Prospects for Artificial Intelligence: Proceedings of AISB93*, Amsterdam, 1993. IOS Press.
58. G. A. Tawney. Feeling and self-awareness. *Psyc. Rev.*, 9(6):570–596, 1902.
59. Jim Torresen, Christian Plessl, and Xin Yao. Self-aware and self-expressive systems. *Computer*, 48(7).
60. J. Wang, D. Brady, K. Baclawski, M. Kokar, and L. Lechowicz. The use of ontologies for the self-awareness of the communication nodes. In *Proceedings of the Software Defined Radio Technical Conference SDR*, volume 3, 2003.
61. Alan F. T. Winfield. Robots with internal models: a route to self-aware and hence safer robots. In Jeremy Pitt, editor, *The Computer After Me*, chapter 16. Imperial College Press/World Scientific Book, 2014.
62. Martin Wirsing, Matthias Hölzl, Nora Koch, and Philip Mayer. *Software Engineering for Collective Autonomic Systems: The ASCENS Approach*, volume 8998 of *Lecture Notes in Computer Science*. Springer, 2015.
63. F. Zambonelli, N. Bicocchi, G. Cabri, L. Leonardi, and M. Puviani. On self-adaptation, self-expression, and self-awareness in autonomic service component ensembles. In *Proceedings of the Fifth IEEE Conference on Self-Adaptive and Self-Organizing Systems Workshops (SASOW)*, pages 108–113, 2011.

Chapter 4
Reference Scenarios for Self-aware Computing

Jeffrey O. Kephart, Martina Maggio, Ada Diaconescu, Holger Giese,
Henry Hoffmann, Samuel Kounev, Anne Koziolek, Peter Lewis,
Anders Robertsson and Simon Spinner

Abstract This chapter defines three reference scenarios to which other chapters
may refer for the purpose of motivating and illustrating architectures, techniques,
and methods consistently throughout the book. The reference scenarios cover a broad
set of characteristics and issues that one may encounter in self-aware systems and
represent a range of domains and a variety of scales and levels of complexity. The
first scenario focuses on an adaptive sorting algorithm and exemplifies how a self-
aware system may adapt to changes in the data on which it operates, the environment in which it executes, or the requirements or performance criteria to which it

J.O. Kephart (✉)
Thomas J. Watson Research Center, Hawthorne, NY, USA
e-mail: kephart@us.ibm.com

M. Maggio · A. Robertsson
Department of Automatic Control, Lund University, Ole Rmers vg 1,
SE 223 63 Lund, Sweden
e-mail: martina.maggio@control.lth.se

A. Robertsson
e-mail: anders.robertsson@control.lth.se

A. Diaconescu
Departement INFRES, Telécom ParisTech, Equipe S3, 46 rue Barrault, 75013 Paris, France
e-mail: ada.diaconescu@telecom-paristech.fr

H. Giese
Hasso Plattner Institute for Software Systems Engineering at the University of Potsdam,
Prof.-Dr.-Helmert-Str. 2-3, 14482 Potsdam, Germany
e-mail: holger.giese@hpi.uni-potsdam.de

H. Hoffmann
Department of Computer Science, University of Chicago, Ry 250, Ryerson Hall,
1100 E 58th St, Chicago, IL 60637, USA
e-mail: hankhoffmann@cs.uchicago.edu

S. Kounev · S. Spinner
Department of Computer Science, University of Würzburg, Am Hubland,
97074 Würzburg, Germany
e-mail: samuel.kounev@uni-wuerzburg.de

S. Spinner
e-mail: simon.spinner@uni-wuerzburg.de

© Springer International Publishing AG 2017
S. Kounev et al. (eds.), *Self-Aware Computing Systems*,
DOI 10.1007/978-3-319-47474-8_4

87

manages itself. The second focuses on self-aware multiagent applications running in a data center environment, allowing issues of collective behavior in cooperative and competitive self-aware systems to come to the fore. The third focuses on a cyber-physical system. It allows us to explore many of the same issues of system-level self-awareness that appear in the second scenario, but in a different context and at a potentially even larger (potentially planetary) scale, when there is no one clear global objective.

4.1 Introduction

This chapter introduces three reference scenarios for which self-awareness plays an important role. The reference scenarios are intended to cover a broad set of characteristics and issues that one may encounter in self-aware systems, and to represent a range of domains and a variety of scales and levels of complexity. They constitute a starting point that will be elaborated further in other chapters, as needed.

The remainder of the chapter is organized as follows. In Sect. 4.2, we explain the criteria that led us to choose this particular set of reference scenarios, including a set of research questions that we wished to expose, and a set of dimensions that we wished to explore.

The first scenario, presented in Sect. 4.3, focuses on an adaptive sorting algorithm and exemplifies how a self-aware individual system element may adapt to changes in the data on which it operates, the environment in which it executes, or the requirements or performance criteria to which it manages itself.

The second scenario (Sect. 4.4) features applications running in a data center environment. It brings to the fore issues of coordination, cooperation, and competition that arise within self-aware applications composed of multiple interacting self-aware elements or components. Moreover, it raises issues of competition and conflict that may arise among multiple self-aware applications, and between those applications and a self-aware entity that represents the interests of the data center owner.

The third scenario (Sect. 4.5) focuses on a cyber-physical system. It allows us to study issues of system-level self-awareness similar to those of Sect. 4.4, but in a different context and at a potentially even larger (potentially planetary) scale, at which there is no one clear global objective. This scenario is built up incrementally in increasing levels of scale and complexity, thereby highlighting different levels of self-awareness. The chapter concludes with a brief summary (Sect. 4.6).

A. Koziolek
Institute for Program Structures and Data Organization, Karlsruhe Institute of Technology, Am Fasanengarten 5, 76131 Karlsruhe, Germany
e-mail: koziolek@kit.edu

P. Lewis
School of Engineering and Applied Science, Aston University, Birmingham, UK
e-mail: p.lewis@aston.ac.uk

4.2 Rationale

The purpose of this section is to explain some of the considerations that led to our choice of reference scenarios, including a set of research questions and dimensions that we wished to explore.

Among the key research questions regarding self-aware systems that we wish our reference scenarios to support are as follows:

- How can self-awareness help a computing system achieve its goals?
- What is the relationship between a system's properties and the type and degree of self-awareness that is most appropriate or beneficial for it?
- What are the costs or drawbacks of self-awareness, and what is its overall net benefit?
- How do different instances of self-awareness operating at different levels of a system interact with or otherwise affect one another, and what is the impact of these interactions upon overall system behavior and performance?

Among the key dimensions of self-awareness that we wished to explore through the reference scenarios were as follows:

- **Goal complexity**. For any given self-aware entity, does its goal concern a single attribute (such as a thermostat that just manages temperature), or is it a multiattribute (as in the data center scenario), where an application owner might strive to optimize multiple application performance criteria (involving response time, throughput, and downtime) while minimizing resource usage (so as to reduce payments due to the data center owner)?
- **Goal alignment**. For self-aware systems that comprise more than one self-aware entity, to what degree do the objectives of the constituent entities align with one another? This is related to whether or not the individual entities are operating explicitly on behalf of one authority, or several.

  - The adaptive sorter scenario represents a simple one-component system with a single purpose.
  - The data center scenario exemplifies a multiplicity of individual goals held among the end users, the application owners, and the data center owner.
  - The various cyber-physical scenarios cover a range of cases, including:
    appliances that have their own individual objectives but may have some consideration for global house-wide objectives built into them;
    smart homes that each seek to minimize cost and maximize power consumption by their owners, potentially creating resource contention and possibly resource shortages; and
    shuttles that are designed to be highly cooperative with one another.

- **Heterogeneity**. Self-aware systems may tend toward homogeneity or heterogeneity in terms of technology and protocols as well as behavior, strategies, self-management capabilities, self-awareness level, degree to which they have adapted effectively to the environment in which they are situated, and timing characteristics [20, 21].

4.3 Adaptive Sorting

What might it mean for software to be adaptive and self-aware? To answer this question, we start by considering as an example the std::sort algorithm included in the C++ Standard Template Library (STL). In its current form, the STL sorting algorithm is neither adaptive nor self-aware. However, there are two important reasons why one might want to endow it with adaptability and self-awareness: coping with the plethora of different hardware architectures on which the algorithm might run and coping with the wide variety of input data characteristics.

First, consider the influence of the hardware architectural features such as cache size, cache line size, and the number of registers on the nature of the optimal sorting algorithm and parameters. In the version of libstdc++ included with GCC 4.3, merge sort was used until the list was smaller than 15 elements, below which insertion sort was used. This choice was established empirically as best for problems of a certain size and type on architectures that were common when the library was originally written. By 2009, architectures had evolved to the point where a higher cutoff was found to be more effective [1]. [1]

Second, consider the influence of data set characteristics such as size and distribution (e.g., standard deviation) upon the optimal sorting algorithm and parameters. Experiments reveal that data sets with small standard deviations favor the quicksort algorithm, while for larger standard deviations the CC-radix sort [17, 29] is the best choice. When the number of keys is increased, the best algorithms for small standard deviation values are multiway merge sort, while CC-radix is best for larger input sizes and higher standard deviation [22].

Recently, researchers have begun to experiment with generating sorting algorithms dynamically, based on the observations of the performance and the execution platform and fine-grained performance tuning [1, 4]. This automatic tuning is usually done through an empirical search [18, 19, 26] that identifies the algorithm (among a set of potential ones) that performs best on the specific deployment machine. Code that dynamically adapts to the characteristics of the input has a significant advantage over other types of optimization [22].

Having established why it is advantageous for a sorter to be capable of adapting to its environment (i.e., the hardware architecture and the data upon which it operates), we now imagine what an adaptive, self-aware sorter might be like.

---

[1] Another notable example where hard-coded parameters have evolved over time to accommodate changes in architecture is the discrete Fourier transform [4, 9].

4.3.1 Scenario

An adaptive, *self-aware sorter* should sense the environment and the input data to be sorted and adapt its behavior accordingly. These requirements have both design-time and run-time implications.

First, consider the design of a self-aware sorter. The designer must anticipate that the sorter could be instantiated in a variety of different environments, including different hardware architectures, or different amounts of compute resources such as CPU, memory, and I/O. The designer must also anticipate that at run-time the user of the sorting algorithm could express goals and constraints in terms of a variety of different high-level attributes, including latency, throughput, and energy consumption and that the data set could vary widely in terms of size or other characteristics that might affect sorting efficiency. The designer must then incorporate her knowledge or expectations into the design of the self-aware sorter. The design must include:

1. means for sensing certain aspects of the environment (e.g., the identity of the operating system, available compute resources, or the data set size);
2. means for controlling certain aspects of the sorter's behavior (e.g., the type of sorting algorithm used, or the amount of memory allocated);
3. means for sensing certain attributes of the self-aware sorter's behavior that might possibly be of interest to the user;
4. knowledge of which environmental aspects and algorithmic behavior attributes can be sensed, and which algorithmic parameters can be controlled;
5. models (or partial models, or hints about the likely functional form of models whose details could be learned at run-time) that capture the dependency of behavioral attributes upon environmental conditions;
6. means for capturing user goals and constraints; and
7. means for using models to optimize control parameters with respect to user goals and constraints

The design goals, run-time expectations (and the ranges into which the user goals fall), and models or model hints should be expressed in a form that can be used by formal verification methods to confirm that the sorter is correct and satisfies the designer's goals and objectives (which include coping with the widest possible set of conditions and user expectations).

Now consider the self-aware sorter at run-time. When instantiated within a specific environment, the self-aware sorter senses the hardware and resources of that environment, assesses the data set that it is being asked to sort, and receives information about the user's goals and constraints with regard to latency, throughput, energy consumption, or other attributes of interest. For example, the user might wish the sorter to minimize CPU and memory usage while maintaining a compute time of no more than 5 s. Given the initial model provided by the designer, its understanding of the environment in which it is situated, its own state and capabilities, and the user's objectives, the self-aware sorter then uses its optimization capability to determine the best sorting algorithm and associated parameters to use, and perform the sort accordingly.

In a more advanced variant of the scenario, the self-aware sorter dynamically searches for new sorting algorithms not contained within its original code base that are more optimal given the current circumstances. Such algorithms might exist in the form of libraries that could be dynamically linked into the code, or a Web service. In order to determine that these new algorithms are likely to be better than any currently used by the sorter, new algorithms should be accompanied by models that predict their likely performance. Such models might be packaged with the algorithms themselves, for example, or provided by a trusted third party that conducts extensive experiments on the algorithms in order to learn models for them.

In an orthogonal variant, models relating environmental conditions and algorithmic parameters to high-level performance criteria might be learned dynamically as the sorter is applied to various data sets over time. If the designer has already provided a model, the model learning might take the form of Bayesian updates to the original model. If the designer has instead provided hints about relevant variables and/or some expectations about the structure of the model, these could be used as a framework or constraint in which the learning would take place. In any case, the learning could be performed by the sorter itself, or it could be done by third parties that do the learning and then make the resultant models available.

Preferably, the design specification should be accessible by the instantiated self-aware sorter. If for some reason the assumptions under which the design was performed and verified are violated, an alert could be created and sent to the designer or the verification algorithm. Upon learning that the original assumptions are violated, the designer would have a chance to redesign the algorithm, or the verification algorithm could be launched automatically and signal the designer if the run-time conditions are such that the algorithm is not sound (or optimal). Moreover, other properties can be taken into account, like software health [28].

4.3.2 Key Questions

- How feasible is it for the designer of a self-aware software component to build in the required sensors, controls, models, and self-regulation mechanisms? Must we invent a new generation of software design tools to help with this task?
- What type of information could a self-aware software component capture at run-time that would support improvements in the design of the next generation of that software? What are the methods by which such information captured from multiple run-time instances of self-aware sorters be integrated into the redesign?
- Is it possible to remove the human designer from the loop, such that the redesign step becomes a type of run-time adaptation? How would this work?

4.4   Data Center Resource Management

As a second reference scenario, we consider self-awareness in the context of a data center. This is an interesting case because data centers involve management of thousands of applications and are therefore several orders of magnitude beyond the self-aware sorter in terms of scale and complexity. Moreover, in this case, there are many different stakeholders instead of just one:

- the *data center owner*, who operates the physical infrastructure, consisting of a large number of physical (and, increasingly, virtual) machines plus network and other computational resources required to run applications. The data center owner seeks to honor its service-level agreements with the application owners while minimizing the costs of building and maintaining the data center.
- multiple *application owners*, who purchase compute resources from the data center owner and use those resources to deploy, run, and manage applications that provide services to the end users. They seek to honor their SLAs with the end users while minimizing what they pay to the data center owner for the use of the physical infrastructure; and
- myriad *end users*, who use the applications provided by the application owners and are concerned only with their own perceived service quality. Web users typically tolerate a waiting time between 2 and 4 s [25], depending upon the type of application (e.g., interactive Web page vs. mail delivery service). There is some price elasticity; that is, the end users may be willing to pay more for better service.

The data center owner, application owners, and the end users may come from different organizations (e.g., in a public cloud) and the usage of the service and the infrastructure may be connected with certain fees. The expectations regarding the quality of service and the fees are defined through service-level agreements (SLAs) between the data center owner and the application owners, as well as SLAs between application owners and their end users.

The need for data centers and the applications that run in them to be adaptive is well-recognized. Many applications are subject to strong time-varying workloads that can (during the so-called flash crowds) reach peaks five times more intense than the average workload [5], causing the resource requirements to increase accordingly [27]. Moreover, unexpected hardware failures occur frequently in data centers [14, 24].

Virtualization is a key technology that has been introduced to enable more dynamic management of resources and applications in data centers. Virtualization flexibly allocates computing, storage, and network resources to applications running in data centers. Data center owners benefit because they can consolidate independent applications onto the same physical hardware, thereby reducing the physical resource and electrical power required to support a given number of applications. Virtualization allows a data center owner to overcommit physical resources; that is, they can allow the allocated virtual machine (VM) resource reservations to exceed the current physical resource capacity, on the assumption that not all virtual machines require the resources at the same time [2, 15]. Application owners benefit because they can dynamically acquire additional computational resources whenever their application workload increases and release those resources back to the data center when it decreases—which is much more efficient and cost-effective than the traditional method of requesting enough dedicated physical resource to satisfy the maximum anticipated demand.

Virtualization enables efficiency and cost-effectiveness for both data center owners and application owners, resulting in savings that can be passed on to the end users. In practice, however, it is challenging to manage virtualization in such a way that objectives are met fairly and efficiently as workloads fluctuate, and goals shift.

One factor that contributes to this challenge is that modern virtualization and middleware platforms provide a wide range of adaptable parameters, such as where virtual machines are placed on physical hosts, the number of VM instances, the size of each VM (e.g., number of virtual CPUs), the scheduling priorities for a VM (e.g., CPU reservations, limits, and shares), and the platform configuration (e.g., thread pools and cache size).

Another factor is that it is difficult to know how changes to the parameters will affect the behavior of the system and its impact on the various stakeholders. Typical cloud management solutions of today (such as Amazon EC2,[2] or CloudStack[3]) use autoscaling techniques to add or remove resources from an application when low-level metrics such as CPU utilization cross a given threshold—a very rough proxy for the metrics of actual interest to the application owners and end users, such as application performance and robustness. These VM management solutions are not only unaware of the high-level goals of the stakeholders, but also they would not know how to manage those goals because they lack models that map from VM management parameters to application-level metrics.

A final factor is that today's VM management systems do not take into account the multiple conflicting goals of the various stakeholders in a principled way. Indeed, the interests of the data center owner and the application owners are often completely at odds with one another; for example, data center owners wish to minimize costs by minimizing use of power and physical resources, while application owners want the higher performance that results from maximizing power and physical resources. Consequently, VM management systems are unlikely to realize trade-offs that are understandable or fair. For example, some modern virtualization techniques attempt to optimize resource allocation at the data center level. The VMware Distributed Resource Scheduler (DRS) [13] balances and distributes the load between physical hosts in a data center by migrating virtual machines. The Distributed Power Management (DPM) controller [13] automatically consolidates VMs if physical hosts are underutilized, placing freed up hosts in standby mode to save energy and rebooting when necessary. While an effort is made to minimize the likelihood that an application will be starved for resource while waiting for a reboot, these controllers do not consider application-performance requirements explicitly.

---

[2]http://aws.amazon.com/en/ec2/.
[3]http://cloudstack.apache.org/.

4.4.1 Scenario

Here, we exemplify how self-awareness could enable more effective use of virtualization from the perspective of the two stakeholders who have the ability to control resources: the application owner and the data center owner.

A hypothetical self-aware controller operating on behalf of the application owner [31] wishes to use an appropriate amount of resource, such that the fees it pays to the data center owner for the use of physical or virtual compute resources are no more than they need to be to satisfy the demand from their end users. To do this, an application controller could take two types of actions. First, it requests virtual computational resources $\mathbf{r}$ from the data center owner (at some cost), and second, it sets the values of the parameters under its control $\mathbf{c}(\mathbf{r})$ to allocate and control the virtual resource $\mathbf{r}$. The virtual resource might, for example, be a week of time on a virtual machine with a CPU capacity of $5 \cdot 10^9$ cycles per second, with 8GB of memory and 80GB of SSD storage.

The application controller's goal is to maximize its revenue from the end-user SLAs, $\pi(\mathbf{V})$, where $\mathbf{V}$ represents the values of the attributes appearing in the SLA. The end-user SLAs would be based upon the application-level metrics, such as average response time (or 95 % response time percentiles), latency, and might include penalties for service disruption. Additional application-level attributes might include elasticity [16] (i.e., the ability to rapidly increase or decrease the allocated resource in response to demand from the end users) and resource stability (guarantees that fluctuations in the compute resource provided to the application will be minimized).[4]

The self-aware controller has a self-model $\mathbf{V}(\mathbf{c}(\mathbf{r}), \lambda)$ that expresses how its performance-attribute values depend upon the control settings and the workload λ. Some methods by which such a model might be learned are discussed in Chap. 12. The self-aware controller then optimizes over all control settings to identify $\mathbf{c}^*(\mathbf{r})$, the setting for which $\pi^*(\mathbf{r}) = \pi(\mathbf{V}(\mathbf{c}^*(\mathbf{r}), \lambda))$ is greatest.

The self-aware controller uses the above procedure to compute $\pi^*(\mathbf{r})$ for all possible values of $\mathbf{r}$. Then, it performs a second optimization over all values of $\mathbf{r}$ to determine the value $\mathbf{r}^*$ that optimizes the net profit $\pi^*(\mathbf{r}) - \gamma(\mathbf{r})$ (the revenue from the end-user SLAs minus the payment to the data center owner for the resources $\mathbf{r}$). It requests compute resources $\mathbf{r}^*$ from the data center owner, and then, when it receives them it allocates and controls those resources according to the optimal control values $\mathbf{c}^*$. Since the model contains a workload-dependent term, it and any optimizations based upon it must be continually updated as the workload fluctuates.

A hypothetical self-aware controller operating on behalf of the data center owner could employ a similar approach involving self-models coupled with optimization, balancing its need to satisfy SLAs that it has in place with each of the application owners against its desire to minimize its own costs for physical infrastructure and

---

[4]The data center owner might minimize such fluctuations by using traditional performance isolation techniques such as physically isolating the compute resources. In contrast to current practice, in which SLAs explicitly mention physical isolation, in our opinion the SLA should be expressed solely in terms of a service guarantee and not in terms of how that guarantee is implemented.

power. Specifically, the data center controller can select a set of control parameters $\mathbf{c}$ that (according to a self-model $\mathbf{r}(\mathbf{c})$) is expected to produce an amount of virtual resource $\mathbf{r}$. Additionally, the choice of control parameters $\mathbf{c}$ implies an increase $\rho(\mathbf{c})$ in the amount of physical resource and power that must be provisioned in order to realize those control parameters. When an application controller requests an amount of virtual resource $\mathbf{r}'$, the data center controller's task is then to find the $\mathbf{c}^*$ that minimizes the effective amortized cost for physical resources and power $p(\rho(\mathbf{c}))$, subject to the constraint that $\mathbf{r}(\mathbf{c}) = \mathbf{r}'$. The data center will then receive a profit of $\gamma(\mathbf{r}') - p(\rho(\mathbf{c}^*))$ from that application owner.

This scenario is somewhat naïve in that it assumes that resource and control settings are instantaneously responsive. This is not true in general; for example, it can take seconds, or even minutes, to allocate new VMs to an existing application, particularly if a physical server needs to be powered on. In a more sophisticated variant of the above scenario, the self-aware application controller would take into account these time lags and compute its resource request proactively by anticipating that more resource is likely to be needed soon. Reinforcement-learning approaches have proven effective in such cases [30].

In yet another variant of the scenario, the agreement between the application owner and the data center owner would be based upon SLAs describing the virtual resource $\mathbf{r}$ provided to the application controller, rather than directly in terms of the resource itself. The attributes appearing in such an SLA would include traditional resource-level metrics such as CPU cycles, memory allocation, and bandwidth, but it would also include metrics describing service disruptions (e.g., downtime) as well as bonuses and/or penalties incurred when the provided resource is more or less than a specified target amount.

In another variant, the data center controller enforces an overall constraint on the amount of physical infrastructure and power consumed across all applications. This necessitates significant changes to the interaction between the data center owner and the application owners. Since the application owners do not decide unilaterally how much resource they will receive, a negotiation process would now be required.

4.4.2 Key Questions

- Which methods are most efficient and effective for learning models that map from controllable parameters and environmental conditions to SLA attributes? Some answers to this question will be provided in Chap. 12.
- In the scenario above, both controllers used a relatively simple predictive model-control approach to govern their actions. More sophisticated approaches are needed to handle situations, where there is a delay between when an action is taken and its effect is manifest, such as reinforcement learning. What are the best techniques for exploiting models to select actions, and under what conditions?
- In the scenario above, the data center owner provided to each application owner the amount of resource that they requested, and the application owners then did their

best to manage within that allocation. One can envision other scenarios in which the data center owner determines the amount of resource, or there is some information exchange or negotiation through which both parties can jointly determine the allocation. What other schemes exist, and how well do they work under various circumstances, from the standpoint of both parties? Some answers to this question can be found in Walsh et al. [31], and in Chap. 13.

- For both the data center owner and the application owners, the terms of the SLA have a profound impact on the behavior of the system. What are some means by which these SLAs can be established in the first place? Must they always be set unilaterally, by the data center owner? Or, might there be a process of negotiation between the data center owner and the application owners, and if so what are some plausible (or perhaps optimal) negotiation mechanisms?
- Would it be feasible to replace SLAs with an auction or other type of dynamic economic mechanism, and if so how would this affect the nature of the algorithms employed by the controllers?

4.5 Cyber-Physical Systems

In this section, we present several scenarios involving cyber-physical systems in which multiple self-aware entities interact within a shared environment. These scenarios allow us to study individual and collective self-awareness, and the relationships between them. As in Frey et al. [8] and Chen et al. [7], the scenarios are organized in order of increasing complexity and scale.

4.5.1 Thermostat

4.5.1.1 Scenario

The first and simplest scenario takes place within a home and involves a single device pursuing a single goal. Specifically, a thermostat strives to maintain a room's temperature within one degree of a value specified by one of the home's inhabitants. The amount of heating or cooling power that must be supplied to the room depends upon the ambient outside temperature, which can vary over the course of a day or a season. Accordingly, the thermostat is equipped with a thermometer that senses the room's temperature, and it uses a simple model to convert the difference between the observed and desired temperature into a signal that controls an actuator that turns the room heating or air-conditioning on or off.

In a more complex variant of the scenario, the thermostat pursues multiple goals simultaneously. For instance, in addition to the temperature goal, the thermostat can be constrained by a power consumption goal, such as a maximum power that may be used to heat or cool the house during a day. Alternatively, a power goal could be defined dynamically by an automatic controller of a local power grid, to which the thermostat is connected. Rather than being defined in terms of a daily threshold, the goal might require that the connected device prioritizes or avoids power consumption. The goal may change at regular intervals depending on the overall state of the power grid—i.e., the current balance between power consumption and production. In many cases, the thermostat's temperature and power goals may conflict with one another, as reaching a higher temperature with respect to the external environment requires the thermostat to consume (switch on) power while the power goal may recommend the opposite (switch off). In more complicated cases, an additional (and potentially conflicting) goal may be given to the thermostat in order to minimize the cost of power consumption for the home owner, while the grid controller could impose fluctuating power prices.

In an orthogonal variant of the scenario, the self-aware thermostat is capable of explaining its state, behavior, and plans. Specifically, if queried, the thermostat would be able to report its actions (past, current, and planned) and the motivations behind them, evaluate its performance with respect to its goal(s), and perhaps even diagnose failures to meet its goals. Such a degree of self-awareness is key to the ability of the thermostat to improve itself, either dynamically at run-time or by collecting observations that would aid in designing the next-generation self-aware thermostat.

4.5.1.2   Key Questions

- How would extending the thermostat's awareness to encompass a broader context, including the presence of humans or the temperature of adjoining rooms, improve its performance and efficiency? How costly would it be to add the requisite sensors, or communication capabilities, or computational power? Would the extra self-awareness warrant this cost?
- How would extending the thermostat's awareness to encompass a broader set of models, such as daily or seasonal external temperatures, models of other rooms in the house, or power price predictions improve its performance or efficiency? How would the costs of such improvements compare to the benefits?
- What are the best means for resolving conflicts among multiple goals?

4.5.2   Smart Home

4.5.2.1   Scenario

This scenario adds to the previous scenario an additional "smart" window shutter and a washing machine, thereby illustrating a case in which several heterogeneous devices pursue different goals within a single environment, under a single authority. Acting upon signals from sensors that sense sunlight and external and internal temperature, and possibly human presence sensors as well, the smart window shutter pursues goals related to the home's lighting and temperature by controlling actuators that rotate the shutter panels individually. In doing so, the smart window controller simultaneously affects both the temperature and the light intensity within the house.

The self-aware washing machine offers different programmes with different on-off cycles and durations, which can be selected by users to run within a specified time frame. When connected to a smart grid, the washing machine may avoid power consumption or price peaks by delaying the washing cycle automatically. Note that, since the shutter's actions affect temperature and the washing machine's, affect power, the introduction of these two self-aware entities into the environment creates the potential for goal conflicts that extend across these devices.

In a more complex version of the scenario, additional thermostats or window shutters are introduced throughout the house, and the user specifies house-wide goals or constraints, such as house temperature and lighting preferences, or power consumption thresholds or costs—thereby requiring cross-device coordination.

Another interesting twist on the scenario considers the consequences of altering the set of sensors or devices installed within the smart home. Individual self-aware devices must adjust to the presence of new sensors or devices that consume power or produce heat, or to the absence of the recently removed sensors or devices. Moreover, any models or controllers that operate at the level of the smart home as a whole must adjust to the changes in power-consumption or power-provision profiles or other characteristics of the newly introduced or recently removed devices.

4.5.2.2   Key Questions

- What conflicts might arise as multiple homogeneous or heterogeneous self-aware devices operating within a single environment attempt to satisfy their individual (and possibly multifarious) goals? For example, how could thermostats cooperate with shutters to manage temperature goals, while simultaneously attending to their respective power and light-intensity goals? How effectively can various negotiation or other mechanisms resolve such conflicts?
- How can a collective of self-aware entities manage micro- and macrogoals simultaneously, such as the power consumption of each device and of the house overall? What are the relative merits of a single central self-aware controller for the home as a whole vs. an arbiter or a fully decentralized arrangement in which global goals are somehow translated into local goals that are combined with the intrinsic goals of the individual controllers?
- How can self-aware entities detect and cope with changes in their environment, such as the addition or removal of sensors or devices?
- How could a self-aware collective (such as a smart home) provide coherent explanations of its behavior and plans, both at an individual and a collective level?

4.5.3   Smart Micro-grid

4.5.3.1   Scenario

Consider a scenario in which several smart homes are interconnected via a smart micro-grid. Not only does this move up a level in the scale from the previous scenario, but also it allows one to explore the situations in which there is no single authority, but rather multiple authorities with interests that may both overlap and conflict. The interests of each smart home owner may be represented by its own independent self-aware controller, while the interest of the power company that owns the micro-grid may also be represented by its own self-aware controller. The interests of these various authorities overlap in some regards; for example, they all desire power service dependability and sustainability. However, they also conflict in other aspects; for example, each home owner desires minimal costs, while the power company wants maximal profits.

Each self-aware controller may act independently of the other and may even choose to leave the power grid at any time. The power grid authority likely plays a role in determining the power consumed by each smart home, but it may be indirect in nature, or shared with the smart homes (e.g., if the allocation depends upon pricing or some type of negotiation). However, it does not have fine-grained over the allocation of power within individual homes; that is the province of the individual smart home controllers.

Other minor variants of the scenario introduce additional entities representing the interests of other independent authorities, such as follows:

- alternative energy generators (e.g., wind turbines and solar plants);
- governmental or other regulatory authorities that may impose general laws (and hence constraints) directly (e.g., restrictions on power consumption by individual homes) or indirectly (e.g., limits on prices charged by the power company);
- entities other than smart homes that consume electric power: businesses, electric cars, etc., and whose behavior are therefore coupled in myriad subtle and unanticipated ways with that of the smart homes (see, for example, [23], on the topic of probabilistic modeling, and Chap. 13).

4.5.3.2   Key Questions

- When multiple self-aware controllers with independent objectives interact in the absence of a central authority, what forms of communication and negotiation ensure most that there is sufficient mutual benefit to warrant the interaction?
- In systems of multiple independent self-aware entities, the learning and adaptation of one such entity induces a behavioral change that affects the experience of those with which it interacts. How is it possible for self-aware entities to learn and adapt in an environment that is always changing due to the learning and adaptation of the other self-aware entities?

- In systems of multiple independent self-aware entities, to what extent is it possible or desirable for self-aware entities to become aware of one another's goals, internal states, and behaviors?
- Given possible restrictions on information access (e.g., due to privacy concerns), what mechanisms and incentives support exchange of useful information among self-aware entities? How might they best employ such information?

4.5.4   System of Autonomous Shuttles

4.5.4.1   Scenarios

As a final cyber-physical systems scenario, consider an intelligent transportation system in which trains of connected railroad cars are replaced by a collection of autonomous shuttles.[5] By operating on demand, autonomous shuttles can be more efficient and tailor their operation more precisely to passenger needs and priorities. For example, managers may request high-speed transport to an urgent meeting, while tourists may request transport within a certain time window for less cost.

A prototype autonomous shuttle system of this nature is under development [11]. In order to separate the hard real-time processing required for reliable switching and reconfiguration from the soft real-time processing required for long-term decision-making, the system features an operator controller module (OCM) containing an arbiter that controls the underlying physical processes. The reflective operator handles the necessary reconfiguration in hard real time. At the same time, a cognitive operator captures the more demanding aspects of self-optimization such as decision making based on run-time models. As depicted in Fig. 4.1, the architecture of a single autonomous shuttle is a hierarchy of OCMs.[6] Optionally, the highest level OCMs within each autonomous shuttle may interact with one another.

In one class of variants, the shuttles operate completely independently, optimizing their own operation without directly sharing any information other than what can be obtained from observation; that is, they have no awareness of one another's models or intent. For example, they might parasitically save energy by following other shuttles when possible to reduce air resistance. In another variant, shuttles compete with another to earn money by transporting passengers or cargo. If the mechanism used to match shuttles with transport requests is an auction, then to form a competent bid the shuttles need to generate good estimates of the time, energy, and expense incurred in meeting specific transport requests, which requires that they learn and/or use models

---

[5]http://www.railcab.de/index.php?id=2\&L=1.

[6]The design of a single autonomous shuttle would be an interesting scenario in itself. See the Mechatronic UML approach [6] for the model-driven development of self-optimizing embedded real-time systems, which includes a notion of UML components for hybrid behavior, real-time statecharts extending UML state machines, and the required tool support [6, 10] and analysis techniques [3, 10–12] developed to be able to design safe autonomous shuttles and their internal hierarchical structure with self-optimization.

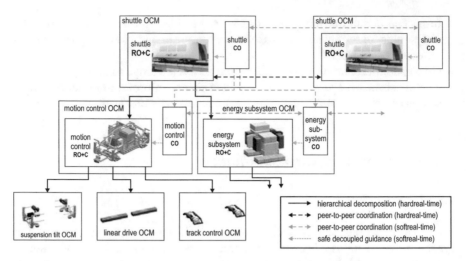

Fig. 4.1 Architecture of the autonomous shuttle as well as their combination (figure taken from [11])

of their own capabilities and costs, as well as a model of the environment in which they operate. Their bids may be placed with or without an awareness of the existence of other shuttles that are vying to serve the same transport requests.

In another class of variants, the shuttles are aware of one another in the sense of possessing or being capable of learning models of other shuttles. Such a degree of awareness could be advantageous, as it affords the possibility of anticipating their likely bids or operational behaviors.

Another dimension to the autonomous shuttle fleet scenario is whether the shuttles coordinate their actions with one another, and if so whether that coordination is achieved through a central coordinator or in a decentralized fashion via messages exchanged among the shuttles (in which case coordination would be an emergent effect). A natural motivation for such coordination would be to optimize transport orders globally across the entire fleet, maximizing its revenue by optimizing quality of service and minimizing its cost by determining which shuttles are in a position to provide the requested service most efficiently. While fleet-level planning would be conducted across the set of shuttles, each shuttle's individual controller would still be responsible for executing the plan, based on its model of its own capabilities along with characteristics of the environment in which it operates.

In the case where shuttles cooperate by explicitly exchanging high-level information with one another, all of the activities of self-aware computing systems discussed by Weyns et al. [32] may be realized, including the following:

- **Learning run-time models jointly.** Consider a fleet of shuttles that cooperates by exchanging monitoring data to learn the characteristics of other shuttles, the characteristics of the environment, or the characteristics of the shuttle fleets. For example, exchanging data on track conditions [6] can help shuttles optimize their travel to any part of the system that has been experienced by at least one shuttle.

- **Sharing goals and joint reasoning**. If shuttles exchange their goals, their planning can take into account what other shuttles are likely to do and might through bilateral or multilateral negotiation arrive at a mutually satisfactory itinerary. For example, they may avoid operating at cross-purposes, e.g., bidding against one another or planning conflicting itineraries.
- **Joint actions**. If shuttles share with one another their plans, they have a chance to detect problems or conflicts and renegotiate or discover a solution that will be more globally beneficial. For example, if a shuttle is no longer able to move on its own, another shuttle may be able to help it by pushing it to the next station.

Also of interest is a competitive scenario that inherits the characteristics of the cooperative shuttle scenario presented above, including the autonomy of individual shuttles and the centralized or decentralized coordination that optimizes plans and schedules over an individual fleet, and imbeds that scenario in a larger one in which fleets compete with one another to serve transport requests. This scenario shares much in common with the scenario in which individual shuttles compete with one another, except that now the competition is at the level of entire fleets rather than shuttles. For example, in the case it becomes interesting to consider the potential advantage that one fleet might gain by learning models of competing fleets.

Finally, the scenario may be extended to a larger-scale and more heterogeneous intelligent-transport system that encompasses automobiles, taxis, bicycles, and other forms of transportation that are represented by self-aware controllers—a diverse milieu that brings together myriad diverse interests and applications (e.g., bus and trucking companies, individual and taxi drivers, traffic management, and city government).

4.5.4.2 Key Questions

- How can a system of autonomous shuttles or other self-aware systems fulfill dependability requirements?
- What coordination mechanisms can permit self-aware systems to satisfy their own individual objectives while functioning competently in a system of systems that contains myriad other self-aware systems that represent multiple diverse interests?
- What forms of information can usefully be shared among self-interested self-aware entities in cooperative settings, or competitive settings, or combinations thereof? Depending upon the type of information shared, how can self-aware entities best avail themselves of such information for making individual decision, or for engaging in negotiation or cooperative planning with other self-aware entities? Under what conditions are the cost and effort worthwhile?

4.6 Conclusion

This chapter presented three broad scenarios, providing some insights into the role of self-awareness in the design of smarter systems. The first scenario, an adaptive sorting algorithm, showed a single-agent adaptation system, where one entity can exploit its knowledge of the system to improve its behavior. The second scenario showed multiple entities in a data center that could benefit from self-awareness to pursue higher level goals. In this case, there is at least a specific data center owner, together with other players. The owner and the players' goals should be fulfilled. The third set of scenarios showed multiple entities that can have conflicting goals, where the owner of the system is unclear or undefined. For all these scenarios, the chapter pointed out challenges and opportunities to be explored.

Acknowledgements This work was partially supported by the Swedish Research Council (VR) for the projects "Cloud Control" and "Power and temperature control for large-scale computing infrastructures," and through the LCCC Linnaeus and ELLIIT Excellence Centers.

References

1. Jason Ansel, Cy Chan, Yee Lok Wong, Marek Olszewski, Qin Zhao, Alan Edelman, and Saman Amarasinghe. Petabricks: A language and compiler for algorithmic choice. In *Proceedings of the 2009 ACM SIGPLAN Conference on Programming Language Design and Implementation*, PLDI '09, pages 38–49, New York, NY, USA, 2009. ACM.
2. Luiz Andre Barroso and Urs Hlzle. *The Datacenter as a Computer: An Introduction to the Design of Warehouse-Scale Machines*. Morgan & Claypool, 2009.
3. Basil Becker, Dirk Beyer, Holger Giese, Florian Klein, and Daniela Schilling. Symbolic Invariant Verification for Systems with Dynamic Structural Adaptation. In *Proc. of the 28th Intl. Conf. on Software Engineering (ICSE), Shanghai, China*. ACM, 2006.
4. Anthony Blake and Matt Hunter. Dynamically generating FFT code. *J. Signal Process. Syst.*, 76(3):275–281, September 2014.
5. Peter Bodik, Armando Fox, Michael J. Franklin, Michael I. Jordan, and David A. Patterson. Characterizing, modeling, and generating workload spikes for stateful services. In *SOCC*, pages 241–252, New York, NY, USA, 2010. ACM.
6. Sven Burmester, Holger Giese, Eckehard Münch, Oliver Oberschelp, Florian Klein, and Peter Scheideler. Tool Support for the Design of Self-Optimizing Mechatronic Multi-Agent Systems. *International Journal on Software Tools for Technology Transfer (STTT)*, 10(3):207–222, June 2008.
7. Tao Chen, Funmilade Faniyi, Rami Bahsoon, Peter R. Lewis, Xin Yao, Leandro L. Minku, and Lukas Esterle. The handbook of engineering self-aware and self-expressive systems. *CoRR*, abs/1409.1793, 2014.
8. Sylvain Frey, François Huguet, Cédric Mivielle, David Menga, Ada Diaconescu, and Isabelle M. Demeure. Scenarios for an autonomic micro smart grid. In *SMARTGREENS 2012 - Proceedings of the 1st International Conference on Smart Grids and Green IT Systems, Porto, Portugal, 19 - 20 April, 2012*, pages 137–140, 2012.
9. M. Frigo and S.G. Johnson. FFTW: an adaptive software architecture for the FFT. In *Acoustics, Speech and Signal Processing, 1998. Proceedings of the 1998 IEEE International Conference on*, volume 3, pages 1381–1384 vol.3, May 1998.

10. Holger Giese, Sven Burmester, Wilhelm Schäfer, and Oliver Oberschelp. Modular Design and Verification of Component-Based Mechatronic Systems with Online-Reconfiguration. In *Proc. of 12th ACM SIGSOFT Foundations of Software Engineering 2004 (FSE 2004), Newport Beach, USA*. ACM, 2004.
11. Holger Giese and Wilhelm Schäfer. Model-Driven Development of Safe Self-Optimizing Mechatronic Systems with MechatronicUML. In Javier Camara, Rogério de Lemos, Carlo Ghezzi, and Antnia Lopes, editors, *Assurances for Self-Adaptive Systems*, volume 7740 of *Lecture Notes in Computer Science (LNCS)*, pages 152–186. Springer, January 2013.
12. Holger Giese, Matthias Tichy, Sven Burmester, Wilhelm Schäfer, and Stephan Flake. Towards the Compositional Verification of Real-Time UML Designs. In *Proc. of the 9th european software engineering conference held jointly with 11th ACM SIGSOFT intl. symposium on foundations of software engineering (ESEC/FSE-11)*. ACM, 2003.
13. Ajay Gulati, Anne Holler, Minwen Ji, Ganesha Shanmuganathan, Carl Waldspurger, and Xiaoyun Zhu. *VMware Distributed Resource Management: Design, Implementation and Lessons Learned*. Mar 2012.
14. Zhenyu Guo, Sean McDirmid, Mao Yang, Li Zhuang, Pu Zhang, Yingwei Luo, Tom Bergan, Peter Bodik, Madan Musuvathi, Zheng Zhang, and Lidong Zhou. Failure recovery: when the cure is worse than the disease. In *HotOS*, pages 8–14, Berkeley, CA, USA, 2013. USENIX Association.
15. James Hamilton. On designing and deploying internet-scale services. In *LISA*, pages 18:1–18:12. USENIX Association, 2007.
16. Nikolas Roman Herbst, Samuel Kounev, and Ralf Reussner. Elasticity in cloud computing: What it is, and what it is not. In *ICAC*, 2013.
17. D. Jimenez-Gonzalez, J.J. Navarro, and J.-L. Larriba-Pey. Cc-radix: a cache conscious sorting based on radix sort. In *Parallel, Distributed and Network-Based Processing, 2003. Proceedings. Eleventh Euromicro Conference on*, pages 101–108, Feb 2003.
18. T. Kisuki, P. M. W. Knijnenburg, and M. F. P. O'Boyle. Combined selection of tile sizes and unroll factors using iterative compilation. In *Proceedings of the 2000 International Conference on Parallel Architectures and Compilation Techniques*, PACT '00, pages 237–, Washington, DC, USA, 2000. IEEE Computer Society.
19. P. M. W. Knijnenburg, T. Kisuki, K. Gallivan, and M. F. P. O'Boyle. The effect of cache models on iterative compilation for combined tiling and unrolling: Research articles. *Concurr. Comput. Pract. Exper.*, 16(2-3):247–270, January 2004.
20. Peter R. Lewis, Lukas Esterle, Arjun Chandra, Bernhard Rinner, Jim Torresen, and Xin Yao. Static, dynamic and adaptive heterogeneity in distributed smart camera networks. *TAAS*, 2015 (to appear).
21. Peter R. Lewis, Harry Goldingay, and Vivek Nallur. It's good to be different: Diversity, heterogeneity, and dynamics in collective systems. In *Eighth IEEE International Conference on Self-Adaptive and Self-Organizing Systems Workshops, SASOW 2014, London, United Kingdom, September 8-12, 2014*, pages 84–89, 2014.
22. Xiaoming Li, María Jesús Garzarán, and David Padua. A dynamically tuned sorting library. In *Proceedings of the International Symposium on Code Generation and Optimization: Feedback-directed and Runtime Optimization*, CGO '04, pages 111–, Washington, DC, USA, 2004. IEEE Computer Society.
23. O.J. Mengshoel, M. Chavira, K. Cascio, S. Poll, A. Darwiche, and S. Uckun. Probabilistic model-based diagnosis: An electrical power system case study. *IEEE Transactions on Systems, Man and Cybernetics, Part A: Systems and Humans*, 40(5):874–885, Sept 2010.
24. Meiyappan Nagappan, Aaron Peeler, and Mladen Vouk. Modeling cloud failure data: a case study of the virtual computing lab. In *SECLOUD*, pages 8–14, New York, NY, USA, 2011. ACM.
25. Fiona Fui-Hoon Nah. A study on tolerable waiting time: how long are web users willing to wait? *Behaviour and Information Technology*, 23(3):153–163, 2004.
26. Shah Faizur Rahman, Jichi Guo, and Qing Yi. Automated empirical tuning of scientific codes for performance and power consumption. In *Proceedings of the 6th International Conference on*

High Performance and Embedded Architectures and Compilers, HiPEAC '11, pages 107–116, New York, NY, USA, 2011. ACM.

27. Charles Reiss, Alexey Tumanov, Gregory R. Ganger, Randy H. Katz, and Michael A. Kozuch. Heterogeneity and dynamicity of clouds at scale: Google trace analysis. In *SOCC*, 2012.

28. Johann Schumann, Timmy Mbaya, Ole Mengshoel, Knot Pipatsrisawat, Ashok Srivastava, Arthur Choi, and Adnan Darwiche. Software health management with bayesian networks. *Innov. Syst. Softw. Eng.*, 9(4):271–292, December 2013.

29. Ranjan Sinha and Justin Zobel. Cache-conscious sorting of large sets of strings with dynamic tries. *J. Exp. Algorithmics*, 9, December 2004.

30. Gerald Tesauro, Nicholas K Jong, Rajarshi Das, and Mohamed N Bennani. A hybrid reinforcement learning approach to autonomic resource allocation. In *2006 IEEE International Conference on Autonomic Computing*, pages 65–73. IEEE, 2006.

31. William E Walsh, Gerald Tesauro, Jeffrey O Kephart, and Rajarshi Das. Utility functions in autonomic systems. In *Autonomic Computing, 2004. Proceedings. International Conference on*, pages 70–77. IEEE, 2004.

32. Danny Weyns, Bradley Schmerl, Vincenzo Grassi, Sam Malek, Raffaela Mirandola, Christian Prehofer, Jochen Wuttke, Jesper Andersson, Holger Giese, and Karl Goeschka. On Patterns for Decentralized Control in Self-Adaptive Systems. In Rogério de Lemos, Holger Giese, Hausi Müller, and Mary Shaw, editors, *Software Engineering for Self-Adaptive Systems II*, volume 7475 of *Lecture Notes in Computer Science (LNCS)*, pages 76–107. Springer, January 2013.

Part II
System Architectures

Chapter 5
Architectural Concepts for Self-aware Computing Systems

Holger Giese, Thomas Vogel, Ada Diaconescu, Sebastian Götz
and Samuel Kounev

Abstract Self-awareness in a computing system is achieved by implementing a model-based learning, reasoning, and acting loop (LRA-M loop). Similar to the feedback loops for self-adaptive software, we argue that the LRA-M loop should be addressed during the architectural design of self-aware computing systems. This allows engineers to explicitly decide and reason about the system's self-awareness capabilities. This chapter, therefore, introduces the relevant architectural concepts to address and make the LRA-M loop visible in the architectural design. Based on these concepts, we discuss how context-awareness, self-awareness, and meta-self-awareness become manifest in an architecture. Finally, we relate the presented architectural concepts to the definition and framework for self-aware computing systems introduced in the previous chapters.

H. Giese (✉) · T. Vogel
Hasso Plattner Institute for Software Systems Engineering at the University of Potsdam,
Prof.-Dr.-Helmert-Str. 2-3, 14482 Potsdam, Germany
e-mail: holger.giese@hpi.de

T. Vogel
e-mail: thomas.vogel@hpi.de

A. Diaconescu
Equipe S3, Departement INFRES, Telécom ParisTech, 46 rue Barrault, 75013 Paris, France
e-mail: ada.diaconescu@telecom-paristech.fr

S. Götz
TU Dresden, Dresden, Germany
e-mail: sebastian.goetz@acm.org

S. Kounev
Department of Computer Science, University of Wrzburg, Am Hubland, 97074 Würzburg,
Germany
e-mail: samuel.kounev@uni-wuerzburg.de

© Springer International Publishing AG 2017
S. Kounev et al. (eds.), *Self-Aware Computing Systems*,
DOI 10.1007/978-3-319-47474-8_5

5.1 Introduction

The vision of self-aware computing as introduced in Chap. 1 promises that self-aware systems achieve their goals in a flexible manner despite the dynamic and uncertain nature of their environments and goals. To achieve their goals, such systems continuously learn and reason about themselves, their environment, and their goals and, if needed, take appropriate actions. For instance, based on their self-awareness, such systems are able to self-adapt at runtime, steer their behavior directly as required, or report to their users to explain what happened.

There are a number of initiatives aiming for more flexible software systems such as autonomic computing [22], self-* systems [3], self-adaptive and self-managing systems [9, 10, 13, 14, 24, 34], organic computing [1, 29], or cognitive computing [21] that advocate a paradigm shift for software from design-time decisions and understanding toward resolving issues dynamically at runtime—typically by equipping the system with a feedback loop [7].

While these approaches traditionally looked only into *reactive* classes of solutions that act at runtime in response to changes without anticipating future changes or reasoning about the long-term future (cf. [17, 24]), recently an additional paradigm shift from a *reactive* to a *proactive* operation can be observed that aims to integrate the ability to learn, reason, and act at runtime (cf. [8, 11, 19]). This trend is well in line with the ideas centered around the notion of self-aware computing [1, 2, 20, 23, 25, 27, 43], runtime models [4–6, 39, 41, 42], and related terms [12, 15, 26, 33] that gained momentum in recent years.[1]

In this chapter, we will look at the solution space for self-aware computing systems with a particular focus on *software architecture* as "a collection of computational components—or simply components—together with a description of the interactions between these components—the connectors" [36, p. 4]. Therefore, this chapter explores which concepts are required to describe architectures of self-aware systems. As introduced by the definition of a self-aware computing system, the concepts we address include runtime *models* of the context and the system itself as well as learning, reasoning, and acting *processes* (cf. Chap. 1). In this context, we consider the prereflective and reflective forms of self-awareness (cf. Chap. 3).

It is important to emphasize that the chapter does not propose a dedicated architectural language for development or a set of well-established, concrete architectures but rather aims to provide an initial basis to compare approaches as well as to explore and discuss the possible solution space. Consequently, the concepts we discuss and capture in the examples in this chapter need not to be relevant for every, but only for specific applications of self-aware computing systems and often only depict a fragment of an architecture rather than a complete architecture. Furthermore, the concepts are the building blocks for such systems but not necessary ingredients. Therefore, they also support modeling architectures of systems that are yet not self-aware. Our goal is to provide an architectural language that allows us (1) to discuss

---

[1] A broader discussion of other related work including also agents and multi-agent systems can be found in Chap. 2 of this book.

the whole spectrum of self-aware computing systems (see Chap. 3), (2) to classify whether a given system is self-aware, (3) to study systems that may evolve into such self-aware computing systems, and (4) to derive steps to adjust the architecture of a non-self-aware system to migrate it into a self-aware system.

Therefore, we do not claim that these concepts are generally relevant for self-aware computing systems. In contrast, they should be considered as a source of inspiration when conducting research or developing an architecture and design for such a system. Future results, experiments, and solutions may then confirm, refine, or even contradict the usefulness of the various concepts we propose. In any of these cases, the purpose of the proposed concepts to start-off research and work on architectures for self-aware computing systems would have largely been fulfilled.

To start-off such research and work, we propose concepts that emerged from the discussions at the Dagstuhl seminar on self-aware computing system and that make the specifics of such systems explicit and visible in the architectural design. We argue that these specifics should become the first-class entities of the architectural design such that they can be properly addressed during development. Similarly, Shaw [35], Müller et al. [28, 30], and Brun et al. [7] argue that feedback loops as the essential characteristic of self-adaptive software should be made explicit and visible in the architectural design, for instance, to also make design decisions explicit and to enable reasoning on the design. Consequently, we borrowed several ideas from approaches of the authors of this chapter. In particular, we borrowed ideas from EUREMA [40], addressing the explicit modeling of feedback loops in the self-adaptive software, as well as from MechatronicUML [18], supporting collaborations on flexible architectures. However, none of these approaches targets self-aware computing systems in particular.[2] In the context of this chapter, applying all of the proposed concepts may lead to a too detailed model that might be considered more like a specific design rather than a general architecture. However, our intention is to be able to express also subtle differences between solutions in *one* notation rather than finding an appropriate compromise between expressiveness and ease of use. Consequently, an important aspect that will need further attention is to determine under which circumstances the proposed concepts are really helpful for architecture modeling and when they are too detailed and rather concerned with the more fine-grained design.

The concepts we propose in this chapter are the foundations for the following chapters. Particularly, Chap. 6 will explore the specific needs of architectures for a single self-aware computing system while Chap. 7 will explore collectives of self-aware systems. Furthermore, Chap. 8 will review the state of the art and contrast it with the proposals of this chapter and of Chaps. 6 and 7. In addition, Chaps. 12 and 13 will target the detailed algorithmic questions of how learning, reasoning, and acting are realized within a single or collective of systems, which is not covered by the chapters on the architectures for self-aware systems.

This chapter is organized as follows: In Sect. 5.2, we introduce the running example we use throughout this chapter as well as basic notational concepts of the UML to

---

[2] A comparison of these related approaches to self-aware computing systems can be found in Chap. 8 of this book.

describe software architectures. Then, we discuss the proposed concepts in terms of elements and relations that are specific to self-aware computing systems in Sects. 5.3 and 5.4. Using these concepts, we describe different cases of self-awareness in Sect. 5.5. In Sect. 5.6, we discuss these concepts concerning architectural views as well as their coverage of the definition and framework of self-aware computing systems (see Chaps. 1 and 3). Finally, we conclude the chapter in Sect. 5.7.

5.2 Preliminaries

In this section, we introduce the running example, a smart home system, that we use to illustrate the architectural and design concepts for self-aware computing systems. Then, we introduce basic notational concepts from the Unified Modeling Language (UML) [32] to describe software architectures, which are extended in this chapter to address the specifics of self-aware computing systems. Finally, we summarize the definition and framework for such systems from Chaps. 1 and 3.

5.2.1 Running Example: Smart Home

To discuss the architectural concepts for self-aware computing systems, we use a running example based on the smart home exemplary scenario presented in Chap. 4. In contrast to the original scenario, we use here a smart home system with a more complicated architecture of prereflective components that control devices in a house and that are coordinated by a *house manager* (see Fig. 5.1).

The house manager reports to the user if something goes wrong (e.g., if failures are detected), self-adapts (e.g., to optimize energy consumption), and actuates the device controllers in the house (e.g., in case of emergencies). Besides a centralized house manager that coordinates the device controllers located in the house, we further consider variants of less hierarchical interaction schemes such as collaborations or self-organization to achieve the coordination among the device controllers.

A house consists of several floors and rooms. Each room is equipped with devices such as sensors to perceive the indoor and outdoor temperature, lighting conditions, and persons, as well as controllers for the *heater* (start or stop heating), *lights* (switch on or off the lights), *windows* (tilt, open, or close the window), and *shutter panels* (open or close the panels). Each controller works independently; for example, one controls the heater based on the temperature and another one the windows based on time. This might result in conflicts such as heating up the room while opening the windows. The task of the house manager is to coordinate the controllers according to some goals. Therefore, the manager aims for (1) self-healing and (2) self-optimization while we leave out other self-* capabilities to keep the example simple.

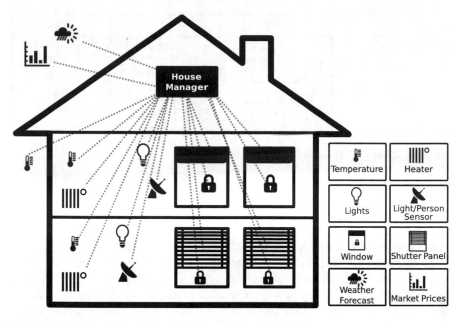

Fig. 5.1 Overview of the smart home system with a centralized house manager

(1) Self-healing:

    a. If a sensor in a certain room is broken, the house manager relies on the sensor data from the neighboring rooms.

    b. If a single point of failure is affected, such as the window cannot be closed any more, a person in the house who is close to the window is notified.

(2) Self-optimization:

    a. The energy consumption should be optimized while achieving the goals such as maintaining a certain room temperature.

    b. Various influencing factors for the optimization can be considered, such as market prices, weather forecasts, government subsidies, and user preferences.

In this chapter, we illustrate the architectural concepts for self-aware computing systems with this example. To discuss a particular concept, we often present a fragment of the example emphasizing this concept instead of a complete architecture.

5.2.2 Architectural Modeling with UML

Before we introduce the architectural concepts that are specific to self-aware computing systems, we provide a summary of UML-based concepts [32] for architecture

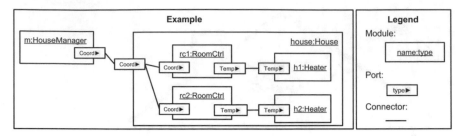

Fig. 5.2 Generic UML elements for architecture modeling

modeling which serve as a basis for this chapter. These UML concepts are modules (e.g., components[3]), ports provided or required by modules, connectors, collaborations, and participation links between modules and collaborations.

Modules have a name and a type and they can be hierarchically composed to *UML hierarchies.* If the name of a module is not relevant, we may omit it (cf. anonymous module). We may also omit the type of a module if it is not relevant for the discussion. Modules may provide or require *ports* that encapsulate functionality and restrict access. Ports are defined by their types. The direction of the arrows (▲, ▼, ►, ◄) within a port denotes whether the port is provided or required by a module.[4] A module provides (requires) a port if the direction of the port's arrow points from the module inward (outward). Provided and required ports of the same type are wired by a *connector* to visualize interactions among the corresponding modules.

The example depicted in Fig. 5.2 shows two modules of different types: m of type HouseManager and house of type House. The manager m coordinates the controllers rc1 and rc2 that are located in different rooms of the house. Therefore, the house is hierarchically decomposed into room controllers each with its own heater to control. The manager requires the port Coord that is provided by the house. Both ports are connected and the manager coordinates the controllers in the house. The house forwards the coordination commands from the manager to the individual controllers that eventually set the temperature to the heaters in the corresponding rooms. The manager's responsibility is to achieve similar temperatures in both rooms.

In addition to modules with their connectors and hierarchical (de)composition, more flexible forms of cooperating behavior can be modeled with *collaborations*. Collaborations are depicted by ellipses and they are wired to the modules that collaborate by *participation links*. For instance, Fig. 5.3 shows a collaboration in which four room controllers agree on a common temperature for each room.

In general, UML hierarchies with shared aggregation and UML collaborations may overlap to some extent. For instance, we may employ collaborations to capture the interaction in a UML hierarchy, but also to capture non-hierarchically struc-

---

[3]Oftentimes the modules may be in fact *components* [38]. However, as components imply a certain degree of encapsulation that might not be the case for the system elements considered in this chapter, we use the more general term of a module here.

[4]This can be seen as simple generalization of the different flow properties for ports in SysML [31].

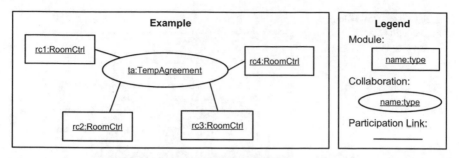

Fig. 5.3 Generic UML elements for modeling collaboration of modules

tured compositions. However, participations of elements in UML collaborations may change rather frequently while memberships in a hierarchy are usually considered more stable and durable (even though such memberships may also change).

5.2.3 Self-awareness Terminology and Framework

The terminology and framework for self-aware computing systems introduced in Chaps. 1 and 3 provide a definition and several dimensions spanning the overall spectrum of such systems. In the following, we briefly summarize the definition and dimensions since they provide the foundation for the architectural concepts of self-aware computing systems, which we discuss in this chapter. At first, we recap the definition of self-aware computing systems given in Chap. 1:

Self-aware computing systems are computing systems that:

1. *learn models* capturing *knowledge* about themselves and their environment (such as their structure, design, state, possible actions, and runtime behavior) on an ongoing basis, and
2. *reason* using the models (e.g., predict, analyze, consider, and plan) enabling them to *act* based on their knowledge and reasoning (e.g., explore, explain, report, suggest, self-adapt, or impact their environment)

in accordance with *higher-level goals*, which may also be subject to change.

Based on this definition, we may sketch a self-aware computing system with the conceptual *learn-reason-act-model (LRA-M)* loop (see Fig. 5.4). This loop shows the relevant aspects of the definition. Particularly, the system collects *empirical observations* of the self and of phenomena outside the self. *Learning* and *reasoning* processes produce and use *models* that capture knowledge derived from the observations. Based on the knowledge, the system may *act* upon itself and on its context. The processes operate according to higher-level *goals* that may dynamically change.

Fig. 5.4   The *LRA-M* loop
introduced in Chap. 1

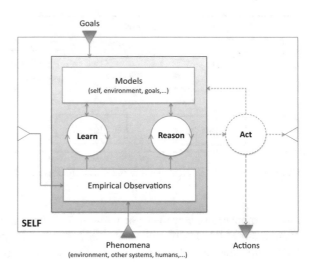

Consequently, the definition and the LRA-M loop introduce the concepts of *empirical data/observations*, *models*, and *goals*, which are used by *learning*, *reasoning*, and *acting processes*. We can elaborate this use relationship by describing the *data flow* within the LRA-M loop. The system observes itself and its environmental context, for which models are learned and used for reasoning and acting. Thus, a system realizing such a loop becomes aware of itself and its context.

These aspects are refined by Chap. 3 providing several dimensions for self-aware computing systems, which we consider as a conceptual framework. This framework covers different levels of self-awareness: A *prereflective self-awareness* level denoting simple subjective observations, a *reflective self-awareness* level if learning and reasoning with awareness models are involved, and a *meta-self-awareness* level where the object of the reflection is a reflective self-awareness process. Moreover, the framework distinguishes a subject (i.e., the *span*) and an object of awareness (i.e., the *scope*) while the span reflects on the scope. In this context, the notion of *action scope* that includes all entities that the system may act directly upon and the notion of *influence scope* that refers to entities upon which the system may only act indirectly are introduced. Finally, the framework refines the notion of awareness by emphasizing different aspects of awareness such as *identity*, *state*, *interaction*, *time*, *behavior*, *appearance*, *goal*, *expectation*, and *belief awareness*.

In the rest of this chapter, we will discuss architectural concepts for self-aware computing systems, which address these aspects and dimensions by applying and extending the generic UML concepts for architecture modeling. To illustrate these architectural concepts, we use the introduced running example.

5.3 Architectural Elements for Self-awareness

In this section, we propose general elements (i.e., building blocks) for describing architectures of self-aware systems, which are motivated by the aspects and dimensions of self-aware computing systems introduced in Chaps. 1 and 3. Thereby, the architectural descriptions target concrete architectures of systems and therefore, the emphasis is on describing specific instance configurations. An overview of the proposed elements is given in the appendix.

5.3.1 System, Environmental Context, and Modules

As depicted in Fig. 5.5a, we may first distinguish a *system* from its *environmental context*. The environmental context, represented by a cloud, is the fragment of the environment (including possibly other systems) scoped by the system's capacities of sensing and exploration. Furthermore, we may distinguish *modules* that represent a system and individual elements that compose the system. Both are depicted by rectangles but a system is illustrated with a bold border in contrast to an individual module having only a thin border. If we do not want to distinguish whether we refer to a system or to a module, we just use a rectangle.

The example shown in Fig. 5.5a describes the SmartHome system with two modules, Controllers and HouseManager, and the environmental context HouseEnvCtx.

(a)   **(b)**

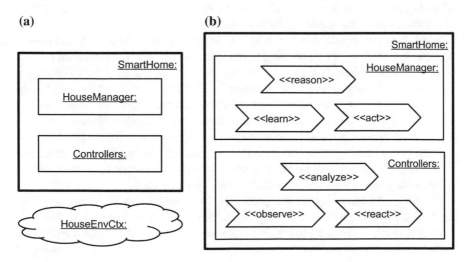

Fig. 5.5 Notation for system, modules, environmental context, and processes

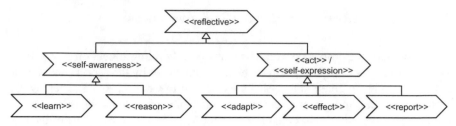

Fig. 5.6 Classification of reflective processes

Fig. 5.7 Classification of prereflective processes

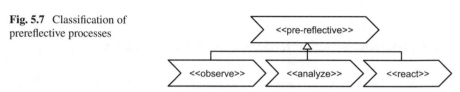

5.3.2 Reflective and Prereflective Processes

We now show how to model processes within the systems and modules. In this context, we will distinguish between processes for prereflective and reflective self-awareness. The former considers basic subjective observations of the system while the latter additionally considers learning and reasoning activities with awareness models. An example is given in Fig. 5.5b. Processes are labeled with ≪learn≫ when they capture how models are learned based on the observations, ≪reason≫ when they analyze the situation or plan actions, or ≪act≫ when they have an external or internal impact and are driven by the results of reasoning.

In the example depicted in Fig. 5.5b, the learning process located in the House-Manager learns about the underlying Controllers module. Then, a reasoning process identifies shortcomings of the Controllers and plans their circumvention. Finally, the act process will enact the planned adaptation by effecting the Controllers accordingly.

These processes can be refined and classified into reflective self-awareness and self-expression (see Fig. 5.6). For self-awareness, we have already introduced the processes of *learning* models and *reasoning* on such models for acting. For self-expression (i.e., acting), we consider processes that have an external influence such as *adapting* the system itself or other systems, *effecting* the context or other systems, and *reporting* to the user or to superordinated system entities.[5]

Similarly, we may classify the processes for prereflective self-awareness (see Fig. 5.7). *Observe* denotes measuring the system itself, other systems, or the environmental context, *analyze* covers simple variants of analysis based on the observations, and *react* describes the reaction to specific situations either directly observed

---

[5]We distinguish adapting and effecting an entity as the former involves changing an entity (e.g., modifying the entity's structure) while the latter denotes interactions between entities that do not require any substantial changes of the entity (e.g., by exchanging knowledge among entities).

or identified by the analysis. Such prereflective processes can be allocated within the systems and modules as illustrated for the Controllers module in Fig. 5.5b.

The classifications of reflective and prereflective processes shown in Figs. 5.6 and 5.7 are derived from the definition of self-aware computing systems (cf. Chap. 1) and should therefore be considered at the conceptual level. In practice, these classifications can be further refined or extended given the specific problem at hand.

5.3.3 Awareness Models, Empirical Data (Models), and Goal Models

As described by the learn-reason-act-model (LRA-M) loop for self-aware computing systems sketched in Sect. 5.2.3, *awareness models (AMs)* and *empirical data (ED)* are used online. To capture the scope that is represented by the model or data, we use the stereotypes ≪ctx≫ in the case of the environmental context and ≪sys≫ in the case of the system itself or parts of it.

AMs are employed online[6] and represent originals outside the system (e.g., the environmental context or other systems) or inside the system (e.g., modules or processes of the self). Such models can be subjective and not a perfect representation of the originals as they might be based on individual measurements as part of specific learning processes. In general, AMs are usually obtained by ≪learn≫ processes and they are subject to ≪reason≫ and ≪act≫ processes. AMs are depicted as blue-shaded, rounded boxes in our notation (see Fig. 5.8).

In the example depicted in Fig. 5.8a, the system has an AM of its environmental context. In Fig. 5.8b, the HouseManager module has an AM of the Controllers module, which is thus a system model. Finally, in Fig. 5.8c, a learning process within the HouseManager module maintains such a system model locally.

Either a single or a group of models is depicted if one or more models are used online. An AM or a group of them can be located within a system, a module, or a process. A group of AMs covers different aspects of the same scope, for instance, a timing aspect to capture the history of AMs. Otherwise, we use completely separate boxes for the AMs if they refer to different scopes.

In addition to AMs, the LRA-M loop addresses *empirical data (ED)* such as sensor data obtained and used by prereflective processes (cf. Chap. 1). Thus, ED is usually obtained by ≪observe≫ processes and subject to ≪analyze≫ and ≪react≫

---

[6]The awareness models (AMs) discussed here overlap with the concept of *models@run.time* [6] when there is a causal connection with the system itself. Our assumption is that not every AM is or needs to be causally connected to the running system. Another view on runtime models considers any models that are used within the system and that either represent (parts of) the system or context for reflection or specify (parts of) the system for execution [40, 41]. In this view, the reflection models correspond to the idea of AMs. In general, we do not restrict the scope of an AM. If an AM represents the context, it usually supports establishing context-awareness while an AM representing (parts of) the system supports establishing self-awareness.

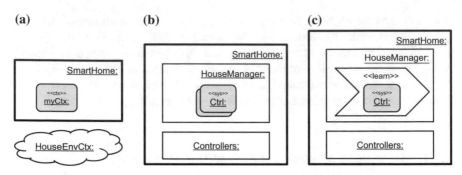

Fig. 5.8 Notation for awareness models within systems, modules, or processes

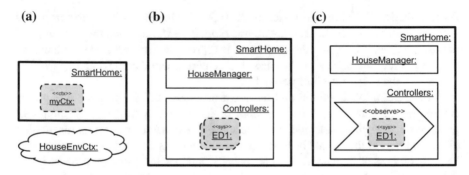

Fig. 5.9 Notation for empirical data within systems, modules, or processes

Fig. 5.10 Notation for goal models

processes. Such data are specified in the notation as blue-shaded, rounded boxes with a dashed border (see Fig. 5.9).

As outlined in the definition of self-aware computing systems in Chap. 1, a self-aware system *is* driven by goals and it *may be* necessary to be able to cope with the changing goals or even the dynamically generated goals. Such runtime goals can be explicitly represented in one or more *goal models (GMs)*. Such models are depicted as red-shaded, rounded boxes stereotyped with ≪goal≫ in the notation (see Fig. 5.10). In our example of Fig. 5.10, the GM describes the criteria indicating the direction that the self-optimization should steer the SmartHome system to, for instance, reducing the energy consumption while considering constraints such as "do not shut down the heater in a room if there is a person in the room".

Runtime goals must be explicitly captured by online GMs. In contrast, design-time goals influence the system during development, for instance, by determining the type of models and processes to be developed. Some of them may not be explicitly represented and they can remain *implicit* in the implementation—if they do not change dynamically. Goals that may change dynamically must be *explicitly* represented to be able to handle such changes. Thus, if a system needs to be goal-aware, then the goals are typically explicitly represented, otherwise not necessarily.

If goals of another system or element are derived by observations, we use AMs rather than GMs to describe these goals. We only use GMs to denote those goals that are imposed on the system either from the outside (e.g., by the user) or from the system itself generating the goals (e.g., based on some observations).

Splitting the system into multiple layers, GMs can be part of each layer though the goals might be of a different kind. Goals in the lowest layer refer to the domain functionality while goals at higher layers refer to awareness such as to the success/failure of lower-layer goals (cf. awareness requirements [37]). For example, a higher-layer goal may prescribe that the controllers have to achieve the desired room temperature in 90 % of the time. The corresponding lower-layer goal prescribes that the desired room temperature should be as close to 22 C as possible.

5.4 Architectural Relations for Self-awareness

Besides the architectural elements for self-aware computing systems discussed in Sect. 5.3, the definition for self-aware computing systems given in Chap. 1 and its refinements in Chap. 3 introduce explicitly or implicitly several relations (cf. Sect. 5.2.3). These relations seem helpful for architectural considerations and they are discussed in the following. An overview of the proposed relations is additionally given in the appendix.

5.4.1 Data Flow Related to Self-awareness

The first relation we introduce is the *data flow* between models, empirical data, processes, modules, other systems, and the environmental context. This is motivated by the data flow that forms the learn-reason-act-model (LRA-M) loop introduced in Chap. 1. As shown in Fig. 5.11, the data flow is represented by a solid black arrow whose direction indicates the direction of the data flow. Thus, the data flow extends the UML connector (see Sect. 5.2.2) by connecting arbitrary elements and representing a flow of data. Note that such a data flow may be realized by quite different technical means such as procedure calls, messages, or flows.

Using the data flow relation, we can describe that a ≪learn≫ process obtains AMs guided by the goals of the self, a ≪reason≫ process uses the AMs and GMs to reason, and finally, that an ≪adapt≫ process uses the AMs to dynamically change a module (see Fig. 5.11a).

Considering our example and Fig. 5.11a, the HouseManager uses the goal model GM, which may prescribe that the desired room temperature should be achieved in 90 % of the time, to learn about the performance of the Controllers module. Learning

(a)

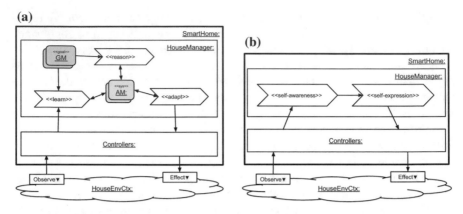

Fig. 5.11 Data flow for self-awareness and self-expression

results in producing a set of awareness models AM describing the Controllers' performance, which are then used to reason about the performance and the achievement of the goals. If the goals are not achieved, the HouseManager may adapt the Controllers module based on the AM, for instance, by changing the control strategy to react more quickly to disturbances of the actual room temperature. For this example, Fig. 5.11b shows an abstraction that only considers the self-awareness (encapsulating the learning and reasoning) and the self-expression (encapsulating the acting) processes while hiding the employed models. Consequently, the figure only captures the data flow between these two processes and the Controllers module.

In general, we can describe detailed views making the data flow between individual processes, models, and modules explicit (see Fig. 5.11a) or abstract views that, for instance, hide the models and the detailed processes (see Fig. 5.11b). Thus, a data flow from or to a module or process may be refined to a data flow from or to an element contained in the module or process. Such contained elements can particularly be AMs and GMs that are used in architectural views to emphasize the role of models in self-aware computing. In this sense, the diagram in Fig. 5.11a refines the one in Fig. 5.11b. It refines the self-awareness and self-expression processes and makes the AMs and GMs explicit. Likewise, we may refine the Controllers module and denote which processes or ED exist within this module.

When refining a module by describing the contained elements such as processes and models, we can emphasize the encapsulation and interactions of these elements by *ports*. A port describes the functionality that is provided or required by modules and connected ports make the interaction among modules explicit. The functionality can be specific to self-aware computing, which we denote by stereotypes. A module can observe (≪O≫) and effect (≪E≫) an element or the context, adapt (≪A≫) an element, or report (≪R≫) to the user or to another element. In this case, the module requires corresponding ports for these functionalities (see Fig. 5.12a). Moreover, if a module can be observed, effected, adapted, or reported to, it provides the correspond-

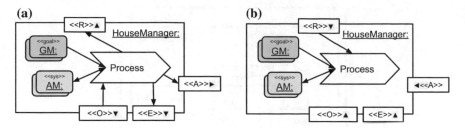

Fig. 5.12 Required (**a**) and Provided (**b**) ports of a module

ing ports (see Fig. 5.12b). Finally, the ports of a module may be connected to the elements contained in this module (e.g., to delegate incoming reports to a process).

In general, we may omit the ports in the diagrams if they are not relevant for the selected architectural view. For instance, a view might emphasize the models and neglect the encapsulation and interaction between modules.

5.4.2 Awareness and Expression Links

Two important aspects of self-aware computing are self-awareness and self-expression. As discussed in Chap. 3, self-awareness has a domain and enables that a subject of the awareness (i.e., the span) reflects about an object of awareness (i.e., the scope) by means of a model employed online. Based on the introduced elements, we can therefore illustrate with an *awareness link* that a scope is represented by a model maintained by a span. Thus, the span is aware of the scope. As shown in Fig. 5.13 by the red bold arrow, usually a model or a group of models represents another module or the context. If we want to abstract the models in an architectural view, we link the scope to a process or module containing the (hidden) models.

Additionally, we may have an *expression link* in the opposite direction. Such a link is denoted by a blue bold arrow pointing from a model maintained by a span to the scope (see Fig. 5.13). Such a link illustrates that the span's self-expression

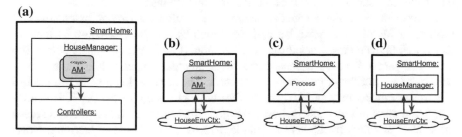

Fig. 5.13 Notation for awareness and expression links

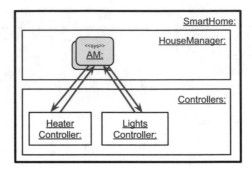

Fig. 5.14 Awareness and expression links with a complex scope

impacts the scope. Again, if we abstract the model in an architectural view, we link the process or module containing the (hidden) model to the scope.

In our example, the HouseManager has an awareness model of the Controllers module as illustrated by an awareness link in the diagram of Fig. 5.13a. Since the HouseManager also adapts the Controllers module, we additionally have an expression link in the opposite direction. For the other three cases in Fig. 5.13, an awareness link illustrates that the context is known by the SmartHome system and represented in an awareness model, by a process of the system, and by a module of the system. These three diagrams also describe that the expression of the corresponding span impacts the context—as visualized by expression links.

According to Chap. 3, the scope of an awareness can be further refined. In our example, a group of awareness models maintained by the HouseManager may be connected via awareness and expression links to dedicated controller modules (see Fig. 5.14). Furthermore, the *aspect* of the reflection for each element in the scope may differ (cf. Chap. 3). We therefore attach stereotypes to the awareness links to distinguish, among others, stimulus awareness (≪sa≫), interaction awareness (≪ia≫), time awareness (≪ta≫), and goal awareness (≪ga≫).

As depicted in Fig. 5.15, besides *direct* awareness (solid red arrow) and expression (solid blue arrow) we consider *indirect* awareness (dashed red arrow) and expression (dashed blue arrow) to address the *action scope* and *influence scope* introduced in Chap. 3. Typical cases where such scopes become relevant is when modules exploit the awareness and expression capabilities of other modules.

In the example of Fig. 5.15a, the Controllers module learns about the context and produces AMs of the context, which is exploited by the HouseManager by feeding its own AMs from these ones through a data flow (black arrow). Consequently, the HouseManger's AMs cover aspects of the environmental context although the House-Manager does not directly observe the context. The same holds for the expression. The HouseManager may indirectly effect the context by adapting the Controllers module. A variant of this example is shown in Fig. 5.15b. The Controllers module observes the context and only maintains ED; that is, it does not perform any learning. However, the HouseManager may (re)use these data to perform the learning and produce

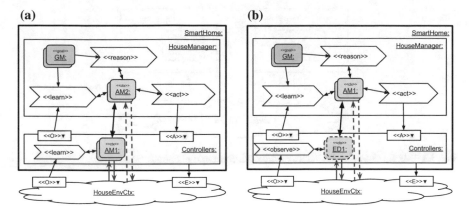

Fig. 5.15   Notation for direct and indirect awareness and expression

Fig. 5.16   Indirect awareness via the environmental context

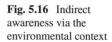
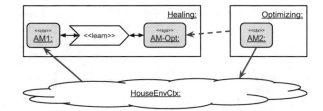

AMs. Thus, in the example, a module such as the HouseManager does not have to perform the observing or learning processes itself but it can rely on the observations or learned information from other modules such as the Controllers.

Another view of indirect awareness is to derive information about a module by observing and learning its environmental context. This is illustrated in Fig. 5.16 showing two modules that do not explicitly interact with each other. However, the Optimizing module effects the environment (see expression link) and the result of its effects may be observed and learned by the Healing module (see awareness link). The resulting awareness model *AM1* is then used to learn about the (behavior of) the Optimizing module. The learned knowledge is captured in the awareness model AM-Opt. Consequently, the Healing module is indirectly aware of the Optimizing module (see indirect awareness link). However, the learned knowledge about the Optimizing module may not be accurate since it is the result of interpreting and speculating about changes in the environment and possible causes of these changes.

As depicted in Fig. 5.17, the fact that a system/module is indirectly aware of another system/module can be realized without having to learn a context and system model. Instead, a phenomenon (bold dot) in the environmental context is connected to the observed system/module with an expression link and to the observing system/module with an awareness link. In the example, the Optimizing module effects the environment (see the expression link), which causes a phenomenon such as a huge increase in the room temperature. This phenomenon is the observable fragment

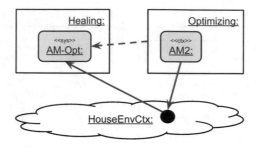

Fig. 5.17 Indirect awareness via a specific environmental phenomenon

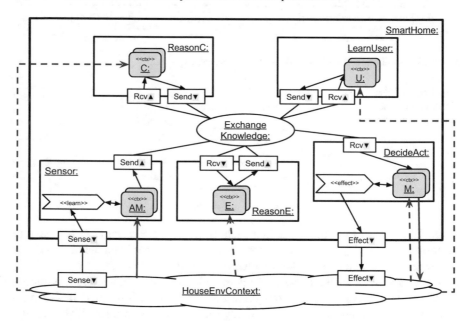

Fig. 5.18 Direct and indirect awareness with collaborations

of the Healing module in the context. The Healing module is directly aware of the phenomenon and, therefore, can be indirectly aware of the Optimizing module.

Finally, the notation can be used similarly to describe direct and indirect awareness if knowledge is obtained through collaborations. This is illustrated in Fig. 5.18 showing the Sensor module that senses and learns about the context, which results in the awareness model AM. This module shares the learned knowledge through the collaboration with the other modules. The ReasonC and ReasonE modules reason about the obtained knowledge independent of each other to identify a heating configuration that is comfortable for the user, respectively, energy-efficient. The LearnUser modules use the obtained knowledge to learn about the behavior of the user. Finally, the DecideAct module obtains the knowledge created by the ReasonC, ReasonE, and LearnUser modules to make a decision of how to adjust the heating configuration in the house and to eventually enact the adjustments. This example illustrates that modules can be indirectly aware of the context by obtaining knowledge about it through a collaboration, one of whose participants is directly aware of the context.

5.5 Self-awareness and Architecture

Based on the elements and relations defined in the preceding Sects. 5.3 and 5.4, we now approach the question of when and how self-awareness is denoted by awareness links in an architecture. In this context, we discuss that not every occurrence of an awareness link needs to result in self-awareness as defined in this book (cf. Chap. 1). In addition, we study the characterization of specific forms of self-awareness such as meta-self-awareness at the architectural level.

In general, it has to be noted that self-awareness is always relative to a given scope. Usually, the scope is the considered system and environmental context. However, we may consider just the context, a particular module of a system, or any other element of a system such as a process.

5.5.1 Self-awareness: Awareness of the Context

One particular aspect of self-awareness for a system is depicted in Fig. 5.19. According to the definition of a self-aware system (cf. Chap. 1), a system must be aware of its environmental context and must have processes capable of learning awareness models and reasoning about the context using the learned models. Furthermore, the system may act upon the models to effect the context. In our example, the SmartHome may have a contextual awareness model of the context capturing information such as the current outdoor temperature and other weather conditions.

Fig. 5.19 Self-awareness: aspect of context-awareness

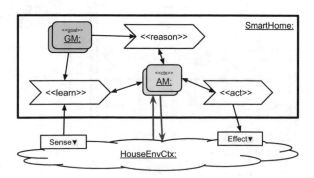

5.5.2 Self-awareness: Awareness of Its Own Elements

A key aspect of self-awareness is that the system is aware of itself or elements of itself, which is illustrated in Fig. 5.20. The elements, a system can reflect on and be aware of, are modules or processes. In contrast, we consider reflecting on an awareness model, empirical data, or a goal model as insufficient since we require the existence of the reflective self-awareness processes in terms of learning, reasoning, and acting.

When a clear *separation* between the element being the scope and the element being the span of awareness is given, this is similar to the *external approach* in self-adaptive software that separates the managing from the managed element [34]. This approach may simplify the treatment of self-awareness. First, it promotes separation of concerns. Second, the scope need not to be altered for realizing self-awareness (maybe besides adding some sensors and effectors) and the capabilities of learning, reasoning, and potentially acting have to be established only in the span. We name this case *external self-awareness*. In contrast, *internal self-awareness* describes that an element can be aware of itself without any architectural separation between the span and the scope. In the context of self-adaptive software, this case is called the *internal approach* [34]. We discuss *internal self-awareness* in the subsequent sections.

Figure 5.20 shows the case of external self-awareness. The HouseManager reflects on the Controllers module using several awareness models that the processes learn, reason, and act upon (Fig. 5.20a). In addition, the learning and reasoning processes take into account the goal model. A variant of this case is shown in Fig. 5.20b, where the HouseManager reflects on a particular process of the Controllers module. Consequently, the scope of awareness can be individual architectural elements.

Moreover, multiple awareness links may exist and jointly describe self-awareness. The scopes of these awareness links may overlap and therefore learning, reason-

(a)   **(b)**

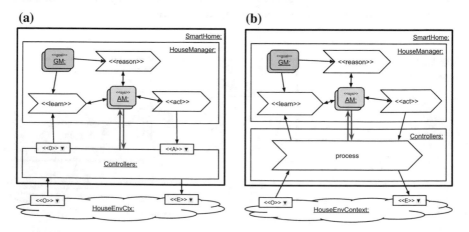

Fig. 5.20 External self-awareness concerning elements of the system

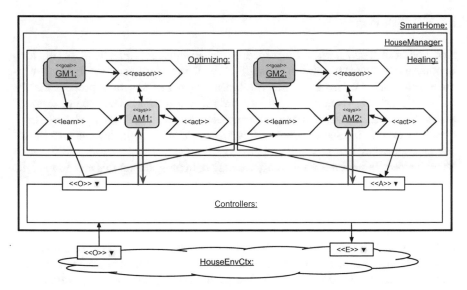

Fig. 5.21 Overlapping self-awareness and self-expression

ing, and acting processes refer to overlapping scopes. This is illustrated in Fig. 5.21 showing the Optimizing and Healing modules that are both aware of the Controllers module. While for the awareness links the overlap is generally not a problem, for the expression links the overlap may require coordination of the individual processes, for instance, to avoid conflicting adaptations (cf. [16, 40]).

As depicted in Fig. 5.21, the HouseManager module consists of two modules, Optimizing and Healing. The former realizes the self-optimization and the latter the self-healing capabilities of the smart home (cf. Sect. 5.2.1). Each of these two modules runs an LRA-M loop with individual awareness models as well as learning, reasoning, and acting processes. The independent learning and reasoning in both modules are not problematic at the conceptual level since the acting processes have to be coordinated. However, from a practical point of view it may be a waste of resources to let the optimization run an expensive reasoning process to optimize a faulty Controllers configuration until this configuration has been healed.

5.5.3 Self-loops and Cyclic Self-awareness

In this section, we discuss the notion of *self-loops* that may occur due to abstraction or internal self-awareness, as well as the related notion of *cyclic self-awareness*. Both notions are neither explicitly covered nor excluded in the Chaps. 1 and 3. However, we consider them here because of their architectural implications.

5.5.3.1 Self-loops

The notion of a *self-loop* is illustrated by the examples of Fig. 5.22. A self-loop denotes that an element is aware of itself; that is, the span and scope of the awareness are not disjoint. For instance, the whole system, a module, or a process can be aware of itself (see examples from left to right in Fig. 5.22). The second example additionally emphasizes that the system maintains an awareness model of itself. Similarly to denoting such kind of self-awareness, if an element acts upon itself, we use an expression link as a self-loop to describe the self-expression. Moreover, if an embedded element has a self-loop, we may optionally depict this self-loop at the level of the embedding element to make it visible at the higher level of abstraction.

Self-loops may occur because of two reasons: abstraction or internal self-awareness. For the first reason, we abstract from fine- to coarse-grained architectural views while during this abstraction step the awareness and expression links can be lost. However, to make self-awareness and self-expression visible in the architectural views, self-loops are used. For instance, the architecture shown in Fig. 5.21 shows that within the SmartHome system, the Optimizing and Healing modules are aware of and act upon the Controllers module. If we abstract from the submodules of SmartHome, we can state that the SmartHome is aware of itself although the awareness is partial since its scope is only the Controllers module. To denote this, we use a self-loop as shown in the leftmost example in Fig. 5.22.

The other reason for occurrences of self-loops is more fundamental and based on design decisions or constraints. In this case, we cannot or do not want to separate the span and scope of the self-awareness in the architectural design. In the context of self-adaptive software, this case is called the *internal approach* [34] as one element performs both the managing and the managed part of the self-adaptation. For a self-aware computing system, this results in situations in which one element is (partially) aware of itself. We call this phenomenon *internal self-awareness*, which is denoted by self-loops as depicted in Fig. 5.22. Likewise, we may use (blue) expression self-loops to denote the self-expression of an element; that is, an element acts upon itself.

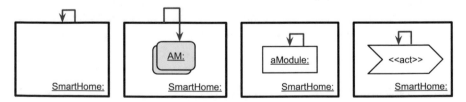

Fig. 5.22 Examples of self-loops

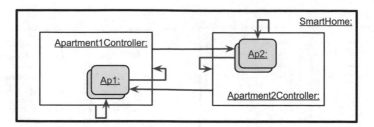

Fig. 5.23   Cycles of awareness links

5.5.3.2   Cyclic Self-awareness

Besides self-loops, another variant is cyclic self-awareness. An example is given in Fig. 5.23 depicting two modules that are aware of each other. This constitutes a cycle since Apartment1Controller is aware of Apartment2Controller and vice versa. In general, longer/bigger cycles involving more than two modules may exist. Moreover, cycles may exist for awareness or expression links such that we may have arbitrary networks of awareness or expression links forming a directed, cyclic graph. Such cycles can complicate achieving stable behavior as modules may continuously be triggered through awareness or expression links. Hence, cycles should be made visible in the architectural design such that they are explicitly handled.

For our example in Fig. 5.23, each apartment controller is aware of itself as well as of the other controller. Based on this awareness, it controls the heating in its own apartment and optimizes the energy consumption.

Similar to self-loops, cyclic self-awareness may occur because of two reasons: abstraction and internal self-awareness. Cyclic self-awareness resulting from abstraction disappears in the architectural design at a more fine-grained level. For instance, Fig. 5.24a shows the refinements of the apartment controllers into heater controller and heater modules that resolve the cycle existing in the more abstract design (cf. Fig. 5.23). The refinements show that Heater1Controller is aware of Heater2 that has no awareness of Apartment1Controller. The same holds the other way around such that there is no cyclic self-awareness present. Having awareness of its own and the other heater, a controller knows about the temperatures in the different apartments and it may act upon this knowledge, especially, to change the heating settings in its own apartment. This example illustrates that a cyclic self-awareness can be resolved when refining the architectural design.

However, there is also the case of internal self-awareness where no refinement of the design exists that resolves the cycles. This is illustrated in Fig. 5.24b showing the persisting cycle of awareness links among the Apartment1Controller and Apartment2Controller, particularly, among their top submodules Heater1Controller and Heater2Controller. These submodules are both aware of each other and each of them can be aware of that the other submodule is aware of it. In this example, a heater controller adjusts the own heater based on the temperature of the own apartment and on the behavior of the heater controller of the neighboring apartment.

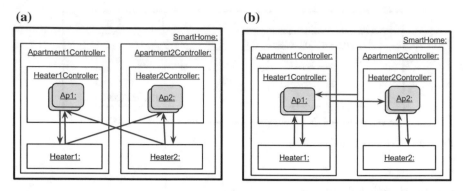

Fig. 5.24 **a** Resolved and **b** Remaining cyclic self-awareness in a refined design

If a cycle of awareness or expression links remains, the depth of the awareness is not clear, that is, the extent to which mutual awareness of the awareness exists. Potentially, there could be an infinite cycle of awareness of awareness, which has to be handled by the reflective learning and reasoning processes. Despite the infinite cycle, the processes have to converge and eventually produce knowledge based on learning and reasoning such that the system may act upon the knowledge.

5.5.4   Meta-Self-awareness

A particular case of self-awareness is *meta-self-awareness*; that is, a system is aware of its self-awareness (see Chap. 3). Considering external and internal self-awareness, we may combine them to describe meta-self-awareness at the architectural level. Such combinations make the meta-self-awareness explicit in the architectural design. However, to actually realize meta-self-awareness, appropriate reflections and LRA-M loops are required, which are able to identify the self-awareness capabilities of the reflected subsystem. In the following, we focus on making meta-self-awareness visible in the architectural design.

At first, we may combine twice the external self-awareness by stacking as depicted in Fig. 5.25. The HouseManagerAdjuster reflects on and is aware of the HouseManager that reflects on and is aware of the Controllers. In particular, the HouseManagerAdjuster is aware of the self-awareness established by the HouseManager.

To make the meta levels of reflective self-awareness visible in the architecture, we may stereotype the system with ≪self-aware≫ if it has self-awareness and with ≪meta-self-aware≫ if it has meta-self-awareness capabilities (see the SmartHome Fig. 5.25). Similarly, we may stereotype modules if they reflect on other system elements. Modules that do not reflect on any other element are *prereflective* and thus stereotyped with ≪prereflective≫ (see the Controllers in Fig. 5.25). Modules that reflect on a prereflective module are *reflective* and thus stereotyped with ≪reflective≫

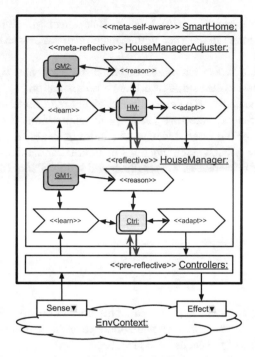

Fig. 5.25 Meta-self-awareness by combining external self-awareness

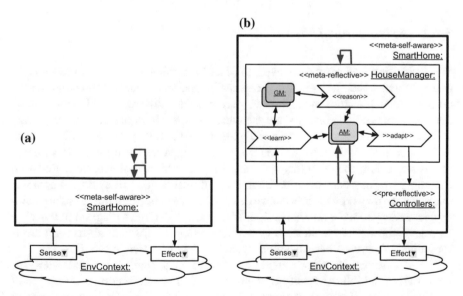

Fig. 5.26 Meta-self-awareness by Combining **a** Twice Internal and **b** Internal and external self-awareness

(see the HouseManager in Fig. 5.25). Modules that reflect on a reflective module are *meta-reflective* and thus stereotyped with ≪meta-reflective≫ (see HouseManagerAdjuster in Fig. 5.25).

A second possible case is that we stack internal self-awareness twice as depicted in Fig. 5.26a. In contrast to the former case, there is no separation between the individual spans and scopes such that we get a compact visual representation of stacking the self-loops for awareness. Likewise, self-loops for expressions (i.e., blue self-loops) are conceivable if the meta-self-awareness includes meta-self-expression.

Finally, we may conceive combinations of internal and external self-awareness to achieve meta-self-awareness. This is illustrated in Fig. 5.26b. In general, the self-awareness relationship is not restricted concerning its depth. Thus, we may apply the external or internal self-awareness more than twice to obtain meta-meta-self-awareness, meta-meta-meta-self-awareness, etc.

5.6 Discussion

In this section, we discuss the proposed architectural concepts for modeling self-aware computing systems. First, we relate them to architectural views and then we discuss the coverage of the needs raised in Chaps. 1 and 3.

5.6.1 Architectural Views

We have introduced several concepts to describe architectures for self-aware computing systems such as modules, processes, goals, and models. Depending on the purpose of architecture modeling, we may consider different architectural views that focus on specific concepts and therefore, on specific dimensions of self-aware systems. In this context, we have already identified the following views/dimensions:

System and Module View: The system and modules form the basic structure of an architecture such that this view provides an architectural overview. However, each diagram may consider a different level of abstraction. To avoid too complex diagrams, we may omit the breakdown of a system or module into further submodules by abstracting from the internal design. We rather expect that a diagram of this view represents the whole architecture while it may support different abstraction levels for individual parts. A basic example of such a view is shown in Fig. 5.5a.

Self-Awareness Process View: In addition to the system and module view, the prereflective and reflective self-awareness processes are an important dimension of the architecture. Therefore, a process view considers processes in addition to or instead of the modules. For a process view and a given level of abstraction, we expect that all processes of the system are covered. A basic example of such a view is shown in Fig. 5.5b.

Self-Awareness and Self-Expression View: This view emphasizes the different awareness models and the empirical data used within a system as well as the awareness and expression links. This view, thus, focuses on the awareness and expression relationships potentially neglecting the processes that operate on the models or data. Basic examples of such a view are shown in Figs. 5.8 and 5.9.

Self-Awareness and Goal View: This view emphasizes the different goals that are used within the system (see Chap. 7 for more architectural concepts concerning goals that may populate the view). This view, thus, focuses on goal models possibly neglecting the processes and the other models and data. However, a goal view can be used together with the process view to show the impact of the goals on the behavior. A basic example of such a view is shown in Fig. 5.10.

Such views help in reducing the complexity in the architecture by focusing on the specific dimensions while abstracting from others. Finally, such views can be combined if multiple dimensions are relevant. For instance, the diagram in Fig. 5.27 uses processes and models to describe the LRA-M loop, thus combining the process and the self-awareness/self-expression views. In Chaps. 6 and 7, we will study in detail the different concepts and views for various architectural styles.

5.6.2 Coverage

We discuss in the following on how the concepts introduced in this chapter cover the needs of architectures for self-aware computing systems. First, we look at the basic needs raised by the definition of self-aware computing systems in Chap. 1 and then at the refined needs raised in Chap. 3.

5.6.2.1 Coverage of the Definition of Chap. 1

How self-awareness manifests in the architecture highly depends on the concrete notion of self-aware computing systems that is employed. Therefore, we first look at the definition of self-aware computing systems given in Chap. 1 and consider the related *Learn-Reason-Act-Model (LRA-M)* loop.

The definition of self-aware computing systems emphasizes that these systems employ *models* for capturing knowledge about themselves and their environment, and that these models are *learned* and used for *reasoning* according to their higher-level *goals*, which may be subject to change. The reasoning enables these systems to *act* (e.g., to report to the user or to self-adapt).

The notation for modeling architectures of self-aware computing systems that we introduce in this chapter considers the concepts of awareness models and goal models as well as learning, reasoning, and acting processes. These concepts allow us to model all the aspects mentioned in the definition as part of an architecture. Moreover, the definition considers models for knowledge that refers to the system itself or to the system's environment. Therefore, we distinguish between system and context-awareness models; that is, we make explicit whether the scope of reflection is the system itself or the context by applying corresponding stereotypes to awareness models. Similarly, we consider further stereotypes to specialize learning, reasoning, and acting processes. For instance, variations of acting such as explore, explain, report, suggest, self-adapt, or impact on the environment are captured by corresponding stereotypes.

Consequently, we may conclude that the notation with its concepts covers all of the aspects mentioned in the definition of self-aware computing systems. These aspects can be interpreted as the basic needs a system has to satisfy to be self-aware. Hence, our notation with its concepts addresses these needs at the architectural or design level and is therefore, a preliminary approach to model architectures and designs of self-aware computing systems.

Besides the definition of self-aware computing systems, Chap. 1 introduces the LRA-M loop as depicted in Fig. 5.4. This conceptual loop illustrates the activities and artifacts that are implemented by a self-aware system. Particularly, the system (i.e., the self) collects empirical observations of itself and the environment uses these observations to learn and reason on models, which eventually enables the system to act upon itself or the environment.

Using the proposed concepts, we can describe the conceptual LRA-M loop. The notation supports modeling the system and the environment as well as refining the system to modules, processes, awareness models, goal models, and empirical data while wiring all of them with data flow connectors. This is sufficient to model the LRA-M loop as depicted in Fig. 5.27. Compared to Fig. 5.4, we extended the LRA-M loop with a prereflective ≪observe≫ process to describe how the empirical data are obtained. That is, this process monitors the self and the environmental context to obtain the empirical observations. These data are used by a learning process to obtain awareness models, which is guided by the goals of the self. The reasoning process uses the awareness and goal models to reason. Finally, the act process may influence the context or the self, for instance, by performing a self-adaptation.

Using the awareness and expression relations of our notation, the essence of the LRA-M loop can be captured in a more abstract way—as depicted in Fig. 5.28a—to illustrate the self-awareness and self-expression of the system. Rather than describing data flows that implement some form of awareness, we model the self-awareness and self-expression in a declarative way by using awareness and expression links. Besides being more abstract, this version is also more explicit than the one in Fig. 5.27 in making the self-awareness and self-expression visible. Thereby, the awareness and expression target the self as well as the context of the self.

In the case of Fig. 5.27, the data flow links are required to form a LRA-M loop that realizes the self-awareness. However, the existence of data flow links does not necessarily imply that self-awareness has really been realized since such links may describe quite different data flows (e.g., at the prereflective level) that do not necessarily lead to self-awareness. Therefore, Fig. 5.28a explicitly denotes the existence of self-awareness by awareness and expression links.

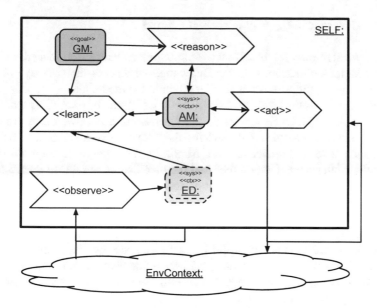

Fig. 5.27 The LRA-M loop modeled with the proposed concepts

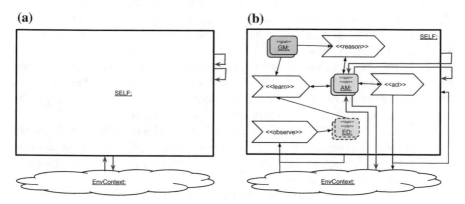

Fig. 5.28 The LRA-M loop extended with awareness and expression links

Finally, we can combine both, the data flow and the awareness/expression links, as shown in Fig. 5.28b. On the one hand, the data flow among processes and models makes the realization of the self-awareness (i.e., the internal design of the system) visible. On the other hand, the awareness and expression links explicitly emphasize the self-awareness and self-expression of the system.

5.6.2.2   Coverage of the Framework of Chap. 3

The conceptual framework for self-aware computing systems as introduced in Chap. 3 proposes various dimensions. In the following, we discuss the coverage of these dimensions by the proposed concepts for architecture modeling.

One dimension is the level of self-awareness, which can be *prereflective* or *reflective*. We address both levels in Sect. 5.3.2 by considering self-awareness processes, especially observe, analyze, and react for the prereflective level as well as learn, reason, and act for the reflective level. Similarly, we support stereotyping of systems and modules depending on the level they are operating on (see Sect. 5.5.4 for the ≪prereflective≫, ≪reflective≫, and ≪meta-reflective≫ stereotypes). In this context, we additionally discussed *meta-self-awareness* by providing stereotypes to label a system as ≪self-aware≫ or ≪meta-self-aware≫.

Concerning goals and goal models introduced in Chap. 1 and addressed here in Sect. 5.3.3, Chap. 3 refines this aspect for self-awareness by discussing the domain of a goal in terms of their span and scope. These refinements are not supported by the architectural concepts proposed here but we will come back to them when discussing collective self-aware systems in Chap. 7.

In general, self-awareness has a domain and enables that a subject of the awareness (i.e., the *span*) reflects about an object of awareness (i.e., the *scope*) (see Chap. 3). This distinction between a span and a scope is addressed by awareness and expression links that connect the span and scope of a self-awareness relationship (see Sect. 5.4.2). A refinement of such relationships in terms of *action scope* that includes all entities that the system may act directly upon and *influence scope* that refers to entities upon which the system may only act indirectly is introduced in Chap. 3. We cover this refinement with direct and indirect expression links (see Sect. 5.4.2). Similarly to the expression links, direct and indirect awareness links are further supported.

We may further refine the awareness links using stereotypes to distinguish, among others, *stimulus awareness* (≪sa≫), *interaction awareness* (≪ia≫), *time awareness* (≪ta≫), and *goal awareness* (≪ga≫). These stereotypes cover different aspects of awareness as discussed in Chap. 3.

Finally, the notion of self-loops discussed in Chap. 3 is addressed by recurrent or cyclic awareness and expression links in Sects. 5.5.3.

5.6.2.3   Summary

The definition and framework for self-aware computing systems (see Chaps. 1 and 3) propose several dimensions that we have discussed previously and that we summarize Table 5.1. These dimensions provide the necessary architectural and design concepts to explore the solution space of self-aware computing system.

Besides these dimensions that are specific to self-aware computing systems, we consider general architectural concepts such as systems, modules, composition/aggregation and collaborations of systems/modules, ports, and connectors to provide the necessary means for describing software architectures. In this context, the dimensions enrich the general concepts, which results in a kind of domain-specific architectural language for the domain of self-aware computing systems.

5.7   Conclusion

In this chapter, we developed basic concepts for describing architectures for self-aware computing systems as defined in Chaps. 1 and 3.

First, we identified the core architectural elements required for self-aware computing systems. In addition to the system and its refinement to modules, the relevant environmental context the system is aware of has to be identified. Furthermore, we noticed and addressed the need to allocate prereflective (observe, analyze, and react) and reflective (learn, reason, and act) self-awareness processes within the architecture. Besides processes representing behavior, the models (e.g., awareness, empirical data, and goal models) have been identified as core ingredients—as they capture the knowledge of self-aware systems—that should be made visible at the architectural level and in the refined design. In addition to all these elements, their linkage is relevant to describe their interactions. The data flow connects modules, processes, and models, which are required for realizing the LRA-M loop and therefore the self-awareness and self-expression. In this context, we aim for making the self-awareness and self-expression explicit by emphasizing when a span is directly or indirectly aware of a scope (cf. awareness link) and when a span directly or indirectly acts upon a scope (cf. expression link).

Based on these concepts we studied how context- and self-awareness can be addressed in the architectural design of self-aware computing systems. Moreover, we discussed specific cases of self-awareness such as multiple overlapping scopes and spans, self-loops, cyclic self-awareness, and meta-self-awareness. Finally, we have shown in Table 5.1 that the proposed architectural concepts cover the needs for self-aware computing systems as raised in Chaps. 1 and 3. The main concepts covering the needs for describing architectures of self-aware computing systems are relevant for individual (see Chap. 6) as well as collectives of such systems (see Chap. 7). The concepts extending the UML offer the necessary elements to discuss specifics of self-aware computing systems such as the LRA-M loop at the architectural level. The sketched use of multiple architectural views provides means to emphasize certain specifics such as the processes, models, or the self-awareness/self-expression in the architecture. Making such specifics explicit in the architectural design supports

Table 5.1 Dimensions and section of this chapter covering each dimension

Dimensions	Section
Dimensions introduced in Chap. 1	
Awareness models	5.3.3
Empirical data	5.3.3
Goal models	5.3.3
Data flow	5.4.1
Awareness of context	5.5.1
Awareness of itself	5.5.2
Dimensions introduced in Chap. 3	
Prereflective self-awareness	5.3.2, 5.5.4
Reflective self-awareness	5.3.2, 5.5.4
Meta-reflective self-awareness	5.5.4
Domain (span and scope) of awareness	5.4.2
Direct and indirect awareness/expression	5.4.2
Aspects of awareness (stimulus, interaction, ...)	5.4.2
Self-loops and cyclic self-awareness	5.5.3

engineers in deciding and reasoning about the system's self-awareness capabilities, which eventually supports development.

In this chapter, we motivated the need for the introduced architectural concepts without an in-depth discussion of their novelty. This discussion will be provided when reviewing the state of the art and research field of architectures for individual and collective self-aware computing systems in Chap. 8.

Acknowledgements This chapter is the result of stimulating discussions among the authors and other participants, especially Peter Lewis, Nelly Bencomo, Kurt Geihs, Kirstie Bellman, Chris Landauer, and Paola Inverardi, during the seminar on Model-driven Algorithms and Architectures for Self-Aware Computing Systems at Schloss Dagstuhl in January 2015 (http://www.dagstuhl.de/15041).

Summary of the Notation

The following table provides a summary of the concepts for modeling architectures of self-aware computing systems. For each concept, its name, syntactic construct (notational element), description, and rationale are listed (Table 5.2).

Table 5.2 Architectural concepts for self-aware computing systems

Name	Syntax	Description	Rationale
System	name:type	A *system* with a name and type. We may omit either its name (anonymous system) or type. It can be hierarchically decomposed into *modules*. Stereotypes such as ≪self-aware≫ and ≪meta-self-aware≫ indicate whether a system is self-aware, meta-self-aware, etc.	The entirety of the modeled system distinguished from the *environmental context*
Module	name:type	A *module* with a name and type. We may omit either its name (anonymous module) or type. It can be hierarchically decomposed into modules. The stereotypes ≪reflective≫ and ≪prereflective≫ indicate whether the module reflects on any other module or not. Stereotypes for higher forms of reflection are ≪meta-reflective≫, ≪meta-meta-reflective≫, etc.	*Modules* are required to decompose a *system* or other *modules*
Environmental context	name:type	An *environmental context* of a *system* describes the fragment of the environment that is scoped by the system's capacities of sensing and exploration. It has a name and type, one of which we may omit	The portion of the overall environment that is relevant for the *system*
Port	type ▾	A *port* describes provided or required functionality of a *system*, *module*, or *context*. It is characterized by its type. The direction of the arrow indicates a required (arrow points outward the element requiring the functionality) or provided (arrow points inward the element providing the functionality) port. Stereotypes indicate the kind of functionality: effect ≪E≫, adapt ≪A≫, observe ≪O≫, and report ≪R≫	A *port* supports encapsulation of elements by making the providing or requiring functionality explicit

(continued)

Table 5.2 (continued)

Name	Syntax	Description	Rationale
Data Flow	⟶	A *data flow* describes the interactions between *systems*, *modules*, *processes*, and *models* by means of exchanging data	*Data flow* connectors make the compositional structure explicit; that is, how elements are wired
Composition	name:type / name:type / name:type	In a *composition* (UML composite structure diagram), we refine modules to other modules while we distinguish between exclusive (solid border of the embedded module) and shared (dashed border of the embedded module) membership of an embedded module	A *composition* allows us to decompose the system into modules and a module into other modules and to distinguish the kind of membership of a contained module
Collaboration	name:type	A *collaboration* describes the cooperating behavior among *systems*, *modules*, and *processes*. The concrete behavior of the cooperation is described within the collaboration	A *collaboration* supports modeling more flexible cooperations among *systems*, *modules*, and *processes* compared to wiring all of the elements using *data flow* connectors
Participation	⸺	A *participation* connects a *system*, *module*, or *process* to a *collaboration* such that the *system*, *module*, or *process* participates in the *collaboration*	A *participation* makes explicit which elements cooperate via a *collaboration* in contrast to directly exchanging data through *data flow* connectors
Process	Process	A *process* describes activities within a *system* or *module* and therefore emphasizes the behavior within these structural elements	Self-aware systems have specific *processes* such as learning *awareness models*, reasoning, or acting that should be made visible in the architecture
Awareness model	name:type	An *awareness model* represents learned aspects of a scope. The scope is often (part of) the *system* itself, other *systems*, or the *environmental context*. In the former case, the model is stereotyped with ≪sys≫, in the latter case with ≪ctx≫. An awareness model has a name and type, one of which can be omitted	An *awareness model* makes explicit that a span maintains a model representing the scope of the awareness

(continued)

Table 5.2   (continued)

Name	Syntax	Description	Rationale
Empirical data	name:type	*Empirical data* represents observations of a scope. The scope is often (part of) the *system* itself, other *systems*, or the *environmental context*. In the former case, the empirical data model is stereotyped with ≪sys≫, in the latter case with ≪ctx≫. An empirical data have a name and a type, one of which we may omit	An *empirical data* model makes explicit that a span collects (sensor) data about a scope
Goal model	≪goal≫ name:type	A *goal model* describes the goals (parts of) the *system* should achieve. Goals are imposed to the system from outside (e.g., by the user) or internally produced. A goal model has a name and type, one of which can be omitted. It is stereotyped with ≪goal≫	Explicit *goal models* are required since self-aware systems are driven by goals and they should be able to handle dynamically changing goals
Awareness link	⟶	An *awareness link* denotes that a span is directly aware of a scope. If a span exploits awareness knowledge about a scope that has been established by another span, the former span is indirectly aware of the scope. Indirect awareness is transitive and can be explicitly represented by dashed awareness links. Awareness links can be specialized by indicating their type: ≪sa≫ for stimulus, ≪ia≫ for interaction, ≪ta≫ for time, and ≪ga≫ for goal awareness	An *awareness link* connects the span and the scope to make explicit which element learns and reasons about which other element, and specifically, which element is the original represented in an *awareness model*

(continued)

Table 5.2 (continued)

Name	Syntax	Description	Rationale
Expression link	⟶	An *expression link* denotes that a span directly impacts a scope. If a span indirectly impacts a scope via another span, the former span can be connected to the scope to make the indirect expression visible. Indirect expressions are transitive and can be explicitly represented by dashed expression links. To specialize the expression type, a link is stereotyped with effect ≪E≫, adapt ≪A≫, observe ≪O≫, or report ≪R≫	An *expression link* connects the span and the scope to make explicit which element acts upon another element

References

1. Anant Agarwal and Bill Harrod. Organic computing. Technical Report White paper, MIT and DARPA, 2006.
2. Anant Agarwal, Jason Miller, Jonathan Eastep, David Wentziaff, and Harshad Kasture. Self-aware computing. Technical Report AFRL-RI-RS-TR-2009-161, MIT, 2009.
3. Ozalp Babaoglu, Mark Jelasity, Alberto Montresor, Christof Fetzer, Stefano Leonardi, Aad van Moorsel, and Maarten van Steen, editors. *Self-star Properties in Complex Information Systems: Conceptual and Practical Foundations*, volume 3460 of *Lecture Notes in Computer Science (LNCS)*. Springer, 2005.
4. Nelly Bencomo, Amel Bennaceur, Paul Grace, Gordon S. Blair, and Valérie Issarny. The role of models@run.time in supporting on-the-fly interoperability. *Computing*, 95(3):167–190, 2013.
5. Amel Bennaceur, Robert France, Giordano Tamburrelli, Thomas Vogel, Pieter J Mosterman, Walter Cazzola, Fbio M. Costa, Alfonso Pierantonio, Matthias Tichy, Mehmet Aksit, Pr Emmanuelson, Huang Gang, Nikolaos Georgantas, and David Redlich. Mechanisms for Leveraging Models at Runtime in Self-adaptive Software. In Nelly Bencomo, Robert France, Betty H.C. Cheng, and Uwe Assmann, editors, *Models@run.time*, volume 8378 of *Lecture Notes in Computer Science (LNCS)*, pages 19–46. Springer, 2014.
6. Gordon Blair, Nelly Bencomo, and Robert France. Models@run.time. *Computer*, 42(10):22–27, 2009.
7. Yuriy Brun, Giovanna Di Marzo Serugendo, Cristina Gacek, Holger Giese, Holger Kienle, Marin Litoiu, Hausi Müller, Mauro Pezzè, and Mary Shaw. Engineering Self-Adaptive Systems through Feedback Loops. In Betty H.C. Cheng, Rogério de Lemos, Holger Giese, Paola Inverardi, and Jeff Magee, editors, *Software Engineering for Self-Adaptive Systems*, volume 5525 of *Lecture Notes in Computer Science (LNCS)*, pages 48–70. Springer, 2009.
8. Radu Calinescu, Lars Grunske, Marta Z. Kwiatkowska, Raffaela Mirandola, and Giordano Tamburrelli. Dynamic qos management and optimization in service-based systems. *IEEE Trans. Software Eng.*, 37(3):387–409, 2011.

9. Betty H.C. Cheng, Rogério de Lemos, Holger Giese, Paola Inverardi, Jeff Magee, Jesper Andersson, Basil Becker, Nelly Bencomo, Yuriy Brun, Bojan Cukic, Giovanna Di Marzo Serugendo, Schahram Dustdar, Anthony Finkelstein, Cristina Gacek, Kurt Geihs, Vincenzo Grassi, Gabor Karsai, Holger M. Kienle, Jeff Kramer, Marin Litoiu, Sam Malek, Raffaela Mirandola, Hausi Müller, Sooyong Park, Mary Shaw, Matthias Tichy, Massimo Tivoli, Danny Weyns, and Jon Whittle. Software Engineering for Self-Adaptive Systems: A Research Roadmap. In Betty H.C. Cheng, Rogério de Lemos, Holger Giese, Paola Inverardi, and Jeff Magee, editors, *Software Engineering for Self-Adaptive Systems*, volume 5525 of *Lecture Notes in Computer Science (LNCS)*, pages 1–26. Springer, 2009.
10. Betty H.C. Cheng, Holger Giese, Paola Inverardi, Jeff Magee, and Rogério de Lemos, editors. *Software Engineering for Self-Adaptive Systems*, volume 5525 of *Lecture Notes in Computer Science (LNCS)*. Springer, 2009.
11. Shang-Wen Cheng, Vahe V. Poladian, David Garlan, and Bradley Schmerl. Improving architecture-based self-adaptation through resource prediction. In Betty H.C. Cheng, Rogerio de Lemos, Holger Giese, Paola Inverardi, and Jeff Magee, editors, *Software Engineering for Self-Adaptive Systems*, volume 5525 of *Lecture Notes in Computer Science (LNCS)*, pages 71–88. Springer, 2009.
12. M.T. Cox. Metacognition in computation: A selected research review. *Art. Int.*, 169(2):104–141, 2005.
13. Rogério de Lemos, Holger Giese, Hausi Müller, and Mary Shaw, editors. *Software Engineering for Self-Adaptive Systems II*, volume 7475 of *Lecture Notes in Computer Science (LNCS)*. Springer, 2013.
14. Rogério de Lemos, Holger Giese, Hausi Müller, Mary Shaw, Jesper Andersson, Marin Litoiu, Bradley Schmerl, Gabriel Tamura, Norha M. Villegas, Thomas Vogel, Danny Weyns, Luciano Baresi, Basil Becker, Nelly Bencomo, Yuriy Brun, Bojan Cukic, Ron Desmarais, Schahram Dustdar, Gregor Engels, Kurt Geihs, Karl Goeschka, Alessandra Gorla, Vincenzo Grassi, Paola Inverardi, Gabor Karsai, Jeff Kramer, Antónia Lopes, Jeff Magee, Sam Malek, Serge Mankovskii, Raffaela Mirandola, John Mylopoulos, Oscar Nierstrasz, Mauro Pezzè, Christian Prehofer, Wilhelm Schäfer, Rick Schlichting, Dennis B. Smith, Joao P. Sousa, Ladan Tahvildari, Kenny Wong, and Jochen Wuttke. Software Engineering for Self-Adaptive Systems: A second Research Roadmap. In Rogério de Lemos, Holger Giese, Hausi Müller, and Mary Shaw, editors, *Software Engineering for Self-Adaptive Systems II*, volume 7475 of *Lecture Notes in Computer Science (LNCS)*, pages 1–32. Springer, 2013.
15. Marco Dorigo, Vito Trianni, Erol Şahin, Roderich Groß, Thomas H. Labella, Gianluca Baldassarre, Stefano Nolfi, Jean-Louis Deneubourg, Francesco Mondada, Dario Floreano, and Luca M. Gambardella. Evolving self-organizing behaviors for a swarm-bot. *Autonomous Robots*, 17:223–245, 2004.
16. Sylvain Frey, Ada Diaconescu, and Isabelle M. Demeure. Architectural Integration Patterns for Autonomic Management Systems. In *Proc. of the 9th IEEE International Conference and Workshops on the Engineering of Autonomic and Autonomous Systems (EASe 2012)*, 2012.
17. David Garlan, Shang-Wen Cheng, An-Cheng Huang, Bradley R. Schmerl, and Peter Steenkiste. Rainbow: Architecture-based self-adaptation with reusable infrastructure. *IEEE Computer*, 37(10):46–54, 2004.
18. Holger Giese and Wilhelm Schfer. Model-Driven Development of Safe Self-Optimizing Mechatronic Systems with MechatronicUML. In Javier Camara, Rogrio de Lemos, Carlo Ghezzi, and Antónia Lopes, editors, *Assurances for Self-Adaptive Systems*, volume 7740 of *Lecture Notes in Computer Science (LNCS)*, pages 152–186. Springer, 2013.
19. Julia Hielscher, Raman Kazhamiakin, Andreas Metzger, and Marco Pistore. A framework for proactive self-adaptation of service-based applications based on online testing. In Petri Mahonen, Klaus Pohl, and Thierry Priol, editors, *Towards a Service-Based Internet*, volume 5377 of *Lecture Notes in Computer Science (LNCS)*, pages 122–133. Springer, 2008.
20. Henry Hoffmann, Martina Maggio, Marco D. Santambrogio, Alberto Leva, and Anant Agarwal. Seec: A general and extensible framework for self-aware computing. Technical Report MIT-CSAIL-TR-2011-046, MIT CSAIL, 2011.

21. John E. Kelly and Steve Hamm. *Smart machines: IBM's Watson and the era of cognitive computing.* Columbia Business School Publishing, 2013.
22. Jeffrey O. Kephart and David M. Chess. The vision of autonomic computing. *Computer*, 36(1):41–50, 2003.
23. Samuel Kounev. Self-Aware Software and Systems Engineering: A Vision and Research Roadmap. In *GI Softwaretechnik-Trends, 31(4), November 2011*, Karlsruhe, Germany, 2011.
24. Jeff Kramer and Jeff Magee. Self-Managed Systems: an Architectural Challenge. In *FOSE '07: Future of Software Engineering*, pages 259–268. IEEE, 2007.
25. Peter R. Lewis, Arjun Chandra, Funmilade Faniyi, Kyrre Glette, Tao Chen, Rami Bahsoon, Jim Torresen, and Xin Yao. Architectural aspects of self-aware and self-expressive computing systems: From psychology to engineering. *IEEE Computer*, 48(8):62–70, 2015.
26. Janet Metcalfe and Arthur P. Shimamura, editors. *Metacognition: Knowing about knowing.* MIT Press, Cambridge, MA, USA, 1994.
27. Melanie Mitchell. Self-awareness and control in decentralized systems (Tech Report SS-05-04). In *AAAI Spring Symp. on Metacognition in Computation*, Menlo Park, 2005. AIII Press.
28. Hausi A. Müller, Mauro Pezzè, and Mary Shaw. Visibility of Control in Adaptive Systems. In *Proceedings of the 2nd International Workshop on Ultra-large-scale Software-intensive Systems*, ULSSIS '08, pages 23–26. ACM, 2008.
29. Christian Muller-Schloer, Hartmut Schmeck, and Theo Ungerer, editors. *Organic Computing - A Paradigm Shift for Complex Systems.* Birkhuser, 2011.
30. Hausi A. Mller, Holger M. Kienle, and Ulrike Stege. Autonomic Computing Now You See It, Now You Don't. In Andrea Lucia and Filomena Ferrucci, editors, *Software Engineering: International Summer Schools, ISSSE 2006-2008, Salerno, Italy, Revised Tutorial Lectures*, volume 5413 of *Lecture Notes in Computer Science (LNCS)*, pages 32–54. Springer, 2009.
31. Object Management Group. OMG Systems Modeling Language (OMG SysML^{TM}), 2015. Version 1.4, formal/2015-06-03.
32. Object Management Group. OMG Unified Modeling Language^{TM} (OMG UML), 2015. Version 2.5, formal/2015-03-01.
33. L.D. Paulson. DARPA creating self-aware computing. *Computer*, 36(3):24, 2003.
34. Mazeiar Salehie and Ladan Tahvildari. Self-adaptive software: Landscape and research challenges. *ACM Trans. Auton. Adapt. Syst.*, 4(2):1–42, 2009.
35. Mary Shaw. Beyond objects: A software design paradigm based on process control. *ACM SIGSOFT Software Engineering Notes*, 20(1):27–38, 1995.
36. Mary Shaw and David Garlan. An Introduction to Software Architecture. volume 2, pages 1–39. World Scientific Publishing Company, 1993.
37. Vítor E. Silva Souza, Alexei Lapouchnian, William N. Robinson, and John Mylopoulos. Awareness requirements for adaptive systems. In *Proc. of the 6th International Symposium on Software Engineering for Adaptive and Self-Managing Systems*, pages 60–69. ACM, 2011.
38. Clemens Szyperski, Dirk Gruntz, and Stephan Murer. *Component Software Beyond Object-Oriented Programming.* Component Software. Addison-Wesley, New York, NY, USA, 2nd edition, 2002.
39. Thomas Vogel and Holger Giese. Adaptation and Abstract Runtime Models. In *Proceedings of the 5th Workshop on Software Engineering for Adaptive and Self-Managing Systems (SEAMS 2010)*, pages 39–48. ACM, May 2010.
40. Thomas Vogel and Holger Giese. Model-driven engineering of self-adaptive software with eurema. *ACM Trans. Auton. Adapt. Syst.*, 8(4):18:1–18:33, 2014.
41. Thomas Vogel, Andreas Seibel, and Holger Giese. The Role of Models and Megamodels at Runtime. In Juergen Dingel and Arnor Solberg, editors, *Models in Software Engineering, Workshops and Symposia at MODELS 2010, Reports and Revised Selected Papers*, volume 6627 of *Lecture Notes in Computer Science (LNCS)*, pages 224–238. Springer, 2011.

42. Eric Yuan, Naeem Esfahani, and Sam Malek. Automated mining of software component inter-actions for self-adaptation. In *Proceedings of the 9th International Symposium on Software Engineering for Adaptive and Self-Managing Systems*, SEAMS'14, pages 27–36. ACM, 2014.
43. Franco Zambonelli, Nicola Bicocchi, Giacomo Cabri, Letizia Leonardi, and Mariachiara Puviani. On self-adaptation, self-expression, and self-awareness in autonomic service compo-nent ensembles. In *Proc. of the Fifth IEEE Conference on Self-Adaptive and Self-Organizing Systems Workshops (SASOW)*, pages 108–113. IEEE, 2011.

Chapter 6
Generic Architectures for Individual Self-aware Computing Systems

Holger Giese, Thomas Vogel, Ada Diaconescu, Sebastian Götz
and Kirstie L. Bellman

Abstract Making computing systems self-aware calls for appropriate architectural designs of such systems that allow developers to explicitly decide and reason about the system's self-awareness capabilities. In this context, a critical issue is the development of appropriate reflections that enable self-awareness and that impact the architectural design. This chapter, therefore, discusses generic architectures for pre-reflective, reflective, and meta-reflective self-awareness as well as various forms of constructing reflections while focusing on an individual system as opposed to a collective of self-aware computing systems. Finally, we discuss the presented ideas with respect to existing control schemes and architectural styles for self-adaptive software that seem to be promising for the architectural design of self-aware computing systems.

H. Giese (✉) · T. Vogel
Hasso Plattner Institute for Software Systems Engineering at the University
of Potsdam, Prof.-Dr.-Helmert-Str. 2-3, 14482 Potsdam, Germany
e-mail: holger.giese@hpi.de

T. Vogel
e-mail: thomas.vogel@hpi.de

A. Diaconescu
Telécom ParisTech, Equipe S3, Departement INFRES, 46 Rue Barrault,
75013 Paris, France
e-mail: ada.diaconescu@telecom-paristech.fr

S. Götz
TU Dresden, Dresden, Germany
e-mail: sebastian.goetz@acm.org

K.L. Bellman
Aerospace Integration Science Center, The Aerospace Corporation,
El Segundo, CA, USA
e-mail: Kirstie.L.Bellman@aero.org

© Springer International Publishing AG 2017
S. Kounev et al. (eds.), *Self-Aware Computing Systems*,
DOI 10.1007/978-3-319-47474-8_6

6.1 Introduction

Research communities such as autonomic computing [1], self-* systems [2], self-adaptive, and self-managed systems [3–7], organic computing [8, 9], or cognitive computing [10] are all arguing for shifting design-time decisions to the run time to better cope with the dynamic and uncertain contexts and requirements. The vision of self-aware computing systems as introduced in Chaps. 1 and 3 argues similarly that *self-aware* systems are better suited for such dynamic and uncertain settings than traditional systems because the system's self-awareness enables capabilities to learn, reason, (self-)adapt, or explain to users what happened. Initial ideas on self-aware computing have already been proposed [8, 11–17] as well as related ideas in the context of run-time models [18–22], meta-cognition [23, 24], and self-organization [25].[1]

The notion of self-aware computing systems as defined in Chaps. 1 and 3 provides the foundation for this chapter to discuss the implications of self-awareness on the architecture. Such a foundation was missing beforehand [26–28] and now allows us to study the architectural design and development of such systems.

In this chapter, we will look at the solution space for self-aware computing systems with the particular focus on the *software architecture* [29] of an individual system. This is motivated among others by Kramer and Magee [30] who argue that the engineering of self-managed systems is an architectural challenge. Therefore, focusing on self-aware computing systems, we will target fundamental questions of how pre-reflective, reflective, and meta-reflective self-awareness can be addressed at the architectural level. Addressing these questions at the architectural level allows engineers to explicitly decide and reason about the system's self-awareness capabilities. In this context, we discuss variants of reflection such as local, hierarchical and centralized, and coordinated reflection as well as their implications on the architecture. Finally, we relate these variants of reflection and the different kinds of self-awareness to existing control schemes and architectural styles that seem to be promising for the architectural design of a self-aware computing system.

The ideas presented in this chapter are based on the architectural concepts for self-aware computing system presented in Chap. 5. These concepts have been derived from the definition and conceptual framework of self-aware computing systems discussed in Chaps. 1 and 3. While we focus on individual systems in this chapter, we study collectives of self-aware computing systems in Chap. 7. Moreover, we skip discussing the state of the art concerning architectures for self-aware computing systems in this chapter, but we come back to it in Chap. 8.

It is important to emphasize that the concepts introduced in Chap. 5 are not a dedicated architectural language intended for development. It rather provides an initial basis to compare approaches as well as to explore and discuss the space of possible architectural solutions. Therefore, the specific architectures or fragments of an architecture we present in this chapter may also include elements of a design to discuss and clarify a certain solution. Our intention is to be able to express and

---

[1] See also Chap. 2 for a discussion of related concepts and research areas.

compare also subtle differences in the architecture or even design rather than having an appropriate compromise between expressiveness and an easy-to-use language. Consequently, the presented diagrams may be too detailed for an architecture as their purpose is to make the comparison possible rather than being a cost-effective step during the development of self-aware computing systems. Hence, the purpose of the presented architectures is to start-off research and work on architectures for self-aware computing systems, while future results, experiments, and solutions may then confirm, refine, or even contradict them.

This chapter is organized as follows: In Sect. 6.2, we introduce the running example and summarize the required terminology. Then, we discuss architectures for pre-reflective (Sect. 6.3), reflective (Sect. 6.4), and meta-reflective (Sect. 6.5) self-awareness. These ideas are discussed with respect to the existing control schemes and architectural styles of self-adaptive systems in Sect. 6.6. Finally, we conclude the chapter with Sect. 6.7.

6.2   Preliminaries

In this section, we introduce the running example that we use to discuss generic architectures for individual self-aware computing systems. Then, we summarize the terminology required for understanding the discussion.

6.2.1   Running Example: Smart Home

To discuss the solution space for architectures and designs of an individual self-aware computing system, we use the running example that has been discussed in detail in Chap. 5. This example considers a smart home system with a set of pre-reflective components controlling devices within a single house. These components are coordinated by a smart *house manager* responsible for the whole house.

The house manager reports to the user if something goes wrong (e.g., if failures are detected), self-adapts (e.g., to optimize energy consumption) and actuates the device controllers in the house (e.g., in the case of emergencies). Besides a centralized house manager that coordinates the device controllers located in the house, we further consider variants of less hierarchical interaction schemes such as collaborations or self-organization to achieve the coordination among the device controllers.

A house consists of several floors and rooms. Each room is equipped with devices such as sensors to perceive the in- and outdoor temperature, lighting conditions, and persons, as well as controllers for the heater (start or stop heating), lights (switch on or off the lights), windows (tilt, open, or close the window), and shutter panels (open or close the panels). Each controller works independently, for example, one controls the heater based on the temperature and another one the windows based on time. This might result in conflicts such as heating up the room while opening the windows.

The task of the house manager is to coordinate the different controllers according to some goals. Therefore, the manager aims for self-healing and self-optimization while we leave out other self-* capabilities to keep the example simple.

A scenario of self-healing is that the house manager relies on the sensor data from the neighboring rooms if a sensor in a certain room is broken or that the house manager notifies a person in the house, who is close to the open window that cannot be automatically closed any more, to manually close the window. A scenario of self-optimization is that the house manager optimizes the energy consumption while achieving the goals such as maintaining a certain room temperature in the house, while it may consider various influencing factors such as market prices, weather forecasts, government subsidies, and user preferences.

In the following, we use this example to discuss architectures of self-aware computing systems. Since the goal of this discussion is to emphasize particular aspects of self-awareness at the architectural level, we will often present only a fragment of the smart home system to illustrate these aspects instead of a complete architecture.

6.2.2   Self-awareness Terminology, Framework, and Notation

The terminology and framework for self-aware computing systems introduced in Chaps. 1 and 3 provide a definition and several dimensions spanning the overall spectrum of such systems. In the following, we briefly summarize the definition and dimensions since they provide the foundation for discussing architectures of individual self-aware computing systems. At first, we recap the definition of self-aware computing systems given in Chap. 1:

Self-aware computing systems are computing systems that:

1. *learn models* capturing *knowledge* about themselves and their environment (such as their structure, design, state, possible actions, and run-time behavior) on an ongoing basis and
2. *reason* using the models (e.g., predict, analyze, consider, and plan) enabling them to *act* based on their knowledge and reasoning (e.g., explore, explain, report, suggest, self-adapt, or impact their environment) in accordance with *higher-level goals*, which may also be subject to change.

Based on this definition, we may sketch a self-aware computing system with the conceptual *Learn-Reason-Act Model (LRA-M)* loop (see Fig. 6.1). This loop shows the relevant aspects of the definition. Particularly, the system collects *empirical observations* of the self and of phenomena outside the self. *Learning* and *reasoning* processes produce and use *models* that capture knowledge derived from the observations. Based on the knowledge, the system may *act* upon itself and on its context. The processes operate according to the higher-level *goals* that may dynamically change.

Fig. 6.1 The *LRA-M* loop introduced in Chap. 1

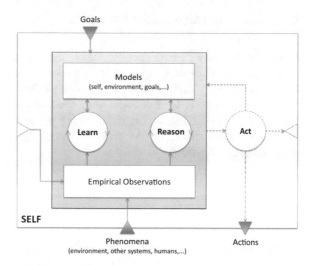

Consequently, the definition and the LRA-M loop introduce the concepts of *empirical data/observations*, *models*, and *goals*, which are used by *learning*, *reasoning*, and *acting processes*. We can elaborate this use relationship by describing the *data flow* within the LRA-M loop. The system observes itself and its environmental context, for which models are learned and used for reasoning and acting. Thus, a system realizing such a loop becomes aware of itself and of its context.

These aspects are refined by Chap. 3 providing several dimensions for self-aware computing systems, which we consider as a conceptual framework. This framework covers different levels of self-awareness: a *pre-reflective self-awareness* level denoting simple subjective observations, a *reflective self-awareness* level if learning and reasoning with awareness models are involved, and a *meta-self-awareness* level where the object of the reflection is a reflective self-awareness process. Moreover, the framework distinguishes a subject (i.e., the *span*) and an object of awareness (i.e., the *scope*), while the span reflects on the scope. In this context, the notion of *action scope* that includes all entities that the system may act directly upon as well as the notion of *influence scope* that refers to entities upon which the system may only act indirectly is introduced. Finally, the frameworks refine the notion of awareness by emphasizing different aspects of awareness such as *identity*, *state*, *interaction*, *time*, *behavior*, *appearance*, *goal*, *expectation*, and *belief awareness*.

These aspects and dimensions are addressed by the architectural concepts and notation that we have discussed in Chap. 5. Particularly, the appendix of Chap. 5 provides a summary of these concepts and notation that we will further use here to model exemplary architectures of individual self-aware computing systems.

6.3   Pre-reflective Self-awareness

In this section, we discuss architectural considerations for the pre-reflective part
of a self-aware computing system. In this context, an important issue is to enable
access to the pre-reflective elements such that reflections of them can be built and
serve as a foundation for self-awareness. We particularly discuss the encapsulated
access in terms of reflection interfaces of the pre-reflective elements as well as the
direct access to these elements. Thereby, we outline variants of the design of the
pre-reflective subsystem.

6.3.1   Encapsulated Access to the Pre-reflective Subsystem

Encapsulating the pre-reflective part of the system requires developing interfaces that
support reflecting upon this part. The reflection may also include acting upon (e.g.,
adapting) this part. The design of such a reflection interface can be quite different. For
instance, a *local reflection interface* provides access to a single pre-reflective module,
a *grouped reflection interface* to a well-defined group of pre-reflective modules, and a
global reflection interface to all pre-reflective modules of the system. Hence, the kind
of reflection interface determines the possible scope of self-awareness. Nevertheless,
there must not necessarily be the need of reflecting upon all pre-reflective modules
even when having a global reflection interface.

Moreover, the pre-reflective part of the system can be structured in a monolithic
or modular manner. Considering a monolithic structure for our running example,
the pre-reflective part consists of a single controller that manages all the devices
in the house. Focusing on the heater device, this example is illustrated in Fig. 6.2
showing one Controller maintaining the room temperature. This Controller uses two
≪observe≫ processes that measure the room and the outdoor temperatures (T°-R and
T°-O). The ≪analyze≫ process relates these measurements to the goal temperature
for the room (Goal T°-R) set by the user and identifies a target temperature (T°) the
heater should achieve. The ≪react≫ process adjusts the heater accordingly based on
the current heater settings (Heater). This adjustment is a simple reaction that updates
the heater's power, either resulting in heating up or down the room.

The pre-reflective processes of the Controller realize atomic functions such as
measuring the temperature, comparing the measurements to the goals, and acting on
devices (e.g., the physical heater). Consequently, the Controller does not perform any
reflection or establish any self-awareness. However, it provides reflection interfaces
allowing other elements to reflect on it (see Fig. 6.2). These interfaces can be kept
rather simple if they offer access only to the goals or the empirical data that is already
measured by the pre-reflective part. In contrast, they are more complicated if they
provide access to the processes capturing (running) behavior. In our example, the
pre-reflective Controller provides two global reflection interfaces. The SetGoals port
supports adjusting the goal temperature as indicated by the delegation connector

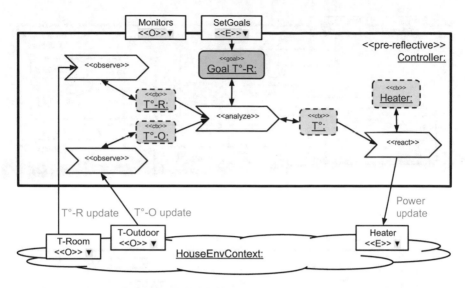

Fig. 6.2 Monolithic and encapsulated pre-reflective part

from the port to the goal model. The Monitor port supports observing all elements of the Controller (to keep the diagram in Fig. 6.2 readable, we omit the delegation connectors from the Monitor port to all elements of the Controller).

In general, any element using a reflection interface must have some understanding of the capabilities of the pre-reflective Controller, for instance, the highest temperature that is achievable. Otherwise, the newly set goals might not be achievable at all. Therefore, besides specifying the access to the pre-reflective part (i.e., what is observable and adjustable), the reflection interfaces should also include a specification of the capabilities, for instance, by constraining the possible adjustments of the pre-reflective part. Finally, the observable information provided by the reflection interface must be sufficient for another element to learn, reason, and act, for instance, to produce new goals. Such aspects influence the design of reflection interfaces.

If we consider a more complex Controller that maintains the room temperature by controlling additional devices such as the windows, further options to react such as opening or closing the windows become available. This is illustrated in Fig. 6.3 showing the Controller using the windows and the heater to achieve its goals.

In such cases, when the pre-reflective part considers different aspects (e.g., multiple controlled devices), we may decompose it into several interacting modules. These submodules may provide local reflection interfaces supporting the observation and adaptation of the locally encapsulated elements. We omit the local reflection interfaces in Fig. 6.3 that, however, shows the delegation of the Controllers' SetGoal port to the goal model encapsulated in the AnalyzeR module. A local reflection interface could be provided by the AnalyzeR module to allow and also restrict adaptation to the goal model but not to the module's process and the empirical data.

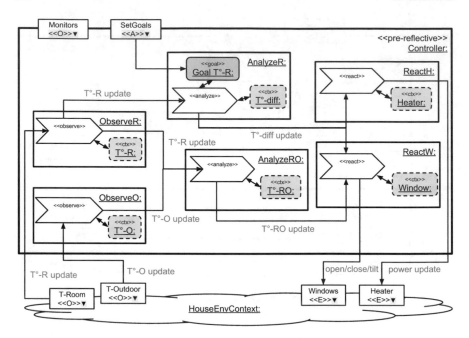

Fig. 6.3 Modular and encapsulated pre-reflective part

The modular Controller functions as follows: The observe processes encapsulated in the individual modules (ObserveR and ObserveO) regularly pull measurements from the room and outdoor thermometers and make them available to other modules. The AnalyzeRO module uses the measured room and outdoor temperatures as input and provides the difference between these as output. In contrast, the AnalyzeR module takes as input the goal temperature and the measured room temperature and provides the difference between these as output. Both analyzers can be triggered whenever new measurements become available such that both may run in parallel and output alternative solutions. These solutions can be executed in parallel with the ReactH and ReactW modules effecting, respectively, the heater and the windows. To avoid conflicts due to concurrent analyses and executions, a coordination mechanism can be employed to determine one of the alternative solutions that is going to be executed. For instance, the analyze strategy that uses the window will not trigger the ReactW module when the difference between the outdoor and room temperatures indicates that changing the window status does not help in reaching the goal. Then, only the other analyze strategy will trigger the ReactH module.

From the perspective of self-awareness, the aforementioned modules are pre-reflective and not self-aware, that is, they simply react to inputs in order to produce outputs. Certainly, we can consider more advanced variants here. For instance, modules can maintain run-time models of several heaters and their performance in time and schedule the heaters accordingly to optimize goal achievement.

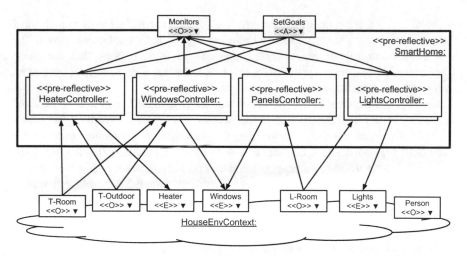

Fig. 6.4 Hierarchical, pre-reflective part with multiple controllers

So far, we considered the case of having a single, pre-reflective controller in the smart home. To further (extend and) modularize the smart home, we may consider different types of controllers. A *heater controller* and a *window controller* sense the indoor and outdoor temperature and control, respectively, the heater or the windows in a room. A *panels controller* senses the lighting conditions in a room and automatically opens or closes the panels of the windows. Using the same observations, a *lights controller* automatically turns the lights on or off.

An instance of each controller type is deployed in each room of the house; hence, there are many controllers running in the SmartHome system that maintain the temperature and lighting conditions of the individual rooms in the house (see Fig. 6.4). Each controller uses some sensor and effector ports provided by devices located in the house, that is, in the system's context. The Person port can be used to locate and identify persons in the house, for instance, to notify them if something goes wrong, such as automatically opening a window does not work. We omit the refined design of each controller, which considers submodules, processes, empirical data, and goal models as it is conceptually similar to the diagrams shown in Figs. 6.2 and 6.3. Finally, the SmartHome system itself provides ports for reflection, particularly to observe the controllers and adjust their goals (e.g., the target temperature of a room).

Having controllers in each room of the house enables *hierarchical control*. For instance, for each room, a module using the reflection interfaces of the SmartHome can individually manage the controllers in the room, while another module can coordinate these room-level modules to achieve the goals for all the rooms at the same floor or even in the whole house. Thus, control can be realized at several hierarchical levels such as the rooms, floors, or the whole house in our example, which supports scalability of control.

In such cases, the reflection interfaces likely have to provide access to additional information such as the structure and topology of the individual controllers in the house. Such information enables reflecting on multiple controllers, their locations, their dependencies, and their interferences, etc., and is required to control the system at multiple hierarchical levels.

Finally, we discussed in Chap. 5 interaction schemes based on collaborations that are more flexible and dynamic than hierarchies. For instance, we may use a collaboration realizing the interaction among the pre-reflective controllers in the house such that they coordinate each other in a self-organizing manner. In such cases, the reflection interfaces have to support reflecting on the collaboration behavior (i.e., how the controllers interact with each other) as well as on the dynamic structure of the pre-reflective part as modules may dynamically join and leave a collaboration.

In general, we may observe that the reflection interfaces can become more complex if we design the pre-reflective part of the system in a more elaborate manner, for instance, by hierarchical decomposition or dynamically collaborating modules.

6.3.2 Direct Access to the Pre-reflective Subsystem

We discussed previously explicit reflection interfaces that allow other elements to reflect and act on the pre-reflective part. While such interfaces can restrict or even hide certain information, we may conceive a direct access to the pre-reflective elements without any encapsulation. In this case, a generic reflection mechanism, for instance, as provided by programming languages, is used to construct reflective views and to act on the system. However, reflecting as well as acting usually happens then at the abstraction level of the program, and no higher-level abstractions are supported. This distinguishes such approaches from approaches with explicit reflection interfaces that may create abstractions.

For instance, Fig. 6.3 shows explicit reflection interfaces to monitor the pre-reflective modules and to set the goals of these modules. However, we may decide to allow other elements to *directly* observe and act upon the pre-reflective part and the contained elements as depicted in Fig. 6.5.

Skipping explicit reflection interfaces lifts any restriction and thus allows many ways to access the pre-reflective elements, which can be beneficial when flexible access is needed. However, such a direct access exposes all the details of the pre-reflective elements, which makes the access more complex than accessing the pre-reflective elements through reflection interfaces.

Summing up, regardless of the design of the pre-reflective part of the system (e.g., monolithic, hierarchical decomposed, or flexibly coordinated by collaborations), we may either define and develop explicit reflection interfaces or generic reflection mechanisms supporting direct access. For the latter case, existing programming languages often support reflection such that they already provide such generic reflection mechanisms. In contrast, reflection interfaces impose development efforts as they need to be developed, particularly if the degree of encapsulation and access as well as the abstraction level of the reflection are specific for the given system.

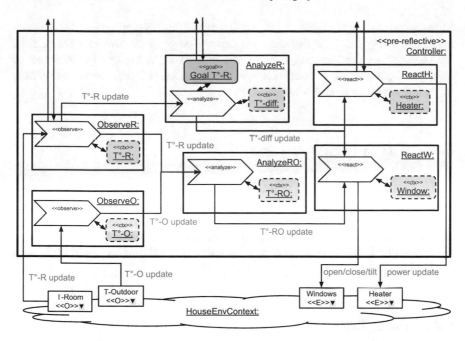

Fig. 6.5 Direct access to the pre-reflective part

6.3.3 Summary

Considering the options for the architecture and design of the pre-reflective sub-system as discussed previously, a decision has to be made whether explicit reflection interfaces or direct access to the pre-reflective elements should be used when developing a system. The decision is crucial since it determines how the reflective subsystem can reflect and act upon the pre-reflective subsystem. Hence, it influences the self-awareness that can be achieved by the overall system.

While a direct and thus a full access to the pre-reflective subsystem can be more powerful and flexible, it does not support any encapsulation, which increases the complexity of the reflection and which avoids any information hiding, for instance, for privacy. However, the experience with self-adaptation and uncertainty of such self-adaptive systems tells us that the adaptation needs cannot be completely anticipated and addressed at design time. This calls for flexible means to realize self-adaptation, which can be in conflict with prescribing the separation between the pre-reflective and reflective elements as well as the reflection interface between them at design time. The same holds for self-aware computing systems, in which the span and scope as well as their interactions may dynamically change. In this context, a direct and full access seems to be more promising.

However, this results in a situation with no clear architectural separation between the pre-reflective and reflective elements. Particularly, there is no encapsulation and controlled access visible at the architectural level. Nevertheless, the underlying dependency that reflective elements depend on pre-reflective elements can be used to structure the elements, for instance, into layers. Additionally, the reflective elements should be able to handle changes of the pre-reflective elements, which calls for more generic or flexible designs.

6.4 Reflective Self-awareness

In this section, we focus on reflective self-awareness, that is, establishing self-awareness by reflecting on the pre-reflective part of the system. Particularly, we discuss the architectural alternatives of local, hierarchical and centralized, and coordinated reflection. In the following, we assume that the pre-reflective subsystem either provides reflection interfaces or allows access to it through a generic reflection mechanism.

6.4.1 Local Reflection

With local reflection, we describe cases in which an element reflects on itself or on individual other elements such that the scope of the reflection is locally constrained and does not cover a global view of the whole system. In general, local reflection can be used for all kind of different concerns such as self-optimization, self-healing, self-configuration, or self-protection and in very different ways. We will consider here self-configuration in a basic form in terms of switching or inhibiting behavior to discuss the inherent problems we have to consider when designing an architecture.

To illustrate these problems, we extend the example of the pre-reflective subsystem of Fig. 6.3. As shown in Fig. 6.6, we introduce an additional module, called ReactionSelect, between the AnalyzeR and the two reaction modules ReactH and ReactW. This new module selects one of the two reaction modules. For instance, to heat up the room temperature, it selects the ReactW module to close the windows instead of the ReactH to turn on the heater. Hence, a selection configures the system such that the selected reaction module will be activated, while the other one will remain idle. To decide on the selection, the module may remember its selection to maintain a history of decisions (see Fig. 6.6). For instance, if it selects the same reaction module several times in a row and if it continuously receives request from the AnalyzeR module—since the target room temperature has not been reached yet—it may try the other reaction module.

In this example, the SelectReact module establishes a basic form of self-awareness by reflecting on its own, which is denoted by an awareness link (see Chap. 5) in Fig. 6.6. On the one hand, the module remembers its selections over time such that it knows about its past behavior. On the other hand, it can evaluate its selections by interpreting the input it receives from the AnalyzeR module. For instance, if the input

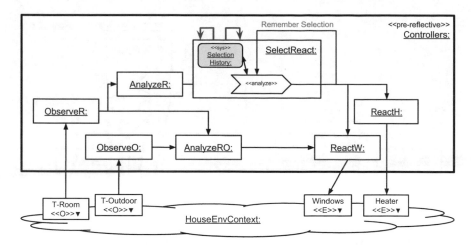

Fig. 6.6 Local reflection to switch between different reactions

continuously demands heating up the room, the SelectReact may conclude that its past selections have not been helpful to achieve the target room temperature and generally the goals. Hence, it may adjust its selection, which is denoted by an expression link (see Chap. 5) in Fig. 6.6. Since the SelectReact module reflects on itself and adjusts itself, we denote the self-awareness and self-expression with self-loops (see Chap. 5) since no other modules or generally elements are involved. Consequently, we may argue that the SelectReact module is self-aware even though the reflection is only local (e.g., remembering the selections and relating them to the input) and does not cover other aspects such as the analysis strategies used by the AnalyzeR module or the goals of the system that are maintained by the AnalyzeR module (see Fig. 6.3). Moreover, the module only performs a very basic form of the LRA-M loop with a simple analyze process but without sophisticated learning and reasoning, which limits the resulting self-awareness.

Such a local reflection can be made explicit in the architecture by positioning the self-aware module at a higher reflection layer. The resulting architecture then employs local layering and reflection, which is illustrated in Fig. 6.7. The SelectReact module receives input from the AnalyzeR module, and it activates or deactivates the ReactW and ReactH modules based on its self-awareness. In this case, the SelectReact module is aware of itself by remembering its selection and maintaining a history of selections (see awareness self-loop in Fig. 6.7) while it directly acts on the ReactW and ReactH modules in terms of activating or deactivating these modules (see expression links pointing to the reaction modules in Fig. 6.7).

A variant of this reflective solution without a dedicated and higher-layer module to coordinate the reactions is based on the idea that the activation of one reaction module inhibits the activation of the other one. This variant is illustrated in Fig. 6.8. The ReactW module is aware of its activation, which is exploited to act on or more precisely inhibit the ReactH module if needed. The direction of the inhibiting depen-

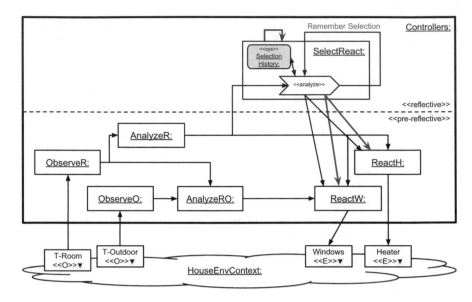

Fig. 6.7 Local and layered reflection to switch between different reactions

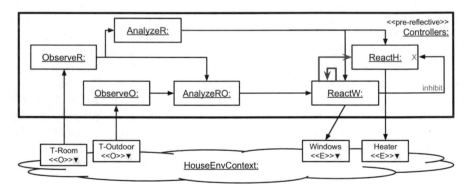

Fig. 6.8 Local reflection to inhibit a reaction

dency is motivated by preferring the ReactW module, which uses the windows to control room temperature, to the ReactH module, which uses the heater, in certain situations since the window-based approach is less expensive in terms of power consumption. The ReactW module activates if there is a small difference between the outdoor and room temperature as determined by the AnalyzeRO module. Otherwise, the ReactW does not activate and inhibit the ReactH module that runs instead.

The ReactW module is able to perform basic analysis whether it is able to handle the input of the AnalyzeRO module. If so, it activates itself, inhibits the ReactH module, and opens or closes the windows. We may argue that such analyses of its own capabilities realize a basic form of self-awareness, particularly awareness of its

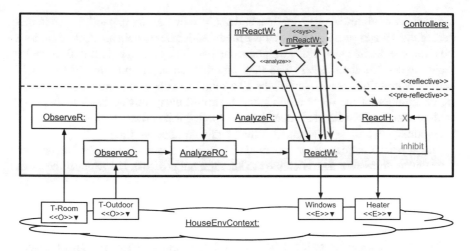

Fig. 6.9 Local and layered reflection to inhibit a reaction

own capabilities (see awareness link in Fig. 6.8). Based on this self-awareness, the module acts on the other reaction modules (see expression link in Fig. 6.8).

Similar to the previous example, we can externalize the inhibiting functionality to a dedicated and higher-layer module, which results in an architectural variant with a clear local separation and layering of the pre-reflective and reflective elements (see Fig. 6.9). The mReactW module reflects on the (capabilities of the) ReactW module and activates or deactivates this module (see awareness and expression links), which indirectly impacts the ReactH module (see indirect expression link in Fig. 6.9).

To discuss cyclic self-awareness and self-expression, we extend this example of inhibiting. More specifically, a cycle exists if the ReactH and ReactW modules inhibit each other as shown in Fig. 6.10 by the cyclic expression links. Each of the ReactH

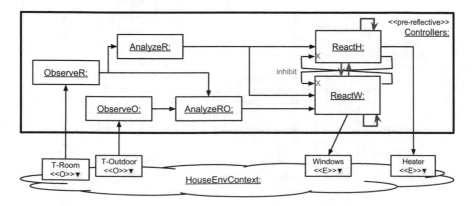

Fig. 6.10 Local reflection and cyclic self-expression

and ReactW modules is able to reflect and analyze on its own capabilities such that each of them is self-aware. If one of these modules decides to activate itself, it inhibits the other one. Such a local self-awareness comes with a certain risk. If both modules decide to activate themselves, then they inhibit each other and none of them will run. To address this issue, one of the two modules should additionally reflect on the capabilities of the other module and it should only activate itself if the other module will not activate itself due to limited capabilities. Hence, preferences over the modules have to be determined, either at design or at run time.

Having such cyclic awareness or expression links, a local layering and separation between pre-reflective and reflective modules are not possible. However, if the cycle is the result of abstraction, we may refine the architecture to resolve the cycle (see Chap. 5 where we conceptually discuss cyclic awareness and expression links, their rationale, as well as cases, in which the cycle can be resolved). Therefore, we will review two alternative cases that refine the architecture shown in Fig. 6.10.

The first refinement introduces modules that are responsible for switching between the different reactions (see Fig. 6.11). Therefore, we refine the design of the reaction modules to separate the switching from the reaction logic. For instance, the mReactH submodule is responsible for switching, while the ReactH submodule performs the reaction in terms of adjusting the heater's settings. The same separation has been done for the reaction module controlling the windows. As emphasized by the awareness and expression links in Fig. 6.11, each of the submodules responsible for the switching is aware of and inhibits the other module's submodule responsible for the reaction. This refinement of the design resolves the cyclic self-expression that existed beforehand (see Fig. 6.10). We may consider the submodules responsible for the switching as local reflective modules that reflect on the corresponding reaction submodules, which establishes self-awareness. Consequently, we can reorganize the

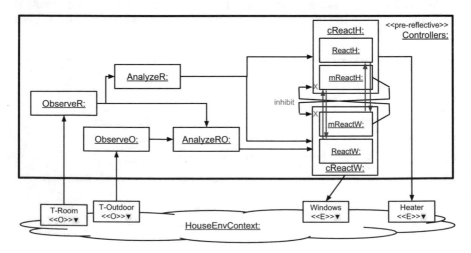

Fig. 6.11 Refined local reflection resolving cyclic self-expression

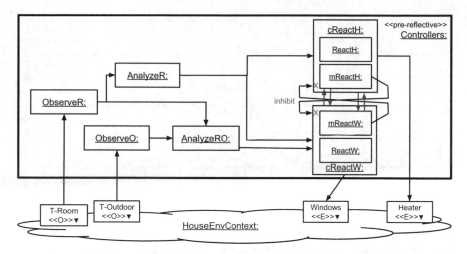

Fig. 6.12 Refined local reflection with cyclic self-awareness and self-expression

architecture by introducing two local layers with the reflective modules located in the higher-layer and the pre-reflective modules in the lower layer.

Nevertheless, cyclic self-awareness or self-expression cannot always be resolved by refining the design. For instance, if each of the submodules responsible for the switching is aware of and inhibits the whole, other reaction module, that is, both submodules for the switching and for the reaction (see Fig. 6.12), the cyclic self-awareness and self-expression remain. In this case, the cycle cannot be resolved by a refinement since it has been introduced by design to have mutually aware modules.

To sum up, local reflection is a basic form of reflection if it is applied to a single, isolated module. However, it may become complex and error-prone when multiple reflective modules are involved. One problem is that reflection often has to cover a sufficiently broad scope to be able to make proper decisions (e.g., it has to know all modules involved in the switching or inhibiting). Another problem exists in the case of multiple reflective modules with non-disjoint action or influence scopes as the modules may compete and perform contradicting actions, which requires coordination. Finally, the boundary between reflective and pre-reflective capabilities can be blurred, which can be addressed by locally structuring modules into layers. In the following, we discuss global layers; that is, the whole architecture is split up into layers to which modules are allocated.

6.4.2   Hierarchical and Centralized Reflection

In this section, we focus on the reflective elements in a self-aware computing system whose architecture is layered. Structuring elements in layers enable hierarchical and centralized reflection in contrast to local reflection discussed previously. To study

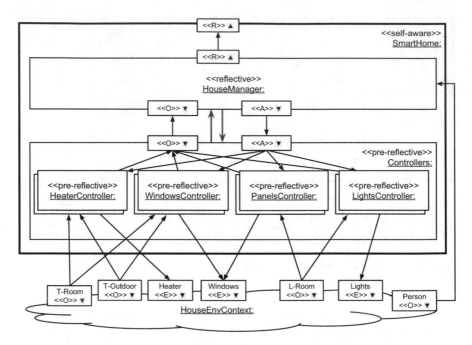

Fig. 6.13 Centralized reflective HouseManager coordinating the Controllers

the reflective elements, we consider the pre-reflective subsystem of our running example as shown in Fig. 6.4. Thus, the subsystem consists of multiple pre-reflective controllers of different types.

To make the overall system self-aware, we equip the controllers with a centralized reflective house manager that coordinates the individual controllers. Therefore, the system is split up into two modules: the reflective HouseManager and the pre-reflective Controllers (see Fig. 6.13).

The HouseManager observes and adapts the controllers. Adaptation can be activating or deactivating a controller as well as selecting one among the given strategies of a controller, for instance, to decide which of the HeaterController or WindowsController as well as which strategy should be used to control the temperature in a specific situation and room. Adaptation can also be more complex such as adjusting the goals, models, or processes and hence the strategies of the individual controllers.

A design of the house manager that addresses self-optimization and self-healing (see Sect. 6.2.1) is shown in Fig. 6.14. This design is monolithic, and it realizes the reflection on the controllers. The house manager is then aware of the controllers, and it may learn and reason about their structure and behavior and adapt them for self-healing and self-optimization purposes (cf. LRA-M loop).

The learning process of the HouseManager learns about the structure and behavior of the Controllers by observing them and representing the learned knowledge in a model (Cs). The reasoning process uses this model to analyze Constraints on this

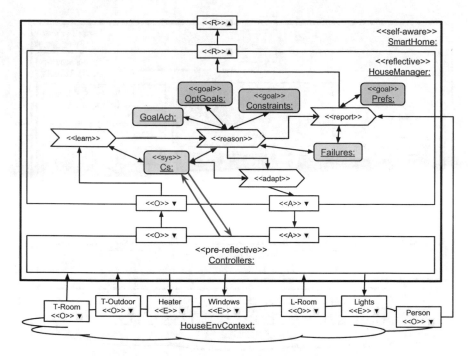

Fig. 6.14 Monolithic design of the centralized reflective HouseManager

model in order to identify failures for self-healing. The identified failures are represented in a model (Failures) and passed to the report process that locates persons in the house by observing the house, selects a person based on preferences (Prefs), and finally reports the identified failures to this person.

Furthermore, the HouseManager addresses self-optimization with respect to the energy consumption. The learning process learns about the behavior of the different controllers with their various strategies to control the devices in the house. The reasoning process analyzes the Cs model whether the controllers achieve the optimization goals (OptGoals) based on their actual performance. This results in a goal achievement (GoalAch) model. If the reasoning identifies the need for adaptation, the adapt process eventually adapts the controllers based on the Cs model that prescribes the adaptation planned by the reasoning process. For instance, the reasoning can determine which controller and strategies are most efficient in achieving the goals such as optimizing the energy consumption while ensuring stable behavior of the controllers. Stable behavior should be achieved by considering the history to avoid thrashing effects such as activating and deactivating a certain controller all the time. Consequently, the reflective house manager is goal-aware, context-aware, interaction-aware, and time-aware.

Since the architecture has a single, centralized reflective module that covers all reflection concerns at once and that has all (relevant) pre-reflective elements in its

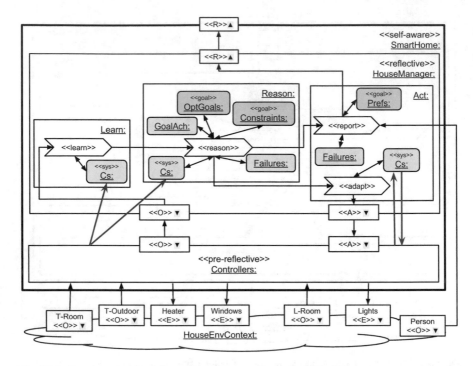

Fig. 6.15 Decomposing the reflective module according to the LRA-M loop

scope, this module can establish global/complete knowledge about the pre-reflective elements. This avoids problems due to limited knowledge obtained by local reflection (see Sect. 6.4.1). By construction, the scope of the reflection can be designed sufficiently broad such that the centralized reflective module can make proper decisions. Moreover, conflicts between multiple reflective modules are excluded by the centralized control. However, the monolithic reflective module can become rather complex and thus its design and development can become difficult.

To address the latter issue, we may decompose the reflective module according to the LRA-M loop while retaining the centralized control. More specifically, we structure the reflective module into three interacting submodules realizing either the learning, reasoning, or acting (see Fig. 6.15).

Another variant of decomposing the reflective module is based on the self-* capabilities. The house manager realizes self-optimization and self-healing such that we may decompose the manager and its LRA-M loop into two LRA-M loops, one for each capability. This is exemplified in Fig. 6.16 showing two modules (Optimization and Healing), each one implementing an LRA-M loop. In a more generalized case, the system may consist of several loops and each of them is decomposed into fine-grained modules representing various learning, reasoning, and acting processes.

In the example of Fig. 6.16, the reasoning processes of the self-optimization and self-healing loops must coordinate to resolve conflicts. A coordination mechanism

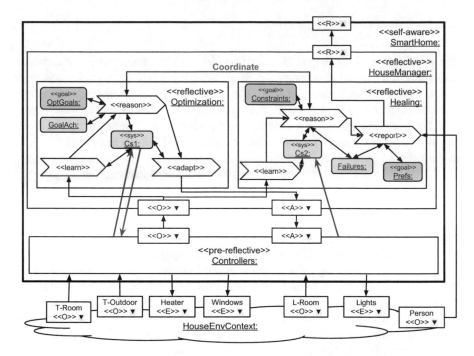

Fig. 6.16 Decomposing the reflective module according to the capabilities

could be as simple as using pre-defined or learned priorities to determine which loop may act and which may not, or as complex as negotiating a compromise taking into account the individually learned models, goals, and reasoning results.

In general, there are many other forms of decomposition such as hierarchies based on the topology of the house. For instance, we may decompose the house manager into multiple modules structured in a hierarchy. Modules of the lowest level in the hierarchy manage the controllers of individual rooms, higher-level modules are allocated to individual floors and coordinate the lowest level modules on this floor, while the module at the highest level coordinate all floor-level modules. Such a hierarchical structure can be imposed on any example discussed so far.

Summing up, centralizing the reflection in a self-aware computing system enables the creation of global knowledge about the pre-reflective subsystem. Hence, the scope of the self-awareness is not necessarily restricted compared to the local reflection. Moreover, having a global view of the pre-reflective subsystem, the reflective module can observe and handle structural changes of the pre-reflective subsystem, for instance, by maintaining an awareness model representing the run-time architecture of this subsystem.

6.4.3 Coordinated Reflection

The architectures and designs discussed previously are rather static and required for centralized control that one pre-planned reflective module learns, reasons, and acts upon all pre-reflective elements. The same holds for architectures adopting hierarchical control although a reflective module learns, reasons, and acts only upon its subordinated modules in the hierarchy. In this context, each reflective module can be modularized by statically decomposing it into submodules, for instance, according to the LRA-M loop or to different capabilities. In the following, we discuss more flexible and dynamic architectures that employ collaborations (see Chap. 5).

One example of such a flexible and dynamic architecture is based on the idea of a *blackboard* through which a dynamic number of modules share relevant knowledge. More specifically, the blackboard is a dedicated module to or from which all the other modules can share or observe information they want to share or to be aware of. When a change occurs, for instance, updates of the goals or modifications of the context, the corresponding information is posted on the blackboard by a observer module. The other modules can retrieve this information from the blackboard, and if they are concerned about this information, they can react and use their learning, reasoning, and acting capabilities. Hence, the other modules may produce and then share more knowledge to the blackboard. As before, the other modules may retrieve this additional knowledge and further contribute to the progressive development of a global solution, that is, to the outcome of the overall LRA-M loop. Consequently, the individual modules of the reflective layer may coordinate and jointly create a reflection of the pre-reflective modules, which establishes self-awareness.

This is exemplified by Fig. 6.17 showing multiple Optimization and Healing modules that coordinate via the Blackboard. In this example, each module sends its observed and learned knowledge to the blackboard and each module may obtain the shared knowledge by participating in the collaboration BlackboardCoord. Individual optimization and healing modules may dynamically join or leave the collaboration. The example could be extended with reasoning capabilities that benefit from the blackboard by only analyzing those chunks of knowledge they are specialized in and then sharing the obtained results to the other modules. Consequently, the individual optimization and healing modules are (directly) aware of the Controllers since they observe and learn about this module. In contrast, the Blackboard module is indirectly aware of the Controllers since it does not observe and learn about this module, but it obtains knowledge about this module through the collaboration.

Thus, the blackboard and the collaboration enable multiple modules to coordinate in creating a reflection of the pre-reflective elements and therefore in jointly establishing self-awareness. The blackboard module serves as a centralized coordinator for exchanging the knowledge, which makes this module a single point of failure and a bottleneck if many modules participate in the collaboration. Therefore, we may even conceive a fully decentralized mechanism to coordinate the knowledge exchange, for instance, in a peer-to-peer fashion. Such a solution avoids a single point of failure and promises to scale with the number of collaborating modules.

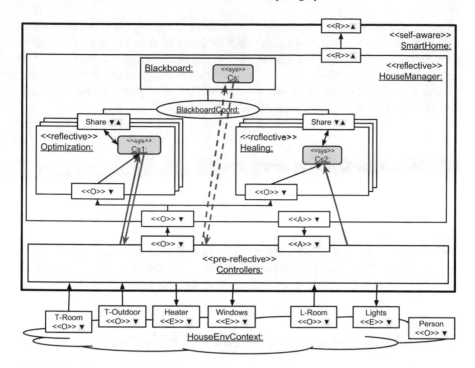

Fig. 6.17 Architecture with a blackboard for coordinated reflection

The solution would only consists of a collaboration that realizes the decentralized protocol for the knowledge exchange.

In Chap. 7, we will discuss in more detail such coordination schemes and their characteristics in the context of collectives of self-aware computing systems.

6.4.4 Summary

Summing up, reflection can be done in three different ways, while the individual ways can be mixed in one architecture. First, reflection can be done locally involving individual modules. These modules can be structured locally into layers to make the reflective and the pre-reflective modules visible in the architectural design. However, such a local layering is not feasible if there exist self-loops of self-awareness that cannot be resolved; that is, distinguishing and separating the reflective and pre-reflective elements from each other are not possible. However, if it is possible, the second reflection scheme can be employed. This scheme globally introduces layers into the architecture, which results in a centralized and possibly hierarchical reflection. In contrast to the local reflection that allows reflective modules to obtain only knowledge of the locally limited scope, the scope of centralized reflection may not be restricted and therefore it may cover all pre-reflective modules. This enables establishing awareness of the global aspects such as the architecture of the pre-reflective subsystem. Third, reflection can be realized by collaborations that need not to be centralized and hierarchical. Thus, the coordination of the reflective modules jointly produces the reflection and establishes self-awareness. Such solutions are more flexible and dynamic compared to centralized ones.

6.5   Meta-reflective Self-awareness

Having discussed pre-reflective and reflective self-awareness in Sects. 6.3 and 6.4, we now focus on meta-reflective self-awareness that is established by higher levels of reflection. Similar to realizing reflection either locally in a centralized manner by layers and hierarchies, or in a decentralized manner by collaborations (see Sect. 6.4), the same approaches also apply to meta-reflection. To avoid repetitions, we focus in the following on the centralized approach and apply it to meta-reflection.

6.5.1   Hierarchical and Centralized Meta-Reflection

To create a meta-reflection in a self-aware computing system, a module reflects on one or more reflective modules. The module realizes an LRA-M loop such that it becomes aware of the reflective modules and their reflection and self-awareness capabilities. Considering the hierarchical and centralized approach to reflection, there is exactly one meta-reflective module, which is illustrated in Fig. 6.18. In general, reflecting and being aware of the reflection and self-awareness capabilities of the system make the system meta-self-aware.

   As shown in Fig. 6.18, the architecture is structured into three layers that are bottom-up pre-reflective, reflective, and meta-reflective. The HouseManagerAdjuster reflects on the HouseManager that reflects on the Controllers. Therefore, the HouseManagerAdjuster learns and reasons whether the HouseManager is capable of achieving the goals taking the energy consumption into account and if necessary adapts the HouseManager. The self-optimization concerning energy consumption performed by the HouseManager might not always works well since external influences such as market prices for energy or user preferences change (e.g., user are willing to pay more during winter to have a "guaranteed" temperature in the house). Such changes might require novel algorithms or techniques for the HouseManager to coordinate the controllers. This should be achieved by the *meta-reflective* module HouseManagerAdjuster whose design is detailed in Fig. 6.19. This module adjusts the coordination mechanism used by the HouseManager to coordinate the controllers based on the currently used mechanism of the house manager (HM) if the energy prices (Prices) or the user preferences (UserPrefs) change. The goal of the adaptation is to make the house manager capable of achieving the goals.

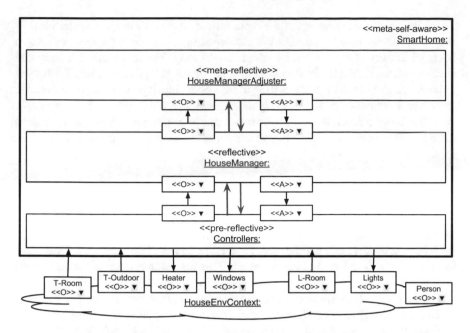

Fig. 6.18 Meta-reflective architecture to establish meta-self-awareness

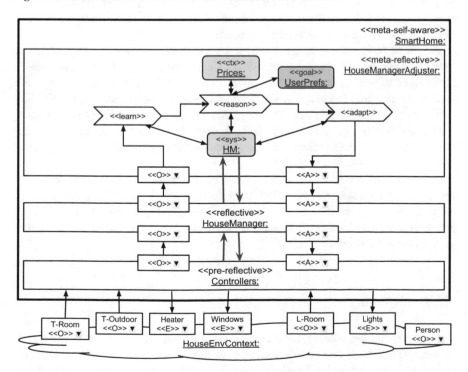

Fig. 6.19 Architecture with a refined design of the meta-reflective module

While the presented design of the meta-reflective HouseManagerAdjuster module is monolithic, we may decompose the module similarly to the reflective modules in Sect. 6.4, for instance, according to the LRA-M loop. Moreover, the reflection and meta-reflection can be realized as well by local or coordinated reflection. With local reflection, a global and strict structuring of the system into layers might not be feasible since the combination of the local layers might not be balanced and homogeneous. With the coordinated reflection, we may decompose the meta-reflective layer into modules that coordinate to jointly create the reflection of the reflective layer.

6.5.2 Hierarchical and Centralized Meta–Meta-Reflection

The same principle to achieve meta-reflection can be used to achieve meta–meta-reflection, that is, we add another reflective layer on top of the meta-reflective layer for a hierarchical and centralized solution. This results in a meta–meta-self-aware system.

For our example, to ensure the long-term evolution of the smart home, for instance, that it does not only consider the market prices as goals (see the HouseManagerAdjuster that controls the HouseManager based on prices) but arbitrary goals (e.g., subsidies by governments that may depend on the country and region where the smart home is located), another reflective layer is added to the system. This additional layer is named HouseManagerEvolution (see Fig. 6.20).

A refined design of the HouseManagerEvolution module is shown in Fig. 6.21. The HouseManagerEvolution module learns about the HouseManagerAdjuster, particularly about its configuration such as which goals, models, and processes (algorithms) are used. If the user provides new goals, for instance, government regulations or subsidies that impact the optimization of the energy consumption, the reasoning process analyzes if and how the HouseManagerAdjuster needs to be adapted to consider these new goals. Based on the reasoning, the HouseManagerEvolution module's adapt process changes the HouseManagerAdjuster.

As discussed previously for the HouseManagerAdjuster module, we may also decompose the HouseManagerEvolution module, for instance, according to the LRA-M loop or to the capabilities of the module. Finally, meta–meta-reflection can be achieved as well by local or coordinated reflection—as discussed for meta-reflection in the previous subsection.

6.5.3 Summary

Summing up, the individual reflection steps in the layered architecture can be realized by local, hierarchical and centralized, or coordinated reflection as well as a combination of those. For higher levels of reflection, it is critical that the reflected layer provides appropriate interfaces or a generic mechanism to reflect upon its reflection

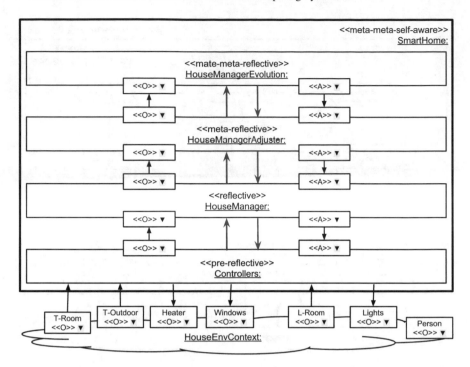

Fig. 6.20 Meta–meta-reflective architecture to achieve meta–meta-self-awareness

and self-awareness. For instance, a centralized meta-reflective module should be able to learn, reason, and act upon the coordinated reflection of the reflective subsystem. Therefore, the subsystem has to enable access to its reflection and self-awareness machinery as realized by the LRA-M loop.

Another interesting observation we made in our example is that with each level of reflection, the layers and their modules become bottom-up more generic. For instance, when a reflective module employs various strategies to coordinate the controllers in the house, a reasoning process in a meta-reflective module must not know any details of the strategies or even of the further underlying layers (e.g., the controllers). In contrast, it may only learn the success rate of the strategies based on the goal fulfillment of the reflective module and adjust the priorities of the strategies accordingly. The reflective module takes the adjusted priorities into account.

6.6   Discussion

Having discussed pre-reflective, reflective, and meta-reflective self-awareness—as introduced by Chap. 3—for individual self-aware computing systems, we will in the following review typical control schemes and architectural styles. In this context, we will discuss the relationship between them and the architectural concepts for

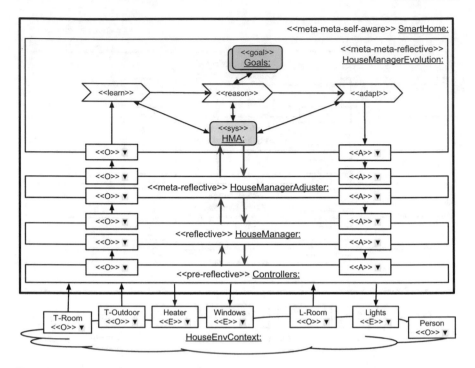

Fig. 6.21 Architecture with a refined design of the meta–meta-reflective module

pre-reflective, reflective, and meta-reflective self-awareness. Therefore, we will particularly model these schemes or styles using the proposed concepts. Furthermore, we discuss how common architectural problems can be identified and addressed for individual self-aware computing systems when employing the suggested architectural concepts.

6.6.1 Control Schemes

As already discussed in Chap. 5, Shaw [31], Mller et al. [32, 33], and Brun et al. [34] argue that feedback loops as the essential characteristic of self-adaptive software should be made explicit and visible in the architectural design. This should make related design decisions explicit, enable reasoning on the design, and support identifying possible problems in the design such as interferences between multiple feedback loops. In the following, we discuss control schemes originating from control theory which emphasize the role and relevance of feedback loops [35–37].

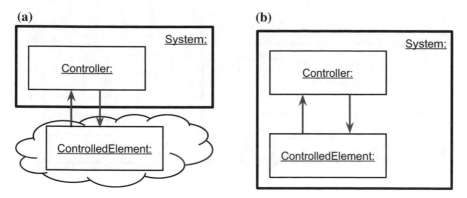

Fig. 6.22 Feedback control at the **a** pre-reflective and **b** reflective level

The idea of *feedback control* is that a controller observes the output and adjust the input of a controlled element in order to compensate external disturbances that influence the controlled element and its output. If the controlled element is outside of the system boundary, it is part of the environmental context (see Fig. 6.22a). The controller is then aware of the system's context, which establishes context-awareness, and it may effect the context, which is illustrated by the awareness and expression links in Fig. 6.22a. If the controlled element is part of considered system, the controller is aware of parts of the system and it may act upon these parts (see Fig. 6.22b and the corresponding awareness and expression links in this figure). Hence, the system is self-aware and may self-express. Thus, we can conclude that feedback control is a possible scheme for setting up a self-aware computing system if the controller realizes an LRA-M loop.

As depicted in Fig. 6.22, the application of the feedback control scheme to self-awareness results in an awareness link from the controlled element to the controller and in an expression link from the controller to the controlled element. Therefore, the feedback control scheme is only applicable if the acting of the controller involves effecting or adapting the controlled element rather than just reporting about the outcome of the learning and reasoning.

The concepts we introduced in Chap. 5 and use in this chapter to describe architectures for individual self-aware computing systems can capture the feedback control scheme in terms of two modules, one being the controller and the other one the controlled element, and the awareness and expression links between them. The controller corresponds to the span and the controlled element to the scope of the self-awareness. Using the proposed architectural concepts and notation, a feedback control loop is represented by (direct or indirect) awareness and expression links between a common span and scope. This representation makes the feedback loop visible and allows us to reason about the feedback loop in the architectural design.

In this context, the controller may dynamically establish the awareness of the controlled element by observing, learning, and reasoning about the element. In contrast, in *feed-forward control*, the controller is not observing the controlled element

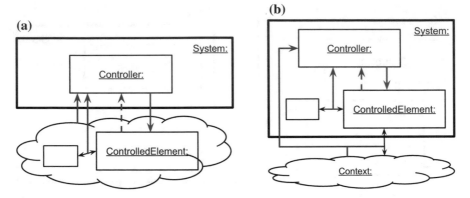

Fig. 6.23 Feed-forward control at the **a** pre-reflective and **b** reflective level

but the disturbances of the context or other elements on this element (see Fig. 6.23). These observations are used to learn, reason, and act upon the controlled element. Such indirect awareness of the controlled element (see indirect awareness links in Fig. 6.23) might require that the controller is equipped with initial awareness knowledge about this element at design time. The observations and learned knowledge enrich this initial awareness at run time. Similar to feedback control, the controlled element can be either part of the context (see Fig. 6.23a) or part of the system (see Fig. 6.23b).

An advanced scheme of feedback control is *adaptive control* that dynamically adapts the control strategy, for instance, based on observations of the controlled element. One specific variant is *model identification adaptive control* (MIAC) that employs a system identification module to observe the controlled element, which impacts the adjustment mechanism that eventually adapts the controller. The MIAC scheme is illustrated in Fig. 6.24 for the case of the controlled element being part of the system. The controller and the system identification are aware of the controlled element (see awareness links in Fig. 6.24), while the system identification acts upon the adjustment mechanism that acts upon the controller that eventually acts upon the controlled element (see expression links in Fig. 6.24). Consequently, the system identification and the adjustment mechanism indirectly act upon the controlled element (see indirect expression links in Fig. 6.24).

Thus, adaptive control is a possible scheme to realize self-awareness and advanced forms of self-expression for self-aware computing systems. Considering the awareness and expression links in Fig. 6.24, we clearly see that the adaptive control scheme employs two feedback loops, one between the controller and the controlled element (i.e., it is the same loop as for feedback control) and one including all of the modules. This second feedback loop is more complicated than the first one since the system identification is aware of but only indirectly effects the controlled element. This indirection is motivated by the fact that the system identification and adjustment mechanism are aware of all the required details of the controller by construction and

Fig. 6.24 Adaptive control
at the reflective level

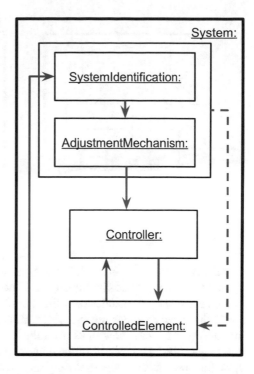

therefore may operate in a feed-forward control manner on the controller. Consequently, the system identification and adjustment mechanism do not observe, learn,
or reason about the controller such that the overall scheme does not result in meta-
self-awareness. Nevertheless, the architectural concepts and notation we propose are
able to cover the adaptive control scheme and make the two feedback loops visible
in the design.

Finally, we discuss the *hierarchical control* scheme that is based on the idea of
divide and conquer. Thus, the elements of the hierarchy are linked with each other in
a tree structure. In general, commands, tasks, and goals to be achieved flow down the
tree, while observations and results flow up the tree. The higher-level elements of the
tree operate at longer time scales than the lower-level nodes. Moreover, the lower-
level elements have rather local commands, tasks, goals, and observations, and their
processes are coordinated by higher-level elements. The coordination performed by
the higher-level elements does not generally override the decisions of the lower-
level elements but rather controls these elements by setting appropriate local goals.
Consequently, the control problem is divided into smaller problems top-down the
hierarchy (e.g., the goals are broken down into smaller ones), while the higher-level
elements do not reflect upon the lower-level elements of the hierarchy. In contrast, the
higher-level elements only take the accumulated observations made by the lower-
level elements into account, but they do not observe these lower-level elements.
Therefore, hierarchical control—although it is very useful to handle complex control
problems—is not implying self-awareness.

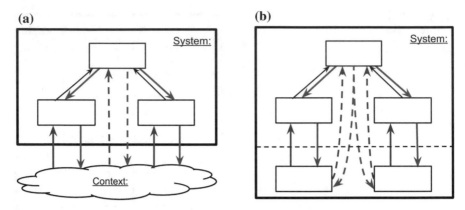

Fig. 6.25 Hierarchical control at the **a** pre-reflective and **b** reflective level

This is illustrated in Fig. 6.25a where the lower-level modules reflect on and act upon the context, while the higher-level modules do not reflect on but only act upon the lower-level modules (see direct awareness and expression links). However, the higher-level modules receive observations of the context from the lower-level modules (see the data flow links from the lower- to the higher-level modules) such that they are indirectly aware of the context (see indirect awareness link). By acting upon the lower-level modules, the higher-level modules indirectly effect the context (see indirect expression link). Overall, this establishes context-awareness but not awareness of the self.

Nevertheless, hierarchical control can be applied in combination with reflection. As shown in Fig. 6.25b, the modules at the lowest level (i.e., those below the dashed line) are pre-reflective and represent the controlled elements. These modules are controlled by a hierarchy of reflective modules (i.e., those modules above the dashed line). In this case, the reflection establishes awareness of the controlled modules that are part of the system, which therefore results in self-awareness. The lower-level reflective modules are directly and the higher-level reflective modules are indirectly aware of the controlled modules. However, the higher-level reflective modules are not reflecting on the lower-level reflective modules (there is no awareness link between them) such that no meta-self-awareness is established. The higher-level modules only receive information from the lower-level modules (see data flow links between them).

This contrasts with meta-self-awareness discussed in Sect. 6.5, which is based on meta-reflection. That is, using the proposed architectural concepts and notation, we may distinguish architectures that are based on reflection, meta-reflection, or meta–meta-reflection and therefore achieve different levels of self-awareness.

Based on the feedback, feed-forward, adaptive, and hierarchical control schemes discussed so far, we may observe common problems when engineering self-aware computing systems, regardless of the specific scheme. A major problem may result from having multiple feedback or LRA-M loops in the system since the individual loops may compete and interfere with each other. One instance of such interferences may occur between the behavior of the controlled elements and the effects of the controller (i.e., of the learning, reasoning, and acting processes) on these elements. Such interferences can usually be circumvented since the (behavior of the) controlled elements are in the awareness scope of the controller. By additionally designing and proving the behavior of the controller, certain guarantees such as stability can be given for the overall system behavior.

Another problem that needs to be addressed is the timescale of each layer whether the system is structured into pre-reflective, reflective, meta-reflective, meta–meta-reflective, etc., layers. Usually, the lower layers are executed much more frequently than the higher layers such that the higher layers only act after the lower layers have stabilized. In terms of self-awareness, we may conceive that higher layers only establish awareness of their lower layers after these lower layers have established an initial awareness of their lower layers. This results in structurally establishing self-awareness bottom-up the layers of the system.

Despite such interferences across layers, there could also exist interferences within one layer if multiple modules have conflicting goals or overlapping action/ influence scopes. In our running example, the pre-reflective controllers located in the smart home may easily interfere, such as one may open the windows, while the other one turns on the heater. The same holds for the reflective or higher layers, in which multiple LRA-M loops may independently act upon the same scope, either directly (i.e., the loops have overlapping action scopes) or indirectly (i.e., the loops have overlapping influence scopes). This calls either for decoupling the scopes by resolving the overlaps or for jointly addressing the overlapping scopes, for instance, by multiple-input multiple-output (MIMO) control.

Finally, a subtle problem is cyclic self-awareness such that a part of the system reflects on another part, and vice versa. An example for cyclic self-awareness was discussed in the context of Fig. 6.12. Such cycles impede reasoning about the control and providing guarantees such that they are typically avoided in the design.

Based on these common problems, we can summarize the phenomena that need to be studied when developing an architecture for self-aware computing systems. These phenomena are illustrated in Fig. 6.26.

(a) *Overlapping expression links*, either direct or indirect ones, denote potentially conflicting actions or influences effecting the same scope. Are these overlapping action or influence scopes properly coordinated to avoid conflicts or generally interferences?

(b) *Stacked reflections* denote that the system establishes different levels of self-awareness (i.e., pre-reflective, reflective, and meta-reflective self-awareness) by stacking LRA-M loops. Such a loop is visible in the architectural design by at least an awareness link and an expression link that can be direct or indirect and that connect the same span and scope. Stacking such loops results in the situation that the scope of a loop corresponds to the span of another loop such that the loops overlap. In such a situation, are the loops sufficiently decoupled from each other, for instance, with respect to their frequencies of operation?

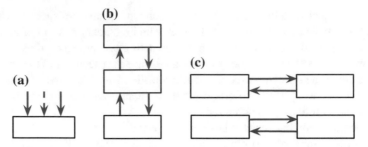

Fig. 6.26 Phenomena to be addressed in the architectural design

(c) *Cyclic reflections* denote cycles of sequences of either awareness or expression links where the scope of one link overlaps with span of another link. Such a cycle may contain direct as well as indirect awareness, respectively, expression links. If such cycles exist, are they properly coordinated to avoid any interferences and to assure termination of the awareness or expression?

In general, these phenomena should not be considered as design errors. However, they can be detected and addressed in the architectural design such that the related problems do not occur. For instance, concerning phenomenon (a), we may design the LRA-M loops in a way that they are executed one after the other in order to avoid conflicts due to concurrently executed adaptations to a common scope. With respect to phenomenon (b), we may merge different levels or adjust the design of individual levels, which supports other frequencies of operation. Concerning phenomenon (c), we may refine the design such that the cycle of awareness or expression links is resolved (cf. the refined design shown in Fig. 6.11 that resolves the cycle of the more abstract design shown in Fig. 6.10).

In general, it is known that *complex systems* are ruled by many interacting feedback loops and that understanding the joint effects of these loops is key to engineer such systems. Consequently, the presented variants of pre-reflective, reflective, and meta-reflective self-awareness that clearly separates the feedback loops in the architectural design are promising approaches to engineer self-aware computing systems since they restrict the design space to schemes that could avoid the problems originating from the phenomena discussed previously.

6.6.2 Architectural Styles: The External and Internal Approaches

Salehie and Tahvildari [7] discuss two architectural styles for self-adaptive software, which are called the *internal* and *external approaches* and which emphasize the importance of the control loop for the architecture. Both approaches are shown in Fig. 6.27. The external approach clearly separates the system under adaptation (i.e.,

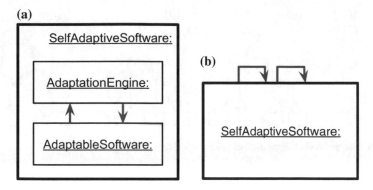

Fig. 6.27 Architectural styles: the **a** external and **b** internal approaches [7]

the adaptable software) from the controller (i.e., the adaptation engine) that performs the adaptation. This separation is identical to the feedback control scheme depicted in Fig. 6.22b. In contrast, there is no clear separation of these two elements in the internal approach such that both are intertwined. According to Salehie and Tahvildari [7], systems adopting the internal approach are difficult to test and maintain as well as often not scalable. In contrast, systems adopting the external approach may benefit from reusing the adaptation engine across applications.

The external approach makes the feedback loop explicit by separating the controller from the controlled element. This can be beneficial for self-aware computing systems since it also makes the self-awareness and self-expression as well as the corresponding span and scope explicit (see awareness and expression links in Fig. 6.27). Otherwise, they remain implicit and can only be pointed out by self-loops since we cannot distinguish the span and scope at the architectural level.

Based on the importance of the feedback loops going along with self-awareness and self-expression (i.e., with awareness and expression links in our notation) and the related architectural phenomena discussed previously (see Fig. 6.26), we further characterize the structure of the awareness and expression links occurring in an architecture. The combination of these links connecting architectural elements forms a graph whose structure impacts the architectural design. Therefore, we discuss in the following architectural styles that are determined by the structure of the graph of awareness and expression links. More specifically, we generalize the external and internal approaches discussed previously.

The *generalized external approach* prescribes *acyclic* graphs of awareness links and of expression links. Examples of this approach are shown in Fig. 6.28. Adopting this approach results in architectures with clearly separated reflection layers that usually form a stack or treelike structure. We distinguish the following cases.

The *stacked external approach* results in a stack of layers, which applies centralized reflection such that a layer of the stack only reflects upon its underlying layers. Thus, the awareness links point bottom-up, while the expression links point top-down the stack. The layers can be either strictly or weakly stacked. A *strict stacking* only

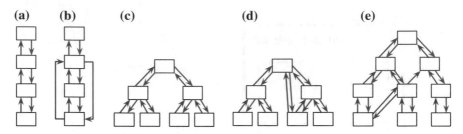

Fig. 6.28 Examples for the variants of the generalized external approach

allows awareness and expression links between neighboring layers (see Fig. 6.28a). That is, each layer is only aware of and effects its adjacently underlying layer. An example for a strict stacking is shown in Fig. 6.20. A *weak stacking* is similar to the strict stacking, but it relaxes the constraint of allowing only awareness and expression links between neighboring layers. As illustrated in Fig. 6.28b, a layer may therefore reflect upon any underlying layer such that the corresponding awareness and expression links may cross more than one layer.

The *hierarchical external approach* results in a treelike structure, which allows the decomposition of lower-level layers. A layer of this tree then reflects upon the underlying layers. Similar to the stacking, the awareness links point bottom-up, while the expression links point top-down the tree. The tree can be structured either in a strict or in a weak hierarchy. A *strict hierarchy* only allows awareness and expression links between neighboring layers of the hierarchy in the subtree (see Fig. 6.28c). That is, each layer is only aware of and effects all elements of the adjacently underlying layer in the subtree. A *weak hierarchy* is similar to a strict hierarchy, but it allows that a layer may also reflect upon any underlying layer in the subtree, not just the adjacently underlying one (see Fig. 6.28d). Consequently, the corresponding awareness and expression links may cross more than one layer in the tree.

The last variant of the external approach is the *acyclic external approach*. It does not prescribe a stack or treelike structure but allows any structure as long as the sequences of awareness links as well as the sequences of expression links are acyclic (see Fig. 6.28e). This generally results in an acyclic graph.

Finally, the *generalized internal approach* does not prescribe any structure at all such that it allows cyclic sequences of awareness links or of expression links as well as self-loops (see Fig. 6.29). Therefore, this approach does not result in architectures with clearly separated reflection layers. Note that the placement of the modules in Fig. 6.29 does not and actually cannot—due to the cycles—follow the sequences of awareness or expression links. In contrast, reflections rather occur locally as well as in an intertwined and a less structured manner such that the design of the self-awareness and self-expression at the system level becomes challenging and requires specific coordination to handle the cycles.

Fig. 6.29 Example of the generalized internal approach

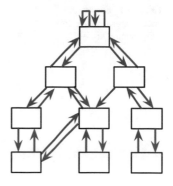

Concerning the phenomena discussed previously (see Fig. 6.26), the strictly layered and strictly hierarchical approaches exclude any overlapping expression links by construction. However, overlapping expression links may occur in the weakly stacked and weakly hierarchical approaches if two or more arbitrary higher layers act upon the same lower layer. It is the responsibility of the developer to address the overlapping action scope, for instance, by implementing an appropriate coordination mechanism. In this context, the architecture helps in identifying and locating the overlapping action scopes. In the best case, these overlaps can be addressed locally, for instance, by coordinating only those modules that directly act upon the same scope. In contrast, the generalized internal approach likely requires to take all elements of the architecture into account since the system-level self-awareness and self-expression emerge from the local reflections dispersed across the architecture.

In general, applying centralized or hierarchical reflection discussed in Sect. 6.4.2 relates to the generalized external approach. That is, the system can be incrementally enhanced with further layers, or its topmost layer can be recursively split up to add additional centralized reflection layers. Such enhancements maintain the structure such as a stack or a tree imposed on the architecture. In contrast, applying local reflections multiple times as discussed in Sect. 6.4.1 likely results in a less structured and intertwined architecture similar to the generalized internal approach. Finally, applying the coordinated reflection as discussed in Sect. 6.4.3 may follow either the generalized external or internal approaches. For the external approach, the coordination will be organized in a separate and potentially additional layer. For the internal approach, such a clear separation will not be achieved and the coordination can be intertwined with other functionalities of the system.

6.7   Conclusion

In this chapter, we have discussed generic architectures for individual self-aware computing systems by investigating how pre-reflective, reflective, and meta-reflective self-awareness becomes manifests in the architecture. At the pre-reflective level, the

Table 6.1 Forms and
phenomena of reflection and
architectural styles

Aspects	Section
Forms of reflection	
Local reflection	6.4.1
Hierarchical and centralized reflection	6.4.2
Coordinated reflection	6.4.3
Phenomena of reflection	
Overlapping expression links	6.6.1
Stacked reflections	6.6.1
Cyclic reflections	6.6.1
Architectural styles	
Stacked external approach	6.6.2
Hierarchical external approach	6.6.2
Acyclic external approach	6.6.2
Generalized internal approach	6.6.2

organization (monolithic, hierarchically decomposed, or flexibly coordinated) of the
pre-reflective modules as well as their provided reflection interfaces is the major
architectural and design aspects to offer a basis for self-awareness. To establish
self-awareness, we discussed various forms of reflection, namely local reflection,
hierarchical and centralized reflection, and coordinated reflection. These forms can
be applied at the reflective and meta-reflective levels. Subsequently, we discussed
the difficulties and pitfalls for architectures of individual self-aware computing systems that are mainly related to the complex dependencies that result from the self-
awareness and self-expression as well as their overlapping actions and influence
scopes. In this context, we particularly discussed the phenomena (overlapping expression links, stacked reflection, and cyclic reflections) that could be identified at the
architectural level and related problems. Finally, we discussed the existing control
schemes and architectural styles for self-adaptive software, which seem promising
for designing architectures of self-aware computing systems. In this context, we generalized the architectural styles to the (stacked, hierarchical, and acyclic) external
and internal approaches targeting self-aware computing systems. Table 6.1 provides
an overview of the discussed forms and phenomena of reflection as well as of the
generalized architectural styles for self-aware computing systems.

Based on this chapter, we can conclude that the proposed architectural concepts
already cover several existing control schemes and architectural styles that seem
promising for self-aware computing systems. However, we are only at the beginning
to understand what is crucial for the architecture of self-aware computing systems
and how architectural styles and decisions impact the self-awareness capabilities of
a system. This calls for future work and experiments to investigate the architectures
for self-aware computing systems, corresponding design spaces and processes, as
well as the relationship between architectures and self-awareness.

Acknowledgements This chapter is the result of stimulating discussions among the authors and other participants, especially Nelly Bencomo, Kurt Geihs, Paola Inverardi, Samuel Kounev, and Peter Lewis, during the seminar on model-driven algorithms and architectures for self-aware computing systems at Schloss Dagstuhl in January 2015 (http://www.dagstuhl.de/15041).

References

1. Jeffrey O. Kephart and David M. Chess. The vision of autonomic computing. *Computer*, 36(1):41–50, 2003.
2. Ozalp Babaoglu, Mark Jelasity, Alberto Montresor, Christof Fetzer, Stefano Leonardi, Aad van Moorsel, and Maarten van Steen, editors. *Self-star Properties in Complex Information Systems: Conceptual and Practical Foundations*, volume 3460 of *Lecture Notes in Computer Science (LNCS)*. Springer, 2005.
3. Betty H.C. Cheng, Rogério de Lemos, Holger Giese, Paola Inverardi, Jeff Magee, Jesper Andersson, Basil Becker, Nelly Bencomo, Yuriy Brun, Bojan Cukic, Giovanna Di Marzo Serugendo, Schahram Dustdar, Anthony Finkelstein, Cristina Gacek, Kurt Geihs, Vincenzo Grassi, Gabor Karsai, Holger M. Kienle, Jeff Kramer, Marin Litoiu, Sam Malek, Raffaela Mirandola, Hausi Müller, Sooyong Park, Mary Shaw, Matthias Tichy, Massimo Tivoli, Danny Weyns, and Jon Whittle. Software Engineering for Self-Adaptive Systems: A Research Roadmap. In Betty H.C. Cheng, Rogério de Lemos, Holger Giese, Paola Inverardi, and Jeff Magee, editors, *Software Engineering for Self-Adaptive Systems*, volume 5525 of *Lecture Notes in Computer Science (LNCS)*, pages 1–26. Springer, 2009.
4. Betty H.C. Cheng, Holger Giese, Paola Inverardi, Jeff Magee, and Rogério de Lemos, editors. *Software Engineering for Self-Adaptive Systems*, volume 5525 of *Lecture Notes in Computer Science (LNCS)*. Springer, 2009.
5. Rogério de Lemos, Holger Giese, Hausi Müller, and Mary Shaw, editors. *Software Engineering for Self-Adaptive Systems II*, volume 7475 of *Lecture Notes in Computer Science (LNCS)*. Springer, 2013.
6. Rogério de Lemos, Holger Giese, Hausi Müller, Mary Shaw, Jesper Andersson, Marin Litoiu, Bradley Schmerl, Gabriel Tamura, Norha M. Villegas, Thomas Vogel, Danny Weyns, Luciano Baresi, Basil Becker, Nelly Bencomo, Yuriy Brun, Bojan Cukic, Ron Desmarais, Schahram Dustdar, Gregor Engels, Kurt Geihs, Karl Goeschka, Alessandra Gorla, Vincenzo Grassi, Paola Inverardi, Gabor Karsai, Jeff Kramer, Antónia Lopes, Jeff Magee, Sam Malek, Serge Mankovskii, Raffaela Mirandola, John Mylopoulos, Oscar Nierstrasz, Mauro Pezzè, Christian Prehofer, Wilhelm Schäfer, Rick Schlichting, Dennis B. Smith, Joao P. Sousa, Ladan Tahvildari, Kenny Wong, and Jochen Wuttke. Software Engineering for Self-Adaptive Systems: A second Research Roadmap. In Rogério de Lemos, Holger Giese, Hausi Müller, and Mary Shaw, editors, *Software Engineering for Self-Adaptive Systems II*, volume 7475 of *Lecture Notes in Computer Science (LNCS)*, pages 1–32. Springer, 2013.
7. Mazeiar Salehie and Ladan Tahvildari. Self-adaptive software: Landscape and research challenges. *ACM Trans. Auton. Adapt. Syst.*, 4(2):14:1–14:42, 2009.
8. Anant Agarwal and Bill Harrod. Organic computing. Technical Report White paper, MIT and DARPA, 2006.
9. Christian Muller-Schloer, Hartmut Schmeck, and Theo Ungerer, editors. *Organic Computing - A Paradigm Shift for Complex Systems*. Birkhuser, 2011.
10. John E. Kelly and Steve Hamm. *Smart machines : IBM's Watson and the era of cognitive computing*. Columbia Business School Publishing, 2013.
11. Anant Agarwal, Jason Miller, Jonathan Eastep, David Wentziaff, and Harshad Kasture. Self-aware computing. Technical Report AFRL-RI-RS-TR-2009-161, MIT, 2009.

12. Henry Hoffmann, Martina Maggio, Marco D. Santambrogio, Alberto Leva, and Anant Agarwal. Seec: A general and extensible framework for self-aware computing. Technical Report MIT-CSAIL-TR-2011-046, MIT CSAIL, 2011.

13. Samuel Kounev. Self-Aware Software and Systems Engineering: A Vision and Research Roadmap. In *GI Softwaretechnik-Trends, 31(4), November 2011, ISSN 0720-8928*, Karlsruhe, Germany, 2011.

14. Peter R. Lewis, Arjun Chandra, Funmilade Faniyi, Kyrre Glette, Tao Chen, Rami Bahsoon, Jim Torresen, and Xin Yao. Architectural aspects of self-aware and self-expressive computing systems: From psychology to engineering. *IEEE Computer*, 48(8):62–70, 2015.

15. Melanie Mitchell. Self-awareness and control in decentralized systems (Tech Report SS-05-04). In *AAAI Spring Symposium on Metacognition in Computation*, Menlo Park, 2005. AIII Press.

16. L.D. Paulson. DARPA creating self-aware computing. *Computer*, 36(3):24, 2003.

17. Franco Zambonelli, Nicola Bicocchi, Giacomo Cabri, Letizia Leonardi, and Mariachiara Puviani. On self-adaptation, self-expression, and self-awareness in autonomic service component ensembles. In *Proc. of the Fifth IEEE Conference on Self-Adaptive and Self-Organizing Systems Workshops (SASOW)*, pages 108–113. IEEE, 2011.

18. Nelly Bencomo, Amel Bennaceur, Paul Grace, Gordon S. Blair, and Valérie Issarny. The role of models@run.time in supporting on-the-fly interoperability. *Computing*, 95(3):167–190, 2013.

19. Amel Bennaceur, Robert France, Giordano Tamburrelli, Thomas Vogel, Pieter J Mosterman, Walter Cazzola, Fbio M. Costa, Alfonso Pierantonio, Matthias Tichy, Mehmet Aksit, Pr Emmanuelson, Huang Gang, Nikolaos Georgantas, and David Redlich. Mechanisms for Leveraging Models at Runtime in Self-adaptive Software. In Nelly Bencomo, Robert France, Betty H.C. Cheng, and Uwe Assmann, editors, *Models@run.time*, volume 8378 of *Lecture Notes in Computer Science (LNCS)*, pages 19–46. Springer, 2014.

20. G. Blair, N. Bencomo, and R.B. France. Models@ run.time. *Computer*, 42(10):22–27, Oct 2009.

21. Thomas Vogel, Andreas Seibel, and Holger Giese. The Role of Models and Megamodels at Runtime. In Juergen Dingel and Arnor Solberg, editors, *Models in Software Engineering, Workshops and Symposia at MODELS 2010, Oslo, Norway, October 3-8, 2010, Reports and Revised Selected Papers*, volume 6627 of *Lecture Notes in Computer Science (LNCS)*, pages 224–238. Springer, 2011.

22. Eric Yuan, Naeem Esfahani, and Sam Malek. Automated mining of software component interactions for self-adaptation. In *Proceedings of the 9th International Symposium on Software Engineering for Adaptive and Self-Managing Systems*, SEAMS'14, pages 27–36. ACM, 2014.

23. M.T. Cox. Metacognition in computation: A selected research review. *Art. Int.*, 169(2):104–141, 2005.

24. Janet Metcalfe and Arthur P. Shimamura, editors. *Metacognition: Knowing about knowing*. MIT Press, Cambridge, MA, USA, 1994.

25. Marco Dorigo, Vito Trianni, Erol Şahin, Roderich Groß, Thomas H. Labella, Gianluca Baldassarre, Stefano Nolfi, Jean-Louis Deneubourg, Francesco Mondada, Dario Floreano, and Luca M. Gambardella. Evolving self-organizing behaviors for a swarm-bot. *Autonomous Robots*, 17:223–245, 2004.

26. Peter R. Lewis, Arjun Chandra, Shaun Parsons, Edward Robinson, Kyrre Glette, Rami Bahsoon, Jim Torresen, and Xin Yao. A survey of self-awareness and its application in computing systems. In *Proc. Int. Conference on Self-Adaptive and Self-Organizing Systems Workshops (SASOW)*, pages 102–107. IEEE, 2011.

27. Jeremy Pitt, editor. *The Computer After Me: Awareness and Self-awareness in Autonomic Systems*. Imperial College Press, 2014.

28. Julia Schaumeier, Jeremy Pitt, and Giacomo Cabri. A tripartite analytic framework for characterising awareness and self-awareness in autonomic systems research. In *Proc. of the Sixth IEEE Conference on Self-Adaptive and Self-Organizing Systems Workshops (SASOW)*, pages 157–162. IEEE, 2012.

29. Mary Shaw and David Garlan. An Introduction to Software Architecture. volume 2, pages 1–39. World Scientific Publishing Company, 1993.
30. Jeff Kramer and Jeff Magee. Self-Managed Systems: an Architectural Challenge. In *FOSE '07: 2007 Future of Software Engineering*, pages 259–268. IEEE, 2007.
31. Mary Shaw. Beyond objects: A software design paradigm based on process control. *ACM SIGSOFT Software Engineering Notes*, 20(1):27–38, 1995.
32. Hausi A. Müller, Mauro Pezzè, and Mary Shaw. Visibility of Control in Adaptive Systems. In *Proceedings of the 2nd International Workshop on Ultra-large-scale Software-intensive Systems*, ULSSIS '08, pages 23–26. ACM, 2008.
33. Hausi A. Mller, Holger M. Kienle, and Ulrike Stege. Autonomic Computing Now You See It, Now You Don't. In Andrea Lucia and Filomena Ferrucci, editors, *Software Engineering: International Summer Schools, ISSSE 2006-2008, Salerno, Italy, Revised Tutorial Lectures*, volume 5413 of *Lecture Notes in Computer Science (LNCS)*, pages 32–54. Springer, 2009.
34. Yuriy Brun, Giovanna Di Marzo Serugendo, Cristina Gacek, Holger Giese, Holger Kienle, Marin Litoiu, Hausi Müller, Mauro Pezzè, and Mary Shaw. Engineering Self-Adaptive Systems through Feedback Loops. In Betty H.C. Cheng, Rogério de Lemos, Holger Giese, Paola Inverardi, and Jeff Magee, editors, *Software Engineering for Self-Adaptive Systems*, volume 5525 of *Lecture Notes in Computer Science (LNCS)*, pages 48–70. Springer, 2009.
35. Wladyslaw Findeisen, Fred N. Bailey, Mieczyslaw Brdys, Krzysztof Malinowski, Piotr Tatjewski, and Adam Wozniak. *Control and Coordination in Hierarchical Systems*. International series on applied systems analysis. J. Wiley, 1980.
36. Karl J. strm and Richard M. Murray. *Feedback Systems: An Introduction for Scientists and Engineers*. Princeton University Press, 2008.
37. Karl J. strm and Bjrn Wittenmark. *Adaptive Control*. Dover Publications Inc., 2 edition, 2008.

Chapter 7
Architectures for Collective Self-aware Computing Systems

Ada Diaconescu, Kirstie L. Bellman, Lukas Esterle, Holger Giese, Sebastian Götz, Peter Lewis and Andrea Zisman

Abstract This chapter aims to discuss the architectural aspects relevant to *collectives of self-aware computing systems*. Here, collectives consist of several self-aware computing systems that interact in some way. Their interactions may, potentially, lead to the formation of a *self-aware collective* of systems. Hence, the chapter defines different types of interactions that can link systems into a collective and then discusses the conditions under which self-awareness can be achieved within such collectives. Furthermore, the chapter identifies some of the most relevant architectural concerns that occur when linking multiple self-aware systems into a (self-aware) collective and defines these in the form of a *generic meta-architecture* for collectives of self-aware systems. Architectural concerns can represent both static and dynamic aspects of system collectives. Static concerns include the self-awareness levels of systems in a collective; the system interrelations, such as competition and cooperation; and

A. Diaconescu (✉)
Telecom Paris Tech, 75013 Paris, France
e-mail: ada.diaconescu@telecom-paristech.fr

K.L. Bellman
The Aerospace Corporation, Los Angeles, CA, USA
e-mail: Kirstie.L.Bellman@aero.org

L. Esterle
Vienna University of Technology, Vienna, Austria
e-mail: lukas.esterle@tuwien.ac.at

H. Giese
Hasso-Plattner-Institut, 14482 Potsdam, Germany
e-mail: Holger.Giese@hpi.de

S. Götz
University of Technology Dresden, Dresden, Germany
e-mail: sebastian.goetz@acm.org

P. Lewis
Aston Lab for Intelligent Collectives Engineering (ALICE),
Aston University, Birmingham, UK
e-mail: p.lewis@aston.ac.uk

A. Zisman
The Open University, Milton Keynes, UK
e-mail: andrea.zisman@open.ac.uk

© Springer International Publishing AG 2017
S. Kounev et al. (eds.), *Self-Aware Computing Systems*,
DOI 10.1007/978-3-319-47474-8_7

several organisation patterns for systems in a collective, such as hierarchy or peer-to-peer designs. Dynamic concerns address changes that may occur over time, with respect to the above-mentioned aspects, based on the experience and learning of systems within the collective. More advanced topics discuss the manner in which the creation of collectives from interrelated systems can be applied recursively, adopting different architectural choices and combinations at each level, and potentially leading to a wide range of variations in the resulting self-awareness characteristics. The chapter concludes by indicating the main contributions and targeted beneficiaries of this chapter and points to the most important challenges to address in future research.

7.1 Introduction

7.1.1 Chapter Overview

Chapter 6 discussed architectural considerations related to individual self-aware systems. The present chapter takes this discussion further by considering multiple self-aware systems that come together to form a *collective*. The key architectural aspects and the associated questions include:

- What are the *types of relations* that can link self-aware systems within a collective (e.g. cooperation, competition or usage)?;
- What are the most common *organisation patterns* for defining the roles and inter-actions among systems in a collective (e.g. hierarchy, peer-to-peer or stigmergy)?; and
- What are the causality relations between the levels of self-awareness of individual systems (local scopes) and those resulting for an entire collective (global scope)?

The above concerns are both orthogonal—in that various combinations are possible, in principle—and interdependent—in that the way in which one aspect is instantiated may depend on the choices made for the other aspects. For instance, a hierarchical organisation is defined differently depending on whether the participating systems are linked via cooperation or competition relations; also, the exact organisational roles would depend on the self-awareness level of each system.

Most of the architectural concerns discussed here, notably including the relation types and organisation patterns, are *not* necessarily specific to self-aware systems. They can be found across related domains such as artificial intelligence, multiagent systems, robotics, autonomic and organic computing systems (cf. Chap. 8). However, since these solutions reoccur across all these domains, they will also, most likely, be relevant when designing self-aware systems.

Also, it is important to note that this chapter does *not* aim to address the *algorithmic* aspects of how self-awareness functions, such as knowledge sharing and distributed decision-making, can be achieved within the collectives of self-aware systems. Some of these algorithmic concerns are tackled in Chap. 13. Here, instead, we focus on the *architectural* aspects of collectives of self-aware systems—e.g. *Where can shared knowledge be stored? Which design patterns* can be used to distribute decision-making logic across systems in the collective? *Which types of relations* among systems can support shared knowledge and collective decision-making?

Finally, this chapter does *not* claim to provide a well-established proposal of concrete architectures for collectives of self-aware systems. This would require extensive experience and validation results, which cannot be the case here. Instead, this chapter is merely aimed to offer a starting point for future research on this topic, based on inspiration that can be drawn from relevant research domains (e.g. Chaps. 2, 8 and 10) and on argumentation about how these could be reused, adapted and built upon for providing concrete designs for self-aware systems and collectives of these.

7.1.2 Chapter Organisation

The remainder of this section provides an overview of the generic *meta-architecture* which defines the three orthogonal dimensions for the architectural concerns identified above: *relation types, organisation patterns* and *self-awareness levels*.

Section 7.2 introduces the main definitions and notations relevant to the architectural aspects of collectives of self-aware computing systems.

Section 7.3 identifies the possible forms of *self-awareness of collectives* and contrasts them with *collectives of self-aware systems*, which lack self-awareness at the collective level. Some of the most promising approaches for engineering such forms of self-awareness into collectives of computing systems are also discussed.

The next three sections detail each meta-architectural concern: self-awareness levels (Sect. 7.4), relation types (Sect. 7.5) and organisation patterns (Sect. 7.6); the latter also shows how architectural organisations can be composed recursively, in order to build more complicated, heterogeneous and multilayered collectives.

Section 7.7 focuses on the *usability* of the meta-architecture, by identifying viable combinations of architectural choices from the meta-architectural space and then proposing a methodology for identifying such choices when designing or adapting collectives of self-aware systems.

Section 7.8 concludes the chapter and identifies major research challenges.

7.1.3 Meta-Architecture Overview

The decentralised architectural style in Chap. 6 showed how self-aware systems could be composed from independent pre-reflective modules. In contrast, this chapter considers these modules are themselves self-aware and may pursue their own goals. We propose a generic *meta-architecture* for such collectives of self-aware systems. It defines a multidimensional space of architectural choices, where each point represents a concrete architecture, with concrete choices (Fig. 7.1).

Fig. 7.1 The three
dimensions of the
meta-architectural space

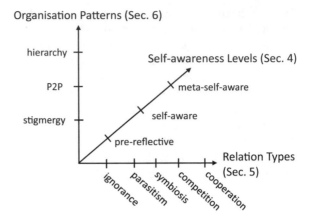

There are three main dimensions related to systems in the collective: their *self-awareness level(s)*; their *relation types*, impacting the way in which they interact; and the *organisational patterns* used for their composition. Specific terminology is defined in Sects. 7.2 and 7.3; the meta-architectural dimensions are detailed in Sects. 7.4, 7.5 and 7.6, respectively; and the valid regions within the meta-architectural space and the way to navigate through them are analysed in Sect. 7.7.

7.2 Definitions and Notations for Collectives

This section defines the basic terms concerning system *collectives*, focusing on those aspects that are of interest when looking into the self-awareness of collectives.

If we consider the definition for self-aware computing systems in Chap. 1 and aim to take the perspective of self-awareness beyond a single system, we must first determine how individual systems can be built and then discuss how they can be linked to each other. To help clarify the discussion on various types of collectives, we employ the notation and concepts introduced in Chap. 5 and depicted in Table 7.1. These are mainly based on the concepts and notation offered by UML, and on their extension, so as to cover the advanced concepts introduced in Chap. 3.

The first possibility for building a system of systems, where a *super-system* is composed of other systems, is via an *UML hierarchy*. While a system most often belongs exclusively to a single super-system, it is also possible to have systems that belong simultaneously to multiple super-systems. Hence, we distinguish between *composition*—representing an embedded component with exclusive membership and depicted with normal border in a UML composite structure diagram—and *shared aggregation*—representing an embedded component with shared membership and depicted with dashed border in a UML composite structure diagram.

Systems that belong to a super-system may be visible to external entities—situated outside the super-system (white-box approach). In this case, the semantics of a UML

Table 7.1 Notations for architectural concepts in self-aware computing systems

Notation	Description
name:type	A **system** with a name and a type. We may omit either the name (cf. anonymous system) or the type. A system can be decomposed into **modules**. Specific stereotypes are used to indicate that a system is ≪self-aware≫, ≪meta-self-aware≫, etc.
name:type	A **module** with a name and a type. We may omit either the name (cf. anonymous module) or the type. A module can be decomposed into (sub-)modules. A module may be stereotyped as ≪pre-reflective≫, ≪reflective≫, ≪meta-reflective≫, ≪meta-meta-reflective≫, etc., depending on the extent to which it reflects upon other module(s)
name:type	An **environmental context** of a **system** represents the part of the environment that is scoped by the system's capacities of sensing and exploration. It has a name and type and we may omit one of them
type ▼	A **port** describes the functionality that is provided or required by a **system**, **module** or **context**. A port is characterised by its type. The direction of the arrow indicates whether the port is required (arrow points outwards the element requiring the functionality) or provided (arrow points inwards the element providing the functionality). Ports can be stereotyped to indicate the kind of functionality: effecting ≪E≫, adapting ≪A≫, observing ≪O≫ and reporting ≪R≫
⟶	A **data flow** describes the interactions between **systems**, **modules**, **processes** and **models**
name:type / name:type / name:type	A **composition** shows modules built from other modules and distinguishes between exclusive and shared membership (solid or dashed border, respectively) of embedded modules.
name:type	A **collaboration** describes the interaction behaviour among **systems**, **modules** and/or **processes**. The concrete behaviour of the interaction is described within the collaboration
⎯⎯	A **participation** connects a **system**, **module** or **process** to a **collaboration** such that the **system**, **module** or **process** participates in the **collaboration**
⟩ Process ⟩	A **process** describes the activities of a **system** or a **module**, hence emphasising its behaviour
name:type	An **awareness model** represents learned aspects from a system's a scope, which is (part of) the **system** itself, **other systems** or the **environmental context**. In the former case, the model is stereotyped with ≪sys≫ and in the other cases with ≪ctx≫. An awareness model has a name and a type, one of which can be omitted
≪goal≫ name:type	A **goal model** describes the goals the **system** or parts of it should achieve. Goals are either imposed to the system from outside (e.g. by the user) or internally produced. A goal model has a name and a type, one of which can be omitted. Finally, a goal model is stereotyped with ≪goal≫

(continued)

Table 7.1 (continued)

Notation	Description
→	An **awareness link** denotes that a span is directly aware of a scope. If a span exploits awareness knowledge about a scope that has been established by another span, the former span is indirectly aware of the scope. Such indirect awareness is transitive and can be explicitly represented by dashed awareness links. Awareness links can be specialised by indicating its kind: ≪sa≫ for stimulus, ≪ia≫ for interaction, ≪ta≫ for time and ≪ga≫ for goal awareness
→	An **expression link** denotes that a span directly impacts (e.g. adapts or effects) a scope. If a span indirectly impacts a scope via another span, the former span can be connected to the scope to make the indirect expression visible. Such indirect expressions are transitive and can be explicitly represented by dashed expression links. To specialise the kind of expression, a link can be stereotyped: effecting ≪E≫, adapting ≪A≫, observing ≪O≫ and reporting ≪R≫

hierarchy is that of a "belongs to" relation between a system and its super-system. Alternatively, systems within a super-system may be (partially) hidden from external entities (grey-box or black-box approach). Here, UML hierarchy takes the additional semantics of *encapsulation*, hence providing a certain degree of isolation to systems embedded within super-systems.

The second possibility for building a system of systems is via a *UML collaboration*. This provides a more flexible form of collective compared to a hierarchy. A system can play different roles in different collaborations, simultaneously. Hence, the semantics of UML collaborations and UML hierarchies with shared aggregation may overlap somewhat. However, UML collaborations also allow to capture compositions that are not hierarchically structured. Furthermore, while system composition in UML collaborations may change rather frequently, membership to a hierarchy is usually considered more durable (even if it can also change).

The UML concepts considered for hierarchy and collaboration from Chap. 5 are limited to direct communication as a means of system coordination and thus are too restrictive to cover collectives as we have them in mind here. Following the design taxonomy introduced in [34], we realise that the core question to ask when considering collectives is whether some *correlation* (resp. *anti-correlation*) is present such that the systems do not behave stochastically independent.

An observed correlation can be a *coupling* that results from shared information at run-time. If no such sharing is present, we may have a correlation but no coupling. For instance, a shared temperature sensor triggers similar behaviours in a number of smart devices and thus couples them. On the other hand, a shared design decision implemented within a number of devices may result in a correlation of their behaviours even in the absence of data sharing at run-time.

If there were *no correlation* at all (which is hardly ever the case in real systems), it would be possible to consider the systems in the collective as completely independent. In such cases, the collective behaviour is the mere superposition of behaviours of the separate systems. This may happen if the systems were completely isolated from each other and their behaviours were not related stochastically in any way.

While in reality systems are rarely isolated completely, often times there is only a *negligible correlation* between them at the *level of abstraction* considered. In such cases, it is possible to consider that the systems in the collective are independent, since the behaviour of the collective is more or less the superposition of the behaviours of the separate systems, at the abstraction level considered. This of course holds as long as certain constraints are fulfilled that guarantee that the coupling can be neglected. For instance, in a "traditional" electric grid, all subsystems (i.e. electric devices) consume electric energy independently, based on their needs, and without considering their collective consumption. As long as the grid's energy supply is able to fulfil all the demands of devices in the collective, the coupling between devices due to energy consumption can be neglected, at this considered abstraction level.

Most often, the design of the collective has to take into account that some correlation occurs among the constituent systems, usually in the form of coupling. These are cases where system correlation cannot be neglected at the considered *level of abstraction*. It may cause either adverse effects that have to be mitigated, or expedient effects from which the collective can benefit (cf. Chap. 13). As a negative example, multiple systems in a collective may try to influence the same environment characteristics in opposite directions, hence destabilising the collective behaviour (e.g. competing feedback loops causing oscillations). As a positive example, multiple systems in a collective may inform each other as soon as they encounter a security threat, hence helping to speed up the transmission of security warnings throughout the collective (e.g. fast convergence due to positive feedback).

Hence, in the following, we will use the UML hierarchy or UML collaboration notations defined above, yet extend their scopes so as to be able to cover the broader notion of collective discussed above. More precisely, we extend these notions so as to *not* require direct communication between the systems in a collective, and to merely assume some sort of correlation (or anti-correlation) instead.[1]

System correlation types within a collective are essential to the resulting behaviour and characteristics of that collective. Correlations imply the extent of information exchanges between systems, as briefly discussed above. Nonetheless, in addition to their mere occurrence, such exchanges typically carry certain semantics—e.g. meaning, intent or utility of interactions. The details of such semantics is specific to each collective, yet some common characteristics can be identified at a more abstract level, depending on the types of *relations* that occur among systems, such as cooperation and competition (cf. Sect. 7.5); and on the types of *organisation patterns* implemented by systems in the collective, such as hierarchy, peer-to-peer and stigmergy (cf. Sect. 7.6).

---

[1] Note that SySML also uses UML concepts that have been introduced originally for software only. It thus uses, for example, a dashed variant of the UML collaboration notation to capture constraints between variables of different systems, as resulting, for instance, from physical laws. In this respect, our usage of UML notation similarly extends the semantics of the employed UML concepts.

When merely concerned with the degree of information exchanges, and hence of system correlation, it suffices to consider system coordination or non-coordination within collectives, as discussed below.

To help characterise different collective types, we rely on a case study of a collective intelligent-transport system, consisting of multiple autonomous shuttles.

Example 7.1 (*Collective Intelligent-Transport System*) This system envisions that traditional railroad transportation operating on predefined schedules and using long trains with many wagons is replaced by autonomous shuttles, for people and goods, that operate on demand and thus avoid overheads and minimise waiting times. Specific demands in terms of time and costs can be addressed via customised solutions— e.g. business managers request high-speed transportation to an urgent meeting, while tourists only ask for transportation within a time window.

One approach to designing collectives is *not* to coordinate its systems, which will operate independently. This implies that there is no communication among the systems, either directly or indirectly. It requires that any system coupling resulting from a shared environment is negligible. Hence, uncoordinated systems are unaware of each other and bound via an *ignorance relation* (cf. Sect. 7.5). Non-coupled correlation may still occur—e.g. time-dependent. For instance, if all systems are programmed to execute a routine at a predefined time, then they will execute in synchrony without any communication among them.

An example where a shuttle is not part of coordination, as there is only negligible coupling with other shuttles, is depicted via a dotted line in Fig. 7.2 for Shuttle2. This notation does not indicate whether a correlation without coupling exists or not.

Example 7.2 (*Uncoordinated Load Balancing*) In the shuttle case study of Example 7.1, the assignment of transportations tasks can be achieved via random shuttle selection. Hence, the selection of shuttle resources only results in negligible coupling among them and ensures a reasonable load-balancing level. Therefore, these solutions are probably more scalable and robust than alternatives that require coordinated selections. However, it can also lead to disadvantageous assignments, which can incur high distances between the start position of the transportation task and the current location of the selected shuttle. It is hence mostly applicable to small regions only.

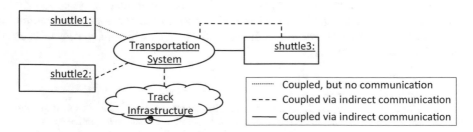

Fig. 7.2 The possible means for communication in a collective and their notation

An alternative approach to designing a collective is to coordinate its systems. This is achieved via some form of communication, including direct or indirect communication, which results in shared information and hence in some form of system coupling. Direct communication can be employed to support various system relation types, such as cooperation, competition or parasitism (cf. Sect. 7.5), which can, in turn, occur within diverse organisation patterns, such as hierarchies and peer-to-peer designs (cf. Sect. 7.6). Indirect communication can include various forms of *sign-based stigmergy*, where it is realised by leaving particular signs in the environment (e.g. pheromones in the case of ants); or forms of *sematectonic stigmergy*, where it results from the modifications of the physical environment (cf. [8]). In this case, we consider that systems implement a stigmergy pattern (cf. Sect. 7.6).

Example 7.3 (*Slightly Coordinated Load Balancing*) A variant of the solution in Example 7.2 involves a random assignment of shuttles to transportation tasks that ensures a low probability of a high distance between the task's start position and the current shuttle location. If shuttle selection only results in negligible coupling, the random nature of the selection makes a reasonable load balancing very likely, while still ensuring better scalability and robustness than solutions based on more advanced deterministic coordination. However, on rare occasions, assignments can still be selected where the distance between the shuttle and its start transport is rather large. Therefore, this scheme is not suitable to settings where a minimum worst-case selection must be guaranteed, like in case of emergency transport.

Based on the system composition concepts introduced above, we can now introduce the term *collective* as the most general notion to denote a composition of systems, where systems are somehow potentially correlated.

Definition 7.1 A *collective of systems* is a group of systems composed via UML hierarchy and/or UML collaboration, in the extended sense concerned with system correlation.

We can further refine such composition as a system of systems, as follows.

Definition 7.2 A *system of systems* (SoS) is a collective where the systems are developed, deployed and managed independently.

Finally, we introduce the concept of distributed system to emphasise that our notion of a collective is independent of the actual system distribution.

Definition 7.3 A *distributed system* is a collective of systems that are deployed on different computational nodes. It is usually assumed that the collective can operate somehow jointly and deal with the temporary unavailability of some of the systems.

7.3   The Self-awareness of Collectives

7.3.1   General Considerations

As noted by many researchers (e.g. [22, 24, 37]), self-awareness can be a property of collective systems, even when there is no single component that is aware of the entire system. This is a key observation for the architecture of self-aware systems: one need not require that a self-aware system possess a global component which is all-knowing. Transferring this idea to collectives of systems, this implies that a self-aware collective does not necessarily require a system that possesses all knowledge and related self-awareness functions over the entire collective.

In this chapter, we deal with a key concept in building and analysing the self-awareness of computational systems: the notion that self-awareness is not only a property which can be observed at the level of an individual component or system, but can be a property of a collective system itself. Architecturally, this can be achieved in several ways. In centralised or hierarchical collectives, it may be that the self-awareness is provided by a dedicated component, or small number of components, responsible for monitoring and reasoning about the collective system as a whole. At the other extreme, self-awareness arises from interactions *among* the systems and components within the collective [24].

Moreover, according to the characterisation of self-awareness, and its various levels, in Chap. 3, a system may be composed of a set of nodes which individually possess various *levels of self-awareness*, and the system is simultaneously able to be characterised in terms of its self-awareness at the level of the collective. Since collectives may be composed themselves, we are able to consider the presence of levels of self-awareness at multiple levels in the hierarchy of such a composition.

One recent example of a collectively self-aware system is the heterogeneous swarm of autonomous underwater vehicles targeted in the COCORO project.[2] For example, Schmickl et al. [29] showed that a group of robots with simple behavioural rules and local interactions may achieve Collective-awareness of a global state, distributed across the individual units. They also demonstrated collective self-awareness at several hierarchical levels: individual, group and swarm levels.

7.3.2   Collective Self-awareness and Self-aware Collectives

An important distinction must be made between two key concepts, which have only subtle differences in wording: (i) *collective self-awareness* and (ii) *self-aware collectives*.

---

[2]http://cocoro.uni-graz.at/drupal/.

- **Collective self-awareness** is a phenomenon where self-awareness is realised in a bottom-up manner, via the interactions of entities within the collective. Thus, the awareness is not present in any one place, but builds up in an aggregated way, where different entities within the collective have an awareness of relevant parts, such that they contribute towards the self-awareness of the whole.
- **The self-awareness of a collective** describes the self-awareness properties (cf. Chap. 3) of a collective system. This may be achieved in various ways, ranging from cases where self-awareness is provided by a single node with a global view, to cases where all nodes feature some self-awareness properties.

7.3.2.1   Collective Self-awareness

First let us recap the definition of *collective self-awareness* from Chap. 3.

Definition: A system is collectively self-aware when it senses, learns, reasons, makes decisions and possibly acts, based on an aggregated self-awareness or a combined contributed self-awareness from (some of) its multiple self-aware entities.

As discussed in Chap. 3, and referring to the five levels of self-awareness proposed in their conceptual model, Lewis et al. [22] describe these as *"systems within a collective that interact with each other only locally as part of a bigger system, [and] might not individually possess knowledge about the system as a whole. Although global knowledge is distributed, each system within the collective can work with other systems, giving rise to the collective itself obtaining a sense of its own state and thus being self-aware at one or more of the five self-awareness levels"*.

When designing such a system, one might be tempted to think that collective self-awareness implies certain constraints about the architecture, contents or behaviour of the collective system. However, any intuition along these lines should be carefully checked. Several aspects should be considered instead:

1. Uniformity of self-awareness capabilities is not assumed. Entities within the collective can (and typically will) have different self-awareness capabilities (with respect to those discussed in Chap. 3), and these may be dynamic in nature.
2. The form and implementation of communication methods, and of sensing, self-modelling and reasoning techniques may also vary and are not prescribed by the presence of collective self-awareness.
3. Collective self-awareness does not necessarily imply the sharing of self-knowledge among entities. This form of interpersonal meta-reflection is sometimes a beneficial capability, but is not implied by the notion of collective self-awareness.
4. Collective self-awareness may be emergent or predesigned (or both). The method of aggregation, collective reasoning and collective action may be predesigned or may emerge, and vary at run-time as the collective behaviour changes.
5. In some cases, only a subset of the entities will contribute to the collective self-awareness, while others will be passive. Again, this may be dynamic across

run-time. We might talk here about the *support of self-awareness*, i.e. those entities which are contributing towards collective self-awareness.

7.3.2.2 Characterising the Self-awareness of Collective Systems

We can also characterise collective self-awareness in terms of the framework for self-awareness introduced in Chap. 3. Notions such as self-awareness scope, span or levels also apply at the collective level. The following list presents levels of self-awareness that are particularly relevant to collective self-awareness.

1. **Collective unawareness**: There is a collective, but entities within it have no awareness of the existence of the collective or of each other.
2. **Other-awareness**: Entities are minimally aware of other entities within the collective. This can be coupled with other individually facing self-awareness levels, such as goal-awareness, and can form intra-reflective capabilities, such as when one entity is aware of another's goals.
3. **Interaction-awareness**: Entities are not just aware of other entities, but also of their interactions within the collective, possibly including themselves. They can also be aware of the type of *relations* between them (Sect. 7.5).
4. **Entity-Collective awareness**: Entities are aware of the state of (part of) the collective, beyond themselves. This forms the beginning of the entities' more aggregate knowledge of the collective as a whole. This may include awareness of the collective goal or overall organisation pattern (Sect. 7.6). Such awareness is still present in individual entities.
5. **Collective-Collective awareness**: Awareness of the state of the collective (or part of it) is present at the level of the collective, despite not being present in any particular entity (as is the case in Entity-Collective awareness). Here, awareness of the collective is itself distributed across its composing entities.
6. **Collective meta-self-awareness**: The collective has an awareness of its own Collective-Collective-awareness. Not only does the collective have (distributed) models of itself, but there is also knowledge of the collective self-awareness processes, such as distributed learning and reasoning.

7.3.2.3 The Elusive Border Between Collectives of Self-aware Systems and Self-aware Collectives

Taking a simplistic view, when several self-aware systems are brought together into a collective system, we have a *collective of self-aware computing systems*.

Let us first consider a case where the systems of a collective possess some self-awareness, but no self-awareness exists at the collective level. This notion, while perhaps intuitive, is somewhat misleading. For the collective to attain higher meta-reflective levels of self-awareness, we would require that it possessed the capability of sensing, learning and reasoning about itself *as a collective*. This is certainly one strong interpretation of the self-awareness of collective systems.

However, at the lower levels of self-awareness, where there is no awareness of the collective itself as an object of awareness, might we expect to find systems in which self-aware systems are aggregated together in some manner such that there was in fact no self-awareness at all manifested at the collective level? Would this, in theory, be possible? It seems unlikely, given that any external actor must interact with the collective through some part of it, and there are by definition some parts which possess such self-awareness capabilities. If we further require that a collective is more than a bag of unrelated entities, and some interaction between the entities is a requirement for collectivism, then it seems highly unlikely that a collective system composed of self-aware entities could exhibit no self-awareness at all.

We have set out here two extremes of, on the one hand, a collective with a (perhaps distributed) model of itself, and on the other hand, a collective which somehow serves to mute the propagation of the self-awareness capabilities of its entities. Of course, in between these two extremes there will be a broad range of self-awareness.

An important question then becomes, given the self-awareness capabilities of individual entities, and their relations and organisation for forming a collective, what can be said about how the self-awareness capabilities aggregate from the various levels present at the entity level, to the levels present at the collective level? Such capabilities may be highly heterogeneous, and the role and connectivity of different reflective processes within the architecture give rise to varied reflective and knowledge-sharing relationships. More concretely, for higher levels of collective self-awareness to emerge at the collective level, we are interested in what self-awareness capabilities need to be present at the entity level, and how these need to be organised. There is no simple answer to this question.

Finally, in some cases, the exact border between these cases of collective self-awareness—self-aware collectives, collective self-awareness and collectives of self-aware systems—may become difficult to establish precisely, just as it can be difficult to establish the exact border between collectives of self-aware systems (this chapter) and self-aware systems composed of pre-reflective components (in Chap. 6).

7.3.3 Approaches for Achieving Self-aware Collectives

7.3.3.1 Overlapping Self-awareness Domains in Collective Systems

While no general answer to the question above exists, one architecture-oriented approach is to consider the self-awareness *scope*, of each constituent system and of the collective, denoting *what* they are aware of, respectively. Two main cases can occur here, depending on whether or not there is an *overlap* among the respective scopes of systems within the collective. Overlapping scopes imply that systems can compare observations between the objects of their awareness, which may be external or internal to the collective. Cases where the systems in the collective are *mutually reflective*—i.e. they can observe each other, belonging each others' self-awareness scopes—may be of particular interest to obtaining some form of collective self-awareness, since mutual reflection can lead to intra-collective meta-reflective behaviour. Might this suffice for a meta-reflective behaviour to emerge at the level of the collective?

7.3.3.2 Examples of Cooperative and Competitive Self-awareness in Self-aware Systems With or Without Overlapping Domains

Self-aware systems may be composed into collectives via *hierarchy* or *collaboration* interconnections (Sect. 7.2). In both cases, their self-awareness scopes may or may not overlap and may or may not include each other mutually. Moreover, in both collective types, coordination among systems can implement various types of *relations*, including cooperation and competition (Sect. 7.5). Via a set of examples from the autonomous shuttle case study (Example 7.1), we aim here to illustrate cases where cooperative or competitive self-awareness can be achieved within a collective, having system self-awareness scopes that may or may not overlap.

Let us first consider examples of systems with non-overlapping scopes.

Example 7.4 (*Collective of Self-aware Computing Systems with Simple Competition*) Shuttles compete to get transport orders and to earn money, by learning their own capabilities and the environment's characteristics. Shuttles are not aware of each other in this case, meaning they do not observe or reason about each other directly.

Example 7.5 (*Collective of Self-aware Computing Systems with Simple Cooperation*) A fleet of shuttles cooperates to get as many transport orders as useful, optimise the quality of the service, and reduce their costs, so as to make a profit for the fleet. Shuttles learn their capabilities and the environment's characteristics. They are not self-aware of each other and do not share their knowledge or reasoning results.

In the examples above, cooperation and competition were achieved without mutual system self-awareness. The corresponding behaviours are hard-coded within shuttles, which are not really aware of their interrelation types. The collective does not feature any Other-awareness or Interaction-awareness. Yet, in the cooperative case, shuttles may feature some form of Entity-Collective awareness, which allows them to reason about how to contribute to the fleet objectives.

Let us now consider examples of systems with self-awareness scopes that do overlap and more precisely that have each other in their self-awareness scopes.

Example 7.6 (*Collective of Self-aware Computing Systems with Competition*) Shuttles compete for transport orders by learning about their own capabilities, the environment and the competing shuttles. They are also aware of each other and learn about competing shuttles by either explicit or implicit self-awareness, via direct or indirect interaction and observation, respectively.

Example 7.7 (Collective of Self-aware Computing Systems with Cooperation) Shuttles cooperate to maximise transport orders, optimise quality of service and reduce costs within their fleet. Shuttles learn about their capabilities, the environment and/or the cooperating shuttles (as before, via direct or indirect interactions).

The examples above extend self-awareness at the collective level, as systems now feature both Other-awareness and Interaction-awareness. Since shuttles are now aware of their interactions, and hence of their cooperation or competition relations, they can use the knowledge acquired about each other from this perspective. As before, shuttles may also feature Entity-Collective awareness, which helps to purposefully contribute to the fleet's objectives.

More complicated cases may occur in collectives if several types of compositions and relation types occur simultaneously, at various levels, as exemplified next.

Example 7.8 (Collective of Self-aware Systems with Competition and Cooperation) Multiple fleets of shuttles compete, while shuttles within each fleet cooperate. Each fleet aims to maximise its transport orders, and quality of service and reduce costs. Shuttles learn about their own capabilities, the environment, cooperating and competing shuttles, their own fleet and/or the competing fleets. This setting represents a collaboration of competing fleets, with each fleet containing, via hierarchy, a cooperating collaboration of shuttles (cf. hybrid compositions in Sect. 7.6.5).

In the example above, self-awareness scopes overlap at various levels—both over other shuttles and other fleets and concern various relation types—shuttles are aware of both cooperation and competing relations—both within their fleet and with other fleets. The Entity-Collective awareness is combined with the Other-awareness since shuttles are aware of other fleets, hence of other collectives.

Finally, the examples above can be extended to systems with meta-self-awareness capabilities, which can lead to various forms of Collective-meta-awareness.

Example 7.9 (Collective of Competing Self-aware Systems with Meta-Self-awareness) Shuttles compete to get orders by learning about their capabilities, the environment and competing shuttles. They also evaluate alternative forms of learning and decide to switch between them and/or tune them. This makes shuttles meta-self-aware.

7.3.3.3 Collective Self-awareness Functions

Let us now consider an alternative approach to collective self-awareness, where the self-awareness processes are achieved *collectively* by the participating systems. We consider here that a collective of systems is self-aware if it fits the definition of *self-aware computing* in Chap. 1 (and Chap. 3), applied to a collective of self-aware systems rather than to a single system. This means that systems within the collective interact with each other in order to learn models of their collective and its environment, to reason about models collectively and to act in accordance with collective goals. In this view, collective self-awareness stems from the self-awareness of systems within the collective and their interactions.[3] Of course, various degrees of collective self-awareness, with different scopes and functions, can be achieved in this manner, depending on the systems involved and their exchanges.

In the following, we will consider two extreme situations featuring partial or complete self-awareness functions at the collective level. A wide range of cases can occur in between these extremes. Firstly, a collective is considered self-aware in a *weak* or *partial* sense if a subset of its systems engage in collective learning, reasoning or acting processes, in accordance with collective goals and with their combined self-awareness scopes only covering part of the collective. Secondly, a *strong*, more complete form of collective self-awareness is achieved by combining all of these capabilities together.

7.3.3.4 Weak Self-aware Collectives

Collective Goals. We first consider a collective of self-aware systems that behaves in accordance with collective goals even though no processes are done collectively.

Definition 7.4 A *collective goal* is a goal that is pursued jointly by several systems in a collective. Each system contributes to the achievement of the collective goal.

Example 7.10 (*Self-aware collectives via collective goals*) All shuttles in the fleet aim to ensure quality services in order to contribute to the fleet's *reputation*—this is the collective goal that can benefit all member shuttles.

Collective Self-awareness Processes. We next assume that there are some information exchanges among the processes of systems within a collective—notably learning, reasoning and acting. We argue that self-awareness in such collective may consequently happen with respect to those processes.[4]

Definition 7.5 *Collective learning* is a learning process that is carried out jointly by systems in a collective. Each system shares the results of its learning function with the other systems, hence contributing to the collective learning process.

Example 7.11 (*Self-aware collectives via system cooperation—Learning*) A fleet of shuttles cooperates by exchanging monitoring data or knowledge to learn about other shuttles, the environment and/or their fleet.

Note that a group of systems that jointly learn about their environment would only form a context-aware collective but not a self-aware collective, since, according to our definition of Chap. 1, system self-awareness is also demanded.

---

[3]Note that cases where a collective consists of systems that are *not* self-aware (or pre-reflective) is outside the scope of this chapter. Chapter 6 discusses such cases instead.

[4]Similar to the sharing of monitoring, analysis, planning, execution and knowledge in [36].

Definition 7.6 *Collective reasoning* is a reasoning process that is carried out jointly by systems in a collective. Each system shares the results of its reasoning function with the other systems, hence contributing to the collective reasoning process.

Example 7.12 (Self-aware collectives via system cooperation—Reasoning) A fleet of shuttles cooperates by exchanging analysis or reasoning results, in order to complement and coordinate their plans and optimise the fleet goals—e.g. maximise the quality of all transports and ensure fairness of order assignments among shuttles.

Definition 7.7 *Collective acting* is an acting process that is carried out jointly by systems in a collective. Each system coordinates its actions with the other systems, so as to contribute to the collective action process.

Example 7.13 (Self-aware collectives via system cooperation—Acting) In a multi-regional fleet, shuttles cooperate by coordinating their actions to fulfil long-distance transport orders. Here, one shuttle fulfils the transport within one region and another within the adjacent region. Exchanges between shuttles can be achieved at a well-known parking location and hence require no prior planning.

Definition 7.8 A *weak self-aware collective of systems* is a collective where collective goals, collective learning, collective reasoning and collective acting are present.

7.3.3.5 Strong Self-aware Collectives

Definition 7.9 A *strong self-aware collective* is a collective where member systems realise all self-awareness aspects—goals, learning, reasoning and acting (i.e. the entire LRA-loop)—at the level of the collective and not at the individual level.

Example 7.14 (Strong self-aware collective via system cooperation—full LRA-loop) The fleet of shuttles cooperate by exchanging monitoring data or knowledge to learn about other shuttles, the environment and/or their overall fleet. They also exchange goals, analysis or reasoning results in order to adjust their behaviours such that the interests of other shuttles, or of the fleet may be taken into account. Shuttles also exchange planned changes and coordinate their actions such that the planned changes of other shuttles or of the fleet are taken into account. The collective learning, reasoning and acting all contribute to achieve the collective goals.

Self-awareness for a collective of systems can be achieved in various ways. Identifying all such viable approaches is outside the scope of this chapter and should be the topic of extensive future research. We exemplified here only some of the most promising ways of achieving collective self-awareness.

Weak and Strong Meta-Self-aware Collectives. A higher level of collective self-awareness may result if systems reflect on their self-awareness, at a collective level.

Example 7.15 (*Self-aware collectives via system cooperation—Meta-Self-awareness*) The fleet of shuttles cooperate by exchanging monitoring data to learn about other shuttles, the environment or the fleet. Also, they sometimes evaluate alternative monitoring schemes, with different detail levels, and decide to switch between these.

Meta-self-awareness can also be a weak or strong form of Definitions 7.8 and 7.9.

7.4 Self-awareness Levels

Capitalising on the notions introduced in Sect. 7.3, this section aims to provide further insights into how combining multiple levels of self-awareness in individual systems may lead to self-awareness characteristics of the entire collective. We investigate both cases of uniform and heterogeneous collectives, composed of systems with similar or diverse self-awareness capabilities, respectively. Within this context, it will become evident that in addition to the actual self-awareness characteristics of the systems involved, the types of their relations and the roles they play within the collective's organisation pattern become critical for establishing the collective's self-aware characteristics. Finally, we look into the collective dynamics, indicating how changes in systems with various self-awareness characteristics may impact the resulting collective self-awareness.

7.4.1 Collective Self-awareness Based on System Self-awareness

We focus here on the way in which various self-awareness levels come about in collectives where systems are interconnected as hierarchies or collaborations. For hierarchical self-aware collectives, an interesting question is whether or not self-awareness is ensured by the top-level system. The type of hierarchy is also important here—i.e. composite, aggregated or encapsulated (cf. Sect. 7.2)—as it impacts the observability of systems beyond the top level. For collaborative collectives, the question extends to all the systems in the collective. Also, if some systems are aware of the self-awareness of the collective, we can have meta-self-aware collectives.

We identify several cases that may occur at recursive levels within a collective:

- (meta-)self-aware collaborative collective of (meta-)self-aware top-level systems;
- (meta-)self-aware hierarchical collective of one (meta-)self-aware system, typically the top-level one, and further systems of any level of self-awareness;
- (meta-)self-aware collaborative collective of pre-reflective systems and at least one (meta-)self-aware system;

- pre-reflective collective of self-aware top-level systems (only local self-awareness);
- pre-reflective collective of pre-reflective top-level systems (out of chapter's scope).

When not all top-level systems in a collective are self-aware, we can still have self-awareness at the collective level, if, for instance, the scopes of the self-aware systems include all the pre-reflective systems within the collective (Fig. 7.3). In case some systems are not covered by the scope of self-aware systems, then we may consider the collective as non-self-aware; as partially self-aware; or even as self-aware (if the partial scope suffices for pursuing the collective's goals).

Let us first consider a collective where top-level systems are self-aware and interconnected via a UML collaboration and where each top-level system is interconnected to its subsystems via a UML hierarchy with encapsulation (Sect. 7.2).

An important question here is how can system designers ensure a certain level of collective self-awareness when joining together top-level systems with either *homogeneous* or *heterogeneous* levels of self-awareness? Homogeneous levels will most likely ensure some form of self-awareness at the collective level—the exact kind will depend on the kind of self-awareness of member systems, the overlap of their scopes and the information sharing among their self-awareness functions.

For instance, if all systems in a collective are State-aware, Behaviour-aware and Interaction-aware and have each other in their scopes, then the collective is also State- and Behaviour-aware; yet not necessarily Interaction-aware or Other-aware with respect to other collectives. As another example, if all systems in a collective are State- and Behaviour-aware with respect to themselves (their scope covers their internal resources) and they exchange their knowledge (cooperation relation), then the entire collective may feature collective State and Behaviour self-awareness, since the underlying learning process is provided collectively. In contrast, if self-aware systems do *not* share information (competition relation), then we can still talk about a *collective of self-aware systems*, yet *without collective self-awareness*.

Based on such considerations, designers can achieve various collective levels of self-awareness by ensuring corresponding levels of self-awareness in the top systems and/or their information sharing.

The question is more complicated when integrating systems with heterogeneous self-awareness levels. In general, we can consider that collective self-awareness may emerge from the individual system levels, their interconnections, scope overlaps, information sharing, relation types and organisation patterns. For instance, we can

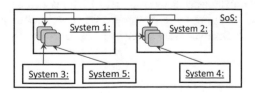

Fig. 7.3 Self-aware systems (1 and 2) include in their scope pre-reflective systems (3, 4 and 5), hence enabling the entire collective to exhibit self-awareness properties

note that a collaborative collective where a single top-level system exhibits self-aware properties and where this system's scope covers all the other systems in the collective should *not* be considered as exhibiting *collective self-awareness* (as defined in Sect. 7.3.2). This is because the self-awareness capabilities of the collective are not provided collectively, but rather by a single system. At the same time, we *can* consider that the collective features some self-awareness properties.

Let us now consider a hierarchical collective with heterogeneous kinds of self-awareness—e.g. one system is State-aware and another one Behaviour-aware of all systems in the collective; the other systems can reason about different models provided by the first systems; all systems send their knowledge and partial reasoning results to a top-level system, which can hence learn from the entire collective. Here, we may talk about collective self-awareness based on systems with different levels and kinds of self-awareness.

More precisely, a collective can feature different self-awareness levels as follows:

- *Stimulus awareness (lowest level)*: at least one system is stimulus-aware, covering all relevant parts of the collective and its environment, and can share these stimuli with other systems in the collective.
- *Interaction awareness*: for any interaction, there is at least one system that is aware of this interaction.
- *Time awareness*: at least one system is time-aware, and aware of all relevant collective events. This can also be achieved via a combination of time-aware systems covering complementary event subsets.
- *State awareness*: may or may not be obtained directly from the aggregated state of the individual systems. This may be because system-level state models may be too fine grained, too heterogeneous and/or lack system interconnection information, and cannot be readily employed for achieving the collective goals.
- *Behaviour awareness*: as with state-awareness, having all top-level systems behaviour-aware, or having systems share behaviour-related information, does not immediately imply that the entire collective becomes behaviour-aware.
- *Appearance-of awareness*: as with state awareness, having all top-level systems being aware of their individual appearance towards an external observer does not make the entire collective-aware of the collective appearance.
- *Goal/Motivation/Intention awareness*: depends on the actual type of goal defined at the collective level. When collective goals emerge through exchanges of local goals, followed by consensus-finding and sharing of results (i.e. bottom-up process), goal awareness at the top-level systems can suffice to also ensure awareness of the resulting collective goal. When collective goals are imposed from outside the collective, systems must have access to them to be collective goal-aware.

7.4.2 Dynamic Self-awareness Changes in the Collective

An additional level of complexity is introduced by collective dynamics, as systems may join or leave the collective at run-time. From the collective perspective, these dynamics can be either intended and hence *expected* (e.g. hibernating resources are required to join the collective to increase performance); or *unexpected* (e.g. system failure). Dynamic changes raise additional questions for system designers:

1. When adding or removing a self-aware system to/from the collective, how does this affect the self-awareness level of the entire collective?
2. When changes are expected, can the collective anticipate the necessary actions to ensure minimum disruption, resource overhead and performance loss?
3. When unexpected changes affect the collective level of self-awareness, will the collective still attain its goals? Or, if interrupted, will it recover?

The answers to these questions depend on the self-awareness implementation. For homogeneous collectives, adding or removing a top-level system may have little influence on the collective self-awareness level. For heterogeneous cases, the impact of such changes highly depends on the self-awareness level of the added or removed system and its interactions with other systems. For example, removing the only interaction-aware system that has all other systems in its scope will cause the entire collective to lose its Interaction-awareness. If the collective can predict the effects of such changes, then it can try to avoid them in order to maintain its self-awareness level. If changes are unexpected, then the collective may attempt to substitute the capabilities of a removed system or to capitalise on those of a new system, so as to maintain or to optimise its performance with respect to collective goals.

7.5 Types of Relations

As described in Sect. 7.2, a collective consists of multiple interconnected systems. Section 7.2 focused on the purely architectural nature of system interconnections, which could be either hierarchical or collaborative, and achieved via direct or indirect communication, or mere correlation. This section concentrates on the semantics that can be attached to such interconnections, associating them with different *relation types*. Relation types are identified with respect to the main self-awareness concerns: *goals*, *knowledge*, *reasoning* and *acting*. Beyond the mere communication, or interference, implied by architectural connections, the associated relation types represent the kind of exchanges between the interconnected systems.

7.5.1 Goals

7.5.1.1 System Goals Versus Collective Goals

Within a collective, goals can be pursued at both the system and collective level. Goals can be either *implicit*, i.e. "hidden" in the system implementation, or *explicit*, i.e. provided as a machine-readable representation. Typically, several collective and system goals are pursued simultaneously. Hence, goals and their interrelations play a major role and must be considered carefully when designing collectives of self-aware systems. Here, we aim to discuss the kinds of relations that can occur between systems depending on the way in which they impact each other's goals, and in which they contribute to collective goals.

Figure 7.4 extends the notation introduced in Chap. 5 to depict how goals can occur at both system level and collective level. Goal interconnections indicate how goals relate to each other. Very generally, and in line with [34], we denote *joint intentions* between systems with compatible goals via the "+" notation attached to a bidirectional relation between their respective goals. As detailed below, this typically represents a *cooperation* relation implemented via direct or indirect communication between the systems. In contrast, we denote *antagonistic intents* between systems with conflicting goals via the "−" notation attached to a bidirectional goal relation. This typically represents a *competition* relation, which may occur via indirect communication or direct negotiation between the systems (also referred to as *contention* in the literature [34]). Finally, we denote the positive or negative impact of a system's goal towards a collective goal via the "+" or "−" notation, respectively, attached to the unidirectional relation between the system and the collective goals and directed towards the collective goal. An arrow in the opposite direction would represent the impact of the collective goal on an individual system goal (not shown).

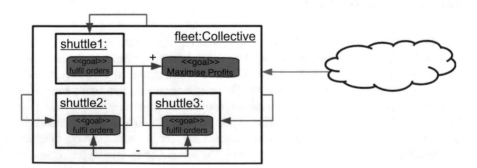

Fig. 7.4 Goals at the individual system level and at the collective level

7.5.1.2 Goal-Oriented Relations

We identify four types of relations based on the positive and negative effects that they have on system goals, namely: (i) *cooperation*, (ii) *competition*, (iii) *parasitism* and (iv) *symbiosis*. A key dimension to consider here is the self-awareness level of the interrelated systems. Therefore, we describe these four relation types for both self-aware (reflective) and pre-reflective cases and illustrate them with examples.

Cooperation denotes that systems help each other to achieve a shared goal. To do this, systems have to have some knowledge about each other—at least if we assume that the systems actively aim for the joint goal. We refer to the case where systems unintentionally operate in a way that leads to a common goal as *emergent cooperation*. In the following, we will use the term cooperation for active cooperation and explicitly indicate emergent cooperation otherwise. In the literature, cooperation is further classified into communicative and non-communicative [10]. The first case covers systems which cooperate by exchanging messages with each other, while the second case denotes systems which merely observe each other's behaviour. Communication may also occur indirectly via observations of changes within a shared environment (i.e. stigmergy). Interestingly, for communicative cooperation, the systems do not need to be aware of each other and of themselves. This is because the cooperation can be encoded into each system's implementation and all systems trust each other. Here, the collective is actually a reactive system.

In case of non-communicative cooperation, systems must feature some awareness of themselves and of the other systems, since the only way to contribute to a shared goal is to analyse the behaviour of cooperators and to plan for corresponding reactions. In more sophisticated cases, cooperating systems may be aware of each other and of their communications (Other-awareness and Interaction-awareness).

Example 7.16 (*Cooperation in the RoboCup Soccer League*) In the kid-size league, teams of four autonomous humanoid robots compete. The relation type between the robots of a team is communicative cooperation as they try to achieve the common goal of winning the game and they can communicate. In contrast, in the small-size league, each team has six robots and a camera to capture the field of play, resulting in non-communicative cooperation among the robots.

Competition occurs in conflicting collectives, where systems pursue conflicting goals. When goals are inherently conflicting, they always end up imposing incompatible actions on shared resources—e.g. different values targeted for a shared resource. Cases may also exist where goals are not inherently in conflict but the strategies the systems select to achieve them may lead to conflicting actions (next subsection). In case of conflicting goals, it is important to differentiate between competition by intent and without intent. The difference lies in the awareness of the competing systems of each other. *Emerging competition* is more likely here, where systems are not aware of each other, but make use of the same resources to achieve their goals. If a system is aware of the other systems and of their goals, then it can either actively compete or engage in negotiations to establish a goal compromise. The former case denotes a special parasitic behaviour of the system, which is actively competing with the others, while being aware of being a parasite. The latter case denotes a special kind of cooperation, as the negotiating systems may share their goals and aim to operate such that each system can achieve its goals. It differs from the cooperation relation discussed above in that the systems do not work together towards a common goal, but towards their own goals. Knowledge exchange between systems may speed up the negotiating process, yet may also be costly in terms of resources and negotiation leverage.

Example 7.17 (*Competition in the RoboCup Soccer League*) Robot teams compete actively, each trying to observe the behaviour of the opposing team; that is, teams are aware of the robots of the other team. Hence, two communicative and actively cooperating collectives form an actively competing super-collective.

Parasitism represents cases where a system uses services of another system to achieve its goals. The difference with cooperation is that systems agree to cooperate to achieve a shared goal, whereas parasitic systems use others without prior consent and possibly in their detriment. Parasitism may be intentional (implying awareness of the other system) or unintentional. Self-awareness can help a collective that contains parasitic systems to reason about their effects and counteract if necessary. If a system uses another, but there is a contract between them, we consider their relation a *negotiated competition*.

Example 7.18 (*Search and Rescue Robots*) In search and rescue scenarios, robots are deployed in the field, each with its own battery. If robots only focus on their goals and do not cooperate, then when a robot uses another robot's battery to charge its own power supply, their relation becomes parasitic.

Finally, **Symbiosis** denotes cases where systems work within a shared environment and have a positive effect on each other, while not pursuing a shared goal. If the positive effect is created on purpose, the systems are related via *negotiated cooperation*. If it is unintentional, the relation denotes an *emergent synergy*.

Example 7.19 (*Symbiosis in Cooperative SLAM*) In simultaneous localisation and mapping (SLAM), robots must jointly create a map of an unknown area—the complete information is aggregated from the partial information collected by each robot. Each robot leaves a (pheromone) trace to avoid remapping the same area; this also benefits other robots, who can also avoid this area.

The relation types identified above are between the goals of systems within a collective. When a self-aware collective has its own goals, the goal-specific relation (a) between each system and the collective and (b) between the relations of systems and the collective must be investigated. A system may have a positive, negative or no effect on the collective goals—of which they may or may not be aware. The collective can also have the same effects on system goals.

7.5.1.3 Goal Decomposition and Emergence

This subsection highlights the architectural considerations on how a system's goals can help or prevent the goal achievement of other systems, or of the entire collective. While the broadness of this topic falls outside the chapter's scope, we mention here briefly how notions of goal decomposition and/or emergence can be used at a generic architectural level to represent and reason about goal interrelations (e.g. [13]). We focus on interrelation between compatible system and collective goals.

Figure 7.5 provides a generic view of how system goals can be interrelated, from an architectural perspective. This view is compatible with the generic notation in Fig. 7.4 and depicts in more detail the semantics of compatible goal relations.

Here, goal decomposition denotes the process of translating and splitting the global goal of a collective into individual goals for each system. This approach can be applied recursively, e.g. through hierarchical systems, to progressively translate higher-level goals into lower-level goals for individual systems and parts. Each system has a set of goals that it aims to achieve, a set of required goals and a set of provided goals. Required goals represent goals that a system needs to obtain from other systems in order to fulfil its own goals. Provided goals are the set of all goals that a system can achieve, either on its own or by relying on required goals (or both). At any time, the system aims to achieve a customised subset of its provided goals, depending on external requests, available resources, environmental context and so on. Each system has to link its required goals to provided goals of other systems. Moreover, a required goal may be indirectly linked to multiple provided goals, which in their composition realise the required goal—via linear composition or emergent goal provisioning.

This straightforward specification of goals allows to compose collective systems by binding required goals of one system to the provided goals of another. Nonetheless, this demands for exact matches between provided and required goals, which is unlikely when systems have not been developed jointly. In consequence, a translation mechanism for the required goals of one system to the provided goals of other

Fig. 7.5 Goal decomposition in collective systems

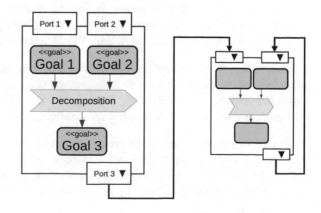

systems is required, via a special-purpose system or part. This translation can be realised: (a) vertically, i.e. lowering the level of abstraction between goals and/or translating their syntax; and/or (b) horizontally, i.e. splitting the domain of the goal. An example for vertical goal decomposition is the translation of the abstract goal of "reduce cost" to the more concrete goal of "reduce execution time on rented virtual machines". The splitting of "maximise energy efficiency of a data centre" to the "maximise energy efficiency of each server within the data centre" is an example for horizontal goal decomposition.

7.5.2 Knowledge

The systems within a collective may have different ways of capturing, representing and reasoning about knowledge of themselves, their parts, their environment and other systems in the collective. In this context, the relation types between systems in a collective describe this knowledge-related aspect. We identify four such relation types: (i) *cooperation*, (ii) *competition*, (iii) *parasitism* and (iv) *ignorance*.

Cooperation denotes systems that assist each other in order to capture and reason about knowledge of the collective and its environment. The systems need to be aware of the type of knowledge that each of them can capture and reason about. The activities related to knowledge capturing and reasoning can be distributed among the cooperative systems. The results of capturing or reasoning of one system may be used by another system to support its capturing and reasoning activities.

Example 7.20 (Smart Home Case Study (Chap. 4)) Washing machines are started at different times depending on their cycles and on the grid load, in order to avoid high costs during consumption peaks. A monitoring system acquires knowledge on power consumption and costs and shares it (cooperates) with a washing machine scheduler to help it decide which cycle to use and when.

Competition occurs between systems in a collective that rival with each other for capturing or reasoning about knowledge. That is, systems may execute incompatible actions on shared resources when capturing and reasoning about knowledge. Also, different systems may acquire knowledge that is inconsistent or incompatible.

Example 7.21 (Thermostat Case Study (Chap. 4)) Several thermometers in a room take different readings, each trying to impose its value as the correct knowledge on room temperature. A processor is introduced to collect all readings, filter outliers and average remaining values to offer more reliable knowledge.

Parasitism occurs when a system uses services or resources of another system to acquire knowledge, reason about knowledge and build models representing the knowledge. This differs from cooperation where the systems agree to work together, since parasitism implies no prior agreement and may be detrimental to its host.

Example 7.22 (Smart Home Case Study (Chap. 4)) Devices in a smart home provide "intelligent reports" about their states and behaviours to the home owners, as well as a global report about the overall power consumption. In this case, the system that produces the overall report uses knowledge from the other devices in the home without necessarily having a previous agreement to make use of the knowledge acquired by the individual systems, i.e. without prior consent.

Ignorance occurs when systems in a collective do not interact with each other by either direct or indirect communication—i.e. they are uncoupled, yet may still be correlated. Hence, there are no direct relations between systems, which are not aware of each other's existence. However, it is still possible to induce or deduce about the existence of other systems by using certain reasoning techniques.

Example 7.23 (Ignorance Between Smart Micro-Grids (Chap. 4)) When smart micro-grids operate in island mode—managing their power autonomously, disconnected from each other and from the main grid—they have an ignorance relation type. The micro-grids do not communicate or influence each other directly in terms of knowledge exchanges or coupled reasoning; they are not aware of each other.

7.5.3 Acting

Based on their goals, knowledge and reasoning, systems in a collective may act differently in order to adapt to internal and external changes. Several relation types correspond to different action-related approaches, of which we identify: (i) *cooperation*, (ii) *competition* and (iii) *ignorance*.

Cooperation occurs when different systems (or their parts) help each other in order to act, in response to internal and external changes. Hence, collective actions form from the actions of cooperating systems; or, the actions of one system are used by another system to support its own actions. Both cases represent a kind of cooperation, where the ability of joint actions is leveraged. This is likely to occur in collectives where individual systems cannot, on their own, perform a task or reach a common goal, but can do so via joint action.

Example 7.24 (Smart Home Case Study (Chap. 4)) When a user sets a temperature goal for a smart home, the thermostats in the home must act together to reach that temperature, since none of them can achieve this alone. They should also coordinate so as to avoid acting in synchrony, in reaction to individually monitored temperatures, which may cause oscillations.

Competition occurs when systems in a collective execute conflicting actions— that is, one system's action is inconsistent with another system's action.

Example 7.25 (Smart Micro-grid (Chap. 4)) A thermostat switches on a heater to reach a temperature; a power manager switches it off to minimise consumption.

Ignorance occurs when systems in a collective act without considering the other systems in the collective. This is most often due to the systems' lack of awareness of each other's existence. Nonetheless, it may also occur between systems that are fully aware of each other, as well as of the mutual consequences of their actions. This may occur when each system's short-term benefits take precedence over the long-term sustainability of the collective, of other systems and even of the acting systems themselves. This can lead to a phenomenon known as "the tragedy of the commons" [15], where the members of a collective, who make use of a shared resource (i.e. a "commons"), individually act to maximise their benefit, but neglect the cumulated effects of all systems and thus minimise the benefit for all members including themselves over the longer term.

Example 7.26 (*Smart Micro-grid (Chap.* 4)) Smart homes do not know about, or may chose to ignore, the other smart homes in the grid. Here, the commons is the shared energy storage of the neighbourhood. If smart homes do not consider the others, in a peak situation when all participants require energy, but the storage capacity is insufficient for all, energy has to be bought from the public power grid, where the costs are shared among all homes. Hence, due to neglecting the demand of other homes, all homes have to pay for the bought energy. If the homes took each other's demands into account, they could schedule their demands to avoid peaks.

7.6 Organisation Patterns

7.6.1 Overview of Organisation Patterns

The *organisation pattern* of a collective of systems defines the generic roles and links among the systems within the collective. No particular assumption is made about the systems' self-awareness levels (Sect. 7.4) or relation types (Sect. 7.5). Also, the organisation pattern does not include any concrete or detailed specification of the systems' behaviours or communication protocols. At the same time, each organisation pattern does feature some generic characteristics, which will, to a certain extent, impact the global behaviour and non-functional properties of the collective.

Several distinctive types of organisation patterns (or design patterns for collectives of systems) can be identified across most domains that deal with system composition. These include hierarchical patterns, peer-to-peer patterns and stigmergic patterns, e.g. [12, 13, 16, 36]. These patterns can be integrated into hybrid designs via two main approaches—by "flat" composition and by embedding. We discuss these briefly below, focusing on their relevance to collectives of self-aware systems and analysing their compatibility with the previous two architectural concerns identified in this chapter—i.e. system self-awareness levels and relation types.

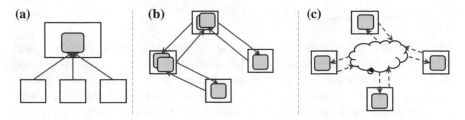

Fig. 7.6 System organisation patterns: **a** Hierarchical; **b** Peer-to-peer; and **c** Stigmergic collective

Each organisation pattern is described with respect to three main concerns:

- *Structure*: the shape specificities of the systems interlinked in a collective;
- *Abstraction level*: the level of granularity of each system's knowledge;
- *Authority level*: the relative ascendancy of each system with respect to the others.

Many other design patterns can apply to collectives of self-aware computing systems, besides the ones discussed here, including various forms of coalitions, teams, congregations, societies, federations, marketplaces, matrices or compounds, as defined for instance in the multiagent systems (MAS) literature [16] (Fig. 7.6).

7.6.2   Hierarchical Collective

7.6.2.1   Overview

A *hierarchical collective* is a multilevel organisation, where systems at different levels are distinguished in at least one of the following ways:

- higher systems detain knowledge over *larger scopes* than lower systems;
- higher systems detain knowledge that is *more abstract* than lower systems;
- higher systems detain *more authority* than lower systems.

In most hierarchical systems, these three characteristics occur simultaneously. However, various combinations of these factors are also possible. Structurewise, hierarchical collectives are shaped as either trees or acyclic graphs. They can be designed via all structural alternatives presented in Sect. 7.2: UML hierarchies (with or without component sharing and with or without encapsulation) or UML collaborations. The notions associated here with hierarchical collectives—i.e. larger scope, higher abstraction and more authority—are both orthogonal and complementary to the structures selected to implement them—i.e. UML hierarchy or UML collaboration. Typically, however, in UML hierarchies, the systems that embed other systems will hold more abstract knowledge, with larger scopes, and more authority compared to the systems they contain. Similarly, in UML collectives with tree structures, the same will apply to systems closer to the tree root, as compared to systems farther from the root.

7.6.2.2 Generic Characteristics

The main advantage of hierarchical collectives lies in the opportunity, via the higher-level systems, for efficient optimisation of global behaviour, based on a global view of the collective problem and application context and/or on a central point of coordination and control. The main disadvantage relates to issues of robustness, like single point of failure, and of scalability, with respect to the size and update frequency of global knowledge maintained, and the number of events processed.

7.6.2.3 Examples and Compatibility with the Other Architectural Concerns

The hierarchy pattern applies to collectives featuring cooperation, parasitism and competition relations. The roles of systems at different hierarchical levels depend on these relations.

Within a hierarchical *cooperation*, the role of higher-level systems is to help coordinate the activities of lower-level systems. They can achieve this by accumulating knowledge about the lower-level systems, like an overall model of the collective, and providing each system with action directives. This knowledge only needs to be detailed in so far as necessary for coordinating the systems to achieve the collective goal(s). Hence, it may be more abstract than the knowledge that systems at the same level have on each other. The extent of a higher system's authority over lower systems is application-specific. Directives may range from strict orders (high authority) to recommendations and simple informative reports (weak authority).

Example 7.27 (Smart Home Case Study (Chap. 4)—Hierarchical Cooperation) A hierarchical organisation helps coordinate device usage within a house in order to avoid power consumption peaks. A central coordinator maintains an overall model of device consumption requirements (abstract knowledge with larger scope), plans consumption schedules and sends directives to devices (higher authority).

Within a hierarchical *competition*, the role of higher-level systems is to implement conflict-resolution among lower-level systems.

Example 7.28 (Smart Grid Case Study (Chap. 4)—Hierarchical Competition) Houses interconnected in a smart grid compete for limited power consumption or for selling their production. A higher-level system regulates power prices based on an overall model of predicted power consumptions and productions (abstract knowledge, with larger scope and no direct authority over the houses' behaviour)—e.g. PowerMatcher [20] and DEZENT [35].

In hierarchical *parasitism*, higher systems use lower systems without accord.

Example 7.29 (Service-Oriented Systems—Hierarchical Parasitism) A service orchestrator selects and coordinates services available via a network in order to provide new composed services, e.g. [23] or [1]. The orchestrator acquires knowledge about the services it uses (abstract knowledge with larger scope), plans their coordination and dictates their execution (higher authority).

By its very nature, hierarchical collectives are incompatible with cases where systems in the collective ignore each other—i.e. via an *ignorance* relation.

7.6.2.4 Sample Usage in Related Areas

The hierarchy pattern has been widely employed across many computing domains related to distributed control, adaptation, planning and so on. Considering our cyber-physical use case in Chap. 4, we can exemplify several contributions that use the hierarchy pattern to integrate smart devices and homes into viable smart grids. In the organic home [2] or in [26], a global house controller acquires knowledge about smart devices (i.e. larger scope), builds an overall model (i.e. more abstract), reasons and sends scheduling directives to devices (i.e. higher authority) [28] and extends this approach to multilevel hierarchies, where higher levels schedule resources for lower levels. Similarly, PowerMatcher [21] uses recursive hierarchies where higher-level aggregators collect bids from lower-level prosumers (i.e. larger scopes and more abstraction) to compute and regulate energy prices (i.e. higher authority). Finally, approaches such as [31] propose to adapt the number of hierarchy layers dynamically, to limit induced overheads depending on the system scale.

7.6.3 Peer-to-Peer Collective

7.6.3.1 Overview

A *peer-to-peer (P2P) collective* consists of systems that are interconnected and has none of the systems play any particular role with respect to the others—with respect to neither authority nor more abstract knowledge over larger scopes. The only constraint on the collective structure is that systems be interconnected directly, i.e. form a connected graph. Each system in a P2P collective may feature different kinds or levels of self-awareness. At the same time, none of the systems is constrained to maintain self-awareness of the entire collective (even if this situation may occur).

7.6.3.2 Generic Characteristics

The decentralisation characteristic of the P2P pattern confers both its advantages, such as robustness and scalability, and its disadvantages, such as latency, difficulty to reach globally optimum solutions with respect to their collective goal(s) or the risk to generate unstable behaviours such as overshoots and oscillations.

7.6.3.3 Examples and Compatibility with the Other Architectural Concerns

The P2P pattern applies to collectives featuring cooperation, parasitism and competition relations.

Example 7.30 (Smart Home Case Study (Chap. 4)—P2P Cooperation) Several heaters communicate to desynchronise their consumption cycles and avoid peaks—e.g. [3]. Self-aware heaters also observe and predict each other's cycles and shift their cycles accordingly without requiring explicit inter-peer communication.

Example 7.31 (Smart Grid Case Study (Chap. 4)—P2P Competition) Smart houses negotiate power sharing and prices directly. Self-aware houses evaluate other houses' trustworthiness, prosumption behaviours or bidding strategies and adapt their techniques in order to minimise their costs (individual goals), while abiding by the collective prosumption constraints (collective goals).

Example 7.32 (Service-Oriented Systems—P2P Parasitism) In some service-oriented technologies, such as Spring[5] and iPOJO,[6] services can find and connect to required services dynamically. Self-aware services can assess the capabilities and reputation of other services, so as to optimise their service choices and hence the services they provide (individual goals). This, in turn, contributes to optimising the services of the entire collective (collective goals), e.g. [5].

Since the P2P pattern implies system interconnections within the collective, it does not apply to collectives of systems that ignore each other (*ignorance* relation).

7.6.3.4 Sample Usage in Related Areas

Considering the cyber-physical use case in Chap. 4, P2P patterns have been employed to implement decentralised multiagent negotiations, such as ContractNet protocol [18] and auction markets [7], or agent games, like the approach in [25].

7.6.4 Stigmergic Collective

7.6.4.1 Overview

A *stigmergic*[7] *collective* consists of systems that do *not* communicate with each other directly but may influence each other indirectly via a shared environment. They may

---

[5]https://spring.io/.

[6]https://felix.apache.org/documentation/subprojects/apache-felix-ipojo.html.

[7]"Stigmergy"—a nature-inspired mechanism for *indirect* coordination among agents or actions. It is achieved by each agent leaving cues, or marks, in a shared environment and reacting to observed

become aware indirectly of each other's existence and adapt their actions accordingly. The collective's structure is only characterised by the lack of direct system interconnections, with no restrictions on system authority or abstraction levels.

7.6.4.2 Generic Characteristics

The advantages of the stigmergic pattern stem from both its decentralisation and lack of direct system communication. In the case of open, dynamic and highly heterogeneous collectives, this pattern circumvents communication compatibility mismatches among systems, since each one only needs to communicate with its environment. As with the P2P pattern, decentralisation helps with robustness and scalability and impedes on the efficiency of global optimisation or stable behaviour.

7.6.4.3 Examples and Compatibility with the Other Architectural Concerns

The stigmergy pattern can occur in cooperative, parasitic and competitive collectives, as well as when systems ignore each other. Depending on their relations, system reactions to changes in the environment can contribute to a shared goal (cooperation), serve another system's goal (parasitism) or conflict with other system goals (competition). When systems ignore each other, they do not observe or react to the other systems' effects on the environment.

Example 7.33 (Smart Home Case Study (Chap. 4)—Stigmergic Cooperation) All heaters aim to achieve a house temperature (collective goal). Each can impact the house temperature (shared environment) and hence influence each other's actions indirectly. Pre-reflective heaters simply react to temperature fluctuations. Self-aware heaters plan their actions based on the predictions of others' behaviour, e.g. to avoid cycle overlaps and temperature overshoots.

Example 7.34 (Smart Home Case Study (Chap. 4)—Stigmergic Competition) Home devices must achieve their respective goals by consuming power from a shared battery. When they observe the battery running low, they speed up their actions to achieve goals before the battery is depleted. If all devices act in this manner, none of them may complete their goals (tragedy of the commons).

Example 7.35 (Smart Home Case Study (Chap. 4)—Stigmergic Parasitism) A heater aims to achieve a temperature in its room (individual goal). It takes advantage of heaters placed in adjacent rooms, which must also achieve their temperature goals, relying on heat transfers across walls and openings. This impacts negatively other

---

(Footnote 7 continued)
accumulated effect of such marks in the environment. Marks can be actual environment modifications, e.g. carvings to form a trail (sematectonic stigmergy), or of signals left in the environment, e.g. pheromone trails (sign-based stigmergy).

heaters' power goals, since they consume more. If a self-aware heater can predict this phenomenon, it may even plan its passivity.

Finally, the stigmergic pattern applies naturally to systems that ignore each other.

7.6.4.4 Sample Usage in Related Areas

Again considering the cyber-physical use case, the stigmergy pattern has been employed for instance in [6, 17] or [3] to determine overall grid loads by observing current frequency. These readings represent the global grid state based on an aggregation of individual prosumptions. Hence, they enable smart devices to react and adapt their prosumption schedules in order to balance global prosumption.

7.6.5 Pattern Composition and Encapsulation

The patterns discussed above can be integrated, via either *composition* or *encapsulation*, to form hybrid designs (within a single collective or a collective of collectives).

In pattern **composition**, some systems must play multiple roles, one for each pattern that they belong to (e.g. [14]). For instance, the hierarchical pattern can be composed with both the P2P and the stigmergic patterns. Here, the hierarchy's "higher-level" system is added to coordinate "lower-level" systems organised as a stigmergic or P2P collectives. Conversely, the higher-level systems of several hierarchies can be organised as a stigmergic or P2P collective. Hybrid designs can capitalise on the advantages of all patterns combined, while avoiding their respective deficiencies.

Example 7.36 (*Smart Home Case Study (Chap. 4)—Composition of Hierarchy with P2P or Stigmergy*) A high-level system coordinates the activities of devices (hierarchy), which negotiate or react to each others' actions (P2P or stigmergy).

Example 7.37 (*Smart Home Case Study (Chap. 4)—Composition of Stigmergy with P2P*) All heaters within a room cooperate via direct communication (P2P) to reach the room temperature. Heaters in different rooms react to each other's influences on global house temperature (stigmergy).

Interesting questions can be raised here with respect to the self-awareness of systems that belong to different patterns simultaneously, including the different types of relations they may entertain with different systems, exercising different roles (Fig. 7.7).

In pattern **encapsulation**, systems are included within super-systems, recursively. Each lower-level pattern is encapsulated within one role of a higher-level pattern (e.g. [14]). This approach has also been identified as "holonic" systems in domains dealing with system complexity—e.g. [30] for complex systems in general, [19] focusing on

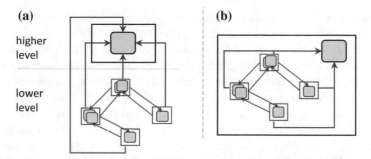

Fig. 7.7 Integration example between Hierarchy and P2P, by: **a** composition; **b** encapsulation

humans and society, [33] for engineering self-adaptive and self-organising systems, [11] and [27] for multiagent systems, [32] for manufacturing, [13] for smart grids, [9] for commons management and [4] for systems of systems.

A higher-level pattern mediates external access to the lower-level patterns it encapsulates, hence impacting their visibility and controllability from the outside (i.e. black-box or grey-box approach). This differs from pattern composition (discussed earlier) where all systems could be observed and accessed directly from any entity within or without pattern composition. Encapsulation implies that external systems cannot really be aware of encapsulated systems and can only speculate about their presence from external observations. This can help address complexity issues (via abstraction) and privacy concerns (e.g. smart homes are managed by a higher-level smart grid, but most devices within each home should be neither visible nor controllable directly from outside the house).

7.7 Developing the Architecture of Collective Self-aware Systems

This section focuses on how to use the architectural aspects discussed so far for developing and maintaining self-aware collectives. We first highlight combinations of meta-architectural aspects that lead to viable architectures. Then, we set the basis of a methodology for navigating the meta-architectural space in order to select valid architectures when developing and evolving self-aware collectives.

7.7.1 Viable Architectures

The meta-architecture introduced in Sect. 7.1.3 comprises three dimensions of variability: system *self-awareness levels* (pre-reflective, self-aware and meta-self-aware—Sect. 7.4); relation types (cooperation, competition, parasitism, symbiosis and ignorance—Sect. 7.5); and organisation patterns (hierarchy, peer-to-peer and stigmergy, which can be composed or encapsulated—Sect. 7.6).

Yet, not all combinations of the choices above lead to a viable architecture. Table 7.2 offers a first attempt to identify such valid combinations. Each row denotes a relation type and each column an organisational pattern among the systems of a self-aware collective. Cells indicate the minimum self-awareness level that is required from the systems to get a viable combination. When this level is "self-aware" we also specify its domain—i.e. span and scope (Chap. 3), where the span denotes *who* is self-aware, and the scope *what* part of the world the self-aware system is aware of. Since any self-aware system has (at least parts of) its *self* in both its span and scope we do not repeat this information in the table.

Notably, we assume that systems do *not* ignore each other, meaning that they explicitly intend to cooperate, compete or be parasitic towards each other. When systems *do* ignore each other, being unaware of each other's existence, the minimum self-awareness level for all systems is pre-reflective (not shown in the table).

Finally, several relation types may occur within an organisation, or a composed organisation, and hence require different self-awareness levels and domains for the systems involved and the roles they play. For instance, in a hierarchy composed with a P2P organisation, a system may compete with the systems at the same level (i.e. its peers) and cooperate with systems at the superior level (i.e. parent systems). Since this occurs quite frequently in real systems, we use this organisation composition when referring to the hierarchy in the table.

Let us now analyse the various table values. If a system *competes* with other systems in a collective that is organised in a hierarchy, then competition typically occurs among the systems situated at the same hierarchical level (i.e. peers). To actively compete, a system needs to be aware of itself and of all the peers it competes with. It is also possible that a parent system competes with its children, in which case the collective goals may suffer, while individual ones better represented. In more subtle cases, child systems cooperate only partially with the parent, in order to reach a compromise between the collective goal and their own goals. Similarly, in P2P organisations, a competing system must be aware of itself and of all the peer systems it competes with. Finally, for a stigmergic collective, a competing system must be aware of its environment in order to observe whether and how other

Table 7.2 Minimal levels of self-awareness per relation type and organisation pattern

	Hierarchy	Peer-to-peer	Stigmergy
Competition	*Self-aware* incl. peers	*Self-aware* incl. peers	*Context-aware*
Parasitism	*Self-aware* incl. children	*Self-aware* incl. peers	*Meta-self-aware*
Cooperation	*Self-aware* incl. peers or children	*Self-aware* incl. peers	*Context-aware*
Synergy	*Self-aware* incl. partners	*Self-aware* incl. partners	*Meta-self-aware*

systems impact it—e.g. monitor the shared resource they compete for. Additionally, systems in stigmergic organisations may highly benefit from meta-self-awareness capabilities, to interpret their observations of the environment as behavioural effects from other self-aware systems and to adjust their competing strategies.

If a system behaves *parasitically* towards others in a hierarchical collective, then the parasitic system is likely to be a parent system (due to the higher authority and/or knowledge) with its hosts being its children. To actively be parasitic, the system must be aware of itself and its hosts. The same holds for P2P organisations, where the hosts are the peers of the parasitic system. In stigmergic collectives, active parasitism requires the system to be meta-self-aware because of the lack of direct communication. The parasitic system has to make indirect use of its host, by learning and reasoning about itself, about the environment and about how the host reacts to changes in the environment imposed by the parasite. Unintended parasitism is also possible and only requires context awareness. However, the parasite cannot easily adapt to its host to continue to take advantage of it when it changes.

For an active *cooperation* between systems in a hierarchical collective, a system must be aware of itself and of either its peers—on the same level, if it cooperates with them—or its children—if it coordinates them to achieve cooperation. In P2P collectives, the same holds for the peer systems. In stigmergic collectives, no direct cooperation is possible, as there is no direct communication. Indirect cooperation can be achieved if systems are context-aware and can determine the correlation between their cooperative behaviour and beneficial changes in the environment. This can happen if systems share a pool of resources, become aware of this fact and proactively try to minimise their resource demands. Systems can benefit from meta-self-awareness to correlate changes in the environment with cooperative behaviour from other self-aware systems, which it cannot observe directly.

Finally, for *synergetic* relations of systems in a hierarchical collective, systems must be aware of themselves and of their partner systems. The same holds for P2P collectives. For stigmergic collectives, all systems must be meta-self-aware.

7.7.2 Navigating the Meta-Architectural Space

This subsection aims to set a methodological basis to help system designers navigate through the meta-architectural space (cf. Sect. 7.1.3). Two cases are distinguished here. Firstly, a new system is designed from scratch. Here, we highlight aspects that architects may consider so that the system architecture reaches a specific area in the meta-architectural space. Secondly, architects may wish to evolve an existing self-aware system and have its architecture transit to a different location in the meta-architectural space. Here, we propose a simple process and highlight necessary system changes and desirable areas within the meta-architectural space.

7.7.2.1   Designing New Collective Systems

When conceiving a new system, one has to first establish the main characteristics of the system's architecture. The main objective here is to reach an area of viable architectures within the meta-architectural space (as discussed in Sect. 7.7.1), which is also compatible with the system's high-level requirements.

This initial proposal does not have the ambition to cover all possible criteria, but rather to offer a general indication on how to approach this vast problem. Therefore, we consider each meta-architectural dimension and provide several examples illustrating possible architectural choices for this dimension. Certainly, these choices cannot be taken in separation for each dimension, but must be considered together and adapted to each other as discussed previously. Hence, for some of the examples, we also provide some correlation hints with choices for other dimensions.

Criteria for *Relation Types*

When it comes to designing a new collective of systems, the architect must consider how systems interact with respect to available resources and services. We can distinguish between collectives where systems try to achieve their own goals and collectives operating towards a common goal.

When a collective uses a common resource pool but each system pursues its own goals, each system may self-govern and aim to optimise its goals over a short term. In this case, new system(s) should be designed to compete with other systems (e.g. a fleet of electrical vehicles that rely on a shared set of charging stations).

When the new system must use services of others to achieve its goals, it must support parasitism, negotiated competition and/or cooperation relations (e.g. a new thermostat in a smart home must use readings from thermometers and act on temperature-impacting devices, such as heaters, air conditioners or windows).

When the targeted collective has a global goal that aims to use common resources optimally in the long run, the new system should be designed to cooperate. If systems belong to different authorities, then the cooperation should be designed so as to find suitable compromises between system goals and the collective goal (e.g. sustainability and fairness)—e.g. electric cars in a fleet may agree to not charge their batteries completely in case of a power shortage, or to allow emergency vehicles to charge first. If all systems belong to the same authority, as may be the case of smart devices joining a smart house, then the cooperation may be designed to prioritise individual or collective goals, at different times, as specified by inhabitants.

Finally, collectives may require that systems support several relation types simultaneously—e.g. cars in a fleet cooperate while competing with cars from other fleets. In advanced cases, a system may even have to switch between relation types, depending on feedback from the environment and/or from other systems. This aspect is heavily related to the system's level of self-awareness, as discussed elsewhere.

Criteria for *Organisation Patterns*

When considering organisation patterns for collectives, the architect is mostly concerned about how systems in the collective are governed and coordinated. The governing authority may belong to the collective, or be external to it.

If the collective belongs to a single authority, then the activities of several systems might need to be coordinated in order to achieve a collective goal, or a compromise among several goals (e.g. coordinating all smart devices within a smart home). Here, a hierarchy organisation can be applied—the architect designs new systems to obey the directives of the high-level governing system. This situation can also impact the requirements on the system's self-awareness level, as discussed elsewhere.

Alternatively, each system governs itself. When systems communicate directly and have the same status (in terms of authority and/or self-awareness levels), they should operate in a P2P manner. When they communicate indirectly, the stigmergy pattern can be applied and new systems enabled with environment-awareness, at a minimum (e.g. a wide range of electric devices switch on and off depending on the power grid's load to help handle prosumption peaks [3]). When the impacts of other systems in the environment are not known, new systems should feature increased levels of (meta-)self-awareness, to determine such knowledge at run-time.

Finally, the new systems may have to be controllable by an external entity while also collaborating with peer systems, directly or indirectly. For instance, a new system joins several organisations at once, including hierarchy, P2P and stigmergy—e.g. a thermostat controlled by a central power manager (hierarchy) negotiates power consumption schedules directly with other devices (P2P) and cooperates indirectly with other thermostats, via the ambient temperature (stigmergy).

Criteria for *Self-awareness Levels*

Designing a collective with a certain self-awareness level can be challenging. It does not always require that all systems possess the corresponding level of self-awareness. Heterogeneous collectives, with systems that have different self-awareness levels, can be highly advantageous.

If the collective has to be Context-aware, Other-aware and/or Interaction-aware (Sect. 7.3.2) with respect to external systems and collectives, the architect must ensure that the systems within the collective possesses the necessary self-awareness levels, kinds and scopes (e.g. Sect. 7.3.3); namely, systems must be Context-aware as well as Collective-aware to differentiate between systems within and without the collective. If these self-awareness functions are to be provided collectively, then the systems must also be designed to support information exchanges (e.g. hierarchical or P2P organisations with cooperation relations and collective goals).

If the architect designs a collective that must be reflective with respect to its internal systems and their interconnections, then (at least some of) the systems should be reflective (with respect to their internal resources) and Interaction-aware (with respect to the other systems). If some of the systems are pre-reflective, then they should be included in the self-awareness scopes of reflective systems.

Collectives that must adapt to dynamic environments, or internal changes, must feature Time-awareness capabilities and be able to track the occurrence of events and actions that may trigger various timers. One solution is to have some of the systems endowed with time-awareness and offer time-related services to other systems (e.g. cooperation or parasitic relations within hierarchy or P2P organisations).

When the validity of a collective depends on its overall state, State-awareness at the collective level may be needed. As before, this can be achieved by endowing all systems with self-reflective capabilities, or having only part of them implement such functions and containing the others in their self-awareness scopes. To obtain the overall collective state, systems may share and merge their local states with each other (cooperation within a P2P organisation), via a centralised entity (hierarchical organisation), or the environment (stigmergy). Combining State-awareness with Time- and Interaction-awareness, the collective may be able to further improve its performance in dynamic environments. This allows systems to react and adapt to actions of other systems in the collective or the environment. In addition, having an understanding of its own actions and impact on internal states and the environment enables a system to reason about its actions a priori and adapt its behaviour.

In some cases, the system has to fulfil multiple, possibly opposing, goals in a highly dynamic environment. Here, it can be beneficial to switch between pursued goals, based on the current collective state and/or the environment. To achieve this, Goal-awareness is required for the collective. A system is able to reason about its current progress towards the goals and to select a goal based on the current state of the collective or the environment. Goal-awareness at the system level (for both themselves and other systems) and of the overall collective may also be useful here.

7.7.2.2   Architectural Transition of Collective Systems

Before delving into this subsection's main topic, we would like to direct the reader's attention to a related Chap. 10, where we discuss how self-awareness can be introduced into existing pre-reflective systems and how self-awareness levels can be increased within reflective systems.

Several phases must be considered when aiming to change the architecture of a collective of self-aware systems. Initially, the current architecture must be analysed and the undesirable shortcomings identified. Next, if limitations can be related to architectural choices, then one must determine the alternatives that would help alleviate them, and carefully consider any new limitations that they may introduce. Architectural changes along one meta-architectural dimension, such as the relation type, may require corresponding changes in the choices made for other dimensions, like the type of organisation and self-awareness levels. Such architectural translation should lead to a new valid architecture within the meta-architectural space.

Furthermore, one should also aim to predict the impacts of the architectural updates on the system requirements and qualities. Before performing the analysis task, a feasibility study should be conducted to determine what needs to be achieved by the collective after the architectural changes. Moreover, the architect has to ensure that there are sufficient resources for performing the actual transition. Finally, this feasibility study has to look into the trade-offs arising between the invested resources, the expected gains and the risks. Only if the analysis produces a positive evaluation should the architect proceed with the next transition step.

Once a new architecture is identified, one must consider how to transfer between the existing architecture and the targeted one. In simple cases, this process can be straightforward—the current collective is interrupted, discontinued and replaced with the new one. In more realistic cases, this transition would have to be progressive, while the collective of systems is still functioning. Here, the transition must be considered carefully and the acceptability of the intermediate states established. Several paths may be possible through the meta-architectural space, linking the current architecture to the new one. The viability of these paths in terms of transfer costs (e.g. time and resources) and risks (e.g. reaching invalid states) must be evaluated. In some cases, even if a targeted architecture would offer several benefits when compared to an existing one, it may be impossible to ensure a smooth transfer path leading to this new collective state (e.g. all transitions pass by a non-viable area).

When the new architecture is achieved, the ensuing characteristics and behaviour of the resulting collective should be evaluated. The architect verifies that the system performs as expected and meets its requirements. This step is similar to the current-state analysis. Failure of the updated collective to meet expectations may trigger another transition process, which may or may not be able to roll back to a previous architecture or to find a more suitable one. Chapter 15 provides an overview on how to measure the self-awareness of a running system.

Transition of Self-awareness Levels

Constraints are often imposed by the capabilities of systems in the collective. For example, if none of the systems provides any communication interfaces, they will be unable to interact with other systems, and hence, it is not possible to achieve Interaction-awareness within the collective, nor with respect to external systems.

Benefits and Risks are at stake when increasing or reducing system self-awareness levels. Reducing self-awareness risks loosing key capabilities that the systems require to achieve collective goals. At the same time, it might also diminish collective complexity, hence facilitating its analysis and maintenance.

Transition of Relation Types

Constraints on viable relations depend on the system-level and collective-level goals, on how knowledge is generated and shared within the collective, and on how decisions and actions are performed throughout the collective. Some relation types are more or less suitable for achieving these aspects. For instance, a collective goal can be difficult to achieve when most systems implement parasitic relations that only serve their own goals. Similarly, collective-level-state knowledge is difficult to achieve whether systems with local state-awareness do not cooperate to share knowledge.

Benefits and Risks when changing relation types depends highly on the systems' goals. As mentioned earlier, certain relations may appear more suitable than others for achieving certain objectives within a context. Nonetheless, considering the uncertainties of systems (especially of self-aware systems of unknown provenance) and of the environment, there is a risk that a promising relation will not provide the expected result and perhaps even worsen the situation. This may be further complicated for run-time transitions where a mixture of old and new relations may destabilise the collective.

Transition of Organisation Patterns

Constraints on organisation patterns are often imposed externally, such as by company regulations in industrial systems. Environmental constraints may also be present. For example, if a collective must supervise a wide area with a large numbers of highly dynamic targets, then centralised organisations, such as wide-scope hierarchies, may be infeasible. The same applies when high robustness and resilience are required, as centralised entities introduce bottlenecks and single points of failure and limit adaptation.

Benefits and Risks may include, on the benefits side, an increase in processing capabilities, a decrease in complexity of the decision process, higher flexibility, faster deployment, better scalability and robustness; and, on the risks side, the opposite aspects, including higher complexity, diminished performance in terms of goal optimisation or adaptation speed, decreased scalability and diminished robustness. The trade-offs between these must be considered carefully, case by case. As discussed earlier, a major additional risk lies in the transfer process between current and targeted organisations, especially when performed online.

7.8   Conclusions

This chapter aimed to bring to the fore the main architectural concerns related to collectives of self-aware systems. It first defined the notion of *collective of self-aware systems*, based on individual systems which are correlated or coupled via UML hierarchy or UML collaboration interconnections. It then discussed the various kinds of self-awareness that can occur at the collective level based on the self-awareness of individual systems and their knowledge exchanges.

The chapter then identified higher-level architectural concerns related to collectives of self-aware systems and their interconnections, notably *self-awareness levels*, *relation types* and *organisation patterns*. These three architectural dimensions were brought together to define a generic *meta-architecture* for collectives of self-aware systems, defining a broad space of possibilities for concrete architectures to be explored. Each dimension was discussed separately and illustrated via examples from the cyber-physical domain. The most likely areas of the meta-architectural space from which viable architectures can be instantiated were also discussed, and an associated methodology for navigating through this space in search of such viable area was proposed.

Since collectives of self-aware computing systems have not yet been built on an extensive scale, the content of this chapter could not be based on previous experience in this domain. Instead, we relied on identifying reoccurring architectural concepts across related domains, such as autonomic and organic computing, artificial intelligence, multiagent systems, self-adaptive and self-organising systems. We then discussed why and how similar architectural concepts would most likely also apply to collectives of self-aware systems and identified the main considerations to be taken into account in this particular case.

The outcome of this chapter should provide an initial and rather abstract base for exploration and validation of concrete architectures for collectives of self-aware computing systems. Future experiments and results with concrete designs will then confirm, refine or even contradict the various aspects of the initial generic meta-architecture described here. Yet, if the present proposal can help offer a generic background of existing architectural considerations, which may help to start off such exploration, even if consequently proven somewhat inaccurate by obtained results, then it would have largely fulfilled its intended purpose.

We hope that this chapter provides a base for future explorations which will help address some of these major questions within this vast research domain.

References

1. M. Aiello, R. Baldoni, A. Lazovik, and M. Mecella. *Self-Steering and Aware Homes*, chapter 7, pages 105–116. IMPERIAL COLLEGE PRESS, 2014.
2. F. Allerding and H. Schmeck. Organic smart home: Architecture for energy management in intelligent buildings. In *Proceedings of the 2011 Workshop on Organic Computing*, OC '11, pages 67–76, New York, NY, USA, 2011. ACM.
3. J. Beal, J. Berliner, and K. Hunter. Fast precise distributed control for energy demand management. *IEEE 7th Intl Cnf on Self-Adaptive and Self-Organizing Systems*, 0:187–192, 2012.
4. G. Blair, Y.-D. Bromberg, G. Coulson, Y. Elkhatib, L. Réveillère, H. B. Ribeiro, E. Rivière, and F. Taïani. Holons: Towards a systematic approach to composing systems of systems. In *Proceedings of the 14th International Workshop on Adaptive and Reflective Middleware*, ARM 2015, pages 5:1–5:6, New York, NY, USA, 2015. ACM.
5. Giacomo Cabri and Franco Zambonelli. *Towards Self-Aware and Self-Composing Services*, chapter 2, pages 21–36. IMPERIAL COLLEGE PRESS, 2014.
6. D. Callaway and I. Hiskens. Achieving controllability of electric loads. *Proc. of the IEEE*, 99(1), 2011.
7. Y. Cheng. Architecture and principles of smart grids for distributed power generation and demand side management. In *Int. Conf. on Smart Cities and Green ICT Systems (SMART-GREENS)*, 2012.
8. G. Di Marzo Serugendo, M.-P. Gleizes, and A. Karageorgos, editors. *Self-organising Software*. Natural Computing Series. Springer Berlin Heidelberg, Berlin, 2011.
9. A. Diaconescu and J. Pitt. *Coordination, Organizations, Institutions, and Norms in Agent Systems X: COIN 2014 International Workshops, COIN@AAMAS, Paris, France, May 6, 2014, COIN@PRICAI, Gold Coast, QLD, Australia, December 4, 2014, Revised Selected Papers*, chapter Holonic Institutions for Multi-scale Polycentric Self-governance, pages 19–35. Springer International Publishing, Cham, 2015.
10. Jim E Doran, SRJN Franklin, Nicholas R Jennings, and Timothy J Norman. On cooperation in multi-agent systems. *The Knowledge Engineering Review*, 12(03):309–314, 1997.
11. K. Fischer. Holonic multiagent systems theory and applications. In Pedro Barahona and JosJ. Alferes, editors, *Progress in Artificial Intelligence*, volume 1695 of *LNCS*, pages 34–48. Springer Berlin Heidelberg, 1999.

12. Sylvain Frey, Ada Diaconescu, and Isabelle Demeure. Architectural integration patterns for autonomic management systems. In *Engineering of Autonomic and Autonomous Systems (EASe'12), 2012 9th IEEE Conference on*, 2012.

13. Sylvain Frey, Ada Diaconescu, David Menga, and Isabelle Demeure. A generic holonic control architecture for heterogeneous multiscale and multiobjective smart microgrids. *ACM Trans. Auton. Adapt. Syst.*, 10(2):9:1–9:21, June 2015.

14. D. Garlan and M. Shaw. An introduction to software architecture. Technical report, Pittsburgh, USA, 1994.

15. Garrett Hardin. The tragedy of the commons. *Science*, 162(3859):1243–1248, 1968.

16. Bryan Horling and Victor Lesser. A survey of multi-agent organizational paradigms. *The Knowledge Engineering Review*, pages 281–316, 2005.

17. N. Jaleeli, L. S. VanSlyck, D.N. Ewart, L.H. Fink, and AG. Hoffmann. Understanding automatic generation control. *Power Systems, IEEE Transactions on*, 7(3):1106–1122, Aug 1992.

18. H.-M. Kim, W. Wei, and T. Kinoshita. A new modified cnp for autonomous microgrid operation based on multiagent system. *Journal of Electrical Engineering and Technology 6-1*, 2011.

19. A. Koestler. The ghost in the machine. 1967.

20. J. K. Kok, C. J. Warmer, and I. G. Kamphuis. PowerMatcher: multiagent control in the electricity infrastructure. In *Proceedings of the fourth international joint conference on Autonomous agents and multiagent systems*, AAMAS '05, pages 75–82, New York, NY, USA, 2005. ACM.

21. J. K. Kok, C. J. Warmer, and I. G. Kamphuis. Powermatcher: Multiagent control in the electricity infrastructure. In *Proc. of the 4th Int. Conf. on Autonomous Agents and Multiagent Systems*, AAMAS'05, pages 75–82, New York, NY, USA, 2005. ACM.

22. Peter R. Lewis, Arjun Chandra, Funmilade Faniyi, Kyrre Glette, Tao Chen, Rami Bahsoon, Jim Torresen, and Xin Yao. Architectural aspects of self-aware and self-expressive systems: From psychology to engineering. *Computer*, 48(8), August 2015.

23. J. Michaux, E. Najm, and A. Fantechi. Session types for safe web service orchestration. *The Journal of Logic and Algebraic Programming*, 82(8):282–310, 2013.

24. M. Mitchell. Self-awareness and control in decentralized systems (Tech Report SS-05-04). In *AAAI Spring Symposium on Metacognition in Computation*, Menlo Park, 2005. AIII Press.

25. A.-H. Mohsenian-Rad et al. Autonomous demand-side management based on game-theoretic energy consumption scheduling for the future smart grid. *IEEE Tr. Smart Grid*, 1(3):320–331, 2010.

26. M. Pipattanasomporn, M. Kuzlu, and S. Rahman. An algorithm for intelligent home energy management and demand response analysis. *IEEE Tr. Smart Grid 3-4*, 2012.

27. S. Rodriguez, N. Gaud, V. Hilaire, S. Galland, and A. Koukam. An analysis and design concept for self-organization in holonic multi-agent systems. In S.n Brueckner, S. Hassas, M. Jelasity, and D. Yamins, editors, *Engineering Self-Organising Systems, 4th Intl Workshop - Revised and Invited Papers*, volume 4335 of *LNCS*, pages 15–27, Hakodate, Japan, 2006. Springer.

28. A. Schiendorfer, J-P. Steghöfer, and W. Reif. Synthesis and abstraction of constraint models for hierarchical resource allocation problems. *Proc. of the 6th International Conference on Agents and Artificial Intelligence (ICAART)*, 2, 2014.

29. T. Schmickl, R. Thenius, C. Moslinger, J. Timmis, A. Tyrrell, M. Read, J. Hilder, J. Halloy, A. Campo, C. Stefanini, et al. Cocoro–the self-aware underwater swarm. In *Proc. Int. Conference on Self-Adaptive and Self-Organizing Systems Workshops (SASOW)*, pages 120–126, Ann Arbor, MI, USA, October 2011. IEEE Computer Society.

30. H.A. Simon. *The Sciences of the Artificial*. MIT Press, 1996.

31. J-P. Steghöfer, P. Behrmann, G. Anders, F. Siefert, and W. Reif. Hispada: Self-organising hierarchies for large-scale multi-agent systems. *Proc. Int. Cnf. on Autonomic and Autonomous Systems*, 2013.

32. M. Ulieru, R.W. Brennan, and S. Walker. The holonic enterprise: a model for internet-enabled global manufacturing supply chain and workflow management, 2002. Integrated Manufacturing Systems, Vol. 13 Iss: 8, pp. 538–550.

33. P. Valckenaers, H. Van Brussel, and T. Holvoet. Fundamentals of holonic systems and their implications for self-adaptive and self-organizing systems. In *SASO Workshops*, pages 168–173. IEEE Computer Society, 2008.

34. H. Van Dyke Parunak, Sven Brueckner, Mitch Fleischer, and James Odell. A Design Taxonomy of Multi-agent Interactions. In Paolo Giorgini, JrgP. Mller, and James Odell, editors, *Agent-Oriented Software Engineering IV*, volume 2935 of *Lecture Notes in Computer Science*, pages 123–137. Springer Berlin Heidelberg, 2004.
35. H.F. Wedde, S. Lehnhoff, C. Rehtanz, and O. Krause. Bottom-up self-organization of unpredictable demand and supply under decentralized power management. In *Self-Adaptive and Self-Organizing Systems (SASO). 2nd IEEE Intl Cnf on*, pages 74–83, Oct 2008.
36. D. Weyns, B. Schmerl, V. Grassi, S. Malek, R. Mirandola, C. Prehofer, J. Wuttke, J. Andersson, H. Giese, and K. Goeschka. On Patterns for Decentralized Control in Self-Adaptive Systems. In Rogério de Lemos, Holger Giese, Hausi Müller, and Mary Shaw, editors, *Software Engineering for Self-Adaptive Systems II*, volume 7475 of *Lecture Notes in Computer Science (LNCS)*, pages 76–107. Springer, January 2013.
37. F. Zambonelli, N. Bicocchi, G. Cabri, L. Leonardi, and M. Puviani. On self-adaptation, self-expression, and self-awareness in autonomic service component ensembles. In *Self-Adaptive and Self-Organizing Systems Workshops (SASOW), 5th IEEE Cnf. on*, pages 108–113, 2011.

Chapter 8
State of the Art in Architectures
for Self-aware Computing Systems

Holger Giese, Thomas Vogel, Ada Diaconescu, Sebastian Götz,
Nelly Bencomo, Kurt Geihs, Samuel Kounev and Kirstie L. Bellman

Abstract In this chapter, we review the state of the art in self-aware computing systems with a particular focus on software architectures. Therefore, we compare existing approaches targeting computing systems with similar characteristics as self-aware systems to the architectural concepts for single and collective self-aware systems discussed in the previous chapters. These approaches are particularly reference architectures and architectural frameworks and languages. Based on this comparison, we discuss open challenges for architectures of self-aware computing systems.

H. Giese (✉) · T. Vogel
Hasso Plattner Institute for Software Systems Engineering at the University of Potsdam,
Prof.-Dr.-Helmert-Str. 2-3, D-14482 Potsdam, Germany
e-mail: holger.giese@hpi.de

T. Vogel
e-mail: thomas.vogel@hpi.de

A. Diaconescu
Telécom ParisTech, Equipe S3, Department INFRES, 46 Rue Barrault, 75013 Paris, France
e-mail: ada.diaconescu@telecom-paristech.fr

S. Götz
Tu Dresden, Dresden, Germany
e-mail: sebastian.goetz@acm.org

N. Bencomo
Aston Institute for Systems Analytics, Aston University, Birmingham, UK
e-mail: nelly@acm.org

K. Geihs
University Kassel, Wilhelmshöher Allee 73, D-34121 Kassel, Germany
e-mail: geihs@uni-kassel.de

S. Kounev
University of Würzburg, Department of Computer Science, Am Hubland,
D-97074 Würzburg, Germany
e-mail: samuel.kounev@uni-wuerzburg.de

K.L. Bellman
Aerospace Integration Science Center, The Aerospace Corporation, California, CA, USA
e-mail: Kirstie.L.Bellman@aero.org

© Springer International Publishing AG 2017
S. Kounev et al. (eds.), *Self-Aware Computing Systems*,
DOI 10.1007/978-3-319-47474-8_8

8.1 Introduction

We studied the architectural dimension of the vision of self-aware computing systems in the previous chapters. Particularly, we discussed generic architectural concepts in Chap. 5, which we used as a basis to investigate architectures for single and collective self-aware computing systems. Therefore, we discussed architectural designs and styles—inspired by control schemes and architectures of self-adaptive software—for prereflective, reflective, and meta-reflective self-awareness and how such systems may construct reflections of themselves and their environment in Chap. 6. We extended this discussion in Chap. 7 for collective self-aware computing systems and how they address prereflective, reflective, and meta-reflective self-awareness at the architectural level with respect to the interactions and the organization of the collective. In this chapter, we discuss the state of the art in architectures for self-aware computing systems by comparing existing approaches with the major ideas presented in Chaps. 5, 6, and 7.

In this context, the self-aware computing paradigm sketched in Chap. 1 emphasizes a development that is already partially supported by a number of research initiatives aiming for more flexible software systems. Examples of such initiatives are autonomic computing [50], self-* systems [5], self-adaptive and self-managed systems [20, 21, 25, 26, 54, 71], organic computing [1, 64], and cognitive computing [49]. All of these initiatives advocate a paradigm shift for software from design-time decisions and understanding toward resolving issues dynamically at runtime.

Such approaches traditionally consider *reactive* solutions that dynamically act in response to changes causing issues (cf. [32, 54]). In contrast, self-aware computing emphasizes anticipating future changes or reasoning about the long-term future and therefore advocates another paradigm shift from a *reactive* to a *proactive* operation that integrates the ability to learn, reason, and act at runtime (cf. [19, 22, 46]). This trend is well in line with the ideas centered around the notion of self-aware computing [1, 2, 47, 51, 57, 62, 81], runtime models [9, 11, 12, 75, 78, 80], and related terms [24, 28, 61, 67]. A broad discussion of such research initiatives with respect to self-aware computing systems can be found in Chap. 2.

In this chapter, we review the state of the art concerning self-aware computing systems with the particular focus on *software architecture* [74]. Moreover, we focus on *specific* approaches—in contrast to research initiatives—and compare them to the architectural concepts for self-aware computing systems discussed in the previous chapters. Thus, we cover the basic architectural concepts (see Chap. 5) and how pre-reflective, reflective, and meta-reflective self-awareness with the related observing, analyzing, and reacting as well as learning, reasoning, and acting processes can be organized at the architectural level for an individual self-aware computing system (see Chap. 6) and for a collective of such systems (see Chap. 7). The specific approaches we discuss in this chapter are either reference architectures or architectural frameworks and languages for software systems that share similarities with self-aware computing systems.

The rest of this chapter is organized as follows. We discuss the state of the art in architectures for self-aware computing systems in three steps. We discuss existing reference architectures in Sect. 8.2, architectural frameworks and languages in Sect. 8.3, and open challenges for architectures of self-awareness computing systems in Sect. 8.4. Finally, we conclude the chapter in Sect. 8.5.

8.2   Reference Architectures

In this section, we discuss existing reference architectures and compare them to the developed architectural concepts for self-aware computing systems. These reference architectures address systems related to self-aware computing. Specifically, we discuss the *MAPE-K* loop from the autonomic computing field [50], the reference architecture for self-managed systems proposed by Kramer and Magee [54], the reference architecture for models@run.time systems proposed by Aßmann et al. [4], the reference architecture from the organic computing field [72], the reference architecture for requirements reflection [10], and finally, architectural principles from artificial intelligence and multi-agent systems.

8.2.1   MAPE-K Loop

Core of autonomic systems, as defined in autonomic computing (cf. Chap. 2), is an entity that realizes the self-* properties [48]. This entity, referred to as *autonomic manager*, can be understood as an executable software unit that implements the adaptation logic in order to continuously meet the system's operational goals.

To structure the principle of operation exhibited by autonomic managers, a reference architecture based on a control loop, referred to as the *MAPE-K loop*, has been proposed [50]. This reference architecture has the advantage that it offers a clear way to identify and classify areas of particular focus, and thus, it is used by many researchers to communicate the architectural concepts of autonomic systems.

The acronym MAPE-K reflects the five main constituent phases of autonomic operations, i.e., *Monitor, Analyze, Plan, Execute*, and *Knowledge* (see Fig. 8.1). Basically, the *Monitor* phase collects information from the sensors provided by the managed system and its context. The *Analyze* phase uses the data of the *Monitor* phase to assess the situation and determine any anomalies or problems. The *Plan* phase generates an adaptation plan to solve a detected problem. The *Execute* phase normally applies the generated adaptation plan on the actual system. A cross-cutting aspect shared among all phases of the loop is the *Knowledge* about the managed system and its context, capturing aspects such as the software architecture, execution environment, and hardware infrastructure on which the system is running. The knowledge may also explicitly capture the operational goals of the system, for instance, the target quality-of-service level the managed system should provide. The representation of the knowledge can take any form, for example, a performance model describing the performance behavior of the system.

Fig. 8.1 MAPE-K (taken
from Chap. 1)

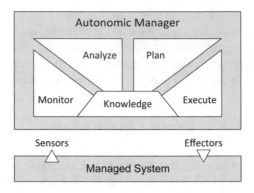

The software engineering community uses a similar feedback loop concept, distinguishing the four phases *Collect*, *Analyze*, *Decide*, and *Act* (cf. [15, 20]). Conceptually, the behavior of these phases is similar to the phases in the MAPE-K loop; however, this concept does not explicitly consider the *Knowledge* part. More details about the use of feedback loops in self-adaptive systems, such as the use of multiple, multi-level, positive, or negative feedback loops, can be found in [15, 20].

The activities or processes of a MAPE-K loop are similar to those of the LRA-M loop realized by self-aware computing systems (see Chap. 1). Nevertheless, the MAPE-K loop does not consider advanced forms of learning and reasoning but rather basic monitoring and analyses of the managed system. Both kinds of loops use runtime models representing parts of the system (especially the managed system in the case of MAPE-K) and goals; however, the MAPE-K loop uses operation-level goals and the LRA-M loop may use higher-level goals.

Separating an autonomic system into an autonomic manager reflecting on a managed system, we may consider the managed system to be the scope and the manager to be the span of awareness. Hence, the managed system is prereflective and the manager is reflective. Hence, systems realizing a MAPE-K loop may achieve reflective self-awareness (cf. Chaps. 3 and 5). With respect to the forms of reflection discussed in Chap. 6, the MAPE-K loop adopts centralized reflection by employing a single autonomic manager. Additionally, hierarchical reflection can be achieved by structuring multiple autonomic managers in a hierarchy [50]. Consequently, the architectural style of MAPE-K is the hierarchical external approach (cf. Chap. 6). Finally, the MAPE-K loop as introduced in [50] does not consider collective systems such that the concepts proposed in Chap. 7 do not apply here.

8.2.2 *Reference Architecture for Self-managed Systems*

Kramer and Magee [54] present a reference architecture for self-managed systems that is inspired by layered robot architectures. As depicted in Fig. 8.2, the architec-

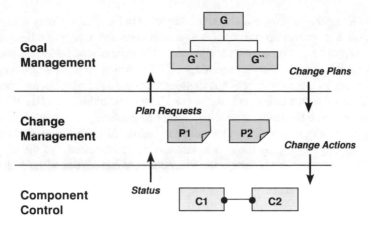

Fig. 8.2 Reference architecture for self-managed systems [54]

ture has three layers and the functionality is distributed among them based on the execution time that increases from lower to higher layers.

First, the *Component Control* layer implements the application functionality using a set of components. This layer reports its status to the next higher layer and supports change actions initiated by the higher layer for reconfiguring its component structure. Particularly, if the component control layer encounters a situation in which it cannot meet the application goals, it reports to the higher layer. In this case or if new goals are introduced by the topmost layer, the *Change Management* layer adapts the component control layer to be able to achieve the (new) goals in the current environmental situation. Therefore, the change management layer contains a set of prespecified plans among which it selects an appropriate one for the current situation. If there is no appropriate plan available, a request is sent to the topmost layer to devise a plan. The *Goal Management* layer is responsible for planning, that is, creating plans to achieve the application goals. Planning is triggered by a request from the layer below or by introducing new goals. Created plans are then provided to the change management layer that enacts such plans by adapting the component control layer.

With respect to self-aware computing systems, this reference architecture is similar to the layered style discussed in Chap. 6. The component control layer is prereflective. The change management layer reflects on the component control layer and is therefore reflective. It typically will have some kind of awareness model of the lowest layer to reason how the lowest layer has to be adapted to execute a certain plan. The goal management layer explicitly maintains the application goals and reflects on the change management layer. For instance, introducing new goals requires new plans as well as potentially adjusted reasoning machinery at the change management layer to cope with new plans and their execution at the component control layer. Therefore, the topmost layer typically uses some awareness models addressing the change management and, by this, also the component control layer.

Considering the reference architecture depicted in Fig. 8.2, we may interpret the arrows pointing bottom-up and top-down as awareness and expression links, respectively. In contrast to our discussion of layered architectures for self-aware systems, the reference architecture by Kramer and Magee [54] does not explicitly address the environmental context, the awareness and expression in terms of models, and processes that achieve such awareness and expression. The same holds for MORPH [13], a recent extension to the reference architecture, that explicitly distinguishes between adapting the configuration (e.g., changing the architectural structure) and adapting the behavior (e.g., changing the orchestration of the components) of the target system. This extension does not change the conceptual characteristics of the architecture with respect to self-awareness.

8.2.3   Reference Architecture for Models@run.time Systems

The models@run.time paradigm promotes the use of models and modeling techniques (e.g., model transformations and code generation) at runtime and can be applied to self-aware computing systems. Traditionally, models are only used during the design of systems with the aim to achieve platform independence, to increase reusability, and generally to improve the efficiency of software development, or as defined by Rothenberg:

> Modeling, in the broadest sense, is the cost-effective use of something in place of something else for some cognitive purpose. It allows us to use something that is simpler, safer or cheaper than reality instead of reality for some purpose. A model represents reality for the given purpose; the model is an abstraction of reality in the sense that it cannot represent all aspects of reality. This allows us to deal with the world in a simplified manner, avoiding the complexity, danger and irreversibility of reality [68].

The challenge posed by models@run.time is, thus, how to transfer existing modeling techniques, which focus on design-time problems, to be applicable to runtime problems. Over the last decade, since the term models@run.time has been coined [12], a considerably large body of knowledge emerged from a vivid research community. The reference architecture proposed in [4] and depicted in Fig. 8.3 summarizes a large subset of this knowledge by showing the major architectural constituents found in most of the approaches employing models@run.time.

A central characteristic of approaches based on the models@run.time paradigm is the distinction between two systems, where one monitors and acts upon the other. The former is often called the managing system and the latter is called the managed system. Some approaches additionally distinguish between the managed system and its environment. The managing system, on the other hand, can often be subdivided into three layers conforming to the reference architecture discussed in Sect. 8.2.2. The bottom layer, interfacing with the managed system, is comprised of models covering different concerns of the underlying managed system. The configuration model, often also simply called runtime model, reflects the current state of the underlying system. Additional models cover the managed system's capabilities (e.g., for adaptation, but

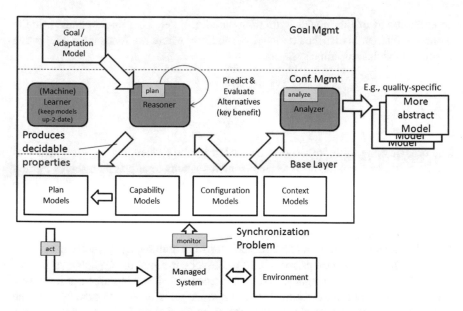

Fig. 8.3 A reference architecture for models@run.time systems [4]

also for use), not only context models focusing specifically on the managed system's environment, but also plan models constituting specifications of how to act upon the managed system. The middle layer consists of three active entities: a reasoner, an analyzer, and a learner. The learner is responsible to keep all models of the lower layer in sync with the managed system. The analyzer provides means to further abstract (i.e., decompose) the managing system, which enables a hierarchical decomposition of models@run.time systems. Finally, the reasoner is in charge of processing the models from the lower layer with the aim of decision making. The reasoner also takes the third layer into account, which typically comprises requirements and goal models. The key benefits of models@run.time systems originate from the position of this reasoner, that is, the fact that this reasoner works on models. The level of abstraction can be adjusted to the respective reasoning task and, thus, allows to reduce the complexity of the reasoning tasks. Moreover, it is possible to use the models for predictions, which, in consequence, enables reasoning about possible, alternative, future states of the system. In summary, the key distinguishing features of models@run.time are predictive reflection and tractability by abstraction.

In comparison with self-aware computing as introduced in Chap. 1, models@run.time systems do not treat self-awareness as a first-class concept. It does, however, focus on the runtime model and observations to keep this model up to date. According to Chap. 6, the reference architecture of models@run.time denotes the hierarchical external reflection style. The concepts introduced in Chap. 7, which allow us to describe how systems can be composed or related to each other, are not an explicit part of the models@run.time paradigm, yet. This might change, due to increased interest in distributed models@run.time, where the focus is on integrating multiple models@run.time systems.

8.2.4 Organic Computing

The organic computing initiative is motivated by the ever-increasing complexity of software systems and the need to enable such systems to adjust themselves to their users and not vice versa. The main objective of organic computing is the "controlled self-organization" [72], that is, the ability of a system to self-adapt in accordance with external influences while at the same time providing guarantees in terms of trustworthy behavior. To reach this goal, the organic computing initiative introduced a novel architectural concept: the observer/controller architecture depicted in Fig. 8.4.

The architecture is comprised of two top-level concepts: the organic system and a human user. While the organic system adheres to the basic input/computer/output principle of computing, the human user imposes goals on the organic system and is able to perceive the system status. The organic system is further decomposed into three major components: the system under observation and control (SuOC), the observer, and the controller. All human interaction is relayed by the controller. Notably, the input/compute/output principle is realized by the SuOC. The observer and controller impose a feedback loop upon the SuOC, where the former observes the SuOC and reports to the latter, which in turn controls the SuOC. An important characteristic of the SuOC is that it is comprised of agents (i.e., autonomous entities). In other words, the SuOC is already a set of self-organizing systems. The observer and controller enhance this system to achieve *controlled* self-organization.

Organic computing differs from the other reference architectures presented in this chapter in its initial situation and its main objective. While most other reference architectures aim at enhancing prereflective systems to become self-aware, in organic

Fig. 8.4 The observe/control loop of organic computing (taken from [72])

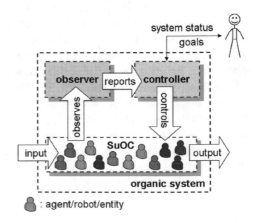

computing the starting point is autonomous systems and the objective is to enhance them such that they are enabled to provide trustworthy behavior. The fundamental idea of models@run.time, which is the use of abstract representations of the runtime system state (see Sect. 8.2.3), is present in organic computing as the link between the observer and controller, which is used to report "an aggregated quantified context (i.e., a description of the currently observed situation)" [72, p.3].

The MAPE-K loop in autonomic computing (see Sect. 8.2.1) can be mapped to the observe/control loop. The observer comprises the monitoring and analysis, while the controller comprises the planning and execution. However, a shared knowledge base is not in the focus of organic computing. Moreover, the LRA-M loop of self-aware computing systems (see Chap. 1) has similarities to the observe/control loop, particularly the external imposition of goals. In contrast to organic computing focusing on the realization of controlled behavior, the focus of self-aware computing is to structure the system under observation and control (i.e., the self) and to realize various forms of behavior such as self-explanation and self-modeling.

With respect to the architectural concepts discussed in Chap. 5, the observation/control loop as a reference architecture (see Fig. 8.4) is described at a higher level of abstraction. Therefore, organic computing systems do not explicitly consider the different levels of self-awareness (i.e., prereflective, reflective, and meta-reflective) although they include at least reflection since the observer and controller as the span reflect upon the SuOC as the scope. In this context, the observe and control links in Fig. 8.4 can be interpreted as awareness and expression links. However, the reference architecture does not detail this reflection such that the potential use of awareness models, empirical data, or goal models is not explicitly covered.

Concerning the forms of reflection discussed in Chap. 6, the organic computing reference architecture realizes—similar to the MAPE-K loop—a hierarchical and centralized reflection as it employs a single observer and controller upon a set of agents. Moreover, the phenomena of overlapping, stacked, or cyclic reflection are not explicitly addressed by the reference architecture. Therefore, the reference architecture primarily adopts the hierarchical external architectural style without explicitly considering the other styles discussed in Chap. 6. Although organic computing targets open and self-organizing systems, the dimensions for collective self-aware systems discussed in Chap. 7 such as collective self-awareness and its levels, weak and strong self-aware collectives, different types of relations between systems of a collective, or the organizational patterns are not considered.

8.2.5   Requirements-Awareness

Traditionally, in requirements engineering (RE) it has been made the assumption that the environmental context is reasonably static and can be understood sufficiently well to permit the requirements model for a solution to be formulated with confidence during design time. However, effectively, environmental contexts are hardly static over long periods, and this can inhibit full understanding.

As discussed before, systems are being produced for environmental contexts that are subject to change over short periods and in ways that are badly understood. In part, this is because the machinery of self-adaptation and autonomic computing has improved, providing a means for systems to dynamically respond to changing contexts. As described in this book, self-awareness and self-adaptivity will become increasingly required properties for software systems. For this to become true, it is crucial that these software systems offer requirements-awareness to discover, reason about, and manage its own requirements that can dynamically change at runtime.

In this context, a key contribution is the seminal work on requirements monitoring [29]. Such monitoring is required because of deviations between the system's runtime behavior and the requirements model, which may trigger the need for an adaptation [8]. Such a deviation needs to be correlated with the state of the environment in order to diagnose the reasons and to perform appropriate adaptations. Where systems have the need to adapt dynamically in order to maintain satisfaction of their goals, RE ceases to be an entirely static, off-line activity and it additionally becomes a runtime activity. This is because design-time decisions about the requirements need to be made on incomplete and uncertain knowledge about the domain, context, and goals. There are clear benefits of being able to revise these decisions at runtime when more information can be acquired through runtime monitoring.

Therefore, requirements need to be runtime entities that can be reasoned over at runtime [10]. Implicit in the ability for a system to introspect (i.e., to be self-aware) on its requirements model is the representation of that model at runtime. The running system provides information as feedback to update the model and to increase its correspondence with reality, which is called causal connection. Analysis of the updated model may detect whether a desired property (e.g., reliability and performance) is violated, causing self-adaptation actions that aim for guaranteeing the goals. Explicit use of computational reflection is a primary means to achieve requirements-awareness. The consequence is that there exists a runtime representation of the requirements model that is causally connected to the running system.

Requirements-awareness enables software systems to revise and re-assess design-time decisions at runtime when more information can be acquired about these by observing their own behavior (i.e., by being self-aware). Two research issues have been identified. One is the evolution of the requirements models and the maintenance of consistency between the requirements and the running systems during this evolution. To do this, it is necessary to specify the abstract adaptation thresholds that allow for uncertainty and unanticipated environmental conditions. The second issue is the need to maintain the synchronization (i.e., the causal connection) between the runtime requirements model and the architecture of the running system as either the requirements or the architecture may change (see Fig. 8.5).

Although requirement-awareness does not explicitly consider different levels of self-awareness, it employs reflection and achieves reflective self-awareness. The element shown in Fig. 8.5 reflects upon a managed system to maintain representations of the system's runtime architecture and requirements. These runtime models correspond to the idea of system-awareness models and goal models in self-aware computing systems (see Chap. 5). In this context, we can interpret the synchronization from

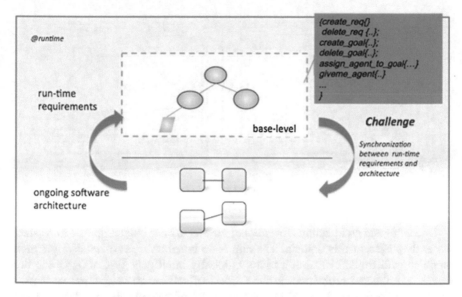

Fig. 8.5 Synchronization between the requirements and the architecture [10]

the running system to the architectural runtime model and then to the requirements runtime model as an awareness link as well as the synchronization in the opposite direction as an expression link. Hence, reflection is considered as a general means to achieve requirements-awareness without detailing possible forms (e.g., local, centralized, hierarchical, or coordinated) or phenomena (e.g., overlapping, stacked, or cyclic) of reflection discussed in Chap. 6. Still, the stepwise synchronization to the architecture and then to the requirements can be seen as a specific form of hierarchical reflection that separates architectural and requirements concerns. Therefore, the basic adopted architectural style in requirements-awareness corresponds to the hierarchical external approach (see Chap. 6).

Finally, establishing requirements-awareness for collective systems is not discussed such that the architectural concepts for collective self-aware computing systems introduced in Chap. 7 do not apply here.

8.2.6 Decentralized Architectures from AI and MAS

In the following, we discuss decentralized architectures from the artificial intelligence (AI) and multi-agent systems (MAS) domains as they could provide inspiration for building self-aware systems. More information on MAS and their progressive transformation into self-aware systems is provided in Chaps. 2 and 10.

(a)   **(b)**

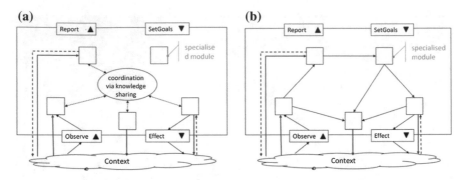

Fig. 8.6 Coordinated architecture with **a** Shared memory or **b** P2P communication

Decentralized architectures for *rational* [1] systems have been proposed in AI since the early stages of this domain. The aim is to integrate a set of relatively simple modules with limited capabilities into a globally intelligent system (e.g., one that solves complicated problems). In the context of self-aware computing systems, a similar approach may be used to integrate a set of prereflective modules into an overall system featuring characteristics of self-awareness.

In general, decentralized architectures consist of a number of independent, specialized modules that execute in parallel and interact with each other. From a self-awareness perspective (cf. Chap. 1), we may distinguish two main cases for such modules. In the first case, modules are rational self-aware entities that pursue individual goals (similar to deliberative agents in MAS), and can have intentional relations with other entities (e.g., cooperation or competition). This case is detailed in Chap. 7 focusing on collectives of self-aware systems. In the second case, modules are non-self-aware (i.e., prereflective according to Chap. 3) such that they are not aware of any individual goals and merely react to inputs in predefined ways (i.e., they are reflexive and context-aware [70], but not reflective). Here, we focus on this kind of systems and their architectures proposed in the literature.

Generally, each module in the system is specialized in detecting and reacting to a set of stimuli. It implements a specific function and provides outputs when it is triggered. Modules may be triggered in parallel and some of their outputs may be conflicting. Hence, coordination becomes an important challenge for conflict resolution and synchronization of modules. Numerous coordination approaches have been proposed, which we categorize into coordination based on *shared memory* (e.g., a blackboard) [43, 66] and coordination based on *peer-to-peer communication* [14], sometimes mediated by control modules [23, 31, 60]. Both variants are illustrated in Fig. 8.6 and will be discussed with respect to their implications on self-awareness.

In a *blackboard-based system*, incoming events are perceived by dedicated modules and placed onto the blackboard. All modules read from the blackboard and each

---

[1]Here, *rational* refers to a system's ability to take the best action for optimizing a performance indicator or a goal. In the context of self-aware computing systems, we focus on rational systems that can learn, represent, and reason about knowledge in order to act and achieve their goals.

one reacts to content it is specialized in (e.g., based on event types or patterns). Thus, each module performs its function and writes its ensuing outputs on the blackboard. This, in turn, may cause a new wave of readings and writings by other modules.

Conflict resolution for incompatible module outputs is performed automatically at the blackboard level using various strategies. For instance, ACT* [3, 65] favors the output of modules triggered by conditions with higher matching degrees and specificities, or it considers each module's success history avoiding repetitive activations from the same module, or finally, it prioritizes outputs related to an active goal. In Soar [65], conflicts represent new problems to be solved by the blackboard. Hence, the blackboard does not control the modules directly with command messages but rather indirectly by transforming individual postings into coherent global results, which, in turn, impact the next wave of module activations.

With respect to *self-awareness in blackboard systems*, each module develops its own knowledge about the particular type of problem it is specialized in. Modules only share and combine the knowledge that is relevant to the problem being solved. Hence, the system only acquires knowledge when developing the solution to each problem. The acquired knowledge is not necessarily saved for later use, and there are no global learning processes based on it. Each module updates, reasons about, and learns from the knowledge shared via the blackboard. This process is cooperative and opportunistic depending on the shared knowledge. However, modules are not necessarily aware of each other's participations (i.e., no interaction-awareness) as they simply react to the changes produced by the others on the blackboard.

With respect to goal-awareness, the global goal to achieve (or problem to solve) can be displayed on the blackboard. In this case, the specialized modules that participate in solving the problem can be aware of the goal. In other cases, the system's execution is merely triggered by information obtained from the environment and displayed on the blackboard. Here, the system's overall goal is implicit in the way in which the modules are selected and implemented. Hence, the specialized modules are not goal-aware and they simply react to the state of the blackboard. Considering state-awareness, all modules are aware of the state of the problem being addressed and of the solution being developed since these are displayed on the blackboard.

The main difficulty in adopting a blackboard solution consists in implementing the blackboard involving several complicated functions that are typical for distributed systems (e.g., synchronization, transactions, security, and communication) and problem solving (e.g., conflict resolution). Increasing system scales exacerbates these issues. Moreover, such a solution typically addresses only one problem at a time. On the positive side, once a blackboard is implemented, it is fairly easy to dynamically add, remove, or update specialized modules. Also, specialists can be fairly simple to implement as they are focused on a specific type of problem.

In *peer-to-peer systems*, specialized modules react independently to events by processing them and sending new events through the system. These new events, in turn, trigger a new wave of module reactions. Hence, a collaboration chain of modules is formed in an opportunistic manner starting with modules observing external inputs (or receiving goals), through modules developing a solution progressively, and ending with modules performing external actions. This allows several solutions to be developed in parallel including conflict-resolution mechanisms.

A notable example of this approach is the multi-layered *subsumption architecture* [14] for robotic systems. Each layer consists of a set of well-integrated reflexes and offers functions of increasing complexity, which eliminates the need for an explicit "intelligent" element to mediate between the robot's perception and action. Examples from the autonomic computing domain also introduce special-purpose controllers in the coordination process (e.g., to resolve conflicts [23, 60]). This is useful in open systems, where modules may dynamically join or leave the system, which might even require decentralized coordination control [26, 31].

With respect to *self-awareness in (controlled) peer-to-peer systems*, knowledge about a problem is only transmitted progressively across the modules that contribute to solving the problem. This forms a problem-specific collaboration chain, which is different from a blackboard, making the knowledge visible to the entire system.

The coordination logic does not necessarily form a reflective (self-aware) or meta-reflective (meta-self-aware) layer. It can be implemented with reflex modules (i.e., they are only stimulus-aware) that do not learn and reason about the modules they coordinate (e.g., [14]). Of course, a more advanced coordination logic that is goal- and time-aware and includes sophisticated learning and reasoning functions can be envisaged. When peer-to-peer systems are goal-unaware, their goals are implicit in the implementations of the specialized modules and their coordination. Nonetheless, goal-aware systems can also be implemented by providing explicit goals to a centralized coordination controller (e.g., an arbiter or scheduler), which can attempt to achieve the goal by controlling (i.e., triggering or inhibiting) various modules [23, 60]. In such cases, the global system is goal-aware even though the individual modules are not. Finally, a goal-aware system can also be achieved by providing the explicit goals to the specialized modules [27]. Here, both the overall system and (some of) its modules can be considered as goal-aware.

With respect to state-awareness, the specialized modules participating in a collaboration chain are only aware of the state of the system and context by receiving related information from other modules or by monitoring the system and context themselves. Except for the action modules at the end of the chain, none of the modules has a complete view of the solution being developed.

An important difficulty with peer-to-peer approaches relates to asynchronous communication and data-formatting standards. However, existing middleware can be used here to address many of these challenges. As with the blackboard, peer-to-peer solutions allow for the dynamic addition and removal of modules and an important advantage can be the ability to develop alternative solutions in parallel.

Finally, in both of the aforementioned approaches, a system can consist of heterogeneous modules with different self-awareness capabilities and levels (e.g., combining prereflective modules with reflective and meta-reflective modules, featuring various learning and reasoning capabilities, and having accumulated knowledge). A major difficulty when constructing and changing such system consists in finding and tuning the correct combination of specialists that together behave coherently to address system-level goals. Also, guaranteeing that such system will behave "as expected" is particularly difficult. In this context, self-awareness capabilities such as learning, reasoning, adaptation, and reporting can be of great help.

In general, the decentralized architectures from AI and MAS can be covered with the architectural concepts introduced in Chap. 5, and they mainly relate to the architectures for collective systems discussed in Chap. 7. The forms, phenomena, and architectural styles of reflection discussed in Chap. 6 usually do not apply to the decentralized architectures from AI and MAS since they only consider individual self-aware systems but not the interaction among multiple systems. In contrast, the concepts introduced in Chap. 7 such as the collective self-awareness with its levels, types of relations/interactions, organizational patterns, and weak/strong self-aware collectives are important aspects of decentralized architectures, but they are often not explicitly covered by AI or MAS architectures.

8.3   Architectural Frameworks and Languages

In this section, we discuss specific approaches to develop computing systems that share similarities with self-aware systems. Focusing on architectures in this chapter, these approaches are mainly architectural frameworks and languages, and we compare them to the architectural concepts for self-aware computing systems introduced in the previous chapters. Specifically, these specific approaches are reflective architectures, Mechatronic UML, MUSIC, EUREMA, MQuAT, and DML.

8.3.1   Reflective Architectures

In 1987, Maes [58] introduced *computational reflection* as a process of reasoning about and/or acting upon oneself. It is an engineered system's ability to reason about its own resources, capabilities, and limitations in the context of its current operational environment. Reflection capabilities can range from simple, straightforward adjustments of another program's parameters or behaviors (e.g., altering the step size on a numerical process or the application of rules governing which models are used at different stages in a design process) to sophisticated analyses of the system's own reasoning, planning, and decision processes (e.g., noticing when one's approach to a problem is not working and revising a plan).

Reflection processes must include more than the sensing of data, monitoring of an event, or perception of a pattern; they must also have some type of capability to reason about this information and to act upon this reasoning. However, although reflection is more than monitoring, it does not imply that the system is "conscious." Many animals demonstrate self-awareness; not only do they sense their environment but they are able to reason about their capabilities within that environment. For example, when a startled lizard scurries into a crevice, rarely does it try to fit into a hole that is too small for its body. If it is injured or tired, it changes the distance that it attempts to run or leap. This adaptive behavior reveals the ability of the animal system to somehow take into account the current constraints of the environment and of its own body within that environment [6, 7].

In order to bring out the ways in which the self-awareness processes and architectures could enhance and further develop reflective architectures, we will quickly overview one approach to implementing computational reflection and the building of reflection processes. By concentrating on what has been built for the Wrappings approach [55, 56], we also want to show how an architecture can have very few fixed relationships and yet still function as an architecture. In fact, because of the lack of fixed relationships with a small amount of guiding infrastructure, the knowledge and the processes used to map resources into appropriate uses for different goals become the foundation for the systems flexible ability to reason potentially about any of its own parts and their use in a goal and hence to have support for the building and utilization of self-models.

Wrappings uses both explicit meta-knowledge and recursively applied algorithms to recruit and configure resources dynamically to "problems posed" to the system by users, external systems, or the system's own internal processing. The problem managers (PMs) algorithms use the Wrappings to choreograph seven major functions: discover, select, assemble, integrate, adapt, explain, and evaluate. Discover programs (or as called in Wrappings, resources) identify new resources that can be inserted into the system for a problem. Selection resources decide which resource(s) should be applied to this problem in this context. Assembly is syntactic integration and these resources help to set up selected resources so that they can pass information or share services. Integration is semantic integration, including constraints on when and why resources should be assembled. Adaptation resources help to adjust or set up a resource for different operational conditions. Explanation resources are more than a simple event history because they provide information on why and what was not selected. Evaluate includes the impact or effectiveness of a given use of this resource. The Wrappings "problem-posing" has many benefits, including separating problems from solution methods and keeping an explicit, analyzable trace of what problems were used to evoke and configure resources. Because all of the resources are wrapped, even the resources that support the wrappings processing, the system is computationally reflective—it can reason about the use of all of its resources. Additional information on the Wrappings approach to reflection and its use in a test bed of robotic cars is found in Chap. 9.

The Wrappings approach considers a more dynamic case to achieve self-awareness than the architectural concepts introduced in Chaps. 5–7. Therefore, it would be required to enrich the architectural concepts, which apply mainly to snapshots of architectures and do not make the dynamical aspects explicit, with support for dynamic architectures as discussed in Sect. 8.4 in order to cover the Wrappings approach. The architectural concepts introduced in Chap. 5 can be relevant for Wrappings, but they are often not explicitly considered. For instance, the different levels of self-awareness (i.e., the prereflective, reflective, and meta-reflective levels) are not explicitly considered, even though they may very well exist in the Wrappings approach. In contrast, the Wrappings approach considers self-models that relate to awareness models and based on the purpose, some of these self-models can be considered as goal models.

For the forms and phenomena of reflection as well as for the architectural styles discussed in Chap. 6 holds that they may temporarily occur in the Wrappings approach, but they are not made explicit and visible at the architectural level. Therefore, local, centralized/hierarchical, and coordinated reflection can be seen as forms of reflection that result from the activities of the problem managers. In specific situations, the resources of a wrapping may be composed such that certain reflection phenomena (e.g., overlapping, stacked, or cyclic reflection) may occur temporarily and certain architectural styles are adopted temporarily. Concerning Chap. 7, the Wrappings approach employs a shared knowledge base such that the concepts of collective self-awareness and weak/strong self-aware collectives are hardly applicable. Likewise, the meta-architecture dimensions (i.e., collective self-awareness levels, types of relations, and organizational patterns) are not suitable for a central knowledge base, but they may be applicable with a distributed knowledge base.

8.3.2   Mechatronic UML

Mechatronic UML [16] is a model-driven development approach targeting self-adaptive embedded real-time systems with substantial mechatronic elements. The core building block for the architectural modeling with Mechatronic UML is the operator–controller module (OCM) [17, 45] depicted in Fig. 8.7.

Fig. 8.7 The operator–controller module as the architectural building block [38]

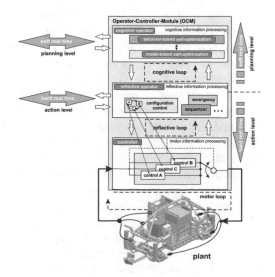

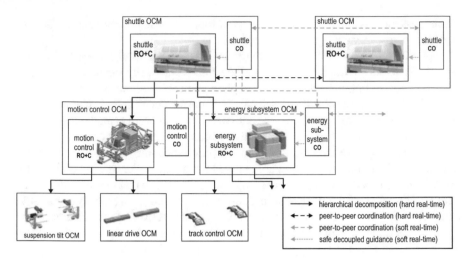

Fig. 8.8 Collaborating hierarchy of OCMs [38]

The OCM is separated into a controller, a reflective operator, and a cognitive operator. While the controller could be seen as the prereflective core describing the regular operation of the system, the two operators realize different forms of reflective self-awareness. The reflective operator realizes self-awareness where learning, reasoning, and acting are limited such that hard real-time guarantees can be given. In contrast, the cognitive operator is decoupled from the hard real-time processing, and therefore, it can use more powerful means for learning, reasoning, and acting. Thus, the two operators separate their tasks based on the required reaction time. The cognitive operator can operate at the same level as the reflective operator by steering the decisions of the reflective operator, but it can also operate at the meta-level if it optimizes parameters of the reflective operator.

As illustrated in Fig. 8.8, we structure multiple OCMs in a hierarchy to construct complex mechatronic systems (e.g., a shuttle). Moreover, collaborations of OCMs at the top level of such hierarchies are used to flexibly compose systems (e.g., multiple shuttles to a convoy). The architectural modeling is supported by hybrid UML components [36] and hybrid, real-time statecharts extending UML state machines [17]. The modeling is complemented with a code-generation scheme that derives an implementation with guarantees that the regular operation and the reconfiguration steps stay within the real-time bounds specified in the models [16, 18, 37]. Therefore, an assurance scheme has been developed for verification [38].

Compared to self-aware computing, Mechatronic UML is tailored for the particular domain of self-adaptive embedded real-time systems with mechatronic elements. The supported architectural concepts indicate that a layered architectural style fits well to the high quality and safety required in this domain. An OCM can be seen as a local-reflective self-awareness module as discussed in Chap. 6 since it has a local feedback loop realized by its two operators. However, the OCM does not make the awareness and goal models as well as the awareness/expression links explicit (cf. Chap. 5). Instead, the reflective operator manages the controller by defining a particular configuration for each operation mode, while the reflection by the cognitive operator is not specified at all in the architecture. Further supporting hierarchies of OCMs (see Fig. 8.8), Mechatronic UML adopts a mixture of local and hierarchical reflection (cf. Chap. 6). Moreover, hierarchies of OCMs can be composed of collaborations (see Fig. 8.8), which partially addresses collective systems as discussed in Chap. 7.

In general, Mechatronic UML suggests a more specific architectural design than the concepts introduced in Chap. 6. Thus, the prereflective and reflective levels of self-awareness are covered by the controller by the reflective and cognitive operators of an OCM, respectively. In contrast, the OCM hierarchies realize hierarchical control and not meta-reflective self-awareness such that the meta-reflective level is not covered. Based on the adopted architecture implied by the OCMs and their hierarchical composition, Mechatronic UML employs local and hierarchical reflection, while it excludes the phenomena of reflection, that is, overlapping, stacked, and cyclic reflection (cf. Chap. 6). Concerning the architectural styles discussed in Chap. 6, Mechatronic UML follows the hierarchical control approach. Concerning the specific concepts for collective self-aware systems introduced in Chap. 7, Mechatronic UML only supports the organizational patterns, particularly in the form of collaborations that combine mechatronic systems (see Fig. 8.8).

8.3.3 MUSIC

The main goal of MUSIC was to simplify the development of adaptive applications that operate in open and dynamic computing environments and adapt seamlessly and without user intervention in reaction to context changes. The main innovations of MUSIC were a comprehensive development framework that consists of a model-driven development methodology with a tool chain for self-adaptive, context-aware applications as well as a corresponding extensible context management and adaptation middleware supporting the development [30, 42]. Context is understood in a broad sense as any information about the user needs and the application execution environment that may vary dynamically and impact the applications. Context parameters can be monitored using appropriate hardware and software mechanisms, called context sensors. MUSIC supports a variety of adaptation mechanisms such as changing configuration and application parameters, replacing components and service bindings, and redeploying components on the distributed infrastructure [33, 69].

In the following, we provide an overview of the main ingredients of MUSIC and an attempt to position MUSIC with respect to the discussion of self-awareness.

To meet the challenges of dynamically adaptive, context-aware applications on mobile devices, MUSIC developed

- an adaptation modeling language which separates self-adaptation and business logic concerns to avoid the surge in complexity;
- generic, reusable middleware components which automate context management and application adaptation based on design-time models that are translated into runtime representations capturing the adaptation options and goals;
- tools which support the development of design models and their transformation into runtime representations for the MUSIC middleware.

An overview of the MUSIC framework is given in Fig. 8.9. The middleware implements a control loop similar to the MAPE-K loop (see Sect. 8.2.1). It monitors the relevant context sensors, and when significant changes are detected, it triggers a planning process to decide whether adaptation is necessary. When this is the case, the planning process finds a new configuration that fits the current context better than the currently used one, and triggers the adaptation of the running application. To do this, the middleware relies on an annotated QoS-aware architecture model of the application which is available at runtime. The model specifies the application dependencies on context information, its adaptation capabilities, and the objective function for adaptation reasoning. The model corresponds to the "Knowledge" component of the MAPE-K loop. The planning process of MUSIC evaluates the utility of alternative configurations, selects the most suitable one for the current context (i.e., the one with the highest utility for the current context which does not violate any resource constraints), and triggers the application adaptation accordingly.

Fig. 8.9 Overview of the MUSIC development framework

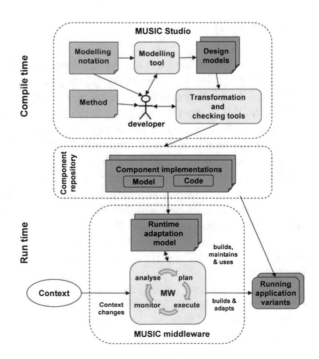

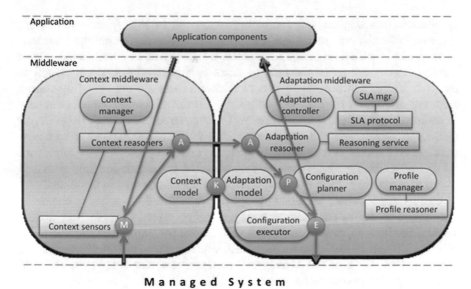

Fig. 8.10 Overview of the MUSIC middleware

An overview of the MUSIC middleware and its adaptation loop is depicted in Fig. 8.10. It shows the main components of the middleware, represented as rounded rectangles, and their mapping to the elements of MAPE-K. The managed system includes the applications, as indicated by the arrows connecting the MAPE-K loop to the application layer, as well as the underlying computing and communication infrastructure. A similar mapping can be done for the LRA-M loop (see Chap. 1) although MUSIC does not support any learning since it controls the applications based on the QoS-aware architecture model resulting from the development.

The context middleware of MUSIC is responsible for monitoring and analyzing context changes and for providing access to context information. It encapsulates the diversity of context information and maintains the context model storing and providing uniform access to both the current state and the history of context data. Moreover, context reasoners may be added to the middleware to perform reasoning on the lower-level context data and derive higher-level information. For example, a reasoner could trigger adaptation planning only when there is major change in the long-term trend of some context parameters rather than on every small value change. With respect to the MAPE-K (LRA-M) loop, the middleware covers the monitoring (collecting empirical data), partially the analyzing (reasoning) of the context, and partially the knowledge (by maintaining context-awareness models).

Thus, the very basic elements of a self-aware system are present in the MUSIC middleware. Even a learning component was considered conceptually in the design of the middleware, but it was not implemented due to project constraints. Despite the support for multi-party adaptation [34], the MUSIC solution focuses on adaptation of applications on a single mobile computing device. The MUSIC framework misses a notion of collective- or group-awareness. This will be a target of our future research.

In general, MUSIC provides a complete model-driven approach rather than a framework focusing on architectural concepts as introduced in Chap. 5. Therefore, the prereflective and reflective levels of self-awareness are not explicitly considered, but they result from the embedded support for self- and context-awareness. In contrast, meta-reflective self-awareness is not covered by MUSIC. However, the QoS-aware architecture and adaptation model of MUSIC can be seen as an awareness and goal model as it captures the system, context, options for adaptation, and the operationalized goals. In contrast, the awareness and expression links with their span and scope are not addressed explicitly but rather embedded in the model.

Using such a model, MUSIC employs centralized reflection and excludes the phenomena of overlapping, stacked, and cyclic reflection (cf. Chap. 6). Employing a single reflection step, the architectural styles discussed in Chap. 6 are not supported by MUSIC. Though MUSIC aims for distributed systems, it realizes a single, centralized reflection step that does not address the architectural concepts for collective self-aware computing systems discussed in Chap. 7.

8.3.4 ExecUtable RuntimE MegAmodels (EUREMA)

EUREMA (ExecUtable RuntimE MegAmodels) [76] is a seamless model-driven engineering approach for the specification and execution of feedback loops for self-adaptive software adopting the external approach (cf. [71]) and a layered architecture. The EUREMA modeling language is used to specify feedback loops, which makes them explicit in the design. The resulting models are kept alive at runtime, and the EUREMA interpreter directly executes these models to run feedback loops.

The specification is done using two types of diagrams as shown in Fig. 8.11 for a self-healing example. A feedback loop diagram (FLD) specifies a feedback loop with its activities (also called model operations such as Update and Repair), control flow among activities, and runtime models. Such models either represent the lower-layer entity to be adapted to achieve model-based adaptation (e.g., the Architectural Model)

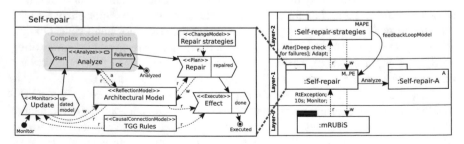

Fig. 8.11 Feedback loop diagram (FLD) and layer diagram (LD) (cf. [76])

or specify the activities (e.g., Repair Strategies determining how the system should be healed if failures occur). An activity and a model are linked in the FLD if the activity accesses the model, for instance, to read, write, or annotate it. A feedback loop can be modularly specified by multiple FLDs. For instance, the analyze activity is defined in a distinct FLD (not shown here) that is invoked by the Self-repair FLD using a complex model operation (cf. left-hand side of Fig. 8.11).

A layer diagram (LD)—as shown on the right-hand side of Fig. 8.11—then structures modules, which are instances of feedback loops as defined in FLDs, in a layered architecture. The lowest layer contains the managed system, in this case the online marketplace *mRUBiS*, that is not specified by EUREMA and thus considered as a black box. This system is adapted by a self-repair feedback loop realized by the two modules :Self-repair and :Self-repair-A. While the latter module is invoked by the former module, the execution of the former module is triggered starting in its initial state Monitor if :mRUBiS emits an RtException event and if more than ten seconds has elapsed since its previous run.

Moreover, EUREMA supports the layering of feedback loops. For instance, the Repair Strategies used by the Self-repair feedback loop will typically not be able to heal all kinds of failures since we cannot anticipate all of them during development. To adjust these strategies, we employ another feedback loop on top (see :Self-repair-strategies in the LD while we omit the related FLD here due to space restrictions) that provides new strategies to the self-repair feedback loop if the currently used one is not able to heal the failures. Hence, the higher-layer feedback loop reflects on the lower-layer feedback loop to analyze its performance and, if needed, to adapt the lower-layer feedback loop to improve the performance. A benefit of EUREMA is that the self-repair feedback loop is specified by a model (see the FLD on the left-hand side of Fig. 8.11) that is kept alive at runtime such that the higher-layer feedback loop can directly use this model to analyze and adapt the self-repair feedback loop. Nevertheless, it is also possible to define activities that maintain a distinct runtime model representing the self-repair feedback loop.

Concerning self-aware systems (cf. Chap. 5), EUREMA supports feedback loops (reflective layers) that reflect on a managed system (prereflective layer) by using abstract runtime models that are causally connected to the system. Such runtime models are similar to awareness models representing the prereflective layer and used by the reflective layer. A major difference is that EUREMA so far does not assume any learning processes, but being an open framework, EUREMA can integrate arbitrary (model-driven) processes and techniques to realize the activities of a feedback loop such as learning, reasoning, and acting of the LRA-M loop.

Moreover, EUREMA explicitly supports meta-self-awareness by layering feedback loops on top of each other. Thereby, the specification, that is, the FLD model of a feedback loop, can be directly used as the awareness model by the higher-layer feedback loop for learning, reasoning, and adaptation. Thus, EUREMA supports coordinated reflection and in particular, centralized reflection (cf. Chap. 6). Moreover, it addresses overlapping and stacked reflections but neglects cyclic reflections. With respect to the architectural styles (cf. Chap. 6), EUREMA fully supports the stacked external approach and partially the hierarchical and acyclic external approach. In contrast, the internal approach is not supported at all since it contradicts the layering of feedback loops. Finally, since EUREMA does not restrict the number of layers and supports adding/removing layers at runtime, the concept of dynamic layers leverages the long-term evolution of the system. Using (temporarily) an additional topmost layer, adaptations for maintenance can be performed [76, 77].

Recently, EUREMA has been extended to support distributed systems. The extension introduces collaborations to EUREMA, which describe the interactions among multiple feedback loops [79]. These collaborations support flexible means to coordinate multiple feedback loops and their runtime models as discussed in Chap. 7 for collectives of self-aware systems and awareness models.

8.3.5   Multi-Quality Auto-Tuning (MQuAT)

Multi-Quality Auto-Tuning (MQuAT) is a model-driven approach to develop and operate self-optimizing software systems using quality-of-service (QoS) contracts and models@run.time [39]. Figure 8.12 depicts an overview of MQuAT.

The principle idea of MQuAT is to develop self-optimizing software in terms of individual software components (i.e., elements of reuse, which explicitly specify what they require and provide). Each component realizes a particular task (e.g., sorting, encryption, or compression) and can have multiple implementations, all providing the same functionality but differing in their non-functional properties (e.g., the time or energy required to perform the task). The non-functional behavior of each implementation is characterized by the developer with QoS contracts [40]. As concrete statements, for instance, about the execution time of a component, depend on the used hardware and the respective input data, which are both unknown during development, these contracts are refined at runtime by benchmarking. That is, the

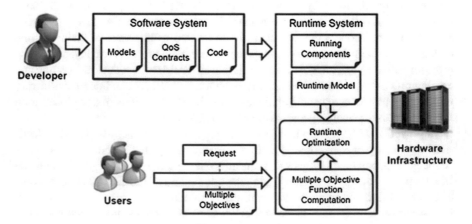

Fig. 8.12 Overview of multi-quality auto-tuning

Fig. 8.13 The role of
models@run.time in MQuAT

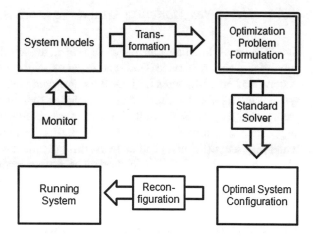

developer has to provide a benchmark for each implementation, which is used at runtime to derive a hardware-specific variant of the contract. When a user poses a request to the system, the input data are known and, hence, the hardware-specific contracts can be refined further to be request-specific. This version of the contracts now contains concrete statements about the non-functional properties of the respective implementation (e.g., the sorting task will take 30 ms on this hardware for this request). Based on these contracts and a runtime model representing the current state of the system, MQuAT generates an optimization problem, which is solved using standard solvers. The resulting solution is translated to a reconfiguration script [41].

This process is depicted in Fig. 8.13 and denotes a particular variant of a self-aware computing system adhering to the models@run.time paradigm and the LRA-M loop as introduced in Chap. 1. The running system is learning by observing itself and its environment with the aim to keep the runtime model of the system in sync with the actual system. This runtime model is reasoned upon by comparing it to QoS contracts to identify adaptation needs. The reasoning is realized by a model-to-text transformation of the runtime model, the design-time models, and QoS contracts to some optimization language (e.g., integer linear programming). Finally, if a better configuration is found, the system acts by reconfiguring itself.

In terms of the concepts for self-aware computing (see Chap. 5), MQuAT enables the development of reflective systems by using an awareness model. If the scheme is applied multiple times, MQuAT can cover the meta-reflective case, too. The awareness model is kept synchronous to its underlying system by collecting empirical data (benchmarking). MQuAT offers a simple variant of goal models in the form of QoS objectives (e.g., minimize energy consumption). Awareness and expression links are not explicitly represented. However, the accuracy of knowledge covered in an awareness model is explicitly captured by the coefficient of determination (R^2). In terms of the concepts introduced in Chap. 6, MQuAT uses coordinated reflection and follows the hierarchical external style. As MQuAT does not aim to support the integration of multiple systems, the concepts introduced in Chap. 7 are not applicable to it.

8.3.6 Descartes Modeling Language (DML)

The Descartes Modeling Language (DML)[2] is an architecture-level modeling language for quality of service (QoS) and resource management of modern dynamic IT systems and infrastructures [53]. DML is designed to serve as a basis for self-aware systems management during operation, ensuring that the system's QoS requirements are continuously satisfied while infrastructure resources are utilized as efficiently as possible. The term QoS refers here to performance (response time, throughput, scalability, and efficiency) and dependability (availability, reliability, and security). The current version of DML is focused on performance and availability; however, the language itself is generic and intended to eventually support further QoS properties.

DML has a modular structure and is provided as a set of meta-models for describing the resource landscape, the application architecture, the adaptation points, and adaptation processes of a system. The meta-models can be used in both online and offline settings for performance prediction and proactive system reconfiguration.

The designers of DML advocate a holistic model-based approach where systems are designed from the ground up with built-in self-reflective and self-predictive capabilities, encapsulated in the form of online system architecture models. The latter are assumed to capture the relevant influences (with respect to the system's operational goals) of the system's software architecture, its configuration, its usage profile, and its execution environment (e.g., physical hardware, virtualization, and middleware). The online models are also assumed to explicitly capture the system's goals and policies (e.g., QoS requirements, service level agreements, and efficiency targets) as well as the system's adaptation space, adaptation strategies and processes. Figure 8.14 presents the DML vision of a self-aware system adaptation loop, based on the MAPE-K loop, in combination with the online models used to guide the system adaptation at runtime. The four phases of the loop are as follows:

Phase 1 (Observe/Reflect): In this phase, the managed system is observed and monitoring data are collected and used to extract, refine, calibrate, and continuously update the online system models, reflecting the relevant influences that need to be captured in order to realize the self-predictive property with respect to the system's operational goals. Here, expertise from software engineering, systems modeling, and analysis, as well as machine learning, is required for the automatic extraction, refinement, and calibration of the online models based on the runtime observations.

Phase 2 (Detect/Predict): In this phase, the monitoring data and online models are used to analyze the current state of the system in order to detect or predict problems such as SLA violations, inefficient resource usage, system failures, and network attacks. Workload forecasting combined with performance prediction and anomaly detection techniques can be used to predict the impact of changes in the environment (e.g., varying system workloads) and anticipate problems before they have actually occurred. Here, expertise from systems modeling, simulation, and analysis, as well as autonomic computing and artificial intelligence, is required to detect and predict problems at different timescales during operation.

---

[2]http://descartes.tools/dml (formerly also known as Descartes Meta-Model (DMM)).

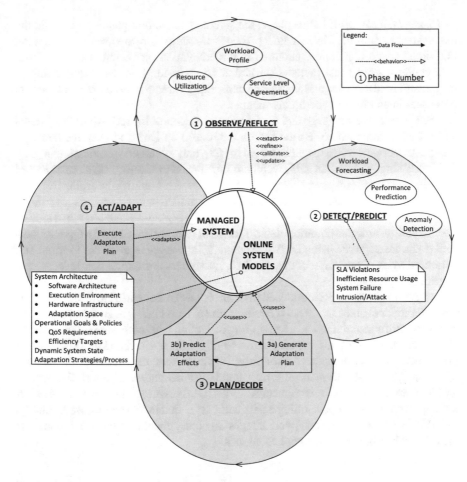

Fig. 8.14 DML system adaptation loop

Phase 3 (Plan/Decide): In this phase, the online system models are used to find an adequate solution to a detected or predicted problem by adapting the system at runtime. Two steps are executed iteratively in this phase: (i) generation of an adaptation plan and (ii) prediction of the adaptation effects. In the first step, a candidate adaptation plan is generated based on the online models that capture the system adaptation strategies, taking into account the urgency of the problem that needs to be resolved. In the second step, the effects of the considered possible adaptation plan are predicted, again by means of the online models. The two steps are repeated until an adequate adaptation plan is found that would successfully resolve the detected or predicted problem. Here, expertise from systems modeling, simulation, and analysis, as well as autonomic computing, artificial intelligence, and data center resource management, is required to implement predictable adaptation processes.

Phase 4 (Act/Adapt): In this phase, the selected adaptation plan is applied on the real system at runtime. The actuators provided by the system are used to execute the individual adaptation actions captured in the adaptation plan. Here, expertise from data center resource management (virtualization, cluster, grid, and cloud computing), distributed systems, and autonomic computing is required to execute adaptation processes in an efficient and timely manner.

DML provides a language and a reference architecture for self-aware IT systems and infrastructures where self-awareness is focused on QoS and resource management. An overview of DML can be found in [53], and a detailed specification in [52].

Concerning the levels of self-awareness introduced in Chap. 3, DML can be used to design self-awareness mechanisms at all three levels: prereflective, reflective, and meta-reflective. The online system architecture models can be seen as awareness models that are learned based on static information (model skeletons) provided at system design-time and empirical data collected at runtime (cf. Chap. 5). Operationalized goals are captured using DML's Strategies/Tactics/Actions (S/T/A) formalism, which includes a basic form of goal models. Awareness and expression links are not explicitly represented.

In terms of the concepts introduced in Chap. 6, DML can be used to design systems with hierarchical and centralized reflection; however, it currently does not explicitly support coordinated reflection. Overlapping reflection is directly supported by using alternative tactics for the same adaptation strategy; the stacked and cyclic reflection phenomena are not considered explicitly; however, they can manifest themselves when applying DML to manage different subsystems and/or layers of the system architecture. In terms of the architectural styles, DML assumes the generalized external approach while not prescribing a particular style that has to be followed. Finally, as DML is not designed to support integrating independent systems, the concepts introduced in Chap. 7 are not applicable to it.

8.4   Open Challenges

Based on the previous sections, we now discuss open challenges for the fundamental architectural concepts introduced in Chap. 5 as well as for the generic architectures of individual and collective self-aware computing systems introduced in Chaps. 6 and 7. We identified different classes of challenges such that we grouped them as follows:

- self-awareness and self-expression,
- encapsulation for self-awareness and self-expression,
- interference, separation, and emergence,
- dynamic architectures, and
- other challenges.

(1) Self-Awareness and Self-Expression

The first group of challenges relates to self-awareness and self-expression. It concerns the complex and potentially cyclic graphs resulting from the awareness and expression links, the support for detailed semantics of such links (cf. Chap. 3), the static knowledge supporting self-awareness, and finally the uncertainty as a main driver for inaccurate and imprecise self-awareness.

Complex and cyclic awareness and expression link graphs: The notation we propose in Chap. 5 allows us to describe direct and indirect awareness and expression links. The graph resulting from the combination of such links can become complex when considering large systems and advanced forms of self-awareness (e.g., architectural elements acting as spans and scopes in various self-awareness relationships that differ in the type of awareness such as stimulus-, interaction-, time-, or goal-awareness). Concepts to describe such complex graphs of awareness and expression links and to understand their implications are currently missing.

Describing the awareness and expression links as a graph supports studying the dependencies between the individual spans and scopes of the awareness and expression. As known from the literature on self-adaptive systems (cf. [15, 63, 73]), not only the individual-awareness or expression links but additionally their interplay that forms feedback loops as well as the interferences of these loops are main challenges for the design of self-adaptive systems. Therefore, means to describe and analyze the interplay and interferences between awareness and expression links are required. In this context, cyclic relationships are a particular challenge, for instance, to guarantee termination, convergence, and an appropriate outcome of the learning, reasoning, and acting processes along the expression and awareness links.

A related challenge is which *detailed semantics of the awareness and expression links* should be covered at the architectural level to achieve separation of concerns. We address the different dimensions of awareness such as time-, interaction-, or state-awareness (cf. Chap. 3) with stereotypes attached to the awareness links (cf. Chap. 5). However, to address the subtle aspects of such dimensions and to enable their analysis, they have to be treated in a much more explicit manner such as describing the specific semantics of the dimensions in a particular case. The same holds for the expression links that only represent the fact that a span impacts a scope without substantiating their semantics such as the extent or kind of impact.

With our notation, we focused on how architectural elements dynamically obtain knowledge by collecting empirical data as well as learning and reasoning about that data (cf. LRA-M loop modeled in Chap. 5). However, we also observed the need to capture *static knowledge* that has been established at design time, embedded into modules, and exploited at runtime (see the discussion of capturing the feed-forward and adaptive control schemes in Chap. 6). Such static knowledge supports self-awareness and it might be enriched by dynamic knowledge at runtime. Hence, means to describe static knowledge along awareness and expression links are required to distinguish it from dynamic knowledge. This further requires means to describe and analyze the composition of static and dynamic knowledge.

Regardless of static or dynamic knowledge, ruling the *uncertainty* that can be tolerated for the runtime models and other elements of the architecture is a major design issue (cf. [35]). Currently, the architectural descriptions do not show the degree of uncertainty that exists in the system as well as the extent to which processes are used to counteract the uncertainty. This calls for specifying or measuring the accuracy and precision of empirical data, awareness models, and actions, which should be supported by reflection interfaces (cf. Chap. 6) as well as how processes address uncertainty in this context. Such information is the basis for determining the uncertainty in the self-awareness of the system, which can be a critical dimension in the design space for self-aware computing systems.

(2) Encapsulation for Self-Awareness and Self-Expression

The second group of challenges addresses the trade-off between the power of self-awareness and self-expression and the need for encapsulation. While strong encapsulation demands explicit and restrictive interfaces, powerful self-awareness and self-expression require generic interfaces for computational reflection with as little encapsulation as possible. Furthermore, concepts for reflection interfaces are required that are able to bridge the abstraction gap between the span and the scope.

Encapsulation and computational reflection: The proposed notation allows us to describe the encapsulation of modules by means of ports and interfaces as well as their links to elements contained in these modules such as awareness models, empirical data, or processes (see Chap. 5). As an alternative, we can model the direct access to a module's internals, which denotes a form of computational reflection. However, in practice a compromise between explicitly encoded access through ports and computation reflection may be needed. Our notation primarily supports the explicitly encoded access, while it lacks concepts to make various forms of computational reflection (e.g., declarative and procedural reflection [58]) explicit.

In this context, finding an appropriate notion for a *reflection interface* (cf. Chap. 6) that separates different levels of reflection such as the prereflective and reflective levels is a crucial challenge. We either have local reflection interfaces where a single interface encapsulates only one monolithic module, which results in a reasonably low complexity for the interface and its realization. However, if a reflection interface covers a group of modules, it becomes more complicated since multiple modules have to be jointly observed and adapted while they and their interconnections may dynamically change (e.g., considering a flexible collaboration of modules). Nevertheless, the increasing complexity of realizing the reflection interface shields the reflecting elements from the complexity of the reflected elements by using the interface. Hence, the design of a reflection interface impacts the complexity of elements performing the reflection and hence establishing self-awareness.

Another dimension that has to be considered for a reflection interface is the degree of *observability* and *controllability*. Observability determines the scope of an awareness link, that is, what can be observed by a span. Controllability determines the action and influence scope of an expression link, that is, what can be directly or indirectly changed by a span. Consequently, this dimension of a reflection interface has to be properly chosen as it determines the system's self-awareness and self-expression capabilities that should be sufficiently powerful to achieve the goals.

To develop a notion of a reflection interface, a promising research direction can be the use of models@run.time [12] serving as interfaces to a managed system.

Finally, the design of the reflection interfaces and the restriction implied by the design may limit the evolution of the system as any reflection can only happen within the anticipated observability and controllability. This might require means to support dynamically adjusting the reflection interfaces to increase (or in certain situation even to decrease) the degree of observability and controllability.

(3) Interference, Separation, and Emergence

This group of challenges targets the existence of multiple awareness and expression links and raises questions of the granularity of self-awareness and self-expression as well as of their separation and dependencies (e.g., interferences). While the separation of different self-awareness concerns such as self-healing or self-configuration is a general problem, the following challenges additionally arise for collectives of self-aware systems: How collective self-awareness can emerge from individual self-awareness? How changes at the individual level can impact the collective level? How concrete architectures for collective self-awareness can be developed?

Achieving a suitable *separation of self-awareness concerns* in an architecture, which reduces the complexity of the problem for individual self-aware systems, is challenging. It is well known from control theory that multiple feedback loops can only be employed if a careful analysis ensures that they are sufficiently decoupled. For self-adaptive software, it has been advocated that feedback loops should be treated as first-class entities in the architectural design and analysis [15, 73]. Likewise, we know from the agent domain that conflicting goals require our attention when designing the agents. Consequently, when multiple awareness and expression links overlap or compete, a suitable approach to study such phenomena at the architectural level is required. However, such an approach is lacking although the concepts introduced in Chap. 5 already go beyond the state of the art (e.g., [44]).

Particularly for emergent architectures, means to ensure the runtime detection and resolution of conflicts are required as such conflicts cannot be necessarily anticipated and addressed by construction. Here, an additional problem may occur since not only feedback loops may compete, but cyclic networks of awareness and expression links may require means to ensure convergent behavior achieving the goals. Addressing such problems at the architectural level is further complicated as *abstraction* may lead to spurious cycles (cf. Chaps. 5 and 6), which requires to identify the right level of detail to identify and understand such problems.

Another challenge is to achieve *collective self-awareness from individual self-awareness* of subsystems. Here, the main question is how the self-awareness at the collective level can emerge from behavior and self-awareness at the individual level. A related challenge is to identify and control the *impact of changes in individual self-awareness on collective self-awareness*. How can such effects be addressed at the architectural level such that the envisioned self-awareness at the collective level is achieved? Finally, it remains an overall challenge of how to translate the answers to the above questions into *concrete architectures for collectives of self-aware systems* that feature the targeted self-awareness levels and can meet their high-level goals.

(4) Dynamic Architectures

Challenges that apply to individual and collective self-aware systems concern the dynamic architecture; that is, the architecture may dynamically change as a result of either external changes or self-adaptation/self-expression. A first challenge is that we lack a notation that is able to capture the architectural dynamics in a comprehensible manner. Furthermore, it is a major challenge to rule the dynamics at the level of individual systems as well as at the level of collectives such that the self-awareness and self-expression mechanisms are able to cope with the dynamics. Moreover, the coherent behavior of individual systems in a collective is crucial since each system may evolve independently without any joint, overall management.

Capturing Dynamics: The proposed notation allows us to model static or snapshots of architectures that show the static existence of self-awareness. However, an architecture can be dynamic by supporting structural changes [59]. The notation proposed in Chap. 5 lacks concepts to make the dynamics and the variability of the architecture explicit. Moreover, it lacks concepts to describe and understand the impact of such dynamics on (the existence and evolution of) self-awareness.

Therefore, the challenge is to cover the *architectural dynamics of an individual self-aware system*, which concerns the establishing of self-awareness, for instance, when prereflective or reflective modules dynamically join or leave the system. In this context, the generalized external approach that separates the reflecting from the reflected modules (cf. Chap. 6) seems to be better suited for handling dynamic cases since it can employ centralized reflection to learn global models of the prereflective layer and hence, it can have global knowledge of this layer and observe its dynamic changes. In contrast, the generalized internal approaches often rely on a precoded wiring among the modules, which might limit the dynamics to local changes. For instance, an architecture adopting the generalized external approach can address such dynamics by employing architectural-awareness models of each prereflective, reflective, meta-reflective, meta-meta-reflective layer, etc. (cf. [76]). In addition, to control the dynamics of each layer, behavior models specifying the architectural dynamics seem to be necessary (e.g., [16]). However, it is not clear whether the ideas of such approaches are generically applicable or whether they are applicable only to specific styles and domains with their implied architectural restrictions such as a strict layering of modules. Generalizing and applying such ideas to other styles and domains are worth investigating.

Moreover, the *variability* in the architecture of self-aware systems should be made explicit to span the solution space, which can be explored and even extended by self-awareness and self-expression. However, this inherent architectural aspect is not addressed by the concepts we proposed in the previous chapters. An extension to these concepts is needed and feature models can be a starting point for that.

In addition to a single, dynamically changing self-aware systems, the *architectural dynamics of a collective self-aware system* is a big challenge including questions of how to dynamically adapt and evolve such a collective to the changing goals, self-awareness levels, internal resources, and execution environment, and of how to *ensure a coherent behavior of collectives* when individual subsystems change.

(5) Other Challenges

Finally, there are aspects and related challenges that we do not address at all with the architectural concepts discussed in Chaps. 5, 6, and 7. For instance, we neglected the aspect of integrating legacy software, enabling reuse, and supporting particular domains with their specific needs and limitations.

The integration of *legacy software* with its architecture, respectively, used middleware/framework is challenging because of having to provide reflections on it. The proposed architectural concepts consider either explicit reflection interfaces or the direct access to the internals of a modules to realize computational reflection. Integrating a legacy software into such an architecture imposes the challenge that the architecture of the legacy software might adopt a different style and does not provide a compatible mechanism to reflect upon it.

Furthermore, to enable *reuse*, some approaches advocate using a generic adaptation mechanism offered by the middleware and only encode the possible solution space and optimization criteria (e.g., MUSIC as discussed in Sect. 8.3.3). How can we cover such approaches at the architectural level—to benefit from the reuse—without embedding the infrastructure/middleware in the architecture? On the other hand, approaches such as Rainbow [32] advocate architectural frameworks that predefine large fragments of the architecture and thus restrict the design space of the system. What is the appropriate granularity of reuse that still provides the freedom to explore architectural choices for individual systems depending on the domain?

Finally, *domain-specific extensions* are required to address the additional constraints and requirements imposed by a particular domain. To realize self-awareness for cyber-physical systems (cf. [16]), sensor networks, or Internet-of-things scenarios, typical domain-specific aspects are predictable real-time behavior, safety issues, or severe resource constraints. For enterprise application, besides the computing part, also humans in the loop play an important role. How can we develop and integrate such domain-specific extensions into a generic framework for self-aware systems?

8.5 Conclusion

In this chapter, we reviewed the state of the art concerning self-aware computing systems with the particular focus on the software architecture. Particularly, we compared state-of-the-art approaches with the fundamental architectural concepts for self-aware systems (cf. Chap. 5), the generic architectures for individual self-aware systems (cf. Chap. 6), and the generic architectures for collectives of self-aware systems (cf. Chap. 7). The approaches we included in the comparison are either reference architectures or architectural frameworks and languages for software systems that share similarities with self-aware computing systems.

The comparison of the proposed architectural concepts with the state-of-the-art approaches demonstrated that the concepts are helpful and oftentimes allow us to make explicit or at least to emphasize specific aspects relevant to self-awareness. Existing reference architectures or approaches often only support such aspects implicitly, for instance, by assumptions. For example, the MAPE-K reference architecture keeps the knowledge part abstract, while we detailed this part. More specifically, we made the awareness models explicit and further linked these models to spans and scopes to denote the self-awareness and self-expression in the architecture.

Moreover, in contrast to the reference architectures and approaches that usually suggest a rather specific architectural style, the proposed concepts support modeling architectures of a broader spectrum ranging from layered architectures with a single centralized self-awareness module to those architectures where self-awareness emerges from the coupled operation of several modules at the level of an individual system up to the level of collectives of systems.

Based on the comparison, we identified open challenges. These challenges showed that the proposed concepts for awareness and expression links are too limited since they do not address analyzing cyclic links, specifying detailed semantics of such links, as well as capturing static knowledge and uncertainty. Furthermore, additional challenges relate to the trade-off between the power of self-awareness and self-expression and the need for encapsulation for reflection as well as to the design and analysis of separating self-awareness and self-awareness concerns. Another group of challenges pointed out the need to address architectural dynamics that result from either external changes or self-expression. Finally, we sketched aspects and challenges that we completely neglected with the proposed architectural concepts. These aspects are legacy software, reuse, and domain-specific extensions for self-aware computing systems.

As future directions, we suggest approaching the open challenges as well as conducting studies to obtain more practical experience with developing architectures for individual and collective self-aware computing systems.

Acknowledgements This chapter is the result of stimulating discussions among the authors and other participants, especially Paola Inverardi and Peter Lewis, during the seminar on Model-driven Algorithms and Architectures for Self-Aware Computing Systems at Schloss Dagstuhl in January 2015 (http://www.dagstuhl.de/15041).

References

1. Anant Agarwal and Bill Harrod. Organic computing. Technical Report White paper, MIT and DARPA, 2006.
2. Anant Agarwal, Jason Miller, Jonathan Eastep, David Wentziaff, and Harshad Kasture. Self-aware computing. Technical Report AFRL-RI-RS-TR-2009-161, MIT, 2009.
3. John R. Anderson, editor. *The Architecture of Cognition*. Harrvard University Press, 1983.
4. Uwe Aßmann, Sebastian Götz, Jean-Marc Jézéquel, Brice Morin, and Mario Trapp. A Reference Architecture and Roadmap for Models@run.time Systems. In Nelly Bencomo, Robert

France, Betty H. C. Cheng, and Uwe Aßmann, editors, *Models@run.time: Foundations, Applications, and Roadmaps*, pages 1–18. Springer, 2014.

5. Ozalp Babaoglu, Mark Jelasity, Alberto Montresor, Christof Fetzer, Stefano Leonardi, Aad van Moorsel, and Maarten van Steen, editors. *Self-star Properties in Complex Information Systems: Conceptual and Practical Foundations*, volume 3460 of *Lecture Notes in Computer Science (LNCS)*. Springer, 2005.

6. Kirstie L. Bellman and Christopher Landauer. Towards an Integration Science. *Journal of Mathematical Analysis and Applications*, 249(1):3–31, 2000.

7. Kirstie L. Bellman, Christopher Landauer, and Phyllis R. Nelson. Systems Engineering for Organic Computing: The Challenge of Shared Design and Control between OC Systems and their Human Engineers. In *Organic Computing*, pages 25–80. Springer, 2008.

8. Nelly Bencomo. Quantun: Quantification of uncertainty for the reassessment of requirements. In *Proceedings of 23rd International Conference on Requirements Engineering (RE)*, pages 236–240. IEEE, 2015.

9. Nelly Bencomo, Amel Bennaceur, Paul Grace, Gordon S. Blair, and Valérie Issarny. The role of models@run.time in supporting on-the-fly interoperability. *Computing*, 95(3):167–190, 2013.

10. Nelly Bencomo, Jon Whittle, Pete Sawyer, Anthony Finkelstein, and Emmanuel Letier. Requirements reflection: Requirements as runtime entities. In *Proceedings of the 32nd International Conference on Software Engineering - Vol. 2*, ICSE '10, pages 199–202. ACM, 2010.

11. Amel Bennaceur, Robert France, Giordano Tamburrelli, Thomas Vogel, Pieter J Mosterman, Walter Cazzola, Fbio M. Costa, Alfonso Pierantonio, Matthias Tichy, Mehmet Aksit, Pr Emmanuelson, Huang Gang, Nikolaos Georgantas, and David Redlich. Mechanisms for Leveraging Models at Runtime in Self-adaptive Software. In Nelly Bencomo, Robert France, Betty H.C. Cheng, and Uwe Assmann, editors, *Models@run.time*, volume 8378 of *Lecture Notes in Computer Science (LNCS)*, pages 19–46. Springer, 2014.

12. Gordon Blair, Nelly Bencomo, and Robert France. Models@run.time. *Computer*, 42(10):22–27, 2009.

13. Victor Braberman, Nicolas D'Ippolito, Jeff Kramer, Daniel Sykes, and Sebastian Uchitel. Morph: A reference architecture for configuration and behaviour self-adaptation. In *Proceedings of the 1st International Workshop on Control Theory for Software Engineering*, CTSE 2015, pages 9–16. ACM, 2015.

14. Rodney A. Brooks, editor. *Cambrian Intelligence: The Early History of the New AI*. MIT Press, 1999.

15. Yuriy Brun, Giovanna Di Marzo Serugendo, Cristina Gacek, Holger Giese, Holger Kienle, Marin Litoiu, Hausi Müller, Mauro Pezzè, and Mary Shaw. Engineering Self-Adaptive Systems through Feedback Loops. In Betty H.C. Cheng, Rogério de Lemos, Holger Giese, Paola Inverardi, and Jeff Magee, editors, *Software Engineering for Self-Adaptive Systems*, volume 5525 of *Lecture Notes in Computer Science (LNCS)*, pages 48–70. Springer, 2009.

16. Sven Burmester, Holger Giese, Eckehard Münch, Oliver Oberschelp, Florian Klein, and Peter Scheideler. Tool Support for the Design of Self-Optimizing Mechatronic Multi-Agent Systems. *Journal on Software Tools for Technology Transfer (STTT)*, 10(3):207–222, 2008.

17. Sven Burmester, Holger Giese, and Oliver Oberschelp. Hybrid UML Components for the Design of Complex Self-optimizing Mechatronic Systems. In J. Braz, H. Araújo, A. Vieira, and B. Encarnacao, editors, *Informatics in Control, Automation and Robotics I*. Springer, 2006.

18. Sven Burmester, Holger Giese, and Wilhelm Schfer. Model-Driven Architecture for Hard Real-Time Systems: From Platform Independent Models to Code. In *Proceedings of the European Conference on Model Driven Architecture - Foundations and Applications (ECMDA-FA)*, volume 3748 of *Lecture Notes in Computer Science (LNCS)*, pages 25–40. Springer, 2005.

19. Radu Calinescu, Lars Grunske, Marta Z. Kwiatkowska, Raffaela Mirandola, and Giordano Tamburrelli. Dynamic qos management and optimization in service-based systems. *IEEE Trans. Software Eng.*, 37(3):387–409, 2011.

20. Betty H.C. Cheng, Rogério de Lemos, Holger Giese, Paola Inverardi, Jeff Magee, Jesper Andersson, Basil Becker, Nelly Bencomo, Yuriy Brun, Bojan Cukic, Giovanna Di Marzo Serugendo, Schahram Dustdar, Anthony Finkelstein, Cristina Gacek, Kurt Geihs, Vincenzo Grassi, Gabor

Karsai, Holger M. Kienle, Jeff Kramer, Marin Litoiu, Sam Malek, Raffaela Mirandola, Hausi Müller, Sooyong Park, Mary Shaw, Matthias Tichy, Massimo Tivoli, Danny Weyns, and Jon Whittle. Software Engineering for Self-Adaptive Systems: A Research Roadmap. In Betty H.C. Cheng, Rogério de Lemos, Holger Giese, Paola Inverardi, and Jeff Magee, editors, *Software Engineering for Self-Adaptive Systems*, volume 5525 of *Lecture Notes in Computer Science (LNCS)*, pages 1–26. Springer, 2009.

21. Betty H.C. Cheng, Holger Giese, Paola Inverardi, Jeff Magee, and Rogério de Lemos, editors. *Software Engineering for Self-Adaptive Systems*, volume 5525 of *Lecture Notes in Computer Science (LNCS)*. Springer, 2009.

22. Shang-Wen Cheng, VaheV. Poladian, David Garlan, and Bradley Schmerl. Improving architecture-based self-adaptation through resource prediction. In Betty H.C. Cheng, Rogerio de Lemos, Holger Giese, Paola Inverardi, and Jeff Magee, editors, *Software Engineering for Self-Adaptive Systems*, volume 5525 of *Lecture Notes in Computer Science (LNCS)*, pages 71–88. Springer, 2009.

23. David M. Chess, Alla Segal, and Ian Whalley. Unity: Experiences with a prototype autonomic computing system. In *Proceedings of the First International Conference on Autonomic Computing*, ICAC '04, pages 140–147. IEEE, 2004.

24. M.T. Cox. Metacognition in computation: A selected research review. *Art. Int.*, 169(2):104–141, 2005.

25. Rogério de Lemos, Holger Giese, Hausi Müller, and Mary Shaw, editors. *Software Engineering for Self-Adaptive Systems II*, volume 7475 of *Lecture Notes in Computer Science (LNCS)*. Springer, 2013.

26. Rogério de Lemos, Holger Giese, Hausi Müller, Mary Shaw, Jesper Andersson, Marin Litoiu, Bradley Schmerl, Gabriel Tamura, Norha M. Villegas, Thomas Vogel, Danny Weyns, Luciano Baresi, Basil Becker, Nelly Bencomo, Yuriy Brun, Bojan Cukic, Ron Desmarais, Schahram Dustdar, Gregor Engels, Kurt Geihs, Karl Goeschka, Alessandra Gorla, Vincenzo Grassi, Paola Inverardi, Gabor Karsai, Jeff Kramer, Antónia Lopes, Jeff Magee, Sam Malek, Serge Mankovskii, Raffaela Mirandola, John Mylopoulos, Oscar Nierstrasz, Mauro Pezzè, Christian Prehofer, Wilhelm Schäfer, Rick Schlichting, Dennis B. Smith, Joao P. Sousa, Ladan Tahvildari, Kenny Wong, and Jochen Wuttke. Software Engineering for Self-Adaptive Systems: A second Research Roadmap. In Rogério de Lemos, Holger Giese, Hausi Müller, and Mary Shaw, editors, *Software Engineering for Self-Adaptive Systems II*, volume 7475 of *Lecture Notes in Computer Science (LNCS)*, pages 1–32. Springer, 2013.

27. Bassem Debbabi, Ada Diaconescu, and Philippe Lalanda. Controlling self-organising software applications with archetypes. In *IEEE International Conference on Self-Adaptive and Self-Organizing Systems (SASO)*, pages 69–78. IEEE, 2012.

28. Marco Dorigo, Vito Trianni, Erol Şahin, Roderich Groß, Thomas H. Labella, Gianluca Baldassarre, Stefano Nolfi, Jean-Louis Deneubourg, Francesco Mondada, Dario Floreano, and Luca M. Gambardella. Evolving self-organizing behaviors for a swarm-bot. *Autonomous Robots*, 17:223–245, 2004.

29. Stephen Fickas and Martin S. Feather. Requirements monitoring in dynamic environments. In *Proceedings of the Second IEEE International Symposium on Requirements Engineering (RE)*, pages 140–147. IEEE, 1995.

30. J. Floch, C. Fr, R. Fricke, K. Geihs, M. Wagner, J. Lorenzo, E. Soladana, S. Mehlhase, N. Paspallis, H. Rahnama, P.A. Ruiz, and U. Scholz. Playing music building context-aware and self-adaptive mobile applications. *Software: Practice and Experience*, 43(3):359–388, 2013.

31. Sylvain Frey, Ada Diaconescu, and Isabelle M. Demeure. Architectural Integration Patterns for Autonomic Management Systems. In *Proceedings of the 9th IEEE International Conference and Workshops on the Engineering of Autonomic and Autonomous Systems (EASe 2012)*, 2012.

32. David Garlan, Shang-Wen Cheng, An-Cheng Huang, Bradley R. Schmerl, and Peter Steenkiste. Rainbow: Architecture-based self-adaptation with reusable infrastructure. *IEEE Computer*, 37(10):46–54, 2004.

33. K. Geihs, P. Barone, F. Eliassen, J. Floch, R. Fricke, E. Gjorven, S. Hallsteinsen, G. Horn, M. U. Khan, A. Mamelli, G. A. Papadopoulos, N. Paspallis, R. Reichle, and E. Stav. A comprehensive

solution for application-level adaptation. *Software: Practice and Experience*, 39(4):385–422, 2009.

34. K. Geihs, C. Evers, R. Reichle, M. Wagner, and M. U. Khan. Development support for qos-aware service-adaptation in ubiquitous computing applications. In *Proceedings of the 2011 ACM Symposium on Applied Computing*, SAC '11, pages 197–202. ACM, 2011.

35. Holger Giese, Nelly Bencomo, Liliana Pasquale, AndresJ. Ramirez, Paola Inverardi, Sebastian Wtzoldt, and Siobhan Clarke. Living with Uncertainty in the Age of Runtime Models. In Nelly Bencomo, Robert France, Betty H.C. Cheng, and Uwe Assmann, editors, *Models@run.time*, volume 8378 of *Lecture Notes in Computer Science (LNCS)*, pages 47–100. Springer, 2014.

36. Holger Giese, Sven Burmester, Wilhelm Schäfer, and Oliver Oberschelp. Modular Design and Verification of Component-Based Mechatronic Systems with Online-Reconfiguration. In *Proceedings of 12th ACM SIGSOFT Foundations of Software Engineering 2004 (FSE 2004)*, pages 179–188. ACM, 2004.

37. Holger Giese, Stefan Henkler, and Martin Hirsch. A multi-paradigm approach supporting the modular execution of reconfigurable hybrid systems. *SIMULATION*, 87(9):775–808, 2011.

38. Holger Giese and Wilhelm Schfer. Model-Driven Development of Safe Self-Optimizing Mechatronic Systems with MechatronicUML. In Javier Camara, Rogrio de Lemos, Carlo Ghezzi, and Antónia Lopes, editors, *Assurances for Self-Adaptive Systems*, volume 7740 of *Lecture Notes in Computer Science (LNCS)*, pages 152–186. Springer, 2013.

39. Sebastian Götz, Claas Wilke, Sebastian Cech, and Uwe Aßmann. *Sustainable ICTs and Management Systems for Green Computing*, chapter Architecture and Mechanisms for Energy Auto Tuning, pages 45–73. IGI Global, June 2012.

40. Sebastian Götz, Claas Wilke, Sebastian Richly, and Uwe Aßmann. Approximating quality contracts for energy auto-tuning software. In *Proceedings of First International Workshop on Green and Sustainable Software (GREENS 2012)*, 2012.

41. Sebastian Götz, Claas Wilke, Sebastian Richly, Georg Püschel, and Uwe Assmann. Model-driven self-optimization using integer linear programming and pseudo-boolean optimization. In *Proceedings of The Fifth International Conference on Adaptive and Self-Adaptive Systems and Applications (ADAPTIVE)*, pages 55–64. XPS Press.

42. S. Hallsteinsen, K. Geihs, N. Paspallis, F. Eliassen, G. Horn, J. Lorenzo, A. Mamelli, and G. A. Papadopoulos. A development framework and methodology for self-adapting applications in ubiquitous computing environments. *J. Syst. Softw.*, 85(12):2840–2859, December 2012.

43. B. Hayes-Roth. A blackboard architecture for control. In *Artificial Intelligence*, volume 26-3, pages 251–321, 1985.

44. Regina Hebig, Holger Giese, and Basil Becker. Making control loops explicit when architecting self-adaptive systems. In *Proceedings of the Second International Workshop on Self-organizing Architectures*, SOAR '10, pages 21–28. ACM, 2010.

45. Thorsten Hestermeyer, Oliver Oberschelp, and Holger Giese. Structured Information Processing For Self-optimizing Mechatronic Systems. In Helder Araujo, Alves Vieira, Jose Braz, Bruno Encarnacao, and Marina Carvalho, editors, *1st International Conference on Informatics in Control, Automation and Robotics (ICINCO 2004)*, pages 230–237. INSTICC Press, 2004.

46. Julia Hielscher, Raman Kazhamiakin, Andreas Metzger, and Marco Pistore. A framework for proactive self-adaptation of service-based applications based on online testing. In Petri Mahonen, Klaus Pohl, and Thierry Priol, editors, *Towards a Service-Based Internet*, volume 5377 of *Lecture Notes in Computer Science (LNCS)*, pages 122–133. Springer, 2008.

47. Henry Hoffmann, Martina Maggio, Marco D. Santambrogio, Alberto Leva, , and Anant Agarwal. Seec: A general and extensible framework for self-aware computing. Technical Report MIT-CSAIL-TR-2011-046, MIT CSAIL, 2011.

48. IBM. An Architectural Blueprint for Autonomic Computing, 2003. White Paper.

49. John E. Kelly and Steve Hamm. *Smart machines : IBM's Watson and the era of cognitive computing*. Columbia Business School Publishing, 2013.

50. Jeffrey O. Kephart and David M. Chess. The vision of autonomic computing. *Computer*, 36(1):41–50, 2003.

51. Samuel Kounev. Self-Aware Software and Systems Engineering: A Vision and Research Roadmap. In *GI Softwaretechnik-Trends, 31(4), 2011*, Karlsruhe, Germany, 2011.
52. Samuel Kounev, Fabian Brosig, and Nikolaus Huber. The Descartes Modeling Language. Technical report, Department of Computer Science, University of Wuerzburg, October 2014.
53. Samuel Kounev, Nikolaus Huber, Fabian Brosig, and Xiaoyun Zhu. A Model-Based Approach to Designing Self-Aware IT Systems and Infrastructures. *IEEE Computer Magazine*, pages 53–61, July 2016.
54. Jeff Kramer and Jeff Magee. Self-Managed Systems: an Architectural Challenge. In *FOSE '07: 2007 Future of Software Engineering*, pages 259–268. IEEE, 2007.
55. Christopher Landauer and Kirstie L. Bellman. Knowledge-Based Integration Infrastructure for Complex Systems. *International Journal of Intelligent Control and Systems*, 1(1):133–153, 1996.
56. Christopher Landauer and Kirstie L. Bellman. New architectures for constructed complex systems. *Applied Mathematics and Computation*, 120(1–3):149–163, 2001.
57. Peter R. Lewis, Arjun Chandra, Funmilade Faniyi, Kyrre Glette, Tao Chen, Rami Bahsoon, Jim Torresen, and Xin Yao. Architectural aspects of self-aware and self-expressive computing systems: From psychology to engineering. *IEEE Computer*, 48(8):62–70, 2015.
58. Pattie Maes. Concepts and experiments in computational reflection. In *Conference Proceedings on Object-oriented Programming Systems, Languages and Applications*, OOPSLA '87, pages 147–155. ACM, 1987.
59. Jeff Magee and Jeff Kramer. Dynamic structure in software architectures. In *Proceedings of the 4th ACM SIGSOFT Symposium on Foundations of Software Engineering*, SIGSOFT '96, pages 3–14. ACM, 1996.
60. Yoann Maurel, Philippe Lalanda, and Ada Diaconescu. Towards a service-oriented component model for autonomic management. *2014 IEEE International Conference on Services Computing*, 0:544–551, 2011.
61. Janet Metcalfe and Arthur P. Shimamura, editors. *Metacognition: Knowing about knowing*. MIT Press, Cambridge, MA, USA, 1994.
62. Melanie Mitchell. Self-awareness and control in decentralized systems (Tech Report SS-05-04). In *AAAI Spring Symposium on Metacognition in Computation*, Menlo Park, 2005. AIII Press.
63. Hausi A. Müller, Mauro Pezzè, and Mary Shaw. Visibility of Control in Adaptive Systems. In *Proceedings of the 2nd International Workshop on Ultra-large-scale Software-intensive Systems*, ULSSIS '08, pages 23–26. ACM, 2008.
64. Christian Muller-Schloer, Hartmut Schmeck, and Theo Ungerer, editors. *Organic Computing - A Paradigm Shift for Complex Systems*. Birkhuser, 2011.
65. A. Newell, P. S. Rosenbloom, and J. E. Laird. Symbolic architectures for cognition. In M. Posner, editor, *Foundations of Cognitive Science*, pages 93–132. MIT Press, 1989.
66. H. P. Nii. Blackboard systems, part one: The blackboard model of problem solving and the evolution of blackboard architectures. In *AI Magazine*, volume 7, pages 38–53, 1986.
67. L.D. Paulson. DARPA creating self-aware computing. *Computer*, 36(3):24, 2003.
68. J. Rothenberg. The nature of modeling. In Lawrence E. Widman, Kenneth A. Loparo, and Norman R. Nielsen, editors, *Artificial Intelligence, Simulation & Modeling*, pages 75–92. John Wiley & Sons, Inc., New York, NY, USA, 1989.
69. Romain Rouvoy, Frank Eliassen, Jacqueline Floch, Svein Hallsteinsen, and Erlend Stav. Composing components and services using a planning-based adaptation middleware. In *Software Composition*, pages 52–67. Springer, 2008.
70. Stuart J. Russell and Peter Norvig. *Artificial Intelligence - A Modern Approach (3. internat. ed.)*. Pearson Education, 2010.
71. Mazeiar Salehie and Ladan Tahvildari. Self-adaptive software: Landscape and research challenges. *ACM Trans. Auton. Adapt. Syst.*, 4(2):1–42, 2009.
72. Hartmut Schmeck, Christian Müller-Schloer, Emre Çakar, Moez Mnif, and Urban Richter. Adaptivity and self-organization in organic computing systems. *ACM Trans. Auton. Adapt. Syst.*, 5(3):10:1–10:32, 2010.

73. Mary Shaw. Beyond objects: A software design paradigm based on process control. *ACM SIGSOFT Software Engineering Notes*, 20(1):27–38, 1995.
74. Mary Shaw and David Garlan. An Introduction to Software Architecture. *V. Ambriola and G. Tortora (ed.): Advances in Software Engineering and Knowledge Engineering*, 2:1–39, 1993.
75. Thomas Vogel and Holger Giese. Adaptation and Abstract Runtime Models. In *Proceedings of the 5th Workshop on Software Engineering for Adaptive and Self-Managing Systems (SEAMS 2010)*, pages 39–48. ACM, 2010.
76. Thomas Vogel and Holger Giese. Model-Driven Engineering of Self-Adaptive Software with EUREMA. *ACM Trans. Auton. Adapt. Syst.*, 8(4):18:1–18:33, 2014.
77. Thomas Vogel and Holger Giese. On Unifying Development Models and Runtime Models. In *Proceedings of the 9th International Workshop on Models@run.time*, volume 1270 of *CEUR Workshop Proceedings*, pages 5–10. CEUR-WS.org, 2014.
78. Thomas Vogel, Andreas Seibel, and Holger Giese. The Role of Models and Megamodels at Runtime. In Juergen Dingel and Arnor Solberg, editors, *Models in Software Engineering*, volume 6627 of *Lecture Notes in Computer Science (LNCS)*, pages 224–238. Springer, 2011.
79. Sebastian Wtzoldt and Holger Giese. Modeling Collaborations in Adaptive Systems of Systems. In *Proceedings of the European Conference on Software Architecture Workshops*, ECSAW. ACM, 2015.
80. Eric Yuan, Naeem Esfahani, and Sam Malek. Automated mining of software component interactions for self-adaptation. In *Proceedings of the 9th International Symposium on Software Engineering for Adaptive and Self-Managing Systems*, SEAMS 2014, pages 27–36. ACM, 2014.
81. Franco Zambonelli, Nicola Bicocchi, Giacomo Cabri, Letizia Leonardi, and Mariachiara Puviani. On self-adaptation, self-expression, and self-awareness in autonomic service component ensembles. In *Proc. of the Fifth IEEE Conference on Self-Adaptive and Self-Organizing Systems Workshops (SASOW)*, pages 108–113. IEEE, 2011.

Part III
Methods and Algorithms

Chapter 9
Self-modeling and Self-awareness

**Kirstie L. Bellman, Christopher Landauer, Phyllis Nelson,
Nelly Bencomo, Sebastian Götz, Peter Lewis and Lukas Esterle**

Abstract The purpose of this chapter is to discuss why self-aware systems must pay special attention to self-modeling capabilities, clarify what is meant by both strong and weak self-modeling, and describe some of the defining characteristics of self-modeling. This chapter is also about self-management via run-time model creation by the operational system, explaining why systems need to build models at run time, what phenomena they need to model, and how they can build models effectively. A system that is expected to operate in a dynamic environment needs to be able to update and occasionally dramatically change its models to maintain synchrony with that environment. We describe several example systems, one rather extensively, to show how the notions apply in practice.

K.L. Bellman (✉) · C. Landauer
Topcy House Consulting, Thousand Oaks, CA, USA
e-mail: bellmanhome@yahoo.com

C. Landauer
e-mail: topcycal@gmail.com

P. Nelson
California State Polytechnic University, Pomona, CA, USA
e-mail: prnelson@cpp.edu

N. Bencomo · P. Lewis
Aston University, Birmingham, UK
e-mail: n.bencomo@aston.ac.uk

P. Lewis
e-mail: p.lewis@aston.ac.uk

S. Götz
TU Dresden, Dresden, Germany
e-mail: sebastian.goetz1@tu-dresden.de

L. Esterle
Alpen-Adria-Universität Klagenfurt, Klagenfurt, Austria
e-mail: lukas.esterle@aau.at

© Springer International Publishing AG 2017
S. Kounev et al. (eds.), *Self-Aware Computing Systems*,
DOI 10.1007/978-3-319-47474-8_9

9.1 Introduction

In this chapter, we explain why we think that self-aware systems must pay special attention to self-modeling capabilities, that is, approaches that the systems can use for building and managing their own models of themselves and their operational environment. These approaches may be as difficult as making choices of what phenomena they will need to model, and choosing modeling methods accordingly, or as seemingly simple as parameterizing models from a much more limited class provided by the designers. We define strong and weak self-modeling and describe some of the defining characteristics of self-modeling. We describe several example applications and other systems, one rather extensively, to tie these seemingly abstract definitions to particular implementations and applications.

We want to stimulate a general discussion within and among the communities that study self-modeling, including autonomic computing [25], models@run.time [9, 19], architecture-based methods [12], software engineering [18], and many others. When the designers have to provide all models to a system, it undercuts its ability to adapt and to operate within new environments (or surprise us with new perceptions or understandings). This chapter defines a collection of considerations and some methods that can be used by the system at run time to model aspects of its operational environment, its own behavior, and concept of operations (how the system is expected to be used by its operators/users/peers, if any).

We do not assume that the system models all aspects of itself or the situation, or even any particular aspect.

We are also especially interested in advanced mathematical methods, such as occuring in data mining, to add new attributes. The self-models are not (usually) the ones we human designers use to model the system; they are the ones the system itself uses to build and analyze its situation and behavior. This chapter will describe some of the new mathematical methods that can be used to produce new candidates for the following aspects of models: model attributes and relationships, system structure and behavior, the retained knowledge, archived and mined, to discover new relationships and patterns, situation awareness, and entities. As the level of self-awareness rises, we expect more of the modeling that supports self-awareness and self-adaptation will be undertaken by the system itself.

9.1.1 Self-modeling

As in all modeling, self-models can be implemented in a wide variety of styles (e.g., rule-based, mathematical, logical, simulation, and other analogies). Indeed, there are many definitions and opinions as to what should be labeled a "model." Self-models are distinguished from others by the following properties; if all of these characteristics are present, we call the self-modeling capability "strong."

1. The system element (which can be an entire system, a subsystem, a component, or a temporary grouping of components) has access to the content and the results of any self-models for the purpose of supporting decisions/actions within that system;
2. The system element uses the self-models to self* (self-control, self-manage, self-heal, self-organize, and so forth);
3. The system element can change the models beyond updating data (where strong implies the additional ability to add or change new parameters, add or change objects, add or change rules, add or change algorithms, etc.);
4. The system element can change what context and use it has for the self-models; it shares the goals for the models with human codevelopers [6] and;
5. The system can reason about its own resources and performance.

To these capabilities, we add that it is very important and very useful to have these additional features:

1. Methods for sharing both the results and the process for determining results (up to whatever given level is desired by human engineers) with both human engineers/users/developers and optionally with other systems/agents, etc.;
2. Methods for self-testing and verification; and
3. Methods for learning, feedback, and self-improvement.

The above characteristics all depend heavily on instrumentation of several sorts:

1. Self-instrumentation so that the system can reason about its own behavior at a granularity effective to its current goals; the ability to change this granularity dynamically is important.
2. Feedback mechanisms that gauge the effectiveness and performance of its actions and application of resources, both on its own internal resources and that may exist in the environment. It is also important to have ways of measuring the desired (and undesired) impacts on the external world (objects and situation).
3. Explicit evaluation criteria on the success of its processing/learning/reasoning.

Clearly from the above statements, self-models and self-modeling are to be distinguished from the automated models that may be built by a system for the purpose of monitoring system performance that are usually intended for review by a human user. The biggest difference with classical models, built to monitor, for example, some performance or state metrics (e.g., network traffic and energy consumption), is that these systems ordinarily have rigidly specified goals for the use of such models, less connection to a diversity of reasoning mechanisms and potential actions/decisions that can result and, perhaps most importantly, do not allow the system itself to change or modify these goals, reasoning methods, and action mechanisms. For adaptive behavior and the ability to cope with complex environments, we believe that it is critical to have dynamic self-models that the system can change autonomously (up to a designer-specified point). These self-models in fact can improve the ability of human users to monitor and suitably control complex systems or agents because such models have the capacity to compactly represent a great deal of system state knowledge, enriched with the system's current reasoning or planning. The system's current reasoning and planning may include such important information on the system's viewpoint as its representation of the user or designer goals, more up-to-date information on the systems current resources, and how it intends to use its resources to map itself to its perceived operational environment. It follows that even though we are emphasizing self-modeling, that is, modeling of the system by the system, this capability presents new opportunities for having models that are of immediate relevance and use by human users working with the system.

9.1.2   Motivation

Self-aware and self-adaptive systems need the ability to build models of many types, because no designer will be able to provide a priori all the models needed for any but the most limited environments, or for changing among sets of operational environments. These models, built from the point of view of the system itself, include models about the situation, the external environment, potentially other agents in the external world, the potential goals and mission given to the system by external institutions or agents, and most critically, the states and current limits on its own resources (e.g., sensors, effectors, and reasoning processes).

In any system of even modest complexity, it is impossible to save all information collected by and known to the system as it operates. Models summmarize prior results, but emphasize various aspects of those results. It is therefore useful to have multiple models at varying levels of granularity and to focus on different aspects of those results in order to provide the most useful view of both results and experience (experience of both the system or component itself and its designers).

Though we can instrument any engineered system for external monitoring, a system will always have quicker, more continuous, and potentially more relevant access to its own internal state. Because the system itself has unique and immediate access to its own internal state and current activation of reasoning and planning mechanisms and other resources, there is an opportunity to have better, more accurate, and more current models of its own state and models of its abilities to execute any given goals and tasks. This is especially true when we want the system to adapt, as much as it is able to, to new requirements, contexts, and situations. Unless the system itself can change its own goals, contexts for usage of resources, models, and reasoning processes, it will inevitably be slowed down by the lag time in communication, in human decision processes and updates, in human intervention and review, and in the lack of knowledge and insight of its human developers. This lag by humans can occur because of such factors as distance (e.g., as is common in space systems or even in downtown surveillance systems in cities), complexity (e.g., system of systems such as emergency response [5], or smart cities), timing requirements (e.g., flight control systems), or unknowns in the operational environment (e.g., surface of Mars).

We believe that self-modeling is one of the differentiating characteristics of self-aware systems, because models seem to be the most convenient operational approach to retaining and using the knowledge of self that is essential for self-awareness. However, as we describe below, these models may be of many types, including rule bases and knowledge bases of different forms, as well as explicit object models, graphs, and other mathematical models.

As we expect with human development, early models are replaced over time with more sophisticated models and modeling processes. We assume that human developers provide initial models, and even early refinements and adaptations as the system are used, but we expect that the systems will take over their own model refinements eventually.

9.2 Background

There is much relevant work on the issues of self-modeling, which draws from many subject domains. Artificial intelligence, psychology, cognitive science, and ethology provide us with many examples of self-modeling as done in natural systems, by both humans and animals (see Chap. 3 for an overview of self-awareness concepts). In biological systems, important properties of self-modeling are supported by play and exploratory behavior, as well as many other perceptual, cognitive, and acting capabilities. Model building is also seen in even primitive animals, as described in ethological and behavioral studies. Some of these model-building processes have been successfully modeled or used to limited extents in computational systems. The next subsections provide some examples.

9.2.1 The DDDAS Program

The following is an example of how to dynamically update data in a model so that a model can be more current; this of course is a first step to much more sophisticated self-modeling. Data-driven dynamic application systems (DDDAS) were first developed by a US National Science Foundation program under the direction of Frederica Darema [13], in order to address the very important challenge of how models could be dynamically updated with current information that was then used by the system to better direct the next data collection and computations of the system. One class of examples focused on firefighting models [34]. In forest fires, there are very complex reasons for a shift in the pattern and direction of a raging forest fire, but correct prediction of such shifts can not only redirect scarce resources, but also save lives. Early models were hindered because even excellent computational models of forest fires have an enormous amount of uncertainty, due to variations in local conditions. Therefore, it is very important to incorporate whatever ground information is available to the models to update the position and direction of the fire. In DDDAS models, the position and characteristics of the fire are updated as much as possible from any ground sensors and aircraft sensors. Then, instead of trying to measure the local conditions (an essentially impossible task), the system infers them from the observed behavior of the fire, which then not only updates the position of the fire and its rate and characteristics, but also prioritizes and directs what sensors and information it needs next.

One of the difficult challenges in DDDAS research was to do more than fitting model parameters to an observed behavior, but rather to do real-time updating of the model structure. Of course, time constraints limit the effectiveness of anything but incremental updates. To that end, a meta-model could be used to enforce appropriate constraints, limiting any search processes to a priori acceptable regions, and suggest appropriate modifications in those regions [24].

9.2.2 Models@run.time

Another community, which can be connected to self-modeling, emerged from model-driven software development (MDSD). The principal idea is to utilize design-time models—starting from goal models derived from requirement analysis up to detailed structural and behavior models—to generate implementation artifacts and thereby to reduce the engineering costs of software systems. To reach this goal, a variety of techniques has been researched, e.g., model transformations and model analysis, to name but a few.

The models@run.time community pushes this idea to the run time of (software) systems by promoting the use of MDSD techniques at run time. The two key principles for models@run.time are as follows: (1) a run-time model, which reflects a certain aspect of a running system for a given purpose, and (2) a causal connection between the running system and the run-time model [9].

Thus, models@run.time represents a part of self-modeling, since a self-model represents part of the system's current state. In contrast to self-modeling, the focus is not how to empower systems to autonomously create, manage, and use models of themselves, their environment, and the interaction between them. Instead, models@run.time focuses in particular on the questions of how to realize the causal connection between the running system and the run-time model and how the run-time model should be characterized, but not on the process of creating the model.

9.2.3 Situation Awareness

The situation awareness community [5, 10, 14] has many important examples of systems with dynamic modeling capabilities that are used in processes to continually improve the ability of a system to reason about a given environment for the purpose of whatever goals and tasks it has been given with respect to that environment. These systems also show the ability to modify some of their objectives and goals. Here, we are using the term "situation" in the technical sense [3], where a situation includes at least the elements that define what we identify as a situation, e.g., objects, events, people, systems, historical and environmental factors, and their current states, e.g., locations, conditions, modes, and actions.

When we add self-awareness to situation awareness, the system is not simply trying to find out what is going on in its environment; instead, it is trying to find out how those changes relate to and impact its own intentions and capabilities. That requires the system to be able to simulate the future effects of those changes, at least in the near term, and to evaluate their impact and assess their utility.

9.2.4   Reflection

Building reflective architectures has given us experience in building reflective processes that reason about a sensor, a computer program, and a strategy or a situation, and many of these reflective processes require the use of models. Within the context of building reflective architectures, we have gained some experience into what self-modeling means and how one might build at least some early forms of self-modeling capabilities [7, 28].

In 1987, Maes [30] defined and implemented "computational reflection" as "the process of reasoning about and/or acting upon oneself." Computational reflection is an engineered system's ability to reason about its own resources, capabilities, and limitations in the context of its current operational environment. Reflection capabilities can range from simple, straightforward adjustments of another program's parameters or behaviors (e.g., altering the step size on a numerical process or the application of rules governing which models are used at different stages in a design process) to sophisticated analyses of the system's own reasoning, planning, and decision processes (e.g., noticing when one's approach to a problem is not working and revising its plan). To be considered as such, the reflection processes must include more than the sensing of data, monitoring of an event, or perception of a pattern; they must also have some type of capability to reason about this information and to act upon this reasoning [5, 7].

The Wrappings approach is one way to implement computational reflection and self-modeling systems. In continuous development since 1988, the approach grew out of work in conceptual design environments for space systems which had hundreds of models and computational components [4]. It amounts to a radical rethinking of the architecture of a running system [27]. The Wrappings approach uses both explicit meta-knowledge (the *Wrappings*, typically defined in one or more knowledge bases) and recursively applied algorithms to recruit and configure resources dynamically to respond to "posed problems" to the system by users, external systems, or the system's own internal processing. The *Problem Managers* (PMs) are algorithms that use the Wrappings to choreograph seven major functions: discover, select, assemble, integrate, adapt, explain, and evaluate. *Discovery* identifies new resources that can be inserted into the system for a problem. *Selection* decides which resource(s) should be applied to this problem in this context. *Assembly* is syntactic integration and helps set up selected resources so that they can pass information or share services. *Integration* is semantic integration, including constraints on when, why, and how resources should be assembled. *Adaptation* helps to adjust or set up a resource for different operational conditions. *Explanation* is more than a simple event history because it provides information on why and what was not selected. *Evaluation* includes the impact or effectiveness of a given use of this resource. The Wrappings "problem-posing" has many benefits, including separating problems from solution methods and keeping an explicit, analyzable trace of what problems were used to evoke and configure resources. Because all of the resources are Wrapped, even the resources that support the Wrappings processing, the system is computationally reflective: It can reason about the use of all of its resources [28].

9.3 CARS: An Extended Example

Wrappings is being used in computational architectures for reflective systems (CARS), an experimental test bed of robotic cars built in partnership with students at California State Polytechnic University, Pomona [7, 26]. The development of self-models, the dynamic substitution of different operational goals and strategies, and adjustments in the uses of sensors and other resources are key parts of how the robotic cars (agents) will be able to participate in four very different types of simple games with the same control infrastructure, as well as adjusting for sensor and component failures. The test bed is experimenting with four games:

1. Follow-the-leader (replicate the trajectory of another with relatively constant distance or time headway);
2. Tag with a pursuer ("It") and evaders;
3. Soccer practice (cars cooperate to bump a ball into a goal); and
4. Push the box (cars must synchronize to push an object that is too large and unwieldy for any one car).

These games have been purposely designed to require a broad range of different and even conflicting game-playing strategies.

The flexibility of the Wrappings approach provides multiple entry points for reflective processes. Given a goal, purpose, or function, a reflective process uses sources of information to do some action, make a decision, or create data that is used by other processes. The goal or function for that reflective process could be built in during design time or assigned dynamically to that reflective process by other programs. It may be in continual use, or it may be recruited or evoked only when certain resources are active or particular conditions exist. The sources of information can be data sets (historical or current), sensor output, internal monitors, other programs' results, and context models. The reasoning process for reflection can be done with an algorithm, decision process, rule base, cognitive model, or planner. The resulting actions are myriad, but include sending messages, setting program or context parameters, recruiting new components, initiating new processes, or instigating a replan or undo process.

Fig. 9.1 Sample car

The cars (agents) in the test bed have different capabilities (e.g., different sizes and shapes, kinds of sensors, engine capacities, and turning ratios). Each car has various sensors, such as video, gyroscopes, magnetometers, accelerometers, wheel or other sensors used for distance traveled, bumper pressure sensors, ultrasound ranging, and infrared sensors. An example of these cars is shown in Fig. 9.1.

In the CARS test bed, we are exploring the different roles of reflection by developing initially four major types of reflection processes that differ primarily in their scope of responsibility: R1 is a reflection on an internal or external sensor; R2 is a reflection about the use, behavior, and performance of a software program; R3 is a reflection on a global characteristic of the system; and and R4 is "a consistency checker" that integrates several other reflection processes. For example, in the CARS test bed, some R2 processes are deciding whether the software programs called "game-playing strategies" are working well enough in the current game context for a specific agent. A strategy is a program that includes a set of rules for playing a game and a reasoner for how to apply these rules to the current game situation. Each agent modifies the parameters of the strategies based on their own capabilities (e.g., their own turning ratio, maximum speed, fuel efficiency, and remaining fuel). Examples of CARS "Tag" strategies include the following:

1. a strategy to keep moving so that one keeps all cars at a distance,
2. identify "It" and hide behind other cars (always keep another car between yourself and "It"), or
3. the energy-minimizing strategy: wait until "It" appears to be approaching you before you move.

The R2 actions include adjusting parameters to the current strategy or posing the problem to select a new strategy.

Each car must actively explore the limits of its own specific capabilities within its environment, a process we call "active experimentation" [5, 8]. To accomplish this, the system must have safe places to "play" and to therefore build the experiences that produce the self-models needed by its reflective processes [8]. Animals invest energy and time in "exploratory behavior" (learning their environment) and "play" (exploring one's own capabilities within that environment) instead of adopting the usual engineering approach of shutting off processes to conserve resources. Clearly, biological systems find value in such experimentation that compensates for the investment of resources.

We thus claim that a system and its agents need ample opportunity for integration of resources within realistic operational environments and with realistic interactions with other entities within that environment. This type of experimentation purposely tests how well certain game-playing strategies fit with an individual agent's own capabilities and is in imitation of the type of self-discovery with which a young child learns how fast they personally can run in water, on sand, or on grass. The agent uses this information to build self-models and to refine game-playing strategies to match its personal capabilities. At the moment, the primitive model-building capabilities in CARS are mostly parameterized templates provided to the agent and adjusted during active experimentation; the parameters (such as turning radius or speed uphill) are in turn used in planning, reasoning, and reflective processes to decide which game strategy will be used in a given game situation. We intend eventually to go beyond such self-parameterization capabilities to enable the system with powerful methods for building new models.

The above description of implementing some basic reflection processes in CARS exemplifies several general principles for reflective architectures. First, there are many types of reflection. There is no single centralized collection of "self-models." However, there is also not a one-to-one mapping between the number of reflective processes and sensors, effectors, or processing elements. Instead, one uses critical functions, requirements, and process entry and exit points to decide where to place the reflective processes. Inserting reflection is an engineering decision depending on requirements (the nature of the decisions and the quality and timing of the performance needed) and the complexity of the system. The lessons learned from biological systems should encourage us to invest enough in instrumentation and reflection to benefit from having many direct and indirect sources of feedback and information.

Play times also offer opportunities to explore responses to unexpected conditions. Such experience is critical to developing trustworthy complex systems, especially autonomous or partially autonomous ones. Because of scale, a complex system cannot test all possible external data conditions with all integration paths, nor analyze all possible side effects. When we add systems that are relatively open or have requirements creep or changing contexts, missions, or technologies, there will never be a chance for the system to do a complete self-discovery and testing. Any design approach for such systems must have two capabilities. First, there must be a strategy for performing continual verification and validation (V&V) [15]. If we allow the system to perform an active role in this continual self-verification and validation, then this continual V&V can be directed by the system to correspond to its most recent experiences and challenges. For example, it can purposely instigate new self-tests or sets of previously constructed benchmarks to correspond to the addition of a new component or a new relationship with another agent. Through non-directed "play," the system can also institute additional tests when it has failed to perform as expected. Second, because no testing will ever be complete, at any given moment, the system must have a robust set of favorite behaviors that it can execute when it needs more time to devise a more specific response. This strategy of "buying time" in a safe configuration is akin to several biological strategies [7]. A weak version of biological strategies exists in technical systems, with an example being "safing" of spacecraft should some anomaly occur.

Deciding, based on experience, what to incorporate into the models developed by a self-aware system requires pairing the results of experimentation with sophisticated cognitive processes. In the next section, we briefly examine some modeling truisms that are especially relevant to self-modeling and then describe how existing computer capabilities and processes both support this self-modeling and also provide opportunities for incorporating advancements that will lead to them becoming part of the powerful repertoire of self-modeling mechanisms.

Our current plan is to use active experimentation to provide extensive raw data for correlating an agent's own capabilities to different operational environments and then to enhance our current methods with the use of advanced data mining/learning algorithms (as described in Sect. 9.5) to help discover new relationships and variables/vectors of interest. To address this challenge, we must deal with representations and language, which we discuss later in Sect. 9.6.

However, we must always keep in mind that modeling failures can and will occur [33]. In our experiments on deducing terrain from movement, we the designers did not realize that the wind had a significant effect on that movement, so the initial and derived models were incorrect and could not easily be fixed. We do not yet expect our systems to identify "unmodeled phenomena," to study them and create wholly new models, so we must expect the designers to verify that the initial models at least have the appropriate set of phenomena, even if their parameters and some interactions are not known at design time.

9.4 Modeling Issues

Many seemingly minor modeling issues especially impact self-models. Whether a complex system is self-aware or not, such systems will each have a repertoire of modeling styles that it recognizes and that it can extend or build new instances of. It also will need processes to decide which style it will use for what data and for what goals/purposes. Even what one think of as "simpler" systems often have much more diversity of models than one might first think, especially when one considers the ways in which data is structured for that application, decisions framed, rules or logic incorporated, and algorithms set up or results presented.

9.4.1 Modeling Questions

We start with a common set of questions relevant to all models and then specifically ask what is different when we address self-models. The purpose of this section is to stimulate the reader to consider many aspects of building models that are currently done by human labor; the challenge for us here is to discover approaches for both automating these aspects and assessing the benefits and costs of doing so.

A common suite of questions about models are

- Models are What?
- Models for What?
- Models of What?
- Models from What?
- Model assurances.

In the rest of this section, we discuss each question in turn.

9.4.1.1 Models Are What?

Starting with the first question, "models are what?" in the most general sense, models are abstractions of phenomena, emphasizing some aspects and ignoring or simplifying others. A self-model, like many other domain-specific and system models, describes what the system can do and cannot do, but it does so from the point of the view of the system itself (as in the Dirty Harry quote "a man's got to know his limitations" [16]).

A model definition is complete, and the model is well-defined, if it can be examined or exercised without reference to any other source information outside the definition. This is especially important in the case of self-models and autonomous systems. In many cases, meta-knowledge about the assumptions, limitations, and correct applications and contexts for use of a given self-model must be available to the system in addition to the self-model, so the system can make proper use of it.

9.4.1.2 Models for What?

As far as the second question, "models for what?", models can be prepared for different purposes. In the case of self-models, we are most interested in the use of models for adaptation, performance improvement, explicit policy representation and management, and system maintenance. Self-models can be used for system modification and behavioral adaptation via either existing rulesets or learning for adaptation to changed conditions or changed capability. They can be used for improvement in performance, when there are appropriate instrumentation (external and internal) and suitable metrics, such as energy consumed, time spent, or even more abstract measures such as degree of safety.

Self-models can be used to enforce policy, such as the constraints on the allowable solutions generated by the planner for a robot interacting with humans (e.g., keeping a certain distance while crossing a room) or for the management of trade-offs and the optimization among competing parameters (e.g., weight and cost, speed of response, and quality). That trade-off space is a map from courses of action to results, which can often be predicted using simulations of hypothetical but possible situations. These models need a good representation of the likely environmental responses, to make the computation more accurate. Much of this modeling can be done in advance, either during design and integration or during periods of active experimentation, so that the resulting map is almost known, and the computation of the likely futures is more like a table lookup than a full-scale simulation.

Lastly, we are interested in the use of models for such maintenance functions as model repair. Since system self-models are personal, they may be incorrect due to limited perception. In some cases, as the system acquires more information, this limited perception may be overcome by additional sources of input, while in other cases, the system may have a repertoire of models that it can substitute into a new context or situation. Still in other circumstances, another agent or system might provide new models to the system or the human developers may have to intervene by upgrading the models.

9.4.1.3   Models of What?

For the third question, "models of what?", aside from modeling its own internal state and current processing capabilities, the system can make models of the system environment, as in situation awareness models, and incorporate into models any knowledge the system has on the rules and policies impacting its CONOPS (concept of operations; see below), and its operational context information. Context information can include aspects of its environment, such as the amounts of radiation in its operational environment or the time of day, as well as other agents and influences. One key type of model for self-aware systems is how the system's current state and capabilities map into its plans and its environment. There can be multiple time and space scales (minimal representable difference), to facilitate quick reasoning. There can be multiple scopes (ranges of possibilities and domains of concern), to facilitate the exploration of possible responses. There can be models of the focus of attention (that is, which aspects of the environment matter more at the current time).

The system can make models of system internals, using computational reflection to examine and affect behavior at many different scales. In the reflective architecture approach used as an example in this chapter, we have long advocated using more than one scale for reflection (as is done in biological systems [8]) and argued that reflective processes must be local, to facilitate historical perspective as well as simplifying the reasoning process.

These internal models will include many aspects, depending on the purpose for the internal models. Hence, some of these internal models will include structure (statics) and behavior (dynamics), which can be especially useful for planners. Often, they must include the system components (parts at a given level of detail) and the interactions and interferences among them. Part of the self-modeling processes will add new interactions and interferences as they become known. There can be models of communication events, including the participants and the locations and times. There can be models of action conflicts, so that the system can perform arbitration among or merging of actions [28].

The system can make models of the CONOPS (concept of operations), which describe how the system is intended to be used by its users within its planned operational environment. These models are important for explaining many aspects of use that are not captured in part-whole models, policy models, or behavioral models. In a sense, they are at the intersection of all of these other models. Some of the types of questions they address are as follows: how the system is being commanded or otherwise tasked, whether the interactions are peer-based, and where there will be online tasks during operation or offline as initial goals. There may be a definition of the expected use, though there is always a consideration about how well that is to be trusted (systems have a long history of being used outside their design space).

The system can make models of its "activity loops" or parallel sequences of processing steps (another important aspect used in reflection, reasoning, and evaluation functions), including additional information recording the decision processes used at each step and any failures that occur. This type of information can be used with extensive instrumentation to engage in detailed anomaly detection, and even fault detection, isolation, and recovery, and then predictively for fault mitigation or prevention. In some cases, fault mitigation may include giving up on a goal or task, accompanied by suitable reports to other agents or human operators. In this latter case, it may be important to not just record the failed goal, but to actually model the purposes and goals, so that the system can reason about what parts of a goal can be accomplished or not and how to change a goal if possible.

It is essential in all of these models to decide what aspects of the modeled objects (internal or external, abstract or concrete) must remain fixed or highly constrained and what can be more variable. The variable parts become essentially the knobs of change that the system can act upon in order to accomplish adaptive responses [6] [8]. This strategy of "allowable variation" is well known in biological systems. For example, in animal behavior, fixed action patterns (genetically encoded pieces of rigid behavior) are interspersed with behaviors that are open to learning and adaptive responses. As an example [36], there is a famous ethological story about the red squirrel raised since it was born in a basement laboratory with no outdoor light to indicate the passage of seasons. Even so, during its first autumn, when given a nut, the red squirrel attempts to dig a hole in the linoleum floor, swish the nonexistent dirt back over the hole with its tail, and tamp it down with its snout, while all the while the nut has actually bounced along the linoleum into a corner. This is taken as a perfect example of genetically fixed behavior, with the rationale being that red squirrels who do not instinctively bury their nuts in the fall will not survive the upcoming winter. However, this example of rigid behavior is punctuated by areas of no fixed behavior. Hence, a red squirrel is dependent upon its experience and learning processes to learn how to open nuts. The explanation for this flexibility is that an animal might be exposed to many new types of nuts in its life, and so there is an advantage to having to learn how to open a nut so that it can take advantage of new food sources.

In a similar fashion, the designers of a system will have to decide what parts of a system's goals and functions they have mechanisms for the system to do itself, and what parts they must prescribe in fixed models and processes. Hence, for any given model of either external or internal objects and processes, the system uses the fixed models and changes and maintains the variable models.

The simplest example of this implementation style can be found in any simple control system, where the only variable parts of the model are the parameters, or in CARS, where the game being played is fixed (for a certain amount of time), and the collection of strategies changes as the individual agents learn how to play better. In fact, a more general way to view this issue is as a hierarchy of timescales, each of which is constant relative to the next. This approach has been shown to be effective in many systems [1].

Eventually, we want it to have sophisticated enough processes to also create and maintain new models. With the self-testing described above, there is also the possibility of detecting a failure in a fixed model and reporting that so the designers can either fix it and redeliver it to the system, or make it variable, so the system can take over its operation. Over time, we would expect to learn how to take our fixed models and make them variable enough for the system to take over its own operation.

9.4.1.4 Models from What?

The next question is "models from what," that is, where do the models come from?

One can imagine that there are contexts in which the designer has built a rigid, fixed self-model for a system that the system uses to make some decisions (a weak kind of self-model, but since the system is using this model of itself to make decisions, we still call it a self-model). Certainly, a more interesting case is when the designers build an initial set of models for the system (representing what we, the human designers and operators, know about what will be relevant to observe and to decide in a given context) that acts as an initial starting point for the system which then has processes for enhancing and modifying that model through experience, reasoning, and learning processes. This, in primitive form, is the strategy shown in the CARS example earlier, where the templates of parameters worth learning are provided by the CARS designers. The most interesting case, of course, is to envision a system that has the right processes to construct the self-model it needs.

In either of these two interesting cases, self-modeling is not exactly the same as run-time model construction, unless the run-time model construction is the models of parts of its own components, behaviors, or intentions. Run-time models often are part of situation awareness, but self-models are part of self-awareness (which of course includes situation awareness, but is much wider in scope).

For example, the camera handoff process in some autonomous surveillance systems [32] (see also Sect. 9.6.2 below) depends on the camera's knowledge of its field of view (which is a self-model), the phenomena in view (which is not, though it is a run-time model), and goals (what is the camera looking for, if anything). One of the interesting challenges in self-modeling systems will be to blend the results from the self-models that the system creates with the models of the system created and provided from outside the system.

We would expect some of the provided models to be slowly varying models for the hardware (to manage failures and other hardware degradation), more quickly varying models for the software, and even more quickly varying models for the current state, including models focused on failure identification. This multiplicity of relevant time scales is a characteristic of some early robot models [1, 21].

9.4.1.5   Model Assurances

Finally, we need to know something about limiting the effects of applying the models, in the form of "model assurances." The designers need to be able to prove, or at least demonstrate with great confidence, that the systems being constructed will not do bad things. Of course, they would also like to demonstrate that the systems will do good things.

The problem is that there are many uncertainties in models, because all models are simplifications, because the system may be too complex for adequate testing, and because the environment is always partly unpredictable and almost always completely uncontrollable by the operational system. When we add systems that can change their operating models, we get to some serious assurance issues. We have addressed some of these issues in our research on self-modeling systems [28], but much more is needed in this area.

9.5   Data Analytics

We claim that advanced mathematical methods are essential to effective self-modeling. One aspect of model building is the ability to incorporate new features or patterns into a model, and to do that, first one has to discover them. Then, one has to have other processes that help relate any discovered pattern or parameter to other objects, situations, and actions. In this section, we describe using data analytics as one way of finding out new patterns and features that might be incorporated into existing models or used to formulate new models, and other advanced mathematical methods to support our ability to relate such new patterns and results to existing ones.

9.5.1   Grammatical Inference

Perhaps the simplest and most easily applied of these methods is grammatical inference [22]. It is about producing a structural description of a sequence of events, based solely on the sequence that is observed. The process can be used for event pattern discovery (to infer patterns that may be important) and for correlations with other patterns to try to get a notion of what the environment is doing and will do. It can also be used to discover the architecture of a running system [35]. The process itself is simple: We assume that the data is made available as a sequence of events (really as a merged collection of separate sequences of events, since we have to assume loosely coupled parallel processes in most interesting applications). The purpose of grammatical inference is to identify behavior "tropes" in a sequence of discrete events. Grammatical inference finds a set of descriptive rules, using several different creation processes: The simplest two are finding common sequences and finding alternatives that occur in a common context. These produce "series–parallel" grammars, but not all context-free grammars (CFGs).

Theorems in the field say that even regular grammars are not recoverable using only positive instances and that any context-free grammar is recoverable with enough positive and negative instances. This poses a problem to any and all audit mechanisms that only see what did happen, because they see no negative instances (i.e., things that did not happen). Therefore, to make use of this process for self-aware modeling, the negative information must also be gathered. This is a part of the purpose of active experimentation.

The purpose of grammatical inference is to identify behavior in discrete events. A useful aspect of the Wrappings approach is that it already defines behavior as a sequence of discrete events within the system, along with the context in which it is being done. It also has a description of why other choices were not made, which gives us negative instances also. As in any engineering application, designers have to choose some level of detail appropriate to the problem and the expected detail of the results.

Structure building processes also need a few more inference rules to get more interesting and complex grammars. Indefinite iteration is seen as consecutive repetitions of a symbol (iteration with an explicit limit is very hard to detect without an enormous amount of training data). With this added rule, this set of rules will identify regular grammars. The last two rules are even more complex: Recursion is the key to context-free grammars, and identification of appropriate context is the key to context-sensitive grammars. There are far fewer theorems about grammar recoverability in these cases.

There is a suggestion for a particular kind of observational modeling, using grammatical inference to determine patterns of recurring behavior and then using some induction to define those "grammars" as (rule-based) programs. Then, continual comparison of their predictions with the actual behavior provides an online check of the correctness of that behavior. This is analogous to the Runge–Kutta 4.5 ordinary differential equation solver, in the sense that there are two versions of the behavior generator, used to assess the correctness of the results. This approach could be used for the environment and the CONOPS models also, not just the self-model.

9.5.2 Other Mathematical Methods

There are other advanced methods that will be useful and still others that may be useful.

- Time Series Analysis: Kalman filter and analogs in other spaces; noise versus clutter (clutter is structured noise; noise is assumed to be random);
- Fractal Dimension and Dynamic Mapping: regime change detection;
- Manifold Discovery: nonlinear maps; and
- Topological Data Analysis.

Some of these advanced mathematical methods can be used to build, assess, and maintain models within these systems. Some of them may be too time-consuming to use, for most purposes, but one of the biological strategies we have noted several times in this chapter is the investment in longer-term processes. Hence, these mathematical methods are like play and exploratory behavior, in that they are investments in the system's improved understanding and hence improved "positioning" with respect to potential changes in its environment or in its tasking. Some of the data mining methods that are currently done off-line by human analysts could be imitated in self-aware systems by allowing background "continual contemplation" [29].

Clearly, time series analysis is already known to be useful, with Kalman filters and analogs in other spaces to help the system distinguish fluctuations from trends (transient changes from changes in character). Here, the designers have to make a careful distinction between noise and clutter (for our purposes, *clutter* is a structured and unwanted data; *noise* is assumed to be random).

Another measurement method that can be very useful is computing the fractal dimension and dynamic mapping of a sequence of measurements, since that is known to be able to identify a regime change. This strategy of using a fractal dimension as a signature for a pattern of events has effectively been used in ethology, geology, the analysis of SAR imagery [31], and recently network intrusion detection applications [2]. This could be of great use in building self-aware models, by becoming an indicator for a point at which the patterns change and the dynamic models have to be rebuilt, since whatever processes governed the measurements up to that point may no longer be relevant.

Analysis of long-term behavior of a measurement, what we call trajectory space analysis, can also benefit from some advanced mathematical methods. In particular, we can define a "trajectory" or "path" space using short sequences of measurements that we call segments and collect many of them over time. Determining the appropriate length of these sequences is an important experiment for each application, and again, active experimentation of some form can be used to determine even these (and other) mathematical parameterizations.

The set of all collected segments lies in a tiny little subspace of the entire space. Manifold discovery and related techniques, using nonlinear maps, can find that subspace and provide constraints on the coordinates in that subspace [11]. These techniques could become an important method for discovering unexpected patterns and new relationships that will go into the self-models.

Finally, topological data analysis can be used to study the behavior of the trajectory space at many scales simultaneously, but there have been as yet no definitive explanations of what we can expect from these advanced uses of topology or examples of results that are not easily discoverable some other way [37].

One of the critical points we would like to emphasize here is that complex self-aware systems will need a repertoire of different analytic methods to build the different kinds of models they will need to use. Since these methods are relatively new, there will have to be a great deal of experimentation by the system designers and the system itself to learn which methods contribute most effectively to which purposes for the models.

9.5.3 Supporting Processes

Many processes in current systems both support self-modeling and are good targets for additional self-aware processes. As noted at the beginning of the chapter, there are many strategies for implementing modeling processes and, by extension, self-modeling processes. One major distinction in such strategies is where one places the resources, such as the instrumentation, the reasoning and decision processes, the monitoring programs, and data transformation procedures for turning data into knowledge that impacts the self-models. One could in fact have generalized versions of all of these types of resources for all system models, as well as specialized versions of each of these types of resources colocated with a given component or subsystem. Although it might be tempting to consider run-time, dynamic, and adaptive modeling processes in systems as exotic and as being a new type of capability, in fact such capabilities have been part of complex systems for a long time.

Consider for example the picture in Fig. 9.2 of a moderately complex system. The architecture is based on the ELF loop (elementary loop of functioning [1]), a very generic choice for reactive systems. The basic cycle goes from the sources of data (live sensors, real-time queries from data bases, and results from other processing systems, all marked "sensors") to a set of programs that process this data (sensory processing, perception), setting it into the appropriate formats for use by the rest of the analysis and at the same time pulling out prioritized data for immediate actions. This processed data goes to update the World Model (which is the system's notion of its current situation and environment, generally captured as models with interaction and change rules), and to Value Judgement, which is providing plan evaluations to the decision processes and the archives for long-term analysis. The decision processes determine actions to be taken. All of these steps are about behaving in the present.

If we were to enhance this system to be self-modeling, then there would be additional links from each of the processing boxes into the sensor box, so that internal behaviors would also be monitored and analyzed. The World Model would also include a system model, an interaction model, and a model of the CONOPS (the concept of operations, which is the definition of how the system is expected to be used). These models would be used to affect the Value Judgements, by refining or

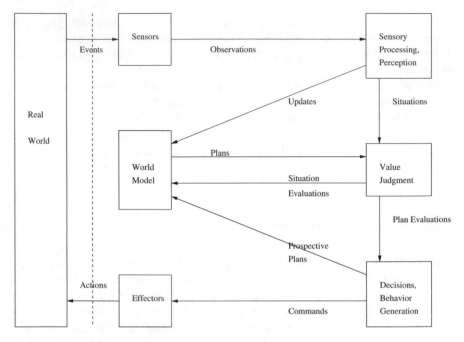

Fig. 9.2 Self-modeling steps

adjusting goals according to the current situation, the decision processes, by changing the data provided by the models and, more fundamentally, the manner in which the models incorporate new data and modify themselves, and even the Sensory Processing, since they may change what is deemed to be important, or even change the manner in which data is collected from sensors and other data sources. In Chap. 10, more strategies for enhancing self-awareness in current systems are discussed.

Hence, although we are focused in this chapter on defining methods to build up and modify self-models, many of our current methods for transforming data into usable forms, evaluating success in plans, and reasoning about results can be adjusted for use in self-modeling self-aware systems.

There are engineering trade-offs for any mixture of these strategies. Parameters considered will include requirements for the speed of local decision-making, uniformity of processing, easing self-verification processes, diversity of specialized processing required, and similar considerations.

9.6 Challenges

There are many challenges as we consider different types of self-models. For example, based on the importance of play and exploratory behavior emphasized above, how do systems build models without having any particular function or goal in mind?

Clearly, in biological systems, experiences attach themselves to existing models, but then in rather a mysterious process, they split off into new models. Hence, models can also be driven bottom-up by the exploratory imperative that is ongoing and continual. This is related to the management of a suite of models of varying resolution and initiative.

This exploratory imperative means that model building and pattern discovery can occur without explicit mapping to a goal or purpose.

Even low-level data patterns can be considered as an early descriptive model (since it supports knowledge building as in mapping a territory, etc.), though they may not be particularly informative. But we must also emphasize how the data patterns become increasingly stronger "models" when tied or mapped to semantics, useful observations, or goals and actions. In increasing order, the levels we consider are as follows:

1. Knowledge building patterns, pure description (CARS Example: blob detected with relative movement);
2. Descriptive with some semantics tying patterns to objects, situations, contexts, etc. (CARS Example: It does not seem to be moving by itself very much, but it does occasionally change position);
3. Descriptive with semantics mapping patterns/observations to uses and purposes, like affordances [20] (CARS Example: It is an obstruction that may allow pushing and may allow hiding);
4. Descriptive model folded in with other existing models, extending those, adding to prediction, but not predictive in itself (CARS Example: It is an obstruction that could be part of an evasion strategy for Tag); and
5. Predictive model based on observations/patterns after experimentation, like the wind example (CARS Example: It could be part of a deception strategy for Tag).

As the picture in Fig. 9.3 shows, sometimes one cannot get the modeling right even with sophisticated modeling and human designers. Some situations are very hard to predict; there are rare events that contradict the designers' assumptions about possible behaviors. In this case, the observations of other agents may become invaluable to the individual system's ability to discover new factors in the environment or to understand what has happened to them and incorporate those new understandings into both models and control actions. For external observers (humans or other systems) to help a system's modeling, it will need other processes and methods for communicating these observations, reasoning about these observations, and incorporating any new insights into the models and control actions. Aside from the use of external observers, another very important challenge will be to develop in self-aware systems the equivalent of what is done in space systems with "safing" behaviors or in animal systems with "holding patterns." These behaviors put the system in the best possible configuration for the given circumstance. In the example above with the car driving up onto the ball, the best the system can do might be to stop all its use of fuel by not trying to drive and to issue an announcement that it will wait for help.

Fig. 9.3 Unmodeled phenomenon

There are many other cases which can prove formidably difficult for both humans and machines to learn from and model correctly. Another example drawn from the CARS test bed was as follows [33]. In order to improve the ability of a car to play the "soccer practice" game by being able to predict the path of the ball, some students made a terrain map. However, the map computed from vehicle position and inclination did not improve the ability to predict the motion of the ball. Furthermore, videos of the ball trajectory for the same initial conditions were not the same. Eventually, the students began to understand that there was an unmodeled effect in the environment: the breeze's effect on a light ball! Unlike the example above with the car driven up on the ball, this effect does not appear as a discontinuity in operation. Could a combination of active experimentation, data analytics, and reflection and modeling identify this case? Could modeling processes determine that one solution for modeling (in this case, a simple polynomial extrapolation) was more effective than a more advanced model?

9.6.1 Language as a Challenge

In the two examples above with the CARS test bed, the observations of potential external observers or the new insights of a self-modeling system to its human developers need to be communicated somehow. But how do the words for these potentially new objects or patterns or occurrences come about? Our technical systems, whether self-aware or not, must ultimately be monitorable and verifiable in their behavior and processing by others. This implies sharing representations or language. But in a self-aware system that is able to change its own models and even introduce new parameters, how can it share terms with us? To address this challenge, we must deal with some initial approaches for creating and sharing representations and language. One very limited approach that we have started to explore for CARS is to let the system generate arbitrarily a term for some new pattern or event that it has identified ("umpyfromp" or "&*^$"), but their definition initially is a collection of context information that is made shareable with the human designer/user. Good starting information could include the following: context information, current associations with other co-occurring systems, agents, or components, and associations with what goals or decisions were being addressed. With Wrappings, such information is automatically generated in its internal control processes. The human can then look at this information and perhaps say "oh this is a new variable called WIND" and add it with suitable content and actions to existing or new models.

9.6.2   The i-Room

The phenomenon of noticing is one of the more mysterious capabilities of biological systems. How can you notice something you were not looking for? This is clearly an important capability for systems that have to operate in the real world. Building systems that notice is an excellent application for self-modeling systems. One of the most difficult issues in model construction is identifying significant events. We try to build systems with sufficient sensors to detect conditions that we think are important (especially the dangerous ones), but we cannot always predict all of them, and we usually cannot afford all the potentially useful sensors (not just for cost, but also weight and data processing time).

The *i-Room* began as a joint NSF project between The University of Southern California (USC) and The Aerospace Corporation and then continued later with The California State University at Pomona. In this project, detailed neurophysiological models of how mammalian visual systems come to notice something [23] were combined with traditional target identification and tracking algorithms, as well as other computational methods for managing the deployment of multiple sensors [17, 32]. The mammalian visual attention system goes a long way toward providing mechanisms that explain noticing, but only for the space of visual cues, not for other domains. It is an active area of research to extend the noticing algorithms to other domains, which is a matter of selecting good features and adapting the change algorithms to them.

The biological mechanisms of noticing can be biased; their attention criteria can be adjusted toward certain features ("look for a white truck" and "look for a motion correlated with your own") and then further adjusted by having the system also assess what is significant or relevant for its own purposes in the current situation.

Part of that is built in (like the parameterized models above), but we would like to leave as much of that as possible to be discovered or determined. We are currently examining an approach that selects information partly by associations of information with decisions and actions needed by system and uses a suite of more powerful data and information mining methods to detect unexpected connections.

9.7 Conclusions and Prospects

In this chapter, we have explained why self-aware systems must pay special attention to self-modeling capabilities, clarified what is meant by both strong self-modeling and weak self-modeling, and described some of the defining characteristics of self-modeling. We also gave some examples of successes and limitations in current self-modeling capabilities. We discussed several advanced end even new mathematical methods and where they may be used for self-modeling, as well as a number of current computational processes in complex systems that can be used to support self-modeling. Lastly, we gave some examples of real-world situations (rare events and unmodeled phenomena) that are formidably difficult, even for human beings to understand and build models for them. In those cases, we offered some lessons learned from biological systems in how they "buy time" and "safe" themselves and have learned preferred behaviors to rely on in the face of enormously complex possibilities.

References

1. James S. Albus, Alexander M. Meystel, *Engineering of Mind: An Introduction to the Science of Intelligent Systems*, Wiley (2001)
2. Daniel Barbara, J. Couto, S. Jajodia, L. Popyack, N. Wu, "ADAM: Detecting Intrusions by Data Mining", *Proceedings of the IEEE SMC Information Assurance Workshop*, West Point, NY (2001)
3. Jon Barwise, *The Situation in Logic*, CSLI Lecture Notes No.17, Center for the Study of Language and Information, Stanford U. (1989)
4. Kirstie L. Bellman, April Gillam, Christopher Landauer, "Challenges for Conceptual Design Environments: The VEHICLES Experience", *Revue Internationale de CFAO et d'Infographie*, Hermes, Paris (September 1993)
5. Kirstie Bellman and Christopher Landauer "Early Work on the BrainPatch, a Reflective Service for System of Systems Integration", *Proceedings SISSY 2015: International Workshop on Self-Improving System Integration*, 08 July 2015, Grenoble, France part of *ICAC2015: The 12th IEEE International Conference on Autonomic Computing*, 07-10 July 2015, Grenoble, France (2015)
6. Kirstie L. Bellman, Christopher Landauer, Phyllis R. Nelson, "System Engineering for Organic Computing", Chapter 3, pp.25-80 in Rolf P. Würtz (ed.), *Organic Computing*, Understanding Complex Systems Series, Springer (2008)
7. Kirstie L. Bellman, Phyllis R. Nelson, "Developing Mechanisms for Determining Good Enough in SORT Systems", *Proc. SORT 2011: The Second IEEE Workshop on Self-Organizing Real-Time Systems*, 31 Mar 2011, part of *ISORC 2011*, 28-31 Mar 2011, Newport Beach, California (2011)

8. Kirstie Bellman, Phyllis Nelson, Christopher Landauer, "Active Experimentation and Computational Reflection for Design and Testing of Cyber-Physical Systems" (poster), *Proceedings CSD&M 2014: The Fifth International Conference on Complex Systems Design & Management*, 12-14 November 2014, Paris, France (2014)

9. Gordon Blair, Nelly Bencomo, and Robert B. France, "Models@run.time", Introduction to Special Issue of *IEEE Computer*, p.22-27 (October 2009)

10. C. A. Bolstad, A. M. Costello, M. R. Endsley, "Bad situation awareness designs: What went wrong and why", *International Ergonomics Association 16th World Congress*, Maastricht, Netherland (2006)

11. Christopher J. C. Burges, *Dimension Reduction: A Guided Tour*, Now Publishing (2010)

12. Shang-Wen Cheng, David Garlan, Bradley Schmerl, "Making Self-Adaptation an Engineering Reality", in Ozalp Babaoglu, Mrk Jelasity, Alberto Montresor, Christof Fetzer, Stefano Leonardi, Aad van Moorsel, and Maarten van Steen (eds.), *Self-Star Properties in Complex Information Systems*, LNCS 3460, Springer (2005)

13. Frederica Darema, "Dynamic Data Driven Applications Systems: A New Paradigm for Application Simulations and Measurements", p.662-669 in Marian Bubak, G.Dick van Albada, Peter M.A. Sloot, Jack J. Dongarra (eds.), *Proceedings ICCS 2004*, Part III, 06-09 June, 2004, Krakow, Poland, SLNCS 3038, Springer (2004)

14. M.C. Dominguez, E. Vidulich, E. Vogel and G. McMillan, " Situation awareness: Papers and annotated bibliography", Armstrong Laboratory, Human System Center, ref. AL/CF-TR-1994-0085, 1994

15. Richard J. Doyle, "Relations Between Resilience and Validation", (presented to) *Workshop on Resilience Space Systems* 01 August 2012, Keck Institute for Space Studies, Caltech (2012)

16. Clint Eastwood, quote from *Magnum Force*, (1973)

17. J. Everist, T.N. Mundhenk, C. Landauer, K. Bellman "Visual Surveillance Coverage: Strategies and Metrics", *Proceedings of SPIE Conference on Intelligent Robots and Computer Vision XXII: Algorithms, Techniques, and Active Vision*, Boston (2005)

18. Erik M. Fredericks, Betty H. C. Cheng, "Automated Generation of Adaptive Test Plans for Self-Adaptive Systems", p. 157-167 in *Proceedings SEAMS@ICSE 2015: The 10th International Symposium on Software Engineering for Adaptive and Self-Managing Systems*, 1819 May 2015, Firenze, Italy (2015)

19. David Garlan and Bradley Schmerl, "Using Architectural Models at Runtime: Research Challenges", *Proc. First European Workshop on Software Architectures*, 21-22 May 2004, St. Andrews, Scotland, p.200-205 in Flavio Oquendo, Brian Warboys, Ron Morrison (eds.), *Software Architecture*, LNCS 3047, Springer (2004)

20. Eleanor J. Gibson, and Anne D. Pick *An Ecological Approach to Perceptual Learning and Development*, Oxford University Press (2000)

21. Rick Hayes-Roth, *Hyperbeings: How Intelligent Organizations Attain Supremacy Through Information Superiority*, Booklocker (2006)

22. Colin de la Higuera, *Grammatical Inference: Learning Automata and Grammars*, Cambridge, Cambridge University Press (2010)

23. L. Itti, C. Koch, "Computational Modelling of Visual Attention", *Nature Reviews Neuroscience*, Vol. 2, No. 3, pp. 194-203 (Mar 2001)

24. Gabor Karsai, Miklos Maroti, Akos Ledeczi, Jeff Gray, "Composition and Cloning in Modeling and Meta-Modeling", *IEEE Transactions on Control Systems Technology*, Vol. 12, No. 2, p.263-278 (March 2004)

25. Jeffrey O. Kephart, David M. Chase, "The Vision of Autonomic Computing", IEEE Computer, Vol.36, Issue 1, p.41-50 (Jan 2003)

26. Christopher Landauer, "Abstract Infrastructure for Real Systems: Reflection and Autonomy in Real Time", *Proceedings SORT 2011: The Second IEEE Workshop on Self-Organizing Real-Time Systems*, 31 March 2011, Newport Beach, California (2011) Morgan Kaufmann (1993)

27. Christopher Landauer, Kirstie L. Bellman, "Generic Programming, Partial Evaluation, and a New Programming Paradigm", Chapter 8, pp. 108-154 in Gene McGuire (ed.), *Software Process Improvement*, Idea Group Publishing (1999)

28. Christopher Landauer, Kirstie L. Bellman, "Self-Modeling Systems", p. 238-256 in R. Laddaga, H. Shrobe (eds.), "Self-Adaptive Software", LNCS 2614, Springer (2002)
29. Christopher Landauer, Kirstie Bellman, "Designing Cooperating Self-Improving Systems", *Proc. 2015 SISSY Workshop: Self-improving Systems of Systems*; 07 Jul 2015, Grenoble, France part of *ICAC 2015: the 2015 Intern. Conf. on Autonomic Computing*, 07-10 Jul 2015, Grenoble, France (2015)
30. Pattie Maes, "Concepts and Experiments in Computational Reflection", pp.147-155 in *Proceedings OOPSLA '87* (1987)
31. A. Marazzi, P. Gamba, A. Mecocci, and E. Costamagna, "A mixed fractal/wavelet based approach for characterization of textured remote sensing images", *Proceedings IGARSS'97: The IEEE International Geoscience and Remote Sensing Symposium*, Vol. 2, p.655-657 (1997)
32. T. N. Mundhenk, J. Everist, C. Landauer, L. Itti, K. Bellman, "Distributed biologically-based real-time tracking in the absence of prior target information", pp. 142-153 in D. P. Casasent, E. L. Hall, J. Roning (eds.) *Proc. SPIE International Conference on Intelligent Robots and Computer Vision XXIII: Algorithms, Techniques, and Active Vision*, SPIE Press (Oct 2005)
33. Phyllis Nelson, "Self-Organized Self-Improvement", (presented to) Dagstuhl Seminar 11181 (2011)
34. Mélanie Catherine Rochoux, *Vers une meilleure prévision de la propagation d'incendies de forêt : évaluation de modèles et assimilation de donnés* (Towards a more comprehensive monitoring of wildfire spread : contributions of model evaluation and data assimilation strategies), Ph.D. Thesis, 21 January 2014, Ecole Centrale Paris, France (2014)
35. Bradley Schmerl, Jonathan Aldrich, David Garlan, Rick Kazman, and Hong Yan, "Discovering Architectures from Running Systems", IEEE Trans. Software Engineering, Vol.32, No.7, p.454-466 (Jul 2006)
36. P. D. Weigl, E. V. Hanson, "Observational Learning and the Feeding Behavior of the Red Squirrel: The Ontogeny of Optimization", *Ecology*, Vol.6, p.213-218
37. Afra Zomorodian, "Topological Data Analysis", p.1-39 in Afra Zomorodian (ed.), *Advances in Applied and Computational Topology*, *Proceedings of Symposia in Applied Math*, v.70, AMS Short Course, Computational Topology, 04-05 January 2011, New Orleans, LA (2011)

Chapter 10
Transition Strategies for Increasing Self-awareness in Existing Types of Computing Systems

Marco Autili, Kirstie L. Bellman, Ada Diaconescu, Lukas Esterle, Massimo Tivoli and Andrea Zisman

Abstract In this chapter, we propose a methodology to analyse the different levels of self-awareness present in distinct types of computing systems and architectures, investigate the level of self-awareness that is already present in those systems and architectures, and describe some transition strategies to increase the level of self-awareness in these systems.

10.1 Introduction

Several types of computing systems and architectures exist and are largely used to support different applications and domains. The level of self-awareness in these different computing systems and architectures may vary and can range from completely self-aware systems to systems and architectures that do not implement any level of self-awareness.

M. Autili · M. Tivoli
University of L'Aquila, 67100 L'Aquila, Italy
e-mail: marco.autili@univaq.it

M. Tivoli
e-mail: massimo.tivoli@univaq.it

K.L. Bellman
The Aerospace Corporation, Los Angeles, CA, USA
e-mail: Kirstie.L.Bellman@aero.org

A. Diaconescu
Telecom Paris Tech, 75013 Paris, France
e-mail: ada.diaconescu@telecom-paristech.fr

L. Esterle
Vienna University of Technology, Vienna, Austria
e-mail: lukas.esterle@tuwien.ac.at

A. Zisman (✉)
The Open University, Milton Keynes, UK
e-mail: andrea.zisman@open.ac.uk

© Springer International Publishing AG 2017
S. Kounev et al. (eds.), *Self-Aware Computing Systems*,
DOI 10.1007/978-3-319-47474-8_10

Based on this variant level of self-awareness, and following from the definition of self-aware computing systems provided in Chap. 1, in this chapter, we (i) propose a methodology to analyse the different levels of self-awareness present in distinct types of computing systems and architectures, (ii) investigate the level of self-awareness that is already present in those systems and architectures, and (iii) describe some transition strategies to increase the level of self-awareness in these systems.

More specifically, the purpose of this chapter is to give readers from diverse computer science communities an entry point for increasing the self-awareness in their respective systems. We do this by pointing out the benefits that additional self-awareness would bring to existing capabilities and systems. We then analyse some systems in terms of their existing capabilities and viewpoints from a self-awareness perspective and show which systems could already support self-awareness. We follow by providing some high-level suggestions for design and implementation strategies for transitioning to a more self-aware system.

It is not possible to provide an exhaustive analysis of the level of self-awareness in all different types of existing computing systems. We analyse some systems and architecture types that are mostly used and that provide a good range of possible different levels. We do not focus on the communities closest to the main topic of this book such as autonomic community, self-adaptive community, and organic computing community. Instead, we focus on some other communities to show how their respective systems could benefit from the concept of self-awareness. We complement the systems discussed in Chaps. 1 and 3 and analyse self-awareness in *legacy distributed systems* (e.g. military and power systems), *service-based systems*, *systems-of-systems*, and *agent-oriented systems*. Due to their current popularity and use, we also analyse the level of self-awareness in some architecture types such as *cloud computing* and *pervasive computing*. It is possible that some of these systems and architecture types already have certain levels of self-awareness, but not necessarily the communities associated with these systems know about these levels.

The remaining of this chapter is structured as follows. In Sect. 10.2, we present an overview of the capabilities and functions of self-aware systems. In Sect. 10.3, we define some questions to support the analysis of systems and architectures in terms of the different levels of self-awareness and discuss about various systems and architectures with respect to these questions. In Sect. 10.4, we present some transition strategies for self-aware service-based and multiagent systems. In Sect. 10.5, we describe an example of how to use the transition strategies proposed in Sect. 10.4 in a smart home service-based system. Finally, in Sect. 10.5, we present some conclusions and open challenges.

10.2 Capabilities and Functions of Self-aware Systems: An Overview

Considering the advantages that self-awareness can bring to computing systems, many existing domains may gain from the introduction of self-awareness abilities into their computing systems. This subsection aims to highlight the main *capabilities* and *functions* of self-aware systems, in order to help the extension process necessary for endowing existing technologies, platforms, or frameworks with self-awareness features.

We consider that a system *capability* represents an ability or a feature that is desirable and useful in itself for achieving the system's goals. For instance, self-optimization, self-repair, self-adaptation, self-configuration, and self-protection are all system capabilities that would help systems to better meet their high-level requirements. For achieving such capabilities, a system must implement a number of *functions*. Such functions are essential building blocks for achieving system capabilities. At the same time, *if taken in isolation*, such functions do not provide desirable or useful system's abilities. For instance, a system's self-monitoring and self-analysis functions are key to all of the aforementioned capabilities. Yet, if provided in isolation, and without being combined with further functions such as planning, runtime system modification, or logging, they would not help the system to meet its requirements.

Certainly, in many situations, the distinction between function and capability will not be clear. We merely make this conceptual distinction here to help the discussion on the advantages that self-awareness can bring at different system levels, in terms of interdependent capabilities and functions. In Sect. 10.4, we will rely on this discussion to identify the capabilities that may be advantageous to acquire for various domain-specific systems; to indicate the capabilities that could be improved by introducing self-awareness support; and to determine the additional functions that such systems may need to introduce for these purposes.

The most common *capabilities* envisaged for self-aware systems include:

- Self-configuration;
- Self-healing, including self-correction and fault management;
- Self-optimization;
- Self-protection, including security insurance;
- Self-adaptation to internal, external, and goal-related changes;
- Self-documentation;
- Self-reporting.

Achieving the above capabilities requires support for various combinations of finer-grained and sometimes interdependent *functions*, including:

- Self-monitoring and context monitoring, including other systems and humans—these functions are required, in various forms and extents, for achieving most of the aforementioned self-* capabilities;
- Self-modification, including dynamic reconfiguration, introduction/updating/removal of components and subsystems, creation or removal of component instances, relocation of instances on different platforms, and dis/connecting services or component instances;
- Data analysis;
- Self-modelling, knowledge acquisition, learning—these are typical self-aware functions, which may rely on finer-grained functions such as data monitoring and analysis;

- Planning and, more generally, finding solutions to problems;
- Reasoning about itself, about others, and about the environment—these are typical self-aware functions;
- Communication with other systems or humans: negotiation, co-operation, usage, and data sharing;
- Identifying the adaptations needed in order to conform to high-level goals—these are typical self-aware functions.

As indicated before, most of the above capabilities and functions can, and have been achieved and used successfully, in other computing domains, without self-awareness support. Nonetheless, in most of these cases, self-awareness can help to improve the range of conditions under which such capabilities and functions apply, as well as the efficiency and the quality of their results.

In short, self-awareness can enable systems to exert their self-* capabilities within a wider range of unexpected changes, for which hard-wired solutions are not readily available. Here, self-modelling and reasoning abilities can ensure a faster and more accurate diagnosis of novel problems and, hence, more appropriate adaptation solutions. Moreover, learning abilities can enable a system to adapt its internal models to changes and to learn from its mistakes, in order to tune and to extend the knowledge of itself and of its environment. Consequently, the system's knowledge and the capability to reason on this knowledge can help to better predict the outcomes of its adaptation actions, within particular contexts, that have not been tested before. This can lead to achieving successful adaptations more efficiently, minimizing necessary trial-and-error iterations or the need for expert human intervention. Finally, the system's awareness of its high-level goals is essential for its ability to find new adaptation strategies or approaches to unexpected situations. Otherwise, the system can only verify and ensure predefined constraints or optimize predefined utility functions.

In addition to achieving its goals successfully, a self-aware system can also help its owners to understand its behaviour and to better administer its resources, environment, and goals. For example, it is possible to extract information from self-aware systems about the reasons and motivations behind certain behaviours and the cases where appropriate solutions to problems could not be identified or applied. This information can be used to suggest external interventions such as adding resources or updating the goals.

10.3 Computing Systems Analysis

In order to analyse the various systems and architectures of our interest, we have defined some questions related to the definition of self-aware computing systems. The process we used to define these questions was based on the independent identification of some questions by the authors of the paper, followed by a collective analysis and discussions of the suggestions of each author. The results of these analyses and discussions are the questions presented below. We have defined questions concerned with the actions associated with *data and information processing*; *knowledge processing: learning, modelling, and reasoning*; *types of knowledge*; and *types of actions*. We present these questions grouped into four corresponding categories, as follows:

Data and Information Processing

- Q1: What type of information can be gathered?
- Q2: When can information be gathered?
- Q3: What are the means for collecting information?

Knowledge Processing: learning, modelling, and reasoning

- Q4: What types of learning processes are available?
- Q5: What types of modelling techniques are available?
- Q6: What types of reasoning techniques are available?
- Q7: When is knowledge acquired (e.g. deployment time vs. runtime)?
- Q8: What are the means by which knowledge is acquired?

Types of Knowledge

- Q9: What type of knowledge is present in the system?
- Q10: What type of knowledge can be learned and how much can be learned?
- Q11: What type of knowledge can the system acquire?
- Q12: What is the scope (span) of knowledge (also with respect to time)?
- Q13: What is the scope (span) of the goal-awareness (also with respect to time)?

Types of Actions

- Q14: What types of actions the system supports (goal-oriented, social, self-adaptive auditing, and reporting)?
- Q15: What types of runtime integration are supported (acting, knowledge processing, information processing)?
- Q16: What types of integration are supported for the results of self-aware processes across the system?

In the following, when necessary, we provide a brief description of each of the different types of systems and architectures of our concern and analyse them with respect to the above questions. For some of the systems and architectures, their brief descriptions are presented in Chap. 2. It is worth noting that for some systems and architectures, not all the questions can be applied and answered.

10.3.1   Existing Distributed Systems Architectures

One of the motivations for early work in self-adaptive and self-aware systems comes from the challenges of managing very large distributed systems such as space, health care, automobile, manufacturing, power grids, and military systems. These systems are characterized by having a very large number and variety types of components (often millions), many diverse users with differing goals and requirements, and distinct managerial policies and organizational concepts of operation (CONOPS). In addition to the challenge of designing such systems (which often takes many years of development, dozens of organizations, and thousands of man-hours testing and ensuring that requirements are met), the evolution and maintenance of these systems also require enormous efforts to keep parts up to date, to insert new technologies and new requirements, and to identify and correct failures. The need for, and the evolution of, system engineering where developed in parallel to these complex systems. Traditional system engineering emphasized a careful sequence in the development process, which could be iterated. These development processes consist of determining requirements and specifications; drilling down from overall system to detailed component design; and climbing back up the development process with component, integration, and overall system test. In such traditional engineering process, the roles for a component are determined a priori, the rigidly and fixed interfaces and protocols among parts are fully tested, and the change processes are carefully managed and restricted [11, 27].

Because of the enormous effort and cost required to develop these large complex distributed systems, at any time during the development, there is usually a combination of both legacy and new software and computer hardware. The physical sensors, effectors, and devices also range from brand new components to obsolete parts that are still being used. Due to this changing mix of new and old components, one often finds that even in a carefully designed and controlled legacy system, there is a patchwork of quick fixes, specially written interfaces and drivers, and other exceptions to standard uses of components. The distributed nature of these systems further complicates the implementations as developers and users locally specialize components or operations to fit their local needs.

This complicated patchwork means that for the most part, a complex distributed system will not have a single style of serving users and processing information. To the contrary, such distributed systems are typified by very diverse roles, functions, and behaviours of their components. For example, a space system has millions of components,[1] some of which serve its intricate communication functions, solar panel deployments, fuel consumption, separate spacecraft and payload movements, housekeeping sensors, guidance, and navigation. A healthcare system may include not only all the equipment and patient monitors in its clinics, and equipment in the laboratories in its hospitals, but also financial services, information services, security, and facility control. The World Health Organization broadens even this definition of a healthcare system to include a variety of associated public health and education outreach programmes [2]. The challenges of integrating these vastly diverse components are further complicated by a number of characteristics that have been well described in the literature [8, 9], namely (i) the resource sharing across users and system components; (ii) the relative openness of environments both in terms of software and equipment from different vendors and in terms of the rapid insertion of

---

[1] According to NASA, the space shuttle had two and half million moving parts alone [1].

new types of components; and (iii) the concurrent ongoing processes creating lots of opportunities for unplanned dependencies and side effects.

The above leads to many challenges for distributed systems. First, one paradoxically has an overly rigid system and at the same time an overwhelming diversity of activities, processes, and events requiring monitoring, management, and conflict resolution. Second, as part of this enormous amount of activity, the human users and development team (as well as the systems' own automated decision processes) can lack perspective over all the events and, with that lack of perspective, fail to notice and respond in a timely fashion to key requirements. Further, within a distributed system, it can be difficult to monitor and respond quickly enough to requests or events. Third, polling the right components for the right data, and understanding the dependencies and implications among the interactions or results, is difficult, given all the concurrent goals and processes. As part of this, it is difficult to discover, select, and set up the right configuration of resources both to identify an event, reason about that request or event, and to respond to it and again—in a timely fashion.

The knowledge collected by such systems and the actions allowed are, therefore, quite diverse. But both the knowledge and the alternative actions are usually completely predefined, and the use of them has been carefully tested for their various uses for specific functions. For example, the sensors used to determine the attitude control are well understood, defined, and tested. The use of sensor data is carefully collected for controlling attitude and for identifying any anomalies.

Comparison Based on the Methodology

Not surprisingly, existing distributed systems have a variety of existing methods for introducing some flexibility and adaptivity into their systems. As noted, they are a patchwork of old legacy and new components. Hence, with the variety of components, there is also a range of methods for adapting and adjusting the behaviour of a component or a set of components (Q5). This flexibility has been introduced in very specific and controlled ways, but the result is that there are still many unknown interactions among components (Q16). In general, learning methods to improve adaptation and responses are not widely used throughout the system (Q4). Any models, rulesets, CONOPS, and actions are predefined at design time (Q1, Q2), and at best, some of the models and actions are parameterized in order to allow some adaptation to changing contexts and operations (Q3). Models and rulesets are not updated in a continual fashion by the system itself as recommended by DDDAS systems [13, 15] (Q3, Q12). However, inputs and results are used to constantly update system models which change the focus and settings of data collection sensors and programs (Q5). This changes data processing programs and decision processes (Q6).

One of the current adaptive mechanisms in large distributed component systems is to support the necessary adaptation by using a large selection of predefined and carefully tested alternative components with their alternative behaviours, solutions, and capabilities (Q14). The challenges in this case are similar to the ones for service-oriented architecture: one must discover, choose, and select among appropriate alternatives for some current event or need, and then determine any necessary local adjustments (to parameters, interfaces, or co-occurring services) (Q16). Self-aware computing can benefit the discovery, selection, and adjustment processes by speeding them up and by making them more context-sensitive and fine-tuned to the current state of the system and the operational context.

Due to diverse activities that occur in large distributed systems, it is easy to lose traceability or perspective over all the ongoing activities in terms of the spatial distribution of all the active components (and their wide-ranging relationships and dependencies) across the system; and over time, unless processes that monitor the likely history leading up to events and the decisions and actions that occurred at each point are created (Q4, Q6, Q8). Self-awareness can support better perspective over all the systems (as in the integration among reflective processes proposed in the Web of reflection [22, 23]) and can support better recording for building a meaningful history, analysis, and evaluation (deciding what causal events led to other events) (Q4, Q6, Q10). This certainly can help the human analyst better understand the situation, as well as any automated reasoning in the machine system.

Most of the adaptive behaviours in existing systems have been carefully segregated from other parts of the system, with the purpose of making that system function more robustly in the face of either failure or the demands of new operational environments. In general, such experiments in adaptivity do not occur in the integration among system components or across the system and its components (Q15). The dynamic integration and configuration described in self-aware computing could potentially benefit the ability of distributed systems to have better and more secure configurations, in response to failure or new requirements.

10.3.2 Service-Based Systems (SBSs)

Comparison Based on the Methodology

By referring to the overview on SBSs reported in Chap. 2, and considering all the questions from Q1 to Q16, the SOC paradigm and the SOA principles do not impose any specific constraints on SBSs for what concerns self-awareness. More specifically, the level of self-awareness of an SBS depends on the way a specific SBS is designed and developed.

As far as **orchestration** is concerned, by its centralized nature, the orchestrator component realizes the whole interaction logic required to achieve a goal. The orchestrator is aware of the goal of the composed system. A straightforward consideration here is that goal-awareness represents the primary knowledge base for orchestration-based systems (Q9). This awareness is global in space (Q12, Q13) in the sense that it concerns all the orchestrated distributed services. The scope of the awareness spans the entire life cycle of the system (Q12, Q13) in the sense that it is acquired at design time (Q7, Q11), and it is used at execution time (Q15).

The basic knowledge of the orchestrator can be enriched, by gathering information at deployment or runtime (Q2) on the resources offered by the execution environment, the system global state, and the intraprocedural interaction behaviour among the orchestrated services (Q1). For instance, the latter represents the typical knowledge that a BPEL-based orchestrator can gather at execution time (Q2) by observation. With respect to the orchestrator, each single orchestrated service is passive and not goal-aware, meaning that it does not have any knowledge in principle. Clearly, this does not prevent an orchestrated service to exploit external resources like monitors (Q3) and (locally) learn the external interaction protocol followed by the orchestrator (Q4, Q11).

As far as **choreography** is concerned, there is no complete/global goal-awareness, since there is no centralized entity (Q9). In particular, although choreography is built based on a given goal, it is realized through goal distribution. This means that, differently from orchestration, the interaction logic required to achieve the goal is not explicitly codified into a single centralized entity; rather, it emerges and can be learned only at runtime (Q2, Q7), through observation (Q6, Q8) of the global collaboration among the choreography participant services (Q7). The latter can be proactive and, due to full distribution, have only knowledge about local views of the goal. In principle, choreography service participants are not aware of the global state, the system architecture, and the ongoing global collaboration among the services. This does not prevent to interpose additional software entities among the participant services such as external coordination entities (Q8), which aim at aggregating/monitoring/interpreting (Q6) at runtime (Q2, Q12) information exchanged through message passing (Q1, Q3), in order to infer some form of global knowledge (e.g. global state, interconnections among the participant services, and flows of exchanged messages (Q11)).

Following the discussion above, for both orchestration and choreography, there is no specific limit on when the knowledge is acquired (Q2, Q7) and on what type of information is gathered at runtime (Q1, Q11). Knowledge can be acquired at either deployment, discovery, binding, or runtimes. The type of gathered information is related to what can be observed from outside directly by the composition code (orchestrator), or by additional resources used as proxies to the participant services and their interaction (choreography). For example, information can range from flows of exchanged messages, to response time of invoked service operations and instance pool of data useful to invoke service operations. Thus, as far as orchestration is concerned, the means by which the knowledge is acquired are related to global monitoring/coordination/mediation/adaptation mechanisms (Q3). In the case of choreographies, knowledge is acquired by aggregating pieces of information coming from distributed resources, i.e. distributed monitoring, coordination, mediation, and adaptation mechanisms (Q3).

Another important aspect is the gap between the gathered information and the different types of knowledge that the system aims to acquire. It depends on the kind of exposed service contracts. It also depends on whether a machine-readable specification of the goal is available and on what this specification predicates (e.g. structure only and structure plus behaviour (functional and/or non-functional)). For instance, as far as choreography-based SBSs are concerned, let us suppose that a BPMN2 choreography diagram specification, G, of the system goal, is available. It is possible to synthesize distributed exogenous controllers that force the global collaboration of the participant services to exhibit only the interactions specified in G (Q14, Q15, Q16). If the system architect is not interested in assessing non-functional properties of the composed system, and if the participant services come with a description of both their signature and interaction protocol, in order to perform the above synthesis, no further processing is required. Rather, if services are provided together with a description of their signature only, then a protocol for interaction learning is required, in order to perform distributed coordination code synthesis (Q14, Q15, Q16).

SBSs do not impose particular constraints and limits on the kind of available acquisition and learning processes (Q3, Q4). Again, they depend on the specific adopted design and development technologies and related modelling notations. Examples in the literature are concerned with service interaction protocols; learning and acquisition of data-oriented information through online (black box) testing [10]; automated synthesis of the required distributed coordination and adaptation logic [3, 20]; and online verification of behavioural properties of the overall service interaction, service discovery, reputation, and trust.

Considering goal-awareness aspects, orchestrations can support self-adaptation of the composition logic to possible goal changes through monolithic or modular/compositional reasoning (Q14–Q16). The ability/inability to perform adaptation in a modular/compositional way depends on how the orchestrator is realized (properties of the composition), on the adopted adaptation technique, and on the type of changes applied, which trigger adaptation. On the other hand, choreographies can be realized to support self-adaptation of the distributed coordination logic to possible goal changes, based on modular reasoning, compositional in the best case (Q14–Q16). Monolithic reasoning is ineffective in this case, often not applicable. Self-adaptation mechanisms can have a layered structure, e.g. coordination/composition layer, adaptation layer, filtering layer, and monitoring layer. Considering design and/or implementation strategies used to implement self-aware mechanisms, the integration and aggregation of related results across the overall system and the composition and integration of business processes realized as composite services are native characteristics of SBSs built via orchestration or choreography.

10.3.3 Systems-of-Systems (SoSs)

Comparison Based on the Methodology

The types of information and actions in systems-of-systems (SoSs) are very similar to those in other large distributed component-based systems with the addition of much more organizational oversight, standards, and policies in regard to authority and access to the various assets in a system. For example, in space systems, only certain groups are authorized to support an asset (e.g. to point the system to a certain direction.) In a hospital system, only some groups or individuals are allowed access to medications under a strict protocol, or are allowed to authorize changes to the patients' medical record.

Systems-of-systems (SoSs) need to be very aware of when different organizational policies are relevant (Q7) and where they can be applied. They also need to understand how their viewpoints (as formed by their specific goals, values, missions, and CONOPS) impact their ability to interface successfully with other organizations (Q15, Q16). For example, how are the viewpoints and capabilities of an SoS hindering the ability of the SoS to perceive solutions that are suitable to all participating organizations in the current situation. Self-aware computing can have processes that specifically reason about the limits of their own sensors, approaches to a problem, and reasoning processes. Furthermore, the extra layer of policies and authorizations required in an SoS (Q9, Q11) also requires much more careful record-keeping and during failures and a complete investigation of what has occurred. The self-aware recording processes can greatly improve the accuracy and detail in the trace of what has occurred, as well as the speed and correctness of the evaluation processes (Q8). The multiple self-monitoring and reporting processes present in an SoS (Q4, Q6, Q8) can also help the system to have better context awareness so that rulesets and policies may be adjusted according to both goals and the context.

There are many other challenges to SoSs because the components of an SoS are not just big components (such as libraries of functions or massive simulations). Rather, the subcomponents are systems themselves, and therefore, they may have many stringent rules on access to any of their internal capabilities. It also means that they may perform changes independently of their roles in a SoS (Q14) and these unannounced or limitedly announced changes could alter some of the carefully predefined protocols and interfaces among the SoS participating systems (Q1). It is already hard in a distributed architecture to keep all the services and interfaces updated by the system. In the case of SoSs, with limited control, limited access, and limited visibility , the problem of keeping agreements, relationships, and interfaces up to date is extremely difficult (Q1, Q2, Q3). Even if permissions are in place, the additional time to go through the security processes of one system could add lag time to many discovery and execution processes. Although self-awareness does not automatically solve these difficult organizational issues, they can make the need for further negotiation and actions more explicit, and rapidly identified, in an ongoing continual fashion when the self-aware processes are distributed in parallel at many levels throughout the system.

However, the next two types of SoS Acknowledged and Directed are especially relevant to our understanding of what reflective and self-integrating processes need to do at the SoS level. The Acknowledged SoS is described as having recognized objectives, a designated manager, and resources for the SoS; however, the constituent systems retain their independent ownership, objectives, funding, and development and sustainment approaches. Changes in the systems are based on collaboration between the SoS and the system. The Directed SoS is described as one in which the integrated systems-of-systems are built and managed to fulfil specific purposes. It is centrally managed during long-term operation to continue to fulfil those purposes as well as any new ones the system owners might wish to address. The component systems maintain an ability to operate independently, but their normal operational mode is subordinated to the central managed purpose.

There are different types of SoSs. For example, in a *Directed SoS* [26], the integrated systems-of-systems are built and managed to fulfil the specific purposes based on a centralized management component. In this case, the SoS is designed in a similar way to a traditional complex distributed system. Although there is a difference in the scope of of the components, there is no difference when considering during design time a large amount of meta-knowledge collected or developed (Q9, Q12). It is important to use specific self-aware computing processes to reason about the types of sensors, feedback, evaluations, and decisions necessary for an SoS (Q4, Q6). Conflicts and issues among participating systems should be corrected in advance together with necessary interfaces, agreements on priorities and operating rules, and resources that embody policies, priorities, authorizations, and agreements (Q1, Q9, Q11).

In another example, in an *Acknowledged SoS* [26], there are recognized objectives, a designated manager, and resources for the SoS. The participating systems retain their independent ownership, objectives, funding, and development and sustainment approaches. Moreover, changes in the systems are based on collaboration between the SoSs and the system. In this case, integration must occur during runtime operations as a result of collaboration, negotiation, and interaction among participant systems (Q15, Q16). To provide a self-aware perspective to these systems, it is important to consider wrapping processes to support dynamic runtime selection and configuration of system components using meta-knowledge about system components and reflective processes provided at design time (Q2, Q9, Q11). However, integration (Q15, Q16) will mostly occur at runtime with no guarantee that the individual systems will have provided all the necessary access to their internal information, state, or functionality. Furthermore, new systems added into a SoS do not have all the necessary knowledge of the goals of the collective, the policies, operational restrictions or context information, or clear input on what is their role within that collective (Q1, Q11).

10.3.4 Multiagent Systems (MASs)

Comparison Based on the Methodology

As discussed in Chap. 2, the type of agents most suitable for comparison with self-aware computing systems are *deliberative agents*, as they must typically possess symbolic representation and learning and reasoning capabilities, in order to achieve well-specified goals. Conversely, *reflex agents* would be closer to pre-reflective entities, as defined in self-aware computing (Chap. 3), as they merely react to stimuli in their environment.

Considering information and knowledge-related aspects (Q1–Q13), there is no particular constraint on the types of knowledge that a deliberative agent may acquire, in principle, either on its own (via learning—Q4) or from an external resource (Q8). This will mostly depend on the agent's type, implementation, and application domain. All agent types are able to collect some information from their environments (Q1), at runtime (Q2). The exact types of information collected will depend on the problem that the MAS system must solve (or the goal to reach). Similarly, the exact means of data collection will be implementation and application-specific (Q3).

Transforming collected information into knowledge, or symbolic models, is typically a capability of deliberative agents. Model-based reflex agents also maintain models of their internal states and external environment, yet mostly as a record of past events and current states that they can react to, rather than as a base for reasoning. When agents acquire knowledge, it occurs during runtime (Q7), though offline knowledge can also be provided. There is no particular constraint on the knowledge representation (Q5), acquisition means (Q8), types (Q9), and scope (Q12); on the kind of reasoning techniques provided—e.g. based on deduction, induction, or abduction (Q6); or on the types of learning processes (Q4) and the types and amounts of knowledge that can be learnt (Q10, Q11).

With respect to goal-awareness (Q13), goal-oriented and utility-based agents do, by definition, have knowledge of the goals that they have to achieve. At the other end of the spectrum, reactive agents are totally unaware of their goals and of themselves as a goal-pursuing entity within an environment. Various options are possible in between these extremes. Concerning the actual *scope* of goal-awareness (Q13), where this applies, an agent either may be limited to knowledge of their local goals, or have a complete view of the global goal pursued by the multiagent system; intermediary cases are also possible.

As with monitoring, all agent types are able to perform some type of action (Q14). Depending on each MAS application, agent actions may include adaptations of their environment, co-operations, or negotiations with other agents, or various reports to users or other agents. Deliberative agents may also represent the results of their actions explicitly and reason upon them for deciding on further actions, while reactive agents will merely act directly depending on their observations (and state in the case of model-based reflex agents) (Q16).

With respect to an agent's self-adaptation—an action that can chiefly profit from self-awareness—even though possible and often provided, this is not a core research topic in the MAS community. Instead, MAS research has focused on the challenge of decentralized problem-solving and on the associated issues of task decomposition and distribution, agent communication, coordination and collaboration, and conflict resolution via negotiation. Within each agent, the focus has been placed on strategy planning and optimization, decision-making, or learning, in order to better fulfil their assigned tasks. Agent self-adaptation mainly occurs when agents change roles within an organization or as they move between organizations. Hence, self-adaptation mainly implies the (de)activation of a behaviour from a predefined set, rather than an actual modification in the agent's internal architecture or implementation. Typical agents are not concerned with maintaining knowledge about their internal structures (Q9–Q12), or adapting their structure based on such knowledge (Q14–Q16). Learning agents can reconfigure their strategies and/or interactions based on experience (e.g. game theoretical or trust-aware agents), in order to optimize their goal achievement (Q14).

In multiagent systems, *integrating* information, knowledge acquisition, reasoning, and action processes, via agent interactions, is quite natural, at the very core of the MAS paradigm (Q15, Q16). Much effort has been spent into this research domain for identifying different types of agent organizations, providing different ways to aggregate agent processes (Q15), and associated results (Q16), across the overall system.

Depending on the type of agent organization, the capabilities discussed above will be distributed differently across the agents and may have different characteristics. For instance, in hierarchic or holarchic organizations, agents placed at the higher levels will have wider knowledge and goal scopes compared to agents at lower levels (Q13). Since they may also have more authority and control, higher-level agents may also feature more sophisticated reasoning and learning capabilities Q4, Q6). In market organizations, the agents' social interaction abilities, such as negotiation, are central to their individual success. Similarly, in organizations formed for goal optimization purposes, such as coalitions, congregations, or federations, social interaction skills are essential. In addition, some organizations such as teams also require global goal-awareness from their participating agents (Q14, Q15).

10.3.5   Cloud Computing

Comparison Based on the Methodology

As discussed in the overview about cloud computing reported in Chap. 2, in this chapter we compare cloud computing with respect to the methodology based on the three service models for cloud computing, namely (a) Software as a Service, (b) Platform as a Service, and (c) Infrastructure as a Service.

As far as self-awareness at the Software as a Service (SaaS) level is concerned, application services share the same abilities that we discussed above for service-based systems (Q1–Q16). However, specifically, considering knowledge-related aspects about the environment, application services do not manage or control the cloud platform (which is transparently managed by the underlying PaaS) including network, servers, operating systems, storage, or even individual application capabilities (Q9, Q12). An exception is found with respect to the limited user-specific application configuration settings. For instance, there is no control or knowledge over the exact location of the provided resources (Q9), and hence, it is not possible to reason based on this information (Q6, Q7, Q10). However, there is the possibility to specify location at a higher level of abstraction (location independence). Application services can have knowledge about resource usage. The cloud platform offers mechanisms to reason on and acts on resource usage through monitoring, controlling, and reporting (Q6, Q8).

At the Platform as a Service (PaaS) level, similarly to what was discussed for the SaaS level, it is not possible to manage or control the cloud infrastructure (which is transparently managed by the IaaS level) (Q9). However, PaaS has control over the deployed applications and possibly configuration settings for the application-hosting environment (Q14).

At the IaaS level, Infrastructure as a Service provides control over operating systems, storage, deployed applications, and hardware components such as host firewalls (Q14).

10.3.6   Pervasive Computing

Comparison Based on the Methodology

Based on the overview about pervasive computing reported in Chap. 2, there is no direct constraint on what kind of information a pervasive system is able to gather from the environment or other systems (Q1). Nevertheless, in most cases, the acquired information is about local context. This is due to limitations in sensing capabilities and to information only being required locally. If multiple entities constitute a pervasive system, information can still be exchanged among these different entities to pursue a common, global goal.

Information can be gathered during runtime (Q2). Information can also be supplied to the system before deployment, allowing for *a priori* information about various factors such as the environment, its own capabilities and resources, or other systems in the environment with which to interact (Q2). As pervasive systems usually possess only limited resources and are also often battery-based, the question on 'how often' is information gathered becomes also quite important. While higher frequencies allow the system to build up a more detailed model of the sensed environment, gathering information often may deplete scarce resources more quickly. One may also be interested to know how long information should be kept within the system. This is highly dependent on the available resources of the pervasive system, but also on the frequency and the amount of information gathered. If the system gathers large amount of data seldom, this might still require too much resources in a short time. In this case, the oldest information might be discarded in favour of newly acquired information.

The type of information that can be gathered highly depends on the system, its implementation, and its capabilities in terms of communicating and sensing (Q3, Q11). In an aggregated system, combining multiple pervasive entities, the information gathered by the individual is used to achieve local goals. The information is gathered in a distributed fashion and only aggregated where needed to achieve the respective goal.

Existing limited resources also affect the available learning methods and their capabilities to self-adapt, self-explain, and self-* (Q4). Therefore, pervasive systems with constrained resources often apply simple rule-based approaches or selection methods (e.g. multiarmed bandit solvers) to switch between predefined learning, monitoring, and reasoning processes (Q6). Alternatively, they often learn based on batches of acquired information in certain predefined intervals, or triggered by certain events (e.g. in cyber-physical systems whenever a user interaction occurs). Meta-learning is usually not employed online due to the limited resources. Nevertheless, pervasive systems do apply simple rule-based approaches or selection methods (e.g.

multiarmed bandit solvers) to switch between predefined learning, monitoring, and reasoning processes. The modelling of information and knowledge within the pervasive system depends on the actual implementation of the system (Q5).

Both information and knowledge can be acquired at deployment and runtime. (Q7). In the case of deployment time, one would refer to this knowledge as *embedded knowledge*. During runtime, *tacit knowledge* can be built internally by simple learning mechanisms, but also pervasive systems may share their knowledge with other systems in their environment, allowing them to increase their knowledge base without having access to the underlying information (Q8, Q9). In most cases, the individual entities receive knowledge about the other individual entities and their capabilities (available and acquirable knowledge, sensing capabilities, and possible actions) in the pervasive system (Q10). Furthermore, pervasive systems are often receiving an initial knowledge base in order to avoid an initial learning phase after deployment. In many cases, modern pervasive systems are deployed with simple learning capabilities in order to refine the initial knowledge over time.

The amount of knowledge that can be learned is similar to the amount of information that can be gathered. Due to resource constraints, knowledge may only be derived based on the available information and is limited by processing power, amount of available memory, or communication bandwidth (Q10). To define the span and the scope of the knowledge, we have to distinguish between *centralized pervasive computing systems* and *distributed pervasive computing systems*, where multiple entities collaborate in order to achieve a common goal. A centralized system can also consist of a global controller, collecting and aggregating information of the individual entities and coordinating them in order to achieve a single goal for the entire system.

In centralized pervasive systems, the central coordination is aware of the global goals and often about the local goals of the individual entities. Nevertheless, the single entity is also aware of its own goals. Furthermore, a pervasive system can be aware of its state and learn about its behaviour and the corresponding effects on its environment. The amount in which a pervasive system is aware of the results of its self-* actions (scope) highly depends on the sensing capabilities of the system (Q12, Q13).

For a distributed pervasive system, goals can be shared among the individual entities through information exchange. However, this is usually done on a per-request basis and does not make the entire system aware of the actual goals of the individual entities. When it comes to an awareness of states, a similar situation occurs where the individual entities are only aware of their local state. Depending on how they have been implemented, individual entities can be aware of the state of their immediate neighbouring pervasive entities through information exchange. They can also receive feedback regarding their self-* actions and their impact on the environment (including other systems). The amount and range of information and knowledge that can be shared define the span regarding knowledge and goal-awareness (Q12 and Q13).

To conclude, a general pervasive computing system does not inherently possess any capabilities to support self-awareness. In a centralized mode, self-awareness could be implemented by the central controller aggregating the information, deriving knowledge, and controlling the individual entities. In a distributed system, self-awareness would be limited to the individual entities, only allowing the self-aware properties to emerge from these individual entities.

10.4   Transition Strategies

In this section, we provide some general strategies to transition an existing system into a more self-aware system. As pointed out before, a self-aware system may be composed of many different types of self-awareness and self-aware components. Hence, there is no single site of self-awareness and no single self-awareness component in most self-aware systems. Therefore, an important part of transitioning a given system into a self-aware system is to analyse the goals and objectives for inserting self-awareness into a given system.

We describe three high-level processes that are meant to stimulate the reader to ask certain kinds of questions and to consider different uses for self-awareness and different types of components that one might want to insert into the implementation of a given architecture. The three high-level processes are shown in the graphs presented in Figs. 10.1, 10.2, and 10.3. This is meant as an overview for a process that would eventually have to consider in detail the specific components of a system and how these components might be implemented in a more self-aware component. The process also needs to consider specific system goals, evaluation criteria for proper performance, types of data sources, and models, and to analyse the requirements for integrating self-aware components into an architecture capable of meeting the system requirements and objectives.

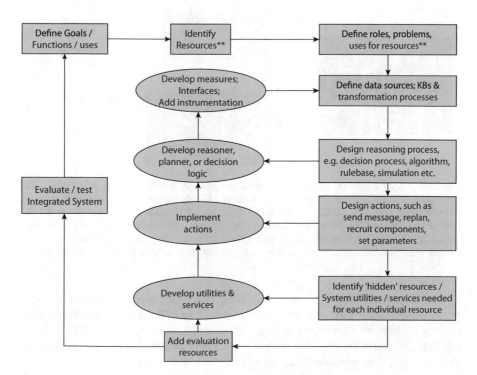

Fig. 10.1 Transition to self-awareness process: per each resource

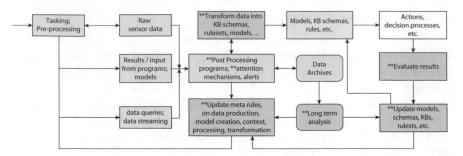

Fig. 10.2 Knowledge transformation steps expanded. *Blue boxes* represent possible insertion points for self-awareness to adjust and adapt transformations, programs, collections, and queries. *Orange boxes* indicate core data flow: collection, processing, and storage. The *green box* represents the knowledge base, model base for both self-models and domain models, etc

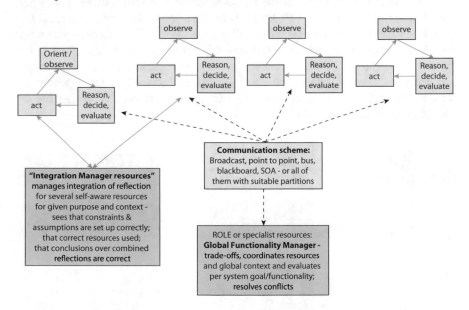

Fig. 10.3 Integration flow: Integration is both a matter of individual resource responsibility and oversight by specialized components; we start with a set of self-aware resources, each with their own instrumentation and monitoring, reasoning and evaluation, and action processes. Each individual self-aware resource "OODA" (Orient/Observe, Decide, and Act) loop set up already. Integration means that the right resources are configured and set up so that they do the right thing in a given context with the correct results and can have combination of predefined actions or reasoning

   The flow chart in Fig. 10.1 starts with the process for generating more self-aware components. The flow chart in Fig. 10.2 lays out some of the typical data sources and the types of processes necessary for using the data and transforming it into knowledge used by the system for all of its diverse purposes. The flow chart in Fig. 10.3 shows some of the major aspects of integrating self-aware processes.

As shown in Fig. 10.1, the process starts as in the design of any system by laying out the basic goals and objectives for a system and identifying all the parts of that system. In the case of transitioning from a traditionally designed system into a self-aware system, it is necessary to concentrate on the objectives that the system should have in terms of self-awareness, as noted in the list of self-awareness benefits. The process considers the types of resources (components) in the system, defines the types of roles these resources play in the system, and defines the goals or requirements for each of these resources, focusing on possible uses for increased self-awareness. For example, in the case of a planner component, it is possible to add a new capability for that planner to reason about the effectiveness of its current plans and to be able to replan according to its reflections on its current areas of weakness. As another example, in the case of security monitoring, in order to increase self-awareness, the security monitors may be extended to negotiate the consistency of their observations. For each resource, after restating roles, goals, and uses and, perhaps, adding some new roles for an increasingly self-aware component, the process consists of identifying the types of knowledge (rulesets or models), reasoning processes, interfaces, and any other supporting programs that would be needed by that resource to do its functions. It is also important to identify the sets of test cases or evaluation resources, in order to evaluate and manage the performance, results, and behaviour of each resource.

The box in Fig. 10.1, defining data sources, is further elaborated in the flow chart in Fig. 10.2. The purpose here is to allow to pull out all the different kinds of data that exist in existing systems and to identify possibly new types of data and knowledge necessary to transform the system into a more self-aware system. Most large complex distributed systems have many types of data sources which need to be archived or stored in some fashion (raising questions on what should be stored and for how long and on whether there is an opportunity for self-awareness to allow more adaptive strategies on deciding what to archive and what can be analysed from an archive). Also, some of the data will need to be treated in different ways in order to transform it into the knowledge needed by both self-aware reasoning processes and other activities within the system. For example, in many existing systems, data from sensors can include sophisticated models and processing programs that are used by the system to determine how to set up and direct sensors for data collection, for postprocessing in order to turn raw data into usable data, and for other programs that filter incoming data for immediate prioritization and alerts. In addition, there may be additional programs that help fuse several sources of data that use the data to update existing models or that create new models. A key advantage of a self-aware system is its potential ability to adapt dynamically to changing situations. Therefore, a requirement for the use of data and knowledge in a self-aware system is the ability to dynamically update existing knowledge (e.g. models, rules, and schemas). The evaluation, feedback mechanisms, and approaches to update all data and knowledge are emphasized in Fig. 10.2. Lastly, as shown in Fig. 10.1, some resources exist in order to help the system manage and evaluate self-aware components. Figure 10.2 presents resources that are necessary to update the meta-knowledge used by the system to adjust its collection processes, its pre- and postprocessing methods, and its transformation processes.

The flow chart in Fig. 10.3 shows the main considerations for integrating across different types of self-aware components. As noted earlier in Chap. 1, a self-aware component has four aspects, namely (i) a goal or purpose for the self-awareness; (ii) a source of data with whatever instrumentation or interface is needed to monitor that source of data; (iii) some type of reasoning process that can be implemented as a simulation, a model, a ruleset, or an algorithm; and (iv) some actions executed by the self-aware component (e.g. send a message, replan, recruit additional resources, and set parameters in another program). This is summarized in each self-aware resource represented as an OODA loop (Orient (focus), Observe (monitor), Decide, and Act).

In order to integrate self-aware components, there are three considerations which can be implemented in different ways. First, there is the need for the self-aware components to communicate with other components, which may or may not be self-aware components. This communication scheme can be a blackboard, a service-oriented architecture, a software bus, or other types of schemes. Furthermore, in large systems, there may be several communication schemes running in either different sections of the system or sometimes in parallel involving overlapping components. If the self-aware components contain certain level of intelligence, then a system may have been designed with all the self-aware components interacting as peer to peer, self-organized, and self-regulated, so that no further types of components are necessary. However, in most complex self-aware systems, there is the need to have two additional types of integration components, as explained below.

An integration manager (IM) resource is a self-aware component with the purpose of managing the integration between several other self-aware resources. For example, in a CAR test bed, one IM resource receives input from the reflective processes of five different types of sensors on the individual robotic car and uses this information to reason about the consistency of the sensor information in order to detect both failures or active cyber attacks. Another IM resource receives input from different self-aware game-playing strategies and uses that information to decide which strategy should dominate in the current game among robotic cars. The IM resource is overseeing how the results from several self-aware resources may be integrated, mitigate conflicts among resources, combine and fuse results, or evaluate whether the correct resources are being recruited. The important point here is that the IM resource is an expert on issues of integration for those specific resources and for a specific goal and situational context.

10.4.1 Transition Strategies in Service-Based Systems (SBSs)

Following the discussion in Sect. 10.3.2, a transition strategy to increase self-awareness of existing SBSs should consider the following enablers.

Automated composition. When third-party services are involved in the composition of a complex SBS, automatic and dynamic synthesis of the services' composition code (i) allows the SBS to dynamically adapt to internal and external conditions according to its goal that, in turn, can be continuously changing and (ii) involves the production of models and related runtime management, capturing knowledge about the SBS, and the ability to perform automated reasoning on the produced models for (self-)adaptation purposes. Note that, according to Sect. 10.1, (i) and (ii) constitute the two fundamental aspects of self-awareness.

Dynamic coordination of service interaction. Composed services cannot be let free to interact in an "uncontrolled" way. Rather, their interaction has to be dynamically controlled, mediated [20], and coordinated [3] in order to allow the composed SBS to achieve the specified goal, even when third-party services are involved in the overall collaboration and might exhibit possible interoperability issues.

Dynamic evolution. The SBS composition and coordination logic has to be produced, or automatically synthesized, in a way that it can continuously evolve in order to dynamically (self-)adapt to new and modified goals (goal changes), as well as changing execution environment.

To achieve the above enablers, the following technical aspects need to be considered.

Machine-readable specification of the SBS's goal. Methods and techniques to transform high-level business goals of an SBS into a machine-readable specification of this SBS have to be applied. For instance, in the early stages of an SBS development process, a domain expert has the responsibility of defining global SBS requirements, in order to help and co-operate with the SBS designer in the production of goal-based models of services and SBSs. This includes the definition of high-level business needs, which can be represented by exploiting state-of-the-art common technologies for requirements specification [5, 24]. Examples include requirement models based on structured natural language, on the usage of "qualifiers" for expressing non-functional attributes, and, specifically concerning choreography-based SBSs, on the exploitation of "task models".

Starting from the semi-formally defined SBS business goal by the domain expert, the SBS designer refines and transforms the business goal into a specification of the SBS that is required to achieve the goal. For instance, in the case of orchestration-based SBSs, the specification can be provided by using BPEL or the BPMN notation. For choreography-based SBSs, the specification can be provided by using BPMN2 choreography diagrams. The designer identifies the activities, the related involved services, and the flow of the services as it is required to achieve the goal (e.g. reserving a taxi from the local taxi company, purchasing digital tickets at the train station, and performing transactions through services based on near-field communication in a shop).

In general, the goal-oriented specification of the SBS must be machine-readable, meaning that it must be able to support automated reasoning for different kinds of analysis, possibly passing through more formal, yet equivalent, models produced through model transformation techniques.

Automated elicitation of enhanced service descriptions. In this case, the knowledge about the involved services is limited. In order to increase the self-awareness of an SBS, involved services should be equipped with detailed behavioural descriptions (functional and non-functional) to allow for automated composition/coordination, dynamic evolution, and goal-oriented reasoning. This does not mean that self-aware SBSs can be built only if the involved services publish such enhanced descriptions. Rather, when these descriptions are missing, model elicitation/learning techniques should be applied in order to automatically explore the behavioural aspects of available services, extract observations, and produce models that abstract the actual service behaviour with the strictly necessary accuracy. For instance, as described in [10], elicitation techniques should be able to synthesize a behavioural model of the services' interaction protocol from their WSDL descriptions [10], with reference to some specific functionality of interest for achieving the SBS goal. In other words, to make the elicitation/learning process feasible at runtime, hence increasing the self-awareness, these techniques should be "opportunistic" and SBS goal-driven.

It is also important to consider third-party, typically black box, services. As introduced in Sect. 10.3.2, an SBS is built through composition of independently developed services; therefore, we are primarily interested in extracting behavioural models of service interaction protocols. One of the challenges is how to measure the behaviour of the model with respect to the SBS goal. The elicited models can be incomplete and/or inaccurate, where incompleteness refers to the behavioural modelling (e.g. less and/or more traces), and the inaccuracy refers to the quantitative modelling (e.g. usage probabilities, response time, and throughput) [25]. Another challenge is related to the problem of eliciting quantitative models in an automatic way, as well as the possibility to elicit partial models referring to a specific goal. Considering the work in [10], we envisage that the same strategy, i.e. coupling static analysis at the interface level with test selection, can be used to obtain partial models relevant to the SBS goal, as well as quantitative models.

Goal-driven elicitation can be very effective, as observed on the Amazon E-commerce WS (AEWS) where we apply the approach in [10] to elicit the AEWS interaction protocol. The experiment considered a goal-independent elicitation versus a goal-driven one [4]. Starting from the AEWS WSDL consisting of 85 XML schema type definitions and 23 WSDL operation definitions, the goal-independent elicitation resulted in an interaction protocol made of 24 states and 288 transitions by using 106 test cases, each executed in 10^{-2} s, e.g. few hours of testing. By considering a goal specification that the user wished to "develop a client for cart management only", the interaction protocol computed was made of 6 states and 21 transitions only. The goal-driven elicitation required the generation and execution of 105 test cases in few seconds of testing.

Addition of autonomous coordination software entities. To increase the self-awareness of SBSs by enabling dynamic service coordination and SBS goal-aware evolution, we suggest to add in the SBS coordination software entities that can be automatically synthesized out of the specification of the SBS goal and the goal-driven description of the involved services. When interposed among the services according to a predefined architectural style (see below), these software entities can use as proxies the services involved in the SBS composition to coordinate their interaction. The coordination entities (called coordination delegates—CDs) enforce the collaboration specified by the machine-readable specification of the SBS goal through protocol coordination. Examples of distributed protocol coordination for choreography-based SBSs can be found in [6, 7]. For orchestration-based SBSs, centralized protocol coordination can be sufficient [28].

In order to design self-aware systems, it is necessary to consider as first-class entities feedback loops that enable adaptiveness [14, 17, 18]. Furthermore, the system engineering process must be rethought, in order to break the traditional division among development phases. This can be achieved by moving some activities from design time to deployment time and runtime [19] and, therefore, allowing exploitation of the models at runtime [12].

Based on the work in the literature, and advancing the notion of CD in [16], our CDs are first-class coordination entities. CDs represent external controllers that realize multiple interacting feedback loops enabling SBS (either choreography or orchestration) evolution at the level of both the supervised services (local evolution) and the emergent collaboration among them (global evolution). In this sense, the SBSs should be considered as autonomic systems. For example, the CDs should manage their internal status and behaviour, as well as relationships with other autonomic elements according to SBS's goal specifications. This enables goal-aware evolution of the SBS to (self-)adapt based on goal changes. Moreover, following the idea behind models at runtime, CDs should manage their own coordination models (CMs).

CDs should also implement a MAPE [17] (Monitor, Analyser, Planner, and Executor) loop. The exact executions in each MAPE phase depend on the specific kind of SBS (e.g. choreography- or orchestration-based) and on the specific realization of CDs. In Sect. 10.5, we present a specific instance of autonomous CDs for choreography-based SBSs that are able to evolve based on goal changes.

Reference architectural style. In the case of increasing self-awareness of existing SBSs, it is important to use a predefined architectural style to support interposing CDs among the services participating in an SBS. Different architectural styles can be used, and they depend on the type of an SBS: choreography- or orchestration-based. For example, referring to the case study described in Sect. 10.5, Fig. 10.4 shows a sample instance of a suitable architectural style for choreography-based SBSs.

CDs use the participant services as proxy in order to coordinate their interaction, when needed. CDs guarantee the collaboration specified by the choreography-based SBS's goal specification through distributed protocol coordination [7]. CDs perform pure coordination of the services' interaction (i.e. standard communication in the figure), in a way that the resulting collaboration realizes the specified choreography. The coordination logic is extracted from the machine-readable goal specification, and it is distributed among a set of CMs that codify coordination information. At runtime, the CDs manage their CMs and exchange this coordination information (i.e. additional communication) to prevent possible "undesired interactions". The latter are those interactions that do not belong to the set of interactions allowed by the choreography-based goal specification and can happen when the services collaborate in an uncontrolled way. The coordination logic embedded in CDs is

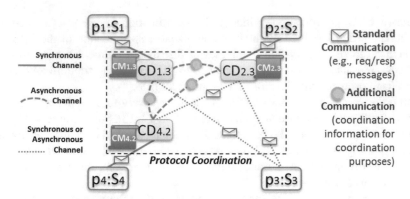

Fig. 10.4 Reference architectural style for choreography-based SBSs

obtained by a distributed coordination algorithm implemented in Java; each CD runs its own instance of the algorithm. Once deployed, CDs support the correct execution and goal-aware evolution of the choreography-based SBS by realizing the required distributed coordination and evolution logic among the participant services.

In summary, at deployment time, for each interface that a service S_i requires from another service S_j, a $CD_{i.j}$, is interposed between S_i and S_j that play the roles of the choreography participants p_i and p_j, respectively. Furthermore, the channel of the service-CD to exchange standard communication is synchronous; the CD–CD channel to exchange standard communication is either synchronous or asynchronous depending on the services' implementation; the CD–CD channel to exchange additional communication (i.e. coordination information) is asynchronous.

10.4.2 Transition Strategies in Multiagent Systems (MASs)

In the case of multiagent systems, agents are defined at a conceptual level, rather than at a technical level. The agent paradigm focuses on generic approaches for distributed problem-solving, rather than particular ways of implementing specific techniques. The specific techniques are developed in a case-by-case basis, depending on each problem domain. The definitions of agents pose no particular restrictions on the design and implementation strategies of their particular capabilities (Sect. 10.3.4). In the case of the development of concrete multiagent systems, numerous approaches have been employed for various agent capabilities ranging from knowledge acquisition, representation, and learning to goal distribution, social interaction, and reflex behaviours. The choices made depend on the problem at hand and on the restrictions imposed by the application domain. Therefore, allowing an agent or a multiagent system to be more self-aware will most likely mean to adopt further capabilities and advanced techniques related to self-aware computing (e.g. knowledge representation, learning, and reasoning). Most of these capabilities have already been proposed, developed, and applied in the MAS and AI domains.

At the same time, multiagent systems may have a lot to gain from extending such capabilities and applying them to the agents themselves, as promoted by the self-aware computing domain. This would enable agents to observe, reason, adapt, and report upon themselves, in addition to applying these functions to their environment and to other agents. Such self-* capabilities would help agents to increase their autonomy, adaptability to changing and unpredictable contexts, and robustness in case of internal failures, as well as improving the agent's goal-oriented strategy, as traditionally applied in MAS.

A transition strategy to increase self-awareness of agents or multiagent systems should consider the following functions:

- self-monitoring and self-adaptation: instrumenting agents, via sensors and actuators, to enable monitoring and adaptation of themselves and/or of other agents;
- self-modelling and self-learning: adding learning and modelling functions to enable agents to use monitoring information for modelling themselves and their environment, so as to accumulate knowledge in an ongoing fashion, at runtime;
- self-configuration/healing/optimization/protection: adding reasoning functions that allow agents to capitalize on the available information and knowledge, so as to achieve their goals and/or collective goals more efficiently, even when their external environments, internal states, and goals change unpredictably. These reasoning functions may concern the agent's internal state, behaviour, and capabilities, as well as other agents, the execution environment, and the goals;
- self-documenting and self-reporting: adding functions that enable an agent to specify formally its current knowledge concerning its state, behaviour, and history, and to communicate this knowledge to external entities, such as other agents or humans;
- dynamic integration of agent resources: adding functions that enable agents to discover and integrate resources at runtime, in order to adapt and enhance their learning, reasoning, and acting strategies, so as to achieve their goals in various execution environments, which may change during runtime;
- dynamic integration of agents: adding functions that enable agents to discover and communicate with each other, to negotiate and coordinate their actions, and to identify and resolve conflicts, in order to help optimize their respective goals and/or to achieve a global goal.

10.5   Example of Transition Strategies: Smart Home Case Study

In this section, we use the Smart Home case study described in Chap. 4 in order to illustrate how our proposed strategies could be used in order to enable goal-aware evolving choreographies. We consider the development of a self-aware Smart Home choreography-based SBS. However, most of the considerations we make below can also be applied to the case of a self-aware Smart Home MAS.

The Smart Home case study involves several devices pursuing different goals within a smart home. It builds on the thermostat use case and introduces an additional smart window shutter and a washing machine, as described in Chap. 4. The smart window shutter can pursue goals related to the home's lighting and temperature. The sensors are sensitive to sunlight and heat, as well as to other sensors and thermometers inside the house. The actuators can rotate the shutter panels (individually) to various degrees. Opening or shutting the window panels can help heat up or insulate the house, respectively. The same actions will also let through or block incoming light, respectively, hence impacting light intensity in the house. The washing machine offers different programs with different lengths and on–off cycles. Users can select any of these and also specify a time frame within which they are to be run. Hence, when the washing machine is connected to a smart grid, the starting of a selected washing cycle can be delayed automatically, to avoid power consumption (or price) peaks, for instance. The new devices may become in conflict with the thermostat, since the shutter's actions can impact temperature and the washing machine impacts power consumption.

As shown in Fig. 10.5, the Smart Home system is designed as choreography of a number of software and services. The choreography specification shown in Fig. 10.5 is given by using BPMN2 choreography diagrams (http://www.omg.org/spec/BPMN/2.0). BPMN2 choreography diagrams model peer-to-peer communication by defining a multiparty protocol that, when put in place by the co-operating parties, allows reaching the overall choreography objectives in a fully distributed way. In BPMN2, a choreography task (e.g. getTemperature) is an atomic activity that represents an interaction by means of one or two (request and optionally response) message

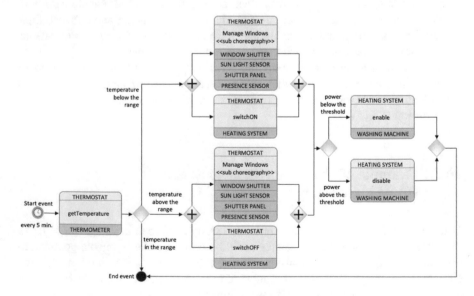

Fig. 10.5 Initial choreography for the Smart Home scenario

exchanges between two participants (e.g. THERMOSTAT and THERMOMETER). Graphically, BPMN2 choreography diagrams use rounded-corner boxes to denote choreography tasks. Each of them is labelled with the roles of the two participants involved in the task and the name of the task. A role contained in the white box denotes the initiating participant. The BPMN2 standard specification employs the theoretical concept of a token that, traversing the sequence flows and passing through the tasks specified by the choreography, aids to define its behaviours. The start event generates the token that must eventually be consumed at an end event. Basically, the BPMN2 choreography diagram in Fig. 10.5 specifies that the Smart Home system periodically (every 5 min) compares the temperature in the house with the one set by the thermostat. If the sensed temperature is in the specified range, then there is nothing to do. If it is below the range, then THERMOSTAT concurrently acts on the actuators of the HEATING SYSTEM and of the other smart devices to increase the temperature in the house, for example, by switching on the heating system and/or opening the window panels. Similarly, if the sensed temperature is above the specified range, then THERMOSTAT concurrently acts on the actuators of the HEATING SYSTEM and of the other smart devices to decrease the temperature in the house. To energy consumption, the Smart Home system checks whether the power consumption is below or above the threshold. If it is below the threshold, then WASHING MACHINE is enabled; otherwise, it is disabled.

Based on Fig. 10.6, suppose that a person wants to move to an even "smarter" Smart Home system by dynamically adapting the Smart Home scenario described above. Consider that for the adapted system, (i) the power consumption of the heating system can be optimized according to the external temperature, and (ii) based on this

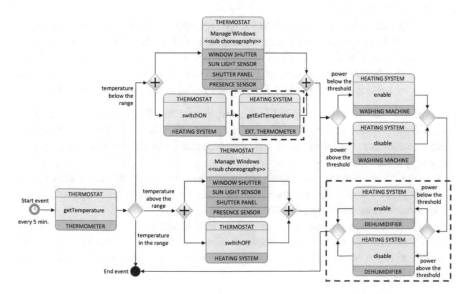

Fig. 10.6 Adapted choreography for the Smart Home scenario

optimization, a dehumidifier can be enabled or disabled. The example shown in Fig. 10.5, and its evolution into the choreography shown in Fig. 10.6, shows how to evolve the coordination logic modular choreography evolution in response to possible changes.

The changes of the goals happen during the lifetime of the system. Following the transition strategy process described in Sect. 10.4, the choreography diagram represents the concrete specification of the system's goal. Thus, on the practical side, the source of this type of changes are the choreography modellers (i.e. software producers, domain experts, and business managers) that modify the current specification of the choreography at runtime, by adding/removing choreography tasks to meet new customers' needs.

Our CDs represent external controllers that realize *multiple interacting feedback loops* enabling choreography evolution at the level of supervised participants (local evolution) and emergent collaboration among them (global evolution). Moreover, following the transition strategy process in Sect. 10.4, CDs distributively co-operate to collect information (knowledge) in the form of CMs, and each CD manages its own CM. CDs implement an "OODA" (Orient/Observe, Decide, and Act) loop. In order to enable choreography evolution without incurring in disruptive interruptions, the CDs' OODA loop makes use of the notion of choreography *quiescent* state (see to [21] for a formal definition of quiescent state).

In our context, a choreography is in a quiescent state with respect to given goal changes if the CDs affected by the change are in a quiescent state. Roughly speaking, a CD is in a quiescent state if (i) the portion of its CM, which is affected by the change, does not involve the current execution state; (ii) it has completed all service-CD and CD–CD interactions required to perform a task, and it has not yet started interactions required for a new task.

After the current choreography-based system specification is changed, a choreography synthesis processor [3] can resynthesize (only) the CMs that are affected by the change and redistribute them to the interested CDs. Moreover, the processor may also synthesize a new choreography deployment model due to CDs' addition, removal, or substitution of their CMs. The following cases can be distinguished:

- The CM of an already deployed CD is substituted when the interactions among the participants controlled by the CD have been modified due to participant service(s) substitution, or specification of new interactions between the already deployed participant services.
- A new CD is added when a new participant has been introduced in the evolved choreography, or new interactions have been specified among existing participants not already controlled by any CD;
- A CD in between two participants is removed when at least one of them is not involved in the choreography anymore. As clarified below, CDs' addition, removal, or substitution of their CMs are handled by specific adaptation rules and related mechanisms.

The CDs' OODA loop is realized as follows:

1. **Orient/Observe**—Each monitor of a CD preprocesses the new CM and choreography deployment model, gathers differences with the previous ones, and informs the CD's observer. By reasoning on the gathered differences, the latter establishes the nature of the change, for example CD addition or removal, or CM substitution.
2. **Decide**—Each planner of a CD selects suitable actions to enable choreography evolution according to the supported adaptation rules, related mechanisms, and the results of the observer. Before executing the required adaptations, a choreography quiescent state has to be reached and kept all throughout the adaptation process. For this purpose, each interested planner communicates with each other to check whether their CDs are all in a quiescent state. If this is the case, the planner activates the executor (see the Act phase below) by providing it with the adaptation plan. Examples of the adaptation plan are substitution of the CM and substitution of one of the two controlled services. The planner waits for the quiescent state to be reached (if possible). Note that the way CD planners are realized points out the distributed nature of the overall OODA loop we realize by means of multiple interacting feedback loops.
3. **Act**—After each executor of a CD is activated by its planner, the executor is in charge of keeping the quiescent state of its CD for the time that is needed to realize the received adaptation plan. First, the executor informs the instance of the distributed coordination algorithm run by its CD to buffer possible incoming service requests. Second, the executor interacts with the needed deployment time and runtime support to reconfigure the current architectural configuration, e.g. by deploying/undeploying services and (re-)establishing the new dependencies. Finally, pending service requests are handled once the adaptation process terminates and after the affected portion of the choreography is re-enacted.

10.6 Conclusions and Open Challenges

In this paper, we have analysed different levels of self-awareness that may exist in several types of systems and architectures. More specifically, we concentrated on legacy distributed systems, service-based systems, systems-of-systems, and agent-oriented systems, as well as cloud computing and pervasive computing architectures. We have also discussed the main capabilities and functions of self-aware systems and provided some transition strategies to be applied to different systems and architectures in order to increase their level of self-awareness. The analysis of the level of self-awareness was performed based on a methodology that we proposed. This methodology consists of using questions related to the definition of self-aware computing provided in Chap. 1. The questions are classified into four categories, namely (a) data and information processing; (b) knowledge processing: learning, modelling, and reasoning; (c) types of knowledge; and (d) types of actions. We have also illustrated the use of the transition strategies in an example of a Smart Home service-based system, as per the case study described in Chap. 4.

The work presented in this paper was developed based on the experience and skills of the authors in all the above systems and architectures, as well as their knowledge and experience with self-aware computing systems. The provided transition strategies were identified based on these experience, skill, and knowledge, but were not evaluated and used in practice. In the future, we plan to evaluate and use these transition strategies in practice, not only in the types of systems and architectures discussed in this paper, but also in other types of systems and architectures. Moreover, the questions described in the paper and used for the analysis of the systems and architectures are not fixed. We believe that with more practical work, these questions will be expanded in order to provide a more complete way of analysing the level of self-awareness in a system, as well as defining the necessary strategies for a system to become self-aware. The work in this paper serves as a starting point on how to incorporate self-awareness in different types of systems and architectures.

Acknowledgements This work has been partially supported by the EC H2020 under grant agreement n. 644178 (project CHOReVOLUTION—Automated Synthesis of Dynamic and Secured Choreographies for the Future Internet).

References

1. Nasa   space   shuttle   era   facts.   http://www.nasa.gov/pdf/566250main_2011.07.
   0SHUTTLEERAfacts.pdf, accessed 2015.
2. World health organisation. http://www.who.int/healthsystems/strategy/everybodys_business.
   pdf, accessed 2016.
3. M. Autili, P. Inverardi, and M. Tivoli. Automated synthesis of service choreographies. *Software, IEEE*, 32(1):50–57, Jan 2015.
4. Marco Autili, Davide Di Ruscio, Paola Inverardi, Patrizio Pelliccione, and Massimo Tivoli. Modelland: Where do models come from? In Nelly Bencomo, Robert France, Betty H.C. Cheng, and Uwe Amann, editors, *Models@run.time*, volume 8378 of *Lecture Notes in Computer Science*, pages 162–187. Springer International Publishing, 2014.
5. Marco Autili, Davide Di Ruscio, Paola Inverardi, James Lockerbie, and Massimo Tivoli. A development process for requirements based service choreography. In *Requirements Engineering for Systems, Services and Systems-of-Systems (RESS), 2011 Workshop on, Trento, Italy, August 30, 2011*, pages 59–62, 2011.
6. Marco Autili, Davide Di Ruscio, Amleto Di Salle, Paola Inverardi, and Massimo Tivoli. A model-based synthesis process for choreography realizability enforcement. In *Fundamental Approaches to Software Engineering - 16th International Conference, FASE 2013, Held as Part of the European Joint Conferences on Theory and Practice of Software, ETAPS 2013, Rome, Italy, March 16-24, 2013. Proceedings*, pages 37–52, 2013.
7. Marco Autili and Massimo Tivoli. Distributed enforcement of service choreographies. In *Proceedings 13th International Workshop on Foundations of Coordination Languages and Self-Adaptive Systems, FOCLASA 2014, Rome, Italy, 6th September 2014.*, pages 18–35, 2015.
8. K.L. Bellman and C. Landauer. Integration science: More than putting pieces together. In *Aerosapce Conference Proceedings, IEEE, Vol. 4*, pages 397–409, 2000.
9. K.L. Bellman and C. Landauer. Towards an integration science: The influence of richard bellman on our research. *Journal of Mathematical Analysis and Applications*, 249(1):3–31, 2000.
10. Antonia Bertolino, Paola Inverardi, Patrizio Pelliccione, and Massimo Tivoli. Automatic synthesis of behavior protocols for composable web-services. In *Proceedings of the the 7th Joint*

Meeting of the European Software Engineering Conference and the ACM SIGSOFT Symposium on The Foundations of Software Engineering, ESEC/FSE '09, pages 141–150, 2009.

11. B. Boehm, S. Lane, S. Koolmanojwong, and R. Turner. In *The Incremental Commitment Spiral Model: Principles and Practices for Successful Systems and Software*, volume Addison-Wesley Professional. 2014.

12. Betty H.C. Cheng, Kerstin I. Eder, Martin Gogolla, Lars Grunske, Marin Litoiu, Hausi A. Müller, Patrizio Pelliccione, Anna Perini, Nauman A. Qureshi, Bernhard Rumpe, Daniel Schneider, Frank Trollmann, and Norha M. Villegas. Using models at runtime to address assurance for self-adaptive systems. In *Models@run.time*, volume LNCS 8378, pages 101–136. 2014.

13. Frederica Darema. Dynamic data driven applications systems: A new paradigm for application simulations and measurements. In *The 4th International Conference on Computational Science, Part III*, pages 662–669, May 2004.

14. Rogério de Lemos, Holger Giese, Hausi A. Müller, Mary Shaw, Jesper Andersson, Marin Litoiu, Bradley Schmerl, Gabriel Tamura, NorhaM. Villegas, Thomas Vogel, Danny Weyns, Luciano Baresi, Basil Becker, Nelly Bencomo, Yuriy Brun, Bojan Cukic, Ron Desmarais, Schahram Dustdar, Gregor Engels, Kurt Geihs, Karl M. Gschka, Alessandra Gorla, Vincenzo Grassi, Paola Inverardi, Gabor Karsai, Jeff Kramer, Antnia Lopes, Jeff Magee, Sam Malek, Serge Mankovskii, Raffaela Mirandola, John Mylopoulos, Oscar Nierstrasz, Mauro Pezz, Christian Prehofer, Wilhelm Schfer, Rick Schlichting, Dennis B. Smith, Joo Pedro Sousa, Ladan Tahvildari, Kenny Wong, and Jochen Wuttke. Software engineering for self-adaptive systems: A second research roadmap. In *Software Engineering for Self-Adaptive Systems II*, volume LNCS 7475, pages 1–32. 2013.

15. C.C. Douglas, J. Beezley, J. Coen, L. Deng, W. Li, A.K. Mandel, J. Mandel, G. Qin, and A. Vodacek. Demonstrating the validity of a wildfire dddas. In *6th International Conference on Computational Science , Part III*, pages 522–529, May, 2006.

16. Amira Ben Hamida, Fabio Kon, Gustavo Ansaldi Oliva, Carlos Eduardo Moreira Dos Santos, Jean-Pierre Lorré, Marco Autili, Guglielmo De Angelis, Apostolos V. Zarras, Nikolaos Georgantas, Valérie Issarny, and Antonia Bertolino. An integrated development and runtime environment for the future internet. In *The Future Internet - Future Internet Assembly 2012: From Promises to Reality*, pages 81–92, 2012.

17. Markus C. Huebscher and Julie A. McCann. A survey of autonomic computing—degrees, models, and applications. *ACM Comput. Surv.*, 40(3):1–28, 2008.

18. IBM. An architectural blueprint for autonomic computing. White Paper 4th Edition, IBM, 2006.

19. Paola Inverardi and Massimo Tivoli. The future of software: Adaptation and dependability. In *Software Engineering, International Summer Schools, ISSSE 2006-2008, Salerno, Italy, Revised Tutorial Lectures*, pages 1–31, 2008.

20. Paola Inverardi and Massimo Tivoli. Automatic synthesis of modular connectors via composition of protocol mediation patterns. In *Proceedings of the 2013 International Conference on Software Engineering*, ICSE '13, pages 3–12, 2013.

21. Jeff Kramer and Jeff Magee. The evolving philosophers problem: Dynamic change management. *IEEE Trans. Softw. Eng.*, 16(11):1293–1306, 1990.

22. Chris Landauer and Kirstie L. Bellman. Knowledge-based integration infrastructure for complex systems. *International Intelligent Control and Systems*, 1(1):133–153, 1996.

23. Chris Landauer and Kirstie L. Bellman. Self-modelling systems. In *Self-Adaptive Software*, volume LNCS 2614, pages 238–256. 2002.

24. Neil A. M. Maiden, James Lockerbie, Konstantinos Zachos, Antonia Bertolino, Guglielmo De Angelis, and Francesca Lonetti. A requirements-led approach for specifying qos-aware service choreographies: An experience report. In *Requirements Engineering: Foundation for Software Quality - 20th International Working Conference, REFSQ 2014, Essen, Germany, April 7-10, 2014. Proceedings*, pages 239–253, 2014.

25. K. Mishra and K.S. Trivedi. Uncertainty propagation through software dependability models. In *Software Reliability Engineering (ISSRE), 2011 IEEE 22nd International Symposium on*, pages 80–89, Nov 2011.

26. A. Sage and C. Cuppan. On the systems engineering and management of systems of systems and federations of systems. *Information-Knowledge-Systems Management Journal*, 2(4), 2001.
27. R Selby. In *Software Engineering: Barry Boehm's Lifetime Contributions to Software Development, Management and Research*, volume Wiley. 2007.
28. Michele Trainotti, Marco Pistore, Gaetano Calabrese, Gabriele Zacco, Gigi Lucchese, Fabio Barbon, Piergiorgio Bertoli, and Paolo Traverso. Astro: Supporting composition and execution of web services. In *Service-Oriented Computing - ICSOC 2005*, volume 3826 of *Lecture Notes in Computer Science*, pages 495–501. Springer Berlin Heidelberg, 2005.

Chapter 11
Synthesis and Verification of Self-aware Computing Systems

Radu Calinescu, Marco Autili, Javier Cámara, Antinisca Di Marco, Simos Gerasimou, Paola Inverardi, Alexander Perucci, Nils Jansen, Joost-Pieter Katoen, Marta Kwiatkowska, Ole J. Mengshoel, Romina Spalazzese and Massimo Tivoli

Abstract Self-aware computing systems are envisaged to exploit the knowledge of their own software architecture, hardware infrastructure and environment in order to follow high-level goals through proactively adapting as their environment evolves. This chapter describes two classes of key enabling techniques for self-adaptive systems: automated synthesis and formal verification. The ability to dynamically synthesize component connectors and compositions underpins the proactive adaptation of the architecture of self-aware systems. Deciding when adaptation is needed and

R. Calinescu (✉) · S. Gerasimou
University of York, York, UK
e-mail: radu.calinescu@york.ac.uk

S. Gerasimou
e-mail: simos@cs.york.ac.uk

M. Autili · A. Di Marco · P. Inverardi · A. Perucci · M. Tivoli
University of L'Aquila, L'Aquila, Italy
e-mail: marco.autili@univaq.it

A. Di Marco
e-mail: antinisca.dimarco@univaq.it

P. Inverardi
e-mail: paola.inverardi@univaq.it

A. Perucci
e-mail: alexander.perucci@graduate.univaq.it

M. Tivoli
e-mail: massimo.tivoli@univaq.it

J. Cámara · O.J. Mengshoel
Carnegie Mellon University, Pittsburgh, PA, USA
e-mail: jcmoreno@cs.cmu.edu

O.J. Mengshoel
e-mail: ole.mengshoel@sv.cmu.edu

N. Jansen
University of Texas at Austin, Austin, TX, USA
e-mail: njansen@utexas.edu

© Springer International Publishing AG 2017
S. Kounev et al. (eds.), *Self-Aware Computing Systems*,
DOI 10.1007/978-3-319-47474-8_11

337

selecting valid new architectures or parameters for self-aware systems often requires formal verification. We present the state of the art in the use of the two techniques for the development of self-aware computing systems and summarize the main research challenges associated with their adoption in practice.

11.1 Introduction

Self-aware computing systems address a rapidly growing need for automation in the management of large, complex computer applications. Made possible by recent advances in the numbers and types of sensors embedded in computing systems, and in the ability to dynamically change system parameters and architectures, self-aware systems are envisaged to be self-reflective, self-predictive, and self-adaptive. As such, self-aware systems need to learn models that encode knowledge about themselves and their environment, and to reason using these models in ways that allow them to self-adjust in response to evolving environments and goals [47].

This chapter presents two classes of key enabling techniques for self-aware systems. First, Sects. 11.2 and 11.3 describe techniques for the *automated synthesis* of self-aware service compositions and self-adaptive connectors, respectively. These synthesis techniques support the run-time modification of software architectures that underpins the adaptation of an increasing number of self-aware computing systems.

Second, Sects. 11.4–11.6 present *formal verification* techniques that support model-based reasoning within self-aware systems. Quantitative verification at run-time, the technique summarized in Sect. 11.4, supports the run-time detection of quality-of-service (QoS) requirement violations in self-aware systems and the selection of new configurations that reinstate system compliance with these requirements. Section 11.5 introduces a technique called *parametric verification*, which is particularly suited for use in a run-time context, to establish the QoS properties of self-aware computing systems. Finally, Sect. 11.6 discusses *run-time verification* based on probabilistic graphical models such as Bayesian networks.

The two classes of techniques—verification and synthesis—are brought together in Sect. 11.7. This section describes how modeling a system and its environment as a

J.-P. Katoen
RWTH Aachen University, Aachen, Germany
e-mail: katoen@cs.rwth-aachen.de

M. Kwiatkowska
University of Oxford, Oxford, UK
e-mail: marta.kwiatkowska@cs.ox.ac.uk

R. Spalazzese
Malmö University, Malmö, Sweden
e-mail: romina.spalazzese@mah.se

stochastic multiplayer game supports the analysis of their interplay, and can be used to drive run-time strategy synthesis for self-aware computing systems.

11.2 From Design-Time to Run-Time Synthesis of Self-aware Choreographies of Software Services

The automated synthesis of the distributed coordination logic that is required to compose software services achieves correctness by the construction of the composed system with respect to specified business goals. State-of-the-art approaches (see [36] and references therein) are static and are poorly suited to the synthesis of service compositions that are able to dynamically evolve in response to changes, e.g., goal changes, QoS degradation, and security policies changes. Focusing on goal changes, this section overviews a novel approach where, together with self-awareness, the integration of design-time and run-time synthesis enables the dynamic evolution of service compositions so as to adapt to possible goal changes. Automatic support is required at design time to synthesize the initial overall logic to exogenously coordinate (in a fully distributed way) the involved services. At run-time, automatic support is then required to achieve self-adaptation, through self-awareness, when re-synthesizing on the fly the portion of the coordination logic affected by the change. For a reasonably complete treatment of alternative approaches in the state of the art, we refer to related work described in [3, 7].

11.2.1 Setting the Context

The Future Internet [31] promotes a distributed computing environment that will be increasingly inhabited by a virtually infinite number of software services. Software systems will be more and more built by composing together software services distributed over the Internet.

Today's service composition mechanisms are based mostly on service orchestration, a centralized approach to the composition of multiple services into a larger application. Orchestration works well in static environments with predefined services and minimal environment changes. These assumptions are inadequate in the Future Internet vision, in which many diverse service providers and consumers keep changing and cannot be coordinated through a centralized approach. In contrast, service choreography is a form of decentralized composition that models the external interaction of the participant services by specifying peer-to-peer message exchanges from a global perspective [3, 7].

The need for service choreography was recognized in BPMN2 (Business Process Model and Notation Version 2.0[1]), the de facto standard for specifying choreogra-

---

[1]http://www.omg.org/spec/BPMN/2.0.

phies, which introduced choreography-modeling constructs. BPMN2 *Choreography Diagrams* model peer-to-peer communication by defining a multiparty protocol that, when put in place by the cooperating parties, allows reaching the overall choreography objectives in a fully distributed way. In this sense, service choreographies differ significantly from service orchestrations, in which one stakeholder centrally determines how to reach an objective through cooperation with other services. Future software systems will not be realized by orchestration only; they will also require choreographies. Indeed, services will be increasingly active entities that, communicating peer-to-peer, proactively make decisions and autonomously perform tasks according to their own imminent needs and the emergent global collaboration.

11.2.2   The Need for Self-adaptation

When third-party participants are involved, usually black-box services are to be reused; a key enabler for the actual realization of choreographies is the ability to automatically compose services, and to dynamically perform exogenous coordination of their interaction. However, in a distributed setting, obtaining the coordination logic required to realize a choreography is non-trivial and error-prone. Accordingly, automatic support for realizing choreographies is needed.

Choreography-based software systems may be in operation for a long time, and it is impractical (if not infeasible) to replace or retry the whole choreography process whenever a change occurs. Instead, choreographies will continuously self-adapt to new and modified goals, e.g., to meet new business requirements, as well as changing execution environment, e.g., to support new technologies. Indeed, in general, many facets can be considered when dealing with software systems that are capable of evolving by adapting their behavior at run-time. The study presented in [2] identifies the multiple facets of (self-)adaptation and classifies them into four groups. These modeling dimensions and their classification help engineers to precisely characterize the types of change that a given system can deal with, and how the system can evolve to face them.

To address the above challenges, this section describes a method for the automatic synthesis of self-adaptable choreographies [3]. The *synthesis processor* used by this method takes as input a BPMN2 choreography diagram together with a set of services discovered as possible candidates to play the choreography roles and automatically generates a set of coordination software entities. When interposed among the services according to a predefined architectural style, these software entities proxify the participant services to coordinate their interaction, when needed. Specifically, coordination entities (called *Coordination Delegates*—CDs) enforce the collaboration specified by the choreography diagram through distributed protocol coordination [7].

The synthesis steps performed by the synthesis processor are described in Sect. 11.2.3. The synthesis processor has been fully implemented within the context of the EU FP7 CHOReOS project as a set of REST services whose open source code is available at http://www.choreos.eu. Moreover, a set of Eclipse plugins that allow for interacting with the REST services according to a predefined development process model is available at `choreos.disim.univaq.it`, and in [4] a tool demo is described on a real CHOReOS case study in the marketing and sales domain. In Sect. 11.2.4, we report on recent enhancements of the CHOReOS synthesis processor that are being developed within the context of the EU H2020 CHOReV-OLUTION project (http://www.chorevolution.eu), a CHOReOS follow-up project. The main aim of these enhancements is to cope with the automated synthesis of adaptive/evolvable choreographies. An explanatory example showing the enhanced synthesis processor at work is given in Sect. 11.2.5.

Following key principles of autonomic computing and related architecture concepts [39], it is widely recognized [27] that, in order to effectively design adaptive systems, feedback loops enabling adaptiveness must become first-class entities. Furthermore, the system engineering process must be rethought in order to break the traditional division among development phases by moving some activities from design time to deployment- and run-time, hence asking for the exploitation of models at run-time [27].

Being inspired by this valuable work in the literature, our enhanced CDs are first-class coordination entities. CDs represent external controllers that realize *multiple interacting feedback loops* enabling choreography self-adaptation at the level of both the supervised participants (local adaptation) and the emergent collaboration among them (global adaptation). In this sense, the choreography-based systems we target are self-aware systems where individual autonomic elements, i.e., CDs, manage their internal status and behavior and their relationships with the other autonomic elements in accordance with the choreography specification.

11.2.3   Method for the Synthesis of Self-adaptable Choreographies

The method presented in this section advances our previous work in [3, 6, 7] by enhancing the synthesis method to also deal with the dynamic evolution of the coordination logic implied by the choreography in response to goal changes.

The synthesis processor takes as input a BPMN2 choreography diagram together with a set of services discovered as possible candidates for the choreography roles and automatically generates a set of coordination entities (i.e., CDs). Figure 11.1 pictorially describes the main steps of the synthesis processor.

Step 1. Software producers cooperate with, e.g., domain experts and business managers to (i) set the business goal (for example, assist travelers from arrival, to staying, to departure); (ii) identify the tasks and participants required to achieve the goal (for example, reserving a taxi from the local taxi company, purchasing digital tickets at the train station, and performing transactions through services based on near-field communication in a shop), and (iii) specify how participants must collaborate through a BPMN2 choreography diagram.

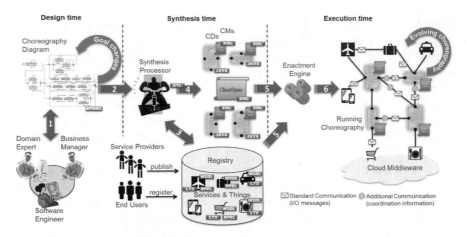

Fig. 11.1 From choreography design to execution and evolution, through automatic synthesis

Step 2. The synthesis processor takes as input the BPMN2 choreography diagram.

Step 3. The synthesis processor queries the registry to discover services suitable for playing the choreography's roles. The registry contains services published by providers (for example, transportation companies and airport retailers) that have identified business opportunities in the domain of interest. As service interfaces description, the synthesis processor assumes WSDL.[2] To describe service interaction behavior, the synthesis processor assumes an automata-based specification, i.e., a Labeled Transition System—LTS, or a BPEL[3] specification.

Step 4. Starting from the choreography diagram and the set of services, the synthesis processor generates a set of CDs through model transformation. The processor also generate the so-called ChorSpec, a specification of service dependencies to be used by the enactment engine (EE) component for deploying and enacting the choreography.

Step 5. The generated CDs, together with the description of the services and their dependencies, serve as an input to the EE for deployment and enactment. The description of the EE is outside the scope of this chapter.

Step 6. Following the dependencies, CDs are then interposed among the participant services needing coordination.

When interposed among the services according to a predefined architectural style (an instance of which is shown in Fig. 11.2), CDs proxify the participant services to coordinate their interaction, when needed.

CDs guarantee the collaboration specified by the choreography specification through distributed protocol coordination [7]. CDs perform pure coordination of the service interactions (i.e., *standard communication* in the diagram) to ensure that the resulting collaboration realizes the specified choreography. For this purpose,

---

[2]http://www.w3.org/TR/wsdl.

[3]https://www.oasis-open.org/committees/wsbpel.

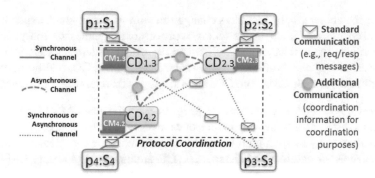

Fig. 11.2 Instance of the predefined architectural style

the coordination logic is extracted from the BPMN2 choreography diagram and is distributed among a set of *Coordination Models* (CMs) that codify coordination information. Then, at run time, the CDs manage their CMs and exchange this coordination information (i.e., *additional communication*) to prevent possible *undesired interactions* [5, 7], and dynamically self-adapt to possible changes in the specified choreography diagram.

11.2.4   Dealing with Choreography Self-adaptation

For choreography-based systems, the choreography diagram represents the concrete specification of the system goal. The source of goal changes is the choreography modeler (i.e., software producers, domain experts, and business managers in Fig. 11.1) who modifies the current specification of the choreography at run time, e.g., by adding/removing choreography tasks to meet new customer needs.

Following the philosophy of models at run time [27], CDs realize multiple interacting feedback loops while managing their own CMs as follows.

CDs implement a MAPE loop [39], i.e., an abstraction of a feedback loop where the dynamic behavior of the managed system is controlled using an autonomic manager. Thus, by following the architectural blueprint for autonomic computing, CDs implement four phases: Monitor (M), Analyzer (A), Planner (P), and Executor (E). Moreover, in order to enable choreography self-adaptation without incurring in disruptive interruptions, the CDs' MAPE loop makes use of the notion of choreography *quiescent* state. For a formal definition of the seminal general notion of quiescent state, we refer to [48]. In our context, a choreography is in a quiescent state with respect to given goal changes if the CDs affected by the change are in a quiescent state. Roughly speaking, a CD is in a quiescent state if (i) the portion of its CM, which is affected by the change, does not involve the current execution state, and (ii) it has completed all service-CD and CD–CD interactions required to perform a task and it has not yet started interactions required for a new task.

After the choreography modelers change the current choreography specification (see goal changes in Fig. 11.1), the synthesis processor re-synthesizes (only) the CMs that are affected by the change and redistributes them to the interested CDs. Moreover, the processor may also synthesize a new `ChorSpec` due to CDs addition, removal, or substitution of their CMs. The CDs MAPE loop is then realized as follows:

1. **Monitors**—each interested monitor pre-processes the new CM and `ChorSpec`, gathers differences with the previous ones, and informs the analyzer.
2. **Analyzers**—by reasoning on the gathered differences, each interested analyzer establishes the nature of the change, i.e., CD addition or removal, or CM substitution.
3. **Planners**—each interested planner selects suitable actions to enable choreography evolution according to the supported adaptation rules, related mechanisms, and the results of the analyzer. Before executing the required adaptations, a choreography quiescent state has to be reached, and kept all throughout the adaptation process. For this purpose, interested planners communicate with each other to check whether their CDs are all in a quiescent state. If it is the case, the planner activates the executor by providing it with the adaptation plan, e.g., the substitution of the CM and, according to a new `ChorSpec`, the substitution of one of the two controlled services. Otherwise, the planner waits for the quiescent state to be reached (if possible). Note that the way CD planners are realized is in line with the distributed nature of the overall MAPE loop, which we realize by the means of multiple interacting feedback loops.
4. **Executors**—after each interested executor is activated by its planner, the executor is in charge of keeping the quiescent state of its CD for the time needed to realize the received adaptation plan. For this purpose, the executor first informs the instance of the distributed coordination algorithm run by its CD (see Sect. 11.2.3) to buffer possible incoming service requests. Secondly, the executor interacts with the EE to reconfigure the current architectural, e.g., by deploying/undeploying services and (re-)establishing the new dependencies. Finally, pending service requests are handled once the adaptation process terminates and after the affected portion of the choreography is re-enacted.

11.2.5 Case Study

We applied our method in a case study from the military domain concerning an instance of an Emergency Deployment System (EDS) inspired by the scenario in [2, 51], which is representative of a large number of modern distributed software applications. We implemented a simulation of this system and used it to validate the approach described in the previous sections. Briefly, starting from a BPMN2 Choreography Diagram specification and following the steps shown in Fig. 11.1, the case study shows that our method is able to automatically synthesize the needed CDs and let them dynamically evolve in response to goal changes without re-synthesizing the whole choreography. A detailed description of the case study, including a report on our findings from this work, detailed results, and related implementation, is available at `choreos.disim.univaq.it/downloads`.

11.3   Synthesis of Self-adaptive Connectors Meeting Behavioral and Quality Requirements

Today's networked environment is increasingly characterized by a wide variety of heterogeneous networked systems (NSs), including, for instance, tablets and smartphones, that dynamically decide to achieve goals through interoperation with other systems. Some independently developed heterogeneous applications running on NSs could interact since they use similar interaction protocols implementing compatible functionalities. However, they can exhibit mismatches in their interaction protocols (e.g., different ordering of messages and/or input/output data, or different formats and granularity of input/output data) preventing them to interact seamlessly. Moreover, applications should obey quality requirements, and this may undermine their ability to seamlessly interoperate. Achieving interoperability requires solving such mismatches and meeting the quality requirements. This asks for the adaptation of the applications through the use of *connectors* (or *mediators*) that are *the only locus where we can act to make the NSs adaptable*.

In this section, we report on the synthesis of connectors that take into account the behavioral and quality constraints (Sect. 11.3.1) and how such techniques can be used to synthesize self-adaptive connectors (Sect. 11.3.2), whereas out of scope of this section are program synthesis, feedback generation in programming, code generation, or frameworks that automatically manipulate specific files.

11.3.1   QB-Synthesis: Quality and Behavioral Connector Synthesis

The research community has devoted significant effort to the synthesis of connectors since when the seminal paper [67] proposed an adaptor theory to characterize and solve the interoperability problem of augmented interfaces of applications. In the Web Service domain, a huge effort has been recently devoted to the description and the automated generation of adaptors, e.g., [55] that is much related to our work. Works [40, 41] describe an approach for the automated synthesis of *functional* (i.e., behavioral) connectors to reconcile application protocol diversities from a behavioral viewpoint. The approach considers NSs as black boxes which expose within their interface the application interaction behavior protocol and an ontological description of exchanged messages and data. By reasoning on the ontology, the approach automatically synthesizes a connector between the considered application protocols allowing interoperability.

Concerning combined approaches taking into account both behavioral and quality issues, two relevant approaches are present in the literature [64, 66]. The first presents an approach to formally specify connector wrappers as protocol transformations, modularizing them, and reasoning about their properties, with the aim to resolve component mismatches. A wrapper is a new code interposed between component interfaces and communication mechanisms, and its intended effect is to moderate the behavior of the component in a way that is transparent to the component or the interaction mechanism.

In [66], the authors propose an approach to automatically derive adaptors in order to assemble correct by construction real-time systems from COTS. The approach takes into account interaction protocols, timing information, and QoS constraints to prevent deadlocks and unbounded buffers. A synthesized adaptor is then a component that mediates the interaction between the components it supervises, in order to harmonize their communication.

Even though the above-described approaches take into account both behavioral and quality issues, they do not take into account self-adaptation, which is considered a challenge for modern systems [27].

To the best of our knowledge, three works contributed to the automated synthesis of self-adaptive connectors meeting both functional and quality requirements, [55] more at middleware level and [29, 54] at application level. This latter presents an automated connector synthesis approach for the interoperability at application layer, taking into account both behavioral and quality interoperability at both predeployment time and run-time. Functional interoperability refers to the applications' behavior and aims at allowing systems to correctly communicate. Non-functional interoperability is about the performance and dependability attributes that must be guaranteed during systems interoperation. The synthesized connector is self-adaptive since it is able to tolerate environment variations and changes within certain ranges. When the environment diverges from the considered assumptions, an adaptation cycle needs to be run according to a provided approach at the cost of re-analysis and synthesis.

11.3.2 QB-Synthesis of Self-adaptive Connector

In this section, we describe a general approach of self-adaptive connectors synthesis (see Fig. 11.3). It is a three-step approach that assumes as input the NS *Applications*, and the QoS properties and requirements of the connected system. A case study that used this approach is described in [29], where the general approach has been tailored on performance properties and applied to a system coming from the e-commerce domain used in CONNECT EU project.[4] In the interest of brevity, we will present only the general approach, and we refer to [29] for details about its application.

---

[4]https://www.connect-forever.eu/.

As a first step, the approach synthesizes (*Functional Synthesis*) a *Functional* connector (satisfying the functional requirements) that allows the input applications to interoperate on the behavioral side. In this step, by choosing among different settings, one could use different state-of-the-art approaches to synthesize connectors, e.g., [41]. Then, the approach carries out the *QoS Analysis* on the connected system (i.e., applications and connector) to ensure that it meets the QoS requirement during interaction. In the literature, one can find many analysis approaches that can be used in this step, such as [9, 24]. This step involves analyzing different connected system's configuration alternatives obtained by applying some adaptation strategies. These strategies might include connector behavior slicing, tuning the upper bound on the number of cycle iterations, and choosing the most convenient deployment configuration (these strategies are better described later in this section). Next, the *Analysis Results* are used to instrument the functional connector so that each possible mediation path is decorated with quantitative information (*Decorated* connector) and is executed only if the current QoS requirement is satisfied. The set of enabled paths associated with a QoS requirement is called *mediator configuration*.

The Analysis Results are thus exploited for two different reasons: The first is to decide (*Reasoning*) what is the current connector configuration to deploy (*Self-Adaptive* connector). The second reason is to select at run-time a new mediator configuration after a QoS requirement change, thus obtaining a new adapted connector. The run-time adaptation is illustrated in the right part of Fig. 11.3 and is described in the following. The approach synthesizes a self-adaptive connector between the applications and (1) the connected system is running. If the QoS requirements change for an application (2), the adaptation process (3) is triggered. The connector, as done in [11], is instrumented with monitoring probes that capture the event and triggers our *Adaptation Engine*. The latter takes as input the decorated connector, the analysis results, and the new QoS requirement. By reasoning on them, the adaptation engine

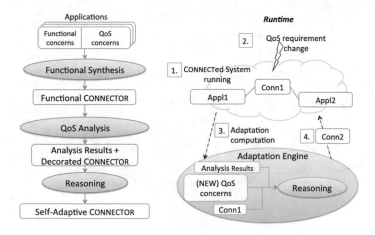

Fig. 11.3 Connector synthesis overview

selects another connector configuration (4) to be properly deployed and run at the end of the ongoing system transaction.

An example of the realization of this process, targeting performance concerns, is proposed in Fig. 11.4 [29]. The process combines (i) the mediator synthesis taking into account the behavioral concerns (upper part of the figure) and (ii) the QoS analysis-based reasoning acting on the intermediary mediator to meet the connected system's performance requirements (bottom part of Fig. 11.4).

The considered approach for the automated synthesis of mediators overcoming interoperability problems between heterogeneous applications, originally introduced in [40, 41], takes as input the systems with compatible affordances, i.e., compatible high-level capabilities in the same domain and comprises three steps: identification of the common language, behavioral matching, and mediator synthesis. The *Identification of the Common Language*, or *Abstraction* (❶ in Fig. 11.4), among the actions and data of the various applications takes as input the applications protocol and the subset of the domain ontology they refer to, and identifies the applications common language by classifying their respective (sub-)ontologies into the application domain ontology through an ontology reasoner revealing the correspondences. The common language makes applications' behavior comparable to reason on them. The *Behavioral Matching* or *Matching* (❷ in Fig. 11.4) checks the applications' behavioral compatibility, i.e., that the two applications can synchronize at least on one trace reaching one of their respective final states by properly reconciling possible mismatches through a mediator. An extensive description of the identified and managed mismatches is given in [63]. Finally, the *Synthesis* (❸ in Fig. 11.4) automatically

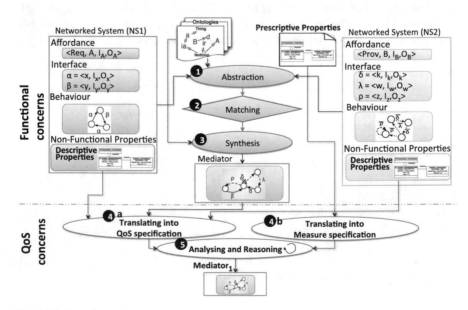

Fig. 11.4 Overview of the connector synthesis

produces a (intermediary) mediator that addresses the identified mismatches, thus enabling the functional interoperation of the two applications.

The QoS analysis-based reasoning takes into consideration QoS concerns during the synthesis. This is done by acting on the intermediary mediator produced before. This reasoning is composed of two steps detailed in the following: Generation of a QoS Model and QoS analysis-based reasoning. The *Generation of a QoS Model* is composed of two activities: The first one, Fig. 11.4 ❹a, takes as input the LTS-based specification of the NSs and of the synthesized mediator, and the *descriptive properties* to generate the QoS Model. To execute QoS analysis, a *measure specification* that defines the QoS indices of interest is required. The second activity, Fig. 11.4 ❹b, translates the *prescriptive property* defining the QoS requirements on the final system into the required *measure specification*. In the *QoS analysis-based reasoning*, from the QoS specification and the measure specification, the QoS analysis is executed. If the composed system satisfies the specified requirements then the mediator is not modified, otherwise it undergoes a reasoning step that tries to obtain a mediator showing better QoS (see Fig. 11.4 ❺). In [29], the performance analysis-based reasoning leverages the Æmilia ADL [10]. As mentioned before, to improve the composed system QoS, we can act on the mediator to slice alternative behaviors, limit the number of execution of cycles, and find out the best deployment. At the end of this step, two scenarios are possible: (i) we obtain a mediator that allows the composed system to meet the QoS requirements; (ii) all the refined mediators obtained by applying the identified strategies do not allow the composed system to meet the QoS requirements. In this case, the approach does not produce a mediator and asks to relax the QoS requirement in order to provide a suitable system.

Adaptation Strategies. The proposed approach tries to act on the mediator to satisfy the quality requirement. Three possible *strategies* are identified and can be applied individually or in combination [29]: (i) *connector behaviors slicing* that can be applied if at least one of the NSs protocols has alternative paths to achieve communication. In this case, the connector behavior is sliced and it mediates only a subset of the NSs communication paths; (ii) *tuning the upperbound on the number of cycle iterations*. If the protocols contain cycles, several bounds are considered in the analysis and only the ones that allow the satisfaction of the QoS requirements are considered in the final synthesized connector. Finally, (iii) *choosing the most convenient deployment configuration* among three possibilities: *all remote* where the mediator and the applications are deployed on separate machines, and *local to NS1* or *local to NS2* where the mediator is deployed on the same machine where either one application or the other is running, NS1 or NS2, respectively. It is worth noticing that the synthesis process generates the *most general* connector that satisfies the functional and non-functional requirements. Most general means that, with respect to the functional mediation, the connector protocol prevents the execution only of the paths that do not satisfy non-functional requirements.

Due to context evolutions, and in particular to run-time changes on the QoS requirements, it might also happen that at run-time the connected system does not satisfy the new requirements. To address this issue, the proposed approach performs a run-time adaptation of the connector based on the three strategies identified above thus obtaining a new connector.

Adaptation Reasoning. Based on the applicable strategies, the reasoning identifies a number of different mediator configurations (# mediator configurations = # possible slicing * # different upper bounds on cycles * # different deployment). For instance, the combination of the strategies in a case study in [29] gave us 54 final configurations to consider and hence 54 corresponding experiments to conduct.

The initial QoS requirement, from the analysis results performed before during the synthesis, can be satisfied by several configurations. Among them is selected the best configuration based on one *policy* or more, e.g., in [29] is selected the admissible configuration that maximizes the user interactions (no mediator slicing and highest upper bound on the number of the number of cycles in the protocol).

This *run-time change in QoS requirement triggers an adaptation*, since the new requirement is not satisfied by the previous mediator configuration. The adaptation is realized by selecting, among all the admissible mediators configurations, the one that better suits the new requirement taking into account the policy (e.g., maximize the user interactions).

11.3.3 Open Issues

Nowadays, it is possible to enable interoperability between heterogeneous protocols leveraging automatically synthesized self-adaptive mediators that let them interact seamlessly. Many automated mediator synthesis methods address the functional facet of the problem. Additionally, a few approaches have recently been proposed to also deal with non-functional aspects and with adaptations of the connector due, for instance, to run-time QoS requirement changes.

However, the behavioral connector synthesis and the quality analysis approaches suffer from the usual limitations of model-based (stochastic) analysis and synthesis (e.g., state explosion). Hence, more efficient methods are needed to make behavioral synthesis and quality analysis widely applicable. Along these lines, a study on how to optimize the designed approaches should be made. This would improve the run-time applicability and scalability of the overall approach for the synthesis of self-adaptive connector that considers both behavioral and quality concerns.

11.4 Quantitative Verification at Run-Time

The integration of formal verification techniques into the reconfiguration of self-aware systems aims to guarantee that these systems continue to meet their requirements as they change over time. The formal verification paradigm overviewed in this section extends the applicability of *quantitative verification* to self-aware systems.

Quantitative verification [49] is a mathematical-based technique for analyzing the correctness, reliability, performance, and other QoS properties of systems characterized by stochastic behavior. The technique carries out its analysis on finite state-transition models comprising states that correspond to different system configurations, and edges associated with the transitions that are possible between these states. Depending on the analyzed QoS properties, the edges are annotated with transition probabilities or transition rates; additionally, the model states and transitions may be labeled with *rewards*. The types of models with probability-annotated transitions include discrete-time Markov chains (DTMCs) and Markov decision processes (MDPs), while the edges of continuous-time Markov chains (CTMCs) are annotated with transition rates.

Given one of these models and a QoS property specified formally in a variant of temporal logic extended with probabilities and rewards, the technique analyzes the model exhaustively to evaluate the property. Examples of properties that can be established using the technique include the probability that a system component operates correctly, the expected reliability of a composite service, and the expected energy consumed by an embedded system. Quantitative verification is typically performed automatically by tools termed *probabilistic model checkers*.

We will illustrate the use of quantitative verification for a dynamic power management (DPM) system with the structure in Fig. 11.5a. This system comprises a *service provider* responsible for handling requests generated by a *service requester* and stored in a finite request queue. The service provider can operate in three different modes—*busy*, *idle*, and *sleep*—that correspond to different power usages and operation rates. Figure 11.5a depicts the power usage of each mode (in watts), the possible transitions between modes, and the energy consumed by each transition (in joules). These values correspond to a Fujitsu disk drive [57].

The DPM system operates as follows. Upon receiving a new request, the service provider automatically transitions to the *busy* mode, if it is in the *idle* mode; otherwise (i.e., if in the *sleep* or *busy* mode), its mode remains unchanged. If the queue contains $q > 1$ requests and the service provider is in the *busy* mode, one of these requests is processed. Upon processing the last request, $q = 0$, the service provider automatically transitions to the *idle* mode. A software power manager controls the transitions between the *sleep* and *idle* service provider modes. In doing so, the power manager considers the state of the system and aims to reduce power use while maintaining an acceptable service level.

Figure 11.5d shows a CTMC model of the DPM system. This model is adapted from [57], and is defined in the high-level modeling language of the probabilistic model checker PRISM [50]. The *RequestQueue*, *ServiceProvider*, and *PowerManager* modules within this model correspond to the similarly named components of the DPM system. The local variables from the RequestQueue and ServiceProvider modules represent the number of requests within the queue (q) and the service provider mode (sp). Synchronization between all modules occurs through the *request* and *serve* actions, which denote requests arriving into the queue and being processed, respectively. The service provider manages the transitions between the *busy* and *idle* operating modes (lines 28–31). In contrast, the transitions between *idle* and *sleep*

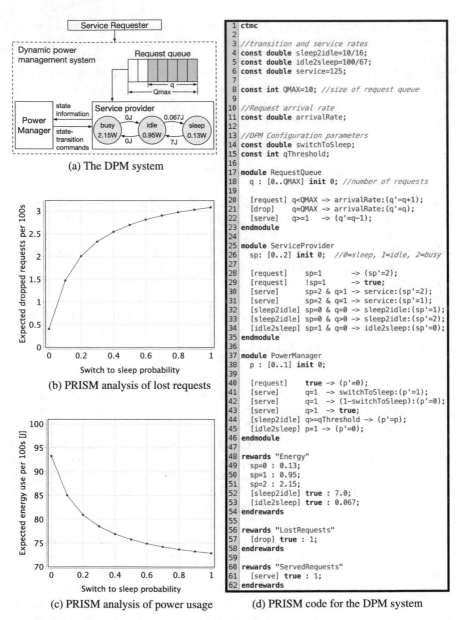

(a) The DPM system

(b) PRISM analysis of lost requests

(c) PRISM analysis of power usage

(d) PRISM code for the DPM system

Fig. 11.5 Modeling and quantitative verification of DPM system properties

are controlled by the power manager through the synchronization of ServiceProvider and PowerManager commands using common actions (lines 32–34 and 44–45). For instance, when the request queue becomes empty, the power manager performs an *idle* to *sleep* transition with probability *switchToSleep* (lines 41–42). Similarly, when the request queue grows to $q \geq qThreshold$ requests, the power manager performs a *sleep* to *idle* transition to ensure that the service provider starts handling requests (line 44).

Finally, CTMC states and transitions are associated with **rewards...endrewards** structures (lines 48–62). The *"Energy"* reward structure encodes the energy consumed by the service provider in each mode and during transitions between modes. The *"DroppedRequests"* and *"ServedRequests"* reward structures associate a reward of 1 with the transitions where requests are dropped due to a full queue and served, respectively. Using these reward structures and a reward-augmented variant of continuous stochastic logic (CSL), it is possible to specify and to analyze the QoS properties of the DPM system. For example, Fig. 11.5b, c depict the expected number of dropped requests and the expected energy use over 100 s of system operation, as a function of the *switchToSleep* probability, when *arrivalRate* = $0.8 \, s^{-1}$ and $qThreshold = 8$. These results were obtained by analyzing the CSL reward properties $R_{=?}^{"DroppedRequests"}[C^{\leq 100}]$ and $R_{=?}^{"Energy"}[C^{\leq 100}]$, respectively.

11.4.1 Application to Self-aware Systems

Extending the applicability of quantitative verification to self-aware systems requires the continual use of the technique at run time [15]. To this end, *quantitative verification at run-time* integrates this formal verification technique into the MAPE (Monitor–Analyze–Plan–Execute) closed control loop of self-aware systems.

Quantitative verification at run-time requires the monitoring of self-adaptive systems and their environment, in order to identify relevant changes and quantify them using fast online learning techniques. These observations are used to continually update a probabilistic model of the system, starting from an initial model provided by the system developers. For example, fast online learning techniques [16, 17, 30] can monitor the changing probabilities of successful service invocation for service-based systems, and thus update DTMC models of these systems. Probabilistic model checking performed at run-time is then used to re-verify the compliance of these updated models with QoS requirements related to the system response time, reliability, cost, etc. If QoS requirement violations are identified or (when the functionality associated with the unsatisfied requirements has not been exercised) predicted, the results of the analysis support the synthesis of a reconfiguration plan. Executing this plan ensures that the self-adaptive system will continue to satisfy its QoS requirements despite the changes identified during monitoring.

To illustrate the use of the technique, suppose that the DPM system from the previous section must comply with the QoS requirements from Table 11.1 in the presence of changes in the request arrival rate. To achieve this compliance, the power manager uses quantitative verification at run-time. Request arrivals are monitored to establish the current request arrival rate. This information is used to continually update the CTMC model from Fig. 11.5d. The updated CTMC model is then verified to identify values for

Table 11.1 QoS requirements for the self-aware DPM system

ID	Informal description	Formal specification
R1	*Performance*: "The expected number of dropped request per 100s of running time should not exceed 0.5"	$R_{\leq 0.5}^{\text{"}DroppedRequests\text{"}}[C^{\leq 100}]$
R2	*Energy use*: "The service provider should consume at most 100 Joules per 100s of running time"	$R_{\leq 100}^{\text{"}Energy\text{"}}[C^{\leq 100}]$
R3	*Utility*: "Subject to R1 and R2 being met, the DPM system must use a configuration that maximizes $utility(switchToSleep, qThreshold) = w_1 S + w_2/E,$ where S is the number of requests served given by evaluating the property $R_{=?}^{\text{"}ServedRequests\text{"}}[C^{\leq 100}]$ and E is the energy used by the service provider per 100s of system's running time. The weights $w_1, w_2 > 0$ express the trade-off between system throughput and battery usage"	find **argmax** *utility(switchToSleep, qThreshold)* such that **R1** and **R2** are satisfied

- the probability *switchToSleep* for setting the service provider to *sleep* mode, and
- the parameter *qThreshold* for switching the service provider to *idle* mode

which ensure that the DPM system meets its QoS requirements for the current request arrival rate. As an example, Fig. 11.6a, b show the results of the quantitative verifi-

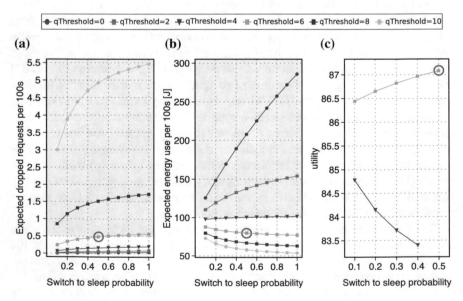

Fig. 11.6 Verification results for **a** requirement **R1** and **b** requirement **R2** from Table 11.1, and **c** *utility* of the valid configurations of the DPM system

cation carried out at run-time when *arrivalRate* $= 0.65\,\text{s}^{-1}$. These results establish the expected number of dropped requests and the energy usage for a range of possible *switchToSleep* and *qThreshold* values. The shaded areas from Fig. 11.6a, b correspond to parameter values (i.e., to power manager *configurations*) that violate requirements **R1** and **R2**, respectively. These configurations are discarded. Next, the *utility* of the remaining, feasible configurations is computed. Figure 11.6c depicts the utility values calculated for the feasible configurations from Figs. 11.6a, b, with $w_1 = 1$ and $w_2 = 2000$ in the utility formula from Table 11.1. The configuration that maximizes the system utility is circled in Fig. 11.6a–c. This configuration is adopted by the power manager when *arrivalRate* $= 0.65\,\text{s}^{-1}$.

11.4.2 Research Challenges

Quantitative verification at run-time is a new area of research. Although successful applications have emerged in QoS optimization for service-based systems [16, 30], reconfiguration of cloud computing infrastructure [43], and adaptive resource management in embedded systems [13], several research challenges remain unsolved.

In particular, the state explosion problem that affects model checking is an even greater challenge for quantitative verification at run-time. In the case of self-aware systems, the probabilistic model checking of an updated model needs to be performed not only with acceptable overheads for the verified system, but also fast enough to support timely self-adaptation, and before the model is rendered obsolete by the next update. Recent research has proposed preliminary approaches to tackling this challenge through *parametric verification* (described in the next section), *compositional* and *incremental* [43] *verification*, and, more recently, *decentralized quantitative verification* [13]. Nevertheless, further research is needed to extend these approaches and to enable the application of the technique to large, rapidly changing distributed systems.

Even when quantitative verification at run-time can be performed very fast for the model associated with a configuration of a self-aware system, the extremely large configuration spaces of many such systems pose a major challenge. The recently proposed search-based software engineering approach to *probabilistic model synthesis* [35] may have the potential to help address this challenge, as it operates without an exhaustive exploration of the configuration space. Assessing the applicability of these solutions to self-aware systems remains an area of future research.

A final key challenge is to ensure that the probabilistic models verified at run-time are accurate. Despite the development of effective techniques for learning the transition probabilities of Markov chains from run-time observations [16, 17, 30], the current use of point estimates for these probabilities may introduce unquantified estimation errors. Quantitative verification with confidence intervals has been introduced recently to address this problem [14], although its use in self-aware systems is yet to be explored.

11.5 Parametric Verification

Many systems that are subject to verification are inherently stochastic. Examples include randomized distributed algorithms (where randomization breaks the symmetry between processes), security (e.g., key generation at encryption), systems biology (where species randomly react depending on their concentration), embedded systems (interacting with unknown and varying environments). A well-known example is the *crowds* protocol, which employs random routing to ensure anonymity. Nodes randomly choose to deliver a packet or to route it to another randomly picked node. In the presence of "bad" nodes that eavesdrop, we could be interested in analyzing probabilistic safety properties such as "the probability of a bad node identifying the sender's identity is less than 5 %."

In the recent past, different automata- and tableau-based *probabilistic model-checking* techniques to prove model properties specified by, e.g., probabilistic ω-regular languages or probabilistic branching-time logics such as pCTL and pCTL* have been developed [38]. Probabilistic model checking is applicable to a plethora of probabilistic models, ranging from discrete-time Markov chains to continuous-time Markov decision processes and probabilistic timed automata, possibly extended with notions of resource consumption (such as memory footprint and energy usage) using rewards (or prices). For instance, PRISM [50] or MRMC [45] are mature probabilistic model checkers and have been widely applied with success.

A major practical obstacle is that these quantitative verification techniques and tools work under the assumption that *all probabilities in models are a priori known*. However, at early development stages, certain system quantities such as faultiness, reliability, reaction rates, and packet loss ratios are often not (or at the best partially) known. In such cases, *parametric* probabilistic models can be used for specification, where transition probabilities are specified as arithmetic expressions using real-valued parameters. In addition to checking instantiated models for fixed parameter values, the important problem of parameter synthesis arises, posing the question which parameter values lead to the satisfaction of certain properties of interest. Parametric models are very natural in adaptive and self-aware software where "continuous" verification frequently amends system models during deployment as well as in model repair, where probabilities are dynamically tuned so as to satisfy a desired property. This section will describe the state of the art in parametric quantitative verification and its usage in model repair.

11.5.1 Parametric Markov Chains

We will first introduce the model at hand. A *parametric discrete-time Markov chain* (pMC) is defined as a usual discrete-time Markov chain (MC), with probabilities given by *rational functions* (fractions of polynomials) over a given set of parameters.

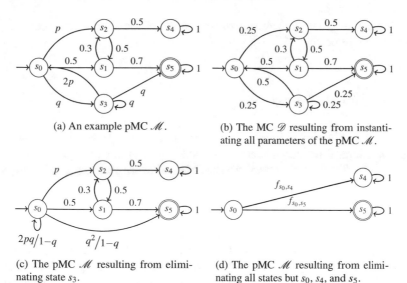

(a) An example pMC $\mathcal{M}$.

(b) The MC $\mathcal{D}$ resulting from instantiating all parameters of the pMC $\mathcal{M}$.

(c) The pMC $\mathcal{M}$ resulting from eliminating state s_3.

(d) The pMC $\mathcal{M}$ resulting from eliminating all states but s_0, s_4, and s_5.

Fig. 11.7 Parametric Markov chains

Consider the example pMC given in Fig. 11.7a. From state s_0 three transitions emerge, one transition carrying probability 0.5 and two parametric transitions with the parameters p and q. In order for these three transitions to form a suitable *probability distribution*, one needs to make sure that the parameters are only instantiated in a way such that all probabilities emanating from s_0 sum up to one. We call such an instantiation a *valuation* of parameters, which is a function mapping from the set of parameters to the real numbers. A valuation inducing probability distributions is called *well-defined*. For instance, the valuation v with $v(p) = v(q) = 0.25$ induces a well-formed MC which is depicted in Fig. 11.7b.

The properties we investigate are the so-called *reachability properties*, i.e., to compute the probability of reaching a dedicated set of target states. For instance, for the MC in Fig. 11.7b, the probability to reach state s_5 from the initial state s_0 is 0.72. For pMCs, this can be solved by computing a rational function over the occurring parameters describing the reachability probability. This means, if the parameters of the function are instantiated by a valuation that is well defined for the original pMC, this will evaluate to exactly the reachability probability of the corresponding instantiated MC. In our running example, the functions describing reachability probabilities from s_0 to s_4 and s_5 are given by:

$$f_{s_0,s_4} = \frac{40p^2 + 20pq + 6p + 3q}{68p^2 + 34pq + 34q^2 + 34p + 17q}$$

$$f_{s_0,s_5} = \frac{28p^2 + 14pq + 34q^2 + 28p + 14q}{68p^2 + 34pq + 34q^2 + 34p + 17q}$$

This example shows that already for very simple benchmarks rather complicated functions might occur.

11.5.2   State of the Art

In 2004, Daws [26] first proposed to represent reachability probabilities in pMCs by means of rational functions, which are obtained by state elimination (as for obtaining a regular expression from automata). The basic idea is to "bypass" a state s by removing it from the model and increasing the probabilities $P(s_1, s_2)$ of the transitions from each predecessors s_1 to each successors s_2 by the probability of moving from s_1 to s_2 via s, possibly including a self-loop on s.

Consider again the pMC in Fig. 11.7a. Assume, state s_3 is to be eliminated. The states that are relevant for this procedure are the only predecessor s_0 and the successors s_0 and s_5. Applying state elimination yields the model in Fig. 11.7c. Moreover, if all intermediate states are eliminated, only transitions directed from initial states to absorbing states remain. The result is depicted in Fig. 11.7d. This is what we call the model-checking result for parametric probabilistic verification.

This technique has been improved by Hahn et al. [37] by directly computing and simplifying intermediate functions, as a major drawback of the state elimination technique is the rapid growth of rational functions. The simplification involves the addition of rational functions where the costly operation of computing the greatest common divisor (gcd) needs to be performed. Jansen et al. [42] further improved the state elimination technique by combining it with SCC decomposition, and a dedicated gcd computation operating on partial factorizations of polynomials. State elimination is the core of the tool PARAM [37] and has recently been adopted in PRISM [50]. The new tool PROPhESY [28] also employs variants of state elimination. These are— to the best of our knowledge—the only available tools for computing reachability probabilities (and expected rewards) of pMCs. For the common benchmarks available at the PRISM Web site [50], PROPhESY performs best on nearly all benchmark instances both for reachability probabilities and expected rewards. In general, for systems with two parameters instances having up to 10 million states can be handled within reasonable time.

With the exception of PROPhESY, the available tools just output the rational function sometimes accompanied by constraints ensuring well-definedness. The problem of parameter synthesis is thereby not addressed directly. Other works consider parameter synthesis of timed reachability in parametric CTMCs [19].

In model repair [8], models refuting a given property are amended so as to satisfy this property. In this setting, parametric MCs are used as underlying model.

11.5.3 Parameter Synthesis

In our setting, a *requirement* is given as an upper bound on reachability probabilities. For instance, for the function f_{s_0,s_5} as in Fig. 11.7d one might give a value $\lambda \in [0, 1]$ such that $f_{s_0,s_5} < \lambda$. Now, to determine whether the requirement is met, one has to consider *all possible parameter valuations* for p and q. These *parameter synthesis* problems are challenging and substantially more complex than verifying standard MCs— just checking whether a pMC is realizable (having a parameter evaluation inducing a well-defined MC) is exponential in the number of parameters.

The tool PROPhESY addresses this problem as follows. To give the user a feasible and usable approach, an (approximate) partitioning of the parameter space into *safe* and *unsafe regions* is computed. Each parameter instantiation within a safe region satisfies the requirement under consideration, while inside the unsafe regions, no instantiation meets the requirement.

This is done in an incremental fashion: After the rational function is computed, the first step is to *sample* the rational function up to a user-adjustable degree. This amounts to instantiating parameter values (determined by dedicated heuristics) over the entire parameter space. This yields a coarse approximation of parts of the solution space that are safe or unsafe and can be viewed as an abstraction of the true partitioning into safe or unsafe parts. A typical sampling result with respect to two parameters can be seen in Fig. 11.8a. Points (or rather parameter instantiations) that satisfy the requirement are drawn green, and the other are red.

The goal is now to divide the parameter space into regions which are *certified* to be safe or unsafe. This is done in an iterative CEGAR[5]-like fashion. First, a region candidate assumed to be safe or unsafe is automatically generated. An *SMT solver* such as Z3 [44] or SMT-RAT [25] is then used to verify the assumption. In case it was wrong, a *counterexample* in the form of a contradicting sample point is provided along which the abstraction/sampling is *refined*, giving a finer abstraction of the solution space. Using this, new region candidates are generated. A very coarse partition into such regions is shown in Fig. 11.8b, a fine partition covering over 90 % of the parameter space is shown in Fig. 11.8c. For the used benchmarks, a covering of over 95 % can be achieved within seconds. After that, it is increasingly costly to determine the rest.

11.5.4 Model Repair

A still open and important problem is how to *automatically and efficiently repair* a MC model that does not meet a certain requirement. This application of parametric models is highly relevant for several applications, for example, in robotics. A first approach was presented by Bartocci et al. [8], based on defining a *nonlinear optimization problem* encoding that the system is changed with minimal cost such

---

[5]Counterexample-guided abstraction refinement.

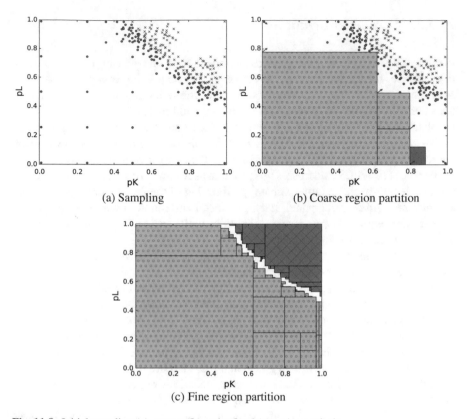

Fig. 11.8 Initial sampling (**a**), coarse (**b**) and refined (**c**) region analysis

that desired property is satisfied. The main practical obstacle of using nonlinear optimization, be it using a dedicated optimization algorithm or using an SMT solver for nonlinear real algebra [44] coupled with a binary search toward the optimal solution, is *scalability*. As the optimization involves costly computations of greatest common divisors of polynomials, approaches like [37, 42] are inherently restricted to small pMCs with just a few parameters.

Recently, Pathak et al. [56] proposed a heuristic approach to model repairs motivated by a robotics scenario. The method starts from an initial parameter assignment and iteratively changes the parameter values by *local repair steps*. To illustrate the basic idea, assume a model in which the probability to reach some "unsafe" states is above an allowed bound. Using model checking, we know for each state the probability to reach "unsafe" states. The higher this probability, the more dangerous it is to visit this state. To repair the model, we iteratively consider single probability distributions in isolation and modify the parameter values such that we decrease the probability to move to more dangerous successor states. The approach is shown to be *sound* in the sense that each local repair step improves the reachability probability towards a desired bound for a repairable pMC.

To illustrate the robotics scenario and the proposed technique, consider a toy example from [56] given in Fig. 11.9a. An object moves between two places (1) and (2) according to the MC $\mathcal{M}_1$. To catch the object, a robot moves between the places according to a strategy modeled by the pMC $\mathcal{M}_2$. With certain parameter domains, this defines the degree of freedom one has to *perturb* the strategy. For these two systems, the synchronous parallel composition is depicted as the pMC $\mathcal{M}$ in Fig. 11.9. Intuitively, the probability to actually catch the ball is the probability to finally reach the states $(1, 1)$ and $(2, 2)$.

Assume now that for some reason it is dangerous to catch the ball at (2). We therefore want to decrease the probability of reaching state $(2, 2)$ in $\mathcal{M}$, say it should be smaller than 0.5. Assume furthermore, an initial valuation of parameters leads to the MC $\mathcal{D}$ depicted in Fig. 11.10a by basically instantiating all parameters with zero. In $\mathcal{D}$, the probability to reach $(2, 2)$ is 0.5, i.e., the requirement is not met.

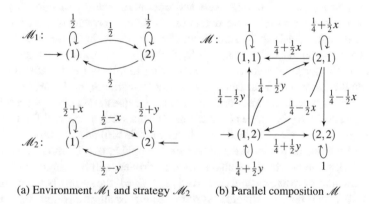

(a) Environment $\mathcal{M}_1$ and strategy $\mathcal{M}_2$ (b) Parallel composition $\mathcal{M}$

Fig. 11.9 Example setting for a robotic application of model repair

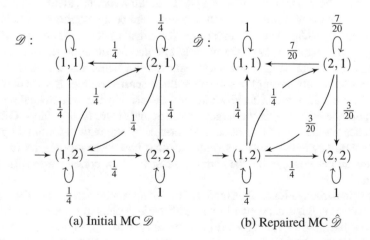

(a) Initial MC $\mathcal{D}$ (b) Repaired MC $\hat{\mathcal{D}}$

Fig. 11.10 Markov chain which is repaired towards satisfaction of the given property

Locally changing the probability distributions towards the requirement means that the reachability probability needs to be decreased. A possible result is the MC $\hat{\mathscr{D}}$ depicted Fig. 11.10b, where the probability to reach $(2, 2)$ is now only $4/9$, which means that the requirement is met. We call $\hat{\mathscr{D}}$ a *repair* of $\mathscr{D}$. Experiments show that this approach is feasible for systems with millions of states.

11.6   Run-Time Verification and Probabilistic Models

The goal of system health management is similar to that of a healthcare system, which aims to keep people healthy. System health management [23], in contrast, focuses on artificial or engineered systems, including aerospace [60, 61], electrical power [52, 58], infrastructure, mobile, and software systems [53, 59], and aims to keep them (and consequently also their users and operators) healthy or safe. Key system health management processes are detection, isolation, prognosis, and mitigation. Detection amounts to asking "Is something wrong or faulty in the system?" Isolation asks "Which components, if any, are faulty?" Prognosis is forecasting, and asks the question "Is the system or any components going to fail soon?" Finally, mitigation focuses on the question "What can I do in order to work around failures?"

The methods used to address each of these four questions, along with their relative importance, vary between applications. In this section, we will focus on general methods—namely probabilistic graphical models [46] and run-time verification [62]—and illustrate them by means of aerospace applications. Unmanned aerial systems (UASs), some of which are also known as drones, will be emphasized.

In general, there are two systems involved [23]. One is the system being monitored, or target. This can be a mechanical system, an electrical power system, a mobile phone, or a software program. Second, there is the monitoring system, or monitor. In our case, the monitor is called a *system health monitor* (SHM). The SHM is typically a computer running adjacent to the system being monitored, and is taking as input sensor readings from the monitored (or target) system. The concept of sensor reading should here be interpreted broadly and can be vibration measurements for a mechanical system, voltage measurements for an electrical power system, or log file entries for a software application. What these sensor readings have in common is that they reflect the target's health status and are used by the system health monitor to compute the estimates of the target's current and future health status. Often, the SHM relies on the use of one or several models, along with algorithms operating on them, and key SHM questions center around how these models are expressed, how they are developed, what they are used for, and how computation with them is performed.

We are in particular focused on models that are represented as probabilistic graphical models using Bayesian networks and arithmetic circuits. Bayesian networks have received substantial attention both from researchers and practitioners, and have been successfully employed for target systems such as electrical power systems and software systems. Sometimes, not only the monitored system is being modeled, but also its sensors. This enables us to distinguish between system failure and sensor failure in the SHM model and thus by the SHM monitor.

Bayesian network models for system health management can be developed manually by developers in collaboration with subject matter experts as well as in a completely data-driven fashion [65]. There are also hybrid development methods, in which the structure of the Bayesian network is constructed manually, while its parameters are estimated from data, perhaps informed by a Bayesian prior. Once a probabilistic graphical model for SHM has been developed, there is the question of deployment. A Bayesian network can be used directly by an SHM monitor for online system health management, or it can be compiled to a secondary model which is then used by the SHM monitor. Data structures for such secondary models include junction trees and arithmetic circuits. Benefits of using a secondary data structure include faster computation, simpler SHM algorithms, more predictable compute time and memory consumption, and lower power consumption. Different computational platforms can be used, including not only CPUs but also graphics processing units (GPUs) [68, 69] and field programmable gate arrays (FPGAs) [61].

Regardless of whether a Bayesian network model or a compiled model is used for SHM monitoring, a posterior distribution $P(H \mid e)$ is computed. Here, e is the input to the model (computed from sensors of the target or monitored system), while H is a set of random variables that reflect the health status of the target system. Each component in the target system is typically represented by a handful of random variables in the SHM model. One random variable among this set can, for example, represent the health status of one component or one subsystem in the target system. The graph structure of the model will reflect dependencies and independencies of the target system, and will also reflect the structure of the problem being solved.

There are at least three central design requirements for UAS SHM in aerospace [61]: unobtrusiveness, responsiveness, and realizability. *Unobtrusiveness* means that the SHM framework must not change the properties of the vehicle.[6] *Responsiveness* means that the SHM framework must operate in real time. *Realizability* means that the SHM framework must easily plug into the existing technology stack of the UAS. One cannot expect that this stack can be easily changed; an SHM component needs to blend into an existing ecosystem without too much "pain."

The above requirements have been met in the novel rt-R2U2 framework [61]. The rt-R2U2 framework is a hybrid or modular one, in which different models are, to a large extent, developed separately but with well-defined interfaces. Typical building blocks of rt-R2U2 are the following: signal processing blocks, temporal logic blocks, Bayesian reasoning blocks, and miscellaneous computing blocks. These blocks can

---

[6]For example, for manned flight, there is a stringent certification requirement. For both unmanned and manned flights, there is typically stringent resource limitations. These resource requirements may vary from aerospace vehicle to aerospace vehicle, but are often concerned with electrical power consumption, weight, and computational needs. These requirements are different from what is often seen in other applications of verification or run-time verification, and impact the techniques developed to meet the requirements.

be connected in a block diagram fashion; thus, a temporal logic block can take as input results from a Bayesian reasoning block and vice versa. Bayesian reasoning blocks, containing arithmetic circuits compiled from Bayesian networks, typically estimate component and sensor state-of-health from noisy and uncertain sensor data. Temporal logic blocks, on the other hand, contain temporal logic formulas that express aerospace safety requirements. Linear Temporal Logic (LTL) and Metric Temporal Logic (MTL) are often used to formalize safety requirements in aerospace. The key benefit of the rt-R2U2 framework is that such temporal formulas can be used for run-time verification, even on a UAS under the three central design requirements discussed above (unobtrusiveness, responsiveness, and realizability).

The rt-R2U2 framework has been successfully implemented and validated using data from the Swift UAS, an unmanned all-electric aircraft at NASA [61]. In the Swift UAS, there is a read-only interface from the bus attached to the main flight computer. This interface is used by the SHM monitor, which is implemented by FPGA. The FPGA is used to compute with an arithmetic circuit (AC) model compiled from a Bayesian network model. In addition, run-time verification methods are being used. These run-time verification techniques are evaluating temporal logic formulas on the FPGA. These temporal logic formulas express flight rules, operational limitations of the Swift UAS, and so forth. Inputs to an AC model can be sensor readings, filtered sensor readings, or outputs of another Bayesian reasoning or temporal logic block. This enables a powerful and flexible system health management capability for the UAS, and we believe it could be a foundation for similar SHM systems outside of aerospace.

11.7   Analysis and Synthesis of Self-adaptation Exploiting Environment Assumptions

During the construction of a self-aware computing system, developers face many decisions about the system's architecture and design. For example, questions such as whether to employ centralized or decentralized decision-making, or whether adaptation should be executed reactively or proactively must be carefully considered.

The answer to these questions can be informed by past experience with similar existing systems, or by prototyping and simulation activities that can provide a good estimation of the behavior of the system at run time. Nevertheless, experience with similar systems may not always be available, and prototyping or simulating (potentially many) system design variants is not cost-effective. Moreover, prototyping and simulation are good at providing estimations of the behavior of a system in the "normal" case, but do not systematically support system analysis in the context of an unpredictable environment (e.g., worst-case scenario).

In this section, we overview a technique to analyze self-adaptive systems that explicitly considers the uncertainty in their operating environment. The approach enables developers to approximate the behavioral envelope of a self-adaptive system by analyzing best- and worst-case scenarios of alternative designs for self-adaptation mechanisms, given some assumptions about the behavior of the operating environment. The formal underpinnings of the approach are based on model checking of stochastic multiplayer games (SMGs) [20], a technique appropriate to analyze the interplay between a self-adaptive system and its environment. SMG models are expressive enough to capture: (i) the inherent uncertainty and variability of the environment and (ii) the competitive behavior between a system and its environment (reflecting the fact that environment changes cannot be controlled by the system).

The underlying idea behind the approach is modeling a system and its environment as players in a SMG, which can either cooperate to achieve a common goal (best-case scenario analysis), or compete against each other (worst-case scenario analysis). Being purely declarative, this technique does not require the availability of specific adaptation algorithms or infrastructure.

This technique is intended to endow developers with a preliminary understanding of the behavior resulting from architecting a self-adaptive system based on a set of coarse-grained design decisions, helping them to narrow down the solution space. Once the coarse-grained architecture of the system has been laid out, it can be refined into more detailed specifications that can be employed to develop prototypes or simulations that require the availability of specific adaptation algorithms and demand more effort to develop, compared to a declarative approach.

The remainder of this section first provides an overview of the technique for model checking SMGs that serves as foundation for analyzing self-adaptation. Next, we describe how model checking of SMGs is applied to compare alternative approaches to proactive adaptation in the context of Znn.com [21], a benchmark system that has been employed to assess different works on self-adaptation. Finally, we discuss the challenges in shifting the technique from design-time analysis to run-time synthesis of adaptation behavior.

11.7.1 Model Checking Stochastic Games

Automatic verification techniques for probabilistic systems have been successfully applied in a variety of application domains that range from power management or wireless communication protocols, to biological systems. In particular, techniques such as probabilistic model checking provide a means to model and analyze systems that exhibit stochastic behavior, enabling reasoning quantitatively about probability and reward-based properties (e.g., about the system's use of resources, or time).

Competitive behavior may also appear in systems when some component cannot be controlled and could behave according to different or even conflicting goals with respect to other system components. In such situations, a natural fit is modeling a system as a game between different players, adopting a game-theoretic perspective.

The approach that we describe in this section builds upon a recent technique for modeling and analyzing SMGs [20]. In this technique, systems are modeled as turn-based SMGs, meaning that in each state of the model, only one player can choose between several actions, the outcome of which can be probabilistic. Players can cooperate to achieve the same goal, or compete to achieve their own goals.

The approach includes a logic called rPATL for expressing quantitative properties of stochastic multiplayer games and reasoning about the ability of a set of players to collectively achieve a particular goal. Properties written in rPATL can state that a coalition of players has a strategy which can ensure that either the probability of an event's occurrence or an expected reward measure meets some threshold. rPATL is a CTL-style branching-time temporal logic that incorporates the coalition operator $\langle\langle C \rangle\rangle$ of ATL [1], combining it with the probabilistic operator $P_{\bowtie q}$ and path formulae from PCTL [12]. Moreover, rPATL includes a generalization of the reward operator $R^r_{\bowtie x}$ from [33] to reason about goals related to rewards. An extended version of the rPATL reward operator $\langle\langle C \rangle\rangle R^r_{max=?}[F \phi]$ enables the quantification of the maximum accrued reward r along paths that lead to states satisfying state formula ϕ that can be guaranteed by players in coalition C, independently of the strategies followed by the other players. An example of typical usage combining the coalition and reward maximization operators is $\langle\langle sys \rangle\rangle R^{utility}_{max=?}[F^c \ end]$, meaning "value of the maximum utility reward accumulated along paths leading to an end state that a player sys can guarantee, regardless of the strategies of other players."

Reasoning about strategies is a fundamental aspect of model checking SMGs, which enables the synthesis of a strategy that is able to optimize an objective expressed as a property including an extended version of the rPATL reward operator. An SMG strategy resolves the choices in each state, selecting actions for a player based on the current state and a set of memory elements [20].

11.7.2   Reasoning About Self-adaptation Using Stochastic Games

The underlying idea behind the approach to analyze self-adaptive systems consists in modeling both the self-adaptive system and its environment as two players of a SMG. The system's player objective is optimizing an objective function encoded in a rPATL specification (e.g., minimizing the probability of violating a safety property, or maximizing accrued utility—encoded as a reward structure on the game). In contrast, the environment can either be considered as adversarial to the system (enabling worst-case scenario analysis), or as a cooperative player that helps the system to optimize its objective function (enabling best-case scenario analysis).

We illustrate the technique in the context of Znn.com [21], a benchmark case study employed to assess different works on self-adaptation.

The main objective of Znn.com is to provide content to customers within a reasonable response time, while keeping the cost of the server pool within a certain operating budget. From time to time, due to highly popular events, Znn.com experiences spikes in requests that it cannot serve adequately, even at maximum pool size. To prevent losing customers, the system can maintain functionality at a reduced level

Fig. 11.11   Znn.com system
architecture

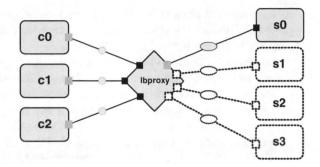

of fidelity by setting servers to return only textual content during such peak times, instead of not providing service to some of its customers. There are two main quality objectives for the self-adaptation of the system: (i) performance, which depends on request response time, server load, and network bandwidth and (ii) cost, which depends on the number of active servers (Fig. 11.11).

When response time becomes too high, the system can execute adaptation tactics to: (i) increment its server pool size if it is within budget to improve performance; or (ii) switch servers to textual mode if the cost is near to budget limit. For simplicity, we consider a simple version of Znn.com that adapts only by adjusting server pool size. Note that different adaptation tactics take different amounts of time until their effects are produced (i.e., they have different *latency*). For example, adapting the system to serve results in textual mode may be achieved quickly if it can be done by changing a simple setting in a component, whereas booting up a server to share the load may take some time. When planning how to adapt, self-adaptive approaches tend to make simplifying assumptions about the properties of adaptation, such as ignoring the time it takes for an adaptation tactic to cause its intended effect.

In the following, we show how SMG analysis can be instantiated to quantify the benefits of employing adaptation latency information in decision-making, comparing latency-aware with latency-agnostic adaptation in Znn.com.

The approach consists of two phases: (i) model specification, consisting of building the game model that describes the possible interactions between the self-adaptive system and its environment and (ii) strategy synthesis, in which a game strategy that optimizes the objective function of the system player is built, enabling developers to quantify the outcome of adaptation in boundary cases.

11.7.2.1   Model Specification

We consider a game for Znn.com played in turns by two players who are in control of the behavior of the environment and the system, respectively:

- *Environment Player*. The environment is in control of the evolution of time and other variables of the execution context that are out of the system's control. During its turn, the environment sets the number of request arrivals for the current time period and updates the values of other environment variables (e.g., increasing the variable that keeps track of execution time).

- *System Player.* During its turn, the system can: (i) trigger the activation of a new server, which will become effective only after the latency period of the tactic expires; (ii) discharge a server (with no latency associated); or (iii) yield the turn to the environment player without executing any actions. In addition, the system updates during its turn the value of the response time according to the request arrivals placed by the environment player during the current time period and the number of active servers (computed using an M/M/c queuing model [22]).

The objective of the system player is to maximize the accrued utility during execution. To represent utility, we employ a reward structure that maps game states to a utility value computed according to a set of utility functions and preferences (i.e., weights). We consider two functions U_R and U_C that map the response time and the number of active servers in the system to performance and cost utility, respectively.

In latency-aware adaptation, a reward structure rIU encoded in the game employs the value of response time $MMc(s, a)$ computed according to the request arrivals a and the number of active servers s during the tactic latency period to compute the value of instantaneous utility as $rIU = w_R \cdot U_R(MMc(s, a)) + w_C \cdot U_C(cps \cdot s)$, where cps is the cost of operating a server.

However, in non-latency-aware adaptation, the instantaneous utility expected by the algorithm during the latency period for activating a server does not match the real utility extracted for the system, since the new server has not yet impacted the performance (although there is an impact on cost, since the server is already active while booting up). In this case, we add to the model a second reward structure rEIU in which the utility for performance during the latency period is based on the response time that the system would have if the new server had completed its activation: $rEIU = w_R \cdot U_R(MMc(s + 1, a)) + w_C \cdot U_C(cps \cdot s)$.

11.7.2.2 Strategy Synthesis

To illustrate how SMG analysis can be employed to compare latency-aware with latency-agnostic adaptation, we describe rPATL specifications that enable quantifying the maximum accrued utility that adaptation can guarantee, independently of the behavior of the environment (worst-case scenario analysis).

- *Latency-Aware Adaptation.* We define the *real guaranteed accrued utility* (U_{rga}) as the maximum real instantaneous utility reward accumulated throughout execution that the system player is able to guarantee, independently of the behavior of the environment player:

$$U_{rga} \triangleq \langle\langle sys \rangle\rangle R^{rIU}_{max=?}[F^c \ t = \text{MAX\_TIME}]$$

This expression quantifies the utility that an optimal self-adaptation algorithm would be able to extract from the system, given the most adverse possible conditions of the environment.

- *Latency-Agnostic Adaptation.* In latency-agnostic adaptation, real utility does not coincide with the expected utility that a self-adaptation algorithm would employ for decision-making. Hence, the analysis is performed in two steps:

  1. Compute the strategy that the adaptation algorithm would follow based on the information it employs about expected utility. That strategy is computed based on an rPATL specification that obtains the expected guaranteed accrued utility (U_{ega}) for the system player:

$$U_{ega} \triangleq \langle\langle sys \rangle\rangle R_{max=?}^{rEIU} [F^c\ t = MAX\_TIME]$$

  For the specification of this property, we use the expected utility reward rEIU instead of the real utility reward rIU (in latency-aware adaptation $U_{ega} = U_{rga}$).
  2. Verify the U_{rga} under the generated strategy. This is done by building a product of the existing game model and the strategy synthesized in the previous step, obtaining a new game under which further properties can be verified. In our case, we quantify the reward for real utility in the new game in which the system player strategy for maximizing expected utility has already been fixed.

The model checking different variants of Znn.com's SMG shows that latency-aware adaptation outperforms in all cases its latency-agnostic counterpart (more details in [18]). Concretely, latency-aware adaptation is able to guarantee an increment in utility extracted from the system, independently of the behavior of the environment (ΔU_{rga}) that increases progressively with higher tactic latencies.

11.7.3 From Design-Time Analysis to Run-Time Synthesis

Although the approach presented in this section is oriented toward obtaining a preliminary understanding of adaptation behavior at design time, its underlying principles can also be tailored to decide how to adapt at run-time by synthesizing system strategies while considering explicitly the behavior of the environment.

The main advantage of using probabilistic model checking at run-time instead of a specific adaptation algorithm is that the adaptation decision is optimal (e.g., over a time horizon), since the model checker selects a strategy that optimizes the system's goal through exhaustive search. However, the current approach has limited scalability, since the interleaving of environment and system transitions can easily lead to an explosion of the state-space. This limitation can be mitigated by carefully choosing the level of abstraction of the model, or representing the behavior of the environment only over a relevant time horizon, for instance. Moreover, we expect that the maturation of this technology will result in the development of efficient run-time synthesis techniques, following the lead of recent advances in efficient quantitative verification at run-time [32, 34].

11.8 Summary

We presented two classes of techniques that support key processes associated with the operation of self-aware computing systems—verification and synthesis. Using probabilistic models ranging from Markov chains and Bayesian networks to stochastic multiplayer games, verification enables self-aware systems to reason about their reliability, performance, cost, and other QoS properties. When changes in the environment or goals render the actual or predicted values of these properties inadequate, the synthesis of connectors and service compositions supports the adaptation of the software architecture of self-aware systems.

Acknowledgements The work concerning the synthesis method described in Sect. 11.2 has been supported by the European Union's H2020 Programme under grant agreement number 644178 (project CHOReVOLUTION—Automated Synthesis of Dynamic and Secured Choreographies for the Future Internet) and by the Ministry of Economy and Finance, Cipe resolution no. 135/2012 (project INCIPICT—INnovating CIty Planning through Information and Communication Technologies).

References

1. Rajeev Alur, Thomas A. Henzinger, and Orna Kupferman. Alternating-time temporal logic. *J. ACM*, 49(5):672–713, 2002.
2. Jesper Andersson, Rogério de Lemos, Sam Malek, and Danny Weyns. Modeling dimensions of self-adaptive software systems. In *SEfSAS*, pages 27–47. 2009.
3. M. Autili, P. Inverardi, and M. Tivoli. Automated synthesis of service choreographies. *IEEE Software*, 32(1):50–57, 2015.
4. Marco Autili, Davide Di Ruscio, Amleto Di Salle, and Alexander Perucci. CHOReOSynt: Enforcing choreography realizability in the future internet. In *FSE'14*, pages 723–726, 2014.
5. Marco Autili, Amleto Di Salle, and Massimo Tivoli. Synthesis of resilient choreographies. In *Software Engineering for Resilient Systems*, pages 94–108. 2013.
6. Marco Autili, Leonardo Mostarda, Alfredo Navarra, and Massimo Tivoli. Synthesis of decentralized and concurrent adaptors for correctly assembling distributed component-based systems. *Journal of Systems and Software*, 81(12):2210–2236, 2008.
7. Marco Autili and Massimo Tivoli. Distributed enforcement of service choreographies. In *FOCLASA'14*, pages 18–35, 2014.
8. Ezio Bartocci, Radu Grosu, Panagiotis Katsaros, et al. Model repair for probabilistic systems. In *TACAS'11*, pages 326–340. 2011.
9. Simona Bernardi, José Merseguer, and Dorina C. Petriu. *Model-Driven Dependability Assessment of Software Systems*. Springer, 2013.
10. M. Bernardo, P. Ciancarini, and L. Donatiello. Architecting families of software systems with process algebras. *ACM TOSEM*, 11:386–426, 2002.
11. A. Bertolino, A. Calabrò, F. Di Giandomenico, et al. On-the-fly dependable mediation between heterogeneous networked systems. In *ICSOFT'11*, pages 20–37, 2012.

12. Andrea Bianco and Luca de Alfaro. Model checking of probabalistic and nondeterministic systems. In *FSTTCS*, pages 499–513, 1995.
13. Radu Calinescu, Simos Gerasimou, and Alec Banks. Self-adaptive software with decentralised control loops. In *FASE'15*, pages 235–251. 2015.
14. Radu Calinescu, Carlo Ghezzi, Kenneth Johnson, et al. Formal verification with confidence intervals to establish quality of service properties of software systems. *IEEE Transactions on Reliability*, pages 1–16, 2015.
15. Radu Calinescu, Carlo Ghezzi, Marta Kwiatkowska, and Raffaela Mirandola. Self-adaptive software needs quantitative verification at runtime. *Communications of the ACM*, 55(9):69–77, 2012.
16. Radu Calinescu, Kenneth Johnson, and Yasmin Rafiq. Developing self-verifying service-based systems. In *ASE'13*, pages 734–737, 2013.
17. Radu Calinescu, Yasmin Rafiq, Kenneth Johnson, and Mehmet Emin Bakir. Adaptive model learning for continual verification of non-functional properties. In *ICPE'14*, pages 87–98, 2014.
18. Javier Cámara, Gabriel A. Moreno, and David Garlan. Stochastic game analysis and latency awareness for proactive self-adaptation. In *SEAMS'14*, pages 155–164, 2014.
19. Milan Ceska, Frits Dannenberg, Marta Z. Kwiatkowska, and Nicola Paoletti. Precise parameter synthesis for stochastic biochemical systems. In *CMSB'14*, pages 86–98, 2014.
20. Taolue Chen, Vojtech Forejt, Marta Z. Kwiatkowska, et al. Automatic verification of competitive stochastic systems. *Formal Methods in System Design*, 43(1):61–92, 2013.
21. Shang-Wen Cheng, David Garlan, and Bradley R. Schmerl. Evaluating the effectiveness of the rainbow self-adaptive system. In *SEAMS'09*, pages 132–141, 2009.
22. R.M. Chiulli. *Quantitative Analysis: An Introduction*. Automation and production systems. 1999.
23. A. Choi, A. Darwiche, L. Zheng, and O. J. Mengshoel. A tutorial on Bayesian networks for system health management. In *Data Mining in Systems Health Management: Detection, Diagnostics, and Prognostics*. 2011.
24. Vittorio Cortellessa, Antinisca Di Marco, and Paola Inverardi. *Model-Based Software Performance Analysis*. Springer, 2011.
25. Florian Corzilius, Gereon Kremer, Sebastian Junges, Stefan Schupp, and Erika Ábrahám. SMT-RAT: an open source C++ toolbox for strategic and parallel SMT solving. In *SAT*, volume 9340 of *Lecture Notes in Computer Science*, pages 360–368. Springer, 2015.
26. Conrado Daws. Symbolic and parametric model checking of discrete-time Markov chains. In *ICTAC'04*, pages 280–294, 2004.
27. Rogério de Lemos, Holger Giese, Hausi A. Müller, et al. Software engineering for self-adaptive systems: A second research roadmap. In *SEfSAS II*, pages 1–32. 2013.
28. Christian Dehnert, Sebastian Junges, Nils Jansen, et al. PROPhESY: A probabilistic parameter synthesis tool. In *CAV'15*, pages 214–231, 2015.
29. Antinisca Di Marco, Paola Inverardi, and Romina Spalazzese. Synthesizing self-adaptive connectors meeting functional and performance concerns. In *SEAMS'13*, pages 133–142, 2013.
30. Ilenia Epifani, Carlo Ghezzi, Raffaela Mirandola, and Giordano Tamburrelli. Model evolution by run-time parameter adaptation. In *ICSE'09*, pages 111–121, 2009.
31. European Commission. Digital Agenda for Europe - Future Internet Research and Experimentation (FIRE) initiative, 2015.
32. Antonio Filieri, Carlo Ghezzi, and Giordano Tamburrelli. Run-time efficient probabilistic model checking. In *ICSE'11*, pages 341–350, 2011.
33. Vojtech Forejt, Marta Kwiatkowska, Gethin Norman, and David Parker. Automated verification techniques for probabilistic systems. In *SFM'11*, pages 53–113, 2011.
34. Simos Gerasimou, Radu Calinescu, and Alec Banks. Efficient runtime quantitative verification using caching, lookahead, and nearly-optimal reconfiguration. In *SEAMS'14*, pages 115–124, 2014.
35. Simos Gerasimou, Giordano Tamburrelli, and Radu Calinescu. Search-based synthesis of probabilistic models for quality-of-service software engineering. In *ASE'15*, pages 319–330, 2015.

36. Matthias Güdemann, Gwen Salaün, and Meriem Ouederni. Counterexample guided synthesis of monitors for realizability enforcement. In *ATVA'12*, pages 238–253. 2012.
37. Ernst Moritz Hahn, Holger Hermanns, and Lijun Zhang. Probabilistic reachability for parametric Markov models. *Software Tools for Technology Transfer*, 13(1):3–19, 2010.
38. Hans Hansson and Bengt Jonsson. A logic for reasoning about time and reliability. *Formal Aspects of Computing*, 6(5):512–535, 1194.
39. Markus C. Huebscher and Julie A. McCann. A survey of autonomic computing – degrees, models, and applications. *ACM Comput. Surv.*, 40(3):1–28, 2008.
40. P. Inverardi, V. Issarny, and R. Spalazzese. A Theory of Mediators for Eternal CONNECTors. In *ISoLA'10*, pages 236–250, 2010.
41. P. Inverardi, R. Spalazzese, and M. Tivoli. Application-Layer Connector Synthesis. In *SFM'11*, pages 148–190, 2011.
42. Nils Jansen, Florian Corzilius, Matthias Volk, et al. Accelerating parametric probabilistic verification. In *QEST'11*, pages 404–420, 2014.
43. Kenneth Johnson, Radu Calinescu, and Shinji Kikuchi. An incremental verification framework for component-based software systems. In *CBSE'13*, pages 33–42, 2013.
44. Dejan Jovanovic and Leonardo Mendonça de Moura. Solving non-linear arithmetic. In *IJCAR*, pages 339–354, 2012.
45. Joost-Pieter Katoen, Ivan S. Zapreev, Ernst Moritz Hahn, et al. The ins and outs of the probabilistic model checker MRMC. *Performance Evaluation*, 68(2):90–104, 2011.
46. D. Koller and N. Friedman. *Probabilistic Graphical Methods: Principles and Techniques*. MIT Press, 2009.
47. Samuel Kounev, Xiaoyun Zhu, Jeffrey O. Kephart, and Marta Kwiatkowska. Model-driven Algorithms and Architectures for Self-Aware Computing Systems (Dagstuhl Seminar 15041). *Dagstuhl Reports*, 5(1):164–196, 2015.
48. Jeff Kramer and Jeff Magee. The evolving philosophers problem: Dynamic change management. *IEEE Trans. Softw. Eng.*, 16(11):1293–1306, 1990.
49. Marta Kwiatkowska. Quantitative verification: models, techniques and tools. In *ESEC/FSE'07*, pages 449–458, 2007.
50. Marta Kwiatkowska, Gethin Norman, and David Parker. PRISM 4.0: Verification of probabilistic real-time systems. In *CAV'11*, pages 585–591, 2011.
51. Sam Malek, Nels Beckman, Marija Mikic-Rakic, and Nenad Medvidovic. A framework for ensuring and improving dependability in highly distributed systems. In *Architecting Dependable Systems III*, pages 173–193. 2004.
52. O. J. Mengshoel, M. Chavira, K. Cascio, et al. Probabilistic model-based diagnosis: An electrical power system case study. *Systems, Man and Cybernetics*, 40(5):874–885, 2010.
53. O. J. Mengshoel and J. M. Schumann. Software health management with Bayesian networks. In *2nd Intl. Workshop On Software Health Management*, 2011.
54. Nicola Nostro, Ronima Spalazzese, Felicita Di Giandomenico, and Paola Inverardi. Achieving functional and non functional interoperability through synthesized connectors. *Journal of Systems and Software*, pages 185–199, 2016.
55. J. L. Pastrana, E. Pimentel, and M. Katrib. QoS-enabled and self-adaptive connectors for web services composition and coordination. *Comput. Lang. Syst. Struct.*, 37(1):2–23, 2011.
56. Shashank Pathak, Erika Ábrahám, Nils Jansen, et al. A greedy approach for the efficient repair of stochastic models. In *NFM'15*, pages 295–309, 2015.
57. Q. Qiu, Q. Wu, and M. Pedram. Stochastic modeling of a power-managed system: construction and optimization. In *Intl. Symp. on Low Power Electronics and Design*, pages 194–199, 1999.
58. B. Ricks and O. J. Mengshoel. Diagnosis for uncertain, dynamic and hybrid domains using bayesian networks and arithmetic circuits. *Intl. Journal of Approximate Reasoning*, 55(5):1207–1234, 2014.
59. J. Schumann, T. Mbaya, and O. J. Mengshoel. Bayesian software health management for aircraft guidance, navigation, and control. In *Prognostics and Health Management Society*, 2011.
60. J. Schumann, O. J. Mengshoel, and T. Mbaya. Integrated software and sensor health management for small spacecraft. In *Intl. Conf. on Space Mission Challenges for Information Technology*, pages 77–84, 2011.

61. J. Schumann, K. Y. Rozier, T. Reinbacher, et al. Towards real-time, on-board, hardware-supported sensor and software health management for unmanned aerial systems. *Intl. Journal of Prognostics and Health Management*, 6, 2015.
62. J. Schumann, A. N. Srivastava, and O. J. Mengshoel. Who guards the guardians? toward V&V of health management software. In *RV'10*, pages 399–404, 2010.
63. Romina Spalazzese and Paola Inverardi. Mediating connector patterns for components interoperability. In *ECSA'10*, pages 335–343, 2010.
64. Bridget Spitznagel and David Garlan. A compositional formalization of connector wrappers. In *ICSE'03*, pages 374–384, 2003.
65. A. Srivastava and J. Han, editors. *Data Mining in Systems Health Management: Detection, Diagnostics, and Prognostics*. Chapman and Hall/CRC Press, 2011.
66. M. Tivoli, P. Fradet, A. Girault, and G. Gößler. Adaptor synthesis for real-time components. In *TACAS'07*, pages 185–200, 2007.
67. Daniel M. Yellin and Robert E. Strom. Protocol specifications and component adaptors. *ACM Trans. Program. Lang. Syst.*, 19, 1997.
68. L. Zheng and O. J. Mengshoel. Exploring multiple dimensions of parallelism in junction tree message passing. In *UAI Application Workshops*, 2013.
69. L. Zheng and O. J. Mengshoel. Optimizing parallel belief propagation in junction trees using regression. In *KDD'13*, pages 757–765, 2013.

Chapter 12
Self-adaptation for Individual Self-aware Computing Systems

Martina Maggio, Tarek Abdelzaher, Lukas Esterle, Holger Giese,
Jeffrey O. Kephart, Ole J. Mengshoel, Alessandro V. Papadopoulos,
Anders Robertsson and Katinka Wolter

Abstract This chapter discusses the role of self-awareness for adaptation at the individual level, when one single entity receives inputs both from itself or some of its components and from the external environment and uses the input to adjust to the current conditions. The chapter reviews the most widely used techniques for

M. Maggio (✉) · A.V. Papadopoulos · A. Robertsson
Department of Automatic Control, Lund University, Ole Römers väg 1,
SE 223 63 Lund, Sweden
e-mail: martina.maggio@control.lth.se

A.V. Papadopoulos
e-mail: alessandro.papadopoulos@control.lth.se

A. Robertsson
e-mail: anders.robertsson@control.lth.se

T. Abdelzaher
Department of Computer Science, University of Illinois at Urbana Champaign,
Urbana, IL 61801, USA
e-mail: zaher@illinois.edu

L. Esterle
Vienna University of Technology, Treitlstrasse 3, 1040 Vienna, Austria
e-mail: lukas.esterle@tuwien.ac.at

H. Giese
Hasso-Plattner-Institut fr Softwaresystemtechnik GmbH,
Prof.-Dr.-Helmert-Str. 2-3, 14482 Potsdam, Germany
e-mail: holger.giese@hpi.de

J.O. Kephart
Thomas J. Watson Research Center, Hawthorne, NY, USA
e-mail: kephart@us.ibm.com

O.J. Mengshoel
Department of Electrical and Computer Engineering, Carnegie Mellon
University, Moffett Field, Pittsburgh, CA, USA
e-mail: ole.mengshoel@sv.cmu.edu

K. Wolter
Institute of Computer Science, Freie Universität Berlin,
Takustr. 9 Raum 149, 14195 Berlin, Germany
e-mail: katinka.wolter@fu-berlin.de

© Springer International Publishing AG 2017
S. Kounev et al. (eds.), *Self-Aware Computing Systems*,
DOI 10.1007/978-3-319-47474-8_12

self-adaptation and identifies the role of self-awareness for each of the techniques and the metrics used to evaluate these techniques. Finally, we pave the way toward the following chapter, which discusses multiple entity adaptation, by introducing the interaction of different self-adaptation techniques at the level of the single individual.

12.1 Introduction

Self-awareness plays a key role in the development of self-adaptation techniques. Indeed, in order for any adaptation technique to be successful, it is necessary to possess some knowledge about the effect of the adaptation strategies. This chapter discusses self-adaptation based on self-awareness at the individual level. This means that one single entity receives inputs both from itself or some of its components and from the external environment and uses the input to adjust to the current conditions.

In order to fully understand the adaptation process, we analyze its drivers. We have identified different drivers for adaptations. First, a system can adjust its behavior because the high-level goals that it was trying to achieve are changed. Aside, it is also possible that the adaptation process is triggered by changes in the system itself or by changes in the environment.

A key role in defining the adaptation process is the technique that is used to build the adaptation strategy. Among the many possible techniques, we focus on three main categories and discuss control theory, machine learning, and optimization research. Moreover, the technique of choice usually determines also how the results are evaluated. We provide here an overview of different methodologies and metrics and discuss the most widely used evaluation techniques.

While the scope of this chapter is limited to a single entity adaptation, we here pave the way toward multiple entities that adjust their behavior, by discussing how a single entity can have multiple adaptation strategies and coordinate among them, to improve the overall behavior.

The chapter is organized as follows. Section 12.2 provides a discussion about why adaptation is introduced into the system and what components of self-awareness drive it. Section 12.3 describes some adaptation techniques, while Sect. 12.4 defines how to evaluate these adaptation techniques. In the end, Sect. 12.5 discusses how multiple adaptation policies can interact in the same entity and Sect. 12.6 concludes the chapter.

12.2 What Drives Adaptation?

In this section, we will describe what are the drivers for self-adaptation.

Self-aware computing systems are characterized by the existence of at least one reflection run-time model where the causal connection [12] realizes some form of learning of the mentioned run-time model. Furthermore, the run-time models allow systems to reason about their behavior and self-adapt in accordance with changing higher-level goals, and thus, these systems are also conceptually characterized by the existence of an evaluation run-time model representing the higher-level goals that may change over time [42]. Accordingly, it has to be emphasized that adaptation in self-aware computing systems is based on reasoning with the run-time models in order to determine adaptation steps that lead to a better fulfillment of the higher-level goals. Consequently, the drivers for adaptation considered are (1) changes in the higher level goals; (2) changes in the system itself or in its run-time model; and (3) changes in the environment. All these different changes are captured by the run-time models and their updates.

For all three cases, the adaptation engine can be based on the reasoning capabilities for the reflection run-time model of the system and environment or for run-time models. Additionally, either static or dynamic knowledge about the adaptation capabilities of the system is added, in the form of a change run-time model. Such a change run-time model may either describe the solution space explicitly or implicitly by describing the possible changes but not the solution space directly. In cases (2) and (3), it determines a solution that takes the changes in the environment and/or system into account and likely better fulfills the evaluation run-time model than the current solution. In case (1), in contrast, possible solutions are determined that fit to the changed evaluation run-time model.

12.2.1 Adapting to Changes in High-Level Goals

Two common ways of expressing high-level goals [20][1] are:

- goal policies, which specify a desired state, or criteria that characterize a set of desired states that are deemed equally desirable; or
- utility-function policies, which specify an objective function, possibly accompanied by a set of constraints. The goal is defined as the desired feasible state or set of feasible states for which the objective function is optimized subject to the set of constraints.

A simple example of a goal policy is "the response time for Gold class should be no more than 1 s." A self-aware entity with such a goal will manage the compute resources at its disposal (CPU, memory, bandwidth, or perhaps higher-level controls such as concurrency levels) to do its utmost to fulfill this goal, along with other goals that may dictate performance metrics for Gold or other service classes, along with other types of criteria that reflect reliability, security, or power consumption considerations. If the entity itself experiences changes in the environment or its

---

[1] While action policies are often used to specify behavior in systems, we do not consider them here because they directly dictate actions that are to be taken if the system is in a given state, typically without mentioning what is the goal or objective to be served by taking that action.

internal makeup, it will modify the control settings in an effort to continue satisfying the goal. Such forms of adaptation are the typical case and are discussed more fully in subsequent subsections. More rarely, the goal itself may be changed dynamically, which will result in adaptation even if the entity does not experience changes in the environment or in its internal makeup. There are two main scenarios under which the goals themselves might change:

1. The end user deliberately modifies one or more of the entity's goals.
2. Another entity in the system modifies the entity's goals (including the entity itself).

In either of these cases, a change to the goals themselves will typically require that the self-aware entity adjust the settings of various system controls in order to satisfy the new set of goals. Thus, the entity will adapt to the new goals, even if the entity itself and the environment in which it is situated remain unchanged.

One entity changing the goals of other entities in the system is itself an adaptive mechanism. If an entity finds it necessary to adapt for any reason, part of its adaptation repertoire may be to place new and different requirements on other entities upon which it depends, and in other words, to effectively modify those other entity's goals. Suppose, for example, that the environment changes in a way that affects only entity A, but not entity B. Entity B will therefore not display an inclination to change its controls in response to the environmental change, but if entity A modifies the demands it places upon B, then B may well change its controls in order to satisfy its new goals. Thus, B will be affected *indirectly* by the environmental change.

Now consider utility-function policies. Environmental or system changes will naturally induce an entity to modify its control settings in an effort to re-optimize the utility in the light of such changes. This form of adaptation will be discussed in more detail in later subsections. Here, we consider adaptation that occurs in response to modifications in the utility function itself. Just as was the case for goal policies, an end user may deliberately change the utility function directly, or else the utility function may be recomputed based upon the (changing) state of another entity's goal or utility function.

The Unity project at IBM Research [39] exemplifies how one utility function can be derived from another. In Unity, an application manager conveyed its resource needs to a resource allocation manager by transforming its utility function (expressed in terms of response time goals) to a utility function (expressed in terms of the number of servers that are made available to the application manager). In this scenario, changes in the environment, such as an increase or decrease in workload intensity, affected the transformation. Consequently, even if the response time utility function remained fixed, the derived resource utility was determined in part by the workload intensity. Regardless of what drove the change to a utility function, the change required adjustments in the control settings—just as was the case for goal policies.

A more subtle form of change in high-level goals occurs in the case of reinforcement learning. Tesauro [39] showed how reinforcement learning could be applied to the Unity example cited above to improve the long-term utility of the system.

Reinforcement learning entails learning a reward function and a policy based upon that reward function. If the system should operate at the same time that it is learning, the fact that the reward function is being learned (and is therefore evolving over time) means that the policy that maps from states to actions is also evolving, i.e., it is not constant over time. One could say that the system's behavior is being driven by an evolving policy (one that bears a lot of similarity to a utility-function policy), and therefore, under these circumstances the system's behavior may change even if the system itself and the environment are stable. (Of course, if the environment is truly stable, then learning may not proceed very well, as the system must experience different states in order to learn the reward function.)

12.2.2 Adapting to Changes in the System

There is also the chance of reacting to *changes in the system*, like the failure of a component. In a production scenario of, for instance, electronic consumer goods, individual quality variations among components and submodules could add up and compromise the total functionality. Using only high-quality/low-variance components makes the product much more expensive and one remedy could be to have intermediate steps of manual or automatic calibration and tuning in the assembly, but this may also add to the total production cost, and one would still need recalibration when components age and change their functionality/performance. An alternative could be to use automatic offset compensation and adaptivity in the design, which then would allow for a range of uncertainties (slowly), time-varying components or even for some malfunctioning submodules. The traditional alternative to adaptivity is to make a so-called robust design which does not need to change with varying components, but may on the other hand be conservative and suboptimal for several of the individual sets of components. The complexity of the control is there traded for performance and overall robustness versus sensitivity.

Finally, adapting to changes in the system may entail changing the algorithms used to achieve goals in view of the new system model. An example is when changes in the system cause certain parameters to become correlated. Hence, controlling these parameters separately (as might be good for separation of concerns) is no longer optimal. To illustrate, consider the data center of the reference scenario specified in Chap. 4, where multiple cooling elements uniformly cool all available space. The operator wants to minimize the total energy cost of cooling. In this case, the amount of energy expended on cooling a server depends only on server load and not server location. Now, imagine that one of the cooling elements fails. The physical space is no longer uniformly cooled. Areas previously cooled by the failed element are now harder to cool (i.e., require more energy to cool). Hence, load allocation now has to consider cooling efficiency. The load allocation algorithm needs to become aware of physical space, such that more load is allocated to servers in cooling-efficient parts of the data center. In other words, by virtue of the change in cooling efficiency resulting from a component failure, new coupling is created between load allocation and cooling that needs to be taken into account to continue to meet the energy-efficiency goal. An adaptation must occur to swap allocation algorithms.

12.2.3   Adapting to Changes in the Environment

As mentioned above, in the *environment-driven changes*, the changes of the evaluation run-time model drive the adaptation. A solution is determined to better fulfill the new evaluation run-time model.

An interesting example of that occurs in systems that must satisfy multiple requirements of different criticality, such as simultaneous requirements on safety and performance. Depending on the state of the environment, the system may choose to enforce a safety goal, a performance goal, or both. In some cases, these goals become at odds, in which case enforcement of one will override enforcement of the other. An adaptive action must be performed by the system in view of the perceived state of both the system and its environment to determine which goals to enforce. Said differently, an evaluation run-time model may exist for each requirement. A switch of models may occur dynamically, causing enforcement of one requirement to take precedence over that of another.

An example, in the context of software performance management, is when an adaptive agent recognizes an unexpected adverse interaction between itself and other adaptive agents, which prompts it to change its normal behavior to continue to attain its high-level goals (such interactions are discussed at more length in Sect. 5.2). To illustrate, consider a data processing agent in some distributed data stream processing workflow. A basic high-level goal of the agent could be to ensure progress such that processing is never stalled as long as more data exists upstream. A more refined operational goal could be to carry out the processing at an optimal level of local resource utilization, such that the agent is neither overloaded nor underutilized. Hence, this agent may exercise back-pressure by throttling the stream of incoming data when local resource utilization is too high and releave the back-pressure when utilization is low.

Ordinarily, the agent's action will regulate utilization around a desired level. In this case, the correlation between changes in back-pressure and resulting changes in utilization should be negative, indicating that the back-pressure is successful at changing utilization in the desired direction. Now assume the agent detects that the correlation between changes in back-pressure and subsequent changes in utilization has become *positive*. This is unusual because it means that decreasing back-pressure now *decreases* utilization rather than increasing it, and vice versa. It is also dangerous because it generates a self-reinforcing loop: Low utilization triggers a decrease in back-pressure by design, but such a decrease triggers further reduction in utilization according to the measured abnormal correlation (for a reason unknown to the agent). This loop may grind progress to a halt as utilization continues to drop in a self-reinforcing manner. The detected unusual condition in the environment (namely, the detected positive correlation between changes in back-pressure and resulting changes in utilization) can thus trigger a reprioritization of goals from optimizing utilization to attaining the presently endangered goal of merely ensuring progress. In the new operation mode, utilization feedback is disconnected, and back-pressure is reset to a fixed open-loop value that attains the progress goal although is suboptimal in terms of resource utilization. In this example, environmental conditions affected the selection of goals, triggering a switch in the run-time model of the system when attainment of higher-level goals (progress) was jeopardized by apparent malfunctions in mechanisms geared to optimize for lower-level goals (optimal utilization). Despite the goal not having changed, the run-time model incorporates the malfunctions and is able to cope with them to keep achieving the goal.

A version of the aforementioned scenario was reported in earlier literature [17], where the unusual positive correlation was triggered by interaction with the Linux anti-receive-livelock mechanism. Specifically, data was received from a network. When the received data rate was very high, the anti-receive-livelock mechanism would switch from interrupt-driven I/O to polling I/O. This switch would trigger a decrease in utilization. Clearly, responding to the decreased utilization by releaving back-pressure would be the wrong thing to do as such an action would only exacerbate the overload and drive the anti-receive-livelock to reduce utilization further. This is how a positive correlation between back-pressure reduction and utilization reduction was triggered. In the adaptive goal reprioritization solution described above, even though the data processing agent was unaware of the reason for the abnormal positive correlation, switching to an open-loop back-pressure scheme to ensure progress would break the vicious cycle and undo the adverse interaction [17]. A separate mechanism was designed to assess when to re-engage the evaluation run-time model geared at optimizing utilization, once progress has been preserved.

A closely related challenge is to ensure system robustness in the presence of software errors. This challenge is especially relevant to systems where different requirements (and thus, different components) have different criticality, as is common for instance in cyber-physical systems. Hence, different components may be validated to a different level of assurance. Errors may occur in less critical components but should not propagate and bring down the system. The most critical requirements in cyber-physical systems are the *safety* requirements. They ensure self-preservation. Violating safety requirements may cause user death or catastrophic physical failures. Subsets of the system that are instrumental to meeting the safety requirements are subjected to a much higher scrutiny in the design and development process and are certified to a higher degree of assurance. These subsets are usually minimal and represent a trusted core. Performance requirements are considered less critical. Often meeting these requirements requires a higher degree of optimization and hence is computationally more involved. Most of the overall system code may be dedicated to computing such value-added performance optimizations. Due to its lower degree of criticality, this code is not certified to the same assurance level as the trusted core and hence can be relatively less reliable. A key adaptation challenge in this context becomes: How to attain performance goals enforced by optimization algorithms that are less reliable (and hence may generate errors) while at the same time robustly guarantee meeting safety goals enforced by components that are intentionally simplified (and hence do not address performance). The answer lies in clever handover schemes between safety operation modes and performance modes (i.e., switching between different evaluation run-time models) depending on current state. This adaptation allows the system to attain performance goals most of the time, while ensuring overall robustness to unexpected failures, making sure that safety requirements are never violated.

To illustrate, consider an implanted smart pacemaker. A key performance requirement is that the pacemaker adapts to user activity. For example, when the user is exercising or is otherwise engaged in vigorous activity, the pacemaker should operate at an elevated rate to ensure a sufficient blood flow. This adaptation can be achieved using implanted accelerometers that measure motion. However, care should be taken to differentiate user motion from ambient motion. For example, heart rate should not be raised when a user is riding a bus on a bumpy road, just because the accelerometers are measuring a high level of motion. Complex signal processing schemes are required. Complexity breeds errors. Incorrect pacing was shown to possibly trigger dangerous conditions such as fibrillation (a potentially fatal condition) in recent work [18]. When onsets of such a condition are detected, the evaluation run-time model is switched to elevate safety over performance, reverting to a simple constant-rate pacing scheme, designed to restore a safe, but not necessarily optimal, heart rate. In this example, the system watches for the dangerous condition in the physical environment (i.e., user heart rate) and adaptively performs the safety override.

Other examples of similar automated overrides (switches in evaluation run-time models) include overrides in collision-avoidance systems in partially autonomous vehicles to prevent imminent collisions, overrides in intravenous fluid infusion pumps to prevent patient overdose (especially when infusing pain medications and sedatives), and thermal emergency overrides in common laptops to prevent physical damage to the processor. In each case, meeting a performance requirement (e.g., optimizing navigation progress, user comfort, or application execution) is adaptively switched for meeting a safety requirement (e.g., avoiding a vehicular collision, avoiding user overdose, or avoiding processor meltdown) when a conflict is detected between the two.

12.3 Adaptation Techniques

This section presents an overview of some of the techniques used to embed self-adaptation in a self-aware system. Among the most commonly used techniques, we survey control theory, machine learning, optimization and operations research, and Markov processes. Other prominent techniques that we do not cover in details are architectural models [16], reflection [25], event-based changes [8], fuzzy rules [44], case-based reasoning [32] and knowledge-based controllers [39].

12.3.1 Control Theory

Control theory in the last century developed a broad family of mathematically grounded techniques for designing objects that make industrial plants behave as expected [2]. These objects, named controllers or regulators, can provide formal guarantees about meeting target specifications, under precise assumptions on the operating conditions. A classical example is the antilock braking system (ABS) in modern vehicles, that detects the wheel lock condition and encapsulates a behavior of most efficient braking; by interpreting the driver's hard braking command, the system adjusts the braking force on the wheel(s) to keep them barely rolling and thereby achieve the highest friction force toward the ground as sliding wheels would decrease the braking force. ABS-brakes can further be utilized in a so-called electronic stability program (ESP) to improve the vehicle's stability under maneuvering. Information from the ABS combined with measurements from a gyroscopic sensor that detects that the direction taken by the car is not aligned with the one given by the steering wheel can distribute the braking on the different wheels so that the vehicle better follows the driver commands.

The presence of a controller already makes the system (composed by the entity to be controlled and the controller itself) self-adaptive in nature. The controller takes care of deciding how the adaptation is performed, by selecting one or more control variables (in the ABS example, the pressure applied to up to three of the wheels). The choice of the control variables depends on measured values of the current conditions of the plant (in the ABS/ESP example, the direction taken by the car), and therefore on the *self-awareness* that the system has about its current state.

Control theory is mainly divided in two broad fields: time-based control and event-based control. The choice often arises from the nature of the system to be controlled, the implementation aspects of the controller and the possibilities to measure and actuate. Whereas physical systems often can be (approximately) described by differential equations, for computing systems with periodic execution times discrete-time representations and difference equations seem to be more appropriate. Event-based modeling is a common formalism to represent these systems. For example, these can be individual arrivals of jobs to a Web server, hybrid systems with switches, sensors signaling when thresholds are passed, etc. While the theory regarding both analysis and design for continuous- and discrete-time systems is well-developed with strong tools available, the case for event-driven system often gets very complex even for low-order systems. However, it was shown in [1] that a simple threshold-based rule can outperform periodic control by a factor of three regarding either state variance or average event rate in a stochastic setting.

It should be noted that outside the control-theoretic community, "adaptation" is often used to describe/denote ordinary feedback control compensating for, e.g., external disturbances and systems which achieve desired set points and references also under unknown load conditions. This is typically solved by introducing so-called integral action on the error between desired and actual/measured levels. The notion of "adaptive control" is in this framework a particular class of feedback control systems, where explicit or implicit estimating of the underlying run-time model is made, and thereby, it influences the parameters (and possibly structure) of the control algorithm. Whereas integral action is a linear operator, adaptive control inherently results in nonlinear feedback control.

The nonlinear adaptation mechanism with respect to unknown or changing system parameters in an a priori defined structure (or a set of structures) could classify as self-aware with respect to this model. Observer techniques and control-theoretic methods for fault detection and isolation is also an example of re-evaluation of system models and corresponding parameters during operation and taking action based on changed performance.

Model-predictive control of non-minimum-phase systems is another example where self-awareness of the system properties and in particular the inevitable transient behavior "in the wrong direction" is important. Such system knowledge is crucial for correct evaluation of performance, where choices of cost function, prediction horizon, and sample-weightings are fundamental factors for successful compensation.

In the area of inference, either as a stand-alone service or as part of a bigger picture, feedback computing can also play a role. For example, Bayesian network inference have been wrapped into a feedback control loop, thereby creating a computational engine that is more aware of its goals (in the specific case, desired completion time) and environment (in the specific case, operating system, and host computer) [28, 33]. This idea has been demonstrated using both non-adaptive [28] and adaptive [33] feedback control techniques.

12.3.1.1   The Data Center Scenario

Time-based control theory has been used to ensure that a computing system would obtain a desired behavior, see for example [9]. Another problem that is related to the single entity is temperature control. In [36], a controller entirely designed with control-theoretic principles (equation-based) was proposed that decides to introduce some idle time in multiprocessor architecture to keep the temperature of the cores below or around a certain threshold. This was not novel, but the use of a pure control-theoretic model allowed to obtain better results with respect to previous contributions.

Timescales, workload, and granularity may influence the choice of modeling. Whereas the arrivals of different new jobs to a server system seem to be well modeled by a discrete-event system, a time periodic sampling may be beneficial for simplifying the model by looking at average behavior within a certain time span. For larger traffic and intensities, the individual events have a small contribution and the main behavior could be characterized by continuous-time flow models. As control and adaptivity most often is based on a process model, not only the action, but the algorithms may change structurally depending on workload conditions.

In the data center scenario described in [9], the use of threshold levels to trigger adjustments is a good example of event-based control, which in a straight forward way addresses and handles the issue of how fast to sample a system not to lose information and not to waste capacity. For increased workload the levels and, e.g., queue lengths quickly increase and then triggers actions via the thresholds. Control action is thus taken much more often than under low workload scenarios, without the need to explicitly change sample times.

12.3.2   Machine Learning

Machine learning can be used to achieve different goals and may also benefit from being adaptive or self-adaptive in order to reach those goals. On the one hand, machine learning algorithms typically have numerous (hyper-)parameters which require appropriate adjustment based on the given context. On the other hand, a system might want to learn about its own performance in order to improve itself over time. This requires the system to learn about its available actions and the corresponding impact of these actions on its own performance. In the following, we discuss both of these situations, where machine learning and self-adaptive as well as self-aware systems intersect.

12.3.2.1   Optimizing Parameters

Many algorithms, including machine learning algorithms, have one or more (hyper-)parameters that substantially impact how they perform. For example, evolutionary algorithms have parameters such as mutation probability, crossover probability, and winning probability [27]. Stochastic local search algorithms have parameters such as a noise step probability, a greedy step probability, and a restart parameter [29]. Reinforcement learning algorithms have parameters controlling their learning or exploration rate, where these parameters either can be constant during computation or can be adapted, which includes self-adaptation.

Evolutionary algorithms (EAs), in particular genetic algorithms (GAs), have the following key components. There is a fitness function f and a population of candidate solutions (or genomes). Selection, using f, decides which candidate solutions survive from the current generation to the next generation. EAs start out with an initial generation, typically randomly initialized. When it comes to their evolutionary operators, EAs vary somewhat. Considering GAs in particular, they typically employ the following two operators, working on a population of bitstrings. The mutation operator changes one candidate solution into another by flipping (changing 0 to 1 or 1 to 0) one or more bits. The crossover operator takes two candidate solutions (the so-called parents) as input, and outputs two different solutions (the so-called children). Generally, a child contains bits from both parents, and the parental bits not found in one child are found in the other child. These two operators, along with selection, are applied in an iterative fashion until a termination criterion is met.

We now consider GAs when applied to optimization problems and in particular optimization of multimodal functions. There are at least three challenges with traditional GAs related to optimization of multimodal functions. These problems, along with potential solutions, are as follows:

1. *Problem of convergence*: A traditional GA will typically convergence to one local optimum, which may not be a global optimum.
   Solution: Use niching (crowding) techniques, for example, generalized crowding [14] to find multiple local optima.
2. *Problem of parameter optimization*: Setting of a GA's parameters in order to optimize performance.
   Solution: Parameter-less or self-adaptive GAs, including self-adaptive generalized crowding [26].
3. *Problem of control*: Lack of control over typical GAs; feedback computing (i.e., feedback control techniques applied in the computer science and computer engineering settings) is not utilized.
   Solution: Integrate feedback computing with evolutionary algorithms [35].

We now discuss each of the above three problems and their corresponding solutions in some more detail.

Solutions to the problem of convergence: Crowding algorithms, which are focused on here, are one class of GAs. Crowding algorithms are focused on preserving diversity—or multiple niches—in the population of candidate solution. For this reason, they are better suited to optimizing multimodal functions than many traditional GAs. Crowding applies in the survival (or selection) stage of a GA and consists of these two phases. First, in the grouping phase, individuals are grouped (paired), often but not necessarily with their offspring, according to a similarity metric. Second, in the replacement (or competition) phase, for each group (pair), one or more winners are picked. The winner(s) remain in the population.

Many crowding algorithms exist, including deterministic crowding, probabilistic crowding, and generalized crowding. As an example, we now study probabilistic crowding. Assume, in probabilistic crowding, that a parent p competes against a child c for survival. Let p_c denote the probability that a child c replaces a parent p in the population. This is the replacement rule for probabilistic crowding: $p_c = f(c)/(f(c) + f(p))$.

Intuitively, the key point in crowding GAs is that competitions (selection) take place between individuals that are close in the search space. In other words, for two bitstrings their Hamming distance is small. This may seem like a minor difference from traditional GAs, but it has a dramatic impact on how the algorithm behaves. In crowding, individuals spread out in the search landscape–diversity is maintained to a larger extent than in traditional evolutionary algorithms. In other words, crowding prevents premature convergence by preserving population diversity through local competitions. Consequently, crowding GAs will often converge to multiple local (global?) optima. In addition, crowding GAs have simple and high-performance implementations, are useful in broad range of settings (including multiobjective and real-valued problems), and have proven useful in different application areas.

Solutions to the problem of parameter optimization: Self-adaptive techniques have been quite popular in evolutionary algorithms. In evolutionary algorithms, self-adaptation typically refers to parameters that "control the behavior of the algorithm" being coded as part of the genome. Thus, the parameters are undergoing the same evolutionary processes, driven by f, as the rest of the genome [26]. The generalized crowding GA (GCGA) builds on probabilistic crowding by introducing a scaling parameter. This scaling parameter ϕ determines the selection pressure in local competitions through a parametric rule $p_c(\phi)$ instead of simply p_c used in probabilistic crowding. However, how to optimize ϕ remains unclear. Adaptive methods, including self-adaptive generalized crowding, address this problem, giving improved optimization performance [26].

Solutions to the problem of control: Recently, the observation has been made that while self-adaptation can improve performance, it does not explicitly communicate the actual external objective or goal to a GA. Such external objective or goals are, on the other hand, important in self-aware systems—see Sect. 12.2. Consequently, the idea of introducing techniques from feedback control into evolutionary algorithms has emerged [35]. A concrete example of this integration is the use of feedback control to enable the GCGA to be better steered or controlled in terms of the number of local optima it computes. The number of local optima is provided as an external objective or goal to this feedback computing GA (FCGA), based on generalized crowding. This method of using feedback computing to control EAs, as demonstrated in the FCGA, has not previously been investigated within the evolutionary algorithms community.

12.3.2.2   Exploring Available Actions

In reinforcement learning, the algorithms try to explore possible actions and their corresponding impact on the performance and on the environment [37]. The main goal is to identify the trade-off between required resources and the achieved performance. In this case, resources include, among others, things such as processing power, consumed energy, required memory, or time to complete a task. Performance is measured as a feedback from the environment. It represents how well the system is able to achieve its goals or performs its given tasks. In reinforcement learning, this exploration of the available actions and their corresponding impact has to be performed only on the feedback available from the environment and its interpretation. This means there is no explicit correction of falsely interpreted feedback or suboptimal behavior [19]. An important problem hereby are the possible dynamics of the environment where the reinforcement learning approach is deployed. While these changes in the environment may be induced by others, they may also be the result of the performed action itself. There is a wide range of approaches in reinforcement learning, where Q-learning [43] and multiarmed bandit solvers [5] are only two examples.

Both approaches introduce various parameters which need to be tuned according to the preferences of the user as well as the application they are used for. In Q-learning, the learning rate defines the importance of the latest information to the system. Even-Dar and Mansour [10] discuss the relationship between the convergence rate to the optimal function and the learning rate in Q-learning. In multiarmed bandit problem solvers, the exploration rate describes the trade-off between exploration of new possibilities and the exploitation of already available information [3]. In addition, reinforcement learning uses a reward function that assigns a stochastic reward for each action in the corresponding state. A person operating a system employing a reinforcement learning algorithm with multiple, maybe even conflicting, objectives might want to tune the learning according to her of his preferences. Introducing a handle parameter in the reward function of a reinforcement learning algorithm allows to steer the learning according to ones preferences. An iterative approach can help to select this handle in order to allow equal exploration of the possible Pareto frontier [41].

12.3.2.3　The Data Center Scenario

In data centers, reinforcement learning is often employed to trade off power consumption and system performance optimally. Furthermore, reinforcement learning techniques are employed in order to allocate resources within data centers accordingly and in a resource and energy aware manner.

In order to optimize the utilization of data centers, Tesauro et al. [38] propose to combine a queuing theory approach with reinforcement learning. Here, an initial queuing model policy controls the system and its utilization. The reinforcement learning trains offline using the data collected during run-time and adapts the queuing model accordingly. Berral et al. [4] employ reinforcement learning to develop models of previous system behaviors. In addition to the optimization of the utilization of the data center, they also use this model to identify the best trade-off between power consumption and performance of the system in future situations.

When using virtualization techniques, one is able to integrate many physical machines into a pool of virtual resources which can be controlled in a central fashion. Reinforcement learning is applied to control resources management and decision making when coordinating multiple tasks with a high degree of dynamics. Yuan et al. [45] propose to use reinforcement learning to introduce energy awareness while controlling the resources of the data center. Similarly, Farahnakian et al. [11] use a consolidation approach among multiple virtual machines to conserve resources and energy during run-time within the data center.

12.3.3　Optimization and Operations Research

Optimization techniques are useful when the underlying system model is known to a sufficient degree of accuracy and when its inputs can be reasonably measured and predicted. Optimization nicely complements feedback control, which is more useful when uncertainty is present, motivating a "trial and error" approach, where adjustments are made that depend on how far the system currently is from desired behavior. Often optimization is used in conjunction with feedback control. Specifically, optimization is used as a feed-forward scheme that attempts to directly set parameters to what is believed to be their optimal values. Feedback is then used to make adjustments around these values in view of actual resulting performance.

It is often the case that an agent has multiple parameters that can be jointly varied. Each of the parameters produces a different effect on desired outputs. The joint setting of these parameters is an optimization problem. A key decision in formulating such optimization problems is to understand whether parameters are coupled (and hence must be jointly optimized) or not (and hence can be optimized separately). The performance advantages of optimizing the parameters jointly compared to optimizing them separately depend on the degree of coupling [31]. Since optimizing different subsystems separately has distinct advantages in terms of computational efficiency and separation of concerns, an adaptive agent might optimize different parameters separately by default, until it detects a mode of operation where coupling has increased, motivating a switch to a joint optimization regime.

Among the optimization-based techniques, one is driven by the operations research and called constraint solving [34]. Constraints are a means to declaratively describe large, particularly combinatorial, problems in the form of variables and constraints that must hold between them. Constraints solver, which employ ideas from artificial intelligence, symbolic computing, computational logic, and operations research, then allow deriving solutions for the problems formulated via variables and constraints. The algorithms employed for constraint solving can be based on combinations and search or algebraic and numeric methods as well as the combination of both. While the technique is very powerful and solvers exist for many problems, solving constraint problems can be time-consuming and in case of contradicting constraints the existence of a solution cannot be guaranteed.

Constraint solving can be employed for adaptation by encoding the current system and environment (in the form of a reflection run-time model) as well as possible adaptations (in the form of the change run-time model) and the higher-level goals (in the form of a evaluation run-time model) into a constraint problem. A constraint solver can then be employed to compute a solution that is optimal concerning the goal and possible adaptations. However, oftentimes the solver results in severe limitations that require that the encoding only approximate the goal fulfillment and adaptation options. The self-awareness comes in here from the fact that the constraint solver can reason over alternative solutions while taking also changing goals into account.

12.3.3.1 The Data Center Scenario

Several data center resource allocation problems can be cast as optimization problems. Examples include load allocation and data storage allocation [24]. The output of the optimizer prescribes settings of various actuators that attain agent goals.

We sketch here how a self-optimization of the deployment and resource allocation for a data center using a constraint solver can in principle be done:

- Encode possible configuration of the deployment, etc., as variables of a constraint problem.
- Encode additional constraints such as upper bounds on the resources to restrict the possible configurations for the deployment and assigned resources as constraints.
- Encode the additive utility function of the different applications running on the data center as a optimization function.
- Use the constraint solver to determine a solution in the permitted configuration space with maximal overall utility.

By repeatedly applying this scheme, the deployment and resource allocation will be optimized by always switching to the optimal configuration according to the constraint problem and its utility function.

The need to repeat the optimization step results from the fact that the application landscape running on the data center or the user load may change, and thus, the utility function and application characteristics encoded into the constraint problem change as well and therefore a different optimal solution exists.

However, there are some limitations of this approach that may be relevant:

- The approach only supports a static view on the configuration space without taking the likelihood of events such as node crashes into account. Therefore, the determined optima may be not very robust and changes may lead to temporarily rather bad configurations until the optimization counteracts a change.
- The efficient solving of the constraint problems usually only works for linear or quadratic optimizations functions. However, in many practical problems the utility functions may be much more complex and then either a longer run-time or a coarse-grained optimization has to be accepted.
- The solver does usually not take into account the old solution, and therefore, it searches the solution space globally. Oftentimes, this procedure results in many required changes to realize the new optima while a more local fix with nearly as good characteristics but less costs concerning the changes is not considered.

There is a subtle trade-off between searching a larger solution space (taken also more costly options in the change run-time model into account) and the quality of the solution. If there are frequent changes that trigger an adaptation and/or the realization costs for particular adaptation steps are high, it is worthwhile to consider limiting the solution space first and then step by step extend it until a solution can be found such that the computation of the solutions takes less time and involves less costly adaptation steps. However, as the most suitable step size and initial size of the solution space may vary depending on the situation, besides an adaptation engine working with fixed step size and initial size of the solution space also a meta-self-aware computing system may be envisioned where an additional adaptation layer on top of the basic adaptation engine steers these two parameters based on its observations of the underlying run-time models and constraint solver as well as their characteristics. In this example, the meta-self-awareness comes from the fact that the adaptation layer on top of the constraint solver can observe which parameter for the step size and the initial size of the solution space work well for which situation. It does so by measuring the average number of extension steps and adjust the parameters accordingly if this number seems to be unnecessary high (resp. the step size seems too small).

Another parameter for the meta-self-awareness may be the frequency with which the system is monitored. Using a stochastic model of the failure frequencies of the nodes, the monitoring frequency can be adjusted to ensure that the self-repair happens frequently enough to reach the availability goals while minimizing the required additional resources [40]. If the stochastic analysis run-time model is derived and reasoned about at run-time, this higher-level adaptation is also capable to handle if the availability goal is adjusted at run-time. Here, the meta-self-awareness comes from the fact that the adaptation layer on top of the monitoring can observe which monitoring frequency is sufficient by employing a stochastic analysis run-time model to achieve the availability goals and adjust the monitoring frequency accordingly.

12.4   Adaptation Evaluation

The problem of evaluating adaptation strategies is non-trivial. There are different methodologies for the evaluation that can be divided into two broad categories. On the one hand, one needs to test the adaptation strategy itself and check that it does the intended thing. In some cases, when control-theoretic approaches are used, a part of this is already done proving the properties of closed-loop systems, such as stability. However, this does not test the controller implementation. The second part is the verification of the adaptation strategy together with the system under control, to understand if the strategy can deliver the promised properties, and to which extent. This should be true, in general, but there might have been model discrepancies that have been overlooked during the design process; therefore, validation is needed despite the analytical guarantees given, for example, by the control theory.

Static analysis and verification techniques can be used to assess both the conformance of the adaptation strategy code to its intended behavior and the absence of numerical errors due to the specificity of different programming languages and execution environments.

There is a growing area of verification theories and tools focusing on real analysis and ordinary differential equations (ODEs). The most recent advancements include satisfiability modulo ODEs and hybrid model checking. The former can be used to verify if a system described by means of a set of ODEs can reach certain desirable (or undesirable) states, within a set finite accuracy [15]. In terms of scalability, satisfiability modulo theory (SMT) approaches over ODEs have been proven to scale up to hundreds of differential equations. Hybrid model checking is instead focused on the verification of properties for hybrid systems, which can in general be defined as finite automata equipped with variables that evolve continuously according to dynamical laws over time. These formalisms are, for example, useful to match different dynamical behavior of a system with its current configuration and can be valuable especially to study and verify switching controllers and the coexistence of discrete-event and equation-based ones. Current hybrid model checkers are usually limited to linear differential equations [13]. The adaptation strategy code usually relies on numerical routines. Using the primitives of general-purpose programming languages to develop complex numerical procedures introduces unavoidable source of uncertainties, including the common issues related to finite numerical precision of their implementations. Some tools (e.g., jpf-numeric) use model checking techniques to identify possible sources of numerical problems for programs implemented with general-purpose languages (e.g., Java) and produce counter examples helping the developer with reproducing and fixing the problems. Moreover, modern SMT tools can be used at compile time to verify the occurrence of numerical problems and automatically provide fixes guaranteeing the final results of the procedures to be correct up to a target precision [7]. When dealing with control-based adaptation strategy, there are techniques able to reduce quantization effects and numerical issues [23].

Once the adaptation strategy is verified alone, it is necessary to verify its implementation, together with the self-adaptive system. This can be done by means of extensive experiments, but the process can be supported by different tools. Each tool comes with its own drawback and guarantees.

For rigorous analysis, one can use tools like the scenario theory [6] to provide probabilistic guarantees on the behavior of the self-adaptive system together with the adaptation strategy. The performance evaluation can be formulated as a *chance constrained optimization problem* and an approximate solution can be obtained by means of the scenario theory. If this approach is taken, the performance of the software system can be guaranteed to be in specific bounds with a given probability. This, for example, allows for quantifying which is the probability that the proposed solution is fulfilling the service level agreements (SLAs) also in the case of failures or unexpected behaviors. This type of analysis requires performing an large number of experiments, varying many sources of randomness in the system, to cover potentially very many cases with the randomized experiments. It is advisable to use this tool when one needs formal guarantees that the implementation meets specific requirements in all the possible conditions and when it is not too costly to experiment with the production ready system. Other types of analysis are based on systematic testing. One common way to validate an adaptation strategy implementation and its system under control is to show statistical evidence, for example, using cumulative distribution functions, or via classical statistical hypothesis test, as done in [22].

Independently of the chosen tool, experiments must be properly designed. Among the various design directions, one needs to define the type of goals, i.e., functional or non-functional, the type of available measurements and how these measurements map to the goals, and objectives of the adaptation strategy. For example, one might be interested in evaluating different autoscalers in cloud systems, and one might have the objective of minimizing over- and under-provisioning of resources and provide probabilistic guarantees on the behavior of the different autoscalers [30].

12.5   Interaction of Different Adaptation Strategies

When multiple software components are present within a self-adaptive entity, each with its own feedback or adaptation mechanism, unexpected interactions between these components may arise that lead to performance degradation of the overall entity. In this section, we discuss examples of such interactions that can occur when the overall entity lacks self-awareness and hence lacks the means to identify the potential for bad interactions. While the section discusses entities composed of multiple coupled components, it is restricted to scenarios, where the components are encompassed within a single entity that can offer a single point of learning and control, and a single scope of self-awareness. This is as distinguished from interactions discussed in the next chapter that focus on multiple entities each with its own learning and control mechanisms and its own self-awareness scope. We first introduce interaction challenges that arise from lack of self-awareness and then present their solutions when the overall entity is aware of its component models and hence can anticipate and centrally resolve undesired interactions.

A particularly incidious form of component interactions is one that results in dynamic instability in the form of self-reinforcing loops. Such loops drive the overall entity away from the desired operating point and into an extreme that features significant performance degradation. Informally, software dynamics (in a control-theoretic sense) arise most often due to delays in response to stimuli. In an adaptive computing system, software components measure and react to various state variables such as latencies, timeouts, error rates (e.g., in communication), resource utilizations (e.g., in energy saving schemes), and event queues. The reactions are not instantaneous, which makes software vulnerable to stability problems if adaptation does not properly account for loop delay.

Software designers are very good at tuning individual components and feedback loops to ensure that they are stable. However, interactions among individually stable components may generate dynamical instability in the system. Consider a scenario where three software components are individually designed, tested, proven bug-free, then put together into one system (the self-adaptive entity), without complete system-wide self-awareness. In other words, the overall entity does not possess a model of all components and does not centrally reason about their joint behavior.

Assume that among other things that each component does: (i) component A measures variable x and affects y, (ii) component B measures variable y and affects z, and (iii) component C measures variable z and affects x. When only a subset of these components is present (or jointly tested), all is well. However, if in some configuration or software state all three components are activated, a *new feedback loop* arises, where x affects y, which affects z, which affects x again. In the absence of entity-wide self-awareness, this loop might not be explicitly considered, since it is a resulting property of the specific component combination and not a design problem with any of the individual components. It represents an unintended side effect of having these components together. Nevertheless, if that loop does not properly respect system dynamics (e.g., if it creates a positive feedback cycle), it may cause instability and degradation. Examples of such cases in real systems are presented below, together with solutions that rely on entity-wide self-awareness.

The first example reports a case where a flow control module caused instability and degraded performance in a certain run-time corner-case in a priority-based service, due to an interaction with the Linux kernel's receive anti-livelock mechanism. In this experiment, a server application was executed on top of Linux, serving incoming job requests of two different priorities over a network. High-priority requests were served first, followed by low-priority requests. When the low-priority queue grew large, a flow controller would exert back-pressure on the upstream workflow stage (of low-priority traffic). Conversely, when the queue was sufficiently depleted, the upstream stage would again be allowed to increase low-priority flow rate. The system mostly performed well. On some occasions, however, a sharp increase occurred in dropped high-priority requests. The high drop rate persisted even though the rate of high-priority requests alone should not have overloaded the system. Further investigation explained that anomalous high-priority drops were attributed to a feature of the NAPI Linux API (kernel 2.6) that prevents livelocks by resorting (for some period of time) to polling-based I/O instead of interrupt-driven I/O under heavy network workload. The shift to polling would disable network interrupts, leading to many dropped requests, and also reducing the utilization. As utilization and arrived requests dropped, the flow controller would consider it safe to ask the downstream workflow stage to increase the low-priority request rate. This would exacerbate the overload problem, leading to more drops. In control-theoretic terms, this is *positive feedback*. The root cause of the problem is the interaction between livelock protection and flow control, each of which contributes different arcs to complete one positive feedback loop. Namely, an increase in incoming low-priority request rate causes the anti-livelock mechanism to react in a way that reduces system utilization, which triggers the flow control mechanism to further increase low-priority request rate, making the problem worse. A solution to this problem relied on self-awareness, which (in this case) refers to understanding components' models within the entity, and monitoring to check that the behavior of each component is conformant with its model. For example, the component models may predict that (i) an increase in low-priority traffic should increase input queue size and (ii) increasing back-pressure upstream should decrease queue size (and vice versa). A run-time monitor should check that this is indeed the case. When a livelock occurs, run-time behavior may deviate from the model. Specifically, contrary to the model, once polling is activated, reducing the back-pressure upstream will result in decreased server queue size (due to packet increased drops at the interface resulting from polling-based I/O). The self-aware entity, having detected this deviation from its model of self, now has the opportunity to take a corrective action. For example, it can adapt by choosing to operate in an open-loop fashion with a safe fixed back-pressure set point for some period of time.

The second example is related to energy consumption. In a multiserver system, an excess of energy consumption was observed because of an adverse interaction between independently designed energy management policies. Imagine scaling up the previous example, such that the server in question is replaced by a set of identical service instances running on different processors. To save energy when load is low, let these processors be equipped with a dynamic voltage scaling (DVS) policy. Furthermore, let a load consolidation policy (that turns processors On/Off) be allowed to put processors to sleep when load is sufficiently below total capacity (consolidating the service on the remaining ones) and turn on processors when load exceeds capacity. In the implementation of this scenario, for some range of workloads, when either policy was used alone, energy savings were observed, but when the two were used together, the energy consumption actually *increased*. Analysis of system logs revealed the reason. The DVS policy, which ran at a higher rate, would check CPU utilization and decrease the processor frequency whenever the utilization was lower than a threshold. The consolidation policy, consequently finding the resulting measured machine utilization high, would turn on an extra processor and rebalance load, thus reducing utilization and causing the DVS policy to further decrease frequency. The cycle continued resulting in more processors turned-on than needed and hence in highly suboptimal energy consumption. The above illustrates the peril of integrating separately designed software components without correspondingly extending the scope to self-awareness, leading to missing possible interactions. In our example, the consolidation policy was designed with no knowledge of the DVS policy. Hence, improper interaction occurred. DVS reacted to lower processor load by reducing frequency and increasing utilization. Consolidation reacted to increased utilization by turning on more processors and reducing processor load, unnecessarily increasing energy consumption. A single self-aware system, on the other hand, would manage both consolidation and DVS as two mechanisms within a joint optimization framework and compute optimal settings for both jointly.

Let us now add to the example above a thermal management policy to prevent processor overheating. This scenario was observed in a machine room, where a number of servers were cooled by a single air-conditioning unit. We observed in the initial implementation that the consolidation algorithm appeared to malfunction when we turned off air-conditioning (i.e., when room temperature temporarily increased). Specifically, during normal operation, all assigned processors had comparable throughput. In one instance, however, when air-conditioning was turned off, we observed that the throughput of the system was unusually low, despite normal input load. The problem, as analysis revealed [21], was due to an interaction between consolidation and thermal management. The consolidation was designed to distribute incoming jobs across multiple worker processors according to their capacity. Capacity was computed dynamically as the ratio of assigned jobs to processor utilization. For example, if 5 jobs results in 50 % utilization, then capacity is $5/0.5 = 10$ jobs. As new jobs arrived, they were bin-packed to the smallest number of processors, after sorting the latter in decreasing capacity order. The consolidation policy did not account for thermal emergency management. In particular, when a processor overheated, it was temporarily put into a sleep mode by a thermal emergency management algorithm. The low utilization (due to sleep) on the machine where emergency management kicked-in caused the load balancer to incorrectly compute its capacity and assign more and more work to it in a futile attempt to increase its utilization. This effect continued until all load was redirected from other machines, causing the overheated machine to get severely overloaded while the remaining machines were turned off.

In general, system-level self-awareness implies that the system should use models that correctly account for its various behaviors. For example, the model for computing component capacity should account for the possibility that components may be asleep due to thermal management.

12.6 Conclusion

In this chapter, we have discussed how a single entity can adjust to fulfill higher-level objectives, using the self-awareness it has of its own status and of the external environment. To introduce the self-adaptation capabilities, we have considered what are the drivers that push a system toward adaptation: higher-level goals and changes in the system or in the environment. Subsequently, the chapter introduced some adaptation techniques. Clearly, many techniques are viable to design an adaptation strategy, but in this chapter, we focused on control theory, machine learning, and optimization. For each of the techniques, we have provided pointers to situations in which they were applied to the data center scenario described in Chap. 4.

The chapter also discussed how to evaluate existing adaptation strategies and eventually how to compare them with one another. Finally, we introduced the concept of multiple adaptation strategies in the same entity, leading the path to the more general problem of multiple and potentially conflicting strategies that will be treated in Chap. 13.

Acknowledgements This work was partially supported by the Swedish Research Council (VR) for the projects "Cloud Control" and "Power and temperature control for large-scale computing infrastructures," and through the LCCC Linnaeus and ELLIIT Excellence Centers.

References

1. Karl Johan Åström and Bo Bernhardsson. Comparison of Riemann and Lebesque sampling for first order stochastic systems. In *Proceedings of the 41st IEEE Conference on Decision and Control*, 2002.
2. Karl Johan Åström and Richard M. Murray. *Feedback systems: an introduction for scientists and engineers*. Princeton university press, 2010.
3. Peter Auer, Nicol Cesa-Bianchi, and Paul Fischer. Finite-time analysis of the multiarmed bandit problem. *Machine Learning*, 47(2-3):235–256, 2002.
4. Josep Ll. Berral, Íñigo Goiri, Ramón Nou, Ferran Julià, Jordi Guitart, Ricard Gavaldà, and Jordi Torres. Towards energy-aware scheduling in data centers using machine learning. In *Proceedings of the 1st International Conference on Energy-Efficient Computing and Networking*, e-Energy '10, pages 215–224, New York, NY, USA, 2010. ACM.
5. Donald A Berry and Bert Fristedt. *Bandit problems: sequential allocation of experiments (Monographs on statistics and applied probability)*. Springer, 1985.

6. Marco C. Campi, Simone Garatti, and Maria Prandini. The scenario approach for systems and control design. *Annual Reviews in Control*, 33(2):149–157, 2009.
7. Eva Darulova and Viktor Kuncak. Sound compilation of reals. In *Proceedings of the 41st ACM SIGPLAN-SIGACT Symposium on Principles of Programming Languages*, POPL '14, pages 235–248, New York, NY, USA, 2014. ACM.
8. Nicolás D'Ippolito. Synthesis of event-based controllers: A software engineering challenge. In *Proceedings of the 34th International Conference on Software Engineering*, pages 1547–1550. IEEE Press, 2012.
9. Xavier Dutreilh, Aurélien Moreau, Jacques Malenfant, Nicolas Rivierre, and Isis Truck. From data center resource allocation to control theory and back. In *Proceedings of the 2010 IEEE 3rd International Conference on Cloud Computing*, CLOUD '10, pages 410–417, Washington, DC, USA, 2010. IEEE Computer Society.
10. Eyal Even-Dar and Yishay Mansour. Learning rates for Q-learning. *Journal of Machine Learning Research*, 5:1–25, December 2004.
11. F. Farahnakian, P. Liljeberg, and J. Plosila. Energy-efficient virtual machines consolidation in cloud data centers using reinforcement learning. In *Parallel, Distributed and Network-Based Processing (PDP), 2014 22nd Euromicro International Conference on*, pages 500–507, Feb 2014.
12. Robert France and Bernhard Rumpe. Model-driven development of complex software: A research roadmap. In *2007 Future of Software Engineering*, FOSE '07, pages 37–54, Washington, DC, USA, 2007. IEEE Computer Society.
13. Martin Franzle and Christian Herde. HySAT: An efficient proof engine for bounded model checking of hybrid systems. *Formal Methods in System Design*, 30(3):179–198, 2007.
14. Severino F. Galán and Ole J. Mengshoel. Generalized crowding for genetic algorithms. In *Genetic and Evolutionary Computation Conference, GECCO 2010, Proceedings, Portland, Oregon, USA, July 7-11, 2010*, pages 775–782, 2010.
15. Sicun Gao, Soonho Kong, and E.M. Clarke. Satisfiability modulo ODEs. In *Formal Methods in Computer-Aided Design (FMCAD), 2013*, pages 105–112, Oct 2013.
16. David Garlan, Shang-Wen Cheng, An-Cheng Huang, Bradley Schmerl, and Peter Steenkiste. Rainbow: Architecture-based self-adaptation with reusable infrastructure. *Computer*, 37(10):46–54, October 2004.
17. Jin Heo and Tarek Abdelzaher. Adaptguard: Guarding adaptive systems from instability. In *Proceedings of the 6th International Conference on Autonomic Computing*, ICAC '09, pages 77–86, New York, NY, USA, 2009. ACM.
18. Zhihao Jiang and R. Mangharam. Modeling cardiac pacemaker malfunctions with the virtual heart model. In *Engineering in Medicine and Biology Society, EMBC, 2011 Annual International Conference of the IEEE*, pages 263–266, Aug 2011.
19. Leslie Pack Kaelbling, Michael L. Littman, and Andrew W. Moore. Reinforcement learning: a survey. *Journal of Artificial Intelligence Research*, 4:237–285, 1996.
20. Jeffrey O Kephart and William E Walsh. An artificial intelligence perspective on autonomic computing policies. In *Policies for Distributed Systems and Networks, 2004. POLICY 2004. Proceedings. Fifth IEEE International Workshop on*, pages 3–12. IEEE, 2004.
21. M.M.H. Khan, Jin Heo, Shen Li, and T. Abdelzaher. Understanding vicious cycles in server clusters. In *Distributed Computing Systems (ICDCS), 2011 31st International Conference on*, pages 645–654, June 2011.
22. Cristian Klein, Alessandro Vittorio Papadopoulos, Manfred Dellkrantz, Jonas Dürango, Martina Maggio, Karl-Erik Årzén, Francisco Hernández-Rodriguez, and Erik Elmroth. Improving cloud service resilience using brownout-aware load-balancing. In *Reliable Distributed Systems (SRDS), 2014 IEEE 33rd International Symposium on*, pages 31–40, Oct 2014.
23. Ian Doré Landau and Gianluca Zito. *Digital Control Systems: Design, Identification and Implementation*. Communications and Control Engineering. Springer-Verlag London, 2006.
24. Shen Li, Shaohan Hu, Raghu Ganti, Mudhakar Srivatsa, and Tarek Abdelzaher. Pyro: A spatial-temporal big-data storage system. In *2015 USENIX Annual Technical Conference (USENIX ATC 15)*, pages 97–109, Santa Clara, CA, July 2015. USENIX Association.

25. Pattie Maes. Concepts and experiments in computational reflection. In *Conference Proceedings on Object-oriented Programming Systems, Languages and Applications*, OOPSLA '87, pages 147–155, New York, NY, USA, 1987. ACM.
26. Ole J. Mengshoel, Severino F. Galán, and Antonio de Dios. Adaptive generalized crowding for genetic algorithms. *Inf. Sci.*, 258:140–159, 2014.
27. Ole J. Mengshoel and David E. Goldberg. The crowding approach to niching in genetic algorithms. *Evol. Comput.*, 16(3):315–354, September 2008.
28. Ole J. Mengshoel, Abe Ishihara, and Erik Reed. Reactive bayesian network computation using feedback control: An empirical study. In *Proceedings of the Ninth UAI Bayesian Modeling Applications Workshop, Catalina Island, United States, August 18, 2012*, pages 44–54, 2012.
29. Ole J. Mengshoel, Dan Roth, and David C. Wilkins. Portfolios in stochastic local search: Efficiently computing most probable explanations in bayesian networks. *J. Autom. Reasoning*, 46(2):103–160, 2011.
30. Alessandro Vittorio Papadopoulos, Ahmed Ali-Eldin, Karl-Erik Årzén, Johan Tordsson, and Erik Elmroth. PEAS: A performance evaluation framework for auto-scaling strategies in cloud applications. *ACM Transactions on Modeling and Performance Evaluation of Computing Systems*, 2016.
31. L. Parolini, B. Sinopoli, B.H. Krogh, and Zhikui Wang. A cyber-physical systems approach to data center modeling and control for energy efficiency. *Proceedings of the IEEE*, 100(1):254–268, Jan 2012.
32. Wenyi Qian, Xin Peng, Bihuan Chen, John Mylopoulos, Huanhuan Wang, and Wenyun Zhao. Rationalism with a dose of empiricism: Case-based reasoning for requirements-driven self-adaptation. In *Requirements Engineering Conference (RE), 2014 IEEE 22nd International*, pages 113–122, Aug 2014.
33. E. Reed, A. Ishihara, and O. Mengshoel. Adaptive control of bayesian network computation. In *Resilient Control Systems (ISRCS), 2012 5th International Symposium on*, pages 106–111, Aug 2012.
34. Francesca Rossi, Peter van Beek, and Toby Walsh. *Handbook of Constraint Programming (Foundations of Artificial Intelligence)*. Elsevier Science Inc., New York, NY, USA, 2006.
35. Jun Shi, Ole J. Mengshoel, and Dipan K. Pal. Feedback control for multi-modal optimization using genetic algorithms. In *Genetic and Evolutionary Computation Conference, GECCO '14, Vancouver, BC, Canada, July 12-16, 2014*, pages 839–846, 2014.
36. Filippo Sironi, Martina Maggio, Riccardo Cattaneo, Giovanni Francesco Del Nero, Donatella Sciuto, and Marco Domenico Santambrogio. ThermOS: System support for dynamic thermal management of chip multi-processors. In *Proceedings of the 22Nd International Conference on Parallel Architectures and Compilation Techniques*, PACT '13, pages 41–50, Piscataway, NJ, USA, 2013. IEEE Press.
37. Richard S. Sutton and Andrew G. Barto. *Introduction to Reinforcement Learning*. MIT Press, Cambridge, MA, USA, 1st edition, 1998.
38. G. Tesauro, N.K. Jong, R. Das, and M.N. Bennani. A hybrid reinforcement learning approach to autonomic resource allocation. In *Autonomic Computing, 2006. ICAC '06. IEEE International Conference on*, pages 65–73, June 2006.
39. Gerald Tesauro, Rajarshi Das, William E Walsh, and Jeffrey O Kephart. Utility-function-driven resource allocation in autonomic systems. In *null*, pages 342–343. IEEE, 2005.
40. Matthias Tichy and Holger Giese. A self-optimizing run-time architecture for configurable dependability of services. In Rogério de Lemos, Cristina Gacek, and Alexander Romanovsky, editors, *Architecting Dependable Systems II*, volume 3069 of *Lecture Notes in Computer Science*, pages 25–50. Springer Berlin Heidelberg, 2004.
41. K. Van Moffaert, T. Brys, A. Chandra, L. Esterle, P.R. Lewis, and A. Nowe. A novel adaptive weight selection algorithm for multi-objective multi-agent reinforcement learning. In *Neural Networks (IJCNN), 2014 International Joint Conference on*, pages 2306–2314, July 2014.
42. Thomas Vogel, Andreas Seibel, and Holger Giese. The role of models and megamodels at runtime. In *Proceedings of the 2010 International Conference on Models in Software Engineering*, MODELS'10, pages 224–238, Berlin, Heidelberg, 2011. Springer-Verlag.

43. Christopher J.C.H. Watkins and Peter Dayan. Q-learning. *Machine Learning*, 8(3-4):279–292, 1992.
44. R.R. Yager and L.A. Zadeh. *An Introduction to Fuzzy Logic Applications in Intelligent Systems*. The Springer International Series in Engineering and Computer Science. Springer US, 2012.
45. Jingling Yuan, Xing Jiang, Luo Zhong, and Hui Yu. Energy aware resource scheduling algorithm for data center using reinforcement learning. In *Intelligent Computation Technology and Automation (ICICTA), 2012 Fifth International Conference on*, pages 435–438, Jan 2012.

Chapter 13
Self-adaptation in Collective Self-aware Computing Systems

Jeffrey O. Kephart, Ada Diaconescu, Holger Giese, Anders Robertsson,
Tarek Abdelzaher, Peter Lewis, Antonio Filieri, Lukas Esterle
and Sylvain Frey

Abstract The goals of this chapter are to identify the challenges involved in self-adaptation (including learning and knowledge sharing) of multiple self-aware systems (or system collectives). We shall discuss the techniques available for dealing with the challenges identified (e.g., algorithms for conflict resolution, collective learning, and negotiation protocols), and which are appropriate given assumptions regarding the collective system architecture. We refer to notions of knowledge, learning, and adaptation; various self-awareness levels; and reference scenarios introduced in Chap. 4.

J.O. Kephart (✉)
IBM Thomas J Watson Research Center, 1101 Kitchawan Rd., Yorktown Heights,
NY 10598, USA
e-mail: kephart@us.ibm.com

A. Diaconescu
Telecom ParisTech, CNRS LTCI, Paris Saclay University, 46 Rue Barrault,
75013 Paris, France
e-mail: ada.diaconescu@telecom-paristech.fr

L. Esterle
Vienna University of Technology, Treitlstrasse 3, 1030 Vienna, Austria
e-mail: lukas.esterle@tuwien.ac.at

H. Giese
Hasso-Plattner-Institut für Softwaresystemtechnik GmbH,
Prof.-Dr.-Helmert-Str. 2-3, 14482 Potsdam, Germany
e-mail: holger.giese@hpi.de

A. Robertsson
Department of Automatic Control LTH, Lund University, SE-221 00, Lund, Sweden
e-mail: Anders.Robertsson@control.lth.se

T. Abdelzaher
Computer Science Department, University of Illinois at Urbana-Champaign,
201 N. Goodwin Ave, Urbana, IL 61801, USA
e-mail: zaher@illinois.edu

P. Lewis
School of Engineering and Applied Science, Aston University,
Birmingham B4 7ET, UK
e-mail: p.lewis@aston.ac.uk

© Springer International Publishing AG 2017   401
S. Kounev et al. (eds.), *Self-Aware Computing Systems*,
DOI 10.1007/978-3-319-47474-8_13

13.1 Introduction

Whereas Chap. 12 dealt with the issues of learning and adaptation by individual self-aware entities, the purpose of this chapter is to explore challenges, opportunities, and methods that arise in the context of learning and adaptation by collectives consisting of multiple self-aware entities. In other words, we treat the issues of learning, adaptation, and self-awareness at the system level. Nevertheless, we are interested in learning mechanisms at at least two levels of abstraction: in the individual systems, which compose the collective, and at the level of the collective itself. An important question concerns how the structure of distributed knowledge, and local learning and adaptation, can affect and give rise to global learning and adaptation behavior. We elaborate upon reference scenarios of Chap. 4 to explore issues of learning, adaptation, and self-awareness at the collective system level in both cooperative and competitive settings.

According to the terminology introduced in Chaps. 3 and 7, we focus on the collectives that are self-aware at the level of individual entities, and which may or may not be self-aware at the level of the collective itself. For the most part, we will assume that there is no entity responsible for coordinating or otherwise managing the collective as a whole in accordance with goals that are described at the level of the collective. In other words, imagine that the entities adapt using the techniques described in Chap. 12, with no conception of or regard for the existence of other adaptive entities in the system. However, in individual agents, the scope of adaptive or other behavior is clearly enabled or limited by its self-awareness. While this is true of the component members of the collective, it is also the case for the collective itself. When considering the case of collective adaptation therefore, two important questions arise: How does distributed self-awareness enable or limit the adaptation at the level of the collective? and, more precisely perhaps: How do different types (cf. Chap. 3) and organizations (cf. Chap. 7) of collective self-awareness impact on the collective adaptation?

Based on the more detailed concepts related to the collectives and self-aware collectives introduced in Chap. 7, we employ UML hierarchies and UML collaborations to denote the collectives of self-aware systems. We also broaden the scope of these concepts by *not* requiring that the direct communication must be present between

A. Filieri
Department of Computing, Imperial College London, 180 Queen's Gate,
London SW7 2AZ, UK
e-mail: a.filieri@imperial.ac.uk

L. Esterle
Department of Computer Engineering, Vienna University of Technology,
Treitlstrasse 3, 1040 Vienna, Austria

S. Frey
Computing and Communications Department,
Lancaster University, Lancaster LA1 4WA, UK
e-mail: s.frey@lancaster.ac.uk

the involved systems, and we only assume that we want to study the correlation (or anti-correlation) between the systems in the collective. These definitions follow the design taxonomy introduced in [36]. In addition, we distinguish the special case where the correlation observed between systems results from information sharing during runtime and thus is a form of *coupling*. Therefore, various additional cases can be covered, including local random behavior of systems in a collective with no coordination, direct forms of coordination of systems in a collective using messages, and indirect forms of coordination of systems in a collective based on stigmergy.

As detailed in Chap. 7, sometimes there is only a negligible correlation between systems at the considered level of abstraction, such that it is possible to consider the systems involved in the collective as independent. In such cases, the behavior of the collective at the considered level of abstraction is more or less the superposition of the behaviors of the separate systems, as long as certain constraints are fulfilled that guarantee that the coupling can be neglected. However, in cases where the design of the collective has to consider that some correlation (usually some coupling) occurs that is not negligible at the considered level of abstraction, this correlation may have either adverse effects, due to the correlation, that have to be mitigated, or expedient effects from which the collective behavior can benefit.

In line with Chap. 7, we will discuss the role that self-awareness and the related coordination has with respect to mitigating or exploiting the correlation between the systems of a collective. For this purpose, we will look into the elements of learning, reasoning, and acting processes making-up the LRA-loop, as per the definition of self-aware computing systems in Chap. 1. In particular, this will include discussions on how to mitigate or exploit the correlation by choosing the right design for the collectives concerning the self-awareness scope (see Chaps. 3 and 7) and coordination approach.

This chapter is structured as follows. Each of the next several sections deals with a general class of collective challenge or opportunity. The first subsection of each section describes one or more scenarios, several of which are the extensions of scenarios introduced in Chap. 4. The focus is upon behavioral phenomena that result from interactions among self-aware entities—many of which are undesirable, but some of which are desirable. In the second subsection of each section, we discuss the approaches that may be taken to cope with or eliminate undesirable phenomena. The third and final subsection discusses ways in which desirable collective phenomena might be encouraged and capitalized upon.

In the first few sections, we consider non-self-aware (or prereflective) collectives in which the entities are individually self-aware, but for which there is no awareness at the level of the collective, and for which no entity is aware of the self-awareness of other entities in the collective. First, in Sect. 13.2, we discuss the interactions among entities whose goals are not in direct conflict, and which act in ignorance of one another's goals, demonstrating the situations in which the actions undertaken to reach their individual goals are in conflict. In Sect. 13.3, we discuss the situations in which the goals among entities are in direct conflict, and in which the entities act in ignorance of or despite the goals of other entities. Next, in Sect. 13.4, we consider the collectives in which the individual entities learn, treating both the case in which they are unaware of one another's existence and, the opposite case, in which they know about (and take into account) one another's existence. Here, we explore the effects that can occur when multiple self-aware entities are all adapting to their environment and to one another simultaneously. Section 13.5 then treats the situations in which the entities coordinate deliberately with one another, either via centralized or decentralized techniques and either based on cooperation or competition relations (cf. Chap. 7). Finally, in Sect. 13.6, we summarize the chapter and make some general observations.

13.2 Actions

In this section, we consider the collectives in which the entities are only *locally* self-aware. That is, they possess an awareness of themselves, but they either do not recognize or otherwise do not account for the behavior, state, or self-awareness of other entities in the system. Additionally, we suppose that the individual goals that govern each individual entity's behavior are not inherently in conflict. Through a series of scenarios, we illustrate negative and positive global behaviors that may occur under such conditions. At the end of the section, we summarize our observations regarding these phenomena and the means that may be taken to ameliorate or eliminate the undesirable global behaviors, or to capitalize on the desirable ones.

13.2.1 Scenarios

We consider two domains in which the self-aware entities strive to realize goals that do not explicitly conflict, but for which the actions taken in service of those goals may cause unintended interactions that result in desirable or undesirable collective effects. First, we describe two scenarios from the cyber-physical system domain (cf. Sect. 4.5 of Chap. 4) involving smart appliances in a smart home. Second, we describe an IT scenario involving the self-aware sorting algorithm (cf. Sect. 4.3 of Chap. 4) plus a power manager.

13.2.1.1 Smart Appliances

Consider the interactions that could conceivably take place between a thermostat and a smart window. The thermostat aims to maintain room temperature within a targeted range, for instance between 21 and 23 °C, while consuming as little power as possible. In the same room, a smart window controller opens the window periodically to maintain the air freshness, and it also opens and closes the blinds to regulate room luminosity. The aforementioned behaviors are governed by the home owner's preferences, along with the environmental conditions (such as the weather and the presence of people in the home).

The goals of the thermostat and the smart window are not explicitly related, but nonetheless their actions can affect one another. For example, if the smart window is open on a cold day, the thermostat may struggle to maintain the targeted temperature; and even if it succeeds in doing so, the heater it controls may consume much more power than it would have had the window stayed shut. Similar issues may occur if the thermostat controls an air-conditioning device during summer months. For example, if the smart window controller opens the blinds on a sunny day to increase the luminosity, this could force the thermostat to choose between consuming extra power to attain the temperature goal, and deliberately falling short on the temperature goal in order to avoid the excessive power consumption. On the other hand, there may be other conditions under which the smart window and the thermostat unwittingly help one another accomplish their respective goals. For example, if the smart window opens the blinds to increase the luminosity on a cold sunny day, the open blinds may help warm the room, allowing the thermostat to attain its temperature goal with less effort than would have been required had the blinds been closed.

13.2.1.2 Adaptive Sorting and Power Management

Consider the adaptive sorting service introduced in Chap. 4, which strives to perform the sort as quickly as possible without exceeding a preset limit on the amount of CPU that should be used. It uses linear regression to adaptively estimate the number of CPU cycles required per basic sort operation, using observations over the last 5 min. Then, it sets the concurrency to a level that is calculated to keep the CPU usage in the neighborhood of 90 %. Consider as well the adaptive power management algorithm introduced in Chap. 12, embodied as a service. It allows a server to use power up to a predefined limit, above which it uses a feedback control mechanism to reduce the chip frequency to a value that is just below that limit.

When taken individually, the sorting service and the power manager are using reasonable approaches to controlling the system, ensuring that it operates efficiently and stably. Each goal is quite reasonably trying to achieve a balance between accomplishing work and reducing resource consumption. However, consider what may happen when the power management algorithm controls the server on which the sorting service is running. Suppose that the power manager detects a slight exceedance in the power and adjusts the chip speed downward. After the chip has been operating at a slower speed for a while, the sorting service will notice a decrease in the rate at which sorting operations are performed, and conclude that the number of operations required per sort has increased. To obtain more resource for sorting, the sorting service adjusts the concurrency level downward. With the decreased concurrency, there is less demand placed on the server, whereupon the power manager decides that it can raise the chip speed. The increased chip speed increases the rate at which the sorting operations are performed, causing a reversal of the logic that was used to decrease the concurrency, and the sorting service now increases the concurrency. This in turn may cause an exceedance of the power limit, beginning the cycle anew. A very related phenomenon was reported by Kephart et al. [22], who observed spon-

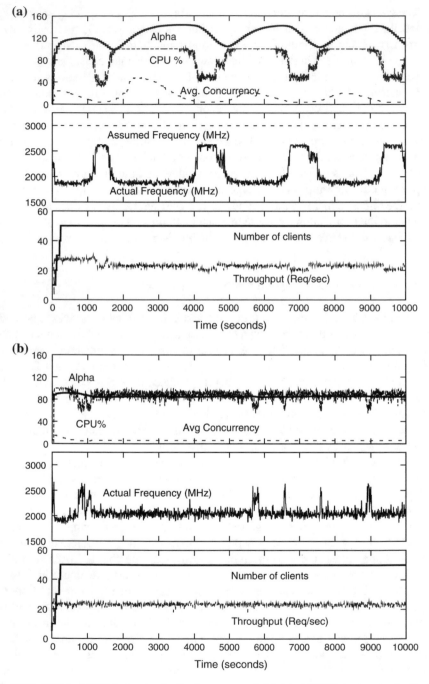

Fig. 13.1 Effect of CPU frequency feedback on system behavior. **a** WXD receives no feedback.
b WXD receives feedback

taneous oscillations generated by an unanticipated feedback loop between a power manager and a performance manager (illustrated in Fig. 13.1).

13.2.2 Mitigating Undesirable Collective Behaviors

The scenarios described in this section exhibited two basic classes of undesirable collective behavior that may occur when two or more self-aware entities attempt to satisfy the goals that are not inherently in conflict, but for which the actions taken in an effort to satisfy those goals may create inadvertent conflicts or misalignments that result in suboptimal behavior:

1. conflicting actions that waste resources and/or thwart attainment of one or more individual goals; and
2. spontaneous instabilities that waste resources and/or thwart attainment of one or more individual goals

We now examine each of these classes in turn, first diagnosing their cause and then (based on that diagnosis) proposing and critiquing various possible approaches to reducing or eliminating these undesirable collective behaviors.

The first class of behavior was exhibited in the scenario involving the thermostat and the smart window. Abstracting from the specifics of that scenario, it is apparent that such phenomena may occur when actions taken by one entity induce an environmental state change that affects the goal of another entity; i.e., the actions taken by the entities are coupled through the impact those actions have on the environment in which both are situated. In more mathematical terms, an action a_e taken by entity e causes the system state S to evolve to state S', and the difference between S and S' matters from the perspective of a second entity ε. In that particular example, when the smart window controller opens the blinds to increase the luminosity, the act of opening the blinds not just causes the luminosity to increase, but also has the side effect of causing the temperature to rise. To the thermostat, the increased luminosity is of no consequence that aspect of the difference between S and S' does not matter to it, but the increased temperature *does* matter, as the thermostat's goal concerns temperature.

The underlying cause of the conflict is that the smart window controller is unaware of two important facts: (a) Opening the blinds affects temperature and (b) the temperature affects the behavior of another adaptive entity. Note that the situation is asymmetric; i.e., the action taken by the thermostat to increase or decrease heating or cooling does *not* affect luminosity, the variable of interest to the smart window controller. Thus, the thermostat's lack of awareness of the existence of the smart window controller and its interest in the luminosity of the room does not contribute to the problem.

What can be done to mitigate this class of collective behavior? In general, an entity A whose actions create a state change that matters to some other entity B must first of all become aware of its impact upon B and second modify its behavior in some way that uses that awareness to reduce or eliminate the conflict. For the thermostat scenario, the smart window controller must somehow become aware that its actions affect the temperature and that temperature matters to some other adaptive entity in the system, and moreover, it must somehow change its behavior to take this new awareness into account.

Many general approaches can be contemplated, some of which we enumerate below. For clarity, all are expressed in terms of the thermostat/smart window scenario, but the generalization should be readily apparent:

1. **Joint control**. Anticipating that they will be used in conjunction with one another, a joint controller is designed to manage the behavior of the smart window and the thermostat (or perhaps the thermostat can be eliminated entirely). The user specifies joint luminosity and temperature goals, along with any trade-offs that may be needed. The joint controller can be situated in either appliance—in fact it could be designed into both, and if both the smart window and the thermostat happen to operate in the same room, then one of the joint controllers can voluntarily turn itself off and let the other take control. The joint controller can also be placed in a dedicated device, which monitors and inhibits other devices when their actions risk causing conflicts. From an architectural perspective, this approach corresponds to a *hierarchy pattern* where devices implement a *cooperation relation* with the joint controller (as discussed in Chap. 7). A valid criticism of this approach is that such conflicts may be difficult to envisage at design time because the heater and window operate a priori in different domains—temperature versus air freshness and luminosity, respectively. Similar issues may occur if an air-conditioning device is added in the summer, as the window may open the blinds on a sunny day to increase the luminosity, which in turn will also cause the temperature to rise.

2. **Distributed control with derived individual goals**. Anticipating that the smart window may be used in an environment where a thermostat is present, the smart window controller is designed to take into account data provided by the temperature sensors located in the room in which it operates. The user specifies joint luminosity and temperature goals, along with any trade-offs that may be needed. The joint goals are transformed into a set of derived goals or policies to be followed by the smart window controller, which if followed are expected to produce nearly the same behavior as would be exhibited by a joint controller. The smart window then operates according to these derived goals, which now take temperature into account. Since devices do not communicate with each other directly but only via their impacts on their joint environment (i.e., temperature), this case corresponds to a solution implementing a Stigmergy pattern (as discussed in Chap. 7). Also, with respect to the relation types identified in Chap. 7, systems implement a *synergy relation* with respect to their goals, since they have positive effects on each-other's goals yet without being explicitly aware of this. At the same time, systems implement ignorance relations with respect to their knowledge and actions, since they are unaware of each other and do not exchange

any direct information to coordinate their knowledge and actions; coordination is provided by-design instead.

3. **Distributed control based upon individual goals derived from global feedback**. The smart window controller is given access to temperature readings as a potentially interesting environmental variable and provided with moment-by-moment readings of a utility variable that indicates the degree to which the overall joint goal of luminosity plus temperature is satisfied. The smart window controller can then learn an association between its actions, the temperature, and the overall utility, and using that model can modify its behavior to try to maximize the joint utility. As in the case above, this corresponds to a Stigmergy pattern, since devices only react to each-other's actions indirectly, via feedback from the environment. The types of relations they implement are also similar to the previous case. The main difference consists in the increased adaptability (e.g., via learning) of this feedback-based case, with respect to the previous one where goals were hard-coded at design time.

4. **Changing one or both strategies**. In the smart home example, the thermostat may choose to achieve a temperature goal by opening the window shutters during a sunny winter day (hence heating by solar energy and saving energy for optimizing a power goal). This, in turn, may conflict with the window shutters' luminosity goal, which would require closing the shutters partially to avoid direct sunlight. If the thermostat chose to switch on its power instead, the conflict would be solved, or more precisely avoided. Such strategy adaptation can be performed either at design time, to avoid conflicts, or at runtime, when the conflict is detected automatically.

In general, the solutions discussed above can be implemented either at design time, when conflicts are being predicted, or during runtime, in cases where systems are able to detect conflicts dynamically (e.g., [20]) and adapt accordingly.

While joint control can certainly solve the problem of conflicting actions, it is impractical under many conditions. It can be extremely difficult for designers to anticipate all of the possible combinations of controllers that could be copresent in a given environment, and to anticipate the couplings that might occur. A more flexible, decentralized solution can be more suitable for unpredictable open environments, where both the initial execution context and the participating devices may change during runtime. Here as well, the levels and kinds of self-awareness that the devices require of each other (Chaps. 3 and 7) will depend on the extent to which device discovery and coordination can be predicted at design time. At the same time, while more decentralization and higher self-awareness capabilities increase the adaptability of devices and of the entire collective, it also increases the overall system complexity and raises several risks (e.g., more unpredictability or decreased performance). Ideally, design-time solutions should be provided to address the aspects that are known and unlikely to change, in order to ensure the desirable outcomes and stable behaviors—e.g., important in a smart home scenario; and self-adaptive solutions with various degrees of self-awareness should be provided to deal with unpredictable aspects—e.g., where a safe, yet perhaps non-optimal solution is better than system failure.

The second class of behavior, spontaneous oscillation, was exhibited in the sorting algorithm/power manager scenario. At a high level of abstraction, one can see that spontaneous oscillation has the same basic cause as the first class, except that the situation is now symmetric rather than asymmetric: Each of the entities induce an environmental state change that affects the goal of the other, thereby creating the potential for an infinite cycle. The environmental coupling in the sorting algorithm and power manager scenario occurs, not through a single-shared resource, but instead through two different environmental variables: The sorting algorithm inadvertently affects power consumption by adjusting concurrency, while the power manager inadvertently affects the computational speed by adjusting chip frequency. A system with such couplings could be modeled to a first degree of approximation as:

$$x'(t) = \alpha y(t)$$
$$y'(t) = \beta x(t), \tag{13.1}$$

from which one can derive $y''(t) = \alpha\beta y(t)$. When the product $\alpha\beta$ is negative (as it is in the case of the power manager and the sorting algorithm), $y(t)$ is sinusoidal; when it is positive, then the solution is a growing exponential (a positive feedback loop that runs amok until something in the system saturates).

For spontaneous oscillations that occur due to couplings to two different environmental variables, we offer the following set of mitigations:

1. **Breaking the feedback loop** by using any of the methods listed above for mitigating asymmetric resource conflicts, such as joint control or distributed control with derived individual goals. Note that applying such a mitigation to just one of the two couplings may suffice to break the feedback loop, but it may leave the system with the asymmetric goal conflict problem, resulting in suboptimal behavior. In such a case, the mitigation may be applied to the second coupling as well.

2. **Giving one or both of the entities knowledge of the variables through which their actions are coupled**, such that it can update its model appropriately. Such a method was employed by Kephart et al. [22] to eliminate the spontaneous oscillation shown in Fig. 13.1. Specifically, the power manager conveyed to the performance manager the chip frequency setting at which it was operating. With this information, the performance manager was able to change its model for the speed at which computations were being performed, enabling it to stop reacting too strongly when the chip frequency was changed. This simple change eliminated the oscillations entirely.

Another case of undesirable synchronization can occur when multiple entities within a collective react in the same way to the same stimuli detected in their shared environment. For instance, if all devices detect a power consumption peak (e.g., by monitoring the frequency of a shared micro-grid), then they may all react simultaneously to reduce their consumptions and to lower the overall load on the grid. This may in turn cause an abrupt fall in overall consumption and risk a blackout. If devices then detect this lack of consumption and start consuming, oscillations may occur and threaten the grid. Similarly, when all thermostats in a room react independently to temperature fluctuations, undesirable oscillations may also occur. Direct coordination may be employed for addressing this issue when dealing with relatively small numbers of devices. Alternatively, randomizing reactions to common events can also be employed when dealing with large-scale collectives. This latter solution has been used [1] for desynchronizing electric devices connected to a shared power grid, as discussed above.

13.2.3 *Capitalizing on Desirable Collective Behaviors*

In other scenarios, global synchronization can be a desirable property of a collective system, which can help achieve a global goal collectively. In such cases, system synchronization helps them achieve goals more efficiently. This is the case for instance in robot swarms where all robots self-synchronize their speeds, and/or their movement directions in order to better achieve some collective goal [33].

In addition, most cases of spontaneous synchronizations can be capitalized upon if some extra design and tuning are introduced to regulate their behaviors. Most often, some form of randomization that is proportional to the number of entities and dependent on the desired aggregated effect can be introduced to obtain lightweight, highly flexible and scalable self-adaptation solutions.

13.3 Reasoning and Goals

In this section, we consider the individual goals that drive the reasoning and subsequent actions of self-aware entities, and discuss the collective behaviors that arise. As in Sect. 13.2, we consider here collectives in which the entities are only *locally* self-aware; that is, they possess an awareness of themselves, but they either do not recognize or otherwise do not account for the behavior, state, or self-awareness of other entities in the system. In contrast to Sect. 13.2, however, here, we suppose that the individual goals that govern each individual entity's behavior are inherently in conflict, either overtly or indirectly through their mutual need for the same limited resource collective. This is because of the following: (i) individual components may themselves differ, for example, in terms of capabilities or resources; (ii) they may be in different locations, and hence be subject to different experiences; and (iii) the individual entities may have different domains, processes, accuracy, or levels of self-awareness. Therefore, learning, adaptation, and knowledge present will all vary between individuals in typical collective systems (e.g., [16, 31]). Through a series of scenarios, we illustrate negative and positive global behaviors that may occur under such conditions. At the end of the section, we summarize our observations regarding these phenomena and the means that may be taken to ameliorate or eliminate the undesirable global behaviors, or to capitalize on the desirable ones.

13.3.1 Scenarios

13.3.1.1 Heater Versus Air Conditioner

As a first, very simple example of direct goal conflicts, consider the case of two (misconfigured) appliances: a heater that aims to maintain temperature above $24\,°C$, and an air conditioner that aims to keep the temperature below $22\,°C$.[1] Several different behaviors might arise in such a situation:

1. If the heater and air conditioner are approximately equal in heating or cooling capacity, and if both operate continually, the system might stabilize at a temperature in between the two set points. Each would labor continually to achieve their goal, wasting enormous amounts of energy in the process.
2. If the heater and the air conditioner are substantially more powerful than the other appliance, and both operate continually, the temperature may stabilize at the set point of the more powerful appliance. As above, tremendous amounts of energy could be wasted in the process.
3. If the heater and air conditioner operate sporadically, each turning off when their set point is met, the system could oscillate: When the heater reaches its goal, it turns off for a while, allowing the air conditioner to start bringing the temperature down. If the air conditioner accomplishes its goal before the heater can turn on, it too will turn off. Then, when the heater turns on, it will once again warm the room—and so the cycle may continue indefinitely, wasting lots of energy. Even if the heater and air conditioner do not act quickly enough to completely reach their set points before the other appliance turns on, significant oscillation (and energy wastage) may occur.

Of course, if one of the appliances were to become aware of the other's goal, it could at least detect the conflict and warn the user about the conflict, in hopes that the user would then rectify the conflict by changing one of the goals.

13.3.1.2 Dishwasher Versus Oven

As a second example of direct conflicts among goals, consider interactions that might take place between a smart dishwasher and a smart self-cleaning oven. The dishes must be washed and the oven must be clean by 9 am, and furthermore, the cost of

---

[1] As ridiculous as it may sound, anecdotally such situations have been observed in industrial buildings, and one basic rule in doing energy audits is to check for this type of conflict.

electricity consumed by these appliances must be minimized. Due to a constraint on the total amount of power that may be consumed by the smart home, the oven (which consumes up to 3 kW) and the dishwasher (which consumes up to 2 kW) may not consume more than 4 kW in total for a period of longer than 5 min (i.e., there is a soft circuit breaker). Each appliance checks every 5 min to ensure that its power consumption is not causing the total power consumption for the house to exceed the limit. Suppose further that the cost of electricity is $0.20 for most of the day, but reduced to $0.10 between midnight and 6 am.

Now imagine that each appliance pursues its own objectives independently, ignorant of the goals (or even the existence) of the other appliance. In an effort to minimize the cost and ensure that their cleaning jobs are done before 9 am, both appliances might turn on automatically as soon as the rates go down, at midnight. After 5 min, each would sense that it is causing the total power to exceed the limit and voluntarily turn itself off. After waiting another 5 min, each would sense that the current power consumption of the house plus what they anticipate adding to that consumption would fall under the limit, and so each would turn itself on again. Five minutes later, each would discover that they are causing the limit to be exceeded again, whereupon each would turn itself off. This oscillatory cycle would continue for a while, until one or the other (probably the dishwasher) finally finishes its job, leaving the other to continue uninterrupted. Alternatively, if the warm-up time for each appliance is longer than 5 min, neither would ever finish their job. In any event, regardless of whether either or both finish cleaning, the continual cycling would potentially shorten the lifetime of both appliances, cause frequent exceedance of the power limit, and create instabilities in total power consumption that might be problematic for neighboring homes. The instability might even affect the electric grid as a whole. If similar smart appliances are installed in many homes throughout the grid, the common electric utility pricing policy (exacerbated further by a propensity for consumers to leave appliance goals at common factory settings) might trigger synchronized instabilities in smart homes throughout the grid.

On the other hand, one can also envision circumstances under which independently acting appliances might function efficiently with no explicit coordination. Suppose that the goals of the two appliances are exactly as described above, but a small bit of randomness is introduced into the algorithms used to realize those goals, such that the oven waits until 12:02 am to turn itself on, while the dishwasher waits until 12:04 am. Consider the dishwasher's perspective first. When the dishwasher wakes up and decides whether to turn itself on, it will decide not to do so, because the extra 2 kW that it will add will cause the total consumption to be too high. Thenceforth, at 5-min intervals, the dishwasher will check again and come to the same conclusion— until the oven finishes its job, at which point the dishwasher will find that it can turn itself on. From the oven's perspective, it will reconsider its state at 12:07 am and find that it is fine to stay on, as the total power consumption for the house remains below the limit (because the dishwasher has decided not to turn on). A similar thought experiment shows that even if the starting times for the two appliances are not randomized, randomizing the time intervals between decisions will also prevent disastrous synchronous power cycles. If some randomness is incorporated into the algorithms, one cannot predict which appliance will turn on first, but whichever one does so will stay on until finished, whereupon the second will turn itself on and then finish. This is an example of a beneficial spontaneous (or emergent) coordination that could occur among two (or even more) self-aware appliances that have no direct awareness of one another.

13.3.1.3 Community of Smart Houses Interacting with Electric Utility

As a third example, we shift our perspective a level up in scale from the smart home. Consider a multitude of smart homes, connected by a power grid owned by a utility that prices energy dynamically according to the supply and demand. Each smart home may have a power manager responsible for ensuring that the overall power consumption of each house does not exceed some limit. As illustrated in the previous scenarios, this may be accomplished by curtailing energy use by various appliances. Note that, in its effort to intelligently manage the consumption of power by household appliances, a smart home's power manager has a slight effect upon the overall demand within the grid and that its level of demand for power in turn affects prices in the grid. Since all homes see and can respond to the same price at the same time, prices and power consumption across all of the homes in the grid are coupled to one another, and one can therefore envision a variety of dynamics that include oscillations in price (price cycles) and power consumption.

As a crude approximation to this coupling, imagine that the aggregate demand for power p is approximately inversely related to the price of power π, while the price π is linearly related to the aggregate power consumption p, i.e.,

$$p'(t) = -\alpha\pi(t)$$
$$\pi'(t) = \beta p(t), \tag{13.2}$$

One can readily see that Eq. 13.2 is essentially identical to Eq. 13.1 and therefore capable of exhibiting the same cyclical dynamics. Such cycles in price and power consumption may hurt both consumers and the electricity provider, as they introduce extra uncertainty into prediction (and therefore planning).

13.3.2 Mitigating Undesirable Collective Behaviors

The heater versus air conditioner scenario exemplifies direct goal conflicts that can result in considerable waste of resources or even spontaneous instabilities in system behavior. Recovering from such a situation requires that the goal conflicts be detected and then resolved in some way. One method by which self-aware entities could recognize that they are involved in a goal conflict with one or more other entities is to recognize that they are consistently failing to meet objectives, and advertise this fact to other entities in the system, along with some information about the variables or metrics that are not behaving according to the expectations. Upon receiving such information, other self-aware entities could check the variables and/or metrics that are most relevant to their function. If there is overlap, the overlapping goals or metrics could be exposed to a human user of the system, or else to some automated authority operating within the system. Once alerted to the conflict, a user may then specify additional goals or preferences that resolve the conflict. One approach to resolving such conflicts is to prioritize some goals higher than others. Another approach is to define a utility function that maps the state (as defined by all of the metrics that matter to the user) to a scalar, in which the system goal is to reach a feasible state that maximizes the utility subject to any constraints that might also be specified. Determining how a self-aware system might exploit models of itself and its environment to elicit additional goals and preferences that suffice to resolve detected conflicts is a worthy research challenge [28, 30].

In the smart homes and power grid scenario, the periodic oscillations in the price and the usage of electric power result from a cause similar to that which drove the spontaneous oscillations in the sorting algorithm and power manager scenario of Sect. 13.2.1. In that case, the sorting algorithm and the power manager each induced an environmental state change that affected the goal of the other. Here, the smart homes each adjust their power consumption in reaction to the electricity price set by the utility, while the utility adjusts its price in response to the aggregate power consumption of the smart homes. All of the mitigation mechanisms discussed in Sect. 13.2.2 apply here. Since the smart homes are a collective rather than a single individual entity, some additional mitigations are possible. For example, the smart homes might collaborate with one another via negotiation or some other mechanism to coordinate with other homes to make the overall consumption more inherently stable, thereby making the prices more stable, which in turn results in less susceptibility to consumption oscillations. Flexible houses with consumption reduction and/or storage capabilities might anticipate peak prices and deliberately consume less energy at times when other households are demanding more, resulting in more stability and lower overall payments to the utility. Houses that are less flexible in their energy consumption might still contribute to scheduling by advertising their consumption predictions, thereby enabling the more flexible houses to schedule their power consumption to avoid oscillations.

In the dishwasher and oven scenario, we also observed spontaneous oscillations. However, the underlying cause is of a different nature, and therefore, the mitigation strategies are necessarily different. The environmental coupling in the sorting algorithm and power manager scenario occurs through two different environmental variables: The sorting algorithm inadvertently affects the power consumption by adjusting concurrency, while the power manager inadvertently affects the computational speed by adjusting a chip frequency. However, in the case of the dishwasher and oven, there is a single environmental variable through which their actions are coupled—a shared resource of which there is a limited supply, electric power.

This situation is closely related to *computational ecosystems*, large-scale, distributed, decentralized computing systems composed of agents that each require a specific type of resource for their operation. Each agent uses exactly one resource at any given moment in time, and asynchronously and independently reconsiders which to use, based upon an expected payoff that depends on their belief about the current usage of that resource by other agents. An agent's belief about the current usage of each resource may not be entirely correct, due to the inherent uncertainty and/or time delays. Kephart et al. [26, 27] showed that in the limit of large numbers of agents, the dynamics of resource consumption in computational ecosystems could be modeled as a differential-delay equation. If the uncertainty is sufficiently large and/or the delay is sufficiently low, the solution to the differential-delay equation is damped oscillations that settle to a fixed equilibrium, but for small uncertainty and/or large delays, the solution may be persistent oscillations, possibly quite complex—even chaotic—in nature. The dishwasher–oven scenario involves only two agents, and for that case, the electricity consumption is best modeled as a difference equation, but the principles and the dynamics are very similar.

For spontaneous oscillations that arise from constraints on shared resources, some possible approaches to stabilizing the system include the following:

1. **Introducing randomness into the actions of the entities**. For computational ecosystems, Kephart et al. [26] showed that introducing randomness into the decision about which resource to use (modeled as softening the decision function for choosing a resource as a function of the usage of all resources) could eliminate oscillations at the expense of shifting the stable operating point to one that is less optimal globally.

2. **Introducing heterogeneity into the goals of the entities**. For computational ecosystems, Kephart et al. [26] also showed that if the agents' resource needs are heterogeneous, then the ecosystem as a whole is much less vulnerable to spontaneous instability; in effect, the agents settle into different niches. Such a strategy is only possible in situations in which the goals of the individual agents may be controllable by a system designer. As above, if this causes the goals to differ from those really intended by the designer, then this greater stability is achieved at the cost of suboptimal behavior.

3. **Reducing information delays**. Since this type of spontaneous instability arises from a differential-delay equation, and the susceptibility to such instability tends to increase with the delay, stability can be restored by reducing the delays in information regarding resource usage (if it is possible to do so).

4. **Endowing entities with an awareness of other entities, and some ability to approximately predict their behavior**. For computational ecosystems in which some of the entities are able to predict the behavior of other entities (or at least the collective behavior of the system as a whole), Kephart et al. [23, 27] showed that the overall behavior may improve provided that the proportion of predictive agents is small. However, the collective behavior can become even more unstable (and strongly suboptimal) if too large a proportion try to predict the collective behavior of the system and act on that basis.

5. **Introducing a resource broker to resolve resource conflicts**. If entities cannot resolve the resource conflicts cooperatively, one or more resource brokers can

be charged with governing resource usage in the system. Rather than each entity placing a direct demand on resource usage, they submit requests to a resource broker that describe the extent to which they need resource, and the broker decides how much resource to allocate to each such entity. Walsh et al. [38] described a system that allocated compute resources, in which each of several application managers could send to a resource broker utility functions describing the value they would realize if they were to as a function of the amount of resource that they might be granted by that broker, and the broker determined the resource allocation by maximizing a (perhaps weighted) sum of utility functions.

13.3.3 Capitalizing Upon Desirable Collective Behaviors

The scenarios of this section focussed exclusively on undesirable collective effects that may occur when multiple self-aware adaptive entities pursue their own goals without considering adaptive goal-driven behavior by other entities operating within the same environment. However, there are conditions under which no serious conflicts will emerge among the goals pursued independently by the self-aware entities. For example, resource conflicts will not emerge if resources are relatively plentiful. If goals do not explicitly conflict, and the actions undertaken to realize those goals do not result in unanticipated couplings, then they may be pursued independently without negative consequences. In such a situation, the system as a whole benefits from the individual adaptive goal-driven behaviors of the individual self-aware entities from which it is composed, as no explicit coordination is needed.

13.4 Learning

A defining characteristic of self-aware entities is that they learn models of themselves and/or the environment in which they are situated, and use these models to reason about what actions to take so as to best realize their goals. Consider for example the various self-aware entities that have appeared in scenarios described in this chapter: smart appliances of various kinds, or a house power manager, or a grid power manager. In all of these cases, and quite generally, default design-time settings cannot encompass the full variability of situations in which an agent will find itself during its lifespan. Moreover, it is often the case that system goals will only be provided by a user at runtime; i.e., they are inherently not predictable by the system designer—and therefore, some sort of learning will be required in order to determine a sequence of actions or behaviors that best realizes the system's goals. Yet another motivation for endowing self-aware entities with an ability to learn is so that they can avoid suboptimal or unstable behaviors resulting from conflicts among actions or goals (as described in Sects. 13.2.2 and 13.3.2). In short, for many different reasons, learning is a must.

A variety of learning mechanisms are described in detail in Chap. 12. The purpose of this section is to explore the impact that learning by multiple individual self-aware entities may have upon the behavior of a collection of self-aware entities that are learning models of themselves and their environments. When multiple self-aware entities are situated within an environment, they typically interact with one another—either directly, or indirectly through the impact their actions have upon the environment. In effect, they form part of one another's environment. Therefore—for better or for worse—whether or not the entities are explicitly aware of one another's existence, their learning algorithms may respond to one another's behavior.

In Sects. 13.2 and 13.3, we considered collectives in which the entities are only *locally* self-aware; that is, they possess an awareness of themselves, but they either did not recognize or they did not otherwise account for the behavior, state, or self-awareness of other entities in the system. In this section, we first treat learning self-aware entities with such limited awareness of other entities, and then, we extend our treatment to agents that are aware of the existence of other self-aware entities, and (in some cases) aware of the fact that those other self-aware entities are learning. While it is possible in some situations to contemplate approaches that model the entire collective as a single learning problem, we give centralized approaches very little consideration here, as they require a global system view [4], which is typically not available to local components. One can approximate a centralized approach in a decentralized setting through the use of joint-action learning [5], but such techniques require strong assumptions about the cooperative nature of the learning problem, or observability of others' actions.

Through a series of scenarios, we shall illustrate negative and positive global behaviors that may occur when agents learn both for the case where they are not directly aware of other self-aware entities and for the case where they are directly aware of other self-aware entities. In either case, very interesting dynamics can be created in systems where agents try to learn simultaneously, as they create moving targets for one another. Several interesting questions arise in this context:

1. How do individual learning strategies of agents influence the environment in which they are situated?
2. Conversely, how should the fact that an individual self-aware entity is a member of a collective affect the choice of learning strategies for that entity?
3. Overall, how does the scope of awareness affect this individual-collective interplay?

At the end of the section, we summarize our observations regarding these phenomena and the means that may be taken to ameliorate or eliminate the undesirable global behaviors, or to capitalize on the desirable ones.[2]

---

[2]It is worth noting in passing that data privacy is a very real issue in systems of self-aware learning agents. With sufficient monitoring accuracy and long enough observation periods, accurate models of user activities can be learnt and exploited for commercial and non-commercial purposes. In the same way, search engines and social media can intrude in the private life of their users, and power utilities would be able to reconstruct their user's life patterns and habits, their usual presence at home and absence periods, the nature and type of their electrical appliances, their usage of these

13.4.1   Scenarios

For our learning scenarios, we extend the smart home scenarios of Sects. 13.2 and 13.3 at three levels: smart appliances, smart homes, and multiple smart homes connected to a smart grid.

13.4.1.1   Smart Appliances

Here, we extend the smart appliance scenarios of Sects. 13.2 and 13.3 to include learning, and explore some issues that may result.

Consider a set of smart appliances operating within a smart home, which may include thermostats and windows in each room, an oven, a dishwasher, and one or more batteries. Each entity is equipped with algorithms and compute resources required for building long-term models. Depending upon the nature of the learning algorithms and the availability of data, such models may range from very elementary to very sophisticated in terms of their complexity and predictive power. For example, a smart thermostat might attempt to learn the temperature preferences and habits of the human occupants of the rooms (perhaps even keyed to each individual). It might further try to learn mappings between the external temperature and the time and effort needed to cool or heat the room. It might even try to augment its models of external temperature by contacting a service to obtain weather forecasts.

The other appliances could exhibit the same broad range in modeling sophistication and awareness of one another's existence and capacity for adapting and learning. A smart dishwasher might learn the consumption patterns of other appliances and schedule its own washing cycles at times when the house's total consumption is expected to be low; a smart battery might learn and anticipate dynamic price variations on energy markets to schedule its load phases to times when prices are low and unload phases when prices are high.

There is also a wide variation in the degree to which the appliances could be aware of one another's existence, and might attempt to develop models of one another's behavior or intent. For example, a smart thermostat that is aware of the existence of other thermostats in other rooms might incorporate into its model the fact that the temperature of the room it is controlling will be affected by not just the external temperature, but also the temperature of neighboring rooms in the house. Given this realization, it would be sensible for the smart thermostat to request from the other thermostats' current temperature readings from nearby rooms. Such information

---

(Footnote 2 continued)

appliances, and down to very specific details such as the multimedia contents they are watching—reconstructed via specific consumption patterns, for instance, of a TV set playing a particular movie. Therefore, the question of the scope of learning—which agents learn about which others and under which conditions—and of the dissemination of the produced knowledge is becoming a critical privacy and security matter. This privacy risk related to the development of self-aware systems must be understood from the earliest design phases. However, as this chapter is concerned with dynamical behaviors, we shall not pursue these important issues further here.

would be useful for both adjusting the demands the smart thermostat places upon the heating or cooling system, but also as data that could be used to adapt its model of how the room temperature depends on the external temperature, the temperatures of nearby rooms, and the heating or cooling effort that it demands. Suppose further that the thermostat is aware of the other thermostats, not just as entities capable of reporting temperature, but as controllers of temperature. Then, it might request not just the current temperature, but also the anticipated demand that the other thermostats intend to place on the house's cooling or heating system.

An even more sophisticated thermostat might try to learn the models employed by the other thermostats by associating reported temperatures with the reported heating or cooling demand, and use this information to anticipate how the other thermostats might respond to its own actions. A yet more sophisticated thermostat might understand that the other thermostats are themselves adaptive and therefore take into account that the models they employ are potentially dynamic. The thermostat might even take into account that its own adaptivity might be anticipated by other thermostats that possess a similarly high scope of awareness, and indeed, this can in principle be taken to an infinite level of regress: "I know that A and B know that I know that they know that I know that .... they adapt and learn."

Self-aware entities that learn are potentially vulnerable to all of the potential pitfalls that have been described in Sects. 13.2 and 13.3. For example, the aggregate demand that thermostats, window controllers, smart ovens, smart dishwashers, and smart batteries place upon electricity consumption may exceed a limit imposed by the user or the utility company, resulting in the resource conflict described in Sect. 13.3. All of the same mitigations described in Sect. 13.3.2 may apply. Of particular relevance is the mitigation strategy according to which entities are endowed with an awareness of other entities and an ability to predict their behavior, as behavior prediction could be based upon a learned model. Another particularly relevant mitigation strategy is the one that introduces a resource broker. In the case of a smart home, the resource broker could be a power usage scheduler that takes into account the power requests from the various self-aware entities (which are derived from the user preferences) and performs some sort of optimization to determine how much and when each appliance may consume power.

Consider what might happen under such circumstances when one or more of the smart appliances have the capacity to learn about the typical daily power consumption profile and reschedule their consumption during low-consumption periods. A typical domestic consumption profile might exhibit peaks in the morning when residents wake up and start their activities, at lunch time, and primarily at night when domestic appliances are used intensively for utilitarian or recreational purposes. In principle, this could enable the smart appliance to optimize its use of power, and if many or all of the smart appliances learn, then the home as a whole could operate very efficiently.

However, one can also contemplate scenarios in which learning by one or more smart appliances has undesirable consequences. To take a specific example, the dishwasher agent might well discover through (via reinforcement learning, for example) that its performance is optimized when it over-reports its consumption needs to a house manager that allocates electric power to the various appliances. Other appliances that are more honest about their electricity needs may suffer, and so may the inhabitants too if they find that the dishes are always washed whenever they want, but the room temperature is often too hot or too cold, and the oven is hardly ever cleaned. In other words, an imbalance in which a single smart appliance learns to optimize its own performance may end up violating global objectives that express trade-offs among tasks performed by the various appliances. Suppose further that one or more smart thermostats and a smart self-cleaning oven also learn that over-reporting their demands secures enough power for them to optimize their performance. Then, these and the other appliances will benefit at the expense of others that do not learn—just so long as their total demand for power does not exceed the limit. However, if all of the appliances learn to over-report their demands—or enough do so that the aggregated demand for power exceeds the limit—then it is easy to imagine that a disastrous form of coevolutionary learning [32] could occur. As each appliance ratchets up its resource estimate in an effort to grab more resource for itself, the other appliances must do so as well, resulting in a never-ending arms race, a destructive feedback loop that makes it impossible for the house's power manager to really know the actual resource requirements. Under such circumstances, the house's power manager might itself learn that the appliances are all lying to it and try to develop its own models of their actual needs based upon their record of actual consumption—and in effect become a central controller that largely or completely ignores the requests made to it by the smart appliances.

Note that the arms race described above could happen without the appliances being aware of one anothers' existence; they would merely be adjusting their actions to maximize their own reward. Now, consider what might happen if self-aware entities were to become aware of one another's existence, without trying to deliberately model one anothers' behavior. A scenario such as this was explored by Kephart and Tesauro [29] in the context of two selling agents (pricebots) that use Q-learning to learn pricing policies that govern the price they should charge for a commodity as a function of the price charged by the other selling agent. The policies did not embody a prediction of the other agent's price; it merely expressed the price that a seller should charge given the other's observed price. The dynamics in this case were surprising. Under some conditions, the pricing policies converged to a well-defined symmetric pair. Under other conditions, they appeared to converge to an asymmetric pair of pricing policies, but when viewed at long timescales these policies proved to be unstable—shifting abruptly to a new pair of policies. One can imagine similar behaviors being exhibited by smart appliances that formulate policies governing how much resource to demand as a function of how much has been requested by other appliances.

Now, consider the case where agents *do* attempt to model one anothers' behaviors [4]. They could do this by observing one anothers' actions, often in response to their own. In some cases, tagging agents according to their type or their membership in a social group may help, as it enables agents to cluster observations about other agents and thereby potentially reduce the time required to learn models of other agents' behavior. Being able to simulate the likely actions of other agents in the system has the potential to let agents anticipate and potentially avoid oscillations or other unfortunate dynamical collective behaviors. For example, the symmetric price policies learned by the two competing Q-learning pricebots studied by Kephart and Tesauro [29] resulted in pricing dynamics with much shorter (and higher-priced) price war cycles than the naïve policy achieved without learning, resulting in a higher profit for both sellers. As another example, Kephart et al. [23, 27] studied computational ecosystems into which some agents were "smart"; i.e., they were endowed with the ability to predict the resource consumption decisions of other agents. Such predictive capabilities could be based upon reinforcement or other forms of learning. The smart agents experienced gains in utility for themselves and even sometimes for the agents whose behavior they were predicting. However, when too many of the agents in the system became smart, the system dynamics changed in such a way that the smart agents could no longer predict them, and the resource usage of the system became highly unstable and inefficient.

The field of game theory provides another family of techniques that self-aware entities may use to learn the behavior of other self-aware entities. In fictitious play, agents use the historical frequency of actions taken by other agents as a model for their behavior and play their best (possibly randomized) strategy against that distribution. Detailed descriptions of NIR and NER and algorithms that exhibit these properties can be found in many references [10, 21]; the basic idea is to use the observed frequency of other agents' actions to converge to a policy (a mapping from an opponent's action to an agent's response to that action) that minimizes the regret that one would feel in hindsight. Depending on the details of the game (the payoffs received by the agents under all possible joint actions), and the details of the learning algorithms, the policies of the players may evolve to various forms of game-theoretic equilibria, such as a Nash equilibrium or correlated equilibria. However, convergence to an equilibrium is not guaranteed. Jafari and Greenwald [21] observed that in the game of "rock, paper, scissors," two agents use a no-regret learning algorithm introduced by Hart and Mas-Colell [19] cycle indefinitely among the various strategies of "rock", "paper" and "scissors", and yet interestingly, the frequency of their play averaged over time does achieve the Nash equilibrium, in which each strategy is played 1/3 of the time. A similar phenomenon was observed by Greenwald and Kephart [17] who studied a probabilistic pricebot scenario in which between two and five seller agents used NER and NIR algorithms to adapt their pricing strategies. The seller agents did not always settle into a stable mixed (probabilistic) strategy, but their long-term empirical frequency of play did coincide with a Nash equilibrium. In some instances, a very long-term period of stability would end spontaneously, and after a very brief transition period, the system would settle into a new Nash equilibrium.

An alternative, less explored approach to self-aware collective learning and adaptation is through the sharing and aggregating of knowledge about global state and progress toward goals. Furthermore, collective adaptation could include adaptation of the architecture of the collective itself, such as to support and optimize such knowledge sharing. A promising direction could be to integrate self-organization mechanisms (e.g., [9]) in order to support such knowledge sharing. Indeed, as agents in a collective learn new architectures based on their self-awareness, more suitable architectures may facilitate more effective collective learning and self-adaptation.

As a final note, it is worth pointing out that the timescale on which learning occurs is typically a good deal slower than that on which operational decisions are made and actions taken. For example, the pricing policies that are learned by Q-learning [29] or by no-regret algorithms [17] evolve on a timescale that is 3 to 6 orders of magnitude slower than the scale on which prices are reconsidered. Therefore, while oscillations can occur both for actions and for the policies that govern those actions, and they may even share similar mathematical bases at some level of abstraction, they are so different in timescale that the shifts in policy can often be too slow to be coupled with the actions themselves.

13.4.1.2   Smart Home

It is also worth considering one or more self-aware entities that could operate at the level of the smart home as a whole. One such entity was already introduced in Sect. 13.4.1.1: a power manager responsible for managing the total power consumption by all of the appliances and other electrical equipment in the house. One can draw an analogy between the power manager and mitigation strategy #5 introduced in Sect. 13.3.2, which entails introducing a resource broker to stabilize systems that are prone to spontaneous oscillation. In this analogy, the various smart appliances could play the role of application managers that each appeal to the power manager for resource. In scenarios where the smart appliances discover that they can increase their resource allocation by exaggerating their resource needs, the power manager might benefit from learning the mapping from an appliance's requests to their actual consumption. It is not clear a priori whether this practice would improve the stability and efficiency, or worsen it. Another form of learning that a power manager might exhibit would be to learn the trade-offs among the various functions provided by the appliances, which could be interpreted as weights on their individual utility functions. While one might think that such weights could be provided explicitly, in practice it is difficult for people to provide them, and therefore, the power manager would more likely have to infer the weights from observations of human behavior.

Another key role that a power manager for the smart home would play is that of an economic software agent that makes purchasing decisions that determine how much power there is to divide among the smart appliances. For this purpose, the power manager could employ various learning mechanisms to build models of the environment in which it is situated, which includes other smart houses in the district, the global behavior of the city grid, and the local and regional weather. Such models would enable the house power manager to predict the consumption patterns in the house and in the local grid with better accuracy. Of special importance in this context would be learning mechanisms that enable the power manager to function competently as an economic player. Each smart home's power manager could then be seen as one economic player among an entire economy consisting of all of the smart homes plus the utility (smart grid). From various works on multi-agent learning in economic systems that have already been referred to in this section [17, 29], it is clear that there is a rich set of dynamical phenomena that can be exhibited in this context.

A few additional observations are worth making here. First, in a related scenario, the power manager might be expanded in scope to be a smart home manager that makes intelligent trade-offs among power consumption, various notions of comfort, and other attributes that matter to the home's occupants. Second, learned models not just are useful for making minute-by-minute decisions about resource allocation, but can also be valuable for making informed decisions about long-term investments, such as more energy storage capacities (batteries), local energy generators (such as solar panels), replacing existing appliances with more efficient versions (e.g., more energy-efficient water heaters or air conditioners or washing machines), or even providing advice to users on their usage patterns (thereby helping the human end user more self-aware with regard to the energy consumption).

13.4.1.3 Smart Grid

At the level of the smart grid as a whole, the self-aware entities could include myriad smart home managers and a resource manager that represents the utility. Having already discussed in the previous scenario the issue of economic learning by the smart home managers, it suffices here to discuss what forms of learning might be valuable to incorporate into the utility resource manager. The utility resource manager might benefit from learning collective generation (e.g., via solar panels) and consumption patterns through their interactions with the smart home managers. Knowledge of the weather, vacation times, and special events that may have a noticeable impact on aggregate demand can help energy providers to provision their capabilities accordingly, on a day-to-day basis. Learning such patterns is also key to anticipating the long-term evolution of the grid, in terms of required production and storage capabilities, and to fine-tune the fair tariffs according to offer and demand. Such global models become key economical and political decision support tools regarding the development of grid infrastructures.

Many of the previously cited advantages and pitfalls of learning in an environment in which other self-aware entities are simultaneously learning apply in the smart grid context as well. One possible form of oscillation that might occur was described in Sect. 13.3.1 (see Eq. 13.2), in which electricity prices and consumption fluctuate at the level of the grid as a whole. Note that this oscillation occurs in the actions; given the observations reported above for Q-learning [29] and no-regret algorithms [17] applied to economically motivated software agents, it may be possible to observe oscillations in the pricing policies themselves, at a much slower timescale. Just as a smart appliance might learn to do a better job of satisfying its individual goal by over-reporting its resource need to the smart home manager, so might the smart home managers try to game the utility resource manager or the other smart home managers by behaving in ways that misrepresent their true needs and interests. In scenarios such as this, one reasonable approach is to create coordination mechanisms that make it difficult or even impossible for smart home managers to game the system. The design of incentive-compatible auctions (such as Vickrey or second-price auctions [37]), which encourage bidders to honestly report their valuations for a good, is motivated by such a goal.

13.4.2   Mitigating Undesirable Collective Behaviors

As has been illustrated several times in this section, learning can be both a cure and a cause of undesirable collective behaviors in self-aware systems. Sometimes, a learning mechanism can be both at the same time curing a problem at one level and introducing a new problem at another, somewhat akin to the infamous efforts of the Cat in the Hat and a succession of Little Cats to get rid of a pink bathtub ring in The Cat in the Hat Comes Back [13] by employing progressively more aggressive methods that only serve to exacerbate the original problem.

In the smart appliances scenario, learning can help appliances to improve their ability to behave in accordance with human preferences, but it can also lead to an arms race in which each appliance tries to grab more resource for itself by overestimating its resource needs. The arms race can occur whether or not the appliances are unaware of one another's existence. This arms race bears some resemblance the resource conflict described in Sect. 13.3, resulting from constraints on shared resources. An important difference is that whereas the resource conflicts of Sect. 13.3 resulted in direction actions by the contending entities to grab resource, in the case described in this section, the actions taken to acquire more resource were more subtle and indirect, since the resource allocations were mediated through the resource broker instead of being obtained directly from the resource. Even more importantly, the dynamics of the system change on a slower timescale, because alterations in the amount of resource requested from the broker are due to learning, and such learning would typically require several resource allocation cycles.

Differences in directness and timescale notwithstanding, some of the mitigation techniques introduced in Sect. 13.3 may still be applied to learning agents. The first two approaches (randomness and heterogeneity) are still applicable in many situations, but of course they still suffer from the drawback that while they may stabilize the system, the equilibrium to which they stabilize is typically suboptimal. The third option, reducing information delays, is potentially of interest, but it is not immediately clear how to apply it in a situation where the unstable dynamics are generated at least as much by the learning process itself as they are by the resource usage. It is conceivable that given that the timescale on which information propagates through the system can profoundly affect the dynamics of that system, such slowing down of the system dynamics from the timescale on which actions take place to the timescale on which policies governing those actions evolve may help reduce or prevent over-reactions and oscillations, but more research would be required to determine whether or not this is the case. The fifth option, introducing a resource broker, appears not to be available as a mitigation in the smart appliances scenario because a resource broker has already been introduced into that scenario.

The fourth option (endowing agents with an awareness of one another, and an ability to predict one anothers' actions) bears more discussion, as it was also discussed as one variant of the smart appliances scenario. In the example of the Q-learning pricebots [29], simultaneous multi-agent learning can result in action policies that converge to an equilibrium, but it can also lead to pseudo-convergence that is punctuated by brief episodes of transition among different near-equilibria that, while less optimal than would be obtained by a benevolent dictator, are still preferable to the case where the agents act in ignorance of one another. However, as noted previously [23, 27], in some cases, efforts to endow agents with awareness of other agents' behavior can succeed only if a sufficiently small proportion of agents possess this awareness. As was discussed in Sect. 13.4.1.1, game-theoretic approaches involving fictitious play or learning algorithms based upon no external regret or no internal regret show some promise, as they can result in convergence to Nash or other game-theoretic equilibria, at least in a time-averaged sense.

In addition to the mitigation strategies discussed in Sect. 13.3.2, another option for avoiding or mitigating undesirable collective behaviors in systems of self-aware learning agents is to introduce mechanisms used in economies to coordinate the actions of self-interested entities, of which auctions are a prime example. Incentive-compatible auction designs (such as Vickrey, or second-price mechanisms) [37] have the potential to eliminate the learning and resource allocation dynamics because they encourage agents to be honest about their resource needs. Such mechanisms are conceptually similar to the idea of using a resource broker to coordinate the actions of multiple self-aware entities, except that they are explicitly designed to handle the systems of self-interested agents, whereas the resource broker concept is inherently designed for cooperative systems in which agents honestly report their resource needs. In a properly designed auction, agents are not just *assumed* to be honest; they are *compelled* to be honest out of self-interest. Auctions are attractive in that they strike a good balance between centralized coordination (which is essentially the joint control mitigation introduced in Sect. 13.2) and independent action by self-aware agents. The number of different auctions' types available to system designers is enormous, ranging at least into the thousands [39], and the mechanisms can become quite complex when agents require multiple types of resource to accomplish their tasks (see various works on combinatorial auctions [35]. Fortunately, there has been some research on how a system designer can translate overall system goals into auction mechanisms that best achieve them [6].

13.4.3   Capitalizing on Desirable Collective Behaviors

A system consisting of self-aware entities that can adapt, learn, and interact with one another without suffering deleterious emergent effects such as those described in Sect. 13.4.1 can exhibit a number of very desirable system-level properties. One important advantage that manifests itself at both design time and runtime is modularity, and the flexibility and evolvability that stem from it. Rather than having to build systems containing predetermined, fixed sets of agents, and controllers designed specifically for that fixed set, one can design each entity individually and be confident that it will settle into the system alongside the other entities that cohabit the same environment, and discover and use the agents, services, or other resources that it needs to satisfy its goals. These qualities enable one to build self-aware systems and applications from self-aware components that were designed before the systems or applications were conceived. At runtime, these capabilities translate into autonomic [25], or self-managing capabilities such as self-configurability, self-healing, self-optimization, and self-protection.

To the extent that the various mitigations discussed in Sect. 13.4.2 prevent or at least reduce suboptimal and/or unstable collective behavior, they enable these natural desirable collective behaviors of self-aware systems to shine through. Several examples of desirable collective phenomena were illustrated in Sect. 13.4.1 alongside the undesirable behaviors, including evolution to Nash or other game-theoretic equilibria (at least in a time-averaged sense) by observing other agents' behaviors. As stated in Sect. 13.4.2, auctions appear to show considerable process as a mechanism that can support favorable collective behaviors, and indeed, the use of economic mechanisms in general seems particularly appropriate and suitable for very large-scale systems, although on the other hand simulations of price war and related behaviors in information economies suggest that economic approaches are not a panacea [24].

13.5 Advanced Coordination with Mutual Awareness

Thus far in this chapter, we have considered scenarios in which adaptive entities within the system learn, reason, and act independently of one another, with various levels of mutual awareness. In this section, we shift our focus to the systems of adaptive entities that learn, reason, and/or act in an explicitly coordinated fashion. While it is not the only rationale, one important reason for coordination is that it can avoid or mitigate undesirable collective behaviors such as those described earlier in this chapter. For example, recall that the following forms of coordination have been introduced earlier in this chapter as methods for mitigating various types of undesirable collective behavior in the adaptive systems:

- Technique 1 (joint control), which was suggested in Sect. 13.2.2 as a means for mitigating the problem of independent controllers taking actions that waste resources and thwart attainment of individual goals;
- Technique 5 (resource broker), which was suggested in Sect. 13.3.2 as a means for mitigating spontaneous oscillations that might arise from constraints on shared resources; and
- Auctions and other economic mechanisms, which were suggested in Sect. 13.4.2 as a means for mitigating undesirable collective behaviors in systems of self-aware learning agents.

This section is organized as follows. First, we illustrate various forms of coordination and resultant collective adaptive behaviors through two scenarios: extensions of the familiar smart home and power grid scenario, and the autonomous shuttle scenario of Chap. 4, which exemplifies large-scale but inherently cooperative adaptive systems. Then, in the second and final subsection, we discuss the pros and cons of these various techniques for achieving system-level adaptation through coordination.

13.5.1 Scenarios

13.5.1.1   Smart Home and Smart Grid

Consider variants of the smart home and power grid scenario in which the entities comprising the system explicitly coordinate with one another [11, 12].

At the level of smart appliances within a single home, appliances (such as a smart window and thermostat) might coordinate their actions with one another through a variety of means. They could submit information about their goals (and perhaps their state) to a central authority such as a joint controller to act on their behalf (as in Technique 1 of Sect. 13.2.2). Another approach is for them to communicate their resource needs to a resource broker (Technique 5 of Sect. 13.3.2), and the resource broker could then provide either an instantaneous power allocation or a power allocation schedule to each appliance. A third approach that avoids a central authority is for the entities to exchange information regarding their proposed actions and perhaps their goals to one another, and to engage in some sort of bilateral or multilateral negotiation [18] to determine which actions (e.g., window opening times and thermostat heating periods that maximize their respective efficiencies while minimizing the negative impacts (for instance, avoiding the window to open during cold weather while the heater is just beginning a heating cycle). In the same vein, the smart oven and dishwasher—and other electrical appliances—can use coordination in one form or another to implement a sophisticated scheduling algorithm taking into account complex constraints on their respective schedules (the dishes have to be cleaned before deadline D, and the oven must run its cleaning cycle for M minutes during the evening, considering that the 7 pm–9 pm slot is reserved for potential cooking on the stove, etc.). When the trade-offs are necessary—for instance, heating must be reduced so as not to exceed a power consumption limit—minimal sacrifices (such as letting the temperature drop more in the living room and the study) can be identified and chosen.

Laws and social norms that encourage or restrict certain types of individual behavior constitute another type of coordination mechanism that can enable a collective to adapt in ways that promote the goals of the collective as a whole. The deviation of Nash equilibria from solutions that maximize societal welfare is a well-known phenomenon in game theory, exhibited in the well-known Tragedy of the Commons /cite-Hardin1968 (in which villagers are compelled through self-interest to overgraze the commons even though they know it will hurt the whole village) and the Prisoner's

Dilemma /citeAxelrod1984. If the villagers in the Tragedy of the Commons scenario were governed by a central authority, that authority could compute a societally better plan, such as rationing the commons equitably among villagers. Similarly, if the prisoners in the Prisoner's Dilemma were permitted to communicate with one another, they could each compute the joint action that maximizes their joint welfare and negotiate an agreement whereby each will execute their contribution to that optimal joint action (which in this case is for both to cooperate). Of course, for this to work they would have to be subject to some authority that either forces or strongly encourages them to hold to their agreement. In the smart home scenario, norms governing power consumption scheduling could resolve resource contention by giving essential appliances (e.g., medical ones) priority over less important ones used for cooking or entertainment. These norms could either be built into the appliances, or they could be enforced by a smart home controller or resource broker.

At the level of the power grid as a whole, smart home managers might use other coordination mechanisms to determine power allocations for individual homes. Since the situation is inherently competitive across different homes, the joint control method of Sect. 13.2.2 is not appropriate, nor is the resource broker as described in Sect. 13.3.2, as it requires that entities communicate their true goals (in the form of utility functions) to the resource broker. On the other hand, auctions and related market mechanisms (which were introduced in Sect. 13.4.2) are inherently suited to competitive situations. For example, suppose house A has planned visitors for the night and expects higher than usual consumption levels. A bid to reserve extra power that night could be placed in a local energy market and matched by a bid to provide power by another house B that has stored extra energy in its smart battery by collecting solar power during the day. Note that communicating bids to a central auctioneer is analogous to sharing utility functions with a resource broker, except that the former approach reveals far less information to competitors. Various forms of negotiation are also appropriate for competitive scenarios such as this.

Might social norms also work at the scale of a power grid? Possibly. For example, in a mutual-assistance smart city, some neighborhoods may adopt norm-oriented solutions to deal with the unpredictability of power production and consumption at a local level and over the long term. Smart houses could agree to offer overproduction to houses that lack power resources at a certain instant, in return for having the favor returned to them in the future, when the situation may be inverted. Such behavior could be regulated based on the mutually agreed norms, and negotiated and updated as needed by the smart houses and/or the users [8]. For instance, participants might agree to only share power when do not intend to use it, or to share overproduction whenever they do not need it for critical tasks. The agents can achieve advanced coordination by specifying and adapting the norms (as in the cited example), in an alternative to market-oriented approaches.

At the largest scales, however, it seems doubtful that social norms could support collective adaptation—but laws certainly could. For example, in the event of an energy shortage, it may be deemed more important for society as a whole to keep hospitals running at the expense of office buildings or sports stadiums. Laws enforcing such prioritization could be implemented by local governments and enforced either in smart devices that control power allocation, or through the more standard practice of threatening legal action against the violators.

13.5.1.2   Autonomous Shuttle Fleet

The autonomous shuttle scenario introduced in Chap. 4 exemplifies a large-scale, inherently cooperative system. In such a situation, coordination mechanisms may be introduced to improve the system's ability to learn, reason, or act.

For example, imagine that the individual shuttles within a fleet each sense aspects of their environment (such as track conditions [3] or traffic conditions) or themselves (such as the number of passengers who embarked or disembarked at each stop, or the remaining battery power), and share their measurements with other shuttles (which could be accomplished via peer-to-peer messages or through a central hub or authority). Sharing such information enables each member of the fleet (or a central authority acting on their behalf) to operate upon more accurate and up-to-date knowledge of system state, and to learn more accurate models of system behavior (cf. [14]).

Members of the fleet might also share with one another their goals (e.g., deadlines or schedules). Based upon this shared information, a central authority could compute an itinerary that optimizes some combination of energy and scheduling goals and constraints (such as avoiding collisions) [2, 15]. This could be thought of as an instance of the joint control method of Sect. 13.2.2 or the resource broker method of Sect. 13.3.2. In addition to avoiding the problems of resource contention and spontaneous oscillation to which the systems of uncoordinated and mutually unaware entities are vulnerable, these and other forms of coordination can avoid problems that arise in systems of entities that possess a high degree of mutual awareness, but whose individual incentives compel them to behave in ways that hurt the collective.

As an inherently cooperative systems, social norms are more likely to be an effective means for coordination than in large-scale competitive scenarios such as the power grid scenario above. For example, a protocol that clearly defines which shuttle has the right of way if two meet at an intersection promotes the societal goal of safe, collision-free operation by the shuttle fleet as a whole.

13.5.2   Coordinated Versus Distributed Adaptation

Much of this chapter has been devoted to cataloging collective behaviors that may ensue when individual entities adapt without awareness of or consideration for actions or goals of other adaptive entities within the system. We have outlined various approaches that can under some circumstances mitigate the more harmful of these collective behaviors. The coordination mechanisms discussed in this section are all designed to avoid these problems by enabling some forms of global computation to be performed over the entire collective—either actively by a central agency such as a joint controller or resource broker, or at design time by a government or other entity that has the power to enforce norms or laws that are calculated to encourage or enforce the individual behaviors that will lead to a desired collective result.

Nonetheless, one should not conclude that coordination mechanisms that enable global computation are preferred universally over more distributed approaches. While centralized approaches may be attractive in principle because they offer the possibility of computing a social optimum, in practice they may suffer from the drawback that they require global knowledge, and (perhaps even worse) computational resources that may scale superlinearly with the number of entities or other variables over which they must compute a solution. Computing a globally optimal solution may be impractical at sufficiently large scale. If the computation involves a game-theoretic calculation, for example, the compute resources required can grow astronomically with the number of players and strategies.[3]

Fortunately, fully distributed and fully centralized approaches to adaptation and control are just two ends of a spectrum. Hierarchical control, in which local controllers operate within a scope that is defined by a higher-level controller (typically at a slower time scale), is often a successful approach. For example, Raghavendra et al. showed that a multi-level hierarchy of controllers using a variety of control techniques at different levels can be effective for data center power management [34].

Moreover, it is worth noting that one could adapt the overall method of adaptation itself in response to observed behavior. In other words, one could contemplate an optimistic approach to designing a adaptive system in which decentralization is attempted, but in which the individual entities are endowed with the ability to monitor their own behavior and perhaps that of their neighbors for signatures of undesirable emergent behaviors. A technique of this nature was employed by Heo and Abdelzaher in their work on coupled feedback control systems [20]. One could even introduce into the system special-purpose watchdog entities that contain signatures of undesirable behaviors. When such signatures are detected, the entities could send their observations to a central authority, or exchange those observations among themselves to determine that they are suffering from a known type of collective behavior. Upon such a determination, the system could introduce into itself an appropriate mitigation, such as one of those described in this chapter.

13.6 Discussion and Summary

Characterizing the vast universe of possible systems of interacting self-aware entities is a daunting task. Rather than attempting a full taxonomy in this chapter, we have mentioned a few non-orthogonal dimensions of that space (borrowing from nomenclature introduced in Chap. 7, where possible) and sampled it rather sparsely with a set of scenarios, many of which are extensions of the reference scenarios in Chap. 4. In order to achieve some measure of coherency, this chapter has been organized

---

[3]More precisely, computing Nash equilibria has been shown to be PPAD-complete, where PPAD is a subclass of NP that contains problems that are suspected of being hard [7].

broadly according to the collections of scenarios that share a common characteristic. However, it should be acknowledged that other groupings that emphasized different dimensions of the space might have been equally coherent, such as arranging them according to the degree of awareness that the self-aware entities have of one another's existence, actions, or goals.

Looking across all of the scenarios covered in this chapter, the many forms of collective behavior exhibited by the system described in those scenarios, and the many approaches proffered for suppressing or fostering these behaviors, we draw some general observations:

- For many reasons, including scalability and evolvability, it is generally desirable to design self-aware systems as collections of adaptive, learning self-aware entities that govern their own actions. While designing joint controllers to manage two or more functions (e.g., smart windows and smart thermostats) can help attain optimality and stability, it is very constraining to try to anticipate all possible pairs or n-way combinations of functions that might be found together in a system.
- Conflicts among self-aware entities can arise under a wide variety of circumstances:
  - The most obvious case is where the goals explicitly conflict; in such a case, the user must somehow clarify how that conflict is to be resolved via a policy or precedence rule, utility function, or other mechanism.
  - Even when goals do not conflict directly, actions guided by goals of different self-aware entities may conflict. One common cause of conflict is contention for a commonly needed resource. Another is via unintended side effects that end up coupling the actions of self-aware entities in unanticipated ways
  - The self-aware entities may conflict with one another directly, or indirectly through their impact on the environment in which they are situated.

- In the common situation where more than one of the self-aware entities learns, each learning agent potentially creates a dynamic environment for other agents and that dynamism creates a need for all self-aware entities to continue learning, further perpetuating the dynamicity of the system. Thus, convergence to stable behavior may be inherently difficult in such systems.
- While many different methods can be used to thwart undesirable collective phenomena, at a sufficient level of abstraction some common themes emerge:
  - introducing randomness or heterogeneity where possible.
  - reducing information delays where possible.
  - engineering individual goals to achieve desired collective behavior (this may be difficult and somewhat against the objective of developing self-aware entities as individual agents that are not necessarily explicitly coordinated).
  - detecting and breaking feedback loops.
  - endowing agents with an awareness of one another's existence, behavior, impact, and/or models.

 – introducing an intermediary such as a resource broker or an auction or other economic/market mechanism (thereby providing a small amount of centralization, or at least localization)

- Conflicts and instabilities that result from learning can bear a mathematical resemblance to conflicts and instabilities that occur among agents that are merely adaptive or reactive (but which do not learn). However, the instabilities tend to originate in the realm of policies that govern actions, as opposed to the actions themselves, and thereafter, the instabilities can occur on a much longer timescale than for non-learning agents.
- Some mitigation strategies entail learning, and yet learning can itself induce instabilities or suboptimal behavior.
- While economic mechanisms such as auctions show promise as general mechanisms for decentralized management of self-aware systems, they too can suffer from instabilities.

Elaborating on the last point somewhat, it is apparent that there is no one panacea. A thread through this chapter has been to better illustrate the advantages of self-awareness and demonstrate mitigation strategies that often relied on information sharing, communication, or learning. It remains to observe that the very mechanisms that improve awareness and help with mitigation often also reduce *robustness* in the presence of failures. The intuitive high-level reason for this conflict lies in the extent of dependencies. Attaining awareness in a multi-agent system often requires one component or agent to receive information (e.g., measurements or state) from another. The receiving component then uses this information in its own algorithms and/or reasoning. This exchange creates a dependency of algorithms in one component on information arriving from another. In turn, this dependency acts as a conduit for failure propagation. When a component fails, those that depend on its outputs may fail as well. The more extensive the web of dependencies, the larger the global fallout from local failures. In the absence of dependencies, components can fail independently without impacting the rest of the system. Hence, in designing adaptive and collectively self-aware systems, it becomes imperative to understand the implications of information exchange (needed to support adaptive behavior and collective awareness) on robustness. Care should be taken not to create information dependencies or functional dependencies that give rise to failure cascades, whereby local component malfunctions propagate along dependency chains to disrupt operation of large chunks of the system.

References

1. Jacob Beal, Jeffrey Berliner, and Kevin Hunter. Fast precise distributed control for energy demand management. In *Self-Adaptive and Self-Organizing Systems (SASO), 2012 IEEE Sixth International Conference on*, pages 187–192. IEEE, 2012.

2. Basil Becker, Dirk Beyer, Holger Giese, Florian Klein, and Daniela Schilling. Symbolic Invariant Verification for Systems with Dynamic Structural Adaptation. In *Proc. of the 28th International Conference on Software Engineering (ICSE), Shanghai, China*. ACM Press, 2006.

3. Sven Burmester, Holger Giese, Eckehard Mnch, Oliver Oberschelp, Florian Klein, and Peter Scheideler. Tool Support for the Design of Self-Optimizing Mechatronic Multi-Agent Systems. *International Journal on Software Tools for Technology Transfer (STTT)*, 10(3):207–222, June 2008.

4. Lucian Busoniu, Robert Babuska, and Bart De Schutter. A comprehensive survey of multiagent reinforcement learning. *Systems, Man, and Cybernetics, Part C: Applications and Reviews, IEEE Transactions on*, 38(2):156–172, 2008.

5. Caroline Claus and Craig Boutilier. The dynamics of reinforcement learning in cooperative multiagent systems. In *Proceedings of the Fifteenth National/Tenth Conference on Artificial Intelligence/Innovative Applications of Artificial Intelligence*, AAAI '98/IAAI '98, pages 746–752, Menlo Park, CA, USA, 1998. American Association for Artificial Intelligence.

6. Vincent Conitzer and Tuomas Sandholm. Self-interested automated mechanism design and implications for optimal combinatorial auctions. In *Proceedings of the 5th ACM conference on Electronic commerce*, pages 132–141. ACM, 2004.

7. Constantinos Daskalakis, Paul W Goldberg, and Christos H Papadimitriou. The complexity of computing a Nash equilibrium. *SIAM Journal on Computing*, 39(1):195–259, 2009.

8. Ada Diaconescu and Jeremy Pitt. *Coordination, Organizations, Institutions, and Norms in Agent Systems X*, volume 9372 of *Lecture Notes in Artificial Intelligence*, chapter Holonic Institutions for Multi-scale Polycentric Self-governance, pages 19–35. Springer International Publishing, 1 edition, 2015.

9. JoseLuis Fernandez-Marquez, Giovanna Di Marzo Serugendo, Sara Montagna, Mirko Viroli, and JosepLluis Arcos. Description and Composition of Bio-inspired Design Patterns: a Complete Overview. *Natural Computing*, 12(1):43–67, 2013.

10. Dean P Foster and Rakesh V Vohra. Calibrated learning and correlated equilibrium. *Games and Economic Behavior*, 21(1):40–55, 1997.

11. Sylvain Frey, Ada Diaconescu, David Menga, and Isabelle Demeure. A holonic control architecture for a heterogeneous multi-objective smart micro-grid. In *Self-Adaptive and Self-Organizing Systems (SASO), 2013 IEEE 7th International Conference on*, pages 21–30. IEEE, 2013.

12. Sylvain Frey, François Huguet, Cédric Mivielle, David Menga, Ada Diaconescu, and Isabelle M Demeure. Scenarios for an autonomic micro smart grid. In *SMARTGREENS*, pages 137–140, 2012.

13. Theodore Geisel. *The Cat in the Hat Comes Back*. Random House, 1958.

14. Holger Giese, Sven Burmester, Florian Klein, Daniela Schilling, and Matthias Tichy. Multi-Agent System Design for Safety-Critical Self-Optimizing Mechatronic Systems with UML. In Brian Henderson-Sellers and J Debenham, editors, *OOPSLA 2003 - Second International Workshop on Agent-Oriented Methodologies*, pages 21–32, Anaheim, CA, USA, Center for Object Technology Applications and Research (COTAR), University of Technology, Sydney, Australia, October 2003.

15. Holger Giese and Wilhelm Schäfer. Model-Driven Development of Safe Self-Optimizing Mechatronic Systems with MechatronicUML. In Javier Camara, Rogrio de Lemos, Carlo Ghezzi, and AntÂnia Lopes, editors, *Assurances for Self-Adaptive Systems*, volume 7740 of *Lecture Notes in Computer Science (LNCS)*, pages 152–186. Springer, January 2013.

16. Harry Goldingay and Peter R. Lewis. A Taxonomy of Heterogeneity and Dynamics in Particle Swarm Optimisation. In Thomas Bartz-Beielstein, Jrgen Branke, Bogdan Filipi, and Jim Smith, editors, *Parallel Problem Solving from Nature PPSN XIII*, volume 8672 of *Lecture Notes in Computer Science*, pages 171–180. Springer International Publishing, 2014.

17. Amy R Greenwald and Jeffrey O Kephart. Probabilistic pricebots. In *Proceedings of the fifth international conference on Autonomous agents*, pages 560–567. ACM, 2001.

18. James E Hanson, Gerald J. Tesauro, Jeffrey O Kephart, and Edward C Snible. Multi-agent implementation of asymmetric protocol for bilateral negotiations. In *Proceedings of the 4th ACM Conference on Electronic Commerce*, pages 224–225. ACM, 2003.

19. Sergiu Hart and Andreu Mas-Colell. A simple adaptive procedure leading to correlated equilibrium. *Econometrica*, 68(5):1127–1150, 2000.
20. Jin Heo and Tarek F. Abdelzaher. Adaptguard: guarding adaptive systems from instability. In Simon A. Dobson, John Strassner, Manish Parashar, and Onn Shehory, editors, *Proceedings of the 6th International Conference on Autonomic Computing, ICAC 2009, June 15-19, 2009, Barcelona, Spain*, pages 77–86. ACM, 2009.
21. Amir Jafari, Amy Greenwald, David Gondek, and Gunes Ercal. On no-regret learning, fictitious play, and nash equilibrium. In *In Proceedings of the Eighteenth International Conference on Machine Learning*, 2001.
22. J O Kephart, H Chan, R Das, D W Levine, G Tesauro, and C Lefurgy. Coordinating multiple autonomic managers to achieve specified power-performance tradeoffs. In *Proceedings of the Fourth International Conference on Autonomic Computing*. IEEE, 2007.
23. Jeffrey O Kephart. Can predictive agents prevent chaos. *Economics and cognitive science*.
24. Jeffrey O Kephart. Software agents and the route to the information economy. *Proceedings of the National Academy of Sciences*, 99(suppl 3):7207–7213, 2002.
25. Jeffrey O Kephart and David M Chess. The vision of autonomic computing. *Computer*, 36(1):41–50, 2003.
26. Jeffrey. O. Kephart, Tad Hogg, and Bernardo A. Huberman. Dynamics of computational ecosystems. *Phys. Rev. A*, 40:404–421, Jul 1989.
27. Jeffrey O Kephart, Tad Hogg, and Bernardo A Huberman. Collective behavior of predictive agents. *Physica D: Nonlinear Phenomena*, 42(1):48–65, 1990.
28. Jeffrey O Kephart and Jonathan Lenchner. A symbiotic cognitive computing perspective on autonomic computing. In *Proceedings of the 2015 IEEE International Conference on Autonomic Computing*. IEEE, 2015.
29. Jeffrey O Kephart and Gerald J Tesauro. Pseudo-convergent q-learning by competitive pricebots. In *Proc. 17th Intl Conf. Machine Learning*, pages 463–470, 2000.
30. Jeffrey O Kephart and William E Walsh. An artificial intelligence perspective on autonomic computing policies. In *Policies for Distributed Systems and Networks, 2004. POLICY 2004. Proceedings. Fifth IEEE International Workshop on*, pages 3–12. IEEE, 2004.
31. Peter R. Lewis, Arjun Chandra, Funmilade Faniyi, Kyrre Glette, Tao Chen, Rami Bahsoon, Jim Torresen, and Xin Yao. Architectural Aspects of Self-Aware and Self-Expressive Systems: From Psychology to Engineering. *Computer*, 48(8), August 2015.
32. Peter R. Lewis, Paul Marrow, and Xin Yao. Resource Allocation in Decentralised Computational Systems: An Evolutionary Market Based Approach. *Autonomous Agents and Multi-Agent Systems*, 21(2):143–171, 2010.
33. Fernando Perez-Diaz, Ruediger Zillmer, and Roderich Groß. Firefly-inspired synchronization in swarms of mobile agents. In *Proceedings of the 2015 International Conference on Autonomous Agents and Multiagent Systems*, AAMAS '15, pages 279–286, Richland, SC, 2015. International Foundation for Autonomous Agents and Multiagent Systems.
34. Ramya Raghavendra, Parthasarathy Ranganathan, Vanish Talwar, Zhikui Wang, and Xiaoyun Zhu. No power struggles: Coordinated multi-level power management for the data center. In *ACM SIGARCH Computer Architecture News*, volume 36, pages 48–59. ACM, 2008.
35. Tuomas Sandholm. Algorithm for optimal winner determination in combinatorial auctions. *Artificial intelligence*, 135(1):1–54, 2002.
36. H. Van Dyke Parunak, Sven Brueckner, Mitch Fleischer, and James Odell. A Design Taxonomy of Multi-agent Interactions. In Paolo Giorgini, JrgP. Mller, and James Odell, editors, *Agent-Oriented Software Engineering IV*, volume 2935 of *Lecture Notes in Computer Science*, pages 123–137. Springer Berlin Heidelberg, 2004.
37. William Vickrey. Counterspeculation, auctions, and competitive sealed tenders. *The Journal of finance*, 16(1):8–37, 1961.
38. William E Walsh, Gerald Tesauro, Jeffrey O Kephart, and Rajarshi Das. Utility functions in autonomic systems. In *Autonomic Computing, 2004. Proceedings. International Conference on*, pages 70–77. IEEE, 2004.
39. M P Wellman, W E Walsh, P R Wurman, and J K MacKie-Mason. Auction protocols for decentralized scheduling. *Games and economic behavior*, 35(1):271–303, 2001.

Chapter 14
Metrics and Benchmarks for Self-aware Computing Systems

Nikolas Herbst, Steffen Becker, Samuel Kounev, Heiko Koziolek,
Martina Maggio, Aleksandar Milenkoski and Evgenia Smirni

Abstract In this chapter, we propose a list of metrics grouped by the MAPE-K paradigm for quantifying properties of self-aware computing systems. This set of metrics can be seen as a starting point toward benchmarking and comparing self-aware computing systems on a level-playing field. We discuss state-of-the art approaches in the related fields of self-adaptation and self-protection to identify commonalities in metrics for self-aware computing. We illustrate the need for benchmarking self-aware computing systems with the help of an approach that uncovers real-time characteristics of operating systems. Gained insights of this approach can be seen as a way of enhancing self-awareness by a measurement methodology on an ongoing basis. At the end of this chapter, we address new challenges in reference workload definition for benchmarking self-aware computing systems, namely load intensity patterns and burstiness modeling.

N. Herbst (✉) · S. Kounev · A. Milenkoski
University of Würzburg, Würzburg, Germany
e-mail: nikolas.herbst@uni-wuerzburg.de

S. Kounev
e-mail: samuel.kounev@uni-wuerzburg.de

A. Milenkoski
e-mail: aleksandar.milenkoski@uni-wuerzburg.de

S. Becker
Technical University Chemnitz, Chemnitz, Germany
e-mail: steffen.becker@informatik.tu-chemnitz.de

H. Koziolek
ABB Ladenburg, Ladenburg, Germany
e-mail: heiko.koziolek@de.abb.com

M. Maggio
Lunds Universitet, Lund, Sweden
e-mail: martina.maggio@control.lth.se

E. Smirni
College of William and Mary, Williamsburg, VA, USA
e-mail: esmirni@cs.wm.edu

© Springer International Publishing AG 2017
S. Kounev et al. (eds.), *Self-Aware Computing Systems*,
DOI 10.1007/978-3-319-47474-8_14

437

14.1 Introduction

Beyond the need for methodologies to assess self-awareness of a computing system, as discussed in Chap. 15, we see an increasing demand for comparisons of self-aware systems on a level-playing field. Established domains in information technology usually come with a set of key performance indicators or metrics, standard scenarios, and measurement rules that taken together form a benchmark. For example, benchmarks of the Standard Performance Evaluation Corporation (SPEC) such as for CPUs, virtualization technology, or enterprise applications enable comparisons and decision making. Our expectation is a growing number of self-aware computing systems that may exhibit similarities in their goals, features, and application domains. We see this as the major reason why benchmarking of self-aware computing systems will become more important in the course of the next years not only to design and improve such systems, but also to reliably compare and select them.

A benchmark usually consists of three major building blocks: The first building block is a set of reliable and intuitive metrics that can be combined to a single-valued score. The second building block is the workload definition as an exact definition of the work that is to be performed by the system under test together with a definition of the load profile over time. The third building block is a well-defined measurement methodology (also known as run rules) that assures repeatable measurements.

As a starting point toward the benchmarking of self-aware computing systems, we propose in Sect. 14.2 an initial set of metrics grouped by the MAPE-K generic control loop. The MAPE-K control loop consists of (i) monitoring, (ii) analyzing, (iii) planning and (iv) executing phases with a central knowledge repository and can be seen as a special case of the self-aware learning and reasoning loop (as defined in Chap. 1). In Sect. 14.3, we review the state of the art in two related fields, self-adaptation and self-protection, identifying commonalities with benchmarking applied to self-aware computing system properties. In Sect. 14.4, we sketch an approach to illustrate how a benchmark can help to improve and better understand a self-aware computing system. In this case, this is achieved by continuously uncovering real-time characteristics of the underlying operating system. In Sect. 14.5, we explain how two new challenges in defining reference workloads can be addressed to build a self-aware computing system benchmark. We focus on modeling load profiles and realistic burstiness.

14.2 Metrics for Self-aware Systems

Existing performance metrics, such as response time or throughput, are not sufficient for benchmarking self-aware computing systems as they do not capture all relevant aspects of self-awareness. Existing benchmarks and metrics often focus on a subset of these aspects (designed, e.g., to evaluate self-adaptive, self-protecting aspects) or use domain-specific refinements of a broader set of metrics that could be suited for self-aware computing systems. In order to make a first step toward closing this gap, we went through a process to identify potential candidates of metrics suited to benchmark self-aware computing systems. Those metrics can then be used to quantitatively evaluate, compare, or analyze self-aware computing systems.

The process we went through was threefold. On the one hand, we identified and adopted existing metrics from systems closely related to self-aware computing systems. In particular, we investigated metrics from self-adaptive computing system evaluation and included them, if suited. Second, we used the MAPE-K reference architecture and used it both as a grouping, as well as inspiration for new metrics. Note that this does not mean in any way that the metrics can only be applied to computing systems implemented in the MAPE-K style. The resulting metrics are meant to be general. Finally, we used the definition of a self-aware computing system given in Chap. 1. We went through all aspects of it and tried to come up with metrics designed to quantify these aspects for any given self-aware computing system.

In the following, we illustrate the resulting list of suggestions for metrics addressing different parts of self-aware computing systems. These suggestions are intended as ideas to influence the development of upcoming benchmarks for self-aware computing systems. Table 14.1 provides an overview of all metrics we identified.

Table 14.1 Metric candidates overview

Goal fulfillment	Monitor	Analyze	Plan	Execute
Proportion of time the system is in a goal fulfillment state	Levels of self-awareness	Number of input sources utilized	Proportion of "correct" decisions made per time unit	Proportion of time the system in an oscillating state
Duration/amount of goal violations per time	Number of monitored internal and external properties	Sophistication of the learning mechanism	Sophistication of the reasoning processes	Duration of an adaptation action
Severity of goal violations	Granularity/precision of sensing the environment	Accuracy of the learned models w.r.t. reality	"Precision and recall" of the selected adaptation actions	Correctness of the adaptation actions
Level of goal fulfillment	Size/length of the historically stored properties	Duration of altering the learning process upon changing goals	Extent/granularity of traceability for reasoning	
	Monitoring frequency			
	Monitoring overhead			
	Completeness of the collected and required information			
	Number of required user inputs per time			

14.2.1 Goal Fulfillment

An initial set of metrics aims at quantifying the extent to which a self-aware computing system is able to fulfill its *goals* over time. The following candidates have been identified:

Proportion of time the system is in a goal fulfillment state: This metric indicates the percentage of the time the system fulfills its goals. The closer this metric is to 100 %, the better the system adapts to changing conditions.

Duration/amount of goal violations per time: This metric captures the overall amount of goal violations over the system's runtime and the durations of time intervals the system spent in a state where at least one goal is violated.

Severity of goal violations: This metric captures, for example, 60 % video quality in an adapting video codec, or 10000 € unnecessarily spent for renting servers.

Level of goal fulfillment: This metric captures, for example, the time in which an autonomous car manages a given track, or the resource efficiency of a cloud infrastructure. This metric captures in addition pure goal fulfillment cases in which a goal can be fulfilled to different degrees.

14.2.2 Quality of the Information Collection (Monitor Phase)

The following metrics aim at quantifying the information needs of a self-aware computing system, i.e., the amount of *monitoring* required for executing its self-awareness functionality.

Levels of self-awareness: This metric classifies the computing system's self-awareness level (cf. Chap. 1); however, this might be hard to measure empirically (awareness of self, internal state; awareness of goals; awareness of self-awareness).

Number of monitored internal and external properties: As an example, a result could be that the computing system uses seven performance counters. The more external properties the computing system needs to track, the more complex and time-consuming the monitoring would normally be.

Granularity/precision of sensing the environment: The metric captures the precision used to sense the environment. Higher precisions require better sensors, but the measurements need more storage space. For example, a system could use a resolution in the range of milliseconds to capture points in time.

Size/length of the historically stored properties: For an example system, the metric could indicate that the collected monitoring data of the last two years is stored and analyzed. The more data is saved, the better the system can reason about its past. However, also the storage requirements increase.

Monitoring frequency: This metric captures the rate at which measurement and monitoring data is collected from the environment (e.g., measurement values per minute).

Monitoring overhead: The metric quantifies the time spent by the system for performing monitoring tasks in contrast to executing other system functions.

Completeness of the collected and required information: The degree to which the data made available to the system about its environment is complete, or can be used to derive all required information, especially important for systems that obtain data about their environment from unreliable sensors.

Number of required user inputs per time (user-in-the-loop): How often the system asks the user for environment data or advice on next steps? The lower this metric is, the more autonomously the system acts.

14.2.3   Quality of the Learning Process (Analyze Phase)

The following set of metrics aim to quantify the system's ability to *analyze and learn* from its observations.

Number of input sources utilized: The metric evaluates how many of the available information sources are actually used in the learning process. It can be defined as number models or views used divided by the total number.

Sophistication of the learning mechanism: This metric captures the effort the system spends on learning. Usually, more effort leads to better behavior, e.g., duration of the evolutionary algorithm (in order to find better solutions, potentially including time bounds). This metric would be specified differently depending on the kind of applied learning algorithm.

Accuracy of the learned models w.r.t. reality: This captures how representative the learned models are of the real-life entities/phenomena they abstract. For example, the amount of real-world states identified by a hidden Markov model or the degree to which a surface explored by a robot matches the real surface. Note that this metric assumes full knowledge of the modeled entities/phenomena.

Duration of altering the learning process upon changing goals: This metric captures the time the learning algorithm takes until it picks up changed system goals and starts to adapt accordingly.

14.2.4   Quality of the Reasoning Process (Plan Phase)

The following metrics aim to capture the *planning* process of a self-aware computing system, i.e., its ability to propose actions that lead to better goal fulfillment.

Proportion of correct decisions made per time unit: The mean number of objectively correct decisions the system makes per unit of time. This metric assumes that the software designers can specify the correct behavior for all situations that arise during the benchmark.

Sophistication of the reasoning: This metric quantifies how smart the system is able to reason. Possible values can be the number of evaluated alternatives for adaptations or the number of surprising positive findings.

Precision and recall of the selected adaptation actions: How many different adaptation alternatives are considered? How many of them are reasonable ones? The concept of precision and recall is, for example, employed for benchmarking self-protecting systems as discussed in Sect. 14.3.2.

Extent/granularity of traceability for reasoning: This metric captures the extent to which a self-aware computing system is able to "explain" its decisions. It can either be binary (is able/is not able to present rationale) or could be defined as degree to which one is able to reproduce the decisions made by the system.

14.2.5   Measure the Adaptation Actions (Execute Phase)

The following metrics quantify the performance of the system in *executing* adaptations.

Proportion of time the system in an oscillating/unstable state: The proportion of time the system spends alternating between two or more states while the environment is in a stable state. This metric is related to a jitter metric that has been proposed in the context of elastic cloud systems and describes the number of missing or superfluous adaptations over time (see Sect. 14.3.1).

Duration of adaptation actions: The time an adaptation action takes, e.g., 5 min to start a new server or 5 s to turn the robot into another direction. This can be approximated by measuring the durations in sub-optimal states as done for elastic cloud systems (see Sect. 14.3.1).

Correctness of the adaptation actions: This metric captures how successful adaptations are. It can be defined as the failure rate of adaptations. This metric also relates to a metric proposed earlier in the context of elastic clouds, namely the average amount of over-/under-provisioned resources (see Sect. 14.3.1).

14.2.6   Summary

The presented metrics are a starting point for the development of new metrics and benchmarks for evaluating the level of self-awareness a system exhibits. They do not provide a formal definition of what to measure, and several of them are domain-specific, i.e., they need to be refined for a concrete self-aware computing system. Furthermore, they have not yet been extensively validated to make sure that they can be used to adequately characterize self-awareness aspects. In addition, aggregate metrics need to be defined to summarize the different sub-metrics producing an overall self-awareness score. This is required to allow easy comparisons of different self-aware computing systems in standardized benchmarks. It is still an open question, how to define weights for the various sub-metrics when aggregating them to produce a single value. Finally, while some metrics are easy to determine and already pretty clear in their definition, other metrics represent dynamic properties. For those metrics, we need a methodology of how to define a representative workload and set up a representative environment in which we execute the system to be evaluated.

14.3   On the State of the Art in Quantifying Self-adaptation and Self-protection

The previous section outlined our proposed metric candidates for characterizing self-aware systems. As indicated, several of these metrics are inspired or adapted from the related fields, self-adaptation and self-protection. In this section, we describe the state of the art in these two fields in detail. In the context of self-adaptation, elasticity of compute clouds is taken as an example. In the context of self-protection, intrusion detection systems (IDSes) are considered.

14.3.1   Quantifying the Quality of Self-adaptation

The system property of self-adaptation is seen in many different fields of applications such as autonomous robots and more. Self-adaptation in the context of elastic resource provisioning in compute cloud resource provisioning is currently a highly discussed topic in academia and industry, and therefore, in the following we use it as an example of a self-adaptation property.

When we talk about elasticity in the context of compute clouds, we refer to the definition given in [17] as follows:

Elasticity   is the degree to which a system is able to adapt to workload changes by provisioning and de-provisioning resources in an autonomic manner, such that at each point in time the available resources *match* the current demand as closely as possible.

Several metrics for elasticity have been proposed during the last years:
(i) The "scaling latency" metrics in [26] or the "provisioning interval" in [8] captures the time to bring up or drop a resource. This duration is a technical property of an elastic environment independent of the demand changes and the elasticity mechanism itself that decides when to trigger a reconfiguration. Thus, these metrics are insufficient to fully characterize the elasticity of a platform.
(ii) The "reaction time" metric in [24] can only be computed if a unique mapping between resource demand changes and supply changes exists. This assumption does not hold especially for proactive elasticity mechanisms or for mechanisms that have unstable (alternating) states.

(iii) The approaches in [2, 9, 10] characterize elasticity indirectly by analyzing response times for significant workload changes or for SLO compliance. In theory, perfect elasticity would result in constant response times for varying workload intensity. In practice, detailed reasoning about the quality of platform adaptations based on response times alone is hampered due to the lack of relevant information about the platform behavior, e.g., information about the amount of provisioned surplus resources.

(iv) Cost-based metrics are proposed in [11, 21, 41, 42] quantifying the impact of elasticity by comparing the resulting provisioning costs to the costs for a peak-load static resource assignment or the costs of a hypothetical perfect elastic platform. In both cases, the resulting metrics strongly depend on the underlying cost model, as well as on the assumed penalty for under-provisioning, and thus they do not support fair cross-platform comparisons.

We select a set of metrics for two core aspects of elasticity: *accuracy* and *timing*. For these metrics, the optimal value is zero corresponding to a perfectly elastic platform. The following assumptions must hold in order to be able to apply the selected elasticity metrics to compare a set of different platforms: the existence of an autonomic adaptation process, the scaling of the same resource type, e.g., CPU cores or virtual machines (VMs), and that the respective resource type is scalable within the same ranges, e.g., from 1 to 20 resource units.

The set of metrics evaluates the resulting elastic behavior as observed from the outside and are thus designed in a manner independent of distinct descriptions of the underlying hardware, the virtualization technology, the used cloud management software, or the employed elasticity strategy and its configuration. As a consequence, the metrics and the measurement methodology are applicable in situations where not all influencing factors are known. All metrics require two discrete curves as input: The demand curve, which defines how the resource demand varies during the measurement period, and the supply curve, which defines how the actual amount of resources allocated by the platform varies.

In the following, we describe the metrics for quantifying the *accuracy* aspect and a set of metrics for quantifying the *timing* aspect as proposed in [18].

14.3.1.1 Accuracy

The under-provisioning accuracy metric $accuracy_U$ is calculated as the sum of areas between the two curves ($\sum U$) where the resource demand exceeds the supply normalized by the duration of the measurement period T, as visualized in Fig. 14.1. Similarly, the over-provisioning accuracy metric $accuracy_O$ is based on the sum of areas ($\sum O$) where the resource supply exceeds the demand.

$$\text{Under-provisioning: } accuracy_U \ [resource \ units] = \frac{\sum U}{T}$$

$$\text{Over-provisioning: } accuracy_O \ [resource \ units] = \frac{\sum O}{T}$$

Thus, $accuracy_U$ and $accuracy_O$ measure the average amount of resources that are under-/over-provisioned during the measurement period T. Since under-provisioning results in violating SLOs, a customer might want to use a platform that does not tend to under-provision at all. Thus, the challenge for providers is to ensure that enough resources are provided at any point in time, but at the same time distinguish themselves from competitors by minimizing the amount of over-provisioned resources. Considering this, the defined separate accuracy metrics for over-provisioning and under-provisioning allow providers to better communicate their elasticity capabilities and customers to select the provider that best matches their needs.

14.3.1.2 Timing

We characterize the *timing* aspect of elasticity from the viewpoint of the pure *provisioning timeshare*, on the one hand, and from the viewpoint of the induced *jitter* accounting for superfluous or missed adaptations, on the other hand.

Provisioning Timeshare

The two accuracy metrics allow no reasoning as to whether the average amount of under-/over-provisioned resources results from a few big deviations between demand and supply or if it is rather caused by a constant small deviation. To address this, the following two metrics are designed to provide insights about the ratio of time in which under- or over-provisioning occurs.

As visualized in Fig. 14.1, the following metrics $timeshare_U$ and $timeshare_O$ are computed by summing up the total amount of time spent in an under- ($\sum A$) or over-provisioned ($\sum B$) state normalized by the duration of the measurement period. Thus, they measure the overall timeshare spent in under- or over-provisioned state:

Fig. 14.1 Illustrating example for accuracy (U, O) and timing (A, B) metrics

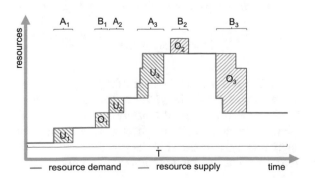

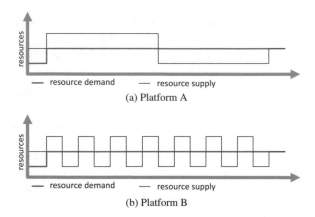

Fig. 14.2 Platforms with different elastic behaviors that produce equal results for *accuracy* and *timeshare* metrics

$$\text{Under-provisioning: } timeshare_U = \frac{\sum A}{T}$$

$$\text{Over-provisioning: } timeshare_O = \frac{\sum B}{T}$$

Jitter

Although the *accuracy* and *timeshare* metrics characterize important aspects of elasticity, platforms can still behave very differently while producing the same metric values for *accuracy* and *timeshare*. An example is shown in Fig. 14.2.

Both platforms A and B exhibit the same accuracy metrics and spend the same amount of time in under-provisioned and over-provisioned states, respectively. However, the behavior of the two platforms differs significantly. Platform B triggers more unnecessary resource supply adaptations than Platform A.

The *jitter* metric captures this instability and inertia of elasticity mechanisms. Low stability increases adaptation overheads and costs (e.g., in case of instance-hour-based pricing), whereas a high level of inertia results in a decreased SLO compliance.

The *jitter* metric compares the number of adaptations in the supply curve E_S with the number of adaptations in the demand curve E_D. If a platform de-/allocates more than one resource unit at a time, the adaptations are counted individually per resource unit. The difference is normalized by the length of the measurement period T:

$$\text{Jitter metric: } jitter \left[\frac{\#adaptations}{time}\right] = \frac{E_S - E_D}{T}$$

A negative *jitter* metric indicates that the platform adapts rather sluggish to changes in the demand. A positive *jitter* metric means that the platform tends to oscillate like Platforms A (little) and B (heavily) as in Fig. 14.2. High absolute values of *jitter* metrics in general indicate that the platform is not able to react on demand changes appropriately. In contrast to the accuracy and timeshare metrics, a *jitter* value of zero is a necessary, but not sufficient, condition for a perfect elastic system.

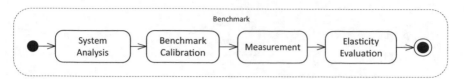

Fig. 14.3 Activity diagram for the benchmark workflow

14.3.1.3   An Elasticity Benchmarking Concept

This paragraph shortly sketches an elasticity benchmarking concept as proposed in [17] and its implementation called BUNGEE[1] in [18]. The generic and cloud specific benchmark requirements as formulated by Huppler [19, 20] and Folkerts et al. [11] are considered in this approach. Figure 14.3 shows the four main steps of the benchmarking process explained in the following:

1. **Platform Analysis**: The benchmark analyzes a system under test (SUT) with respect to the performance of its underlying resources and its scaling behavior.
2. **Benchmark Calibration**: The results of the analysis are used to adjust the load intensity profile injected on the SUT in a way that it induces the same resource demand on all compared platforms.
3. **Measurement**: The load generator exposes the SUT to a varying workload according to the adjusted load profile. The benchmark extracts the actual induced resource demand and monitors resource supply changes on the SUT.
4. **Elasticity Evaluation**: The elasticity metrics are computed and used to compare the resource demand and resource supply curves with respect to different elasticity aspects.

The results of an exemplary benchmark run are plotted in Fig. 14.4, and the computed elasticity metrics are shown in Table 14.2.

14.3.2   Quantifying the Quality of Self-protection

We consider self-protection as a distinct property of self-aware systems. Under self-protection, we understand continuous system protection against malicious activities (e.g., intrusion attempts and resource exhaustions) by performing actions countering these activities in real time; that is, self-protection may be understood as one of the high-level goals that a self-aware system may have (see Chap. 1). A typical self-aware system performs actions countering malicious activities by utilizing common security mechanisms, such as intrusion detection and prevention systems, access control systems, performance isolation mechanisms for preventing deliberate resource exhaustions, and so on. In this section, we provide an overview of metrics

---

[1]BUNGEE Cloud Elasticity Benchmark: http://descartes.tools/bungee.

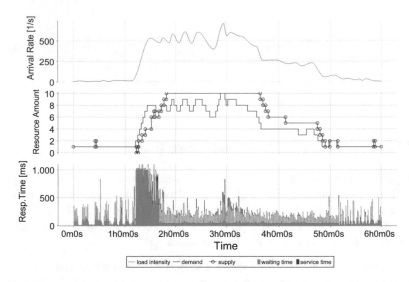

Fig. 14.4 Resource demand and supply curves for an exemplary benchmark run on a public cloud

Table 14.2 Metric results for an exemplary benchmark run

acc_O [#res.]	acc_U [#res.]	ts_O [%]	ts_U [%]	$jitter \left[\frac{\#adap.}{min}\right]$
1.053	0.180	51.9	8.1	−0.033

for quantifying properties of intrusion detection systems, which often play a key role when it comes to self-protection. We also discuss the relevance of the considered metrics in the context of self-protection.

14.3.2.1   Quantifying Properties of Intrusion Detection Systems

Intrusion detection is a key enabling technology for self-protection. This is because the timely and accurate detection of intrusion attempts (i.e., security breaches) enables timely reaction in order to stop an ongoing attack, or to mitigate the impact of a security breach.

We distinguish between two categories of metrics for quantifying properties of intrusion detection systems (IDSes): *performance-related* and *security-related* metrics. By performance-related metrics, we refer to metrics that quantify the non-functional properties of an IDS under test, such as attack detection delay, capacity, or resource consumption. By security-related metrics, we refer to metrics that quantify the attack detection accuracy of an IDS, such as true and false positive rates.[2] Because of their relevance when it comes to self-protection, we focus on metrics that

---

[2]We refer the reader to Chap. 22 for in-depth discussions on these metrics.

quantify the attack detection delay as well as on security-related metrics that express the false positive rate.

Attack detection delay. The attack detection delay (also known as "attack detection and reporting speed") is typically evaluated in the context of IDSes coupled with attack response mechanisms (see, e.g., the work of Sen et al. [39]). Given that attack response mechanisms perform actions countering attacks detected by IDSes, the fast detection and reporting of attacks by an IDS is crucial for the timely prevention of attacks, which, in turn, is crucial for effective self-protection.

The attack detection delay can be quantified as the time needed for an IDS to issue an alert after an attack has occurred. However, the way in which attack detection delay is quantified may depend on the type of employed IDS. For instance, the attack detection delay is often considered in the context of distributed IDSes. A distributed IDS is a compound IDS consisting of multiple intrusion detection sub-systems (i.e., nodes) possibly deployed at different sites that communicate to exchange intrusion detection-relevant data, for example, attack alerts. Each node of a distributed IDS typically reports an ongoing attack to the rest of the nodes when it detects the attack. The immediate detection and reporting of attacks by each IDS node is crucial for the timely detection of coordinated attacks (i.e., attacks targeting multiple sites in a given time order). Therefore, the attack detection speed in the context of distributed IDSes is typically evaluated by measuring the time needed for an IDS to converge to a state in which all its nodes are notified of an ongoing attack, as done by Hassanzadeh et al. [16] and Sen et al. [39].

Attack detection accuracy. The benefits of evaluating IDS attack detection accuracy are manifold. For instance, one may compare multiple IDSes in terms of their attack detection accuracy in order to deploy an IDS that operates optimally in a given environment, thus reducing the risks of a security breach. The security research community has developed multiple metrics for quantifying the attack detection accuracy, such as the *basic* metrics false and true positive rates. The false positive rate $\alpha = P(A|\neg I)$ quantifies the probability that an alert generated by an IDS is not an intrusion, but a regular benign activity; the true positive rate $1 - \beta = 1 - P(\neg A|I) = P(A|I)$ quantifies the probability that an alert generated by an IDS is really an intrusion.[3] There are also *composite* metrics, that is, metrics that combine the basic metrics in order to enable the analysis of relationships between them, such as a ROC (receiver operating characteristic) curve [28] and the metrics developed by Gaffney and Ulvila [12] and Gu et al. [13].

The measure of false positive rate is important when it comes to evaluating the attack detection accuracy of an IDS employed as part of a system featuring self-protection—such an IDS may exhibit high false positive rate and cause the triggering of many unnecessary actions countering attacks (e.g., shutting down targeted network services or sub-systems), which may have negative effects. For example, the system may incur high performance costs or become unavailable to users mistakenly labeled as users performing malicious activities. We now discuss the composite

---

[3] A denotes an alert event (i.e., an IDS generates an attack alert); I denotes an intrusion event (i.e., an attack is performed).

"expected cost" (C_{exp}) metric developed by Gaffney and Ulvila [12]. This metric is a representative *cost-based* metric. Under cost-based metrics, we understand metrics designed to quantify costs, such as performance or financial costs, incurred by a system performing actions countering activities labeled as malicious by an IDS. Cost-based metrics characterize the impact of the false positive rate and are therefore relevant in the context of this work.

Gaffney and Ulvila combine ROC curve analysis with cost estimation by associating an estimated cost with each IDS operating point (i.e., an IDS configuration that yields given values of the true and false positive rates). A ROC curve is a two-dimensional depiction of the accuracy of a detector as it plots true positive rate against the corresponding false positive rate. Gaffney and Ulvila introduce a cost ratio $C = C_{\alpha}/C_{\beta}$, where C_{α} is the cost of an IDS alert when an intrusion has not occurred, and C_{β} is the cost of not detecting an intrusion when it has occurred. To calculate the cost ratio, one would need a cost analysis model that can estimate C_{α} and C_{β}.

C_{exp} for a given IDS operating point can be calculated as $C_{exp} = Min(C\beta B, (1 - \alpha)(1 - \beta)) + Min(C(1 - \beta)B, \alpha(1 - B))$.[4] This formula can be obtained by analyzing (i.e., "rolling back") a decision tree whose leaves are costs that may be incurred by an IDS (i.e., C_{α} and C_{β}). For more details on the analytical formula of the "expected cost" metric, we refer the reader to [12].

Using C_{exp}, one can identify an optimal IDS operating point (i.e., an IDS configuration that yields optimal values of both the true and false positive detection rates) in a straightforward manner. The identification of an optimal IDS operating point is a common goal of IDS evaluation studies. A given operating point of an IDS is considered optimal if it has the lowest C_{exp} associated with it compared to the other operating points. In Fig. 14.5, we depict a ROC curve annotated with the minimal C_{exp} for an IDS such that $1 - \beta$ is related to α with a power function (i.e., $1 - \beta = \alpha^k$). In Fig. 14.5, we depict values of $1 - \beta$ such that $\alpha = 0.005, 0.010, 0.015$, and $k = 0.002182$. We obtain the values of α and k from the work of Gaffney and Ulvila [12]. Further, we assume a base rate $B = 0.1$ and a cost ratio $C = 10$ (i.e., the cost of not responding to an attack is 10 times higher than the cost of responding to a false alert).

Because of the negative effects that IDSes exhibiting high false positive rates may have, the research and industrial communities have designed IDS false alert filters. A typical false alert filter detects false alerts issued by an IDS and blocks their delivery. For instance, the de facto standard network-based IDS Snort [37] features suppression of alerts.[5] Besides technical benefits, false alert filters bring usability-related benefits; that is, they reduce the cognitive overhead incurred on IT security officers who deal with IDSes on a daily basis, an issue acknowledged by many researchers (e.g., Komlodi et al. [23]). Meng et al. [29] have proposed a cost-based metric called "relative expected cost" (C_{rec}), which enables the quantification

---

[4] $1 - \alpha = 1 - P(A|\neg I) = P(\neg A|\neg I); \beta = 1 - P(A|I) = P(\neg A|I); B$ is the base rate (i.e., prior probability that an intrusion event occurs—$P(I)$).

[5] See, for example, http://manual.snort.org/node19.html#SECTION00343000000000000000.

Fig. 14.5 Quantifying costs using the expected cost metric

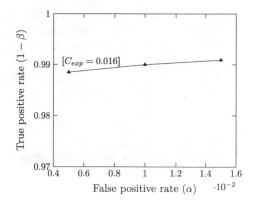

of costs incurred by IDSes that use false alert filters. C_{rec} is based on the "expected cost" metric (C_{exp}) [12]; however, in contrast to C_{exp}, C_{rec} quantifies costs associated with the accuracy of an IDS's false alert filter at classifying alerts as true or false. Values of C_{rec} can be associated with each IDS operating point on a ROC curve. We refer the reader to the work of Meng et al. [29] for more details on the "relative expected cost" metric.

Cost-based metrics require cost analysis models for estimating costs, such as C_α and C_β. However, such models can be difficult to construct in practice since they assume the availability of parameters that might not be easy to measure (e.g., man-hours). Further, cost-based metrics are not objective—they quantify the attack detection accuracy of an IDS based on a subjective measure (i.e., cost). However, cost-based metrics may be of significant value when the relationships between the different attack detection costs (e.g., cost of missing an attack and cost of a false alert) can be estimated and when such estimations would be considered as sufficiently accurate by the IDS evaluator for a particular IDS evaluation study. For instance, given a statement such as *"a false alarm is three times as costly as a missed attack,"* a cost-based metric would be crucial to identify an optimal IDS operating point.

Open challenge. Many modern environments exhibit self-adaptivity, a trait of self-awareness (see Chap. 1), in terms of on-demand provisioning of resources to computing nodes with respect to changes in the workload intensity. An example is a virtualized cloud environment that has *elastic* properties; that is, the hypervisor governing the environment may provision on-demand (i.e., hotplug) CPU and memory resources to virtual machines (VMs). With the increasing adoption of virtualization technology, the practice has emerged to deploy IDSes in virtualized environments. For instance, a network-based IDS, such as Snort [37], deployed in a designated, secured VM may tap into the physical network interface card used by all VMs. Therefore, it can monitor the network activities of all guest VMs at the same time while being isolated from, and transparent to, potential malicious VM users.

Existing metrics for quantifying IDS attack detection accuracy are defined with respect to a *fixed* set of hardware resources available to the IDS. Their values express the properties of the IDS for a specific hardware environment in which the IDS is expected to reside during its lifetime [15]. However, many modern virtualized environments (e.g., cloud environments) have elastic properties; that is, resources can be provisioned and used by VMs, on demand during operation. Elasticity may have an impact on the measured attack detection accuracy of an IDS deployed in a virtualized environment. For example, the measured attack detection accuracy of a network-based IDS under test may depend on the number of dropped packets by the IDS in the time intervals when attacks have been performed. Large amounts of dropped packets in such intervals due to lack of resources may manifest themselves as low IDS attack detection accuracy.

Based on the above, we believe that the use of conventional metrics may lead to inaccurate measurements in cases where the on-demand provisioning of resources to the VM where an IDS under test resides has significant impact on the IDS's attack detection accuracy.[6] This, in turn, may result in the deployment of misconfigured or ill-performing IDSes in production environments, increasing the risk of security breaches. We argue that novel metrics and measurement methodologies for measuring the attack detection accuracy of IDSes deployed in virtualized environments are needed. Such metrics and methodologies should take into account the behavior of a given IDS under test as its operational environment changes. As a result, they would allow to quantify the ability of the IDS to scale its attack detection efficiency as resources are allocated and deallocated during operation. Metrics for quantifying IDS attack detection accuracy that takes elasticity of virtualized environments into account are discussed in detail in Chap. 22.

14.4 Enhancing Self-awareness by Benchmarking

In some context, self-awareness may be used mainly to dimension the system. The knowledge of some relevant properties (like the latency of a job for real-time systems) guides the choice of the hardware to be used for a specific task. This is especially crucial where, for space limitations, the amount of computing capacity that can be inserted into the physical space is limited.

In the automotive domain, for example, processors take care of multiple jobs at the same time. Some of these jobs are high-priority ones, like the cruise control. Some other jobs have lower priority, like the entertainment system. Obtaining the awareness of how much computing capacity is needed for each of the required tasks can simplify the resource allocation and the entire design process. Applications can be packed in the same physical cores, to save space and minimize the amount of necessary hardware. While the system is running, the same awareness can guide scheduling and resource allocation decisions, minimizing energy and performance loss.

---

[6]Under conventional metrics, we understand existing IDS attack detection accuracy metrics, which do not take elasticity of virtualized environments into account.

14.4.1   Unveiling the Real-Time Properties of Schedulers

The design principles that are followed when developing resource management techniques in operating systems include *simplicity, low overhead/memory footprint*, and *efficiency*. Operating systems schedulers are usually developed following these principles and guidelines. Once a scheduler is developed, its performance is tested with a set of benchmarks. However, these benchmarks usually check the functionality of the schedulers and the correctness of their behavior from a functional point of view, while the ability to provide real-time guarantees is rarely properly quantified.

The real-time community has put a great effort in developing efficient scheduling algorithms and, more in general, resource management policies to respond to a broad variety of application models, types of execution platforms, etc. Unfortunately, a large share of these results remains confined to the theory and is not implemented into operating systems. In fact, operating system developers are resistant to the adoption of real-time methods and algorithms, mostly because general purpose operating systems must function in a more complex scenario than the one abstracted in real-time models, while real-time scheduling algorithms tend to respond to specific problems and needs.

In an attempt to close the gap between these two worlds (the implementation side and the theoretical algorithm side), one can basically follow two strategies: (1) simplifying the development of schedulers and providing tools that reduce the implementation burden; (2) abstracting relevant quantities that can describe the behavior of schedulers based on the execution of real tasks. This latter solution unveils the real-time properties of tasks when they are executed on top of the real implementation of scheduling policies. In turn, this introduces *self-awareness* in the system. The developer now has more information about the execution of tasks and is provided with relevant data that can be used to design the system (for example, for hardware dimensioning).

rt-muse[7] in an application-independent tool that takes as input a model of a multi-threaded application, where each thread is constructed by basic elements called *phases* and produces as output an analysis of what happens when the threads are executed on a real Linux platform.

Phases can be selected from a library that includes pure computation, resource locking, and memory usage. The tool is also extensible, and the effort to create new phases (possibly needed to capture application-specific behaviors) is minimal. The results of the experiments are reproducible, as the tool relies only on tools that are integrated in the Linux kernel. rt-muse records execution traces of the benchmark application. The recorded traces are analyzed, providing both per-thread metrics and aggregated features such as the bandwidth and the delay of the computing capacity given to the application. The analysis is based on plug-ins, each one providing some desired real-time feature. The usage of plug-ins enables both the configuration of the analysis procedure and the development of additional analysis methods. Currently, rt-muse supports three types of analysis. The runmap analysis is aimed at providing migration-relevant information and execution maps, unveiling how the computing

---

[7]https://github.com/martinamaggio/rt-muse/.

resources are utilized. The statistical plug-in approximates the empirical data about the execution times of the threads with probability distributions. The supply analysis produces abstractions of the computing capacity based on the concept of a supply function [3, 25].

rt-muse executes the multi-threaded program directly on the hardware and transfers the data via a UDP network connection, to avoid generating logging overhead on the machine that is executing the threads.

The tool was used to discover interesting facts about the behavior of Linux scheduling classes. In Linux terms, SCHED_OTHER is the standard algorithm in Linux, called Completely Fair Scheduler (CFS). The main advantage of using this algorithm is to enforce fairness among the running threads. Threads that have the same characteristics should receive an approximately equal amount of CPU. A set $\mathscr{T} = \{\tau_1, \ldots, \tau_6\}$ of 6 threads was run using rt-muse. All the τ_i threads have the same characteristics. Their job is composed by one single phase $\phi_{i,1}$ which simply executes some mathematical instructions. In other words, every thread executes a certain number of mathematical operations for each job, and jobs are run one after the other without stopping. The scheduling parameters of all the threads belonging to $\mathscr{T}$ are the same: The threads affinity mask contains three CPUs, [1, 2, 3], avoiding the execution on CPU #0. The experiment lasted 100 s, and rt-muse was recording the start time of each job. Ideally, one would expect that six threads with the same characteristics, running on three cores, would receive similar budgets, possibly obtaining each half of a CPU.

Table 14.3 reports the amount of CPU α_i' that is used by each thread as estimated by the tool and the delay in executing the thread δ_i'. The last three columns correspond to the share of consumed CPU.

The allocated computing capacities α_i' are almost all equal to each other, except α_6' which is noticeably larger than the others. A possible explanation could be in the longer time τ_6 executed over the same CPU. Although other interfering operating system threads could be easily accommodated on CPU #0, which is not used by the set $\mathscr{T}$, still the overall delivered bandwidth is $\alpha_*' = 2.641862$, quite less than the full 3 CPUs dedicated to $\mathscr{T}$.

Table 14.3 Threads scheduled by SCHED_OTHER

τ_i	CPU USAGE		CPU SHARE		
	α_i'	δ_i'	#1	#2	#3
τ_1	0.412	0.591	0.062	0.614	0.324
τ_2	0.410	1.314	0.191	0.332	0.476
τ_3	0.409	1.398	0.009	0.440	0.551
τ_4	0.413	1.839	0.159	0.302	0.539
τ_5	0.413	0.684	0.109	0.545	0.346
τ_6	0.567	3.985	0.834	0.062	0.104

From this experiment, a developer would learn that the Completely Fair Scheduler in Linux is in fact not that fair among threads and that to enforce real-time guarantees on the computation capacity offered to the threads, it is better to use real-time scheduling policies such as SCHED_RR and SCHED_FIFO. In subsequent experiments with the tool, however, it was discovered that despite both SCHED_RR and SCHED_FIFO, timing properties, they do not enforce any type of fairness among the threads and the push/pull migration system that they use has quite many defects [27].

14.5   Addressing the Challenges in Defining Reference Workloads for Benchmarking Self-aware Computing System Properties

Benchmarking is a critical step for effective capacity planning and resource provisioning, and consequently may guide the design of self-aware systems. An effective benchmark should evaluate the system responsiveness under a wide range of client demands from low to high, but most benchmarks are designed to assess the system responsiveness under a *steady* client demand. If systems are provisioned for steady *peak* loads to avoid the deleterious effects of sudden workload surges, they consistently suffer from low resource utilizations [4], which results in ecosystems that are energy inefficient and wasteful. In addition, system behavior under high yet steady client demand may actually be very different than under varying or bursty conditions [30, 32]. Because of its tremendous performance implications, variability and burstiness must be accounted in the design of self-aware systems and must be incorporated into benchmarking.

Burstiness in workloads can be broadly defined as workload surges that occur aperiodically, with various frequencies and (usually) short duration. In cloud computing, for example, virtual machine (VM) workloads have been observed to be highly bursty [5, 31, 44]. For a typical Web server, burstiness can be an outcome of the flash crowd effect, where a Web page linked by a popular blog or media site suddenly experiences a huge increase of the number of hits. Consider also the case of an auction site (e.g., eBay) where users compete to buy an object that is going to be soon assigned to the customer with the best offer, but also in e-business sites as a result of special offers and marketing campaigns. Generally, if variability or even burstiness in the workload is observed, it can be catastrophic for performance, leading to dramatic server overloading, uncontrolled increase of response times and, in the worst case, service unavailability [30–32].

Standard benchmarks lack the ability to produce a representatively varying load profile with burstiness because user arrivals are defined by a Poisson process, i.e., they are always assumed to be independent of their past activity and independent of each other. Exponential interarrival times are incompatible with the notion of burstiness for several reasons:

Temporal locality: Intuitively, under conditions of burstiness, arrivals from different sources cannot happen at random instants of time, but they are instead condensed in short periods across time. Therefore, the probability of sending a request inside this period is much larger than outside it. This behavior is inconsistent with classic distributions considered in performance engineering of Web applications, such as Poisson, hyper-exponential, Zipf, and Pareto, which all miss the ability of describing temporal locality within a process.

Variability of different time scales: Variability within a traffic surge is a relevant characteristic for testing peak performance degradation. Therefore, a benchmarking model for burstiness should not only create surges of variable intensity and duration, but also create fluctuations within a surge. This implies a hierarchy of variability levels that cannot be described by a simple exponential distribution and instead requires a more structured arrival process.

Lack of aggregation: In standard client–server benchmarks, each thread on the client machines uses a dedicated stream of random numbers; thus, interarrival times of different users are always independent. This is indeed representative of normal traffic, but fails in capturing the essential property of traffic surges: Users act in an aggregated fashion which is mostly incompatible with independence assumptions.

In the following subsections, we shortly outline an approach to model variable load profiles and present a methodology that addresses the above points and provides a seamless way to incorporate burstiness into benchmarks.

14.5.1 Modeling of Load Intensity Patterns

Many modeling approaches include concepts to define workload intensity by attaching this information to modeled workload scenarios. Examples can be found in the SPE approach by [40] and in UML-SPT [34]. UML-SPT supports scenarios with open and closed workloads that are parameterized by specifications of arrivals (occurrence patterns), or a population with a think times distribution (external delay). The allowed attribute values include the definition of probability distributions and different arrival patterns—namely bursty, bounded, and periodic. Other approaches to be mentioned in this context are the CSM [36] and MARTE [35].

We conclude from reviewing the above-mentioned approaches that a load intensity profile definition is a crucial element to complete a workload characterization. The observed or estimated arrival process of transactions (on the level of users, sessions, or requests/jobs arrivals) needs to be specified. As basis to specify time-dependent arrival rates or interarrival times, the extraction of a usage model should provide a classification of transaction types that are statistically indistinguishable in terms of their resource demanding characteristics.

A *load intensity profile* is an instance of an arrival process. A workload that consists of several types of transactions is then characterized by a set of load intensity profile instances.

Load intensity profiles are directly applicable in the context of any open workload scenario with a theoretically unlimited number of users, but are not limited to those in [38]. In a closed or partially closed workload scenario, with a limited number of active transactions, the arrival process can be specified within the given upper limits and zero. Any load intensity profile can be transformed into a time series containing arrival rates per sampling interval.

For a load profile to be representative of a given application domain, it has to be a mixture of (i) one or more (overlaying) seasonal patterns, (ii) long-term trends including trend breaks, (iii) characteristic bursts, and (iv) a certain degree of noise. These components can be combined in an additive or multiplicative manner over time as visualized in Fig. 14.6.

At early development stages, load intensity profiles can be estimated by domain experts by defining synthetic profiles using statistical distributions or mathematical functions. At a higher abstraction level, the Descartes Load Intensity Model (DLIM) allows to descriptively define the seasonal, trend, burst, and noise elements in a wizard-like manner [22]. DLIM is supported by a toolchain named LIMBO [1].

A good starting point for a load intensity profile definition at the development stage is to analyze the load intensity of comparable systems within the same domain.

We identify the following open challenges in the field of load profile description and their automatic extraction:

- Seasonal patterns may overlay each other (e.g., weekly and daily patterns) and change in their shape over time. Current load profile extraction approaches do not fully support these scenarios.
- Based on meta-knowledge or clustering techniques, seasonal patterns can be classified and extracted into separate models, e.g., a model for ordinary working days, for public holidays, and for weekends, which would result in more accurate load profile extraction.

Fig. 14.6 Elements of load intensity profiles as proposed in [22]

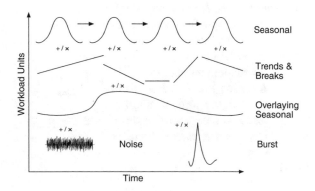

14.5.2   Markov Arrival Processes for Modeling Burstiness

A Markov arrival process (MAP) can be seen as a simple mathematical model of a time series, such as a sequence of interarrival times, for which we can accurately shape distribution and correlations between successive values. Correlations among consecutive think times are instrumental to capture periods of the time series where think times are consecutively small and thus a surge occurs, as well as to determine the duration of the surge.

We use a class of MAPs with two states only, one responsible for the generation of "short" interarrival times implying that users arrive in closely spaced arrivals, possibly resulting in surges, while the other is responsible for the generation of "long" interarrival times associated to periods of normal traffic. In the "short" state, interarrival times are generated with mean rate λ_{short}; similarly, they have mean rate $\lambda_{long} < \lambda_{short}$ in the "long" state. In order to create correlation between different events, after the generation of a new interarrival time sample, our model has a probability p_{short} that two consecutive times are short and a different probability p_{long} of two consecutive think times being both long. The values of p_{short} and p_{long} shape the correlations between consecutive interarrival times and are instrumental to determine the duration of the traffic surge. The two probabilities p_{short} and p_{long} are independent of each other.

In order to gain intuition on the way this model works, we provide the following pseudocode to generate a sample of n_t interarrival time values $Z_1, Z_2, \ldots, Z_n, \ldots, Z_{n_t}$ from a MAP parameterized by the tuple $(\lambda_{long}, \lambda_{short}, p_{long}, p_{short})$:

function: MAP_sample($\lambda_{long}, \lambda_{short}, p_{long}, p_{short}, n_t$)
/* initialization in normal traffic state */
active_state = "long";
for $n = 1, 2, \ldots, n_t$
/* generate sample in current state */
    Z_n = sample from exponential distribution
       with rate λ_{active_state};
/* update MAP state */
    r = random number in [0, 1];
    if $active\_state$ ="long" **and** $r \geq p_{long}$
       $active\_state$ = "short";
    else if $active\_state$ ="short" **and** $r \geq p_{short}$
       $active\_state$ = "long";
    end
end

Figure 14.7 summarizes the traffic surge model described above. Note from the pseudocode that the problem of variability of different time scales is solved effectively in MAPs by the fact that if the MAP is in a state i, then the samples are generated by an

Fig. 14.7 Model of traffic
surges based on regulation of
interarrival times

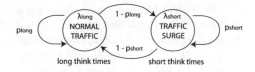

exponential distribution with rate λ_i associated with state i. This creates fluctuations within the traffic surge. The probability of arrivals inside the traffic surge is larger than outside it, thanks to the state change mechanism that alters the rate of arrival from λ_{long} to λ_{short}.

Summarizing, we propose to generate interarrival times in such a way to periodically enter into a state "short" that facilitates the formation of burstiness because here users have smaller interarrival times and thus submit requests more often. The parameterization of the MAP requires only to assign λ_{short} and $\lambda_{long} < \lambda_{short}$ to describe the interarrival times, respectively, during flash crowds and normal user activity periods, together with the probabilities p_{short} and p_{long} of consecutive interarrival times being both short or both long, respectively. Once that these four parameters have been set up, the benchmark can generate interarrival time samples using the above pseudocode. For more details on MAPs, we direct the interested reader to [6, 7].

Yet, the problem that is not solved is the quantification of burstiness. The *index of dispersion* as a regulator of the intensity of traffic surges. The index of dispersion I is a measure of burstiness in networking and service engineering [14, 30]. Consider a sequence of values (e.g., think times, interarrival times, and service times) with variability quantified by the squared coefficient of variation (SCV), where the difference in magnitude between consecutive values is summarized by the lag-k autocorrelations[8] ρ_k. Assuming that SCV and ρ_k do not change over time, then the index of dispersion is the quantity $I = SCV \left(1 + 2 \sum_{k=1}^{\infty} \rho_k\right)$. For finite length sequences, this value can be estimated accurately, without resorting to an infinite summation, using the methods outlined in [14]. The index of dispersion I has the fundamental property that it grows proportionally with both variability and correlations, thus can be immediately used to identify burstiness in a workload trace.

When there is no burstiness, the value of I is equal to the squared coefficient of variation of the distribution, e.g., $I = SCV = 1$ for the exponential distribution, while it grows to values of thousands on bursty processes. Thus, a parameterization of I spanning a range from single to multiple digits can give a good sense of scalability between workloads with "no burstiness" and workloads with "dramatic burstiness"; for examples of workloads and their index of dispersion, we direct the interested reader to [31].

Now the question becomes: How should the MAP process be parameterized in order to regulate burstiness using the index of dispersion as a measure? We present here a case study that considers a **closed system** and show how to determine a

---

[8]Recall that the lag-k autocorrelation coefficient is a normalized measure of correlation between random variables X_t and X_{t-k}, with position in the trace differing by k lags. For a trace with mean μ and variance σ^2, $\rho_k = E[(X_t - \mu)(X_{t-k} - \mu)]/\sigma^2, k \geq 1$.

parameterization (λ_{long}, λ_{short}, p_{long}, p_{short}) that produces a sequence of surges in the traffic. We assume that the user gives the desired values of the mean interarrival time $E[Z]$ (typically, in closed systems terminology, this value can be considered as the mean user "think time" before a request is sent to the system and of the (desired) index of dispersion I). Again, using typical closed system terminology, we assume that we have N circulating users in the system. For example, for a typical Web server, N corresponds to the maximum number of client connections. One needs to also consider the average service demand $E[D_i]$ of each server i that can be estimated from utilization measurements [43]. This measure is important to provide, because the purpose of the benchmark is to keep the average system utilization to less than 100 %, i.e., the system is never in over-saturation.

A MAP can fully define the think/interarrival time distribution other than the mean $E[Z]$ starting by the following parameterization equations:

$$\lambda_{short}^{-1} = (\textstyle\sum_i E[D_i])/f, \tag{14.1}$$

$$\lambda_{long}^{-1} = f \max(N(\textstyle\sum_i E[D_i]), E[Z]]). \tag{14.2}$$

Here, $f \geq 1$ is a free parameter, N is the maximum number of client connections considered in the benchmarking experiment, $\sum_i E[D_i]$ is the minimum time taken by a request to complete at all servers, and $N(\sum_i E[D_i])$ provides an upper bound to the time required by the system to respond to all requests. Equation (14.1) states that, in order to create surges, the think times should be smaller than the time required by the system to respond to requests. Thus, assuming that all N clients are simultaneously waiting to submit a new request, one may reasonably expect that after a few multiples of λ_{short}^{-1} all clients have submitted requests and the architecture has been yet unable to cope with the traffic surge. Conversely, (14.2) defines think times that on average give to the system enough time to cope with any request, i.e., the normal traffic regime. Note that the condition $\lambda_{long}^{-1} \geq f E[Z]$ is imposed to assure that the mean think time can be $E[Z]$, which would not be possible if both $\lambda_{short}^{-1} > \lambda_{long}^{-1} > E[Z]$ since $f > 1$, and in MAPs, the moments $E[Z]$, $E[Z^2]$, ... are

$$E[Z^k] = \frac{p_{long}}{p_{long} + p_{short}} \lambda_{short}^{-k} + \frac{p_{short}}{p_{long} + p_{short}} \lambda_{long}^{-k}. \tag{14.3}$$

The above formula for $k = 1$ implies that $E[Z]$ has a value in between of λ_{short}^{-1} and λ_{long}^{-1}, which is not compatible with $\lambda_{short}^{-1} \geq \lambda_{long}^{-1} \geq f E[Z]$. According to the last formula, the MAP parameterization can always impose the user-defined $E[Z]$ if

$$p_{long} = p_{short} \left(\frac{\lambda_{long}^{-1} - E[Z]}{E[Z] - \lambda_{short}^{-1}} \right), \tag{14.4}$$

condition which we use in the modified TPC-W benchmark to impose the mean think time.

In order to fix the values of p_{short} and f in the above equations, we first do a simple search on the space ($p_{short} \geq 0$, $f \geq 1$) where at each iteration we check the value of the index of dispersion I and lag-1 autocorrelation coefficient ρ_1 from the current values of p_{short} and f. We stop searching when we find a MAP with an I that is within 1 % of the target user-specified index of dispersion and the lag-1 autocorrelation is at least $\rho_1 \geq 0.4$ in order to have consistent probability of formation of surges within short time periods.[9] The index of dispersion of the MAP can be evaluated at each iteration as[10] [6, 7, 33]:

$$I = 1 + \frac{2\, p_{short}\, p_{long}\, (\lambda_{short} - \lambda_{long})^2}{(p_{short} + p_{long})(\lambda_{short}\, p_{short} + \lambda_{long}\, p_{long})^2}, \tag{14.5}$$

while the lag-1 autocorrelation coefficient is computed as

$$\rho_1 = \frac{1}{2}(1 - p_{long} - p_{short})\left(1 - \frac{E[Z]^2}{E[Z^2] - E[Z]^2}\right), \tag{14.6}$$

where $E[Z^2]$ is obtained from (14.3) for $k = 2$. We direct the reader to [31] for a case study that illustrates how to generate arrival processes with various degrees of burstiness within the TPC-W benchmark.

14.6 Conclusion and Open Challenges

In this chapter, we proposed a set of metrics for describing self-aware computing system properties and grouped them by the MAPE-K paradigm. This set of metrics can be seen as a first step toward building benchmarks for self-aware computing systems, consisting of a well-defined measurement methodology (run rules), representative workloads, and metrics.

The central remaining challenge is to properly evaluate the behavior of self-aware systems with this set of metrics, in other words to build a level-playing field for fair comparisons of self-aware system properties. This includes the challenges to define reference systems/behavior, and design measurement processes for repeatable and fair results. Ideas on how these challenges could be tackled can be found in related areas of research such as self-adaptive systems, autonomic computing, and similar. Starting from Sect. 14.3.1, we presented central aspects from related areas that may become relevant for benchmarking self-aware computing systems. As a more philosophical outlook and discussion on how self-aware system properties can be assessed, we refer the reader to Chap. 15.

---

[9]The threshold 0.4 has been chosen since it is the closest round value to the maximum autocorrelation that can be obtained by a two-state MAP.

[10]Note that Eq. (14.5) slightly differs in the denominator from other expressions of I, such as those reported in [14], because here we consider a MAP that is a generalization of an MMPP process.

References

1. LIMBO: Load Intensity Modeling Framework. http://descartes.tools/limbo, 2015.
2. Rodrigo F Almeida, Flávio RC Sousa, Sérgio Lifschitz, and Javam C Machado. On Defining Metrics for Elasticity of Cloud Databases. In *Proceedings of the 28th Brazilian Symposium on Databases*, 2013.
3. Enrico Bini, Marko Bertogna, and Sanjoy Baruah. Virtual multiprocessor platforms: Specification and use. In *Proceedings of the 2009 30th IEEE Real-Time Systems Symposium*, pages 437–446, 2009.
4. Robert Birke, Mathias Björkqvist, Lydia Y. Chen, Evgenia Smirni, and Ton Engbersen. (big)data in a virtualized world: volume, velocity, and variety in cloud datacenters. In *Proceedings of the 12th USENIX conference on File and Storage Technologies, FAST 2014, Santa Clara, CA, USA, February 17-20, 2014*, pages 177–189, 2014.
5. Robert Birke, Andrej Podzimek, Lydia Y. Chen, and Evgenia Smirni. State-of-the-practice in data center virtualization: Toward a better understanding of VM usage. In *2013 43rd Annual IEEE/IFIP International Conference on Dependable Systems and Networks (DSN), Budapest, Hungary, June 24-27, 2013*, pages 1–12, 2013.
6. Giuliano Casale, Eddy Z. Zhang, and Evgenia Smirni. Kpc-toolbox: Best recipes for automatic trace fitting using markovian arrival processes. *Perform. Eval.*, 67(9):873–896, 2010.
7. Giuliano Casale, Eddy Z. Zhang, and Evgenia Smirni. Trace data characterization and fitting for markov modeling. *Perform. Eval.*, 67(2):61–79, 2010.
8. Dean Chandler, Nurcan Coskun, Salman Baset, Erich Nahum, Steve Realmuto Masud Khandker, Tom Daly, Nicholas Wakou Indrani Paul, Louis Barton, Mark Wagner, Rema Hariharan, and Yun seng Chao. Report on Cloud Computing to the OSG Steering Committee. Technical report, April 2012.
9. Brian F. Cooper, Adam Silberstein, Erwin Tam, Raghu Ramakrishnan, and Russell Sears. Benchmarking cloud serving systems with YCSB. In *Proceedings of the 1st ACM symposium on Cloud computing*, SoCC '10, pages 143–154, New York, NY, USA, 2010. ACM.
10. Thibault Dory, Boris Mejías, Peter Van Roy, and Nam-Luc Tran. Measuring Elasticity for Cloud Databases. In *Proceedings of the The Second International Conference on Cloud Computing, GRIDs, and Virtualization*, 2011.
11. Enno Folkerts, Alexander Alexandrov, Kai Sachs, Alexandru Iosup, Volker Markl, and Cafer Tosun. Benchmarking in the Cloud: What It Should, Can, and Cannot Be. In Raghunath Nambiar and Meikel Poess, editors, *Selected Topics in Performance Evaluation and Benchmarking*, volume 7755 of *Lecture Notes in Computer Science*, pages 173–188. Springer Berlin Heidelberg, 2012.
12. John E. Gaffney and Jacob W. Ulvila. Evaluation of intrusion detectors: a decision theory approach. In *Proceedings of the 2001 IEEE Symposium on Security and Privacy*, pages 50–61, 2001.
13. Guofei Gu, Prahlad Fogla, David Dagon, Wenke Lee, and Boris Skorić. Measuring intrusion detection capability: an information-theoretic approach. In *Proceedings of the 2006 ACM Symposium on Information, computer and communications security (ASIACCS)*, pages 90–101, New York, NY, USA, 2006. ACM.
14. R. Gusella. Characterizing the variability of arrival processes with indexes of dispersion. *IEEE JSAC*, 19(2):203–211, 1991.
15. Mike Hall and Kevin Wiley. Capacity verification for high speed network intrusion detection systems. In *Proceedings of the 5th International Conference on Recent Advances in Intrusion Detection (RAID)*, pages 239–251, Berlin, Heidelberg, 2002. Springer-Verlag.
16. Amin Hassanzadeh and Radu Stoleru. Towards Optimal Monitoring in Cooperative IDS for Resource Constrained Wireless Networks. In *Proceedings of 20th International Conference on Computer Communications and Networks (ICCCN)*, pages 1–8, August 2011.
17. Nikolas Roman Herbst, Samuel Kounev, and Ralf Reussner. Elasticity in Cloud Computing: What it is, and What it is Not (short paper). In *Proceedings of the 10th International Conference on Autonomic Computing (ICAC 2013)*. USENIX, June 2013.

18. Nikolas Roman Herbst, Samuel Kounev, Andreas Weber, and Henning Groenda. BUNGEE: An Elasticity Benchmark for Self-adaptive IaaS Cloud Environments. In *Proceedings of the 10th International Symposium on Software Engineering for Adaptive and Self-Managing Systems*, SEAMS '15, pages 46–56, Piscataway, NJ, USA, 2015. IEEE Press.

19. Karl Huppler. Performance Evaluation and Benchmarking. chapter The Art of Building a Good Benchmark, pages 18–30. Springer-Verlag, Berlin, Heidelberg, 2009.

20. Karl Huppler. Benchmarking with Your Head in the Cloud. In Raghunath Nambiar and Meikel Poess, editors, *Topics in Performance Evaluation, Measurement and Characterization*, volume 7144 of *Lecture Notes in Computer Science*, pages 97–110. Springer Berlin Heidelberg, 2012.

21. Sadeka Islam, Kevin Lee, Alan Fekete, and Anna Liu. How a Consumer Can Measure Elasticity for Cloud Platforms. In *Proceedings of the 3rd ACM/SPEC International Conference on Performance Engineering*, ICPE '12, pages 85–96, New York, NY, USA, 2012. ACM.

22. Jóakim V. Kistowski, Nikolas Herbst, Daniel Zoller, Samuel Kounev, and Andreas Hotho. Modeling and extracting load intensity profiles. In *Proceedings of the 10th International Symposium on Software Engineering for Adaptive and Self-Managing Systems*, SEAMS '15, pages 109–119, Piscataway, NJ, USA, 2015. IEEE Press.

23. Anita Komlodi, John R. Goodall, and Wayne G. Lutters. An Information Visualization Framework for Intrusion Detection. In *CHI '04 Extended Abstracts on Human Factors in Computing Systems*, page 1743, New York, NY, USA, 2004. ACM.

24. Michael Kuperberg, Nikolas Roman Herbst, Joakim Gunnarson von Kistowski, and Ralf Reussner. Defining and Quantifying Elasticity of Resources in Cloud Computing and Scalable Platforms. Technical report, Karlsruhe Institute of Technology (KIT), 2011.

25. Hennadiy Leontyev, Samarjit Chakraborty, and James H. Anderson. Multiprocessor extensions to real-time calculus. *Real-Time Syst.*, 47(6):562–617, December 2011.

26. Zheng Li, L. O'Brien, He Zhang, and R. Cai. On a Catalogue of Metrics for Evaluating Commercial Cloud Services. In *Grid Computing (GRID), 2012 ACM/IEEE 13th International Conference on*, pages 164–173, Sept 2012.

27. Martina Maggio, Juri Lelli, and Enrico Bin. Analysis of os schedulers with rt-muse. In *RTSS@Work (Real-Time Systems Symposium Demo Session)*, 2015.

28. Roy A. Maxion and Kymie M.C. Tan. Benchmarking anomaly-based detection systems. In *Proceedings of the International Conference on Dependable Systems and Networks (DSN)*, pages 623–630, 2000.

29. Yuxin Meng. Measuring intelligent false alarm reduction using an ROC curve-based approach in network intrusion detection. In *IEEE International Conference on Computational Intelligence for Measurement Systems and Applications (CIMSA)*, pages 108–113, July 2012.

30. Ningfang Mi, Giuliano Casale, Ludmila Cherkasova, and Evgenia Smirni. Burstiness in multi-tier applications: Symptoms, causes, and new models. In *ACM/IFIP/USENIX 9th International Middleware Conference (Middleware'08)*, Leuven, Belgium, 2008. The preliminary paper appeared in the HotMetrics 2008 Workshop.

31. Ningfang Mi, Giuliano Casale, Ludmila Cherkasova, and Evgenia Smirni. Injecting realistic burstiness to a traditional client-server benchmark. In *Proceedings of the 6th International Conference on Autonomic Computing, ICAC 2009, June 15-19, 2009, Barcelona, Spain*, pages 149–158, 2009.

32. Ningfang Mi, Qi Zhang, Alma Riska, Evgenia Smirni, and Erik Riedel. Performance impacts of autocorrelated flows in multi-tiered systems. *Perform. Eval.*, 64(9-12):1082–1101, 2007.

33. M. F. Neuts. *Structured Stochastic Matrices of M/G/1 Type and Their Applications*. Marcel Dekker, New York, 1989.

34. Object Management Group, Inc. UML Profile for Schedulability, Performance, and Time (SPT), version 1.1. http://www.omg.org/spec/SPTP/1.1/, 2005.

35. Object Management Group, Inc. UML profile for MARTE: Modeling and Analysis of Real-Time Embedded Systems, version 1.1. http://www.omg.org/spec/MARTE/1.1/, 2011.

36. Dorin Bogdan Petriu and C. Murray Woodside. An intermediate metamodel with scenarios and resources for generating performance models from UML designs. *Springer Software and System Modeling (SoSym)*, 6(2):163–184, 2007.

37. Martin Roesch. Snort - Lightweight Intrusion Detection for Networks. In *Proceedings of the 13th USENIX conference on System Administration (LISA)*, pages 229–238. USENIX Association, 1999.

38. Bianca Schroeder, Adam Wierman, and Mor Harchol-Balter. Open versus closed: A cautionary tale. In *Proceedings of the 3rd conference on Networked Systems Design & Implementation (NSDI '06)*, pages 18–18. USENIX Association, 2006.

39. Jaydip Sen, Arijit Ukil, Debasis Bera, and Arpan Pal. A distributed intrusion detection system for wireless ad hoc networks. In *16th IEEE International Conference on Networks (ICON)*, pages 1–6, 2008.

40. Connie U. Smith and Lloyd G. Williams. *Performance Solutions: A practical guide to creating responsive, scalable software*. Addison-Wesley, 2002.

41. Christian Tinnefeld, Daniel Taschik, and Hasso Plattner. Quantifying the Elasticity of a Database Management System. In *DBKDA 2014, The Sixth International Conference on Advances in Databases, Knowledge, and Data Applications*, pages 125–131, 2014.

42. Joe Weinman. Time is Money: The Value of "On-Demand", 2011. (accessed July 9, 2014).

43. Qi Zhang, Ludmila Cherkasova, and Evgenia Smirni. A regression-based analytic model for dynamic resource provisioning of multi-tier applications. In *Fourth International Conference on Autonomic Computing (ICAC'07), Jacksonville, Florida, USA, June 11-15, 2007*, page 27, 2007.

44. S. Zhang, Z. Qian, Z. Luo, J. Wu, and S. Lu. Burstiness-aware resource reservation for server consolidation in computing clouds. *IEEE Trnascations on Parallel and Distributed Systems*, 27(4):964–977, 2016.

Chapter 15
Assessing Self-awareness

**Lukas Esterle, Kirstie L. Bellman, Steffen Becker, Anne Koziolek,
Christopher Landauer and Peter Lewis**

Abstract This chapter discusses the importance of assessing self-awareness of a system and different approaches and aspects on how to enable a human as well as a machine to perform such an assessment. The chapter also elaborates on the different requirements and constraints for an assessment. Furthermore, this chapter outlines how these requirements and constraints limit the accuracy of defining the capabilities of an assessed system and the corresponding degree of self-awareness.

15.1   Introduction

An essential part of self-awareness is the ability to assess ones current state, current situation, and to reason about how one can map from ones current state into the current situation, given ones goals and capabilities. Hence self-assessment in many forms becomes a foundation for self-awareness. Included in the self-awareness of one's capabilities relevant to a given goal is the ability to identify the capabilities

L. Esterle (✉)
Technische Universität Wien, Vienna, Austria
e-mail: lukas.esterle@tuwien.ac.at

S. Becker
Technische Universität Chemnitz, Chemnitz, Germany
e-mail: steffen.becker@informatik.tu-chemnitz.de

K.L. Bellman · C. Landauer
Aerospace Corporation, El Segundo, CA, USA
e-mail: kirstie.l.bellman@aero.org

C. Landauer
e-mail: chris.landauer@aero.org

A. Koziolek
Karlsruhe Institute of Technology, Karlsruhe, Germany
e-mail: anne.koziolek@kit.edu

P. Lewis
Aston University, Birmingham, UK
e-mail: p.lewis@aston.ac.uk

© Springer International Publishing AG 2017   465
S. Kounev et al. (eds.), *Self-Aware Computing Systems*,
DOI 10.1007/978-3-319-47474-8_15

and limitations one has to be self-aware to be able to reflect on one's components and behaviors. Hence, human beings will be quick to identify for one the capabilities they have to monitor and to reason about their own system. Unless provided with special external sensors, they will quickly tell you that they cannot tell you the state of individual brain neurons or even major blood arteries, but that they can tell you a great deal about where an object is touching them on their skin. They can tell you that they can reason about an action plan, but that their motivation for certain goals is sometimes less clear. They can tell you what they heard or saw (with errors in both when compared to an external recording), but they may not be able to report why something caught their attention. And so the list goes on. In practice, these abilities are fundamental to a human's (or a system's) ability to reason about what they know, how well their reasoning is going or where their reasoning or information may be flawed.

In a similar fashion, there are various situations requiring a computational system embedded in a dynamic environment to determine its performance and capabilities. Nevertheless, it might also be required to identify the system's properties of self-awareness. In this case, the system is not trying to define how good it is able to achieve certain goals but what it is able to do in order to achieve these goals at all. There are various situations where an assessment of a system is beneficial or even required. One of the most prominent situations is in case of (self-)explanation. Here the system is required to justify its own behavior. This can happen *a priori* as well *a posteriori* achieving a certain goal or performing a specific task. *A priori* might allow a user or another system to decide if the respective system might be able to perform a certain task. A posteriori this information might be used in order to reason about why a system failed or succeeded in achieving a specific goal/task. However, assessment is a pivotal process for self-adaptation of systems embedded in a dynamic environment or deployed for a new, unknown mission. Without the ability to assess the capabilities of a system, reasoning about the chances of success as well as improving one's own behavior in order to achieve certain goals becomes impossible. This makes assessment a foundational process for any self-aware system.

In order for a system to be able to reason about its own capabilities, it has to be aware of its own abilities which are based on functions, actuators, and mechanisms. In a similar fashion, a system might need to be able to assess the level of self-awareness of another system. Alternatively, a cooperative system might want to be able to make a statement about its own level of awareness when this is requested by another system. We therefore distinguish between *internal assessment* and *external assessment*. We define an assessment as an internal assessment whenever a system assesses its own level of self-awareness. In contrast, external assessment is done from the outside, where a system or a human assesses another system by posing different questions and observing the corresponding response. In external assessment we may not be able to consider all systems to be cooperative or trustworthy. Furthermore, the response a system might give to a posed question is most probably ambiguous. For that reason, external assessment may request the result of an internal assessment but additionally requires techniques to assess other systems without their explicit consent. Therefore, we will also propose approaches similar to the imitation game proposed by Turing

[8] also known as the Turing test. While in the imitation game, a machine should try to trick a human assessor into believing to interact with another human, we will try to illustrate approaches to allow an assessor to identify specific levels, processes, or accuracy of self-awareness. In a similar fashion, we are not trying to find out whether a system is self-aware per se but what state of self-awareness this system might have.

The result of such an assessment would allow the system to reason about the minimal and the maximal capabilities of the assessed system. Furthermore, a system able to assess its own level of self-awareness would be able to indicate possible limitations in capabilities to other systems. Conversely, other systems may make assumptions based on such indications. Only by having an understanding of the current level of self-awareness, the system is able to perform appropriate actions in order to adapt its own level of self-awareness in coordination with an operator.

In Part I of this chapter, we discuss some of the issues in developing artificial systems with some of these essential self-assessment capabilities. We will initially consider the differences, benefits, and drawbacks between assessments performed by humans and assessments performed by a machine. Afterwards, we will outline the problems and benefits of the so-called black-box and white-box assessments. Finally, we present an overview of different axes of assessing self-awareness such as domain, level, or processes. We will specially focus on the indicators for the various levels of self-awareness. In all cases, we will propose general approaches and present constraints for white-box as well as black-box assessment. In Part II, we acknowledge that some areas of self-assessment overlap with the traditional areas of verification and validation in assessing whether one's performance or behavior is meeting well enough one's goals and requirements. In this latter section, we discuss some of the relevancy of current methods and some of the shortfalls of our traditional methods for assessment and self-assessment in self-aware systems.

Part I: Essentials of Self-assessment Capabilities

15.2   Human Versus Machine

An important aspect of assessing the level of self-awareness of a system is whether it is done by the system itself or by a human. While internal assessment can only be performed by the system itself, external assessment may also be performed by an operator or user of the system. Both approaches have the benefits and drawbacks. Internal assessment can only be performed by the system itself. However, this requires trust from the humans and other machines in the assessment process as well as the truthful information by the assessing system.

Table 15.1 presents the differences/difficulties/benefits between having a human perform the assessment and enabling machines to perform the assessment of the self-awareness of another machine. While a machine might be able to perform an assessment with very high accuracy, a human can also use his/her intuition to reason about the state of self-awareness of a system. Nevertheless, the assessing human

Table 15.1 Differences between human assessor and a machine performing the assessment

Human	Machine
Accurate and intuitive	Accurate
Slow	Fast
Only external assessment	Internal and external assessment
Trusted	Doubted

Table 15.2 Overview of trade-offs between assessor and assessment technique

	Assessor	
	Human	Machine
External (assessment of another)	Comparative behavior based on intuition and self-comparison	Objective measures of behavior in different circumstances, responses etc.
Internal (self-assessment)	Self-reflection, qualia, phenomenology	Reflection, introspection, self-measurement

requires certain expert knowledge to perform the assessment in the first place and only with this experience he/she will have this intuition. It is expected that a human assessor with the help of analyzing tools will require much more time than a machine on its own. Even though a human is able to self-reflect, we are interested in the assessment of computing systems. Hence, without explicit access to the internals (e.g. program code) of the machine, the human is only able to perform external assessment while the machine can perform internal as well as external assessments (also cp. Table 15.2). As already discussed, the assessment performed by a machine requires trusting the machine in the first place in order to rely on the information of the outcome.

While a precise determination of the actual level of self-awareness might be desired, the assessor, independent of being a human or a machine, may only be able to define the boundaries of the self-aware capabilities of the system to be measured.

15.3   Black-Box Versus White-Box Assessment

When performing an assessment, we have to distinguish not only who performs the assessment, but also what information the assessor has about the system. We distinguish between assessments where the assessor has knowledge of internal structures, mechanisms, or internal results of the system on the one hand and on the other where we can only observe the system from the outside (Table 15.3). We call these approaches white-box and black-box assessment, respectively.

Table 15.3 Summary of black-box versus white-box assessment and the corresponding implications when performing the assessment

Assessment type	Summary	Implications
Black box	Assessment based on observable behavior only. Can be based on experimentation, probing and in-situ observation	Reasoning might be unreliable. Observations might need to be quite extensive. Can be done without the explicit consent of the assessed system
White box	Assessment also involves inspection of the machinery and models present at run time	Does require access to the system and its internals. Can be very reliable. Might require a lot of effort

15.3.1 White-Box Assessment

When having knowledge of the internal structures of a system, one of the most common approaches is to perform a code inspection. In this case, we are not referring to a code review process as known from software engineering, but analyzing the actual code of the system in order to understand the level of self-awareness.

- code inspections
- benchmarking
- model checking
- data flow analysis
- function header analysis
- analysis of description of functions and methods

In white-box assessment, the assessor requires knowledge of the interna of a system. These interna can range from very detailed, such as actual code, to abstract, where the assessor only has access to the description of methods and functions.

White-box assessment may include code inspections where a person tries to determine the self-aware capabilities of a system not only by analyzing its code and processes but also by performing tests and analyzing the created data-structures information and knowledge within the system.

15.3.2 Black-Box Assessment

In contrast to white-box measurement, black-box measurement would refer to determining the level of self-awareness through probing the system from the outside and analyzing its behavior. Black-box measuring allows us to determine the level of self-awareness without accessing the actual code of the system, and therefore, we can do this during runtime or even enable other systems to perform the assessment. Nevertheless, black-box measurement is less accurate as we can only infer the level based on the observed behavior of the system upon performed tests. In addition, a black-box measurement for a given system may not allow us to determine a level of self-awareness at all. More precisely, a tester might either be able to determine a level, which might not correspond to the actual level of the system, or no self-awareness at all even though the system might in fact be self-aware. Identifying the aspects of self-awareness becomes more complicated when multiple self-aware systems come together in a single collective operating towards a common, high-level goal. The architecture and the accompanying benefits and drawbacks of such systems are described in Chap. 7.

When measuring, we might be interested in two different spans of the self-awareness: on the one hand, in the individual levels of the different entities of the collective and on the other hand in the overall self-aware level of the entire collective integrating the individual self-awareness aspects. This gives rise to a fundamental question about where and how the level of self-awareness in a collective is brought about? We can identify two possible answers:

1. The collective level of self-awareness is the aggregation of the individual entities forming the collective. In this case, a white-box measurement of the individual systems (entities of the collective) could be performed in order to determine the individual aspects and hence infer the self-awareness of the entire collective.
2. The collective level of self-awareness emerges from the combination of the different systems. In this case, the collective as a whole needs to be assessed.

While the different aspects can not always be measured using quantitative methods, we will discuss different qualitative characteristics of a system possibly possessing a certain aspect of self-awareness. We will shed light on single systems as well as multiple systems interacting with each other in either a cooperative or competitive manner.

15.4   Axes of Assessing Self-awareness

This section gives an overview of the different axes of assessable dimensions of a self-aware system. We will furthermore outline on how this assessment can be approached when using a white-box and black-box technique. These different approaches can be implemented by a human assessor as well as a machine given the necessary requirements are fulfilled. Nevertheless, there is no universal recipe to perform an assessment and hence the steps of the individual assessment have to be adapted for the purpose of the individual system to be assessed.

15.4.1 Domain of Self-awareness

For the domain of self-awareness one can inspect the span and the scope for each awareness link. This may range from very simple domains where the span as well as the scope only contain a single entity to more complex domains involving a larger number of entities for both sets. The most complex domains involve dynamically changing sets for the span and the scope not allowing to pinpoint the sets at a specific point in time. This can include the definition of entities becoming member during runtime of either set as well as the maximum and minimum number of members at any point in time of span and scope. In closed sets for span and scope, where the members of both sets do not change over time, the measurer might be able to define a complete graph of the awareness links between the different entities. This would allow to employ graph theoretical approaches in order to asses the flow of information and knowledge or the flow of computation.

15.4.2 Level of Self-awareness

When assessing the levels of self-awareness with white-box measuring, one has to assess the processes and data structures. If a system has no learning and modeling capabilities, it can only be a pre-reflective self-aware system. When the system builds up a model of its own actions and their impact on the environment and itself, we can assume this system to be reflective self-aware. In a further granularization, what the models represent allows the measurer to determine the exact scope of the level (e.g. interaction aware, time aware, state aware,...).

The following three subsections discuss the important aspects an assessor has to watch out for in order to determine the corresponding level of awareness of the assessed system. For the assessment approaches, we consider both, black-box and white-box assessments.

15.4.2.1 Assessing Pre-reflective Self-aware Systems

Pre-reflective self-aware systems are only aware of the individual stimuli a system receives from the environment through its sensors or its communication interfaces.

White-box assessment: The system has to have some kind of input mechanism such as sensors or a communication interface. In addition, this input has to be processed in some way by the system. Examples for such processing can include direct mapping as done in the Braitenberg vehicle, where the sensor directly influences the actuator, or simply counting the number of messages received via a communication interface.

Black-box assessment: Black-box assessment of pre-reflective systems if extremely difficult if not even impossible. While one might be able to observe a reaction based on a given stimuli, not each input stimuli will trigger such a reaction observable from the outside.

15.4.2.2   Assessing Reflective Self-aware Systems

Reflective self-aware systems are able to build models about themselves and their environment. In addition, these systems are also able to reason about these models allowing them to improve their performance over time.

Interaction-awareness: Interaction-awareness requires to system to interact with other systems or the environment in general. If the system is completely isolated, it can not be interaction-aware.

White-box assessment: The system has methods to keep track of interactions with another machine or system. This does not require the system to keep track of the content or the type of interaction.

Black-box assessment: The interaction of a system is based on the other system it is interacting with. In a black-box assessment, the assessor should be able to observe different behavior of the system based on the partner it is interacting with.

Time-awareness: The system has to be operational over a certain period of time. If the system only operates once momentarily, the system cannot be time-aware.

White-box assessment: The system is able to store previously acquired data and to perform analysis of this historical data. It is not relevant how this data is modeled internally.

Black-box assessment: A time-aware system is able to learn about previous experiences and to reason about this knowledge. It is not defined what type of experiences and to what extent this is learned and how this reasoning needs to be implemented. A time-aware system should possess at least one out of two properties: (i) improve its own performance over time by exploiting previously learned knowledge or (ii) deal with dynamic changes in the environment. The first property allows the system to exploit its knowledge in order to achieve a given goal faster or with better results according to the goal-function. The second property allows the system to unlearn previous information and hence increase its flexibility, robustness, as well as its scalability. Furthermore, the system also might be able to make some sort of predictions about the future and is able to adapt before actual changes occur. Determining time-awareness can be difficult as impacts of actions of the systems, as well as results of this time-awareness, may only show after long periods (days, weeks, or even months) of observation.

State-awareness: State-awareness requires the system to keep track of its own state or the state of other, external systems at any time. It is not necessary that the system can predict future states but every current state needs to be clearly defined. While externally observable states are very similar to appearance-awareness of external entities, state-awareness also includes the awareness about usefulness, stability, and validity of the current state of a system.

White-box assessment: The system requires the ability to keep track of its own internal state or state of external entities. To identify the states of external entities, the system does not need to have access to the internal state information of the external entity. An black-box assessment of the external entity can be sufficient.

Black-box assessment: In black-box assessments of state-awareness, the assessor has to consider not only the externally observable state information of the system but also the context of the system in order to define its stability, validity, and usefulness. For example, a standard RGB visual sensor in completely dark environment is not useful.

Behavior-awareness: Behavior-awareness allows to reason about the reaction to certain situations or actions of the system itself or an external entity. In contrast to time-awareness and interaction-awareness, behavior-awareness requires the system to keep track of the relation between actions, current context and environment, and corresponding impact over time.

White-box assessment: The system needs to be able to keep track of its own actions, the current context and environment, and the corresponding impact of its actions on the environment. Implemented methods to reason about the behavior allow predictions as well as improvements of the system over time.

Black-box assessment: The system learns the results and impacts of previous actions. Having this knowledge allows to make changes in order to improve future behavior in case of a similar situation given this is deemed necessary by the system. Behavior-awareness might be hard to detect from the outside as unexpected changes in the behavior of the system might be acconted for by an exploration strategy to find better actions for a given situation.

Appearance-awareness: Appearance-aware systems have knowledge about their own appearance and/or the appearance of other, external entities. This information allows them to reason about the capabilities of the system not only in its current state but also how it might change in order to exhibit other/different/new capabilities.

White-box assessment: There is an internal representation of what the system looks like. This can range from rough descriptions of general features such as color and shape to very detailed descriptions where the system can exactly locate sensors and actuators on its own external surface and even describe them accurately.

Black-box assessment: An appearance-aware system is able to distinguish itself from another system given that all systems look differently. At the same time, it would recognize itself in a mirror next to another system. Assuming that multiple systems might look the same, the appearance-aware system would recognize any similarly looking system as itself. From a robotics perspective, appearance-aware systems do know about the general location of their external sensors and actuators, allowing them to give a description of these relative locations to another system/robot.

Goal-awareness: Goal-aware systems have knowledge about the different goals within the system. This does not mean, that the corresponding system has a goal-function alone but requires the system to be aware of the pursued goal(s) as well as its current performance towards achieving these available goals. Furthermore, the system might even be able to weigh its own goals and change these weights based on the current situations during runtime in order to fulfill multiple goals as good as possible simultaneously.

White-box assessment: The system has an internal representation of goals and its own progress towards achieving them. Additionally, the system might have function in order to weigh the goals during runtime and hence prioritize different goals at certain times.

Black-box assessment: The system should exhibit its awareness of different goals and its own progress of achieving them. The behavior of the systems changes based on the actual goal it is pursuing. This does not mean other goals are discarded, but rather the behavior changed in order to pursue another specific goal. Even while other goals are pursued, the progress of achieving previous goals should not be decreased. In order to perform an black-box assessment on this level of self-awareness, the assessor needs a notion of pursued goals of the system.

15.4.2.3 Assessing Meta-Reflective Self-aware Systems

Meta-reflective self-aware systems are aware of its reflective abilities. In addition, the system is able to switch between their different reflective approaches during runtime based on the given requirements.

In Chap. 9, we describe an approach to integration infrastructure called "Wrappings" [5], that inherently includes reflection, and that allows the reflection processes themselves to access and assess their own processing steps, along with those of all other processes (how deeply and how extensively this is done in a given system is a design decision, subject to engineering judgment, but in principle, all processes in the system can be so examined). The information available to these processes includes the context in which they were selected and the reason for which they were selected (called the "problem" in the Wrapping approach), so the reflective process can assess how well the resource served the purpose, how well the selection process connected the original purpose to an applicable resource (ordinary reflection interests), and how well the assessment process went (meta-reflection). The information also includes the selection criteria, so the reflective process can determine why other resources were not selected, and, in particular, why the system responded with a failure because no resource could address the problem. It was a fundamental design decision that the computational resources that perform the reflective processes (monitoring and reasoning about this wealth of available behavioral data) on system operations are themselves part of system operations, so we get meta-reflection for free (in terms of conceptual architecture, though not, of course, in computation time).

15.4.3 Processes of Self-awareness

The process of self-awareness describes the span of self-awareness generating and reasoning about a model of a specific scope to achieve certain goal(s). As discussed in Chap. 3, span describes the system(s) being self-aware and scope the entities the span is aware about. Furthermore, the self-awareness process encapsulates **learning** the model, **reasoning** about it, and **acting** accordingly in order to achieve the system's goals.

To identify these **processes of self-awareness**, the assessor can analyze the behavior of the system and might be able to identify learning, reasoning, acting processes, as well as processes of joint types. Nevertheless, often it will not be easy to clearly identify those processes as this highly depends on the implementation and the separation of the different processes. In general, learning will create an initial model of the acquired information and adapt it over time. Reasoning process will analyze this model but not adapt or change it. Acting processes will perform actions and are—depending on the level of self-awareness—triggered by a reasoning process. Processes of joint types will combine multiple processes at once. However, these three processes have to be performed in a specific order. In addition, the learning, reasoning, and acting process might be performed multiple times in a single self-aware process.

White-box assessment: In white-box assessments, functions reacting on input already indicate very simple levels of self-awareness. Processes building a model already indicate more advanced self-awareness. If these models are adapted over time and these changes kept track of, it might be an indication of advanced processes. Nevertheless, for a self-aware system, there are also reasoning processes required. These are often indicated by an adaption of the system itself (e.g. learning parameters, how knowledge is exploited, etc.). The generated model gives an indication of the scope of the self-aware system. However, this model alone might not be enough to identify the scope at runtime as it might not yet be complete. A formal analysis to identify the actual scope is possible if the entire possible scope is known.

Black-box assessment: In black-box assessments, the assessor may not be able to identify the actual learning and reasoning approaches implemented in the system. Based on observation, the assessor might be able to perform a very good approximation based on the behavior of the system on certain inputs. However, the assessor might be able to identify the order in which learning, reasoning, and acting occurs as well as the scope and the span of the self-aware process.

15.4.4 Accuracy of Self-awareness

Accuracy of self-awareness can only be determined in white-box measurements. Here the assessor is required to analyze and compare the generated models with the real world. This becomes more difficult in dynamic environments as the analysis is required to be done online. Alternatively, the ground truth information can be employed for evaluation of the accuracy. Nevertheless, the acquisition of the ground truth has to be at least of the same precision as the corresponding model and requires to be taken at the same or higher frequency.

Part II: Applying Verification and Validation Methods to Self-aware Systems

The lifecycle of a self-aware system will depart from traditional software development life-cycles in a number of important ways—it may not be possible to fully specify the requirements for the system at design time and hence to test it in traditional fashions. In fact one of the motivations for highly adaptive and self-aware systems is their ability to monitor, manage, learn and substantially change themselves when placed in new operational environments and when given new capabilities (such as in relatively open system of systems) and new goals. However, having said that, there is no excuse for the developer of a self-aware system not to do many of well-known steps of developing any complex system, with some additional design activities. Hence, instead of having a fixed set of requirements, the designer of the self-aware system must make some careful decisions as to what is to be fixed by the human developer and what must be developed into a self-modifiable process by the self-aware system. Further, the developer must decide all the monitoring, reasoning, learning and other change methods available to the self-aware system. In the sophisticated case, the self-aware system will be able to develop new change methods (e.g., what is monitored, what is modeled and what is learned) for itself. A particularly important case for autonomous systems and self-aware system is the ability to determine some set of its own goals and requirements.

15.5 Validate Design Decisions

As mentioned above, developers need to make some careful decision as to what is to be fixed by the human developer and what self-modifiable capabilities the system shall have. For assessing the quality of self-aware systems, these decisions needs to be assessed and validated. Possible validation questions include the following

- Will it be feasible for the designed system to adapt and achieve its goals under the expected environmental conditions?
- What are the quality properties (performance, reliability, ...) of the designed system in different environmental conditions and states?
- How well can the system be understood and adapted by developers when maintaining the system?

We can distinguish two types of validation questions: First, whether the system will be able to achieve its goals (be they quality goals or functional goals). Second, what quality the system will have in terms of other quality characteristics that are not addressed by the goals that the system is aware of (such as performance, reliability, and maintainability in the examples above).

As self-awareness and self-adaptation manifest in the system's behavior over time, the timing of this behavior is of particular importance when validating the design. A self-aware system can become useless if awareness is achieved too late, after a window of possible action has already closed. In our example, after the system detects performance issues, it needs to be able to reason and react fast enough to avoid actual violations of performance goals, such as violations of service level agreements. Possibly, if the load increases suddenly and steeply, the system might not be able to adapt fast enough to always fulfill performance goals. Thus, when designing this system, it is important to understand the boundaries of the environmental conditions in which the system can successfully reason and adapt to fulfill its goals.

Another particular validation question is the stability of the reasoning and adaptation mechanisms. Here, stability as in control theory is desired: The system shall not continuously move in a circle of reasoning or adaptation and thus show oscillating behavior.

15.5.1 Evolution

A system might contain different levels of self-adaptation and self-awareness mechanisms. Just like the human body, it might combine adaptation loops with quick reaction time to handle short-term fluctuations of the load and avoid performance goal violations (using actions such as CPU frequency scaling) with more long term reasoning and acting on optimality of the performance and energy trade-off, for example (using actions such as VM re-deployment). Just like the human body, it might be desirable to restrict self-awareness and complex reasoning on the higher levels with longer reaction time (as also reflected in the multi-level observer/controller architecture of organic computing [7]).

Combining different levels of self-adaptation and self-awareness obviously makes designing self-aware systems harder, as designers need to take the lower-level adaptation capabilities into account when designing higher-level self-awareness models, reasoning, and actions. Figure 15.1 shows how self-awareness and self-adaptation loops (shown in black) may vary in "size": From quick reactions, e.g. to changing workload, to longer, automated re-optimization loops. In addition to the two loops mentioned here, different intermediate loops might be considered with varying degrees of self-awareness.

As any software system, also self-aware systems need to be evolved and changed over time by human designers to cope with such new, unexpected requirements that were not considered while the system was initially designed and built (some systems, such as space systems, that are not reachable after deployment are an exception here, although even these systems often evolve in terms of code being reused in later projects). This adds another dashed loop to Fig. 15.1.

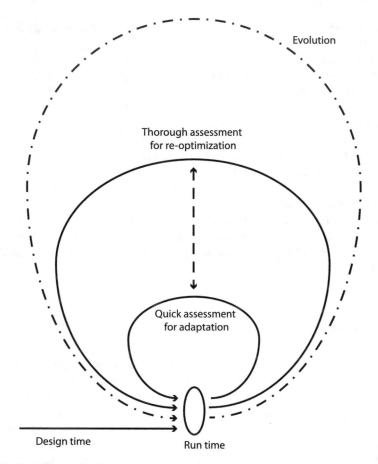

Fig. 15.1 Decision-making loops

15.5.2 Design-Time Assessment

Validating self-aware systems at design time is a rather new area in the development of such systems. Hence, not many approaches exist so far which address this concern. In principle, the validation at design time seeks to analyze the quality of the system based on its design. The design is typically captured in models of the system and its self-awareness mechanism which allow formal analyses to be performed. For example, software architects create models that model the system and its self-awareness mechanism using modeling languages like the UML2 [6], the Palladio Component Model [3], MechatronicUML [2], etc. In a second step, software architects enrich these models using quality annotations, like resource demands, worst-case execution times, message sizes, loop counts, failure rates, etc. which are then used during the analysis step.

In principle, the existing analysis methods can be categorized into two main categories: approaches, which test or simulate the self-aware mechanism in certain, specified environmental situations on the model level. This is related to system testing, as it just analyses the system in specific situations and evaluates how to system copes with these situations without any option to generalize the gained insights for other situations. Often, simulation-based approaches are used here, where the system model is simulated for each environment under test. For example, if we simulate how a cloud system reacts to a specific burst workload situation to learn about its capability to master this situation, it would be such an approach.

In the second category, we find approaches which try to validate that the system's self-awareness mechanism is capable of managing any kind of situation the model is able to reflect. Such analyses are often based on model checking techniques. The main drawback of these techniques is that the state space in combination with the large variety of operational environments is typically very large. As a consequence, model checking may fail due to memory or time constraints. In such cases, these approaches often limit themselves to checking a subset of the overall state space which still may lead to a larger coverage than simulation-based approaches. For example, if we would model check a cloud system's behavior for any initial situation and any type of burst workload we could guarantee correct behavior (e.g., minimized resource usage) in all cases.

15.5.2.1   Situational Quality Analyses

In order to verify whether a self-adaptation mechanism fulfills its requirements, model-based verification approach could simulate certain self-adaptation use cases. In this type of analysis, software developers simulate a model of the self-adaptation mechanism to explore how it reacts to predefined test cases. Based on the results, the developers can then evaluate to which extend the mechanism fulfills its requirements. Furthermore, they can also fine tune the behavior of the self-adaptation mechanism.

A representative of this type of approach is SimuLizar [1]. SimuLizar has been designed to model and analyze self-adaptive business information systems. It has been extended and applied in the domain of elastic cloud computing systems in the EU FP7 project CloudScale.[1]

SimuLizar uses the component-based performance and reliability modeling language PCM [3]. The PCM already provides modeling constructs to model the structure of a component-based system, its quality relevant behavior, its deployment, and its usage context. SimuLizar extends these core viewpoints and adds an adaptation viewpoint which describes under which conditions the system performs which adaptations and what their effect will be. Furthermore, a usage evolution viewpoint characterizes the evolution of the system's environment over time, e.g., the frequency and extend of workload bursts or the overall workload evolution trend.

---

[1]http://www.cloudscale-project.eu.

All the models described above have an operational semantics which allows to simulate the models w.r.t. their performance and reliability impact. SimuLizar leverages this semantics and simulates the system under the specified usage evolution. As a result, software developers gets metrics for some of the self-adaptive or self-aware metrics outlined in Chap. 14. For example, they can analyze the mean time to quality repair, or the overall system costs for used resources.

15.5.2.2   Global Quality Analyses

In global quality analyses, the verification approach has to check the system against a specification of environments and their changes. Afterwards, you have a guarantee that the system will be able to work correctly in those environments. The main concern is the huge state space which might cause the model checker to fail due to a lack of memory or time.

One approach in this category is the verification approach for mechatronic systems [4] specified in the MechatronicUML modeling language. In this approach, the model checker looks at all adaptations the system can perform. Then all system configurations (i.e., a running system as a result of an adaptation) are verified to comply with the specified constraints. In this way, it is guaranteed that - no matter which adaptations are performed - the system will always satisfy a set of constraints. Typically those constraints are safety constrains, i.e., they specify that the system does not execute any harmful behavior.

15.6   Summary

There are various reasons why one might want to assess the degree of self-awareness within a given system. First, an operator might want to make a statement about the systems capabilities with respect to self-awareness in order to market the corresponding system better. Second, an architect needs to know the capabilities of another system in order to allow a system to be developed to interact with this other system accordingly. Third, individual components might want to react to requests of other systems about their own degree of self-awareness or be able to assess other systems during runtime.

In this chapter, we discussed the different aspects required in order to successfully assess the degree of self-awareness of a given system. We outlined the difference between having a system assessed by a human or another machine. Additionally, we also discussed the differences between an internal assessment, i.e. where the system analyses its own capabilities and tries to identify its own degree of self-awareness, and external assessment, i.e. where an external assessor tries to identify the capabilities of a system. For any of these cases, we further distinguished between white-box, where the assessor has access to internal information such as structures, code, and models, and black-box assessment, where the assessor can only observe the system from the outside and can infer on the degree of self-awareness based on the outputs of the system. We presented a road-map of the most important aspects for different levels of self-awareness and how to identify those aspects using white-box and black-box assessment. A short summary of the most important techniques and models on how to assess self-awareness of a system concludes the chapter.

Finally, we discussed challenges and initial approaches to verify and validate the correctness of self-aware software systems. At design time, we have classified the approaches into test-based and global verification depending on the completeness of the inspected potential environments they system is supposed to react to. The ideas in this chapter help software architects to design, verify, and optimize self-aware systems. This helps to ensure that those systems show correct behavior not only in their normal functions but also in the behavior of the self-awareness mechanism. However, still a lot of open issues are left. For design time verifications, one of the most severe issue is the huge state space such systems, their self-awareness mechanisms, and all possible system environments form. Exhaustive testing as well as simulation is here close to impossible. Instead, it will become crucial to define equivalence classes of behavior and methods to identify representative test cases which allow model-based or real testing of the systems but still guarantee a good test coverage.

References

1. Matthias Becker, Steffen Becker, and Joachim Meyer. SimuLizar: Design-Time Modelling and Performance Analysis of Self-Adaptive Systems. In *Proceedings of Software Engineering 2013 (SE2013), Aachen*, 2013.
2. Steffen Becker, Stefan Dziwok, Christopher Gerking, Wilhelm Schäfer, Christian Heinzemann, Sebastian Thiele, Matthias Meyer, Claudia Priesterjahn, Uwe Pohlmann, and Matthias Tichy. The mechatronicuml design method - process and language for platform-independent modeling. Technical Report tr-ri-14-337, Heinz Nixdorf Institute, University of Paderborn, 2014. Version 0.4.
3. Steffen Becker, Heiko Koziolek, and Ralf Reussner. The Palladio component model for model-driven performance prediction. 82:3–22, 2009.
4. Christian Heinzemann and Steffen Becker. Executing reconfigurations in hierarchical component architectures. In *Proceedings of the 16th International ACM Sigsoft Symposium on Component-based Software Engineering*, pages 3–12. ACM, 2013.
5. Christopher Landauer. Infrastructure for Studying Infrastructure. In *Workshop on Embedded Self-Organizing Systems*, Berkeley, CA, 2013. USENIX.
6. Object Management Group (OMG). Unified Modeling Language (UML), Infrastructure Specification – Version 2.4.1, August 2011.
7. Hartmut Schmeck, Christian Müller-Schloer, Emre Çakar, Moez Mnif, and Urban Richter. Adaptivity and self-organisation in organic computing systems. In Christian Müller-Schloer, Hartmut Schmeck, and Theo Ungerer, editors, *Organic Computing - A Paradigm Shift for Complex Systems*, volume 1 of *Autonomic Systems*, pages 5–37. Springer Basel, 2011.
8. Alan M. Turing. Computing Machinery and Intelligence. *Mind*, LIX(236):433–460, 1950.

Part IV
Applications and Case Studies

Chapter 16
Run-Time Models for Online Performance and Resource Management in Data Centers

Simon Spinner, Antonio Filieri, Samuel Kounev,
Martina Maggio and Anders Robertsson

Abstract In this chapter, we introduce run-time models that a system may use for self-aware performance and resource management during operation. We focus on models that have been successfully used at run-time by a system itself or a system controller to reason about resource allocations and performance management in an online setting. This chapter provides an overview of existing classes of run-time models, including statistical regression models, queueing networks, control-theoretical models, and descriptive models. This chapter contributes to the state of the art, by creating a classification scheme, which we use to compare the different run-time model types. The aim of the scheme is to deepen the knowledge about the purpose, assumptions, and structure of each model class. We describe in detail two modeling case studies chosen because they are considered to be representative for a specific class of models. The description shows how these models can be used in a self-aware system for performance and resource management.

S. Spinner (✉) · S. Kounev
Department of Computer Science, University of Würzburg, Am Hubland,
97074 Würzburg, Germany
e-mail: simon.spinner@uni-wuerzburg.de

S. Kounev
e-mail: samuel.kounev@uni-wuerzburg.de

A. Filieri
Department of Computing, Imperial College London,
180 Queen's Gate, London SW7 2AZ, UK
e-mail: a.filieri@imperial.ac.uk

M. Maggio · A. Robertsson
Department of Automatic Control, Lund University,
Ole Römers Väg 1, 223 63 Lund, Sweden
e-mail: martina.maggio@control.lth.se

A. Robertsson
e-mail: anders.robertsson@control.lth.se

© Springer International Publishing AG 2017
S. Kounev et al. (eds.), *Self-Aware Computing Systems*,
DOI 10.1007/978-3-319-47474-8_16

485

16.1   Introduction

Modern data centers provide advanced mechanisms to dynamically change the amount of physical resources (compute, storage and network resources) allocated to deployed applications. The allocation of resources has a strong influence on the performance of an application (measured by the end-to-end response time and throughput) as experienced by its end users. In order to achieve a certain level of performance, e.g., specified in a service-level agreement (SLA), the application requires a certain amount of physical resources. However, this resource requirement depends on many performance-influencing factors, including the current workload, the application implementation, the configuration of underlying layers (such as middleware systems, operating systems, or virtualization), and external services invoked by the application. As a result, the relationship between resource allocations and application performance is highly *nonlinear* for most practical systems and subject to *frequent changes* (e.g., time-varying workloads and dynamic system reconfigurations).

Self-aware systems for online performance and resource management in data centers need to learn models that capture the complex relationship between resource allocations and application performance, taking into account the various performance-influencing factors. Based on these models, self-aware systems will help to increase resource efficiency while ensuring a certain level of application performance in data centers (see also the reference scenario on data center resource management in Chap. 4, as they enable to reason and act based on models capturing knowledge about the system's performance behavior). All factors expected to change over time should be explicit parameters of such models, so that a self-aware system is able to evaluate the impact of changes in these factors on the application performance in advance and proactively reconfigure itself when necessary to improve resource efficiency or avoid SLA violations.

In this chapter, we give an overview of different classes of models that have been used at system run-time for online performance and resource management and discuss their applicability for building self-aware systems, where self-awareness is considered with respect to the system's performance and resource management behavior. Furthermore, we present two candidate models in more detail showing how these models can be used as abstractions of practical systems supporting allocation decisions in data centers.

In the past, there has been comprehensive work on offline, design-time models for comparing different design alternatives and for offline capacity planning purposes (e.g., queueing models and Petri nets). These models are also partially applicable in online scenarios, as we will see later. On the other hand, we see fundamental differences between design-time and run-time models [27]:

1. At design time, we can use time-intensive, computationally expensive techniques (e.g., discrete-event simulation) to analyze a model. At run-time, the analysis is often time-critical, and the analysis overhead is an important factor. Therefore, it is often necessary to decide on a model abstraction level and an analysis technique that provides a trade-off between accuracy and overhead.

2. Design-time models are usually constructed manually based on experiments in dedicated test environments or traces from a production system covering a limited period of time. Run-time models should be constructed automatically from monitoring data of the production system. The system should be continuously monitored, and changes in the system should be automatically reflected in the models.
3. At design time, it is usually possible to explore a large space with many degrees of freedom. In contrast, a run-time model should be specifically targeted at the degrees of freedom that can be changed at system run-time in order to limit the search space.
4. Run-time models should be able to reflect the layered architecture of applications in data centers (virtualization, operating system, and application) and support to answer performance-related questions relevant to the different layers (e.g., the data center owner often has different goals from those of the application owner). Design-time models are optimized for their usage in different phases of the software life cycle (e.g., design, development, or in production).

In this chapter, we focus on the different classes of run-time models and their solution techniques that can be used to analyze such models. Chapter 17 will introduce techniques to automatically extract models from running applications and update these models when the system changes.

16.2   Run-Time Models

This section provides an overview of existing classes of run-time models and shortly introduces their main aspects. The different classes of models are compared along the dimensions described in Sect. 16.2.1. The classes of run-time models are then presented in Sects. 16.2.2–16.2.6.

16.2.1   Dimensions for Classification

The classification of the run-time models is based on the following five dimensions:

- *Abstraction level*: We distinguish between the following abstraction levels for describing a system: black-box, coarse-grained, and fine-grained [27]. A *black-box* model describes the functional relationship between the inputs and outputs of a system without any knowledge of the system internals. A *coarse-grained* model includes information on the internal architecture of a system (e.g., components, resources, and control flow between components). A *fine-grained* model may include additional descriptions of the component internal behavior (e.g., forks and synchronization, and dependencies on input parameters). The abstraction level can influence the analysis accuracy and the types of questions that can be answered by a model. For example, predicting the influence of deployment changes on the performance requires a representation of the internal system architecture in the model.

- *Model structure*: This describes the main elements of the modeling formalism. In particular, we discuss which of these elements can be automatically determined at run-time (i.e., *online*) and which of them are specified manually at design time (i.e., *offline*).

- *Input and output parameters*: A performance model can be seen as a generic function $y = f(x)$ that calculates a vector of output parameters y from a vector of input parameters x. The output parameters are typically certain performance metrics of the system (e.g., response time, throughput, or resource utilization). The input parameters determine the types of questions that can be answered by a performance model. Typical input parameters are, for instance, workload intensity or number of replicated server instances. In case of dynamic models, where the function also depends on previous outputs, f is a transfer function that maps the input signal x (time-based or frequency-based) to an output signal y. The function itself may not have a closed-form solution.

- *Model inference*: When learning models at run-time, certain techniques are required to determine the model structure and the values of internal model parameters (e.g., service demands of queueing networks). We list state-of-the-art techniques for model inference here and refer the reader to Chap. 17 for details.

- *Model analysis*: Depending on the class of models, different techniques for model analysis are available. We distinguish between *analytical solution* (exact or approximate) and *simulation*. Given that the available time for model analysis is often limited at run-time, fast closed-form or analytical solutions are preferable. However, in certain situations, simulations may also be feasible.

16.2.2 Regression Models

Regression techniques can be used both for model inference (e.g., for model identification or model parameter estimation), as well as for extracting a regression model that can be applied directly for performance prediction (e.g., extra- and interpolating measured data). In this section, we focus on the latter.

Abstraction level: Regression models are mainly used for black-box modeling of a system, where no information (or very limited information) on the internal behavior and the system structure is available.

Model structure: Different types of regression models are available. Linear models are often insufficient to describe the performance of a system (e.g., the function between the incoming workload and the response time of a system is highly nonlinear). Nonparametric regression approaches (e.g., multivariate adaptive regression splines (MARS) [17], classification and regression trees (CART) [8], M5 trees [39], cubist forests [29]) do not require a decision on the model function to be made a priori (linear vs. polynomial vs. exponential).

Input and output parameters: Regression models directly fit a function describing the relationship between one or several output parameters and multiple input parameters. In theory, all measurable quantities can be used as input or output parameters. Common candidates for output parameters in the context of performance and resource management are response time, throughput, resource utilization, or power consumption. Input parameters could be, for instance, workload intensity, resource allocation, or resource utilization.

Model inference: Linear regression models are typically learned with least-squares regression or robust regression schemes. Nonparametric regression models require specialized model inference algorithms [8, 17, 29, 39].

Examples: Curtois and Woodside use regression splines to derive resource functions for the CPU demand of TCP/IP communication [12]. Noorshams et al. [35] use a similar approach to create black-box models of storage systems.

16.2.3   Queueing Network Models

Queueing networks (QNs) constitute a classical formalism for the performance analysis of computer systems. A QN consists of a set of interconnected queues. Each queue consists of a waiting line and one or multiple servers. Incoming jobs to a queue need to wait as long as all servers are occupied by other jobs. Each job consumes a certain amount of service time at a server. While QNs are traditionally used for predicting the performance of a system for offline capacity planning, they also provide a powerful formalism for online performance and resource management.

Abstraction level: QNs are well suited to describe a system as a black box (i.e., the complete system is represented by a single queue) or on a coarse-grained level (i.e., individual servers or individual resources are modeled as separate queues). While traditional QNs can describe the control flow between queues, they lack the expressiveness to describe more fine-grained behavior, such as, software synchronization aspects or the hierarchical layering of systems. Extended QN formalisms have been proposed to overcome these limitations, e.g., extended queueing networks or layered queueing networks (LQNs). These extended formalisms also support fine-grained models. It is possible to distinguish between different workload classes in order to obtain per-class performance measures.

Model structure: A QN definition consists of the workload description, the queue descriptions, and the service demands. The workload description defines a set of workload classes. For each workload class, the type (open vs. closed) and the workload intensity are specified. The workload intensity is either the arrival rate for open workloads or the number of users and their think time for closed workloads. Each queue description consists of a scheduling strategy (e.g., processor sharing or first-come-first-serve), a maximum capacity, and a number of servers (i.e., the level of parallelism). The service demand D at a queue is defined as $D = V \cdot S$, where V is the visit count of jobs of a workload class at the queue and S is the service time consumed during each visit.

When using QNs at run-time, usually a hybrid approach is chosen where some of the model elements are determined offline and others are updated online. In existing appproaches, the workload classes, scheduling strategies, maximum capacities, and service time/inter-arrival distributions are mostly set offline at design time. The number of queues and the number of servers at each queue may be derived easily online from structural information about the system. Workload intensities, service demands, and visit counts are ideally updated online based on monitoring data because their values often change during system operation.

Input and output parameters: In theory, all parameters of the workload description (e.g., workload intensity and transaction mix), the queue descriptions (e.g., scheduling strategies), and the service demands are potential input parameters. However, when using QNs for performance and resource management at run-time, most of these parameters are kept fixed, and only a small subset is varied at a given point in time. Typical examples for variable input parameters are the workload intensity, which is varied to predict the impact of changes in the workload, or the number of queues, typically varied to predict the effect of a horizontal scaling action. The output parameters of a QN are performance measures for the complete system as well as for individual queues. These measures are response time, throughput, utilization, average number of users in the system, and queue length. Depending on the employed analysis technique, the results may include mean values, percentiles, or complete distributions of relevant metrics such as response time.

Model inference: A key parameter of QNs is the service demand of a request/job at a queue (also referred to as resource demand). In practical systems, service demands often cannot be observed directly. Therefore, extensive research has been done to estimate service demands using statistical techniques (e.g., least-squares regression, Kalman filters, and optimization techniques) based on indirect measurements (for an overview see the survey by Spinner et al. [41]). Other work uses independent component analysis to automatically group requests into workload classes based on their service demands [40]. Complete frameworks for model inference have been proposed for QNs in [31] and for LQNs in [21].

Model analysis: A broad set of techniques for solving QNs are available with different degrees of accuracy and computational complexity. Operational analysis and bounds analysis provide closed-form equations to quickly calculate average performance measures of individual queues [5]. Mean value analysis [5] can be used to obtain accurate or approximate average measures for QNs with closed workloads. Assuming certain distributions and scheduling strategies, analytical solvers based on Markov chain analysis [5] can provide fast and accurate results (including percentile measures). However, they often suffer from a state-space explosion. Fluid analysis [6] can overcome these limitations; however, it is only an approximative technique. With discrete-event simulation, it is possible to analyze any type of QN; however, its computational complexity is prohibitive in many run-time scenarios.

Examples: Menascé et al. [32] propose an SLA controller based on a QN to optimize a system configuration periodically. Chen et al. [11] use QNs to optimize the allocation of applications to servers. Bennani and Menascé [4] use the results of an analytically solved QN to improve the deployment of applications in data centers.

Pacifici et al. use QNs for performance management of cluster Web services [38]. Zhang et al. [46] model multi-tier applications with QNs for resource allocation purposes. Urgaonkar et al. [43] also use QNs and predict the response times of a multi-tier application at run-time using approximative mean value analysis. Li et al. [30] use LQNs for the run-time management of cloud applications. Mistral [23] is a resource management framework for virtualized environments that is based on LQNs.

16.2.4   Petri Net Models

Petri nets are a mathematical formalism to describe the behavior of distributed and parallel systems. A basic Petri net consists of a set of places, transitions, and tokens. Each transition is connected to a number of input places and a number of output places. A transition requires a certain number of tokens in each input place. When this condition is met, a transition is enabled and may fire. When firing, the transition consumes the required tokens and produces new ones in the output places. The firing order of enabled transitions is by default non-deterministic.

In order to capture timing aspects of systems, stochastic Petri nets have been proposed introducing transitions with a probabilistic firing delay. In this section, we focus on queueing Petri nets (QPNs) [2] as an extension of the stochastic Petri nets including so-called queueing places to model scheduling aspects.

Abstraction level: QPNs support black-box, coarse-grained, and fine-grained models. QPNs can be used to model the fine-grained control flow within individual components including synchronization aspects in parallel systems. QPNs also support different token colors to distinguish between different types of requests.

Model structure: A QPN is an 8-tuple $(P, T, C, I^-, I^+, M_0, Q, W)$ [2]. P is a set of places and T a set of transitions. The color function C assigns a set of supported colors to each place and each transition. I^- and I^+ are the backward and forward incidence functions defining the firing of transitions. M_0 is the initial marking of tokens to places. Q contains a queue description similar to that of QNs for each queueing place. W assigns firing weights to each transition. Existing uses of QPNs at run-time are focusing on online updates of the service time parameters of queueing places (contained in Q) and the initial marking of the QPN (e.g., to specify the number of concurrent users). In [36], also the structure of the QPN is updated at run-time as well to reflect changes in the system architecture (horizontal scaling). Based on an initial offline model, all parameters of the QPN are updated online in this case.

Input and output parameters: All elements of the QPN 8-tuple can be considered as input parameters. However, typical questions for online performance and resource management (e.g., horizontal scaling of servers) require adaptations to only a few of those parameters. Therefore, it may be beneficial to define specific input parameters for the available reconfiguration options (e.g., number of replicated instances) of a system and define a mapping to the respective QPN elements. QPNs support the same output parameters as QNs on a system of a per-place level, namely response time, throughput, utilization, number of users in the system, and queue length. In addition, it is also possible to determine the usage of software resources (e.g., thread or connection pools).

Model inference: The same techniques used for QNs to estimate service demands can be applied to QPNs.

Model analysis: While QPNs support a range of qualitative analyses, these are irrelevant for online performance and resource management. Quantitative analysis can be done based on Markov chain analysis [2]. However, for many practical applications, one has to resort to simulation [42] due to a state-space explosion.

Examples: In [36], QPNs are used to schedule jobs in the context of the Globus grid computing framework such that performance requirements are satisfied.

16.2.5   Control-Theoretical Models

Control theory offers a principled approach and a set of guidelines for how to create a control system. Its applications spread in many engineering domains most of which interact with the physical world, such as an industrial plant and chemical processes. In general terms, a *controller* takes inputs form the *sensors* that measure the environment, determines a sequence of actions that drive the plant toward its intended behavior, and executes these actions through the *actuators*. The major advantage of using control theory is the access to a broad set of mathematically grounded techniques that can provide formal guarantees on the effectiveness and robustness of the controlled system [14, 16]. Examples of such guarantees are stability (i.e., the ability of reaching an area close to the desired goal and not leaving that area if the conditions are unchanged), quantified settling time, and the absence of overshoots (possibly corresponding to costly overprovisioning).

Despite the potential benefits of control-theoretical solutions for software adaptation and resource management, their usage in practice is challenged by the difficulty of abstracting software behaviors through convenient mathematical formalisms [16]. This challenge is twofold: On the one hand, classic software design models are often inadequate to capture the relevant time dynamics for control; on the other hand, control theory was originally developed around the physical world, whose dynamics are subject to the laws of physics, while software behavior can be arbitrarily more complex in general.

Abstraction level: Finding the right level of abstraction and identifying the proper set of sensors and actuators are in general challenging [16]. A number of ad hoc solutions for specific problems or architectures have been proposed in literature (see related work surveyed by Filieri et al. [16]), as well as some attempts toward the automatic synthesis of controllers [14, 15].

In the following, we briefly review the two most common classes of models enabling the application of control-theoretical techniques: dynamical and hybrid system models.

16.2.5.1 Dynamical System Models

Dynamical system models consist of equations that describe the dynamic behavior of objects in a system. Objects are assumed to have input variables and output variables and a certain internal behavior.

Model structure: A dynamical system can be modeled in two different ways, depending on the physical nature of the model. Continuous-time models are represented in the form of ordinary differential equations (ODEs), while discrete-time models in the form of Difference Equations. In the control of computing entities, we are usually interested in discrete-time models (since in a computer there is usually no continuous-time physics).

Input and output parameters: A discrete-time dynamical system is described by the equations

$$\begin{cases} x(k+1) = f\left(x(k), u(k), d_x(k)\right) \\ y(k) \quad\;\; = g\left(x(k), u(k), d_y(k)\right) \end{cases} \tag{16.1}$$

where $x \in \Re^{n_x}$, $u \in \Re^{n_u}$, and $y \in \Re^{n_y}$ are referred to as the state, input, and output vectors, respectively, and $d_x \in \Re^{n_x}$ and $d_y \in \Re^{n_y}$ the state and output disturbance vectors, respectively. The two functions $f(\cdot, \cdot, \cdot)$ and $g(\cdot, \cdot, \cdot)$ are real-valued vector functions of proper dimensions. The number k is an integer index counting the time instants—not necessarily evenly spaced in time. In a more general form, $f(\cdot, \cdot, \cdot)$ and $g(\cdot, \cdot, \cdot)$ could depend on an arbitrary number of real-valued parameters, possibly time-varying. The term "step k" denotes the time span between the k-th and the $(k+1)$-th instants.

The first equation in (16.1) is called the *state equation*, and dictates what the system state will be in the end of step k given what it is at the beginning, and what happens to the system input. The system inputs are assumed to be captured by the values of u and d_x at the beginning of the time step. The state equation represents the dynamic system's character as *difference* equations, i.e., owing to the contextual presence of two subsequent index values. In other words, the state equation gives the system "memory of the past" and explains why the same action generally yields different effects depending on the system condition when it is applied. The input vector u represents *manipulated variables* that can be used to influence the system's behavior, while the state disturbance d_x accounts for any input other than u, i.e., for any external entity that actually influences the system state, and that in some cases can possibly be measured, but never manipulated.

The second equation in (16.1) is called the *output equation*. It is not dynamic, as shown by the presence of a single index value k, while the state equation highlights the relationship between what the values at time $k+1$ and the values at time k are. In most problems of interest, the output equation describes what one measures (vector y) to represent the system's behavior. The disturbance vector d_y represents possible alterations of the measurements, e.g., due to noise, but *not* of the actual evolution of the system state.

Model inference: Dynamical system models can either be derived from first principles, yielding so-called white-box models, where all parameters are given by already known constants, or models where there is a need to identify or estimate (possibly online) parameters and structure. Gray-box models are those that contain structural information like known nonlinearities such as saturation elements and have parameters that need to be identified empirically to make the model complete, whereas black-box-models do not have any a priori structure imposed. Several different system identification methods in both time and frequency domain can be used: either indirectly via so-called nonparametric identification methods such as transient response, correlation methods, and spectral analysis, or directly with parameter estimation methods from linear regression and time-series analysis, such as (N)ARMAX, instrument variable, and prediction error (PE) methods [22]. From input-output data, mixed deterministic–stochastic systems can be found, capturing both the (deterministic) process model dynamics as such and the influence of e.g., (stochastic) disturbances. Linear system models can be represented in several different but equivalent forms, e.g., characterized by their impulse or step responses, by their transfer function, or written in a state-space model form. For the latter, efficient numerical algorithms for subspace state-space system identification (so-called N4SID-algorithms) have been derived [20, 45]. The well-known Kalman / Kalman–Bucy filtering [24] can be used for both state estimation and parameter estimation, and several of the parameter estimation methods mentioned above can be formulated in recursive algorithms, allowing online estimation of model parameters, for instance, in adaptive control algorithms and observers.

Model analysis: In synthesis, dynamical system models are descriptive. They can be used for reasoning (in the sense that you can use them to build an understanding of the current situation and to predict what is going to happen in the future). The abstraction level can (theoretically) be chosen arbitrarily, *but* the models should describe phenomena that can be quantified, which means that, for example, it might not be possible to detail the behavior of the system at a specific granularity level because it is impossible to find the correct equations for it. In general, higher abstraction levels are easy to solve, while for more detailed ones, the number of state variables increases significantly. The mathematical foundations including differential and difference equations, control theory, identification theory, and also machine learning could be used to fine-tune the model parameters. These models are quantitative, in the sense that they only describe things that can be turned into numbers, but they cannot, for example, describe the difference in two software architectures. They are mainly used to: (a) build an understanding of the systems (for example, using system identification can give insight on how the system behaves) and (b) control the system to ensure that it has the desired behavior. The models are mainly online ones, but the structure can be prescribed offline (for example, determining that there is a linear relationship between the value of the states at time $k + 1$ and the same values at time k). Coefficients can be identified online, or the entire structure itself can be identified online.

16.2.5.2   Hybrid System Models

Model structure: In contrast to the pure discrete-event systems of the types described in Sects. 16.2.3 and 16.2.4, where all evolutions of states are caused by discrete events in time, event-based systems in general may be formulated within the hybrid automaton framework [1, 19]. The latter supports both discrete events, for instantaneous transitions between a set of steps, and time-driven dynamics, comprising continuous- and/or discrete-time dynamics, evolving within each step. As special cases, they can therefore describe the models in previous chapters where either the evolution within each step is trivial/non-changing or the system can be satisfactorily modeled and described as difference or differential equations without any transitions to other steps.

This modeling framework can be used to model a large class of systems and has appeared in slightly different forms in various domains, however, often with different foci. In automatic control, the focus is often on the continuous behavior, whereas in computer science, the emphasis often concerns the discrete aspects.

By being able to accurately capture system behavior comprising both sequencing and events, like turning on and off computers in large server farms, and the dynamic evolution, like approximate fluid models at high load, within the same framework, this model class has large potential to both describe and predict system behavior relevant for resource allocation and accurate performance monitoring.

However, in general, it is very hard to find analytical solutions to a hybrid system consisting of mixed discrete events and continuous dynamics. A restricted (but still powerful and useful) subclass is linear piecewise hybrid systems [7, 33]. As a note of warning, using hybrid automata for modeling, a system may easily introduce undesired or false behavior, even if it may seem reasonable from a physical point of view. After a transition to a new step (caused, e.g., by an event triggering a guard function or governed by high-level sequencing), the dynamics of the new active step may be re-initialized. This switching may thus cause a discontinuous right-hand side of an ordinary differential equation which then typically results in lack of existence or lack of uniqueness of solutions [25].

Input and output parameters: Usually, parameters are the transition probabilities from one state to another or follow a deterministic scheduling based, e.g., on timing.

Model inference: Due to the higher complexity, these issues may be difficult to discover in the modeling phase. However, hybrid systems are sometimes intentionally modeled without uniqueness to incorporate uncertainty.

Model analysis: As shown in a simple example from [18], a hybrid model of a bouncing ball, where each contact between the ball and the ground causes an impulse according to the Newtonian law of change of momentum, will create an infinite number of mode switches in finite time, called Zeno behavior. It is therefore important to incorporate inherent delays in, e.g., context switching to avoid similar, but erroneous analysis as above, caused by too idealistic scenarios in the modeling.

16.2.6   Descriptive Meta-Models

The previously described model classes are based on rigorous mathematical foundations, whereas the focus of this class of models lies in greater model expressiveness and interpretability. Two representatives of this class of models are SLAstic [44] and the Descartes Modeling Language (DML) [28].

Abstraction level: Descriptive modeling languages may be defined at different abstraction levels allowing to model a system at a black-box, coarse-grained, or fine-grained level of detail. They may also support hybrid models with mixed abstraction levels (e.g., DML [28]).

Model structure: The model structure is described in a meta-model. The meta-model describes the available model elements (i.e., classes and their attributes) and the relationships between them (i.e., containment and association). Meta-models based on OMG's Meta-Object Facility (MOF) standard [37] are most commonly used (e.g., UML is an example of a modeling language defined using a MOF-based meta-model). Compared to mathematical formalisms (e.g., QNs or QPNs), descriptive meta-models typically introduce a more extensive set of different model elements with richer semantics. The model elements should be direct abstractions of real-world hardware or software entities (e.g., servers, software components, program loops and branches) in order to support the understandability of the model.

The improved model interpretability is beneficial in both offline and online scenarios: There is a large number of tools for creating graphical and textual editors for MOF-based modeling languages, simplifying the creation of a model of a system and lowering the barrier for less experienced users. In the online case, the additional meta-information provided through different model elements helps to create richer visualization of the learned model enabling self-expressiveness of the system. Furthermore, meta-models allow to enforce additional constraints on the structure of the models avoiding errors when creating models manually or programmatically.

Input and output parameters: The input parameters are usually not defined by the employed meta-model itself, but are rather highly dependent on the used model analysis method. The meta-model may provide high-level goal descriptions from which low-level input parameters are derived (e.g., DML comes with a special query language [28]). The available output parameters also depend on the model analysis method.

Model inference: It is possible to extract meta-model-based performance models from monitoring data. As shown in [10], even very fine-grained architecture-level performance models can be extracted using practical monitoring tools with an acceptable overhead. However, this requires fine-grained instrumentation capabilities in the system.

Model analysis: The model analysis is typically supported either through *model-to-model transformations* into one of the previous mathematical formalisms (e.g., QNs or QPNs) or by direct simulation. The benefit of using a descriptive modeling language is the flexibility to use different mathematical solution techniques depending on the analysis goal without the need to maintain different models.

16.3 Modeling Case Studies

16.3.1 Control-Theoretical Models

In this subsection, we present a control-theoretical model that captures the maximum response time of a cloud application. The model is primitive, yet useful, and has been applied to develop control strategies to keep the maximum response time bounded [26].

Cloud applications serve multiple users through the Internet. Their computations are generally separated into independent and stateless user requests processed by the system [13]. An essential requirement of these applications is that requests should be processed in a time-sensitive way; otherwise, unsatisfied users may abandon the service [34]. Therefore, having a model for the maximum time consumed to generate a response is quite useful.

We assume that the maximum response time of a Web application, measured at regular time intervals, follows the equation:

$$\begin{cases} x(k+1) = \alpha(k) \cdot u(k) + \delta t(k) \\ y(k) \quad\;\; = x(k) \end{cases} \tag{16.2}$$

i.e., the maximum response time $y(k)$ of all the requests that are served between time index k and time instant $k+1$ depends on a time-varying unknown parameter $\alpha(k)$ and can have some disturbance $\delta t(k)$ that is a priori unmeasurable. $\alpha(k)$ takes into account all the variations that can happen in a controlled way, $u(k)$. These include, for example, booting of a new machine or a resource upgrade. In Eq. (16.2), $\delta t(k)$ is an additive correction term that models variations that do not depend on something that can be changed by the user. These include, for example, variation in retrieval time of data due to cache hit or miss. If $\alpha(k)$ is considered as a time-invariant parameter α, and its time dependency is not present, the state equation of the proposed model is linear and so is the output equation. Otherwise, the equation can be seen as a linear parameter-varying (LPV) one and treated accordingly.

This model is quite trivial, but it captures the application behavior enough for a control action to be useful [26]. A controller should aim at canceling the disturbance $\delta t(k)$ and selecting the value of $u(k)$ so that the maximum response time would be equal to the desired value.

16.3.2 Descartes Modeling Language

The Descartes Modeling Language (DML) [28] is a descriptive modeling language for online performance and resource management formalized by a set of metamodels based on OMG's Meta-Object Facility (MOF). The goal of the modeling language is to provide common abstractions for describing performance- and resource management-related aspects of modern dynamic IT systems, infrastructures, and services. DML was designed from the beginning to support the design of systems exhibiting self-awareness with respect to performance and resource management aspects. As such, the formalism is intended to build reflective models (see Chap. 6) capturing knowledge about the static structure and dynamic behavior of a self-aware system. In the following, we focus on this part of DML. On top of that, DML also provides means to model the high-level goals specified in service-level agreements (SLAs) and the processes to derive intermediate- and low-level goals from the high-level ones (for details see Chap. 17).

16.3.2.1   Blue Yonder System

Figure 16.1 depicts an excerpt of a DML model in a UML-like notation. The model was created in the context of an industrial case study in cooperation with Blue Yonder GmbH & Co. KG, a leading service provider in the field of predictive analytics and big data. The modeled system (called Blue Yonder system) provides forecasting services used by customers for predicting, e.g., sales, costs, and churn rates. These services are based on compute-intensive machine-learning techniques and subject to customer SLAs. In this case study, the DML models were used to predict the resource requirements for a given usage scenario and optimize the resource allocation to reduce Blue Yonder's operating costs.

Application Architecture: The application architecture of the adapted system is modeled after the principles of component-based software systems. A software component is defined as a unit of composition with explicitly defined provided and required interfaces. For convenience, we also use the term *service* to refer to a signature of a software component's interface. A typical Blue Yonder system (depicted in Fig. 16.1) consists of three main software component types: the gateway server (GW), the prediction server (PS), and a third party component, the database (DB). The GW is the communication endpoint to the Blue Yonder system. Users can invoke a set of different services via HTTP (train, predict, and results). The GW receives historical data for training a prediction model, parses it, and generates a job, which is put into the GW's queue and scheduled for processing. Then, an active PS takes the job from the queue, processes it, and stores the results in the database. After training, a user can invoke the predict service to calculate a forecast based on the trained prediction model. The user sends the data for which the forecast should be made to the GW. The GW reads the data and generates one or several jobs—depending on the size of the data—which are scheduled for processing. These jobs are again processed by one or several PS, and the results are stored in the database for retrieval by the user (results service).

The control flow within the components is modeled in Fig. 16.1 using a fine-grained behavior abstraction level specifying the sequence of performance-relevant actions (e.g., internal actions, external calls, branches, and loops). For instance, the predict service of the GW first executes two internal actions (parsePredicti onJobs and schedulePredictionJobs) requiring a certain amount of CPU

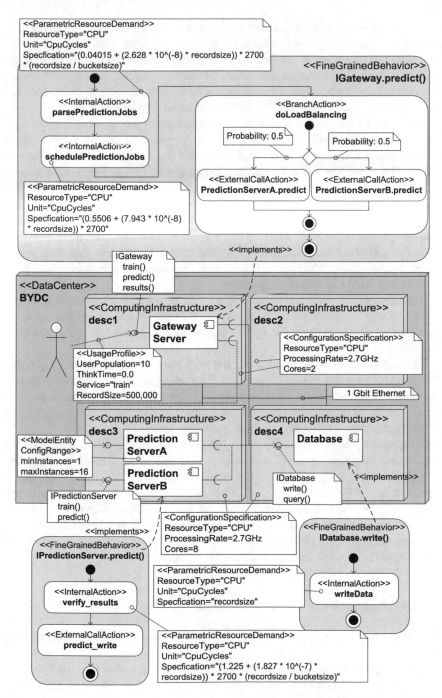

Fig. 16.1 Resource landscape, application architecture, deployment, and adaptation points of the Blue Yonder system

cycles, which depends on the record size. The record size is an input parameter of the system. The load-balancing behavior is modeled using a probabilistic branch with external call actions to the corresponding PS instances. DML supports multiple (possibly coexisting) behavior abstraction levels: fine-grained, coarse-grained (i.e., the service behavior as observed at the component boundaries), and black-box (i.e., a probabilistic representation of the service response time behavior).

Resource Landscape: The resource landscape meta-model is used to describe the structure and properties of the environment shared by the deployed applications. It includes a description of both the physical and the logical resources of the system environment. The example resource landscape in Fig. 16.1 consists of a data center with four different servers (represented by computing infrastructure). Each computing infrastructure is associated with a configuration specification describing the available resources. As the system is compute-intensive, only CPUs are modeled. However, it is also possible to specify other types of resources, such as storage, network, and software resources. Additionally, the container hierarchy (e.g., hypervisor, virtual machine, and middleware services) including configuration information (e.g., memory and bandwidth) may be specified.

Deployment: To capture the interactions of the resource landscape and the application architecture, one must model the connection between hardware and software. Each component instance in the system is assigned to a computing infrastructure instance.

Usage Profile: To model user interactions with the system (i.e., the usage profile), DML provides a usage profile meta-model. The usage profile of the `train` service describes a closed workload specifying a user population and think time. In addition to this, the usage profile also specifies the sequence of system calls and values for system parameters used in the system (e.g., record size).

Adaptation Points: The adaptation points model marks the elements of the resource landscape and the application architecture that can be adapted (i.e., reconfigured) at run-time. Adaptation points can be either associated with model parameters (e.g., number of CPU cores) or with model entities (e.g., a software component). In the example model, the adaptation point ModelEntityConfigRange is associated with a component specifying the minimum and maximum number of instances of this component that are allowed. In the example, the PS component is instantiated twice (`PredictionServerA` and `PredictionServerB`).

16.3.2.2   Application in Self-aware Systems

We now discuss *learning* and *reasoning* processes that can be implemented using DML.

Learning: We distinguish between *model structure extraction* (e.g., components, interfaces, or control flow) and *model parameterization* (e.g., resource demands or branching probabilities). The model structure may be extracted using techniques described in Chap. 17. All model parameters (e.g., branching probabilities and resource demands) can be flagged as either *explicit* or *empirical* in DML. Empirical model parameters need to be learned based on monitoring data while explicit ones are specified in advance. Thus, it is possible to specify some model parameters based on expertise knowledge in advance while others are learned at system runtime.

Reasoning: DML can be used to predict the impact of changes in the workload or in the system configuration on the performance and the resource usage of the application. By intention, DML is a purely descriptive model optimized for high expressiveness and good understandability. In order to enable performance predictions, DML relies on mathematical analysis techniques based on existing stochastic modeling formalisms, such as layered queueing networks (LQNs) and queueing Petri nets (QPNs). In [9], three different model-to-model transformations are defined providing different levels of prediction speed and accuracy: (a) bounds analysis uses operational analysis from queueing theory to determine asymptotic bounds on the average throughput and response time, (b) an LQN solver enabling the fast analytical solution of models, and (c) a QPN solver that allows to obtain predictions based on simulation. The benefit of the transformation approach is that it provides the flexibility to switch between different prediction techniques depending on the prediction goals. The prediction goals comprise the requested performance metrics, the required accuracy, and time constraints.

16.4   Conclusions

16.4.1   Open Challenges

While the described classes of run-time models already provide a foundation for self-aware performance and resource management, we still see several open challenges requiring further research:

- The analysis of models at run-time in a self-aware system is often subject to hard constraints on the analysis time. If the solution from a model is not available in time, it may be too late for a system to react to changes in its environment. Furthermore, the decision-making may require the exploration of multiple alternatives requiring multiple analyses of a model. Therefore, there is a need for fast and flexible analysis techniques especially for coarse- and fine-grained models (e.g., queueing network and Petri net models). This requires advances in optimizing existing analysis algorithms (e.g., by pre-computing certain parts of a model before an analysis request) as well as novel approaches to automate the decision, which analysis algorithm is to apply in a given prediction scenario.
- A model is always an abstraction of a real system capturing only a subset of factors influencing the performance of the system. Many factors are often not represented explicitly in the model in order to simplify the model solution or because of being difficult to quantify. Therefore, the resulting performance predictions are always subject to a certain level of uncertainty. New techniques to estimate the uncertainty

of model solutions are necessary for a system to be able to take uncertainty into account in its decisions.

- In addition to performance goals, a self-aware system may be subject to constraints and goals with respect to other properties (e.g., reliability, security, energy consumption, or costs). Further models of different types are needed to evaluate and predict such properties under varying system workloads and configurations. Thus, more work is necessary to integrate the different types of models with each other and improve the support for trade-off decisions. Descriptive architecture-level models are beneficial here as additional analyses for different quality attributes can be supported using model-to-model transformations. This has been shown to be beneficial for design-time models (e.g., Palladio Component Model [3]).
- Existing approaches to model-based performance and resource management often either assume the availability of a complete model of the system in advance (e.g., created offline during design and implementation of a system) or at least a model template with relevant parameters estimated at run-time. Only few works consider also the inference of the model structure at run-time. Self-aware systems typically run in dynamic, constantly changing environments. In such environments, learning and maintaining a model automatically at run-time are crucial. Furthermore, it is often not safe to assume that a self-aware system has a global view of its environment. The system may need to interact with other systems to obtain the required information for building models of the environment.

16.4.2 Summary

In this chapter, we surveyed existing classes of run-time models for performance and resource management that can be used to support the design of systems with self-aware performance and resource management mechanisms. In particular, we considered regression models, stochastic performance models (QNs and QPNs), control-theoretical models, and descriptive meta-models. These models vary in their abstraction level, their model structure, their input and output parameters, as well as supported model inference and analysis techniques. In general, one can distinguish between *predictive models* (regression, stochastic performance models, or control-theoretical models) and *descriptive models*. The prediction models have a rigorous mathematical foundation optimized for fast and efficient model solution. They are typically purpose build for answering certain pre-defined questions using a certain analysis technique. In contrast, descriptive models are optimized for greater model expressiveness and interpretability. This class of models can help to abstract from the details of model analysis techniques and thus support a greater variety of analysis techniques by using model-to-model transformations into different prediction models. The decision which analysis technique to use can then be done at run-time depending on the high-level goals of a self-aware system.

References

1. R. Alura, C. Courcoubetisb, N. Halbwachsc, T.A. Henzingerd, P.-H. Hod, X. Nicollinc, A. Oliv-eroc, J. Sifakis, and S. Yovinec. The algorithmic analysis of hybrid systems. *Theoretical Computer Science*, 138(6):3–34, Feb 1995. doi:10.1016/0304-3975(94)00202-T.
2. Falko Bause. Queueing petri nets-a formalism for the combined qualitative and quantitative analysis of systems. In *Petri Nets and Performance Models, 1993. Proceedings., 5th International Workshop on*, pages 14–23. IEEE, 1993.
3. Steffen Becker, Heiko Koziolck, and Ralf Reussner. The Palladio component model for model-driven performance prediction. *Journal of Systems and Software*, 82:3–22, 2009.
4. Mohamed N. Bennani and D. Menascé. Resource allocation for autonomic data centers using analytic performance models. In *ICAC '05: Proceedings of the Second International Conference on Automatic Computing*, pages 229–240, Washington, DC, USA, 2005.
5. Gunter Bolch, Stefan Greiner, Hermann de Meer, and Kishor S Trivedi. *Queueing networks and Markov chains: modeling and performance evaluation with computer science applications*. John Wiley & Sons, 2006.
6. Maury Bramson. A stable queueing network with unstable fluid model. *The Annals of Applied Probability*, 9(3):818–853, 1999.
7. M.S. Branicky. Stability of hybrid systems: state of the art. In *Proceedings of the 36th Conference on Decision and Control*, pages 120–125, San Diego, California USA, December 1997.
8. Leo Breiman, Jerome Friedman, Charles J Stone, and Richard A Olshen. *Classification and regression trees*. CRC press, 1984.
9. Fabian Brosig. *Architecture-Level Software Performance Models for Online Performance Prediction*. PhD thesis, Karlsruhe Institute of Technology (KIT), Karlsruhe, Germany, 2014.
10. Fabian Brosig, Nikolaus Huber, and Samuel Kounev. Automated Extraction of Architecture-Level Performance Models of Distributed Component-Based Systems. In *26th IEEE/ACM International Conference On Automated Software Engineering (ASE 2011)*, 2011.
11. Yiyu Chen, Amitayu Das, Wubi Qin, Anand Sivasubramaniam, Qian Wang, and Natarajan Gautam. Managing server energy and operational costs in hosting centers. In *Proceedings of the 2005 ACM SIGMETRICS International Conference on Measurement and Modeling of Computer Systems*, SIGMETRICS '05, pages 303–314, New York, NY, USA, 2005. ACM.
12. Marc Courtois and Murray Woodside. Using regression splines for software performance analysis. In *Proceedings of the 2Nd International Workshop on Software and Performance*, WOSP '00, pages 105–114, New York, NY, USA, 2000. ACM.
13. Roy T. Fielding and Richard N. Taylor. Principled design of the modern web architecture. *ACM Trans. Internet Technol.*, 2(2):115–150, May 2002.
14. Antonio Filieri, Henry Hoffmann, and Martina Maggio. Automated design of self-adaptive software with control-theoretical formal guarantees. In *Proc. of the 36th Intl. Conference on Software Engineering*, pages 299–310, 2014.
15. Antonio Filieri, Henry Hoffmann, and Martina Maggio. Automated multi-objective control for self-adaptive software design. In *Proceedings of the 10th Joint Meeting of the European Software Engineering Conference and the ACM SIGSOFT Symposium on the Foundations of Software Engineering*, ESEC/FSE 2015. ACM, 2015.
16. Antonio Filieri, Martina Maggio, Konstantinos Angelopoulos, Nicolas D'Ippolito, and Ilias et al. Gerostathopoulos. Software engineering meets control theory. In *Proc. of the 10th Intl. Symposium on Software Engineering for Adaptive and Self-Managing Systems*, 2015.
17. Jerome H Friedman. Multivariate adaptive regression splines. *The annals of statistics*, pages 1–67, 1991.
18. Sven Hedlund. *Computational Methods for Optimal Control of Hybrid Systems*. PhD thesis, Department of Automatic Control, Lund University, Sweden, May 2003.
19. T.A. Henzinger. The Theory of Hybrid Automata. In *Proceedings of the Eleventh Annual IEEE Symposium on Logic in Computer Science (LICS)*, pages 278–292, 1996.
20. B. L. Ho and R. E. Kalman. Effective construction of linear state-variable models from input/output functions. *Regelungstechnik*, 14:545–548, 1966.

21. Tauseef A. Israr, Danny H. Lau, Greg Franks, and Murray Woodside. Automatic generation of layered queuing software performance models from commonly available traces. In *Proc. of the 5th Intl. Workshop on Software and Performance*, pages 147–158, 2005.
22. Rolf Johansson. *System Modeling and Identification*. Prentice Hall, Englewood Cliffs, New Jersey, January 1993.
23. Gueyoung Jung, M.A. Hiltunen, K.R. Joshi, R.D. Schlichting, and C. Pu. Mistral: Dynamically managing power, performance, and adaptation cost in cloud infrastructures. In *Distributed Computing Systems (ICDCS), 2010 IEEE 30th Intl. Conf. on*, pages 62 –73, 2010.
24. R. Kalman and R. Bucy. New results in linear filtering and prediction theory. *Trans ASME, J. Basic Eng., ser. D*, 83:95–107, 1961.
25. H.K. Khalil. *Nonlinear Systems*. Pearson Education. Prentice Hall, 2002.
26. Cristian Klein, Martina Maggio, Karl-Erik Årzén, and Francisco Hernández-Rodriguez. Brownout: Building more robust cloud applications. In *Proceedings of the 36th International Conference on Software Engineering*, pages 700–711, 2014.
27. Samuel Kounev, Fabian Brosig, and Nikolaus Huber. The Descartes Modeling Language. Technical report, Department of Computer Science, University of Wuerzburg, October 2014.
28. Samuel Kounev, Nikolaus Huber, Fabian Brosig, and Xiaoyun Zhu. Model-Based Approach to Designing Self-Aware IT Systems and Infrastructures. *IEEE Computer Magazine*, 2016. Accepted for Publication.
29. M. Kuhn, S. Witson, C. Keefer, and N. Coulter. Cubist Models for Regression. http://cran.r-project.org/web/packages/Cubist/vignettes/cubist.pdf. Last accessed: Jul 2015.
30. Jim Li, John Chinneck, Murray Woodside, Marin Litoiu, and Gabriel Iszlai. Performance model driven QoS guarantees and optimization in clouds. In *Proc. of the 2009 ICSE Workshop on Software Engineering Challenges of Cloud Computing*, pages 15–22, 2009.
31. Awad M. and Daniel A. Menascé. Dynamic Derivation of Analytical Performance Models in Autonomic Computing Environments. In *Proceedings of the 2014 Computer Measurement Group Performance and Capacity Conference (CMG)*, Nov 2014.
32. D. Menascé, Honglei Ruan, and Hassan Gomaa. Qos management in service-oriented architectures. *Performance Evaluation*, 64(7-8):646–663, August 2007.
33. V.S. Borkar M.S. Branicky and S.K. Mitter. A unified framework for hybrid control. In *Proc. IEEE Conf. Decision and Control*, pages 4228–4234, Lake Buena Vista, FL, Dec 1994.
34. Fiona Fui-Hoon Nah. A study on tolerable waiting time: how long are web users willing to wait? *Behaviour and Information Technology*, 23(3):153–163, 2004.
35. Qais Noorshams, Dominik Bruhn, Samuel Kounev, and Ralf Reussner. Predictive Performance Modeling of Virtualized Storage Systems using Optimized Statistical Regression Techniques. In *Proc. of the ACM/SPEC Intl. Conf. on Performance Engineering*, pages 283–294, 2013.
36. Ramon Nou, Samuel Kounev, Ferran Julia, and Jordi Torres. Autonomic QoS control in enterprise Grid environments using online simulation. *Journal of Systems and Software*, 82(3):486–502, March 2009.
37. OMG. Meta Object Facility (MOF) Version 2.5, 2015.
38. G. Pacifici, M. Spreitzer, A. Tantawi, and A. Youssef. Performance Management of Cluster-Based Web Services. *IEEE Journal on Selected Areas in Communications*, 23(12):2333–2343, December 2005.
39. John R Quinlan et al. Learning with continuous classes. In *5th Australian joint conference on artificial intelligence*, volume 92, pages 343–348. Singapore, 1992.
40. Abhishek B Sharma, Ranjita Bhagwan, Monojit Choudhury, Leana Golubchik, Ramesh Govindan, and Geoffrey M Voelker. Automatic request categorization in internet services. *SIGMETRICS Perform. Eval. Rev.*, 36(2):16–25, Aug 2008.
41. Simon Spinner, Giuliano Casale, Fabian Brosig, and Samuel Kounev. Evaluating Approaches to Resource Demand Estimation. *Performance Evaluation*, 92:51 – 71, October 2015.
42. Simon Spinner, Samuel Kounev, and Philipp Meier. Stochastic Modeling and Analysis using QPME: Queueing Petri Net Modeling Environment v2.0. In *Proc. of the 33rd Intl. Conf. on Application and Theory of Petri Nets and Concurrency*, pages 388–397, 2012.

43. Bhuvan Urgaonkar, Giovanni Pacifici, Prashant Shenoy, Mike Spreitzer, and Asser Tantawi. Analytic modeling of multitier internet applications. *ACM Trans. Web*, 1(1), May 2007.
44. André van Hoorn. *Online Capacity Management for Increased Resource Efficiency of Component-Based Software Systems*. PhD thesis, University of Kiel, Germany, 2014.
45. P. van Overschee and B. de Moor. *Subspace Identification for Linear Systems—Theory, Implementation, Applications*. Kluwer Academic Publishers, Boston-London-Dordrect, 1996.
46. Qi Zhang, Ludmila Cherkasova, and Evgenia Smirni. A Regression-Based Analytic Model for Dynamic Resource Provisioning of Multi-Tier Applications. In *Proceedings of the Fourth International Conference on Autonomic Computing*, page 27ff, 2007.

Chapter 17
Online Learning of Run-Time Models for Performance and Resource Management in Data Centers

Jürgen Walter, Antinisca Di Marco, Simon Spinner, Paola Inverardi and Samuel Kounev

Abstract In this chapter, we explain how to extract and learn run-time models that a system can use for self-aware performance and resource management in data centers. We abstract from concrete formalisms and identify extraction aspects relevant to performance models. We categorize the learning aspects into: (i) model structure, (ii) model parametrization (estimation and calibration of model parameters), and (iii) model adaptation options (change point detection and run-time reconfiguration). The chapter identifies alternative approaches for the respective model aspects. The type and granularity of each aspect depend on the characteristic of the concrete performance models.

17.1 Introduction

In order to become self-aware, systems require an internal representation of themselves. According to the definition of self-aware computing systems given in Chap. 1, such systems

1. *learn models* capturing *knowledge* about themselves and their environment (such as their structure, design, state, possible actions, and run-time behavior) on an ongoing basis and

J. Walter (✉) · S. Spinner · S. Kounev
Department of Computer Science, University of Würzburg, Am Hubland,
97074 Würzburg, Germany
e-mail: juergen.walter@uni-wuerzburg.de

S. Spinner
e-mail: simon.spinner@uni-wfuerzburg.de

S. Kounev
e-mail: samuel.kounev@uni-wuerzburg.de

A. Di Marco · P. Inverardi
University of L'Aquila, Via Vetoio 1, 67010 Coppito (AQ), Italy
e-mail: antinisca.dimarco@univaq.it

P. Inverardi
e-mail: paola.inverardi@univaq.it

© Springer International Publishing AG 2017   507
S. Kounev et al. (eds.), *Self-Aware Computing Systems*,
DOI 10.1007/978-3-319-47474-8_17

2. *reason* using the models (e.g., predict, analyze, consider, and plan) enabling them to *act* based on their knowledge and reasoning (e.g., explore, explain, report, suggest, self-adapt, or impact their environment)

in accordance with *higher-level goals*, which may also be subject to change. In this chapter, we focus on learning performance models of IT systems and infrastructures that can be used for online performance and resource management in data centers. As stressed in the definition, the term "learn" does imply that some information based on which models are derived is obtained at system run time, while also additional static information built into the system at design time can be employed as well. Typically, a system may be built with integrated skeleton models whose parameters are estimated using monitoring data collected at run time. Once an initial model is available, it is subjected to continuous updates at run time to reflect any changes in the system itself and/or in the environment during operation.

A performance model is any abstraction of the system and its environment capturing knowledge that can be used to reason about the performance of the system. One main challenge in learning performance models is that the built models should present a right level of abstraction since it has to be detailed enough to guarantee accurate performance results while maintaining the adequate abstraction to be resolvable at run time. The learned models, also called extracted models, can be descriptive, prescriptive, and predictive models (see Chap. 1). Note that this classification is not mutually exclusive. One major challenge of the performance model learning is to find the right level of abstraction such that the constructed models are detailed enough to support accurate performance analysis, while at the same time, they can be solved with reasonable overhead.

Approaches to automatically construct analytical performance models, such as queueing network(s) (QNs), are very popular (e.g., [36, 38, 39]). Often, in such approaches, performance models are learned in a testing phase and applied at run time. However, the constructed models are rather limited since they abstract the system at a very high level without capturing its architecture and configuration explicitly. For example, such models offer no means to express a change in the configuration of the virtualization platform, which may have a significant impact on the performance of system. Moreover, they often impose restrictive assumptions such as a single workload class or homogeneous servers. Furthermore, the model structure is typically assumed to be static. The structure is either derived by hand or tied to a specific application scenario (e.g., n-tierWeb applications [1] or MapReduce jobs [47]), and only model parameters are derived using run-time monitoring data [29]. Furthermore, extraction case studies are often limited to certain technologies, e.g., Java EE systems [10], or certain specific target platforms like Oracle WebLogic server offering a proprietary monitoring infrastructure [8]. There is a lot of existing work on the extraction and maintenance of performance models. However, the extraction process often includes non-automated manual subparts or a priori knowledge about the system. Few solutions support a full automation and provide portability beyond one or two case studies.

In this chapter, we focus on gray-box or white-box models as they contain structural and causal information (see Chap. 16), whereas black-box models do not have any a priori structure imposed. In contrast to white-box models, black-box models serve as interpolation of the measurements and lack information that is required for system adaptation (i.e., resource management at run time). Hence, black-box model extraction, e.g., using genetic optimization techniques [15, 44], is not considered in the following. There are numerous performance modeling formalisms in the literature (cf. Chap. 16), and due to their high number, we cannot discuss the extraction process separately for each of them. However, most performance models provide a common set of features that have to be extracted, which allows us to abstract from the concrete modeling formalisms. We propose to structure the model extraction and maintenance into the following three disciplines, namely: (i) model structure, (ii) model parametrization (estimation and calibration of model parameters), and (iii) model adaptation options (change point detection and run-time reconfiguration). We focus on the extraction of architectural performance models, as they provide the highest flexibility and potential for realizing the general idea of self-aware computing in data centers. Such models combine the descriptive and semantic aspects of architectural models, such as the Unified Modeling Language (UML), with the prediction capabilities of analytical models, like QN. Nonetheless, most of the techniques we present are not restricted to architectural performance models. In this chapter, we use the following acronyms:

APM   Application performance management
DML   Descartes Modeling Language
EJB   Enterprise JavaBeans
Java EE Java Enterprise Edition
LQN   Layered queueing network(s)
QN   Queueing network(s)
QPN   Queueing Petri Net(s)
PMF   Performance Management Framework
S/T/A   Strategies/Tactics/Actions
UML   Unified Modeling Language

The remainder of this chapter is structured as follows: Sect. 17.2 discusses crosscutting concerns for model extraction. Section 17.3 explains possibilities for system structure extraction. Section 17.4 discusses parametrization of models with resource demands and branching probabilities. Section 17.5 is about system and model adaptation. Section 17.6 concludes the chapter and discusses future work.

17.2 Crosscutting Concerns

The learning of performance models requires several issues to be taken into account in order to guarantee the correctness of the process and its efficiency.

Data Collection   Performance models are parameterized by means of monitoring data. Disseminated commercial application performance management (APM) tools are, e.g., Dynatrace, AppDynamics, NewRelic, and Riverbed Technology [9]. Additionally, free and open source performance monitoring tools exist, e.g., Kieker [9]. Typically, trace data are collected from the running system and are used to estimate model parameters, e.g., request arrival rates, service resource demands, or control flow parameters like routing probabilities. Problems that might follow include the following:

- The collected data may be more fine-grained than the performance model parameters; thus, an aggregation step may be needed.
- The measurement overhead may significantly influence the system.

Modeling Abstraction and Formalism   The constructed performance models have to be modified and evaluated online. This poses requirements on the models themselves. The choice of a suitable performance model of the system becomes one of the most important and critical steps. Indeed, the models should be as flexible as possible supporting dynamic adaptation when the system is reconfigured or its architecture evolves, and at the same time, they should support efficient performance analysis at run time. In many cases, these two characteristics may be incompatible. The model flexibility requires detailed models that support changes, such as *reparameterization* based on online monitoring data or *modification* in terms of their topology, in order to reflect a new system configuration. The efficient performance analysis requires models that can be solved in a *short* amount of time. This implies that in many cases only models having analytical/numerical solution may be usable at run time. The challenge here is to design performance models expressive enough to describe different resource allocations and system configurations with respect to their performance behavior, but still having numerical/analytical solution.

Online Evaluation   In order to control the state space explosion, system performance models should be as expressive as possible, omitting irrelevant details about individual system component behavior. This is important for lightweight and fast model evaluation. Of course, there is a trade-off between the simplicity of models and their support for detailed feedback facilitating online decision making.

17.3 Model Structure

The learning of model structure involves extracting information about the software components of the system as well as information about resource landscape in which the system is deployed. The learning of inter-component interactions is covered in the next section since it includes dynamic aspects. Although different types of software components exist, for pragmatic reasons, we consider a component simply as an element of the software architecture providing one or more services. Software systems that are assembled from existing prepackaged components may be represented by the same components in a performance model [45]. Examples of components are as follows: Web services, Enterprise JavaBeans (EJBs) in Java Enterprise Edition (Java EE) applications [7, 8, 10], or `IComponent` extensions in .NET. Apart from building performance models of systems assembled from prepackaged components, previous research on architecture extraction targeted system reengineering scenarios. Examples of reverse engineering tools and approaches in this area are FOCUS [17], ROMANTIC [25], Archimetrix [43], or SoMoX [3]. These approaches are either clustering-based, pattern-based, or a combination of both. Components are identified from a reengineering perspective which does not necessarily correspond to deployable structures of the current implementation. Furthermore, the choice of an appropriate granularity is important. The complexity of a component decomposition can be reduced by merging subservices. However, there is no rule that can be automatically applied to solve the granularity problem. To allow automated learning of the system structure, the system and its components should provide information about their boundaries. If no predefined component boundaries are provided, component identification requires manual effort. In general, the following guidelines can be applied in case of component-based systems implemented using an object-oriented programming language: (i) Classes that implement component interfaces form components, (ii) all classes that inherit from a base class belong to the same component, and (iii) component A that uses component B $\rightarrow$ A is a composite component containing B. Compared to component extraction, the automated identification of hardware and software resources in a system environment is already supported by industrial software tools. For instance, [26] or [46] provide such functionalities. An open issue is to define common interfaces for resource extraction. This would greatly improve the integration of different tool chains supporting interoperability. Deployment information can be extracted using event logs containing identifiers for software components and resources. The extraction process creates one deployment component for each pair of software component and resource identifier. Summing up, there are still many open research questions and a lack of tool support for a full automation of the extraction of information about the system structure. However, many semiautomatic solutions have already been proposed and successfully applied in case studies.

17.4 Model Parameterization

Model parameterization includes the determination of resource demands, determination of the inter-component interactions (control flow), and the extraction of load profile. In performance models, component resource demands are key parameters required for quantitative analysis. A resource demand describes the amount of a hardware resource needed to process one unit of work (e.g., a user request, a system operation, or an internal action). The granularity of resource demands depends on the abstraction level of the control flow in a performance model. Resource demands may depend on the values of input parameters. This dependency can be either captured by specifying the stochastic distributions of resource demands or by explicitly modeling parametric dependencies.

The estimation of resource demands is challenging as it requires the integration of application performance monitoring solutions with resource usage monitors of the operating system in order to obtain resource demand values. Operating system monitors often provide only aggregate resource usage statistics on a per-process level. However, many applications (e.g., Web and application servers) serve different types of requests with one or more processes.

Profiling tools [20, 21], typically used during the development to track down performance issues, provide information on call paths and execution times of individual functions. These profiling tools rely on either fine-grained code instrumentation or statistical sampling. However, these tools typically incur high measurement overheads, severely limiting their usage in production environments and leading to inaccurate or biased results. In order to avoid distorted measurements due to overheads, [33, 34] propose a two-step approach. In the first step, dynamic program analysis is used to determine the number and types of bytecode instructions executed by a function. In a second step, the individual bytecode instructions are benchmarked to determine their computational overhead. However, this approach is not applicable during operation and fails to capture interactions between individual bytecode instructions. APM tools enable fine-grained monitoring of the control flow of an application, including timings of individual operations. These tools are optimized to be also applicable to production systems.

Modern operating systems provide facilities to track the consumed CPU time of individual threads. This information is, for example, also exposed by the Java Runtime Environment and can be used to measure the CPU resource consumption by individual requests as demonstrated for Java in [10] and at the operating system level in [2]. This requires application instrumentation to track which threads are involved in the processing of a request. This can be difficult in heterogeneous environments using different middleware systems, database systems, and application frameworks. The accuracy of such an approach heavily depends on the accuracy of the CPU time accounting by the operating system and the extent to which request processing can be captured through instrumentation.

Over the years, a number of approaches to estimate the resource demands using statistical methods have been proposed. These approaches are typically based on a combination of aggregate resource usage statistics (e.g., CPU utilization) and coarse-grained application statistics (e.g., end-to-end application response times or throughput). These approaches do not depend on a fine-grained instrumentation of the application and are therefore widely applicable to different types of systems and applications incurring only insignificant overheads. Different approaches from queuing theory and statistical methods have been proposed [42], e.g., response time approximation least-squares regression, robust regression techniques, cluster-wise regression, Kalman filter, adaptive filtering, Bayesian estimation, optimization techniques, support vector machines, independent component analysis, maximum likelihood estimation, and Gibbs sampling. These approaches differ in their required input measurement data, their underlying modeling assumptions, their output metrics, their robustness to anomalies in the input data, and their computational overhead. A detailed analysis and comparison are provided in [42], where a library for resource demand estimation—LibReDE—is described.

We identify the following areas of future research on resource demand estimation:

1. Current work is mainly focused on CPU resources. More work is required to address the specifics of other resource types, such as memory, network, or I/O devices. The challenge with these resource types is, among others, that resource utilization is often not as clearly defined as for CPU, and the resource access may be asynchronous. For instance, utilization of a storage I/O device w.r.t. throughput is hard to quantify since the maximum input/output operations per second of a device is workload dependent itself.
2. Comparisons between statistical estimation techniques and direct measurement approaches are missing. This would help to better understand their implications on accuracy and overhead.
3. Most approaches are focused on estimating the mean resource demand. However, in order to obtain reliable performance predictions, it is also important to determine the correct distribution of the resource demands.
4. Modern system features (e.g., multi-core CPU, dynamic frequency scaling, virtualization) can have a significant impact on the resource demand estimation.

The extraction of information about the interactions between components differs for design time and run time. At design time, models can be created based on designer expertise and design documents as proposed in [14, 37, 40, 41]. The automated extraction of structural information based on monitoring logs has the advantage that it tracks the behavior of the actual product as executed at run time. An *effective architecture* can be extracted which means that only executed system elements are extracted [27]. Furthermore, run-time monitoring data enable to extract branching probabilities for different call paths [6, 10]. The approaches for the extraction of information about inter-component interactions by [5, 23, 27] use monitoring information based on probes injected in the beginning of each response and propagated through the system.

17.5   Adaptation

Software systems and surroundings are continuously subject to change (e.g., hardware breakdown and workload increase or decrease). Therefore, performance models have to be maintained up-to-date, and the system has to be adapted to guarantee the satisfaction of performance requirements. In this section, we face the problem of maintaining performance models in online scenarios, continuously refining and calibrating them the performance models to allow them to better fulfill the purpose for which they are used. First of all, in Sect. 17.5.1, we discuss adaptation points which specify what may be changed within a system. Section 17.5.2 is about detection of changes in the system (e.g., hardware breakdown) and its surroundings (e.g., work-load). Section 17.5.3 is about model-based reconfiguration in general, followed by the description of two exemplary reconfiguration frameworks in Sect. 17.5.4.

17.5.1 Adaptation Points

To support suitable automatic adaptations of a self-aware system, it has to be defined what, in the system, can be subject to change and what not. First, one has to define what changes shall or can be detected. Secondly, one has to define how the system may adapt itself. Therefore, it is necessary to identify adaptation points in the system and, respectively, in its model. The points where the system architecture can be adapted can be formalized in an adaptation point meta-model, as proposed in [24]. Therefore, this submodel reflects the boundaries of the systems configuration space; i.e., it defines the possible valid states of the system architecture. The adaptation points at the model level correspond to adaptation operations executable on the real system at run time, e.g., adding virtual CPUs to VMs, migrating VMs or software components, load-balancing requests, variation of algorithms, or the size of a thread pool. In general, the detection of the change points cannot be executed automatically since they are typically limited by constraints imposed by the execution environment, design choices (e.g., the usage of monolithic component/service), or even by business issues (e.g., in case of Infrastructure as a Service, we have a maximum amount of resources that we can use fixed by the contract). Adaptation point models are application specific, and research on adaption point extraction is in its infancy. For example, the authors are not aware of an extraction mechanism that says whether a component may be replicated or not.

In the future, guidelines or semiautomatic approaches should improve adaption point model creation. However, whenever identified and formally specified, such adaption points can enter the online adaptation mechanisms in order to select actions respecting them and hence to be considered in the adaptation.

17.5.2 Detection of Changes

To detect changes in the system and its surrounding, monitoring infrastructures can be used to capture the occurrences of relevant events. Even in large and distributed systems, it is possible to generate, combine, and filter huge amounts of events to timely detect changes in the behavior of the systems. Among existing monitoring infrastructures, it is worth to mention Glimpse [4], a flexible monitoring infrastruc-ture, developed with the goal of decoupling the event specification from the monitor-ing and analysis mechanism. Glimpse was initially proposed to support behavioral learning, performance and reliability assessment, security, and trust management. Many changes can be detected directly using event logs, e.g., deploy and undeploy or allocation and deallocation of hardware resources [22]. In such cases, an incoming event triggers a model update directly. However, there are changes in the real world that require changes in the model that cannot be mapped to an event directly. For instance, the behavior of software components often depends on the parameters that are not available as input parameters passed upon service invocation. Such parameters are not traceable over the service interface, and tracing them requires looking beyond the component boundaries [6]. For example, parameters might be passed to another component in the call path and/or they might be stored in a database structure queried by the invoked service. Moreover, the behavior of component services may also depend on the state of data containers such as caches or on persistent data stored in a database. For example, databases often behave differently for different load levels due to caching behavior. Such changes, non-traceable by events, require a continuous periodic surveillance of the system and a validation and adaptation of the model both with respect to its structural [22] and parameterization aspects [18]. Note that the prediction of workload changes is covered in detail in Chap. 18. So we refer the interested reader to that chapter.

17.5.3   Adaptation Mechanisms

Besides externally driven changes, systems may proactively change according to model-driven reconfigurations based on predictive analysis. This system-triggered change idea is close to the self-aware computing vision as it includes deduction of future states. The automated and dynamic nature of the reconfiguration process poses new challenges on the decision step that aims at choosing the next system configuration in order to overcome the observed problem. Most approaches use predetermined strategies coded in the application or in the reconfiguration framework [16]. However, in QoS management, a predetermined schema of decision can prevent the implementation of smart alternatives more suitable to effectively overcome the observed problems. Compared to purely measurement-based approaches, the use of predictive system performance models enables proactive adaptation operations. It allows the choice of the system reconfiguration alternative that is predicted to satisfy the performance requirements of the system [11, 12, 19, 35].

In case of self-aware resource management in data centers, a general framework observes the software application during its execution to monitor performance attributes of the software application. Whenever the performance constraints are no longer satisfied, the adaptation management process will start. The monitoring data is evaluated in order to identify the performance problem and the portion of the system affected by it. Such information is used to plan changes in the system configuration in order to overcome the observed problem. Whenever a new system configuration is determined, the changes are enacted and the system configuration is modified accordingly. Such general framework has been realized in different application domains (e.g., in service-oriented software, in cloud computing, and in component-based systems).

While at design time the full design space can be explored [31], it is not possible to explore all design alternatives at run-time. Instead of a full exploration, greedy approaches select the most promising configuration candidates for evaluation. Moreover, models for run-time application must be often less detailed than design time models in order to reduce the effort for the evaluation of a single alternative. This simplification may have impact on the accuracy of the measured performance indices. However, the evaluation has to be only sufficiently accurate to select a suitable reconfiguration alternative. While it can be shown that adaptation mechanisms are able to select the best alternatives, there are some major open issues in online model adaptation.

1. When should the reconfiguration be performed? The condition that triggers the adaptation process is a very critical issue in run-time performance management. It influences the execution frequency of the reconfiguration loop. Conditions that are verified too often lead to a high overhead: The management framework can consume more resources than the application itself. Conversely, conditions that rarely trigger the reconfiguration can prevent a timely management of performance problems. The critical issue here is to determine the best trade-off between computational overhead and timely resolution of performance problems.

2. Cost-benefit analysis for the next reconfiguration step. In order to be effective, the reconfiguration process must actually improve the performance of the managed system. Indeed, complex systems must address several non-functional requirements. The risk of having a degradation of some other non-functional property (e.g., security) related to the reconfiguration is avoided by allowing only a controlled set of configuration alternatives, which are decided by the developer according to the risks associated with the reconfiguration. Moreover, at each reconfiguration step, the costs to place the system in the new selected configuration should be considered during the selection. This can be achieved by combining the result of the model evaluation provided by the solver with a coefficient representing the cost of the reconfiguration process.

3. Extensive search for the best reconfiguration versus finding a sufficient reconfiguration very fast.

Whenever a system and the corresponding performance model are adapted, the monitoring infrastructure that supports the adaptation framework could be subject to adaptation itself. For example, deploying some components may require redeploying the measurement probes as well; dynamic binding of a different service would also change the catch and monitor event. As a consequence, an adaptable monitoring infrastructure able to reflect the system changes must be used. An example of such a flexible monitoring infrastructure can be found in [28]. However, this opens a wide research area that is out of scope of this chapter.

17.5.4   Model-Based Adaptation Frameworks

In this section, we discuss two frameworks for model-based system adaptation at run time. Section 17.5.4.1 presents the Performance Management Framework [11] and Sect. 17.5.4.2 the Strategies/Tactics/Actions [24] framework. Extraction of system structure and calibration will be mostly left out for complexity reasons.

17.5.4.1   Performance Management Framework

Performance Management Framework (PMF) [11] is an environment that focuses on run-time management of performance requirements of complex software systems. It monitors the current performance of the application, and when some problem occurs, it chooses a new configuration based on the feedback provided by the online evaluation of the performance models corresponding to different reconfiguration alternatives. The main characteristic of PMF is the heuristic mechanism to generate such alternatives. Differently from other approaches, it does not rely on a fixed repository of predefined configurations but on a reconfiguration policy defined as a suitable combination of basic reconfiguration rules. Such basic reconfiguration rules guarantee the validity of the final reconfiguration policy with respect to external constraints (e.g., usage of legacy systems and usage of resources).

The reconfiguration policy is evaluated on the data retrieved by the online monitoring (that represents a snapshot of the current system state), thus generating a number of new configurations. Once such alternatives have been generated, and the online evaluation is carried out to predict which one is most suitable to solve the observed problem.

The PMF approach is based on: (i) monitoring of the running system to collect data, (ii) dynamic reconfiguration to change the running configuration, and (iii) model-based performance analysis to decide the next system configuration among the available ones. Figure 17.1 outlines the PMF process and its flow of activities. PMF observes the software application during its execution to monitor the performance attributes of the software application. Whenever the performance constraints are no longer satisfied, the adaptation management process is triggered. The monitoring data is evaluated in order to identify the performance problem and the portion of the system affected by it. This information is used to plan changes in the system configuration in order to overcome the observed problem. Whenever a new system configuration is determined, the changes are enacted and the system configuration is modified accordingly.

At PMF, the initial performance model is specified by performance specialists. The next ones instead are generated on-the-fly by modifying the current performance model applying the devised reconfiguration policies. The information collected during the monitoring phase is used to evaluate the predictive performance model(s). All design alternatives are represented at the same level of abstraction and the actual data are observed through the same abstractions thus providing a uniform workbench to

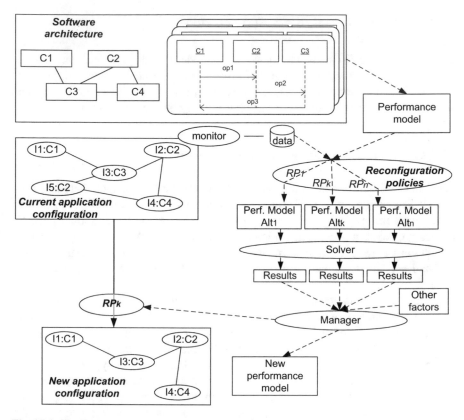

Fig. 17.1 The Performance Management Framework (PMF)

consistently evaluate different alternatives. The empirical experimentation case study described in the following shows that PMF is able to chose the best alternative among the generated ones.

Application of PMF on SIENA Publish/Subscribe Middleware

In [11], PMF has been used to dynamically reconfigure the SIENA middleware [13] topology depending on the *utilization* and *throughput* of SIENA routers. According to the general publish/subscribe model, the SIENA architecture (depicted in Fig. 17.2) defines two main entities: (*i*) the *clients* and (*ii*) the *event service*. Clients may be both *publishers* (i.e., objects of interest) and *subscribers* (i.e., recipients) that express their interest in certain kinds of events by supplying a *filter*. The event service, composed of one or more servers interconnected in a hierarchical fashion (shown in Fig. 17.3), forms a store-and-forward network that is responsible for delivering events from publishers to the subscribers that submitted a filter matching the respective events.

The performance of a SIENA network depends on the performance of each SIENA server within the event service and of the SIENA network topology. The performance of a SIENA router depends on the number of stored filters, as well as on the traffic

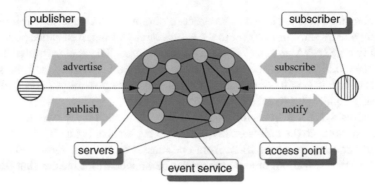

Fig. 17.2 SIENA architecture

Fig. 17.3 A possible configuration for the SIENA network

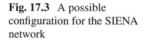

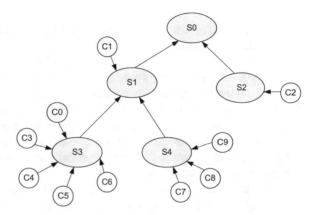

generated by the clients connected to it. The SIENA network topology affects the routing of subscriptions and publications and thus the global performance of the middleware.

Indeed, since these indices are correlated with the utilization law, in the experimental setup of SIENA publish/subscribe middleware [11], we use the routers' utilization as a basis to decide when a reconfiguration has to be performed.

Due to the event dispatcher rules and the dynamism of the network, it can happen that one or more routers are overloaded and degrade the performance of the whole network. For example, a router might be the access point of too many clients or it might be the root of a large subnetwork, while other routers are unloaded (in this case, the hierarchical structure is not balanced). When a SIENA router is overloaded (i.e., its utilization is high), we aim to reconfigure the network in order to prevent critical performance scenarios. The possible policies to reconfigure the network are specified as follows:

Moving SIENA clients—One or more SIENA clients are moved from the overloaded SIENA router to the unloaded one(s). This policy aims at balancing the workload among the routers. Note that, in order to obtain a significant improvement, the receiving routers must not belong to the subhierarchy of the overloaded router.

Changing SIENA routers' internal parameters—The router implementation allows the modification of the number of its internal threads satisfying the service requests of external software entities. In this way, it is possible to add (software) processing capabilities to each router.

Changing SIENA routers topology—One or more routers are switched from the overloaded router to the unloaded ones. This policy aims at balancing the workload among the routers switching them from one master to another. Again, to reach an improvement, the reconfigured routers must be attached to a master that does not belong to the subhierarchy of the overloaded router.

Adding/removing SIENA routers—The last possible reconfiguration policy is to remove/add router instances in order to increase/decrease the processing capacity of the network. Of course, we add new router instances if we need more (software) processing capacity, whereas we remove router instances whenever there are too many routers with respect to the needs.

The online adaptation of the performance model has to respect the changing requirements of the software system the model represents. Moreover, a reconfiguration is normally not intended to change the application functionality (e.g., the substitution of a component with a new one providing different services). This restriction is necessary since functional changes in the application would normally imply a redesign of the performance model, and not only a change in its topology or in some parameters. Consequently, the reconfiguration process could not be realized in a completely automated manner.

In line with the above observations, in PMF [11], the allowed model reconfigurations are of two kinds: They may change internal parameters of software components (such as the number of threads or other features defined by the component developer); they may change the system topology by adding/removing component and/or connector instances. To relax this restriction, the online reconfiguration of models should rely on a database containing several different implementations of a component together with their performance models. When the reconfiguration policy requires the substitution of an implementation of a component, the adaptation of the performance model is done by replacing the submodel of the first implementation with the one of the new implementation retrieved from the database.

PMF has been the first approach in the literature to self-adapt system that uses performance models at run time. In PMF, the predictive models are used to support the decision of how to reconfigure the system to overcome performance problems observed through the monitoring. In this way, the selected reconfiguration guarantees the performance requirement satisfaction until both system and environment characteristics do not change considerably.

17.5.4.2   S/T/A Adaptation Framework

In this section, we illustrate how an architectural performance model of a software system (modeled with the Descartes Modeling Language (DML) described in Chap. 16 or [30]) can be updated and kept in sync with the real system using the Strategies/Tactics/Actions (S/T/A) adaptation framework [24]. We demonstrate this based on an industrial case study. The example model was created as part of a cooperation with Blue Yonder GmbH & Co. KG, a leading service provider in the field of predictive analytics and big data. The modeled system (called Blue Yonder system) provides forecasting services used by customers for predicting, e.g., sales, costs, and churn rates. These services are based on compute-intensive machine-learning techniques and subject to customer SLAs. In this case study, the DML models were used to predict the resource requirements for a given usage scenario and optimize the resource allocation to reduce costs. Figure 17.4 depicts an excerpt of a DML model in a UML-like notation. Blue Yonder system consists of three types of components: `Gateway Server`, `Database`, and `Prediction Server`. These components run on a heterogeneous resource environment composed of low-cost desktop computers and high-end machines. The `Prediction Server` provides two services: `train` and `predict`. The `train` service infers a mathematical model for the available historical data. The `predict` service uses this model to return forecasts.

To enable performance predictions, services have to be equipped with model variables (e.g., branching probabilities, resource demands). For model parameterization, DML supports a hybrid approach: All model variables can be declared as either *explicit* or *empirical*. The model parameters in the example model in Fig. 17.4 are all explicit, i.e., the values of the parameters are defined at model creation time. Empirical model parameters need to be learned based on monitoring data. Thus, it is possible to specify some model parameters based on expertise knowledge in advance, while others can be learned from monitoring data collected at system run time. Further, the model in Fig. 17.4 includes an example for an adaptation point. Adaptation points can be either associated with model parameters (e.g., number of CPU cores) or with model entities. In the example model, the adaptation point (see `ModelEntityConfigRange`) is associated with a component specifying the minimum and maximum number of instances of this component that are allowed. In the example, the `PS` component is instantiated twice (`PredictionServerA` and `PredictionServerB`). The depicted configuration can be changed using adaptation processes. Figure 17.5 shows a schematic representation of an adaptation process for the Blue Yonder system. The objective is to keep the response time below a certain SLA (while at the same time optimize the resource efficiency). In order to achieve this objective, the adaptation mechanism uses the following strategies: `FindDeployment`, `ReduceDeployment`, and `ConsolidateDeployment`. The `FindDeployment` strategy launches new `PS` instances until all customer SLAs are fulfilled. It contains two different tactics starting the new `PS` instances on low-budget machines or on high-end machines, respectively. `ReduceDeployment` removes unnecessary `PS` instances from machines to save operating costs, e.g., if

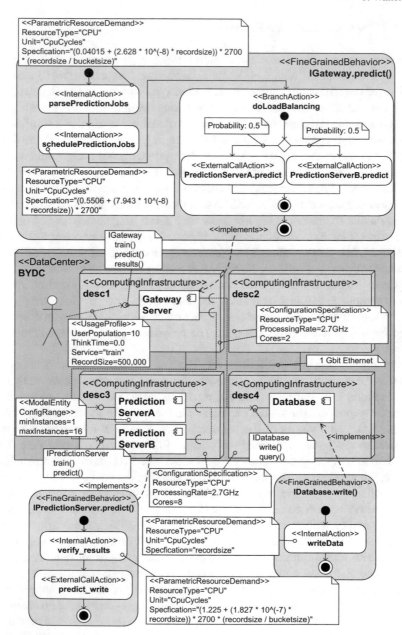

Fig. 17.4 Excerpt of the DML Blue Yonder system model

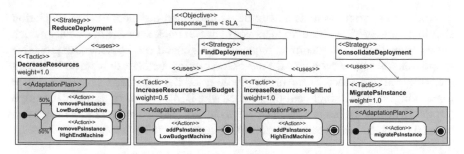

Fig. 17.5 Adaptation process for the Blue Yonder system

the workload of a customer has decreased. Finally, `ConsolidateDeployment` migrates `PS` instances between machines with the goal to improve efficiency.

If a strategy contains different tactics to reach a certain objective, S/T/A assigns weights to the tactics, which are dynamically updated based on their predicted impact. The tactic with the highest weight is always applied first until the objective is reached or the tactic's weight is decreased, and another tactic becomes the tactic with the highest weight. An educated setting of initial weights may speed up convergence; however, it is not required.

The reconfiguration planning step ends when the adaptation process has determined a series of reconfigurations that results in all application objectives being fulfilled. The reconfigurations are then applied on the real system. Thus, the model-based adaptation ensures that all reconfigurations are first applied on the model level, and their impact is predicted before applying them on the real system.

DML can be used to predict the impact of changes in the workload and system configuration on the performance and resource usage of the application. DML is a descriptive model designed for high expressiveness and good understandability. In order to enable performance predictions, DML relies on mathematical analysis techniques based on existing stochastic modeling formalisms, such as (layered) queueing network (LQN) and Queueing Petri Net (QPN). In [6], three different model-to-model transformations are defined providing different levels of prediction speed and accuracy: (a) Bounds analysis uses operational analysis from queueing theory to determine asymptotic bounds on the average throughput and response time, (b) an LQN solver offering fast analytical model solution, and (c) a QPN solver supporting the analysis of larger models using simulation. The benefit of the transformation approach is that it provides the flexibility to switch between different prediction techniques depending on the prediction goals. The prediction goals comprise the requested performance metrics, the required accuracy, and the time constraints. In [6], an algorithm is described that automatically selects a suitable transformation depending on the prediction goals. This algorithm is able to tailor the input model and remove parts that are not relevant for predicting the requested performance metrics. Thus, the model complexity can be reduced to speed up the analysis.

Another important issue is how to determine when the model-based adaptation should be triggered. At Blue Yonder, users have to book services in advance which allows to predict future incoming requests. In a general setting, enabling proactive adaptations of a system requires the use of forecasting methods to predict changes in the workload (described by the usage profile in DML). Chapter 18 introduces such forecasting methods, which can be combined with DML to detect changes in the usage profile. If workload changes are detected, the previously described mechanisms can be used to determine whether and how the system should be reconfigured.

17.6   Conclusion and Open Challenges

In order to be self-aware, a system needs to create an internal model representation of itself. The extraction of performance models yields an abstraction of the real system capturing only a subset of factors influencing the performance of the system. We briefly discuss the open challenges for completely automating the model extraction process. Existing research on automated model extraction is mostly based on small case studies, and the majority of approaches proposed in the literature have not yet been validated in the context of large real-life systems. Improvements can be achieved by developing extraction tool benchmarks (which are currently missing) and by defining specific extraction tool design goals. Existing model extraction approaches differ in accuracy, granularity, and update behavior. So far, there are almost no comparisons between different approaches. Besides this, we identify the following challenges for performance model extraction:

- Testing whether the extracted model accurately reflects the system behavior. The assessment of validity and accuracy of extracted models is often based on trial and error. An improvement would be to equip models with confidence intervals that provide hints on their validity.
- Models may become outdated if they are not updated as the system evolves. Change point detection mechanisms are required to learn when models get out of date and when to update them.
- Devise guidelines or semiautomatic approaches for the extraction of adaptation points to derive actions for online adaptation.
- Current performance modeling formalisms barely ensure the traceability between models and the systems they represent. Explicit traceability information should be stored as part of the models.
- The automated inspection of the system under test often requires technology-specific solutions. One approach to enable tools that are less technology-specific might be a definition of self-descriptive resources using standardized interfaces.
- A system can be modeled at different granularity levels. Extraction approaches usually support only one. Automated identification of an appropriate model granularity level and model reduction techniques are promising research areas.

- The automated identification and extraction of parametric dependencies in call paths and resource demands would enable significant improvements in the prediction accuracy of extracted models. Basic approaches, based on static code analysis, have been proposed in [32].
- Model extraction should support parallelism (multi-core systems and asynchronous calls) [31].

Acknowledgements This work is supported by the German Research Foundation (DFG) in the Priority Programme "DFG-SPP 1593: Design For Future-Managed Software Evolution" (KO 3445/15-1).

References

1. Mahmoud Awad and Daniel A. Menascé. *Computer Performance Engineering: 11th European Workshop, EPEW 2014, Florence, Italy, September 11–12, 2014. Proceedings*, chapter On the Predictive Properties of Performance Models Derived through Input-Output Relationships, pages 89–103. Springer International Publishing, Cham, 2014.
2. Paul Barham, Austin Donnelly, Rebecca Isaacs, and Richard Mortier. Using Magpie for request extraction and workload modelling. In *Proceedings of the 6th Symposium on Operating Systems Design & Implementation (OSDI'04)*, pages 18–18. USENIX Association, 2004.
3. Steffen Becker, Michael Hauck, Mircea Trifu, Klaus Krogmann, and Jan Kofron. Reverse engineering component models for quality predictions. In *Proceedings of the 14th European Conference on Software Maintenance and Reengineering (CSMR '10)*, pages 199–202. IEEE, 2010.
4. Antonia Bertolino, Antonello Calabrò, Francesca Lonetti, and Antonino Sabetta. Glimpse: A generic and flexible monitoring infrastructure. In *Proceedings of the 13th European Workshop on Dependable Computing*, EWDC '11, pages 73–78, New York, NY, USA, 2011. ACM.
5. Lionel C. Briand, Yvan Labiche, and Johanne Leduc. Toward the reverse engineering of UML sequence diagrams for distributed Java software. *IEEE Transactions of Software Engineering*, 32(9):642–663, 2006.
6. Fabian Brosig. *Architecture-Level Software Performance Models for Online Performance Prediction*. PhD thesis, Karlsruhe Institute of Technology (KIT), Karlsruhe, Germany, 2014.
7. Fabian Brosig, Nikolaus Huber, and Samuel Kounev. Automated extraction of architecture-level performance models of distributed component-based systems. In *Proceedings of the 26th IEEE/ACM International Conference On Automated Software Engineering (ASE 2011)*, 2011.
8. Fabian Brosig, Samuel Kounev, and Klaus Krogmann. Automated Extraction of Palladio Component Models from Running Enterprise Java Applications. In *Proceedings of the 1st International Workshop on Run-time mOdels for Self-managing Systems and Applications (ROSSA 2009)*. ACM, 2009.
9. Andreas Brunnert, Andre van Hoorn, Felix Willnecker, Alexandru Danciu, Wilhelm Hasselbring, Christoph Heger, Nikolas Herbst, Pooyan Jamshidi, Reiner Jung, Joakim von Kistowski, Anne Koziolek, Johannes Kroß, Simon Spinner, Christian Vögele, Jürgen Walter, and Alexander Wert. Performance-oriented DevOps: A research agenda. Technical Report SPEC-RG-2015-01, SPEC Research Group — DevOps Performance Working Group, Standard Performance Evaluation Corporation (SPEC), 2015.
10. Andreas Brunnert, Christian Vgele, and Helmut Krcmar. Automatic Performance Model Generation for Java Enterprise Edition (EE) Applications. In MariaSimonetta Balsamo, WilliamJ. Knottenbelt, and Andrea Marin, editors, *Computer Performance Engineering*, volume 8168 of *Lecture Notes in Computer Science*, pages 74–88. Springer Berlin Heidelberg, 2013.

11. Mauro Caporuscio, Antinisca Di Marco, and Paola Inverardi. Model-based system reconfiguration for dynamic performance management. *Journal of Systems and Software*, 80(4):455–473, 2007.
12. Valeria Cardellini, Emiliano Casalicchio, Vincenzo Grassi, Stefano Iannucci, Francesco Lo Presti, and Raffaela Mirandola. MOSES: A framework for qos driven runtime adaptation of service-oriented systems. *IEEE Trans. Software Eng.*, 38(5):1138–1159, 2012.
13. Antonio Carzaniga, David S. Rosenblum, and Alexander L. Wolf. Design and evaluation of a wide-area event notification service. *ACM Trans. Comput. Syst.*, 19(3):332–383, 2001.
14. Vittorio Cortellessa, Antinisca Di Marco, and Paola Inveradi. *Model-based software performance analysis*. Springer-Verlag, 2011.
15. Marc Courtois and Murray Woodside. Using regression splines for software performance analysis. In *Proceedings of the 2nd International Workshop on Software and Performance (WOSP '00)*, pages 105–114. ACM, 2000.
16. Antinisca Di Marco, Paola Inverardi, and Romina Spalazzese. Synthesizing self-adaptive connectors meeting functional and performance concerns. In Marin Litoiu and John Mylopoulos, editors, *Proceedings of the 8th International Symposium on Software Engineering for Adaptive and Self-Managing Systems, SEAMS 2013, San Francisco, CA, USA, May 20–21, 2013*, pages 133–142. IEEE Computer Society, 2013.
17. Lei Ding and Nenad Medvidovic. Focus: A light-weight, incremental approach to software architecture recovery and evolution. In *In Proceedings of the Working IEEE/IFIP Conference on Software Architecture (WICSA '01)*, pages 191–200. IEEE, 2001.
18. Ilenia Epifani, Carlo Ghezzi, Raffaela Mirandola, and Giordano Tamburrelli. Model evolution by run-time parameter adaptation. In *Proceedings of the 31st International Conference on Software Engineering, (ICSE 2009)*, pages 111–121. IEEE, 2009.
19. Carlo Ghezzi, Valerio Panzica La Manna, Alfredo Motta, and Giordano Tamburrelli. Performance-driven dynamic service selection. *Concurrency and Computation: Practice and Experience*, 27(3):633–650, 2015.
20. Susan L. Graham, Peter B. Kessler, and Marshall K. Mckusick. Gprof: A call graph execution profiler. *SIGPLAN Not.*, 17(6):120–126, 1982.
21. Robert J. Hall. Call path profiling. In *Proceedings of the 14th International Conference on Software Engineering (ICSE '92)*, pages 296–306. ACM, 1992.
22. Robert Heinrich, Eric Schmieders, Reiner Jung, Kiana Rostami, Andreas Metzger, Wilhelm Hasselbring, Ralf Reussner, and Klaus Pohl. Integrating run-time observations and design component models for cloud system analysis. In *Proceedings of the 9th Workshop on Models@run.time co-located with 17th International Conference on Model Driven Engineering Languages and Systems (MODELS 2014), Valencia, Spain, September 30, 2014.*, pages 41–46, 2014.
23. Curtis E. Hrischuk, C. Murray Woodside, Jerome A. Rolia, and Rod Iversen. Trace-based load characterization for generating performance software models. *IEEE Transactions of Software Engineering*, 25(1):122–135, January 1999.
24. Nikolaus Huber, André van Hoorn, Anne Koziolek, Fabian Brosig, and Samuel Kounev. Modeling Run-Time Adaptation at the System Architecture Level in Dynamic Service-Oriented Environments. *Service Oriented Computing and Applications Journal (SOCA)*, 8(1):73–89, March 2014.
25. Marianne Huchard, A. Djamel Seriai, and Alae-Eddine El Hamdouni. Component-based architecture recovery from object-oriented systems via relational concept analysis. In *Proceedings of the 7th International Conference on Concept Lattices and Their Applications (CLA 2010)*, pages 259–270, 2010.
26. Hyperic. Hyperic (2014). http://www.hyperic.com, 2014.
27. Tauseef Israr, Murray Woodside, and Greg Franks. Interaction tree algorithms to extract effective architecture and layered performance models from traces. *Journal of Systems and Software*, 80(4):474–492, 2007.
28. Gregory Katsaros, George Kousiouris, Spyridon V. Gogouvitis, Dimosthenis Kyriazis, Andreas Menychtas, and Theodora Varvarigou. A self-adaptive hierarchical monitoring mechanism for clouds. *Journal of Systems and Software*, 85(5):1029 – 1041, 2012.

29. Samuel Kounev, Konstantin Bender, Fabian Brosig, Nikolaus Huber, and Russell Okamoto. Automated simulation-based capacity planning for enterprise data fabrics. In *Proceedings of the 4th International ICST Conference on Simulation Tools and Techniques (SIMUTools '11)*, pages 27–36. ICST (Institute for Computer Sciences, Social-Informatics and Telecommunications Engineering), 2011.

30. Samuel Kounev, Fabian Brosig, and Nikolaus Huber. The Descartes Modeling Language. Technical report, Department of Computer Science, University of Wuerzburg, 2014.

31. Heiko Koziolek, Steffen Becker, Jens Happe, Petr Tuma, and Thijmen de Gooijer. Towards Software Performance Engineering for Multicore and Manycore Systems. *SIGMETRICS Perform. Eval. Rev.*, 41(3):2–11, December 2013.

32. Klaus Krogmann. *Reconstruction of Software Component Architectures and Behaviour Models using Static and Dynamic Analysis*. PhD thesis, Karlsruhe Institute of Technology (KIT), Karlsruhe, Germany, 2010.

33. Michael Kuperberg, Martin Krogmann, and Ralf Reussner. ByCounter: Portable runtime counting of bytecode instructions and method invocations. In *Proceedings of the 3rd International Workshop on Bytecode Semantics, Verification, Analysis and Transformation*, 2008.

34. Michael Kuperberg, Martin Krogmann, and Ralf Reussner. TimerMeter: Quantifying accuracy of software times for system analysis. In *Proceedings of the 6th International Conference on Quantitative Evaluation of SysTems (QEST) 2009*, 2009.

35. Moreno Marzolla and Raffaela Mirandola. Performance aware reconfiguration of software systems. In Alessandro Aldini, Marco Bernardo, Luciano Bononi, and Vittorio Cortellessa, editors, *Computer Performance Engineering - 7th European Performance Engineering Workshop, EPEW 2010, Bertinoro, Italy, September 23–24, 2010. Proceedings*, volume 6342 of *Lecture Notes in Computer Science*, pages 51–66. Springer, 2010.

36. Daniel A. Menascé, Mohamed Bennani, and H.Honglei Ruan. On the use of online analytic performance models, in self-managing and self-organizing computer systems. In *Self-star Properties in Complex Information Systems*, pages 128–142, 2005.

37. Daniel A. Menascé and Hassan Gomaa. A method for design and performance modeling of client/server systems. *IEEE Transactions of Software Engineering*, 26(11):1066–1085, 2000.

38. Daniel A. Menascé, Honglei Ruan, and Hassan Gomaa. QoS management in service-oriented architectures. *Perform. Eval.*, 64(7-8):646–663, 2007.

39. Adrian Mos. *A framework for adaptive monitoring and performance management of component-based enterprise applications*. PhD thesis, Dublin City Universit, 2004.

40. Dorin C. Petriu and C. Murray Woodside. Software performance models from system scenarios in use case maps. In *Proceedings of the 12th International Conference on Computer Performance Evaluation, Modelling Techniques and Tools (TOOLS '02)*, pages 141–158. Springer-Verlag, 2002.

41. Connie U. Smith and Lloyd G. Williams. *Performance Solutions: A practical guide to creating responsive, scalable software*. Addison-Wesley, 2002.

42. Simon Spinner, Giuliano Casale, Xiaoyun Zhu, and Samuel Kounev. LibReDE: A library for resource demand estimation. In *Proceedings of the 5th ACM/SPEC International Conference on Performance Engineering (ICPE '14)*, pages 227–228. ACM, 2014.

43. Markus von Detten. Archimetrix: A tool for deficiency-aware software architecture reconstruction. In *Proceedings of the 2012 19th Working Conference on Reverse Engineering (WCRE '12)*, pages 503–504. IEEE Computer Society, 2012.

44. Dennis Westermann, Jens Happe, Rouven Krebs, and Roozbeh Farahbod. Automated inference of goal-oriented performance prediction functions. In *Proceedings of the 27th IEEE/ACM International Conference on Automated Software Engineering (ASE)*, pages 190–199, 2012.

45. Xiuping Wu and Murray Woodside. Performance modeling from software components. In *Proceedings of the 4th International Workshop on Software and Performance (WOSP '04)*, pages 290–301. ACM, 2004.

46. Zenoss. Zenoss (2014). http://www.zenoss.com, 2014.

47. Zhuoyao Zhang, L. Cherkasova, and Boon Thau Loo. Automating platform selection for mapreduce processing in the cloud. In *Cloud and Autonomic Computing (ICCAC), 2015 International Conference on*, pages 125–136, Sept 2015.

48. Anne Koziolek, Heiko Koziolek, and Ralf Reussner. PerOpteryx: automated application of tactics in multi-objective software architecture optimization. In Ivica Crnkovic, Judith A. Stafford, Dorina C. Petriu, Jens Happe, and Paola Inverardi, editors, *Joint proceedings of the Seventh International ACM SIGSOFT Conference on the Quality of Software Architectures and the 2nd ACM SIGSOFT International Symposium on Architecting Critical Systems (QoSA-ISARCS 2011)*, pages 33–42. ACM, New York, NY, USA, 2011.

Chapter 18
Online Workload Forecasting

Nikolas Herbst, Ayman Amin, Artur Andrzejak, Lars Grunske,
Samuel Kounev, Ole J. Mengshoel and Priya Sundararajan

Abstract This chapter gives a summary of the state-of-the-art approaches from different research fields that can be applied to continuously forecast future developments of time series data streams. More specifically, the input time series data contains continuously monitored metrics that quantify the amount of incoming workload units to a self-aware system. It is the goal of this chapter to identify and present approaches for online workload forecasting that are required for a self-aware system to act proactively—in terms of problem prevention and optimization—inferred from likely changes in their usage. The research fields covered are machine learning and time series analysis. We describe explicit limitations and advantages for each forecasting method.

N. Herbst (✉) · S. Kounev
University of Würzburg, Würzburg, Germany
e-mail: nikolas.herbst@uni-wuerzburg.de

S. Kounev
e-mail: samuel.kounev@uni-wuerzburg.de

A. Amin
Swinburne University of Technology, Melbourne, Australia
e-mail: aabdellah@swin.edu.au

A. Andrzejak
Heidelberg University, Heidelberg, Germany
e-mail: artur.andrzejak@informatik.uni-heidelberg.de

L. Grunske
Humboldt-Universität zu Berlin, Berlin, Germany
e-mail: lars.grunske@informatik.hu-berlin.de

O.J. Mengshoel · P. Sundararajan
Carnegie Mellon University, Pittsburgh, CA, USA
e-mail: ole.mengshoel@sv.cmu.edu

P. Sundararajan
e-mail: priya.sundararajan@west.cmu.edu

© Springer International Publishing AG 2017
S. Kounev et al. (eds.), *Self-Aware Computing Systems*,
DOI 10.1007/978-3-319-47474-8_18

18.1   Introduction

The purpose of online workload forecasting, as discussed here, is to predict the future workload of a computing system. Forecasting the future workload is central in the context of self-aware systems as defined in Chap. 1. The quality of such forecasts will, along with the future state of the computing system itself, have a profound effect on the quality of the services provided to users by the computing system. Online workload forecasting is similar to other forecasting problems in related areas of technology, science, and business. These related problems can inspire and inform our forecasting objectives, which center on workloads in data centers, including private and public clouds.

Online workload forecasting plays a crucial role in monitoring and managing the resources in data centers, an environment where self-aware computing can provide significant value. Specifically, as the workload offered to a data center increases or decreases, data center resources can be scaled accordingly. An important consideration is to carefully balance resource consumption, on the one hand, and response time, on the other hand. With the increasing ubiquity of cloud computing, smartphones, wearable computing enabled by clouds, PaaS, SaaS, virtual machines, and related technologies, online workload forecasting clearly has a key role to play.

Different stakeholders clearly have different goals and concerns when it comes to data center resource management. Three main types of stakeholders, along with their goals and concerns, should be considered. *End users* focus on the availability, performance, and utility of their applications and their supporting cloud services. A *data center owner* is typically concerned about cost, associated with both buying the equipment and running the data center (energy cost, for example, can be very high). One component of cost optimization is to carefully perform re-balancing of services in cloud data centers [60]. The *app owner* is in the middle and purchases resources from the data center owner for hosting one or more applications that provide services to the end users. An app owner tends to focus on supporting and pleasing a potentially broad range of users while not incurring too much cost with the data center owner. Workload forecasting can play a key role in helping to meet the goals of each of these three stakeholder groups.

In the presence of seasonal (or cyclic) patterns or long-lasting trends, forecasting results still need to be accurate and reliable. Intuitively, there are several complications making forecasting difficult, including abrupt events, randomness, seasonal variation, and trend changes. Seasonal or cyclic behavior includes the diurnal cycle, which is a pattern that repeats every 24 h around the world, impacting how computers, mobile devices, the Internet, and the Web are used. For example, the traffic or load of social networking Web sites often shows a clear diurnal pattern [13, 47]. In addition, there may be weekly cycles, due to the fact that people's behavior on weekdays is typically quite different from their behavior on weekends. Both daily and weekly seasonality patterns, as well as other types of cyclic load variations, can have a dramatic impact on data center load. Obvious examples of these include holidays and other events that occur on an annual or multi-annual cycle. In addition to these temporal patterns, there are strong empirical indications that humans follow clear spatial and social patterns [13].

That being said, there are issues beyond cyclic behavior, namely trends, abrupt events, and randomness. As examples of trends, we can consider the steady increases in various prices, for example, stock market prices or housing prices. Examples of abrupt events include, for example, crashes in stock markets, strong earthquakes, rain in arid climates, and reaction to headline news on the Web [44, 55]. Finally, there is probabilistic, random, statistical, or stochastic behavior.

In the following Sect. 18.2, we discuss preprocessing actions that are relevant for forecast methods in general. In Sects. 18.3 and 18.4, we describe forecast methods from the machine learning and the time series analysis domains that are applicable in the context of workloads mentioning explicit advantages and limitations of each. Section 18.5 presents the state of the art of applying forecast methods in the IT workload domain.

18.2 Process of Modeling and Data Preprocessing

Online workload data is typically represented in the form of a time series $(\mathbf{w}_0, \mathbf{w}_1, \ldots)$, i.e., a sequence of scalar or vector values $\mathbf{w}_i$ ordered by timestamps, indicating the sampling times. The forecasting of future values in this time series is performed as an evaluation of a so-called *forecasting function* f (or *model*). Such function utilizes as its input raw and/or preprocessed data known at the instant of the forecast computation. Such data can include historical workload data, system-related measurements, external data or signals, as well as past forecast values.

For example, the load of a public Web server can be expressed as its CPU utilization over the last minute, i.e., the portion of time the server was busy. A corresponding forecast function f might use the load values of the last hour of this and other servers in a cluster (historical workload data), currently available RAM and number of users on this server (application-related measurements), time of the day and day of the week (external data), and error of the forecast values in the last hour as input.

More formally, a time series forecasting function f can be expressed as follows:

$$y_t = f(x_t, x_{t-1}, \ldots, x_{t-L}, y_{t-1}, y_{t-2}, \ldots, y_{t-L}), \tag{18.1}$$

where y_t is the current prediction, $y_{t-1}, \ldots, y_{t-L}$ are past predictions, and x_t and $x_{t-1}, \ldots, x_{t-L}$ denote the vectors of current and past observations, respectively [58]. The observations include raw and/or preprocessed workload data and other types of data listed above. The parameter L specifies how much historical information is used as model input. In general, using all available data (i.e., setting L close to t) is hardly feasible as this would greatly increase model dimensionality, leading to spurious and probably inaccurate results due to overfitting.

The forecasting functions (or models) are typically either models based on machine learning (Sect. 18.3) or auto-regressive models including hybrid models (Sect. 18.4). As a prerequisite for forecasting, we may need to prepare data as well as to train (fit) the model for a particular application scenario. We explain in detail the data preparation process in the remainder of this section. Model fitting depends strongly on the type of the predictive function and is discussed in Sect. 18.3 and 18.4.

18.2.1 Overview of Modeling Steps

Projects in time series forecasting typically consist of two phases: the *modeling phase* and the *deployment phase*. The purpose of the modeling phase is to understand the data at hand, to engineer features, and to train a predictive model, or a set of those. In the deployment phase, a production environment, these models are used for computing forecasts.

18.2.1.1 Modeling Phase

This is typically an exploratory process with multiple iterations. The key steps of modeling are the following:

- Extraction and transformation of raw data into relational format. Examples include parsing of log data with format conversion and import into spreadsheets, into an SQL database, or into a distributed file system such as HDFS. In several cases, corrective measures are needed prior to import to handle malformatted input lines or values, or to eliminate illegal characters.
- Cleaning of relational data by removing outliers and handling missing values is the next step. In many cases, more extensive preprocessing steps such as median filtering and normalization take place.
- Feature engineering is a more advanced form of data preprocessing. It can be understood as the creation of derived time series, which exposes and represents forecasting-relevant information in a form accessible to the modeling algorithms. An example is to extract *time* until host load exceeds, e.g., 50 % for more than one minute, and use the corresponding time series as additional input for the modeling algorithm. Even sophisticated modeling approaches, such as support vector machines (see Sect. 18.3), could hardly derive this information from the raw data. Another popular and automatic approach to feature engineering is dimensionality reduction, which can create new attributes (e.g., in case of principal component analysis (PCA) [25]) and remove irrelevant ones in a single step. Feature engineering is typically an essential but complex component of the modeling phase, known to be decisive for the overall success. We discuss this in detail in Sect. 18.2.2.
- Computation of a prediction target is needed when forecasting some derived signals instead of "raw" data. For example, for regression, we might want to forecast a difference from the current value one hour in advance instead of absolute host load. In the case of classification, target values must be quantified to represent them by symbolic elements from a fixed set of values, e.g., value intervals [7].

- Preprocessed data is then split into training, validation, and testing sets. The first two data sets are used in the subsequent model fitting step, while test data is necessary for evaluating model accuracy.
- Model fitting on the training data is the actual core of the modeling phase. In machine learning, typically a collection of algorithms such as decision trees, SVMs, and others (Sect. 18.3) are investigated. For auto-regressive methods (Sect. 18.4), model coefficients are fitted by, e.g., least-squares methods [25]. This step can be computationally demanding but can be easily automated by leveraging available libraries such as WEKA [68], MATLAB toolboxes, and Python libraries (e.g., SciPy learn).
- Trained models are validated using test data sets (i.e., "out-of-sample" data not used in the fitting step). For time series data, the cross-validation approach [68] frequently used for evaluation is not suitable and can lead to overoptimistic results. Instead, so-called walk-forward testing known from the financial industry can be used [38]. Multiple types of evaluation metrics are commonly used to estimate the forecasting error, for example, mean-squared error or mean absolute error. In case of classification, the confusion matrix or F_1-score [25] is commonly used.

As noted above, obtaining an accurate model typically requires several iterations, where the steps from feature engineering until validation are repeated. A lot of manual effort is spent for programming extraction and optimization of features, while other steps can more easily be automated.

18.2.1.2   Deployment Phase

In this phase, the trained prediction functions are used for performing predictions in a production setting. It is typically dominated by a software engineering effort during which an automated prediction pipeline is created. The pipeline is used to process data streams or data batches for scenarios where the availability of forecast result is not time-constrained. Several aspects need to be considered here:

- Robust functions for efficient computation of derived features need to be implemented. Such functions must be able to handle corrupt data and missing values (if the model cannot handle them) to ensure that the data forecasting subsystem does not break down for non-standard inputs.
- Another essential issue—especially for long-term forecasting—is the correction of a so-called concept drift. Concept drift refers to the modeled process changing after some time and the prediction function becoming less accurate [51]. The corrective measure includes monitoring the accuracy of the forecasting function online and retraining it if an error exceeds a critical threshold [6]. In more severe cases, it may be necessary to repeat the feature engineering step, especially if the currently used features do not capture the essential information anymore, or new raw data types became available.

18.2.2 Feature Engineering

Feature engineering is the (partially manual) process of considering the raw data and identifying suitable derived values that become components of the vectors $\mathbf{x}_i$ serving as input for the forecasting function in Eq. (18.1).

In the case of time series, designing and implementing features is particularly challenging since data can contain useful sequence information, e.g., event patterns or periodical fluctuations. In most scenarios, it is recommended to include data (or derived values) from the "past" relative to the time of sampling, in addition to information sampled at a given time instant. Typically, manual feature engineering (possibly supported by automated methods such as feature selection) is needed both to specify the amount of historical data (value of L in Eq. (18.1)) and to identify significant historical data values.

Below, we give examples of typical features in the context of time series. However, a multitude of other approaches to preprocessing time series data exist. As an interesting example, Symbolic Aggregate approXimation (SAX) [39] converts time series values into a sequence of symbols from a finite set (essentially, the values are quantized according to their distance to the series mean value). This allows using more advanced methods for feature generation like identification of frequent patterns in the temporal behavior.

18.2.2.1 Aggregated Values

A simple yet effective approach is to compute aggregates for each of the components of the observation vector $\mathbf{x}_i$. Such aggregates can include simple or exponential moving averages, maximum or minimum values in a (sliding) time window, medians over such a time window, and combinations thereof [51]. To capture different timescales, multiple features with different time window sizes (or other parameters) can be used. Since the number of candidate features can be large, typically feature selection [68] is also used to identify most informative raw data and derived features.

18.2.2.2 Exposing Periodic Patterns

Features exposing periodic patterns in temporal data are particularly relevant when hosts are subjected to recurrent demand fluctuations, e.g., due to periodic patterns in user behavior. It may be essential to consider multiple timescales. For example, a load of a host in a Web server cluster is likely to depend on the load for the last few minutes, the time of the day (business hours versus night hours), and day of the week.

Moreover, for an online retailer such as Amazon, considering week of the calender year might also be of value (e.g., Cyber Monday or Black Friday sales peak). Features exposing periodical patterns over multiple timescales can be implemented in several ways. A straightforward approach is to subsample past data by using only vectors $\mathbf{x}_{t-k}, \mathbf{x}_{t-2k}, \mathbf{x}_{t-3k}, \ldots$, where k is the targeted cycle period. This can be done for different values of k, e.g., 24 h, one week, one month, and so on.

A more sophisticated option is to use calendar methods [57]. Here, one computes load averages over the same hour of a day or week, over the same day of a month, etc. In the former case, one could obtain 24 feature "groups" (each group with all components of the observation vector $\mathbf{x}_i$), one per each hourly slot in a day, and in the latter case, 7 feature groups, one per day of the week.

If periodic patterns in data exist, features can be used to represent them directly and thus greatly facilitate the learning of an accurate model. In contrast, using consecutive raw historical values over a prolonged historical period is unlikely to exploit periodical patterns in data and only increases the risk of overfitting.

18.2.2.3   Downsampling with Feature Selection

A more automated method of feature generation for time series is to select vectors of past observations (and even components of these vectors). This can be done using standard feature selection approaches such as forward search with a wrapper method [68]. For example, forward search has been used in conjunction with model-based evaluation in [58]. Given a set of already selected k feature groups derived from $\mathbf{x}_{t-i(1)}, \mathbf{x}_{t-i(2)}, \ldots, \mathbf{x}_{t-i(k)}$, a next feature group derived from $\mathbf{x}_{t-i(k+1)}$ is added only if a candidate feature set $\mathbf{x}_{t-i(1)}, \mathbf{x}_{t-i(2)}, \ldots, \mathbf{x}_{t-i(k)}, \mathbf{x}_{t-i(k+1)}$ gives rise to a more accurate model (fitted on the training data and evaluated on the validation data set). To identify an optimal value of index offset $i(k + 1)$, all values between $i(k + 1)$ and L can be evaluated, which might be computationally costly.

18.3   Predictive Models Based on Machine Learning

18.3.1   Bayesian Networks

A Bayesian network (BN) is a directed acyclic graph whose vertices are random variables, and the directed edges denote the dependency relationship among the random variables. Bayesian networks are well suited for systems where we need to make predictions under uncertainty [49]. Formally, a BN is defined as $B = (G, P)$, where G is a directed acyclic graph and P is the set of probability distributions associated with $G's$ nodes. The graph is denoted by $G = (\mathbf{X}, \mathbf{E})$, where $\mathbf{X} = \{X_1, X_2, \ldots, X_n\}$ is the node set and $\mathbf{E}$ is the edge set. If there is an edge from X_i to X_j, then $(X_i, X_j) \in \mathbf{E}$ and we denote X_i as the parent of X_j. $pa(X_j)$ denotes the set of all parents of X_j. The key property of BNs is the *conditional independence* of the variables from any of their non-descendants, given the value of their parent variables, i.e., given the value of $pa(X_j)$, X_j is conditionally independent of all its non-descendants. A BN factorizes a joint distribution $\Pr(\mathbf{X})$ as shown below:

$$P(\mathbf{X}) = \prod_{j=1}^{n}(P(X_j \mid pa(X_j)))\qquad(18.2)$$

For example, a set of random variables can be used to predict network traffic. Let us consider a Bayesian network model with the following random variables: resources assigned (R), workload (W), cloud service level (C), user experience (U), and energy consumed (E). Using probability theory, we can compactly represent the relationship among these random variables: $P(W)$, $P(R)$, $P(C|W, R)$, $P(U|C)$, and $P(E|R)$.

Modeling phase: Let $\mathbf{E} \subset \mathbf{X}$ be the variables under observation (we call them evidence variables), and let **e** denote their observed values (evidence). For the purpose of cloud performance prediction, a BN can be learned from data. Two of the many dimensions to consider are as follows: (i) whether the BN's graph structure is known or not and (ii) whether the data is complete or not. For learning, if the data is complete, maximum likelihood estimation can be used. For incomplete data, the expectation maximization algorithm (EM) [16] can be used. EM is found to be computationally expensive for difficult BNs. An age-layered approach (ALEM) [48] has been developed to speed up EM. ALEM has been extended to the MapReduce framework [56]. The ALEM strategy was found to achieve gains in parameter quality and run-time. After BN learning, the different types of queries as mentioned above can be answered using the inference algorithm.

Deployment phase: For online load forecasting, a Bayesian network can help to solve different probabilistic queries. The process of solving the probabilistic queries is called inference. The inference algorithms assume that the nodes in **E** are clamped to values **e**. Computation of *most probable explanation (MPE)* amounts to finding a most likely assignment (y) to all of the non-evidence variables $\mathbf{R} = \mathbf{X} - \mathbf{E}$, or MPE($\mathbf{R}$). Computation of marginals amounts to inferring the *most likely value (MLV)* over one query variable $\mathbf{Q} \in \mathbf{R}$. Computation of the *maximum a posteriori probability (MAP)* generalizes MPE computation and finds a most probable instantiation over some variables $\mathbf{Q} \subseteq \mathbf{R}$, MAP($\mathbf{Q}$, **e**). Different BN inference algorithms [41] can be used to perform the above computations.

Example: Di et al., have used a Bayesian model to predict the host load in a cloud system [18]. Their model predicts the mean load over a long-term time interval as well as the mean load in consecutive future time intervals. The experiments are based on a Google trace with over 10 K hosts and millions of jobs. The results suggest that this Bayesian method improves the load prediction accuracy by 5.6–50 % compared to other state-of-the-art methods based on moving averages, auto-regression, and noise filters.

Limitations:

- There is no universally accepted method for constructing a BN from data.
- It takes some effort to design a BN by hand.
- For large and complex BNs, posterior probabilities can be expensive to compute.

Advantages:

- The graphical structure of BNs is very intuitive and easy to understand for people who are not familiar with the domain.
- BNs provide a theoretical framework for handling missing data. Missing data is marginalized out by summing or integrating over all the possibilities of the missing values.
- BNs can handle both discrete and continuous variables in the same model.
- BNs provide a theoretical framework for handling expert knowledge using prior probabilities.

18.3.2   Neural Networks

Neural networks (NNs), often referred to as artificial neural networks (ANNs), are inspired by the way the human brain learns and processes information. ANNs consist of a large number of neurons interconnected in layers. The first layer consists of input neurons where input data is fed into the neural network. The input neurons send the data to the next layer, which consists of hidden neurons. The activity of the hidden neurons is determined by the input data, the weights in the interconnections between the input neurons, and the hidden neurons and the activation functions. The output layer consists of output neurons whose behavior is determined by the hidden neurons and weights in the interconnections between the hidden neuron and the output neuron. The complexity of learning in a neural network depends on the number of layers, the interconnection patterns between different layers, the learning process for updating the weights, and the activation function that converts input to output. A single-layer neural network or perceptron consists of a single layer of output neurons. The inputs are fed directly to the output neurons through a series of weights. A multi-layer perceptron (or a deep neural network) consists of many hidden layers of neurons, with each layer fully connected to the next one.

Modeling phase: In order to train an ANN in a supervised manner to perform a task, we must adjust the weights of each interconnection in such a way that the error between the desired output and the actual ANN output is minimized. Backpropagation is the most widely used algorithm for determining the error derivative of the weights ($\frac{dW}{dt} = 0$). ANN learning algorithms fall into two broad categories: heuristic techniques (variable learning rate backpropagation, resilient backpropagation) and numerical optimization techniques (conjugate gradient [33], quasi-Newton [17]).

In a supervised learning setting, input data along with its desired output data (x, y) is fed to the network. The task of the network is to find a mapping function $f : X \rightarrow Y$. For workload forecasting, the network can be trained at fixed intervals depending on the nature of the load variation (i.e., batch learning, e.g., hourly, seasonally or annually). In an unsupervised setting, the task of the learning algorithm is to update a sequence of functions $f_1, f_2, \ldots, f_t$ in such a way that the prediction (x_{t+1}, y_{t+1}) depends on the previous function f_t and the current data (x_t, y_t).

Large memory is needed if the current prediction depends on all previous functions $f_1, f_2, \ldots, f_t$ and data $(x_1, y_1), (x_2, y_2), \ldots, (x_t, y_t)$. For online workload prediction, adaptive neural networks can be used, i.e., learning and operating at the same time.

Deployment phase: After training, the learnt ANN model is used for prediction. The test data is given as input to the input neurons. The learned weights are used to predict values at the output neurons. For online workload forecasting, we first train the ANN for a limited time of historical workload data. The trained ANN is then used to forecast the future workload.

Example: An ANN-based framework (PRACTISE) has been proposed for online prediction of computed loads such as CPU utilization, memory utilization, disk usage, and network bandwidth [71]. PRACTISE uses an online updating module that monitors the prediction errors periodically. If the errors suddenly surge, then the neural network model is retrained. Experiments were done using traces from IBM data centers. PRACTISE is able to efficiently capture the peak loads in terms of their intensities and timing, in contrast to classic time series models.

Limitations:

- Neural networks are difficult to design. One must determine suitable number of nodes, hidden layers, and activation functions.
- The output values do not come with a confidence measure.
- Neural networks are a "black box." During training, there is no easy way to ensure how the domain-specific information is being used.
- Training typically requires significant computational resources.
- Neural network models can be prone to overfitting.

Advantages:

- Neural networks can implicitly detect nonlinear patterns in the training data.
- The static, nonlinear function used by neural networks provides a method to fit the parameters of a particular function to a given set of data.
- A wide variety of ANN architectures and activation functions can be used to fit a given set of data.

18.3.3 Decision Trees

A decision tree [53] is a tree-structured directed graph, where the goal is to predict the leaf nodes based on several attributes. If the target leaf node is continuous, then the decision tree is called a regression tree. If the target leaf node takes categorical values, then the decision tree is called a classification tree.

Modeling phase: For example, consider the data vector $(x, y) = (x_1, x_2, x_3, \ldots, x_k, y)$. Here, the target is y and it depends on the values of the attributes

$(x_1, x_2, x_3, \ldots, x_k)$. Each interior node in the decision tree corresponds to an attribute X_i with value x_i. The edges emanating from node X_i are labeled with possible values of the attribute. Each leaf represents the value of the target given the values of the attribute as we traverse the path from the root to the leaf node. A decision tree can be constructed by recursively partitioning the training data into subsets based on the attributes. The first step is to choose the attribute that best splits the given training data. The measure of goodness of split (score) is based on the impurity of child nodes. The best attribute to split on is the one that produces smaller impurity and thus more skewed label distribution at the child nodes. Examples of goodness-of-split measures include information gain and Gini index.

Deployment phase: After constructing the decision tree, it can be used for prediction. Consider a test data vector $(x, y) = (x_1, x_2, x_3, \ldots, x_k, y)$. Our goal is to predict the target y. The test data X is classified by passing it through the tree starting at the root node. The test at each internal node along the path is applied to the attributes of X_i to determine the next arc along which X should go down. The label at the leaf node at which X ends up is output as its classification.

During online learning, it is preferable to update the existing decision tree as new training instances arrive without needing to build a new decision tree. Utgoff proposed an incremental decision tree (ID5R) [65]. The ID5R algorithm updates the tree at each node based on the "best" split according to the new training instance. This leads to efficient re-structuring of the subtrees without the need to re-iterate through the past training examples.

Example: Decision trees are used for both long-term (yearly) [23] and short-term (every 15 min) [52] forecasting. Ding [23] uses decision trees for long-term forecasting of energy consumption. The attributes consist of 14 key factors that contribute to energy consumption including primary, secondary, and tertiary GDP, residential energy consumption, industry output, financial revenue, and economic index. Ding's improved decision tree method outperforms traditional forecasting methods such as linear regression and exponential curves.

Limitations:

- Overfitting the training data can happen if the training data is small or noisy. Post-pruning is often performed to avoid overfitting.
- The accuracy of the model depends on the higher-order interactions of the input variables.
- Finding an optimal decision tree is an NP-complete problem [35]. Many decision tree algorithms employ a heuristic-based approach (such as information gain) to guide the search in the hypothesis space. Each split depends on the previous splits, so an error in a higher split is propagated down toward the leaves.

Advantages:

- The decision tree can clarify the relationship between the factors influencing the forecast and possible forecasting.

- The decision tree extracts the decision rules from the data set, which are stored in a knowledge base and used for forecasting.
- A large variety of extensions to the basic algorithm have been developed. These include algorithms to handle missing data, real-valued attributes, post-pruning methods, and incremental learning.

18.3.4 Support Vector Machines

The support vector machine (SVM) is a supervised algorithm where the goal is to predict the value of a target given the values of the attributes. It can be applied to both real-valued and categorical data that are linearly or nonlinearly separable. SVM is a robust classification and regression technique. SVM works by finding the optimal separating hyperplane that maximizes the margin of the attributes. A hyperplane can be defined by an intercept term b and a normal vector $\mathbf{w}$ perpendicular to the hyperplane. A hyperplane can be written as the set of points $\mathbf{x}$ (also called support vectors) satisfying the equation $\mathbf{w}^T\mathbf{x} = -b$.

Modeling phase: Consider a data set $D = \{(\mathbf{x}_i, y_i)\}$, where each $\mathbf{x}_i$ is a point and y_i is the class label. For example, in a 2-class classification problem, the class labels are $y_i = +1$ and $y_i = -1$. Our goal is to learn a mapping function: $y_i = f(\mathbf{x_i}, \{\mathbf{w}, b\})$. The linear SVM classifier can be written as $y_i = sign(\mathbf{w^T x_i} + b)$. A value of $+1$ indicates one class and -1 indicates the other class. The maximum margin is given by $\frac{2}{\sqrt{\mathbf{ww^T}}}$. We want to maximize this margin, which is equivalent to minimizing $\frac{\mathbf{w^T w}}{2}$, subject to the constraints $(\mathbf{w^T x_i} + b) \geq 1$ if $y_i = 1$ and $(\mathbf{w^T x_i} + b) \leq 1$ if $y_i = -1$. Now we have a quadratic optimization problem, and we need to solve for w and b.

In real world, training data can be nonlinear. For nonlinear SVMs, we map data to a rich feature space and construct hyperplanes in that space. Formally, we pre-process the data: $\mathbf{x} \leftarrow \Phi(\mathbf{x})$. Then, we learn the classifier: $f(\mathbf{x}) = \mathbf{w}\Phi(\mathbf{x}) + b$. But the dimensionality of $\Phi(\mathbf{x})$ can be large, making it computationally difficult to solve for $\mathbf{w}$ and b. So we use kernel functions $K < x_i, x_j >$. The kernel functions and parameters have to be carefully chosen as this would influence the performance of the SVM model. The resulting high-dimensional space from the kernel functions can make the data linearly separable, even though it was not linearly separable in the original attribute space.

Deployment phase: After training the model, it is used to predict the labels of the test data. During online prediction, as one receives new data $(\mathbf{x})$, the model uses the learnt weights to predict the label. Online training can happen either in batch for a set of test cases or per test case based on the results of the prediction. Several online SVM algorithms have been developed [9, 43].

Example: Support vector machines (SVM) have been applied for measurements of CPU utilization, memory utilization, disk space usage, communication latency, and bandwidth [50]. SVN-based forecasts are found to be more accurate and outperform the existing methods based on metrics such as mean absolute error and mean-squared error among others. Hu et al. [34] have explored different machine learning models for multi-step-ahead prediction of grid resources. Their experiments indicate that epsilon-support vector regression and nu-support vector regression achieve better performance than backpropagation neural network, radial basis function neural network, and generalized regression neural network.

Limitations:

- Difficult determination of the regularization parameters, kernel parameters, and choice of kernel.
- Sensitive to skewed distributions.
- Computationally expensive training process.

Advantages:

- Both simple (few dimensions) and complex (many dimensions) classification models can be learned.
- Model is robust to small training data sets.
- SVM employs sophisticated mathematical methods to avoid overfitting.

18.4 Predictive Models Based on Time Series Analysis

18.4.1 ARIMA Models

Auto-regressive integrated moving average (ARIMA) models were originally proposed by Box and Jenkins [10], and they are commonly used to fit linearly dependent time series data and forecast their future values. ARIMA models have been successfully applied in many fields such as financial and economic forecasting [54]. In addition, some researchers have applied these models to forecast the future values of QoS attributes [2, 3, 12, 28] or for estimating system reliability [4].

The time series $\{z_t\}$ is said to be generated by an auto-regressive integrated moving average (ARIMA) model of orders p, d, and q, denoted by ARIMA(p, d, q), if it satisfies:

$$\Phi_p(B)y_t = \Theta_q(B)\varepsilon_t \qquad (18.3)$$

where y_t is a stationary time series (of the original non-stationary time series $\{z_t\}$) computed by using d differences as $y_t = (1 - B)^d z_t$ and $B^d z_t = z_{t-d}$. In addition, $\{\varepsilon_t\}$ is a sequence of independent normal errors with zero mean and variance σ^2. The auto-regressive polynomial is $\Phi_p(B) = \left(1 - \phi_1 B - \phi_2 B^2 - \cdots - \phi_p B^p\right)$ with order p and $\Theta_q(B) = \left(1 + \theta_1 B + \theta_2 B^2 + \cdots + \theta_q B^q\right)$ is the moving average polynomial with order q. The auto-regressive and moving average coefficients are $\Phi = \left(\phi_1, \phi_2, \cdots, \phi_p\right)^T$ and $\Theta = \left(\theta_1, \theta_2, \cdots, \theta_q\right)^T$, respectively. The model (18.3) can be rewritten as

$$y_t = \sum_{i=1}^{p} \phi_i y_{t-i} + \sum_{i=1}^{q} \theta_i \varepsilon_{t-i} + \varepsilon_t \qquad (18.4)$$

where y_{t-i} for $i = 1, \ldots, p$ are the past stationary observations, ε_t is the current error, and ε_{t-i} for $i = 1, \ldots, q$ are the past errors.

To forecast one step ahead, we shift from t to $t + 1$:

$$y_{t+1} = \sum_{i=1}^{p} \phi_i y_{t+1-i} + \sum_{i=1}^{q} \theta_i \varepsilon_{t+1-i} + \varepsilon_{t+1} \qquad (18.5)$$

and similarly we can forecast multi-step-ahead values.

If the original time series $\{z_t\}$ is stationary, then there are no differences used and $\{z_t\}$ is said to be generated by an auto-regressive moving average (ARMA) model of orders p and q and denoted by ARMA(p,q). In addition, most of the existing nonlinear time series models are normal extensions for ARIMA models, including SETARMA models [61], introduced in Sect. 18.4.3.

Limitations:

- ARIMA models are generally used as black box models. Insights are limited to the values of p, q, and d.
- Model selection and identification of ARIMA parameters is time-consuming.

Advantages:

- ARIMA defines a family of models that can be (automatically) selected and parametrized to provide accurate forecasts.
- ARIMA is usable as a black box model.
- ARIMA is fast when used for prediction once model and parameters are selected.

18.4.2 GARCH Models

The auto-regressive conditional heteroscedastic (ARCH) models were introduced by Engle [24] to model high volatility by describing the dynamic changes in time-varying variance as a deterministic function of past errors. These models have become widely accepted for financial time series with volatility clustering and turn out to be an important tool in the field of financial forecasting [45] but also have been applied to software systems [2].

Engle formally defined the ARCH model for a conditional variance σ_t^2 of the dependent variable y_t as follows:

$$\sigma_t^2 = \alpha_0 + \alpha_1 \varepsilon_{t-1}^2 + \cdots + \alpha_m \varepsilon_{t-m}^2, \qquad (18.6)$$

where $\varepsilon_t = y_t - \sum_{i=1}^{p} \phi_i y_{t-i} - \sum_{i=1}^{q} \theta_i \varepsilon_{t-i}$, and m and α_i for $i = 0, \ldots, m$ are the ARCH model order and coefficients, respectively.

A generalization of the ARCH model (GARCH) where additional dependencies are permitted on lags of the conditional variance was introduced by Bollerslev [8]. In the GARCH model, the conditional variance is more general than in the ARCH model and can be written as follows:

$$\sigma_t^2 = \alpha_0 + \sum_{i=1}^{r} \alpha_i \varepsilon_{t-i}^2 + \sum_{j=0}^{m} \beta_j \sigma_{t-j}^2 \tag{18.7}$$

with these constraints

$$\alpha_0 > 0, \ \alpha_i \geq 0, \ \beta_j \geq 0, \ and \ \sum_{i=1}^{r} \alpha_i + \sum_{j=0}^{m} \beta_j \ < \ 1. \tag{18.8}$$

Limitations:

- Inherits all ARIMA limitations (Sect. 18.4.1).
- Model selection and construction are more expensive compared to ARIMA models.

Advantages:

- Inherits all ARIMA advantages (Sect. 18.4.1).
- Can be used on time series with high volatility.

18.4.3   SETARMA Models

Self-exciting threshold auto-regressive moving average (SETARMA) models were first introduced by Tong and Lim [61] and further studied by Tong [62], Lim [46], and Cook and Broemeling [14]. Tong [62] reports that threshold effects can arise in many scientific fields and the SETARMA models are able to characterize this because of their attractive features such as limit cycles. Consequently, the SETARMA models have been found useful in many real-life applications including economics, population biology, hydrology, and software [3, 63].

The SETARMA model is a generalization of the ARMA model in the nonlinear domain, and its main idea is to start with a linear ARMA model and then allow the parameters to vary according to the past values of the time series data. In order to explain the idea, let l disjoint intervals be defined as $R_j = [r_{j-1}, r_j)$ for $j = 1, 2, \ldots, l$, and let an integer d_p be known as the delay parameter. For the time series $\{y_t\}$, each interval R_j defines a "regime," in the sense that, the time series value y_t is said to follow the regime j if $y_{t-d_p} \in R_j$. Accordingly, a SETARMA model is defined as a piecewise linear structure that follows a linear ARMA model in each j alternative regime, for $j = 1, 2, \ldots, l$, and switches among the different regimes based on the threshold values determined by the past values of the time series data.

A SETARMA model of order $(l; p_1, p_2, \ldots, p_l; q_1, q_2, \ldots, q_l)$ or SETARMA $(l; p_1, p_2, \ldots, p_l; q_1, q_2, \ldots, q_l)$ can be written as follows:

$$y_t = \mu^{(j)} + \sum_{i=1}^{p_j} \phi_i^{(j)} y_{t-i} + \sum_{s=0}^{q_j} \theta_s^{(j)} \varepsilon_{t-s} + \varepsilon_t^{(j)} \quad if \quad r_{j-1} \le y_{t-d_p} < r_j \quad (18.9)$$

where $\phi_i^{(j)}$ and $\theta_s^{(j)}$ $(i = 1, 2, \ldots, p_j; s = 1, 2, \ldots, q_j; j = 1, 2, \ldots, l)$ are model parameters, and $\left\{ \varepsilon_t^{(j)} \right\}$ $(j = 1, 2, \ldots, l)$ are a sequence of independent normal errors with mean zero and variance σ_j^2. The ordered constants $-\infty = r_0 < r_1 < \cdots < r_l = \infty$ are known as the thresholds.

When q_j equals zero (for $j = 1, 2, \ldots, l$), the SETARMA model is reduced to the self-exciting threshold auto-regressive model which is denoted by SETAR $(l; p_1, p_2, \ldots, p_l)$. Similarly, the self-exciting threshold moving average model, SETMA $(l; q_1, q_2, \ldots, q_l)$, is a special case of SETARMA when p_j equals zero (for $j = 1, 2, \ldots, l$). If the auto-regressive orders and moving average orders are the same for all regimes and equal to p and q, respectively, the SETARMA model (18.9) takes the form as follows:

$$y_t = \mu^{(j)} + \sum_{i=1}^{p} \phi_i^{(j)} y_{t-i} + \sum_{s=0}^{q} \theta_s^{(j)} \varepsilon_{t-s} + \varepsilon_t^{(j)} \quad if \quad r_{j-1} \le y_{t-d_p} < r_j, \quad (18.10)$$

which is SETARMA(l, p, q) where p and q are repeated l times. Similarly to bi-linear models and exponential auto-regressive models, it is easy to show that the ARMA(p, q) model is a special case of the SETARMA model (18.10) when l equals one, which implies that the SETARMA models are natural extensions of the ARMA models.

Limitations:

- Inherits all ARIMA limitations (Sect. 18.4.1).
- Model selection and construction are more expensive compared to ARIMA models.

Advantages:

- Inherits all ARIMA advantages (Sect. 18.4.1).
- Can be used on nonlinear time series.

18.4.4 Cubic Smoothing Splines

Cubic smoothing splines (CS) can be fitted to univariate time series data to obtain a linear forecast function that estimates a trend [37]. The smoothing parameters are estimated using a likelihood approach enabling the construction of confidence intervals. This method is an instance of the $\mathrm{ARIMA}((p, d, q) = (0, 2, 2))$ model as described above with a restricted parameter set that does not impair the forecast accuracy. This method is suitable for extrapolation of trends, but seasonal patterns are not captured. In steep parts of a time series, the method overestimates the trend—accordingly the method should only carefully be applied to time series data with bursts, high noise ratio, or strong seasonal patterns. It has been observed that the computation time rises for more data points without an observable improvement in forecast accuracy.

Limitations:

- In the presence of bursts or dominating seasonal patterns, the method is likely to overestimate the impact of an extrapolated trend.
- Forecast accuracy may not increase with more historical data.

Advantages:

- Simple model that is easy to understand.
- Gives good trend estimates in many cases.
- Only needs a few historical values and has a low computational overhead.

18.4.5   Extended Exponential Smoothing

Extended exponential smoothing (ETS) is based on the state space approach and can explicitly model a trend, a season, and a trend component in individual exponential smoothing equations that are combined in the final forecast [36]. The component combination can be modeled either as additive or multiplicative. In addition, damping the influence of one of these components is possible. The forecasting process starts in the first step by selecting an optimized model instance before the parameters of the individual exponential smoothing equations are estimated. Having the model and the parameters adapted to the time series data, point forecasts and confidence intervals are computed. This method is able to detect and capture sinus-like seasonal patterns that are contained at least three times in the time series data. In the presence of more complex seasonal patterns, the ETS often fails to model those and returns quicker with a worse forecast accuracy compared to other methods.

Limitations:

- Positive time series values are required.
- May fail to model complex and overlapping seasonal patterns.
- User needs to decide whether a seasonal pattern and trend component should be modeled as additive or multiplicative.

Advantages:

- Established approach with various implementations available.
- Reasonable model complexity and computational overhead.

18.4.6 tBATS Innovation State Space Modeling Framework

The *tBATS* innovation state space modeling framework [15] extends the ETS state space model. The goal of *tBATS* is the better handling of more complex seasonal effects by making use of a trigonometric representation of seasonal components based on Fourier transformations, by the incorporation of Box–Cox transformations and use of ARMA error correction. *tBATS* relies on a method that reduces the computational burden of the maximum likelihood estimation. We observed examples of higher forecast accuracy compared to the ETS method, while computation time stayed in the same range.

Limitations:

• Positive time series values required.

Advantages:

• Improved capability to handle complex seasonality compared to the classical ETS approach (Sect. 18.4.5).

18.4.7 Model Selection and Conclusion

Before constructing a forecasting model, the given time series data should be checked for fulfillment of the various model assumptions. For example, a time series for an ARIMA model should satisfy the following assumptions: *serial dependency*, *normality*, and *stationarity*. Consequently, before using any model, statistical tests are needed to check for these assumptions. If they are not satisfied, a suitable transformation is required to align the data with the assumptions. Traditional statistical tests include the runs test for serial dependency, the Kolmogorov–Smirnov (K-S) test for normality, and the KPSS test for stationarity [26]. For achieving normality and stationarity in the variance, Box–Cox transformations [10] can be used, and differences in non-stationary time series can be used to produce stationary series in the mean. To determine whether GARCH model should be used, the time series has to be checked for volatility and for dynamic changes in time-varying variance as a deterministic function of past errors. The common statistical test for volatility is the Engle's test [24]. The selection of a SETARMA model is recommended for a nonlinear time series, which can be tested with the Hansen test [31]. The cubic smoothing splines are basically an ARIMA$((p, d, q) = (0, 2, 2))$ model, and thus, this model can be used whenever the ARIMA assumptions are satisfied. For the extended exponential smoothing approach, the same model assumptions as for ARIMA need to be satisfied. The tBATS approach includes a Box–Cox transformation and accordingly can cope with non-normality. Besides the required assumption checking, rules based on common statistical measures such as seasonality, normality, linearity, kurtosis, and skewness can also be derived for model selection or ranking. A detailed approach for rule derivation and a set of general rules for a subset of methods are given in [67]. In practice, different forecast approaches are applied concurrently and either the result that is more likely to be accurate or a weighted combination of the different results is used. This technique is also known as ensemble forecasting or boosting. An example can be found in [32].

18.5 Applications of Workload Forecasting

In this section, we discuss the applications of workload forecasting. Further applications and a broader view on workload characterization can be found in a recent survey [11]. It is worth noting that methodology as well as applications strongly resembling workload forecasting can be found in the domain of managing electricity supply [42]. Short-term forecast (hours to one day ahead) of demand on electric power is of particular interest to power suppliers [42].

18.5.1 Load Forecasting for Data Centers, Grids, and Cloud Environments

Load forecasting is used in this domain in a variety of ways including system and performance scaling, optimization of resource utilization, and its sharing, estimation of the run-time of tasks, and others. For a more recent overview, see [59], a survey focusing on job run-time prediction, but also discussing applications and methods related to workload prediction in computational grids.

The Network Weather Service (NWS) [69] is one of the first and most widely known systems for load forecasting in grid environments. It uses an ensemble of simple prediction methods and selects the one that performed best in the recent time frame. It can forecast the usage of CPU, network, and memory of a single server on a short time frame.

Peter A. Dinda has contributed a series of early works in this domain [20, 21]. He typically uses simple auto-regressive models (e.g., AR) since in his evaluation, they compare favorably, e.g., to BM and LAST models. He evaluates two applications of host load forecasting: estimation of running times of jobs [20] and real-time scheduling for interactive applications where new jobs are assigned to resources with minimum expected load [22]. The results of the evaluation show the clear benefits of using a prediction-based strategy. In [21], also a forecasting method based on wavelet analysis is introduced.

In [1], the authors use a combination of seasonal load variation modeling and Markov model-based meta-predictors for CPU and network load forecasting within a wide range of time horizons: from several minutes to more than a week. The motivating applications are grid scheduling and support for infrastructure maintenance.

The approach in [73] also targets the prediction of running times of grid tasks. The application scenario is CPU load prediction. The forecasting technique is a combination of polynomial fitting (essentially, a variant of auto-regressive methods) and detection of similar patterns; the latter method helps to exploit periodicity in the signal.

In [70], forecasting the future load of a grid system is achieved by combining an auto-regressive model (AR) enhanced by confidence interval estimations with two filtering techniques: Savitzky–Golay smoothing filter and Kalman filter. The potential application of this approach is forecasting task run-time and guiding scheduling strategies.

Workload analysis, performance modeling, and capacity planning in the context of data centers are considered in [27]. In [40], a model is proposed to capture groups of VMs that behave in frequent and repeatable patterns. The targeted application domains are capacity management and VM placement in a data center. Other works targeting such scenarios and environments include [30] and [29].

The authors of [19] propose an approach to predict host load in a Google cluster with 10,000+ hosts. The method includes an exponentially segmented pattern model and a Bayes' method exploiting a feature engineering and selection process.

Another approach of workload management in the context of video streaming is presented in [72], where the characteristics of workload burstiness are captured. In this way, they can model workload spikes caused by demand for a few very popular video clips.

18.5.2 Forecasting for Web-Based Systems

Optimizing the performance, resource usage, quality of service (QoS), and costs of complex multi-tier applications is another domain where host load prediction plays an essential role.

In [64], an analytical model of a multi-tier Internet application based on a network of queues was introduced, where the queues represent different tiers of the application. This model can accurately predict response times even in complex workload scenarios, including caching.

The issue of predicting future resource loads under constraints in Internet-based systems is addressed in [5]. The authors propose a two-step approach that first obtains a representative view of the load trend from measured raw data and then applies a load prediction algorithm upon this data. The envisioned application scenarios are load balancing and load sharing, overload and admission control, and job dispatching and redirection.

In [66], the topic of allocating servers to each of the Web sites in a data center with shared resources is considered. The constraints here are maintaining the QoS levels in different classes and optimizing server usage, while maintaining cost-efficiency. The proposed solution is based on a Web server load prediction schema based on a hierarchical framework with multiple timescales.

18.6   Conclusion and Open Challenges

The ability to forecast external behavior that impacts a self-aware system (e.g., amount of arriving work) becomes a crucial feature for a self-aware system if it should not only react to changes in its environment, but also prepare for likely changes to maintain or increase goal compliance. In this chapter, we presented an overview of workload forecasting methods based on machine learning and time series analysis. We discussed the common methodological process and reviewed related work in the area of workload forecasting. We see this as a first step toward enabling self-aware systems to become proactive.

Besides the general challenge to apply meaningful forecasting techniques in an autonomic manner within self-aware systems, several open challenges exist in this field. One open challenge is forecasting for highly dynamic applications. As an example of a highly dynamic application, consider a cloud-based start-up company with a cloud-based smartphone app that all of a sudden becomes extremely popular. It is extremely hard to forecast the medium- to long-term growth and the corresponding computational load for such an app. In contrast, it is relatively easy to forecast the short-term diurnal variation in demand, although this pattern will vary depending on the nature of the app. For example, a location-based social networking Web site such as Brightkite or Gowalla often has higher traffic around dinner and lunch [47], while the data center load of a travel-oriented app like Waze may peak slightly before and after typical meal times.

References

1. S. Akioka and Y. Muraoka. Extended forecast of CPU and network load on computational Grid. In *IEEE International Symposium on Cluster Computing and the Grid, 2004. CCGrid 2004*, pages 765–772, April 2004.
2. Ayman Amin, Alan Colman, and Lars Grunske. An Approach to Forecasting QoS Attributes of Web Services Based on ARIMA and GARCH Models. In *proceedings of the 19th International Conference on Web Services*, pages 74–81. IEEE, 2012.
3. Ayman Amin, Lars Grunske, and Alan Colman. An automated approach to forecasting qos attributes based on linear and non-linear time series modeling. In Michael Goedicke, Tim Menzies, and Motoshi Saeki, editors, *IEEE/ACM International Conference on Automated Software Engineering, ASE'12, Essen, Germany, September 3-7, 2012*, pages 130–139. ACM, 2012.
4. Ayman Amin, Lars Grunske, and Alan Colman. An approach to software reliability prediction based on time series modeling. *Journal of Systems and Software*, 86(7):1923–1932, 2013.
5. Mauro Andreolini and Sara Casolari. Load Prediction Models in Web-based Systems. In *Proceedings of the 1st International Conference on Performance Evaluation Methodolgies and Tools*, valuetools '06, New York, NY, USA, 2006. ACM.
6. A. Andrzejak and J.B. Gomes. Parallel Concept Drift Detection with Online Map-Reduce. In *2012 IEEE 12th International Conference on Data Mining Workshops (ICDMW)*, pages 402–407, December 2012.
7. Artur Andrzejak and Luis Silva. Using Machine Learning for Non-Intrusive Modeling and Prediction of Software Aging. In *IEEE/IFIP Network Operations & Management Symposium (NOMS 2008)*, Salvador de Bahia, Brazil, April 2008.

8. T. Bollerslev. Generalized autoregressive conditional heteroskedasticity. *Journal of Econometrics*, 31(3):307–327, 1986.
9. Antoine Bordes, Seyda Ertekin, Jason Weston, and Léon Bottou. Fast kernel classifiers with online and active learning. *J. Mach. Learn. Res.*, 6:1579–1619, December 2005.
10. George E. P. Box and Gwilym M. Jenkins. *Time Series Analysis: Forecasting and Control.* HoldenDay, San Francisco, 1976.
11. Maria Carla Calzarossa, Luisa Massari, and Daniele Tessera. Workload characterization: A survey revisited. *ACM Comput. Surv.*, 48(3):48:1–48:43, February 2016.
12. Bice Cavallo, Massimiliano Di Penta, and Gerardo Canfora. An empirical comparison of methods to support QoS-aware service selection. In *proceedings of the 2nd International Workshop on Principles of Engineering Service-Oriented Systems*, pages 64–70. ACM, 2010.
13. E. Cho, S. A. Myers, and J. Leskovec. Friendship and mobility: user movement in location-based social networks. In *Proc. of KDD-11*, pages 1082–1090, 2011.
14. Peyton Cook and Lyle D Broemeling. Analyzing threshold autoregressions with a Bayesian approach. *Advances in Econometrics*, 11:89–108, 1996.
15. Alysha M. De Livera, Rob J. Hyndman, and Ralph D. Snyder. Forecasting time series with complex seasonal patterns using exponential smoothing. *Journal of the American Statistical Association*, 106(496):1513–1527, 2011.
16. A. P. Dempster, N. M. Laird, and D. B. Rubin. Maximum likelihood from incomplete data via the em algorithm. *Journal Of The Royal Statistical Society, Series B*, 39(1):1–38, 1977.
17. John E Dennis, Jr and Jorge J Moré. Quasi-newton methods, motivation and theory. *SIAM review*, 19(1):46–89, 1977.
18. Sheng Di, Derrick Kondo, and Walfredo Cirne. Host load prediction in a google compute cloud with a bayesian model. In *Proceedings of the International Conference on High Performance Computing, Networking, Storage and Analysis*, SC '12, pages 21:1–21:11, Los Alamitos, CA, USA, 2012. IEEE Computer Society Press.
19. Sheng Di, Derrick Kondo, and Walfredo Cirne. Google hostload prediction based on Bayesian model with optimized feature combination. *J. Parallel Distrib. Comput.*, 74(1):1820–1832, 2014.
20. P.A. Dinda. Online prediction of the running time of tasks. In *10th IEEE International Symposium on High Performance Distributed Computing, 2001. Proceedings*, pages 383–394, 2001.
21. P.A. Dinda. Design, implementation, and performance of an extensible toolkit for resource prediction in distributed systems. *IEEE Transactions on Parallel and Distributed Systems*, 17(2):160–173, February 2006.
22. Peter A. Dinda. A Prediction-Based Real-Time Scheduling Advisor. In *16th International Parallel and Distributed Processing Symposium (IPDPS 2002), 15-19 April 2002, Fort Lauderdale, FL, USA, CD-ROM/Abstracts Proceedings*, 2002.
23. Qia Ding. Long-term load forecast using decision tree method. In *Power Systems Conference and Exposition, 2006. PSCE '06. 2006 IEEE PES*, pages 1541–1543, Oct 2006.
24. R.F. Engle. Autoregressive conditional heteroscedasticity with estimates of the variance of united kingdom inflation. *Econometrica*, pages 987–1007, 1982.
25. J Friedman, T Hastie, and R Tibshirani. *The elements of statistical learning.* 2001. 00571.
26. Jean Dickinson Gibbons and Subhabrata Chakraborti. *Nonparametric statistical inference.* CRC, 2003.
27. Daniel Gmach, Jerry Rolia, Ludmila Cherkasova, and Alfons Kemper. Workload Analysis and Demand Prediction of Enterprise Data Center Applications. In *Proceedings of the 2007 IEEE 10th International Symposium on Workload Characterization*, IISWC '07, pages 171–180, Washington, DC, USA, 2007. IEEE Computer Society.
28. Manish Godse, Umesh Bellur, and Rajendra Sonar. Automating QoS Based Service Selection. In *proceedings of the IEEE International Conference on Web Services*, pages 534–541. IEEE, 2010.
29. Zhenhuan Gong and Xiaohui Gu. PAC: Pattern-driven Application Consolidation for Efficient Cloud Computing. In *2010 IEEE International Symposium on Modeling, Analysis Simulation of Computer and Telecommunication Systems (MASCOTS)*, pages 24–33, August 2010.

30. Zhenhuan Gong, Xiaohui Gu, and J. Wilkes. PRESS: PRedictive Elastic ReSource Scaling for cloud systems. In *2010 International Conference on Network and Service Management (CNSM)*, pages 9–16, October 2010.
31. Bruce Hansen. Testing for linearity. *Journal of Economic Surveys*, 13(5):551–576, 1999.
32. Nikolas Roman Herbst, Nikolaus Huber, Samuel Kounev, and Erich Amrehn. Self-Adaptive Workload Classification and Forecasting for Proactive Resource Provisioning. *Concurrency and Computation - Practice and Experience, John Wiley and Sons, Ltd.*, 26(12):2053–2078, 2014.
33. Magnus R. Hestenes and Eduard Stiefel. Methods of Conjugate Gradients for Solving Linear Systems. *Journal of Research of the National Bureau of Standards*, 49(6):409–436, December 1952.
34. L. Hu, X. L. Che, and S. Q. Zheng. Online system for grid resource monitoring and machine learning-based prediction. *IEEE Transactions on Parallel and Distributed Systems*, 23(1):134–145, Jan 2012.
35. Laurent Hyafil and Ronald L. Rivest. Constructing optimal binary decision trees is np-complete. *Information Processing Letters*, 5(1):15–17, 1976.
36. Rob Hyndman, Anne Khler, Keith Ord, and Ralph Snyder, editors. *Forecasting with Exponential Smoothing: The State Space Approach*. Springer Series in Statistics. Springer-Verlag Berlin Heidelberg, Berlin, Heidelberg, 2008.
37. Rob J Hyndman, Maxwell Leslie King, Ivet Pitrun, and Baki Billah. Local linear forecasts using cubic smoothing splines. Monash Econometrics and Business Statistics Working Papers 10/02, Monash University, Department of Econometrics and Business Statistics, 2002.
38. Charles D. Kirkpatrick II and Julie Dahlquist. *Technical Analysis: The Complete Resource for Financial Market Technicians*. FT Press, November 2010.
39. Eamonn J. Keogh and Jessica Lin. Symbolic Aggregate approXimation (SAX) Homepage.
40. A. Khan, X. Yan, Shu Tao, and N. Anerousis. Workload characterization and prediction in the cloud: A multiple time series approach. In *2012 IEEE Network Operations and Management Symposium (NOMS)*, pages 1287–1294, April 2012.
41. Daphne Koller and Nir Friedman. *Probabilistic Graphical Models: Principles and Techniques - Adaptive Computation and Machine Learning*. The MIT Press, 2009.
42. Ali Lahouar and Jaleleddine Ben Hadj Slama. Random forests model for one day ahead load forecasting. In *Renewable Energy Congress (IREC), 2015 6th International*, pages 1–6, March 2015.
43. Pavel Laskov, Christian Gehl, Stefan Krüger, and Klaus-Robert Müller. Incremental support vector learning: Analysis, implementation and applications. *J. Mach. Learn. Res.*, 7:1909–1936, December 2006.
44. Jure Leskovec, Lars Backstrom, and Jon Kleinberg. Meme-tracking and the dynamics of the news cycle. In *Proceedings of the 15th ACM SIGKDD International Conference on Knowledge Discovery and Data Mining*, KDD '09, pages 497–506, New York, NY, USA, 2009. ACM.
45. WK Li and K Lam. Modelling asymmetry in stock returns by a threshold autoregressive conditional heteroscedastic model. *The Statistician*, pages 333–341, 1995.
46. KS Lim. On the stability of a threshold ar(1) without intercepts. *Journal of Time Series Analysis*, 13(2):119–132, 1992.
47. O. J. Mengshoel, R. Desai, A. Chen, and B. Tran. Will we connect again? machine learning for link prediction in mobile social networks. In *Proc. of Eleventh Workshop on Mining and Learning with Graphs*, Chicago, IL, August 2013.
48. Ole J Mengshoel, Avneesh Saluja, and Priya Sundararajan. Age-layered expectation maximization for parameter learning in bayesian networks. In *Proc. of the Fifteenth International Conference on Artificial Intelligence and Statistics*, 2012.
49. J. Pearl. *Probabilistic Reasoning in Intelligent Systems: Networks of Plausible Inference*. Morgan Kaufmann, San Mateo, CA, 1988.
50. Hema Prem and N. R. Srinivasa Raghavan. A support vector machine based approach for forecasting of network weather services. *Journal of Grid Computing*, 4(1):89–114, 2006.

51. Dorian Pyle, Text Design, Morgan Kaufmann Publishers, Sixth Floor, and San Francisco. *Data Preparation for Data Mining*. 1999. 01347.
52. Jian qiang Li, Cheng lin Niu, Ji-Zhen Liu, and Jun jie Gu. The application of data mining in electric short-term load forecasting. In *Fuzzy Systems and Knowledge Discovery, 2008. FSKD '08. Fifth International Conference on*, volume 2, pages 519–522, Oct 2008.
53. J. R. Quinlan. Induction of decision trees. *Mach. Learn.*, 1(1):81–106, March 1986.
54. YC Raymond. An application of the arima model to real-estate prices in hong kong. *Journal of Property Finance*, 8(2):152–163, 1997.
55. E. Reed, A. Ishihara, and O. J. Mengshoel. Adaptive control of apache web server. In *Proc. of Feedback Computing '13*, San Jose, CA, June 2013.
56. Erik B Reed and Ole J Mengshoel. Scaling bayesian network parameter learning with expectation maximization using mapreduce. *Proc. of Big Learning: Algorithms, Systems and Tools*, 2012.
57. Jerry Rolia, Xiaoyun Zhu, Martin Arlitt, and Artur Andrzejak. Statistical Service Assurances for Applications in Utility Grid Environments. *Performance Evaluation Journal*, 58(2+3):319–339, November 2004.
58. D. Ruta and B. Gabrys. Neural Network Ensembles for Time Series Prediction. In *International Joint Conference on Neural Networks, 2007. IJCNN 2007*, pages 1204–1209, August 2007.
59. S. Seneviratne and S. Witharana. A survey on methodologies for runtime prediction on grid environments. In *2014 7th International Conference on Information and Automation for Sustainability (ICIAfS)*, pages 1–6, December 2014.
60. P. K. Sundararajan, E. Feller, J. Forgeat, and O. J. Mengshoel. A constrained genetic algorithm for rebalancing of services in cloud data centers. In *8th IEEE International Conference on Cloud Computing, CLOUD*, pages 653–660, 2015.
61. H. Tong and K.S. Lim. Threshold autoregression, limit cycles and cyclical data. *Journal of the Royal Statistical Society. Series B (Methodological)*, pages 245–292, 1980.
62. Howell Tong. *Threshold models in non-linear time series analysis*, volume 21. Springer, 1983.
63. Howell Tong. *Non-linear time series: a dynamical system approach*. Oxford University Press, 1990.
64. Bhuvan Urgaonkar, Giovanni Pacifici, Prashant Shenoy, Mike Spreitzer, and Asser Tantawi. An Analytical Model for Multi-tier Internet Services and Its Applications. In *Proceedings of the 2005 ACM SIGMETRICS International Conference on Measurement and Modeling of Computer Systems*, SIGMETRICS '05, pages 291–302, New York, NY, USA, 2005. ACM.
65. Paul E. Utgoff. Incremental induction of decision trees. *Mach. Learn.*, 4(2):161–186, November 1989.
66. T. Vercauteren, P. Aggarwal, Xiaodong Wang, and Ta-Hsin Li. Hierarchical Forecasting of Web Server Workload Using Sequential Monte Carlo Training. *IEEE Transactions on Signal Processing*, 55(4):1286–1297, April 2007.
67. Xiaozhe Wang, Kate Smith-Miles, and Rob Hyndman. Rule induction for forecasting method selection: Meta-learning the characteristics of univariate time series. *Neurocomput.*, 72(10-12):2581–2594, June 2009.
68. Ian H. Witten and Eibe Frank. *Data Mining: Practical machine learning tools and techniques*. Morgan Kaufmann, San Francisco, 2nd edition, 2005. 23937.
69. Rich Wolski, Neil T. Spring, and Jim Hayes. The Network Weather Service: A Distributed Resource Performance Forecasting Service for Metacomputing. *Future Gener. Comput. Syst.*, 15(5-6):757–768, October 1999.
70. Yongwei Wu, Yulai Yuan, Guangwen Yang, and Weimin Zheng. Load Prediction Using Hybrid Model for Computational Grid. In *Proceedings of the 8th IEEE/ACM International Conference on Grid Computing*, GRID '07, pages 235–242, Washington, DC, USA, 2007. IEEE Computer Society.
71. J. Xue, F. Yan, R. Birke, L. Y. Chen, T. Scherer, and E. Smirni. Practise: Robust prediction of data center time series. In *Network and Service Management (CNSM), 2015 11th International Conference on*, pages 126–134, Nov 2015.

72. Hui Zhang, Guofei Jiang, K. Yoshihira, and Haifeng Chen. Proactive Workload Management in Hybrid Cloud Computing. *IEEE Transactions on Network and Service Management*, 11(1):90–100, March 2014.

73. Yuanyuan Zhang, Wei Sun, and Yasushi Inoguchi. Predicting Running Time of Grid Tasks Based on CPU Load Predictions. In *Proceedings of the 7th IEEE/ACM International Conference on Grid Computing*, GRID '06, pages 286–292, Washington, DC, USA, 2006. IEEE Computer Society.

Chapter 19
State of Practice of Non-self-aware Virtual Machine Management in Cloud Data Centers

Lydia Y. Chen, Robert Birke and Evgenia Smirni

Abstract Hardware virtualization is the prevalent way to share data centers among different tenants. In this chapter, we present a large-scale characterization study that aims to better understand the state of the practice, i.e., how data centers in the private cloud are used by their customers, how physical resources are shared among different tenants using virtualization, and how virtualization technologies are actually employed. Our study focuses on IBM corporate data centers as a major infrastructure provider and reports on their observed usage across a 19-day period. We aim at answering two key questions in virtual machine management: (i) whether the VM are dynamically adjusted according to the system state given the high flexibility in resizing virtual resources, and (ii) what type of self-learning policy governing the VM migration can be found in real data centers given a plethora of studies on VM migration. Our study illustrates that there is a huge tendency in over-provisioning resources while being conservative to several possibilities opened up by virtualization (e.g., migration and co-location), indicating the lack of autonomic VM management and a great potential for developing self-learning systems.

19.1 Introduction

Data centers are the backbone of the infrastructure of contemporary cloud environments where application executes in the form of virtual machine (VM) instances. This makes the management of VMs, such as provisioning, de-provisioning, and migration, central to the data center operation. Naturally, each VM instance varies in

L.Y. Chen (✉) · R. Birke
IBM Research Zurich, Zurich, Switzerland
e-mail: YIC@zurich.ibm.com

R. Birke
e-mail: bir@zurich.ibm.com

E. Smirni
College of William and Mary, Williamsburg, VA, USA
e-mail: esmirni@cs.wm.edu

© Springer International Publishing AG 2017
S. Kounev et al. (eds.), *Self-Aware Computing Systems*,
DOI 10.1007/978-3-319-47474-8_19

terms of its required virtual hardware resources and its degree of multiplexing with other VM instances over time. Multiplexing VMs, while very desirable to optimize data center usage and operation cost, may come at a performance cost. In the case of public clouds, computing capacity is provided to users in the form of pre-configured VM sizes, which are usually selected such that the capacity matches the peak VM usage. In a private data center, the system administrator has a higher control over the execution of applications and the resource requirements, and perhaps a better chance to utilize the data center such that different VMs are consolidated efficiently. An important feature is the possibility of easily suspending, restarting, and migrating VMs on different hardware to better meet the performance and application service level objectives.

The ability of the data center to gracefully deal with persistent workload fluctuations strongly depends on its ability to dynamically manage VMs, i.e., reconfigure and migrate VMs. There is a rich literature on the costs of dynamic reconfiguration, consolidation [2, 8, 10, 12], and migration [5, 9, 11], but most experimental works report on small-scale and easily controllable hardware environments. Yet, there is no clear view of the current state of the practice of VM management at today's cloud data centers.

In this chapter, we aim to conduct a detailed characterization study of VM usage in corporate data centers in the private cloud. Our objective is to provide a better understanding on how autonomic and self-adaptive today's VM management is. Due to the fact that VM management policies are not well documented and kept via word of mouth among system administrators, we resort to a black box approach, i.e., leveraging spatial variability of VM resource usages and timings of VM on/off and migration. We inspect multiple corporate data centers geographically dispersed across different countries and continents and used by more than three hundred customers from a variety of industries, including banking, industrial, automotive, retail, and media. The trace data focus on a specific time window of 19 days ranging from September 1 to September 19, 2012. Our data set provides insights into a broad range of both physical and virtual hardware configurations running a diversity of operating systems and applications. The data centers considered here are within a private cloud, i.e., their tenants and applications are stable.

Specifically, we start out our analysis by presenting the complexity of VM resource management, which scales nonlinearly with the number of VMs consolidated on physical boxes, and the amount of different resources involved. Our main analysis focuses on answering two key questions related to self-learning VM management: (i) whether VM resources are provisioned adaptively to harvest the flexibility offered in the Cloud, and (ii) whether VMs are dynamically consolidated on boxes via turning on/off and migrating VMs. Our findings show that VM resources, i.e., number of CPU and memory, can be rather static over time, and the consolidation landscape indeed changes but follows specific timings and spatial patterns, indicating a low degree of self-awareness in VM management. In particular, VMs are turned on and off, following specific time patterns, and this activity is highest during midnight, ditto for VM migration. There is a strong tendency for the VMs to not migrate and even if they do, they migrate to a restricted set of physical servers with the same hardware characteristics, and in particular with smaller numbers of CPUs and memory sizes.

This chapter is organized as follows. Section 19.2 presents an overview of the collected data. Section 19.3 illustrates the complexity of VM resource management. The dynamics of VM resource provisioning and consolidation plan are summarized in Sect. 19.4. Characterizations of VM life cycle and migration are summarized in Sects. 19.5 and 19.6, respectively. Discussion and conclusions are given in Sect. 19.7.

19.2 Data Collection

We survey 90 k VMs hosted on ≈8 k physical servers from different data centers in the world, serving over 300 corporate customers over a 19-day period starting September 1, 2012. Thanks to these sheer numbers, we can deduce meaningful statistics. These systems are used by different industries and are based on various operating systems. The virtualization technologies used are from major vendors, such as VMware and IBM.

Due to the nature of the trace data available to us, our study has some limitations. Although the trace data identify unique VMs (via a unique VM id), we are unaware of the exact applications each VM runs due to business confidentiality. We are also not aware of the response time of each VM at a transaction level (if the application is transaction-based), but we are aware of the end-to-end time of an application. In addition, the trace data are only collected in 15-min periods, i.e., this is the finest available data granularity.

While a 15-min sampling interval may be considered relatively long and may compromise the completeness of the data set with respect to extremely frequent events, we argue that it actually has a negligible effect given the typical liveness and migration characteristics of most VMs in this data set. Our evaluation suggests that provisioning and de-provisioning as well as migration are much less frequent than data sampling in the vast majority of cases. We direct the interested reader to our previous work on the same data set focusing on the evolution of data center resource demands across a 2-year period [3] and on seasonal patterns to enhance autonomic resource allocation policies [4].

For the purpose of the work presented in this chapter, we collect two types of virtualization statistics, namely on *virtual resource provisioning* and on *VM deployment*. Virtual resource provisioning focuses on the amount of virtual resources assigned to each VM, whereas VM deployment focuses on how physical resources are shared by VMs on a physical server. We concentrate on the number of VMs and on their virtual CPU and virtual memory capacity demands, and how those are shared (or multiplexed) on their physical counterparts where the VMs are deployed. Throughout this chapter, we use the terms *server* and *host* to denote a VM's physical counterpart. We also use the generic terms *processor* and *CPU* interchangeably to denote a thread slot visible to the operating system.

A physical server equipped with multiple physical CPUs (PCPU) and sufficient physical system memory (PMEM) hosts multiple VMs. Each VM in turn is configured with multiple virtual CPUs (VCPU) and virtual system memory (VMEM) of a certain size. The total number of VCPUs is independent of the number of PCPUs on a physical server. A VCPU can use only up to one PCPU at a time, whereas a PCPU *may* be shared by multiple VCPUs. Similarly, the total size of VMEM used by the VMs is independent of the available PMEM.

VM deployment may be static or dynamic, i.e., a VM may be bound on a physical server throughout its lifetime or not. We focus on the dynamic handling of the VMs over the entire period by looking at VM life cycles (on/off patterns) and VM migrations. We consider a VM on, if the VM is running and its activity is traced during the 15-min sampling interval; we consider the VM off otherwise. Naturally, on/off periods and migration can be intertwined: That is, a VM can be turned off and then turned on at different physical hosts. In such cases, we consider that both the VM life cycle and migration occurred. Live migrations are also possible: That is, a migration without the VM being suspended or turned off.

For a better understanding on how and what we measure (see Fig. 19.1). The figure illustrates an example of VM dynamic behavior over time. The VM first runs on server A, then B, and then C, i.e., two migrations occurred. When the VM is migrated from server A to server B, it is also turned off during three time intervals. Migration from B to C has no gaps, either because of live migration or because the off time is hidden by the sampling interval. Based on this example, we further illustrate the four basic time intervals we measure: the on and off times—the sum of all consecutive time periods in which the VM is in the same on or off state; the host time—the time spent by the VM on the same physical server irrespective of being on or off; and the migration time—the off time between changing physical hosts, which can be zero.

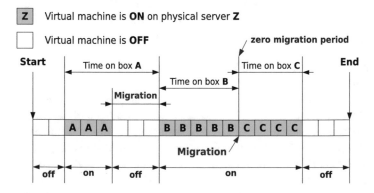

Fig. 19.1 The definition of VM on, off, host, and migration times

19.3 Resource Allocation and Consolidation

In this section, we give an overview of the complexity of virtual machine management, which increases nonlinearly with respect to the number of resources, virtual
machines, and physical servers. In particular, we present the amount of CPU and
memory equipped at virtual machines and physical servers, and most importantly,
their dependency due to consolidation.

19.3.1 Physical Resources at Boxes

In this subsection, we present statistics on the physical resources, in particular on
processors and memory, available in today's servers. In Fig. 19.2, we give an overview
of the physical resources available. Figure 19.2a shows the histogram of PCPUs
per server. The histogram reflects the availability of commercial configurations. In
the most common case (i.e., 34.5 %), servers have eight PCPUs. Other common
configurations are 12, 16, and 32 PCPUs. The PMEM configurations have a wider
range (see Fig. 19.2b). The highest peaks in the histogram are between 2 GB and
50 GB and account for 56 % of servers. Overall, servers have abundant resources with
on average 14.95 PCPUs and 60.6 GB of PMEM. Even some high-end machines exist
with 64 PCPUs and 1 TB of PMEM. In addition, there is a non-negligible portion of
"resource limited" servers with 4 PCPUs and less than 2 GB of PMEM. Figure 19.2c
gives a sense on how balanced the physical servers are in terms of processors and
memory by presenting the histogram of the ratio between these two resources. The
average value is 3.98 GB per CPU.

The main message from Figs. 19.2 and 19.4 is that today's servers have very
powerful computational capacity (on average 15.95 PCPUs) and a reasonable size of
memory (on average 60.6 GB of PMEM), making room for resource sharing by VMs
(on average 10.8 per server). These servers not only present plenty of opportunities for
VM consolidation but also underline the challenges in VM management, particular
toward the direction of self-awareness.

19.3.2 Virtual Resources at Virtual Machines

The complexity of VM management arises from the amount of resources provisioned
in each VMs. Figure 19.3a illustrates that VMs use mostly few VCPUs. Most VMs
have either 1 VCPU (39.5 %), 2 VCPUs (40.6 %), or 4 VCPUs (17.2 %).

Similar observations hold for the VMEM size (see Fig. 19.3b): most of VMs
(87.2 %) have between 1 and 9 GB of VMEM with specific peaks around 2, 4, and 8
GB. We would like to point out that small, medium, and large instance types at Amazon EC2 have 1, 2, and 4 VCPUs and 1.75, 3.5, and 7 GB of VMEM, respectively [1].

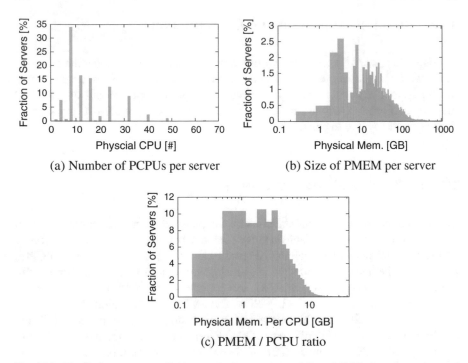

(a) Number of PCPUs per server   (b) Size of PMEM per server

(c) PMEM / PCPU ratio

Fig. 19.2 Physical resources available on today's servers: **a** number of CPUs, **b** memory size, and **c** ratio of memory (size) per CPU. Note the log-scale on the x-axis for **b** and **c**, to better illustrate the higher densities that are associated with smaller memory requirements

Indeed, our data confirms that those are the most popular VM configurations. Finally, as indicated by the different histogram shape in Fig. 19.3c, the memory/processor ratio is scaled down: on average 2.3 GB of VMEM per VCPU. Overall, our key observation is that VMs are "smaller" than physical servers, in terms of number of CPUs and memory. In addition, as reported in Sect. 19.4, the daily averages and percentile values are remarkably stable across time. One can use these statistics to size VM resources, especially within cloud solutions.

19.3.3   Virtual–Physical Dependency by Consolidation

The most challenging part in unrevealing the state of practice in today's VM management lies at the virtual–physical dependency, introduced by consolidation. The prior work has developed various self-adaptive and self-learning VM consolidation policies. In this subsection, we present the landscape of consolidation in the wild and highlight the overall system complexity with respect to resource multiplex ratios.

Figure 19.4 gives an overview of consolidation levels on the various physical machines. Figure 19.4a shows the discrete data histogram of the empirical density

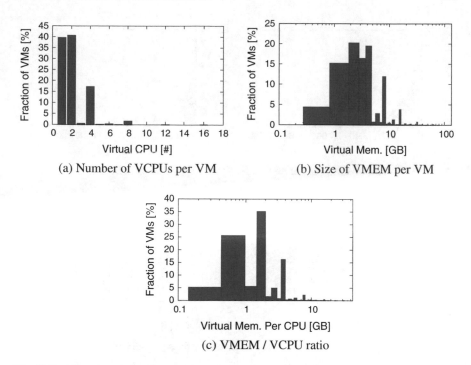

Fig. 19.3 Allocation of virtual resources per VM: **a** number of VCPUs, **b** memory size, and **c** ratio of memory size per VCPU. Note the log-scale on the x-axis for **b** and **c**, to better illustrate the higher densities that are associated with smaller memory requirements

of the number of VMs per physical server. The figure shows that 10 % of servers host one VM, i.e., there is no consolidation, whereas 90 % of servers host at least two VMs. The average number of VMs hosted on a physical server is 10.8, but this average can be deceiving. Indeed, the CDF counterpart of Fig. 19.4a (not reported here due to lack of space) shows that the 95th percentile is 31.

For completeness, we present two more histograms. The first one is the histogram of the number of VMs handled by the same management entity, i.e., an external entity used to monitor and deploy the VMs such as *vSphere* from VMware (see Fig. 19.4b). In general, a manager handles many VMs: on average 173.3 VMs. Since central VM managers can become the bottleneck, such information can be useful for capacity planning of management units.

Figure 19.4c depicts the histogram of the number of different enterprises sharing the same physical server. We see that there is almost no flexibility here: 96.5 % of servers host VMs all belonging to the same enterprise. This further confirms that the statistics presented in this paper are mostly from private clouds.

Next, we turn our analysis to the overall resource multiplex ratios, i.e., CPU and memory, across physical servers. We start with how VCPUs compete for PCPUs on the physical host. Figure 19.5a shows the histogram of the ratio between the total

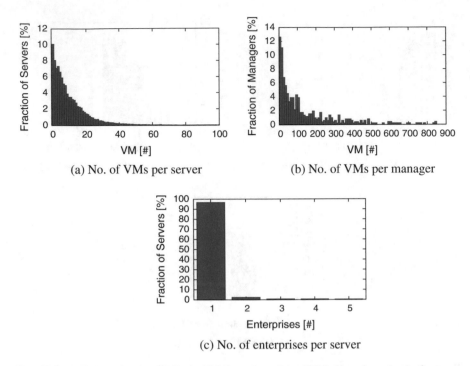

(a) No. of VMs per server   (b) No. of VMs per manager

(c) No. of enterprises per server

Fig. 19.4 Statistics related to VM consolidation: **a** number of VMs hosted on physical servers, **b** number of VMs under a managing unit, and **c** number of different enterprises running VMs in a single physical server

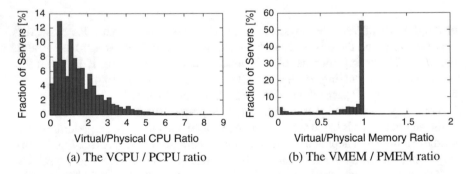

(a) The VCPU / PCPU ratio   (b) The VMEM / PMEM ratio

Fig. 19.5 Comparison between the amount of virtual and physical resources per physical server. Note the log-scale on the x-axis for **b** to better illustrate the higher densities that are associated with smaller memory requirements

number of all VCPUs from all VMs and the number of PCPUs of the underlying hosting physical server. If such a ratio is less than 1, then the VCPUs are likely not able to "stress" the PCPUs: That is, the server is under-populated. Therefore, ratios greater than one are necessary but not sufficient conditions for processor resource

Table 19.1 Statistics for VM consolidation: number of VMs per server, number of VMs per managing units, and the number of different enterprises' VM per server

	Mean	Std. dev	Percentiles (%)			Figure
			5	50	95	
VMs/Server	10.82	11.03	1.00	7.00	31.00	19.4a
VMs/Manager	173.26	301.11	3.00	76.00	631.00	19.4b
Clients/Server	1.06	0.42	1.00	1.00	1.00	19.4c
PCPU	14.95	9.54	4.00	12.00	32.00	19.2a
PMEM	60.58	69.62	3.75	40.00	175.50	19.2b
PMEM/PCPU	3.98	3.13	0.58	3.28	9.79	19.2c
VCPU	2.07	1.33	1.00	2.00	4.00	19.3a
VMEM	4.76	5.74	0.99	3.75	15.88	19.3b
VMEM/VCPU	2.30	1.93	0.50	2.00	4.82	19.3c

contention. Roughly, 35.2 % of servers are under-populated, 4.3 % even with ratios lower than 0.1, while the rest of the servers have ratios greater than 1 and up to 8.25. Overall, the average is 1.56 VCPUs per PCPU. This is not surprising considering that efficient physical resource sharing is in fact the purpose of virtual environments' existence.

Next, we study how the PMEM is multiplexed among the VMEMs allocated to each VM. To this end, we compute the ratios between the sum of all VMEMs and the PMEM of the underlying physical server. Figure 19.5b depicts such ratios and illustrates that it is rare for VMs to request more than the available PMEM.

We summarize the statistics discussed in this section in Table 19.1. Overall, the complexity of VM management at data center is very high due to a large amount of virtual and physical resources involved and a high degree of consolidation. Moreover, the presented data show that over population of VCPUs is a prevailing condition, which is expected, especially considering the main motivation for virtualization— efficient consolidation of resources. The degree of over-subscription is roughly at 50 %, indicated by the mean value of VCPU/PCPU in Table 19.1. Such values can be used to further guide the design of self-adaptive VM consolidation policies. On the opposite, memory is never over committed, i.e., the total VMEM requested is just below the PMEM of the hosting server. Resource multiplexing is more conservative for memory than for CPU, hinting a simpler performance requirement in developing a self-learning VM management systems.

19.4 Dynamics of VM Management

In this section, we present a bird view on the dynamics of VM management, particularly focusing on the spatial variability of resource provisioning and consolidation plan. As pointed out earlier, VM management policies are typically kept by word of mouth among system administrators without much formal documentation. We thus resort to a black box approach to uncover the state of practice for self-aware VM management systems, i.e., to infer the policy via observing the resource allocations and consolidation plans. We conjecture that as the data center workloads show strong time of the day effect and seasonality, self-adaptive VM management policies can thus dynamically resize VM resources and change consolidation plan over time. To change the consolidation plan in a private cloud data center where the VM population is rather constant, there are two basic operations associated with it: turning on/off VMs and migrating VMs. We dive into the current practices of VM on/off and migration in Sect. 19.6, whereas here we look at the evolution of VM sizes.

Similar to the earlier sections, we focus on CPU and memory. In Fig. 19.6a, we present the percentiles of the virtual CPUs per VM as a function of the observation day. The statistics are quite stable across time. On average, each VM uses 2 VCPUs, while the 95th percentile is equal to 4, concluding that in most applications multithreading is limited. In Fig. 19.6b, we show the average virtual memory used per VM across the time line of the observation period. The percentiles of average memory remain fairly constant, indicating stability in resource consumption requirements. Both observations implicitly point to that most VMs do not change their resource allocation during the observation period, even though workloads fluctuate greatly over time, and there exits a high flexibility in resizing VMs. Another observation worth mentioning is that resource utilization, particularly CPU, is fairly low, arguing for a strong incentive to improve the resource provisioning plan. In Sect. 19.6, we show how CPU and memory are actually affected when VMs are turned on/off and migrated.

As for the consolidation plan, we gather the time evolution of consolidation factors, i.e., the number of VMs consolidated on a server over time. Due to the large number of servers in this data set, we focus on different percentiles of consolidation factors. Figure 19.6c presents the daily time evolution of the average number of VMs per server. The figure also depicts the 5th, 50th, and 95th percentiles of the number of VMs per server. These values are fairly constant, with small variations from day to day, especially for 5th and 50th percentiles. We note that 95th percentile shows a stronger variation, indicating that the consolidation plan across physical servers indeed changes at a smaller scale. Consequently, we argue that at a macroscale the overall consolidation plan for data centers does not change. In other words, consolidation management is rather static in a macroscale, indicating inactive practices in self-aware management systems. The figure further corroborates the high degree of sharing of VMs per server and further highlights the complex dependency in designing a self-learning management system.

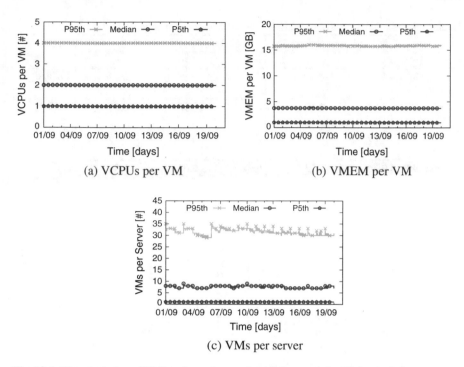

Fig. 19.6 Time evolution of VM configurations and numbers across the 19-day period

19.5   Life Cycle of VMs

The ease of commissioning and decommissioning VMs together with the promise of performance isolation contributes to the popularity of using VMs in data centers. The fluctuations of the VM population strongly depend on whether the data center is a part of the public or of a private cloud. High churn rates of VMs are expected in public clouds. Since the trace data that we use in our study came from data centers within privately administered clouds, our observations are bound to the private clouds only. In this section, we focus on the frequencies at which VMs are turned on and off, the durations of the on/off times, and whether VMs are bound to the physical servers where they execute or not. Table 19.2 provides an overview on the main statistics for all empirical densities shown in this section.

19.5.1   VM On/Off Frequencies and Times

We start by reporting on the number of on and off states for each VM across the observation period of 19 days. Naturally, the numbers of on and off states are tightly related, since an off (on) state is always going to be followed by an on (off) state,

Table 19.2 Statistics for VM on/off during the 19-day observation period

	Mean	Std. dev.	Percentiles (%)			Figure
			5	50	95	
Freq. ON (#/days)	1.58	4.65	0.05	0.16	10.53	19.7a, b
Freq. OFF (#/days)	1.54	4.65	0.00	0.16	10.53	19.7a, b
Time ON (days)	0.39	1.91	0.01	0.01	1.19	19.7c
Time OFF (days)	0.25	1.13	0.01	0.04	1.00	19.7c

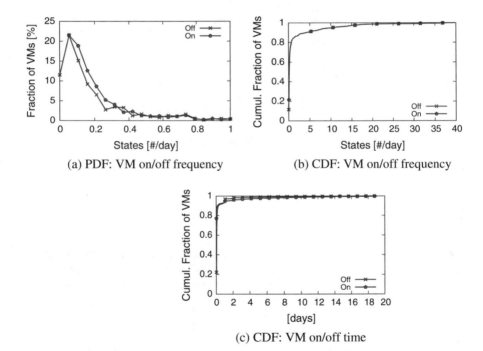

(a) PDF: VM on/off frequency   (b) CDF: VM on/off frequency

(c) CDF: VM on/off time

Fig. 19.7 Statistics related to VM on/off cycles: **a**, **b** daily frequency, and **c** duration

respectively. Provided that we observe each VM over a fixed time interval, the number of off states might be at most the number of on states ±1, depending on whether we observe a leading or trailing offstate which may not have a corresponding on state. Figure 19.7a presents the frequencies of on and off states during the 19-day observation period, computed over the set of all VMs. As expected, the lines are almost overlapping with few deviations (e.g., the starting points of the two curves). In the rest of this section, we only comment on the frequency of the off states.

One can immediately see that most of the frequency mass is located at the beginning. To better illustrate the results, Fig. 19.7a shows the PDF of the initial part only, while Fig. 19.7b shows the complete cumulative density function (CDF), including its tail. 11 % of VMs have *zero* observed off states, i.e., these VMs were continuously operating during the 19-day interval. The absence of off samples suggests that these VMs have never been turned off, and we treat them as if they are turned on once. Further, 23 % of VMs only have one observed off state throughout the 19-day interval or, estimating based on the observation period, only 0.053 off states per day. For the remaining VMs, the density functions rapidly decay into a long tail which extends almost to the maximum possible value given by our 15-minutes sampling interval, i.e., 48 times per day. This suggests that the VM stayed on for one sampling interval and off for the subsequent one throughout the whole observation period. Figure 19.7b shows the complete CDF that illustrates the presence of a long tail, i.e., there are at least 2 % of cases where the number of on/off states per day is more than 20. Note also that the two CDF curves nearly completely overlap.

Next, we focus on how long a VM stays in either the on or off state. We call the durations of the on (off) state the on (off) times. Figure 19.7c presents the CDFs of the on and off times across all VMs. Again, the line corresponding to the off time is either roughly overlapping or above the line corresponding to the on time. This indicates that off periods are in general shorter than on periods, also reflected by the mean values of Time ON and Time OFF in Table 19.2. In general, we see that for almost 90 % of the VMs the on/off times are less than a portion of the day, while a small percentage corresponds to very long on/off durations.

19.5.2   More on VM On/Off Timings

Here, we provide information about the specific times when VMs are turned on and off. Figure 19.8 presents the empirical frequencies of the fraction of VMs that are turned on and turned off as a function of the time of the day across the entire 19-day period. For each time period, two bins are reported—one that corresponds to on and one that corresponds to off. Graphs are stacked on top of each other in order to illustrate the relationship of on and off frequencies. Remarkably, there is a strong repeating pattern on the frequencies of on/off time periods (see Fig. 19.8a), i.e., it appears that the timestamps that VMs are set to on state are repetitive, featuring a daily spike. For the rest of the time periods, the fraction of VMs that are turned on or off is more or less stable. To further investigate this, we plot the frequencies of the on and off for 24 h, across all days. Indeed, the spikes in Fig. 19.8a now correspond to one frequency (see the leftmost part of Fig. 19.8b). The figure clearly shows that almost 12 % of all VMs in the entire time period are started at midnight, while almost 6 % of VMs are shut down in the same time period and 3 % right before this time (see the leftmost and rightmost parts of the top graph in Fig. 19.8b). Such repeatable patterns clearly point to routine VM deployment of perhaps maintenance work.

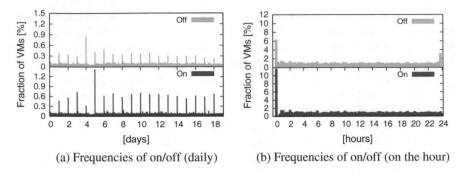

(a) Frequencies of on/off (daily)   (b) Frequencies of on/off (on the hour)

Fig. 19.8 Fraction of VMs that are turned on and off at specific timestamps: **a** across the entire observation period and **b** across 24 h

19.5.3 Virtual Resource Characteristics of VM On/Off

Here, we look at how the virtual resource demands change during the VM on/off switching and whether on/off states depend on the VM resource configurations. In particular, we look at the number of VCPUs assigned to the VM right before the VM is switched off, and the number of VCPUs assigned to the VM right after it is switched on. Due to the space limitation, we skip the presentation of those two figures. Results are reported as a function of the average daily switching frequency. The figures are scatter-plots, i.e., on the x-axis, we plot how many times the VM is switched off daily, and on the y-axis, we plot the VCPUs assigned to it before it is switched off (and right after it is switched on). Each data point in those plots is associated with a VM on/off and essentially represents the average VM on/off frequency of this VM and number of VCPUs considered. At the first glance, the number of VCPUs assigned to a VM seems to be identical before switching off and right after switching on. Also, it is not clear whether VMs with larger numbers of VCPUs are switched on/off more frequently than VMs with small numbers of VCPUs. To better understand the changes of VCPUs, we plot in Fig. 19.9a the difference of VCPUs assigned to a VM before it is switched off and after it is switched on as a function of the average daily switching frequency. For VMs that are switched on and off often (see values that correspond to large x-axis values), this difference is zero; while for few VMs, there are differences, but these differences are still small (see left side of Fig. 19.9a).

Figure 19.9b reports similar results for the allocated VMEM, again as a function of the frequency of on/off states. The figure confirms the same behavior as the one observed for VCPUs: VMs with high on/off frequencies tend to use the same amount of VMEM, while those with low frequencies tend to be less stable in their resource demands (see the left side of Fig. 19.9b).

To conclude, this subsection presents relevant statistics related to the life cycle of VMs, which point to the observation that data centers are still handled in a quite conservative way, i.e., VMs are switched on/off with low frequency at off-peak times, probably in an attempt to not disrupt working solutions and to avoid the increase in

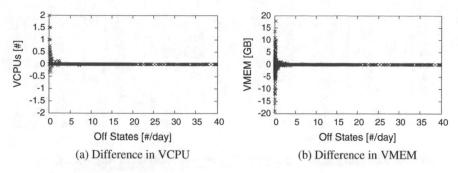

(a) Difference in VCPU   (b) Difference in VMEM

Fig. 19.9   VCPUs and VMEM scatter-plots as a function of average VM on/off frequency

management complexity. Furthermore, these statistics can be used as follows: (i) to shed light on what the current practices are and to fill the gap between academic research and field practice, and (ii) as a valuable input to create reference workloads that mimic today's common practices.

19.6   VM Migration

In this section, we focus on one of the most important features of virtualization: migration. Migration plays an indispensable role in bridging two key aspects of virtualization: dynamic server consolidation and scalable resource provisioning. Most of the existing migration studies are done within controlled environments of small scale [5–7, 11]. Here, our data allow to provide the big picture on current migration practices in the private cloud. First, we focus on the frequency of how often VMs actually migrate and how much this frequency varies from VM to VM. Second, we are interested in isolating observable migration patterns, trying to see whether VMs migrate regularly. Finally, we also report on how many physical servers the VMs migrate on. In this section, we concentrate on the large-scale characteristics of VM migration, without attempting to evaluate its performance impacts.

19.6.1   Migration Frequency and Inter-Migration Times

In the following, we split the data into two sets and draw the empirical distribution functions for (i) the entire set of VMs, which we call *full set*, and (ii) the set of VMs that migrated at least once, referred as *migration-only set*.

Figure 19.10a shows the frequency of VM migration, i.e., how often a VM is migrated between physical servers. The main plot zooms on the initial part of the PDF across VMs. This illustrates the fact that most VMs are unlikely to migrate: 78 %

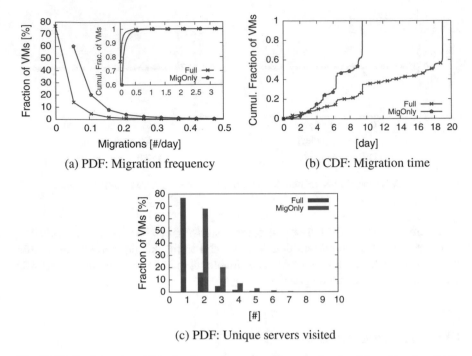

(a) PDF: Migration frequency   (b) CDF: Migration time

(c) PDF: Unique servers visited

Fig. 19.10 Statistics about VM migration: **a** how often it happens in a day, **b** how long does it take to migrate, and **c** how many different servers a VM visits

of them never migrated throughout the whole 19 days, i.e., the migration frequency was equal to zero. However, as shown in the inlet of Fig. 19.10a, the right tail of the CDF also includes few VMs that migrated more than three times per day.

Figure 19.10b shows the cumulative frequencies of the average residence time of a VM on a physical server before migrating to another server. This is an alternative representation of the results shown in Fig. 19.10a, confirming that most VMs exhibit relatively long inter-migration times. In particular, only about 3 % of VMs belonging to the migration-only set have inter-migration times of 2 days or less. There are four peaks of increasing intensity at 3.8, 4.8, 6.3, and 9.5 days, which are influenced by the length of the observation period and correspond to fractions of 19 days. The full set is skewed even more towards longer inter-migration times, due to the considerable number of VMs that never migrate and remain active for the whole 19 days. This can be seen from the big jump at the end of the CDF. Since the full set includes the migration-only set, the full set's density function exhibits the same jumps scaled in intensity as the one corresponding to the migration-only set.

The main message is that most VMs (78 %) never migrate. Furthermore, Fig. 19.10a, b both point towards rather long periods between migrations. In particular, the highest peaks are either just slightly shorter than a week, i.e., 6.3 days for 10 % of migrating VMs, or just slightly longer than a week, i.e., 9.5 days for 28 % of migrating VMs.

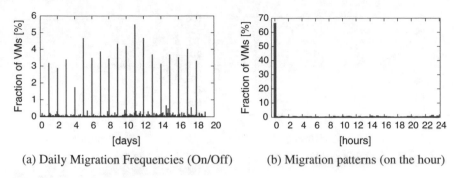

(a) Daily Migration Frequencies (On/Off)   (b) Migration patterns (on the hour)

Fig. 19.11 Fraction of migrating VMs: **a** across the entire 19 days, **b** across 24 h

19.6.2   Migration Timings and Patterns

Herein, we focus on VMs experiencing migrations, particularly their timings of occupancies and spatial patterns on underlying servers. Figure 19.11a reports on the fraction of VMs that migrate across the entire 19-day period. The figure shows a strong repetitive pattern: most migrations occur at specific timestamps that appear to repeat across the entire 19-day period. Figure 19.11b shows the same information but as an aggregate for 24 h. It clearly shows that almost 70 % of all VM migrations occur at midnight.

Regarding the spatial patterns of migration, i.e., *where* VMs migrate, we look at (i) the number of distinct physical servers visited and (ii) the probability of transition among those servers. Figure 19.10c shows the PDF of the number of distinct physical hosts visited by a VM over the 19 days. A value of one means that the VM stayed on the same physical host for the whole 19 days. Again, we observe that 78 % of VMs do not migrate, which is consistent with our previous results. Even considering the *migration-only* set, the set of physical servers visited by a VM is relatively small: 68 % of VMs visit only two servers.

19.6.3   Resource Characteristics of VM Migration

To get a sense of how physical resources are related to VM migrations, we provide scatter-plots (see Fig. 19.12 a, b). The former illustrates the similarities of the physical servers before and after VM migration, and the later illustrates the similarities of the physical memory available before and after migration. Using these two figures, we are able to answer the question about what type of machines tend to have VM migrations.

The x-axis in Fig. 19.12 represents the average migration frequency per VM per day. The y-axis in Fig. 19.12a, b represents the number of physical CPUs and memory on physical hosts. Each data point in those plots is associated with a VM migration and essentially represents the average VM migration frequency of this VM and the

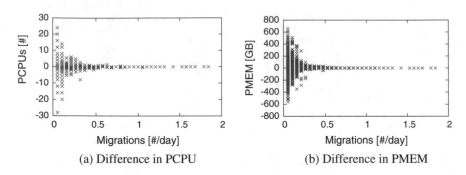

Fig. 19.12 Differences in the machine configurations before and after migration: PCPU and PMEM

physical memory of the host considered. Note that due to discrete values of the number of CPUs, there is a severe overlapping of the plotted points. A single point at the left side of the scatter-plot could represent a very large number of VMs, because of the overlapping effect. Due to a smaller number of VMs with high migration frequency, there are few points on the right side of the figure. One can see that VMs with low migration frequency tend to reside on machines with a wide range of CPU resources, whereas VMs with higher migration tend to reside at machines with 10 to 20 CPUs. An interesting observation is that VM migrations tend to happen on machines with smaller numbers of CPUs. In other words, the bigger the machines are, the less frequently their hosted VMs migrate. One can observe the difference in the number of PCPUs on servers, which VMs reside before and after their migration. On the one hand, there is no difference in physical servers before and after migration, in terms of their average number of CPUs. On the other hand, due to a wide spectrum of server configurations for VMs with low migration frequency, the difference in terms of the number of CPUs spreads in a wider range in the left side of the figure. Overall, VMs are observed to migrate among machines equipped with similar numbers of CPUs.

The number of points in Fig. 19.12b appears higher than in Fig. 19.12a, due to a higher number of different memory sizes available than the number of CPUs in servers. Similar to the CPU trend, one can observe that servers with bigger memory experience less migrations. VMs with high migration frequency tend to be hosted on machines with around 100 GB of physical memory. VMs that migrate a lot tend to migrate to servers with the same physical memory as compared to those who do not migrate that often.

To summarize, in this section, we provided a description of contemporary migration processes in data centers. Consequently, the statistics presented here can be used to validate the basic assumptions about workload migration patterns. Other uses are also possible, e.g., the frequency of VM migrations can be used to estimate how much additional load the underlying data center network infrastructure has to handle or the knowledge of existing migration patterns can be useful when it comes to improving

Table 19.3 Statistics for migration: frequency, inter-migration times, and number of unique servers visited

	Mean	Std. dev.	Percentiles (%)			Figure
			5	50	95	
Freq. all (#/days)	0.02	0.07	0.00	0.00	0.10	19.10a
Freq. MigOnly (#/days)	0.11	0.12	0.05	0.05	0.31	19.10a
Time all (days)	13.76	6.12	2.00	17.52	19.00	19.10b
Time MigOnly (days)	7.18	2.51	2.51	8.51	9.51	19.10b
#Servers all	1.36	0.80	1.00	1.00	3.00	19.10c
#Servers MigOnly	2.01	2.24	1.00	1.00	6.00	19.10c

VM placement strategies. Finally, Table 19.3 summarizes the main statistics for the plots presented in this section.

19.7 Conclusions

In this chapter, we present a detailed characterization study of virtualization management in today's data centers, based on vastly diversified systems. We focus on uncovering whether the state of practice of VM management is self-aware and self-adaptive, with respect to the workload dynamics. We particularly focus on the time variability of resource allocation of VM and consolidation plans, whose changes are triggered by turning on/off and migrating VMs. Moreover, we show the common characteristics of VM lifetimes and their migration patterns, including migration frequency and transition probabilities across different physical servers. The presented statistics provide an overview of how VM management policies are employed in practice. Our findings illustrate that conservative approaches are the prevailing ones: most VMs never migrate, and those who migrate do not do this often. In addition, VMs tend to migrate with specific spatial patterns, i.e., the transition probabilities from certain physical servers to certain others depict strong affinities among physical servers. Distinct patterns are also found at times when the majority of VMs are turned on and when they mostly migrate (at midnight), pointing to the prevalence of routine applications (perhaps maintenance ones). We also reported on the durations of VM on and off periods and saw that a significant percentage of VMs are continuously on versus those which are switched on and off. All in all, most statistics presented suggest that VM management policies lack self-awareness and self-adaptation and strongly argue the need for a self-tuning VM management in cloud data centers.

Acknowledgements This chapter is based on the paper with the title "State of the practice in data center virtualization: Toward a better understanding of VM usage," appeared in the Proceedings of Dependable Systems and Networks (DSN), 2013, pp. 1–12.

References

1. Amazon EC2. Last visited on: Apr 4th, 2016.
2. Danilo Ansaloni, Lydia Y. Chen, Evgenia Smirni, and Walter Binder. Model-driven consolidation of java workloads on multicores. In *DSN*, pages 1–12, 2012.
3. Robert Birke, Lydia Y. Chen, and Evgenia Smirni. data centers in the cloud: A large scale performance study. In *IEEE CLOUD*, pages 336–343, 2012.
4. Robert Birke, Lydia Y. Chen, and Evgenia Smirni. Usage patterns in multi-tenant data centers: a temporal perspective. In *ACM ICAC*, pages 161–166, 2012.
5. Christopher Clark, Keir Fraser, Steven Hand, Jacob Gorm Hansen, Eric Jul, Christian Limpach, Ian Pratt, and Andrew Warfield. Live migration of virtual machines. In *NSDI*, 2005.
6. Daniel Gmach, Jerry Rolia, and Ludmila Cherkasova. Selling t-shirts and time shares in the cloud. In *CCGRID*, pages 539–546, 2012.
7. Daniel Gmach, Jerry Rolia, Ludmila Cherkasova, Guillaume Belrose, Tom Turicchi, and Alfons Kemper. An integrated approach to resource pool management: Policies, efficiency and quality metrics. In *DSN*, pages 326–335, 2008.
8. Sriram Govindan, Arjun R. Nath, Amitayu Das, Bhuvan Urgaonkar, and Anand Sivasubramaniam. Xen and co.: communication-aware cpu scheduling for consolidated xen-based hosting platforms. In *VEE*, pages 126–136, 2007.
9. Gueyoung Jung, Kaustubh R. Joshi, Matti A. Hiltunen, Richard D. Schlichting, and Calton Pu. A cost-sensitive adaptation engine for server consolidation of multitier applications. In *Middleware*, pages 163–183, 2009.
10. Pradeep Padala, Kai-Yuan Hou, Kang G. Shin, Xiaoyun Zhu, Mustafa Uysal, Zhikui Wang, Sharad Singhal, and Arif Merchant. Automated control of multiple virtualized resources. In *EuroSys*, pages 13–26, 2009.
11. Akshat Verma, Gautam Kumar, Ricardo Koller, and Aritra Sen. Cosmig: Modeling the impact of reconfiguration in a cloud. In *MASCOTS*, pages 3–11, 2011.
12. Timothy Wood, Gabriel Tarasuk-Levin, Prashant J. Shenoy, Peter Desnoyers, Emmanuel Cecchet, and Mark D. Corner. Memory buddies: exploiting page sharing for smart colocation in virtualized data centers. In *VEE*, pages 31–40, 2009.

Chapter 20
Self-awareness of Cloud Applications

**Alex Iosup, Xiaoyun Zhu, Arif Merchant, Eva Kalyvianaki,
Martina Maggio, Simon Spinner, Tarek Abdelzaher,
Ole Mengshoel and Sara Bouchenak**

Abstract Cloud applications today deliver an increasingly larger portion of the information and communications technology (ICT) services. To address the scale, growth, and reliability of cloud applications, self-aware management and scheduling are becoming commonplace. How are they used in practice? In this chapter, we propose a conceptual framework for analyzing the state-of-the-art self-awareness approaches used in the context of cloud applications. We map important applications corresponding to the popular and emerging application domains to this conceptual

A. Iosup (✉)
Delft University of Technology, Delft, The Netherlands
e-mail: A.Iosup@tudelft.nl

X. Zhu
Futurewei Technologies, Santa Clara, CA, USA
e-mail: xiaoyzhu@yahoo.com

A. Merchant
Google, Inc., Menlo Park, CA, USA
e-mail: aamerchant@google.com

E. Kalyvianaki
Imperial College of London, London, UK
e-mail: Evangelia.Kalyvianaki.1@city.ac.uk

M. Maggio
Lund University, Lund, Sweden
e-mail: mmartimay@gmail.com

S. Spinner
University of Wuertzburg, Wurzburg, Germany
e-mail: simon.spinner@uni-wuerzburg.de

T. Abdelzaher
University of Illinois at Urbana Champaign, Champaign, IL, USA
e-mail: zaher@illinois.edu

O. Mengshoel
CMU Silicon Valley at the NASA Ames Research Center, Moffett Field, PA, USA
e-mail: ole.mengshoel@sv.cmu.edu

S. Bouchenak
INSA Lyon, Lyon, France
e-mail: sara.bouchenak@insa-lyon.fr

© Springer International Publishing AG 2017
S. Kounev et al. (eds.), *Self-Aware Computing Systems*,
DOI 10.1007/978-3-319-47474-8_20

575

framework and compare the practical characteristics, benefits, and drawbacks of self-awareness approaches. Last, we propose a road map for addressing the open challenges in self-aware cloud and datacenter applications.

20.1   Introduction

Cloud computing is the information and communications technology (ICT) paradigm under which services are provisioned by their users on demand, with payment covering only what is actually used. Cloud users can today lease infrastructure, platform, software, and others "as a service," from commercial clouds such as Amazon, Azure, Google, and SAP. Governments and entire industries are building large-scale datacenters that are and will increasingly host cloud computing applications. At the same time, data become an integral part of cloud computing: By 2017, over three quarters of our personal and business data will reside in datacenters, according to a recent IDC report [32]. Cloud applications, often consumed by users as services, already represent over 10 % of the entire ICT market in Europe [15]. Netflix, whose users consume a large fraction of the global Internet traffic, relies on ICT services from Amazon Web Services (AWS).[1] The market, growing in size, diversity of applications, and sophistication, already exceeds hundreds of millions of users and, as a consequence, $100 billion worldwide [10]; the cloud market will likely contribute over 100 billion euro to the European GDP in 2020 [15]. At this scale and with this importance, human management of datacenter resources is prohibitively expensive and, often, too error-prone. Thus, the use of self-awareness techniques to manage cloud applications is increasingly more present. In this chapter, we analyze the use of self-awareness in cloud computing and its applications.

Cloud applications raise a complex management challenge, derived from the goals of three main stakeholders: application users, application operators, and cloud operators. Each of these stakeholders has different requirements, which are often conflicting. For example, application users could demand that an interactive application is always responsive, even under bursty arrivals of user-issued requests. To meet this demand, application operators could require that enough capacity is always provided by cloud operators, yet only want to pay for what is actually consumed. Tension arises between performance and other requirements, including the cost of operations. As a consequence, the management challenge is to optimize non-trivial efficiency metrics and to meet complex service-level agreements (SLAs), to an extent that already exceeds the capabilities of human management.

We investigate in this chapter the current state of self-awareness in cloud computing and in particular datacenter-based cloud applications. Our goals are to introduce practical cases of self-awareness in such applications; to present a conceptual framework for analyzing state-of-the-art self-awareness approaches used in practice; to map the already important and emerging application domains to the conceptual

---

[1] Details: https://aws.amazon.com/solutions/case-studies/netflix/.

framework of self-awareness approaches used in practice and analyze the similarities and differences, benefits, and costs of self-awareness approaches; and to identify and analyze the open challenges in self-aware cloud applications and propose a road map for advancing the state of the art. The main contribution is structured as follows.

In Sect. 20.2, we introduce a framework for the analysis of self-awareness techniques used in cloud computing and its applications. Our framework consists of a structured way to analyze the types of applications, problems, and approaches for which self-awareness is relevant in practice. The framework also structures the analysis of directions for future research. Although the framework is currently built for the analysis of self-awareness in cloud applications, and thus is adapted to the operational conditions in cloud computing (metrics, stakeholders, etc.), the framework could be extended to other domains. We show the usefulness of this framework by applying it in practice, with the results presented in the next sections.

In Sect. 20.3, we focus on eight popular or emerging application domains, with an important commercial, scientific, governance, and other societal impact. Although any application domain is applicable, the market volume and the number of users, today or in the foreseeable future, are important criteria for selecting the application domains for this chapter. Among the selected applications are business applications, compute-intensive and data-intensive batch processing, data stream processing, online gaming, partial processing, and cyber-physical applications. Some of these applications, such as online gaming, partial processing, and cyber-physical applications, are emerging in terms of number of users and adoption of cloud technology. We also include in this section the workloads generated by the datacenters themselves, which can be seen as overhead, but are already consuming large amounts of resources and must meet complex, albeit internal, SLAs.

In Sect. 20.4, we identify ten types of problems that are already addressed by self-awareness techniques, including recovery planning, resource autoscaling, runtime architectural reconfiguration and load balancing, fault tolerance in distributed systems, energy proportionality, workload prediction, performance isolation, diagnosis and troubleshooting, discovery of application topology, and intrusion detection and prevention. Some of these problems, such as autoscaling, energy proportionality, performance isolation, and intrusion detection and prevention, have developed a new form or even appeared specifically in the context of cloud computing.

In Sect. 20.5, we identify and analyze seven types of self-awareness approaches used in practice: feedback control-based techniques, metric optimization with constraints, machine learning-based techniques, portfolio scheduling, self-aware architecture reconfiguration, stochastic performance models, and other approaches. Although none of these approaches are unique to cloud computing, their adaptation to cloud computing and its applications is non-trivial.

In Sect. 20.6, we identify and analyze four directions for future use of self-awareness approaches for cloud computing and its applications. We focus on directions that are not only needed for practical applications, but for which we can envision the next research steps and that the results of this research can be put in practice in the following 3–5 years.

Our survey of applications, problems, self-awareness approaches, and open challenges in self-awareness is by far not exhaustive. However, we study for each broad type with existing popularity and likely future impact. Moreover, we envision that the approach we take in this work will also be useful for studying other types.

This chapter is the result of original work by the authors, and in particular, the survey started during the Dagstuhl Seminar 15041, "Model-driven Algorithms and Architectures for Self-Aware Computing Systems."

20.2   Overview of the Framework

We propose a framework for understanding the practice of using self-awareness techniques in managing and scheduling of cloud applications. This framework follows the structure of a natural discussion about the field, with three main questions and a format for answering them that is conductive to surveying the field. The first question focuses on specific applications: *Which cloud applications raise the challenges that self-awareness techniques are particularly good in addressing?* Answering this question requires an understanding of the nature and characteristics of self-awareness challenges that affect such cloud applications. Thus, the second question is, *Which are the important self-awareness challenges for cloud applications?* A third question is, *Which are the self-awareness approaches that address the self-awareness challenges in this context?* Last, a fourth question focuses on the future: *Assuming a research horizon of 3–5 years, what are the most promising directions for future research in enabling self-aware cloud applications?*

Answering the first three questions is sufficient to yield a survey of cloud applications whose self-awareness challenges are addressed or resolved in practice by self-awareness approaches (techniques, methods, best practices, or even entire methodologies). For example, mapping all the different <application–challenge–approach paths> can create a survey of the entire space. Then, it is easy to group together applications raising the same challenge; similarly, self-awareness approaches that address the same challenge can be grouped together. The survey is practical, in that a complete "application–challenge–approach" path can be directly considered by the practitioner.

The first three questions in our framework are also necessary. There are hundreds of application *types* commonly used in software engineering practice, as indicated, for example, by the extensive taxonomy of Forward and Lethbridge [21]. Thus, surveying without the guidance of specific applications provided by the first question could lead to a variety of self-awareness challenges and approaches, all with the merit of being applicable, but without much proof of use in cloud context. Without the specific problems provided by the second question, the self-awareness techniques could be used in a variety of cases, limited only by the creativity of the designer and by the difficulty of proving their benefit for practical use. Thus, limiting the survey to the set of challenges that are currently addressed in the context of cloud applications is necessary; we address this through the combined expertise of the authors regarding the field. Last, although many self-awareness techniques already exist, not all have yet been applied to cloud settings. Thus, surveying could go well beyond the scope of the third question, and generic techniques that may not work well (enough) in practice will also be surveyed.

The framework also structures the analysis of directions for future research. We leverage here the collective expertise of the authors, in which important questions are proposed by individuals and discussed by the community. By iterating this process, we believe the community can propose and refine its own most important goals. The results of the first iteration are shared with everyone interested to help the community make progress, through the text in Sect. 20.6.

20.3   Types of Applications

In this section, we present the following eight types of applications that already benefit from the use of self-awareness techniques.

1. Enterprise applications,
2. Computing-intensive batch processing,
3. Data-intensive batch processing,
4. Data stream processing,
5. Workloads generated by datacenter operations,
6. Online gaming,
7. Partial and delayed processing,
8. Cyber-physical applications.

Each of these selected applications is already popular, generates a significant amount of revenue, is critical to the operation of many businesses, uses a significant amount of resources, or is promising to emerge as such; often, the applications we select have a combination of these characteristics.

20.3.1   Enterprise Applications

Description: We reuse the definition of enterprise applications proposed by Shen et al.: "the user-facing and backend services, generally supporting business decisions and operations and commonly contracted under strict SLA requirements, whose downtime or even just low performance will lead to reduced productivity, loss of revenue, customer departure, or even legal actions. These workloads include enterprise multi-tier applications, and business-critical workloads that often include applications in the solvency domain or other decision-making tools. Other applications that characterize business-critical workloads are email, collaboration, database, ERP, CRM, and management services, when used in conjunction with other workloads" [71].

20.3.1.1 Multi-tier Enterprise Applications

Application components: Multi-tier enterprise applications refer to those Web-based business applications that each comprises a collection of cooperating components, organized as multiple logical tiers. The most common three-tier architecture consists of a presentation tier, an application tier, and a database tier. The presentation tier receives requests from the clients, and the application tier handles the business logic and in turn interacts with the database tier to obtain and store persistent data. Examples of such applications including enterprise resource planning (ERP) and customer relationship management (CRM) are often subject to an interactive workload. Different types of requests often incur different loads on the system (e.g., read- vs. write-intensive transactions and compute- vs. data-intensive workloads). The multi-tier architecture makes it challenging to implement self-awareness schemes for such applications, as there may be complex control flows between the different tiers, and each tier may have different resource requirements and performance bottlenecks. With the trend toward service-oriented architectures, the different tiers are often split into different services, making the control flow even more complex.

Metrics of interest: *Availability*—the percentage of time the application service remains up and running; *reliability*—the ratio of successful requests to the total number of requests; *performance*—characterized by such metrics as throughput (requests/sec) and request–response times; *resource* (CPU, memory, I/O) *utilization* of the underlying system; and *cost*—metrics related to financial or energy cost.

Typical problems: They are performance isolation and service differentiation, trade-off between multiple metrics of interest, diagnosis and troubleshooting, dynamic load balancing, end-to-end service-level assurance, and autoscaling of resources.

Typical self-aware elements: Metric optimization [50], machine learning [57, 77], feedback control [36, 50, 67], stochastic performance models [5, 73], and statistical estimation [47] are the main approaches researchers have applied to help create self-aware multi-tier applications.

20.3.1.2 Business-Critical Applications

Application components: Business-critical workloads often include not only applications that provide support for decision-making, such as Monte Carlo simulations and financial and other types of modeling applications programmed as tightly coupled parallel jobs of relatively small size, but also the regular management services described in Sect. 20.3.1.1. It is typical for the system user to not specify the applications, due to privacy and business secrecy. Instead, users request service expressed only in SLA terms, e.g., number and size of virtual machines, generally provisioned for long periods of time and operated by the users of IT team. The current practice in the datacenter is to require engineering confirmation for the most important provisioning and allocation decisions, especially at the initial installation of the long-running virtual machines. Self-aware resource management and scheduling tools [75] provide advice that engineers may take into account.

Metrics of interest: Various traditional metrics include latency and throughput, and reliability and system load. Risk-related metrics are the risk score [75], which expresses the risk of significant underperformance and thus penalties paid by the service operator to the service user, and loss of trust.

Typical problems: Reduce the risk of performance degradation; use resources efficiently; and avoid system overload and unavailability.

Typical self-aware elements: They are portfolio scheduling [75], topology-aware resource management [75],[2] prediction of runtimes and resource occupancy, and bin-packing-based optimization [27].

20.3.2   Compute-Intensive Batch Processing

Description: Compute-intensive batch processing includes workloads where computation, rather than data I/O and movement, consumes the largest portion of the runtime and of the consumed resources and is thus the main focus of resource management and scheduling. This type of applications has evolved much over the past few decades, from select few users running large parallel jobs on supercomputers (late 1980s–early 1990s), to practically every research and engineering laboratory running in multi-cluster grids many small, independent tasks [33], integrated through scripts into mostly compute-intensive jobs (mid-1990s to today). These bags of tasks (BoTs), which are effectively conveniently parallel implementations of scientific and engineering workloads (e.g., simulations), have emerged as a response to the shift from expensive supercomputers that offered high performance and availability, to commodity hardware that crashes often. Since the early 2000s, workflows of inter-dependent tasks, where dependencies are expressed programmatically and intertask data transfers occur through batch transfers of (typically POSIX) files, have also become increasingly more common in practice [33, 35].

20.3.2.1   Compute-Intensive Batch Processing in Clusters

Application components: Workloads include bags of predominantly sequential tasks and small-scale parallel jobs (in engineering and research laboratories).

Metrics of interest: They are throughput, response time/bounded slowdown, makespan for BoTs, and normalized schedule length for workflows.

Typical problems: Problems are increased throughput, reduced response time and, in particular, the (bounded) slowdown/makespan for BoTs and the (normalized) schedule length for workflows and balance performance and cost.

---

[2]Commercial products in this domain are scarce. Notable products include VMware's open-source Project Serengeti http://www.vmware.com/hadoop/serengeti.

Typical self-aware elements: They are traditional techniques for dynamic and adaptive scheduling and resource management. Flagship projects include Condor, Globus, and, more recently, Mesos.

20.3.2.2   Compute-Intensive Batch Processing in and Across Datacenters

Application components: At the scale of entire datacenters and in multi-datacenter environments, that is, on the order of 10,000 to over 100,000 machines, load is submitted by thousands of users. Workloads come from scientific computing, financial, engineering, and other domains and are dominated by bags of tasks of highly diverse sizes and resource demands [33].

Metrics of interest: User metrics are similar to those in the cluster context, but also include aggregate measures of the fraction of deadlines and throughput goals satisfied under extreme conditions such as large-scale failures and flash crowds. It includes energy costs. Metrics interesting to datacenter administrators include scalability, availability, load balance, and achievable utilization.

Typical problems: It includes load balancing, particularly across data centers, handling dynamic load variations, likely due to normal bursty behavior, time-of-day effects, and failures, and enabling high resource utilization without adverse impact on performance and with performance isolation across the workloads of many diverse users.

Typical self-aware elements: It includes resource management that is aware of dynamic loads, service-level objectives, and failure/maintenance issues. Examples include automatic job queue reconfiguration [17], self-aware job managers [33], and large-scale datacenter management systems [66].

20.3.3   Data-Intensive Batch Processing

Description: There is a plethora of application domains including commercial applications, retail, and science domains that generate big data (large volume, high variety, low veracity, etc.). Data-intensive batch processing involves systems to process sets of big data without interactive data processing sessions. Such processing is performed by a cluster of compute nodes of data that are typically stored on distributed storage, with intermediary results stored in memory or on disks local to each node. The nodes collectively execute software that coordinates the distribution and computation of the datasets across the cluster according to the processing semantics. We classify these systems into the following two categories.

20.3.3.1 MapReduce-Based Data-Intensive Batch Processing

Application components: MapReduce is a popular programming model for developing and executing distributed data-intensive and compute-intensive applications on clusters of commodity computers. A MapReduce job is an instance of a running MapReduce program and is comprised of map and reduce tasks. Tasks are executed according to the programming model, but embed functions (code) provided by the user. High performance and fault tolerance are two key features of typical MapReduce runtime environments. They are achieved by automatic task scheduling; data placement, partitioning, and replication; and failure detection and task re-execution.

The MapReduce model has proven to be versatile in industry, where it is used for many big data tasks including log processing, image processing, and machine learning. For example, MapReduce has been used to learn conditional probability tables of Bayesian networks (BNs). Both traditional parameter learning (complete data) and the classical expectation–maximization algorithm (incomplete data) can be implemented within the MapReduce model [6].

Metrics of interest: Metrics include performance metrics such as job response time and throughput (jobs/minute) and data input and output (IOPS); reliability— measured as the ratio of successful MapReduce job requests to the total number of requests; various cost metrics; and other low-level MapReduce metrics related to the number, length, and status (i.e., success or failure) of MapReduce jobs and tasks.

Typical problems: Performance and dependability guarantees, and trading-off between multiple metrics of interest. Chains and workflows of MapReduce jobs are useful, but could be difficult to manage and troubleshoot. Vicissitude workflows of MapReduce jobs lead to diverse challenges, by stressing different system resources at different or even the same time. Workloads can be dominated by a few MapReduce jobs, used periodically or in bursts.

Typical self-aware elements: They are performance models and management [68] and self-aware architecture reconfiguration [25].

20.3.3.2 Other Data-Intensive Batch Processing

Application components: It includes many programming models for data-intensive batch processing and they are significantly different from MapReduce that exists today: Spark, Naiad, Ciel, etc. Such systems rely on functional, imperative, or dataflow models to express computations and may be general or highly specialized.

Metrics of interest: Metrics are response time, recovery time, and cost. Some of these systems, such as Naiad, are also designed to support low-latency results, to provide support to process data and deliver results in near real time.

Typical problems: They are handling workload variations and data recovery after machine failures and synchronization of data state when processing spans many nodes. For graph processing, not only the algorithm but also its input dataset affect the performance significantly, but predicting it is challenging. Autoscaling is very challenging, due to the possible need to transfer large state.

Typical self-aware elements: They are recovering from failures and scaling to additional nodes to handle workload variations and arbitrary computation.

20.3.4 Data Stream Processing

Description: We observe an avalanche of data continuously generated from various sources such as sensor networks, business operations, Web applications, and social networks. There is a pressing need to process such data in real time. For example, several companies such as Facebook and LinkedIn used to analyze their daily Web logs to better support their operations [64], but are shifting to real-time analysis.

Application Components: Data stream processing (DSP) involves the real-time processing of data that are continuously generated from several distributed sources at time-varying rates. Data analysis is represented via user queries that describe the type of processing users who wish to operate over source data. DSP queries are typically represented by directed dataflow graphs where vertices correspond to operators and directed edges indicate the flow of data among operators. Each operator typically corresponds to certain parts of the query processing—often associated with well-defined semantics such as joins, aggregates, and filters. Finally, queries are deployed on a cluster of nodes, referred to as data stream processing systems (DSPSs).

Metrics of interest: Primarily, query performance on a DSP is measured via the delivery of low-latency and high-throughput results, regardless of the workload demands and their time-based variations.

Typical problems: Problems are dynamic workload and operator diversity (e.g., different semantics), load balancing in datacenters (e.g., System S, SPQR [38], and Soda), architectural reconfiguration, and performance isolation in cloud environments [7, 28, 60].

Typical self-aware elements: They are optimization models for resource allocation and placement [38] and CPU-based heuristics to trigger scale-out operations [7].

20.3.5 Workloads Generated by Datacenter Operations

Description: Unlike the other applications described in this section, this workload is created by the system itself, as response to real-input workloads, in particular to give probabilistic operational guarantees. Typical workloads here are the product of backup, logging, checkpointing, and recovery systems. Although needed to meet declarative specifications of the availability, durability, and recovery time requirements, these workloads cause significant reliability-related overheads that need minimization. For example, on the order of 20% of the resources are currently wasted on failures and spent for recovery in large-scale infrastructure [14].

20.3.5.1 Addressing Failures in the Datacenter

Application components: They are implementing data redundancy for availability and disaster tolerance results in some of the largest workloads in datacenters, especially regarding data transfer and storage. Resources consumed may include disk and tape capacity and bandwidth; CPU and memory for redundancy operations (such as encoding); and network bandwidth within and across datacenters.

Metrics of interest: Metrics are availability (expected fraction of time that a desired data object will not be accessible); durability (annual data loss rates, MTTDL); amount of data lost during failures (e.g., how far a checkpointed system will need to rewind); and recovery time (how long it will take to recover back to a normal operating state).

Typical problems: Problems are recovery planning by selecting the combination of redundancy techniques to meet reliability requirements; designing a schedule of backup operations to fit resource availability and limit interference with other workloads; and designing a schedule of recovery operations after a large-scale failure while enabling diagnosis (see Sect. 20.4.1).

Typical self-aware elements: Automated designers combine multiple resilience techniques to meet the reliability and recovery requirements within resource limitations. Both deterministic and stochastic models [42] are used to represent the monitored workload levels and changes, component failure rates, and the reliability provided by the resilient system. Design methods include machine learning-based techniques, mathematical optimization, and meta-heuristic techniques [24, 40].

20.3.5.2 Addressing Failures at Exascale

Application components: Future exascale machines, which will exceed 1 exaflop sustained performance (so, 2–3 orders of magnitude larger than today's Top500 machines), exacerbate the problems and pose important scale challenges to the aspects observed in Sect. 20.3.5.1. Checkpointing and other mechanisms designed for this scale operate with waves or hierarchies of periodic or triggered operations, either partial or for the entire system, that affect CPU, memory, network, and storage resources.

Metrics of interest: Same as for Sect. 20.3.5.1; also energy and human resource costs (e.g., does recovery require human resources?).

Typical problems: Recovery planning and general automatic recovery approaches are the key challenges in the field, possibly aided by advanced workload prediction, with current approaches leading to poor energy proportionality (high energetic cost). Containment, including performance isolation, is important, because correlated (e.g., cascading) failures can cause significant problems to other components and applications than affected by the original failure. Diagnosis and troubleshooting pose important challenges, because at this scale applications can have over a million concurrent threads of execution and are very difficult to debug; even error identification and reporting are important challenges in exascale systems.

Typical self-aware elements: Include various methods, surveyed in a recent overview of the field [72], among which: stochastic performance models, to trade-off re-computation of results for stored backups and checkpoints; and, from another research community, redundancy of execution [2], of all or of critical tasks, and on all or a selection of more reliable resources, to reduce the effects of failures efficiently.

20.3.6   Online Gaming

Description: Hundreds of online games (OGs) entertain over 250,000,000 online players in a global market that generates over 30 billion euros yearly. Massivizing, which means to scale efficiently while meeting strict SLAs, is the biggest challenge of massively multiplayer online games (MMOGs). We consider here only the resource management for the in-game virtual world, excluding external processes such as gaming analytics (similar to Sects. 20.3.3 and 20.3.4) and game-content generation (not standardized). There are many types of online games, among which the most popular are online social games (OSGs); first-person shooters (FPSs) and real-time strategy games (RTSs); and massively multiplayer online role-playing games (MMORPGs).

Metrics of interest: In general, it includes response time, cost of operation, performance variability impact as aggregate performance penalty (own metric), time- and space-varying reliability, or availability.

Typical problems: Problems are reduced cost, balanced cost performance, impact of performance variability, and unavailability at critical time or for the critical component.

20.3.6.1   Datacenter-Based Approaches

Application components: The most popular OSGs (e.g., the Farmville series and the Clash of Clans) have over 100 million daily active users, and hundreds of OSGs attract over 1 million daily active users. OSGs use multi-tier Web applications (described earlier) with hundreds of thousands to millions of concurrent yet short-lived user sessions. Their populations can fluctuate significantly over time, especially during initial deployment and after their peak popularity is gone [55]. MMORPGs (e.g., World of Warcraft and Destiny) commonly use geographically distributed clusters of servers to support (multi-)hour game sessions. FPS games, e.g., the Call of Duty series, and RTS games, e.g., the StarCraft and DotA series, typically use servers to run independent game instance that run for a few tens of minutes; often, these servers are hosted by gaming-friendly datacenters.

Typical self-aware elements: They are self-aware provisioning of resources from datacenters, especially in hybrid clouds, using workload prediction and modeling; cost-aware operation; portfolio scheduling [69]; and availability on demand [70].

20.3.6.2   Offloading of Mobile Interactive Applications

Application components: An emerging application in this space is that of mobile games that use clouds as offloading target. The structure of such an application is typically a workflow or dataflow, where tasks have interdependencies and typically execute iteratively (the input–update–synchronize cycle common in game design). Some or all tasks can be offloaded to the cloud. For example, cloud gaming applications could offload all update tasks to the cloud and stream back to the mobile device a video rendering of the current game status.

Metrics of interest: They are general metrics plus energy costs and metrics relating to more complex costs of operation (e.g., roaming and other special rates).

Typical problems: Problems are the general online gaming problems plus focus on energy.

Typical self-aware elements: Applications may offload only (a part of) computation, data acquisition, or another resource-consuming part. Several, but not many, feedback and reconfiguration techniques and stochastic performance models address which part to offload, where, and how already exist [56, 76].

20.3.7   Partial and Delayed Processing

Description: Cloud applications have functional requirements on the computations they should perform and non-functional requirements on the additional properties they should have. Some of these requirements can be expressed as incremental requirements on application behavior. For example, the accuracy of the answer and the reliability of the operation could be bounded in stages. In partial processing, applications can gradually downgrade user experience to avoid system saturation.

Partial and *delayed* processing addresses such requirements. For example, recommendation engines used by online shops to offer end users suggestions of similar products are often highly demanding on computing resources [46]. Using a partial input instead of the entire database of choices can lead to acceptable recommendations for both users and system. With delayed processing, applications can extend their response time to cope with overload conditions [37] or dynamically vary resource allocations to batch processing jobs to increase the overall utilization [51].

Metrics of interest: Typically, they are (bounded) response time: the latency experienced by the users or the latency to deliver results in real-time data stream processing and also reliability and cost to produce the results.

Typical problems: In addition to the traditional requirements, it includes dynamic loads and variable number of users, making dynamic resource provisioning necessary [62], unexpected events and potential failures, such as large load spikes, software and hardware failures, and lack of performance isolation during workload consolidation.

Typical self-aware elements: For partial processing, enable and disable optional components on the fly, which leads to bounded response time [13, 44] and ability to address multiple failures [45]. Stochastic performance models can help in analyzing the trade-offs in the use of content versus capacity requirements, in the use of content versus response time, and in the use of (iterative) response accuracy versus response time.

In some cases, extending the response time slightly (e.g., a few seconds every hour) is typically unnoticeable for users, but solving this optimization problem with flexible constraints can significantly reduce the impact of overloads [37, 51].

20.3.8 Cyber-Physical Applications

Description: In cyber-physical system (CPS) applications [61], a computing system interacts with the physical world in some non-trivial manner. While originally exemplified by closed embedded systems, such as industrial automation, the scope of CPS applications has grown over the years to include larger open systems such as disaster response, medical applications, energy management, and vehicular control.

Metrics of interest: There are two often conflicting evaluation metrics for CPS applications: safety and performance. Attaining higher performance often requires greater coupling between components, but such coupling introduces complexity and pathways for failure propagation, which may compromise safety.

Typical problems: A self-aware architecture should offer ways to meet both safety and performance requirements despite the conflict between them. Adaptation is needed to attain good trade-offs, as discussed in the examples below.

20.3.8.1 Medical Applications

Application components: Consider a future implanted smart insulin pump for a diabetes patient. Multiple control mechanisms may be present that take measurements of activity levels from accelerometers and measurements of sugar levels in the bloodstream to modulate insulin delivery. While inner control loops will run locally, there is an opportunity to perform some predictive optimization in the cloud based on the context derived from user location, synchronized calendar, and other factors. Decisions on where to execute which functionality at what time may be revisited dynamically to adapt to different networks and patient conditions, as well the current control objectives (see Sect. 20.5.1 for detail).

Metrics of interest: The safety requirement may specify that the pump shall never overdose the patient (which could be fatal). A performance requirement may specify that the pump should predictively adapt its output depending on the person's activity and food intake. The predictive aspect is key, because the human body has too large of a response time for purely reactive (feedback) control schemes to offer a tight sugar regulation.

Typical Problems: Attaining better predictions requires exploitation of more information. Acquisition of this additional information comes at the cost of having to connect to other less reliable subsystems (e.g., the cloud), creating dependencies that may act as pathways for failure propagation and hence safety violations. Hence, a conflict manifests between performance and safety.

Typical self-aware elements: The need to reconcile safety and performance gives rise to a new type of adaptation, where the system toggles between meeting performance objectives and meeting safety objectives, depending on the current state. In the nominal (normal operation) state, the system optimizes performance. However, when the system approaches boundaries of safety, the objective switches to enforcement of safety, even if performance is affected. This approach is commonly referred to as the simplex architectural pattern. For example, when the insulin pump observes large deviations in patient's blood sugar levels, it may switch to a simple PID control mode based only on trusted local sensors and disconnect itself from the less reliable cloud inputs that might be offering bad predictions.

20.3.8.2   Vehicular Applications

Application components: Vehicles are an interesting and emerging case study for CPSs. Up until now, development has focused on making the individual more autonomous. While this trend continues, we believe there will be an increasing emphasis on (i) the communication between vehicles of different degrees of autonomy; (ii) careful sharing of CPS information resources; and (iii) system health management [8].

Metrics of interest: Safety requirements might be that a vehicle shall avoid hitting other vehicles or pedestrians; traffic signs shall be obeyed. Performance requirements could be to minimize fuel consumption and travel time.

Typical problems: Better performance may be achieved by exploiting global information, typically from a cloud service. The service might include a database of all traffic signs, estimates of current traffic conditions, and a schedule of traffic signals. This information can be used to plan itineraries and driving speeds such that fuel, trip time, and other passenger preferences are optimized. To ensure safety, however, only reliable sensors that are local to the car should be used in making decisions. However, these sensors have only a local view and may miss various performance optimization opportunities.

Typical self-aware elements: To attain a good trade-off between safety and performance, a local override mechanism is needed to take control when a safety requirement is about to be violated. For example, if the perceived state at an approaching intersection is different from that reported by the cloud (e.g., light is red, not green), the local override should take over and manage the car based on local sensors only. The idea is to use the subset of most reliable information only, when the system state is close to a safety violation boundary, while exploiting additional less reliable sources for optimization in other states.

20.4   Types of Problems

In this section, we identify the following ten types of problems that affect cloud applications and that can benefit from the use of self-awareness techniques:

1. Recovery planning,
2. Autoscaling of resources,
3. Runtime architectural reconfiguration and load balancing,
4. Fault tolerance in distributed systems,
5. Energy proportionality and energy-efficient operation,
6. Workload prediction,
7. Performance isolation,
8. Diagnosis and troubleshooting,
9. Discovery of application topology, and
10. Intrusion detection and prevention.

20.4.1   Recovery Planning

Context: Enterprise storage systems are designed to be resilient to failures, but when a large failure occurs—for example, a datacenter-level failure—recovery is a complex process and frequently involves some application downtime. It is important to recover the most important applications quickly; but *What is the sequence of recovery operations that will minimize the damage?* [40] and *What can prevent the failure from reactivating?* [72]

   Problem: When an enterprise storage system experiences a large failure, critical applications must be recovered quickly, even at the expense of additional downtime for less important applications. Administrators are under stress and have little time to design the best sequence of recovery operations, and the default methods may be far from optimal, since each failure can be different. Preventing the reoccurrence of the failure, for example, by isolating, reconfiguring, or micro-rebooting the failed component, also requires careful planning. A self-aware recovery system that understands the failures, the criticality of the applications to be restored, and the possible recovery options can propose or automatically execute a customized recovery plan.

   Expected Advancement: By codifying the recovery operations, the cost of downtime for applications, and what is needed to bring each application backup so that future failures are also avoided, it is possible to model many possible recovery plans. An automated system can select an optimal schedule that balances recovery targets with cost and resource waste.

   Expected Impact on Application Types: A recovery planning optimizer should be integrated with the overall mechanisms for managing backups, failures, and related workloads in datacenters (see Sect. 20.3.5.1). Clearly, the availability of resources (e.g., interdatacenter bandwidth) impacts the recovery process and should be planned accordingly. In the other direction, the design of the backup and restore mechanisms should be visible to the recovery planner in a way that enables introspection, modeling, and updates when the mechanisms or the applications change.

20.4.2   Autoscaling of Resources

Context: Many applications are subject to time-varying workloads. For instance, workloads of Internet and enterprise applications typically contain time patterns (e.g., day vs. night and seasonal effects), long-term trends (e.g., increasing customer base), and bursts (e.g., flashcrowds of interest for content).

Problem: As a consequence of time-varying workloads, sizing a system for the expected peak workload is very inefficient (by orders of magnitude!) and may be infeasible if the workloads are hardly predictable. Therefore, a system should be able to dynamically acquire and release the resources (e.g., number of replicated VMs) as required for serving the current workload with a certain level of performance. Target levels for the application performance may be specified in service-level agreements (SLAs). Cloud computing provides the required flexibility to dynamically change the amount of resources allocated to applications. However, scaling controllers in state-of-the-art cloud platforms are following simple trigger-based approaches (e.g., if "utilization is above a given threshold, add one VM"), lacking knowledge about the structure and behavior of the application. Moreover, few are able to respond to rapid, bursty load transitions [23]. Scaling controllers when data processes require non-trivial management, for example for big data processing (see Sect. 20.3.3) are even more difficult to design [25].

Expected Advancement: A certain self-awareness of the system is required to take acceptable or even optimal decisions about when to scale an application vertically or horizontally and by what amount of resources; about which part of an application to scale if the application is comprised of multiple tiers, components or tasks, or concurrent threads of execution; about which (part of the) application to ensure against the risk of underperformance or failure; etc. Ideally, the self-aware system will be able to enforce high-level objectives as specified in SLAs (e.g., end-to-end response times and maximum risk of SLA breaches).

Expected Impact on Application Types: Autoscaling affects resource provisioning in both multi-tier enterprise applications (Sect. 20.3.1), component-based applications such as data-intensive batch processing (Sect. 20.3.3), data stream processing (Sect. 20.3.4), and datacenter-based online gaming (Sect. 20.3.6.1). This allows the autoscaled applications to meet their quality-of-service goals in spite of increased workload demands.

20.4.3 Runtime Architectural Reconfiguration and Load Balancing

Context: For many of the applications we describe in Sect. 20.3, the conditions they are operating under can change at runtime. These include workloads from users or other systems interacting with the application, resource usage patterns of the application itself, component failures from the hosting platform, and competing demands from other applications sharing the same infrastructure.

Problem: In contrast to autoscaling, which keeps the same architecture while changing the scale of the system, architectural reconfiguration is a family of techniques that reconfigure some architectural components of the overall system. When workload changes occur, the current architecture of the system may become obsolete. For example, even if individual virtual clusters can autoscale, the overall architecture of how the virtual clusters are deployed on the physical infrastructure also needs self-aware capabilities. A self-aware architecture should reconfigure and manage its components, for example, by resizing its queues and changing their scheduling policies or by changing the paths for sharing loads between different queues.

Another common problem in managing a cluster of resources (e.g., servers or storage devices) is how to automatically balance the load across the cluster. This involves migrating workloads from one server or device to another quickly and without any downtime to the applications. Load balancing can also happen among multiple clusters running similar or different workloads.

A further complication can arise in datacenters with thousands of hosts and services where some services have affinity or antiaffinity constraints. For example, a service and its backup service should not reside on the same host (*antiaffinity*), while it is preferred to have a user interface service and its corresponding DB service on the same host (*affinity*). It is a challenge to maximize the utilization of the servers while providing a high-quality user experience and not violating these constraints.

Expected Advancement: Runtime reconfiguration and load balancing typically require solving an online optimization problem, whose objective involves specific performance or availability metrics. First, for each type of applications, such metrics need to be identified, collected, and calculated in real time. Second, we need to develop techniques for quantifying the cost of each reconfiguration step (e.g., an architectural change or a VM migration) and for weighing the cost against the benefit of the reconfiguration. Third, we need frameworks for dealing with the fundamental trade-off between faster response and stability. Finally, advances on load-rebalancing optimization under affinity or antiaffinity constraints are expected, especially with the ever-increasing scale and complexity of such problems.

Expected Impact on Application Types: Runtime reconfiguration benefits especially applications which are not negatively impacted by the duration and other costs of reconfiguration. Among such applications are batch processing applications, either compute-intensive (Sect. 20.3.2) or data-intensive (Sect. 20.3.3), and some data stream processing applications (Sect. 20.3.4).

20.4.4   Fault Tolerance in Distributed Systems

Context: Due to ever-increasing scale and complexity, hardware and software faults (which lead to errors, which *may* lead to a failure) in cloud computing infrastructures are the norm rather than the exception [4]. This is why many from the application classes introduced in Sect. 20.3 include fault tolerance techniques, such as replication, early in their design.

Problem: Failures in cloud infrastructures are often correlated in time and space [22, 79], which means that a failure may affect tens to hundreds of nodes, or even entire datacenters. Therefore, it may be economically inefficient for the service provider to provision enough spare capacity for dealing with all failures in a satisfactory manner. When correlated failures occur, the service may *saturate*, i.e., it can no longer serve users in a timely manner. This in turn leads to dissatisfied users that may abandon the service, thus incurring long-term revenue loss to the service provider. Note that the saturated service causes infrastructure overload, which by itself may trigger additional failures, thus aggravating the initial situation. Hence, a mechanism is required to deal with rare, cascading failures that feature temporary capacity shortage. The main problem is to maintain bounded response times in the presence of failure, while wasting an acceptable amount of resources (today, about 20 % of the entire capacity, but the goal for exascale systems is to waste under 2 % [72]). The problem of fault handling also includes a component about preventing fault reoccurrence, which includes the elements of diagnosis, troubleshooting, isolation, and (micro-)rebooting [72].

Expected Advancement: Advances are expected in the use of control theory with the brownout approach, in smart load balancing using knowledge gained with control, in self-checking and self-diagnosing, and in self-reconfiguration and in smart decisions about micro-reboots. Using these techniques, the applications perform better at hiding faults from the user, as measured in the number of timeouts a user would observe.

Expected Impact on Application Types: This problem affects request–response applications (Sect. 20.3.7).

20.4.5   Energy Proportionality and Energy-Efficient Operation

Context: A problem tightly related to autoscaling is one of energy proportionality. Workloads in many applications are becoming more data-centric. In other words, the data volume, and not the algorithmic complexity, is becoming the primary contributor to resource consumption. Single-pass algorithms are used on most streaming data, and their complexity is largely linear in the data size. Moving data across machines is therefore very expensive, compared to the cost of data processing.

Problem: It is hard to design systems where resources operate at capacity all the time. Necessarily, some resources will not be fully utilized. Solutions such as autoscaling could become prohibitively expensive if they involve frequent data movement. On the other hand, in the absence of autoscaling, some machines will not be fully utilized. This operating mode exposes a problem with most current datacenter hardware, namely energy proportionality (or, rather, lack thereof). A server that is only 30 % utilized may be using 80 % of the energy needed at full load. One needs to design solutions where energy consumption shrinks proportionally to load.

Expected Advancement: Attaining energy proportionality in data-centric applications is challenging. It requires algorithms that minimize unnecessary data movement, while performing autoscaling. These algorithms must amortize cost of data movement over time [49]. The latter may require a prediction of future data access patterns [39].

Expected Impact on Application Types: Energy proportionality will benefit both data-centric multi-tier enterprise applications and stream processing applications by allowing them to operate in a more energy-efficient manner while minimizing the need for data movement.

20.4.6 Workload Prediction

Context: The increased volume of data involved in modern cloud applications suggests that initial data placement will play a big role in application performance and energy consumption. Improper placement will create future load imbalance (e.g., if many popular items are collocated) or needlessly increase the energy consumption (e.g., if infrequently accessed items are placed together with some frequently accessed ones, thus preventing machines from being turned off). Chapter 18 discusses these issues in further detail, from both a time series and a machine learning perspective.

Problem: In (nearly) stateless services, such as those serving static Web pages, a load balancer can rectify the imbalance simply by distributing future requests in a more equitable fashion. In applications where moving data is costly, it is harder to predict computing load because such load has a substantial data affinity. Hence, data placement dictates where computation runs. Getting the placement right in the first place becomes important. This motivates techniques for predicting future access patterns to data items at the time these items first enter the system and are stored [39].

Expected Advancement: Self-awareness techniques can understand and represent efficiently the state of the system. Collecting and summarizing the monitoring data at the scales expected for cloud computing infrastructures and workloads is challenging, yet needed. Proper data access pattern prediction techniques will minimize the need for moving data unnecessarily and hence improve both performance and energy consumption of datacenters. For example, data predicted to be of no further interest could be moved proactively to servers that operate in more aggressive energy-saving modes, or are in places that are harder to cool, hence saving energy.

Similarly, data predicted to be popular could be partitioned among a sufficient number of servers, reducing the chances of developing hotspots and needing to relocate some of the data to other machines. To conclude, increasing awareness for the lowest possible cost is an important trade-off that remains largely unexplored.

Expected Impact on Application Types: Most cloud computing applications will benefit from some forms of workload prediction.

20.4.7 Performance Isolation

Context: Support for multi-tenancy is an important feature of clouds. For example, SaaS offerings are typically implemented by multi-tenant application architectures. Multi-tenancy means that different tenants from separate organizations are sharing the same application instance and see their own tenant-specific view of the data and functionality. Thus, the operator of a SaaS provider can increase the efficiency compared to running separate application instances.

Problem: The tenants of a cloud service may, unwillingly or even willingly, affect the operation of the system and thus each other. If one tenant exceeds its shared portion, or if the services are oversubscribed and the rightful tenants access the service simultaneously, the performance as experienced by the other tenants can fluctuate or even depreciate significantly. Likely because of (lack of) performance isolation, not only SaaS, but also PaaS and IaaS clouds, can experience a high variability in the performance of their service [34].

Expected Advancement: To ensure performance isolation in such disruptive scenarios, per-request admission control is required that automatically throttles users exceeding their quota to avoid breaking the SLAs of other tenants.

Expected Impact on Application Types: Multi-tier enterprise applications in a cloud environment need both performance isolation among different application instances (e.g., on IaaS) [50, 58] and among different tenants of the same application instance (e.g., on SaaS) [47].

20.4.8 Diagnosis and Troubleshooting

Context: When an application or service goes down or fails to reach the service-level objective (SLO) regarding its end-to-end performance, one needs to engage in the process of diagnosis and troubleshooting.

Problem: The key problem is to identify the faulty component that has caused the failure, or the associated performance bottleneck that has led to the service degradation. This can be challenging due to the increasingly more complex and distributed nature of modern applications, their growing space of configurations, the typically time-varying workload demands, and the applications' dependency on a variety of hardware resources, such as processors, memory, storage, and network I/O devices, and software resources, such as locks, threads, and connection pools.

Expected Advancement: Traditionally, maintenance personnel, system administrators, or datacenter operators perform diagnosis and troubleshooting manually, using a combination of logs, performance charts, best practices menus, and their domain knowledge, which is time-consuming and error-prone. With the utilization of self-awareness techniques, we should build management services that can automatically determine the likely causes of failures or performance problems [43, 77, 78].

Expected Impact on Application Types: Applications from enterprise multi-tier systems to networked cyber-physical front ends can benefit from automatic diagnosis and troubleshooting, resulting in shorter durations of failures or service-level violations, and reduced cost in management and operations. Prior work addresses system health management, including diagnostic and prognostic capabilities [52, 63, 65], application troubleshooting [43], and troubleshooting uncoordinated self-aware managers [30].

20.4.9 Discovery of Application Topology

Context: Automatic discovery of application topology or runtime architecture is a required feature for any mature application performance monitoring or management solutions, according to the Gartner's APM Conceptual Framework.

Problem: The problem here is to automate the process of identifying the relationship and dependency among individual application components at runtime, as well as how they are mapped to the physical infrastructure (e.g., servers), with no or only minimum input from human operators.

Expected Advancement: To solve the above problem, one needs to implement real-time, fine-grained tracing of individual transactions as they traverse through the execution paths of the application. Such monitoring solutions can be passive or require instrumentation at the kernel, middleware, or application level. Statistical techniques for inferring correlations or discovering dependencies are often needed.

Expected Impact on Application Types: Having access to an accurate application topology can help diagnose or debug the performance degradations and discover the hidden performance bottlenecks in multi-tier enterprise applications (Sect. 20.3.1.1) during their operation or help identify the potential root causes of observed failures through event correlation.

20.4.10 Intrusion Detection and Prevention

Context: In cloud environments, different applications coming from diverse organizations may share the same physical resources. Depending on the cloud service model (IaaS, PaaS, or SaaS), the datacenter owner has different levels of control over the executed application and their configuration. Vulnerabilities in the infrastructure software (e.g., hypervisors) or in shared services (e.g., storage services) can be exploited to widen an attack from any application to any other virtual machine in the same infrastructure. For instance, attackers may rent virtual machines (in case of public clouds) or exploit vulnerabilities of applications (e.g., private Web site) to get access to sensitive data (e.g., e-commerce system with credit card data) in other virtual machines in the same cloud environment.

Problem: The detection and prevention of attacks in a cloud environment require a classification of cloud workloads (either using application or using network probes) into benign and malicious ones. False positives can result in unnecessary actions countering attacks, which may have negative effects on the applications.

Expected Advancement: A self-aware system automatically learns to distinguish between benign and malicious workloads and can filter out false positives. Furthermore, the system is able to react to attacks and adapt itself to ensure its self-protection capabilities. For more detail on quantifying the self-protection capabilities of self-aware systems, we refer the reader to Chap. 14.

Expected Impact on Application Types: All application types running in a cloud are potential targets for attacks. Prior work in this area aimed at automatic workload anomaly detection and at enabling self-healing capabilities of systems.

20.5   Types of Approaches

In this section, we identify and analyze the following seven types of self-awareness approaches used in practice to address the problems identified in the previous section.

1. Feedback control-based techniques,
2. Metric optimization with constraints,
3. Machine learning-based techniques,
4. Portfolio scheduling,
5. Self-aware architecture reconfiguration,
6. Stochastic performance models, and
7. Other approaches

20.5.1   Feedback Control-Based Techniques

Description: Control theory is a branch of mathematics that studies how to influence the behavior of dynamical systems [48]. Based on a formal model of the target system in the form of equations (for time-based control) or automaton (for event-based control), control theory provides principles for how to synthesize a controller that would regulate the behavior of the system and obtain prescribed properties.

Expected Impact: Although control theory was invented to deal with physical systems, the same principles have been successfully applied to many different application domains in computing systems [29], including resource allocation [36, 50], application performance via bounded response times [37, 44], reliability [19], fault tolerance [7, 45], stream processing [38], and big data [18].

Details: A controller should provide the following properties [12, 20]:

- *Setpoint Tracking*. A setpoint refers to the goals to be achieved. For example, a system is considered responsive when its user-perceived latency is subsecond.
- *Transient behavior*. This concerns *how* the setpoint is reached by the system.
- *Robustness*. The controller should be able to cope with inaccurate measurements, delayed data, or other uncertainties not captured in the system model.
- *Disturbance rejection*. The closed-loop system should reach its goal in spite of other disturbing actions happening simultaneously in the system.

These properties are often translated into the corresponding control properties of stability, no overshooting, quick settling time, and robustness to model errors and disturbances.

Use Cases: There have been many published studies of developing self-awareness capabilities using feedback control-based techniques.

One broad application area has been resource management in computing systems. For example, [36] describes a control-based approach to assign CPU resource shares of virtualized Web server applications. This approach emphasizes the CPU allocation around periods of workload changes and uses H^∞ filters to minimize the maximum controller error. The work also extends previous work on optimal configurations for CPU resource entitlement of virtualized multi-tier Web applications. More recently [67], a control theoretic approach was described to provide performance, dependability, and cost guarantees for online cloud services, with time-varying workloads. The approach is validated through case studies and extensive experiments with online services hosted on Amazon EC2. One case study demonstrates SLA guarantees for a cluster-based multi-tier e-commerce service. In [50], application managers automatically learn a quantitative model that correlates app-level performance with resource utilizations and use control theory to derive the optimal resource control settings (limits, reservations) for individual virtual machines such that the multi-tier application can achieve its performance target. Finally, [20] generalizes and automates core allocation based on various metrics. The approach provides formal guarantees on the application behavior in spite of external disturbances like additional load on the machine. This shows the versatility of feedback control as an approach for building self-aware and self-adaptive systems.

Another broad application area for feedback control is cyber-physical systems (see Sect. 20.3.8). Feedback control is central in smart grids [16], intelligent transportation, modern critical care units, etc. Parameters and offsets of local loops might be obtained from remote repositories. The critical need for these applications typically requires continued, correct operation even in the presence of connectivity problems to the cloud, bad data, and other failures, which often lead to joint investigation of control and safety.

20.5.2   Metric Optimization with Constraints

Description: System design, configuration, and management decisions often come down to a choice between various options. Self-aware systems can reason about the impact of different choices, but that still leaves the question of which choice best achieves the system goal. Optimization techniques require first a formal specification of the system objective and the constraints under which the system operates and then a solution that attempts to optimize the objective. Solution methods can be exact or approximate, depending upon the situation, but the explicit specification of goals is essential.

Expected Impact: Using the optimization techniques for system decisions has several advantages [41]. First, it guarantees clarity: System decisions often come down to choosing between conflicting goals, and specifying an objective forces the designer to explicitly choose how much weight to assign to them and secondly when approximate solution techniques are used. It enables a quantitative evaluation of how far the results are from the optimal. Thirdly, it allows the use of the enormous toolbox of optimization techniques that already exist, allowing the system designer to focus on the design aspects.

Details: System designer sometimes use ad hoc heuristics to make system decisions, because there may be conflicting, sometimes intangible requirements that are hard to quantify, and because the heuristics often produce results that are "good enough." However, it is then unclear what "good enough" means, or if the heuristics in fact achieve it. Expressing the trade-offs into a common currency—whether execution time, throughput, monetary cost, or a utility function—enables a definition of goodness. A wide variety of optimization techniques can be applied, depending on the formulation and requirements: mathematical optimizations, such as linear programming or mixed integer programming; constraint programming, if only a feasible solution is required; meta-heuristic techniques such as simulated annealing or genetic algorithms, when the optimization problem cannot be solved exactly in the available time; or other approximate optimization techniques that bound the error in the resulting solution.

Use Cases: Examples of the use of optimization in systems include Maestro [54], where online optimization was used with feedback control to provide performance differentiation between applications in a disk array, and Janus [3], where off-line optimization was used to determine allocation of flash resources to workloads. Meta-heuristic techniques have been used for finding the sequence of recovery operations to use after a failure to minimize the cost of the downtime [40] and for designing a redundancy configuration for large enterprise storage systems, in order to minimize the overall cost of the system including operating overheads and potential downtime costs.

Another example from the commercial world is the VMware Distributed Resource Scheduler (DRS) [27], a widely used feature in the VMware vCenter management software. DRS manages a set of virtual machines running on a cluster of physical hosts and performs dynamic load balancing to avoid hotspots and improve application performance, by solving an online optimization problem with hill-climbing heuristics and by taking into account the cost/benefit trade-off of each move.

Finally, this approach can be applied to the applications described in Sect. 20.3.4. For example, the SQPR query planner [38] allocates physical resources of hetero-geneous clusters to data stream processing queries. SQPR models query admission, allocation, and stream reuse as a single-constrained optimization problem and solves an approximate version to achieve scalability. The SQPR approach monitors the resource utilization across the cluster and performance progress of running queries to decide on queries' placement and allocation. SQPR adapts to operating conditions through continuous monitoring and modeling of cluster and queries' performance. SQPR uses an off-the-shelf optimization solver for optimal solutions.

20.5.3   Machine Learning-Based Techniques

Description: Machine learning is the science of using data to "uncover an underlying process" [1]. More specifically, it involves designing, implementing, and validating a set of algorithms that can extract insights from data regarding the relationships among objects and events, often captured in the form of statistical models.

Expected Impact: Besides the successful application of machine learning to financial applications, e-commerce, and medical applications, there has been a great deal of research in the past decade on leveraging machine learning-based techniques to creating self-awareness for business-critical applications (Sect. 20.3.1).

Details: Supervised learning, unsupervised learning, and reinforcement learn-ing are the three main types of machine learning approaches. They are commonly applied to perform clustering, classification, and prediction, using a variety of statis-tical models, including decision trees, regression models, neural networks, Bayesian networks, or support vector machines.

A system that utilizes machine learning typically has the following components:

- *Sensors*. Software or hardware modules that measure and collect metrics of interest for the target system or process.
- *Preprocessor*. Raw data collected from systems are rarely perfect. It is not uncom-mon to have missing data from certain components or during certain periods of time, or data corrupted during collection. Such data need to be "cleaned up" or aggregated before being fed into an analysis engine.
- *Analyzer*. This is where statistical learning algorithms are being run, on top of the collected data, to extract relationships and to build models that can represent the learned behavior in a concise form.
- *Reporter/Predictor*. This is where the insights gained from data are presented to human operators in the forms of alerts, charts, or dashboards. Alternatively, the model learned can be used to generate predictions for the target system or metrics, or to recommend remediation actions.

Use Cases: In [9], tree-augmented Bayesian network (TAN) models are learned on top of instrumentation data collected from a three-tier Internet service to automatically identify the top system-level metrics that have likely contributed to the observed violation of service-level objectives (SLOs).

In [57], an autoscaling system employs reinforcement learning to automatically learn the performance behavior of a multi-tier application when instances of an elastic tier are added or removed and then uses the knowledge to scale the application horizontally as its workload demand varies over time.

20.5.4   Portfolio Scheduling

Description: Traditional scheduling policies are designed a specific workload and sometimes even for specific applications within a workload; in practice, reuse of old and adoption of new scheduling policies happens rarely. Instead, portfolio scheduling, which is a self-aware and self-expressive technique, considers a set (portfolio) of scheduling policies, from which it selects at the appropriate moments (e.g., periodically) the policy which promises the best results for the current and expected conditions. In this way, the portfolio scheduler combines the strengths of each individual policy in its portfolio, which also means that designers of scheduling policies can focus on simpler policies that do not need to address every type of workload.

Expected Impact: Portfolio schedulers promise to deliver performance at least as good as any of their constituent policies, without poor performance when the workload changes. In this context, performance includes traditional performance metrics, such as application response time and system utilization, and non-traditional metrics, such as availability, cost performance efficiency [11], and risk of SLA violations [75].

Details: The concept of portfolio scheduling derives from economics, where stock brokers can use portfolio theory to select policies for managing their stocks, to balance risks and rewards. For cloud applications, portfolio scheduling uses the following four-stage iterative process. In the configuration stage, the portfolio scheduler is equipped with a set of scheduling policies. Then, the portfolio scheduler goes through a selection stage, which results in the selection of an optimal policy; through an application stage, which results in applying the optimal policy to the current scheduling problem (queue) and in monitoring the results; and through a reflection stage, where stale policies are possibly eliminated and the portfolio can compare its operation relative to the goals of the system. The next cycle can be triggered periodically or, if enough resources allow for timely completion of stages, whenever an event can lead to system reconfiguration (e.g., at the arrival of a new request in the system).

Use Cases: Portfolio scheduling has been used for business-critical applications, with a focus on reducing the risk of SLA violations [75]. The selection stage is simulation-based, online, and applied after each arrival of a job and periodically. The optimal policy, from the policies included in the portfolio, is then applied until the next selection occurs. The results obtained by applying this portfolio scheduler on the workloads of a real cloud provider indicate not only that this portfolio scheduler is better than its constituent policies, but also that the initial configuration of the portfolio is very important.

Portfolio scheduling has been used for online gaming applications, but only tested under laboratory, albeit realistic, conditions [69]. Here, the portfolio is configured with various typical online scheduling policies, but also with an optimal solver of a linear integer problem; in the selection stage, the portfolio is given a limited amount of time to decide.

20.5.5 Self-aware Architecture Reconfiguration

Description: Self-aware architecture reconfiguration is a family of techniques that can reconfigure at runtime the architecture of the system or of the application.

Expected Impact: The generality of this approach is an advantage, but also makes the actual impact difficult to predict in advance. By affecting the essence of the entire system, this approach can affect every metric and virtually every application. When applied to applications, this approach can change the operational characteristics of the application. This approach addresses the runtime architectural reconfiguration problem.

Details: By monitoring the environment and the (queued) workload, by predicting the performance of the system or application, and by reflecting on the overall goals of the system or application, self-aware architecture reconfiguration leads to changing of not only operational characteristics (queue size and policy, structure of application components), but also the way in which the system or application operates (e.g., how queues share load).

Use Cases: Koala-C [17], which services the Dutch research cloud DAS4, creates a system with multiple queues, which can be instructed to shed load to only one other or a group of other queues. Each queue is aimed to run jobs of a specific runtime (job size). If a job scheduled by a queue does not finish in the time allocated for that queue (exceeds the job size for that queue), it is stopped and moved to a queue of larger size. The approach does not require any prior knowledge about the input workload. Instead, each job is submitted to the queue(s) servicing the shortest job; larger jobs traverse progressively the chain of queues, with probabilistic guarantees in terms of performance and wasted resources. (Queues can also be equipped with autoscaling mechanisms.) Another use case [31] is that of the cloud provider Blue Yonder: Through a parameterized application performance model, a set of modeled adaptation points, and an adaptation model, the Blue Yonder applications can adjust their resources to workload changes and can share the resources between the customers.

20.5.6   Stochastic Performance Models

Description: Stochastic performance models (e.g., queueing networks) enable the prediction of the expected system performance in terms of throughput, response time, and utilization for a given workload. In a self-aware system, these models are automatically created and maintained in the learning phase.

Expected Impact: In contrast to machine learning- or feedback control-based techniques, they promise the ability to predict also the performance for previously unseen workloads or configurations which are significantly different to the current operating point. Stochastic performance models have been applied to dynamically reconfigure enterprise multi-tier applications for autoscaling [73] and performance isolation [47].

Details: Classic queueing networks model the computing at processing resources (e.g., CPU, hard disk, and network). Furthermore, extended formalisms, such as layered queueing networks or queueing Petri nets, are able to capture the influence of passive resources (e.g., software or memory resources). In Chap. 16, a more extensive discussion of stochastic performance models can be found.

Use Cases: In [47], the authors describe a request admission controller for multi-tenant applications (e.g., SaaS application) that enables performance isolation and SLA differentiation between tenants. Using a combination of statistical estimation of resource demands and operational analysis from queueing theory, the admission control is able to determine the current resource usage of individual tenants and determine which requests are admitted and which are delayed.

In [73], a controller for vertical CPU scaling of virtualized applications is presented based on a layered queueing network. The model is dynamically parameterized based on monitoring data from the system and also captures contention effects due to hypervisor scheduling. By using the performance model, oscillating reconfigurations are avoided and the parameters can be estimated automatically at runtime.

20.5.7   Other Approaches

A number of other approaches have been developed by related fields, such as design science [59]. Although these approaches do not share the entire spectrum of characteristics of, for example, control-based systems, they can be seen as proto-self-awareness approaches. We enumerate in the following several of these approaches.

Other approaches for autoscaling: For data-intensive batch processing, which typically has large state, autoscalers such as Amazon Elastic, MapReduce, and FAWKES [25] use various types of system feedback to decide on scaling. Amazon's approach is based on the topology-aware S3 storage. Focusing on application semantics, FAWKES considers various types of VMs, including VMs that store data transiently or permanently. These approaches consider the MapReduce programming model, which has not been designed to enable interactive processing (e.g., for fast decision-making) or tightly coupled data items (e.g., for graph processing).

In the area of data stream processing, systems such as Apache S4 and Storm exploit intraquery parallelization to scale out operators and eventually handle demanding resource requirements per operator. There are two main challenges in operators' parallelization to support a scalable DSPS, i.e., how to handle operators' state and when to scale out/in. Existing research has shown that simple heuristics to detect violations on resource-based thresholds can be used to horizontally scale out to additional stream processing operators to handle the excess load [7, 28]. When handling operator state, most systems focus on the parallelization of stateless operators. In [7, 60], different generic approaches to manage the parallelization of both stateful and stateless operators are introduced. In [18], an advanced approach to handle operator state alongside specialized programming primitives is discussed.

Other approaches for runtime architectural reconfiguration and load balancing: Better load balancing within a cluster of compute nodes [27] or storage nodes [26], or between clusters [17], can lead to avoiding hotspots and to improving the performance of many types of applications, including compute-intensive scientific applications (Sect. 20.3.2), business-critical applications (Sect. 20.3.1), and batch processing applications (Sect. 20.3.2). Reconfiguring the system partitions, not only in scale but also in the way they interact, can greatly benefit batch workloads where long and short jobs can coexist [17]. A genetic algorithm for load rebalancing (GALR) was proposed to deal with affinity or antiaffinity constraints [74]. In experiments running the PlanetLab dataset in a cluster up to 300 hosts, GALR performs close to optimality in load rebalancing, within 4–5 s.

Other approaches for fault tolerance in distributed systems: Experimental results demonstrated that using brownout [44] and smart load-balancing [13] application can tolerate more replica failures and that the novel load-balancing algorithms improve the number of requests served with optional content and thus the revenue of the provider by up to 5 %, with high statistical significance [45]. Various self-testing and self-diagnostic techniques exist (e.g., SMART, which is a commercial technology for hard disks), but self-repair through self-reconfiguration and self-rebooting is still a largely open field.

20.6   Open Challenges for Self-aware Cloud Applications

In this section, we focus on identifying and analyzing directions for future research in developing self-aware cloud applications. We ask questions that we find challenging, yet promising, that is, whose answers we foresee being put in practice in the next 3–5 years.

To what extent are self-awareness techniques necessary for cloud applications? Currently, non-self-aware techniques are prevalent in the management of increasingly large cloud datacenters and their applications. Uncertainty about the need and possible gains limits the adoption of self-awareness techniques for this setting.

Anecdotal evidence such as that gathered in this chapter and the existing small controlled experiments conducted by scientists provide some evidence of the benefit of using self-awareness techniques, but on their own still cannot provide the needed strong evidence. Instead, inspired by the evolution of related fields, it would be beneficial to collect and share many operational traces from real-world deployments into an open-access Trace Archive and to provide a layer of fundamental understanding and knowledge by analyzing and sharing quantitative information such as the frequency of self-aware decisions and metrics about their impact. Large-scale experimental comparisons of self-aware and non-self-aware techniques, published as both technical material and open-access data, could provide a useful complement and further the acquisition of fundamental knowledge.

How can self-aware computing and communications enable or improve upon emerging applications for increasingly capable mobile devices—including smartphones, wearable devices, and IoT devices? Today's cloud architecture, which relies on the use of a "dumb pipe" sitting between it and a smart edge including increasingly capable mobile devices, is likely to be a productive area for future research [53]. In particular, there is a fundamental limitation in how much power a wearable or handheld device can consume before it becomes "too hot to wear" or "too hot to handle." Consequently, off-loading to an external computing platform, currently a cloud, becomes attractive. However, given the current Internet and telecom system architectures, data from apps need to cross a dumb pipe before it reaches the cloud. This can be a severely limiting factor, when it comes to supporting emerging applications that need low-latency, high-bandwidth communications. Examples of such emerging applications include rich media (including video), unmanned vehicles, and gaming.

How can self-aware computing learn and maintain knowledge of itself if it is subject to frequent releases? The development of many popular Internet applications (e.g., Facebook and Netflix) is characterized by very short release cycles (e.g., daily). The term DevOps is often used to describe approaches and processes to align development and operation of software systems with the goal of continuous delivery of new versions with new or changed functionality. As a result, such software systems are often in transient phases where different versions of software run in parallel.

How can self-aware computing learn the characteristics of the workloads and update the allocation of their resources in a distributed manner with global coordination for efficient use of datacenter resources? Current cloud datacenters span thousands of physical servers and host tens of thousands of virtual machines running different workloads. Managing such large systems while satisfying individual workload performance requirements and making efficient use of cluster resources is an open challenge. Current scalable approaches use either distributed scheduling (e.g., Mesos) or optimistic resource allocation using shared state (e.g., Omega [66]). However, such approaches cannot guarantee global scheduling optimality with respect to multiple (possibly competing) goals across all resources and workloads in the datacenter.

Can self-aware computing offer techniques for fully automated root cause analysis (RCA) that can be applied to a variety of management operations in the cloud? Over the past decade, the wide deployment of monitoring solutions in datacenters and access to real-time telemetry have advanced the art in diagnosis and troubleshooting. At the same time, *automated RCA* still remains an unsolved puzzle for operators. This is mainly due to the large number of hardware (compute, storage, networking) and software (OS, hypervisor, container, middleware, application) components that can potentially contribute to an observed failure or performance drop and the complex interactions among them. Furthermore, typical statistical analysis and learning approaches discover correlations and not causality between different metrics or events, and hence, it can only provide hints for the real root cause.

20.7 Conclusion

Cloud computing and its applications are already an important branch of ICT, with interesting benefits and challenges. Due to sheer scale, but also to the increasing sophistication of both their stakeholders and their infrastructure, clouds and their applications are increasingly relying on self-aware management techniques. In this chapter, we have proposed a systematic framework to explain existing self-awareness approaches and to facilitate the analysis of self-awareness in the future.

Our framework proposes a structured way to analyze the types of self-awareness approaches used in practice, in cloud computing and its applications. The framework focuses on the types of applications, problems, and approaches relevant to self-awareness. The framework also structures the discussion and the analysis of open challenges.

In this chapter, we have used the framework to analyze seven types of self-awareness approaches used in practice: feedback control-based techniques, metric optimization with constraints, machine learning-based techniques, portfolio scheduling, self-aware architecture reconfiguration, stochastic performance models, and other approaches. We conduct a systematic survey of self-awareness techniques. We focus on eight types of applications, among which most are already established, whereas applications such as online gaming, partial processing, and cyber-physical applications are still emerging. We analyze ten types of traditional and novel problems. Novel, we focus on problems that have developed beyond their traditional scope or even emerged altogether in the space of cloud computing, such as autoscaling, energy proportionality, performance isolation, and intrusion detection and prevention. We also identify four open challenges for self-awareness in cloud computing and its applications.

The future of this work is in facilitating, for the authors and for the self-awareness community at large, work addressing the open challenges. We also hope the framework will be used for analyzing other self-awareness approaches, new problems, and new applications.

Acknowledgements This work is partially supported by the Dutch STW/NWO Veni personal grant @large and Vidi personal grant MagnaData, by the Dutch national program COMMIT and COMMissioner subproject, by the Dutch KIEM project KIESA, by a generous ERO gift from Oracle, by the European FP7 research project AMADEOS Grant Agreement 610535 on Systems of Systems, by the Swedish Research Council (VR) for the projects "Cloud Control" and "Power and temperature control for large-scale computing infrastructures," and through the LCCC Linnaeus and ELLIIT Excellence Centers.

References

1. Yaser S. Abu-Mostafa, Malik Magdon-Ismail, and Hsuan-Tien Lin. *Learning From Data*. AML-Book, 2012.
2. Orna Agmon Ben-Yehuda, Assaf Schuster, Artyom Sharov, Mark Silberstein, and Alexandru Iosup. Expert: Pareto-efficient task replication on grids and a cloud. In *IPDPS*, 2012.
3. Christoph Albrecht, Arif Merchant, Murray Stokely, Muhammad Waliji, François Labelle, et al. Janus: Optimal flash provisioning for cloud storage workloads. In *USENIX ATC*, 2013.
4. Luiz Andre Barroso and Urs Hölzle. *The Datacenter as a Computer: An Introduction to the Design of Warehouse-Scale Machines*. Morgan & Claypool, 2009.
5. Jean Arnaud and Sara Bouchenak. *Performance and Dependability in Service Computing*, chapter Performance, Availability and Cost of Self-Adaptive Internet Services. IGI, 2011.
6. Aniruddha Basak, Irina Brinster, and Ole J. Mengshoel. MapReduce for Bayesian network parameter learning using the EM algorithm. In *Proc. of Big Learning: Algorithms, Systems and Tools*, 2012.
7. Raul Castro Fernandez, Matteo Migliavacca, Evangelia Kalyvianaki, and Peter Pietzuch. Integrating scale out and fault tolerance in stream processing using operator state management. In *SIGMOD*, 2013.
8. Arthur Choi, Adnan Darwiche, Lu Zheng, and Ole J. Mengshoel. A tutorial on Bayesian networks for system health management. In A. Srivastava and J. Han, editors, *Data Mining in Systems Health Management: Detection, Diagnostics, and Prognostics*. Chapman and Hall/CRC Press, 2011.
9. Ira Cohen, Moises Goldszmidt, Terence Kelly, Julie Simons, and Jeff Chase. Correlating instrumentation data to system states: A building block for automated diagnosis and control. In *OSDI*, 2004.
10. Louis Columbus. Roundup of cloud computing forecasts and market estimates, 2015. Forbes Tech Report, 2015.
11. Kefeng Deng, Junqiang Song, Kaijun Ren, and Alexandru Iosup. Exploring portfolio scheduling for long-term execution of scientific workloads in iaas clouds. In *SC*, 2013.
12. Yixin Diao, Joseph L. Hellerstein, Sujay Parekh, Rean Griffith, Gail E. Kaiser, and Dan Phung. A control theory foundation for self-managing computing systems. *IEEE J. on Selected Areas in Communications*, 23(12):2213–2222, 2006.
13. Jonas Dürango, Manfred Dellkrantz, Martina Maggio, Cristian Klein, Alessandro Vittorio Papadopoulos, et al. Control-theoretical load-balancing for cloud applications with brownout. In *CDC*, 2014.
14. E.N. Elnohazy et al. System resilience at extreme scale. White paper. Defense Advanced Research Project Agency (DARPA) report, 2009.
15. European Commission. Uptake of cloud in europe. Final Report. Digital Agenda for Europe report. Publications Office of the European Union, Luxembourg, 2014.
16. Xi Fang, Satyajayant Misra, Guoliang Xue, and Dejun Yang. Smart grid; the new and improved power grid: A survey. *IEEE Communications Surveys Tutorials*, 14(4):944–980, 2012.
17. Lipu Fei, Bogdan Ghit, Alexandru Iosup, and Dick H. J. Epema. KOALA-C: A task allocator for integrated multicluster and multicloud environments. In *CLUSTER*, 2014.

18. Raul Castro Fernandez, Matteo Migliavacca, Evangelia Kalyvianaki, and Peter Pietzuch. Making state explicit for imperative big data processing. In *USENIX ATC*, 2014.

19. Antonio Filieri, Carlo Ghezzi, Alberto Leva, and Martina Maggio. Self-adaptive software meets control theory: A preliminary approach supporting reliability requirements. In *ASE*, 2011.

20. Antonio Filieri, Henry Hoffmann, and Martina Maggio. Automated design of self-adaptive software with control-theoretical formal guarantees. In *ICSE*, 2014.

21. Andrew Forward and Timothy C. Lethbridge. A taxonomy of software types to facilitate search and evidence-based software engineering. In *Conference of the Centre for Advanced Studies on Collaborative Research*, page 14, 2008.

22. Matthieu Gallet, Nezih Yigitbasi, Bahman Javadi, Derrick Kondo, Alexandru Iosup, and Dick H. J. Epema. A model for space-correlated failures in large-scale distributed systems. In *Euro-Par*, 2010.

23. Anshul Gandhi, Mor Harchol-Balter, Ram Raghunathan, and Michael A. Kozuch. Autoscale: Dynamic, robust capacity management for multi-tier data centers. *ACM Trans. Comput. Syst.*, 30(4):14, 2012.

24. Shravan Gaonkar, Kimberly Keeton, Arif Merchant, and William H. Sanders. Designing dependable storage solutions for shared application environments. *IEEE Trans. Dependable Secur. Comput.*, 7(4):366–380, 2010.

25. Bogdan Ghit, Nezih Yigitbasi, Alexandru Iosup, and Dick H. J. Epema. Balanced resource allocations across multiple dynamic mapreduce clusters. In *SIGMETRICS*, 2014.

26. Ajay Gulati, Chethan Kumar, Irfan Ahmad, and Karan Kumar. BASIL: Automated IO load balancing across storage devices. In *FAST*, 2010.

27. Ajay Gulati, Ganesha Shanmuganathan, Anne Holler, Carl Waldspurger, Minwen Ji, and Xiaoyun Zhu. VMware Distributed Resource Management: Design, implementation, and lessons learned. *VMware Technical Journal*, 1(1), 2012.

28. Vincenzo Gulisano, Ricardo Jimenez-Peris, Marta Patino-Martinez, Claudio Soriente, and Patrick Valduriez. Streamcloud: An elastic and scalable data streaming system. *IEEE Trans. Parallel Distrib. Syst.*, 23(12):2351–2365, 2012.

29. Joseph L. Hellerstein, Yixin Diao, Sujay Parekh, and Dawn M. Tilbury. *Feedback Control of Computing Systems*. John Wiley & Sons, 2004.

30. Jin Heo and Tarek Abdelzaher. Adaptguard: Guarding adaptive systems from instability. In *ICAC*, pages 77–86, 2009.

31. Nikolaus Huber, Jürgen Walter, Manuel Bähr, and Samuel Kounev. Model-based Autonomic and Performance-aware System Adaptation in Heterogeneous Resource Environments: A Case Study. In *ICCAC*, 2015.

32. IDC. Worldwide and regional public it cloud services: 2013-2017 forecast. IDC Tech Report. [Online] Available: www.idc.com/getdoc.jsp?containerId=251730, 2013.

33. Alexandru Iosup and Dick H. J. Epema. Grid computing workloads. *IEEE Internet Computing*, 15(2):19–26, 2011.

34. Alexandru Iosup, Nezih Yigitbasi, and Dick H. J. Epema. On the performance variability of production cloud services. In *CCGrid*, 2011.

35. Gideon Juve, Ann L. Chervenak, Ewa Deelman, Shishir Bharathi, Gaurang Mehta, and Karan Vahi. Characterizing and profiling scientific workflows. *Future Generation Comp. Syst.*, 29(3):682–692, 2013.

36. Evangelia Kalyvianaki and Themistoklis Charalambous. A Min-Max framework for CPU resource provisioning in virtualized servers using H-infinity Filters. In *CDC*, 2010.

37. Evangelia Kalyvianaki, Themistoklis Charalambous, Marco Fiscato, and Peter Pietzuch. Overload Management in Data Stream Processing Systems with Latency Guarantees. In *Feedback Computing*, 2012.

38. Evangelia Kalyvianaki, Wolfram Wiesemann, Quang Hieu Vu, Daniel Kuhn, and Peter Pietzuch. Sqpr: Stream query planning with reuse. In *ICDE*, 2011.

39. Rini T. Kaushik, Tarek Abdelzaher, Ryota Egashira, and Klara Nahrstedt. Predictive data and energy management in greenhdfs. In *IGCC*, pages 1–9, 2011.

40. Kimberly Keeton, Dirk Beyer, Ernesto Brau, Arif Merchant, Cipriano Santos, and Alex Zhang. On the road to recovery: Restoring data after disasters. In *EuroSys*, 2006.
41. Kimberly Keeton, Terence Kelly, Arif Merchant, Cipriano A. Santos, Janet L. Wiener, Xiaoyun Zhu, and Dirk Beyer. Don't settle for less than the best: Use optimization to make decisions. In *HotOS*, 2007.
42. Kimberly Keeton and Arif Merchant. A framework for evaluating storage system dependability. In *DSN*, 2004.
43. Mohammad M. H. Khan, Hieu Khac Le, Hossein Ahmadi, Tarek F. Abdelzaher, and Jiawei Han. Troubleshooting interactive complexity bugs in wireless sensor networks using data mining techniques. *ACM Trans. Sen. Netw.*, 10(2):31:1–31:35, 2014.
44. Cristian Klein, Martina Maggio, Karl-Erik Årzén, and Francisco Hernández-Rodriguez. Brownout: Building more robust cloud applications. In *ICSE*, 2014.
45. Cristian Klein, Alessandro V. Papadopoulos, Manfred Dellkrantz, Jonas Durango, Martina Maggio, et al. Improving cloud service resilience using brownout-aware load-balancing. In *SDRS*, 2014.
46. Joseph A. Konstan and John Riedl. Recommended to you. *IEEE Spectrum*, 2012.
47. Rouven Krebs, Simon Spinner, Nadia Ahmed, and Samuel Kounev. Resource usage control in multi-tenant applications. In *CCGrid*, 2014.
48. William S. Levine. *The control handbook*. The electrical engineering handbook series. CRC Press New York, 1996.
49. Shen Li, Shiguang Wang, Fan Yang, Shaohan Hu, Fatemeh Saremi, and Tarek Abdelzaher. Proteus: Power proportional memory cache cluster in data centers. In *ICDCS*, pages 73–82, 2013.
50. Lei Lu, Xiaoyun Zhu, Rean Griffith, Pradeep Padala, Aashish Parikh, Parth Shar, and Evgenia Smirni. Application-driven dynamic vertical scaling of virtual machines in resource pools. In *NOMS*, 2014.
51. Luo Mai, Evangelia Kalyvianaki, and Paolo Costa. Exploiting time-malleability in cloud-based batch processing systems. In *LADIS*, 2013.
52. Ole J. Mengshoel, Mark Chavira, Keith Cascio, Scott Poll, Adnan Darwiche, et al. Probabilistic model-based diagnosis: An electrical power system case study. *IEEE Trans. on Systems, Man and Cybernetics, Part A: Systems and Humans*, 40(5):874–885, 2010.
53. Ole J. Mengshoel, Bob Iannucci, and Abe Ishihara. Mobile computing: Challenges and opportunities for autonomy and feedback. In *Feedback Computing'13*, 2013.
54. Arif Merchant, Mustafa Uysal, Pradeep Padala, Xiaoyun Zhu, Sharad Singhal, and Kang G. Shin. Maestro: quality-of-service in large disk arrays. In *ICAC*, 2011.
55. Alexandru-Corneliu Olteanu, Alexandru Iosup, and Nicolae Tapus. Towards a workload model for online social applications. In *ICPE*, 2013.
56. Alexandru-Corneliu Olteanu, Nicolae Tapus, and Alexandru Iosup. Extending the capabilities of mobile devices for online social applications through cloud offloading. In *CCGrid*, 2013.
57. Pradeep Padala, Anne Holler, Lei Lu, Xiaoyun Zhu, Aashish Parikh, and Madhuri Yechuri. Scaling of cloud applications using machine learning. *VMware Technical Journal*, 2014.
58. Pradeep Padala, Kai-Yuan Hou, Kang Shin, Xiaoyun Zhu, Mustafa Uysal, Zhijui Wang, Sharad Singhal, and Arif Merchant. Automated control of multiple virtualized resources. In *Eurosys*, 2009.
59. Ken Peffers, Tuure Tuunanen, Marcus A. Rothenberger, and Samir Chatterjee. A design science research methodology for information systems research. *J. of Management Information Systems*, 24(3):45–77, 2008.
60. Zhengping Qian, Yong He, Chunzhi Su, Zhuojie Wu, Hongyu Zhu, et al. Timestream: Reliable stream computation in the cloud. In *EuroSys*, 2013.
61. Ragunathan Rajkumar, Insup Lee, Lui Sha, and John Stankovic. Cyber-physical systems: The next computing revolution. In *DAC*, 2010.
62. Charles Reiss, Alexey Tumanov, Gregory R. Ganger, Randy H. Katz, and Michael A. Kozuch. Heterogeneity and dynamicity of clouds at scale: Google trace analysis. In *SOCC*, 2012.

63. Brian Ricks and Ole J. Mengshoel. Diagnosis for uncertain, dynamic, and hybrid domains using bayesian networks and arithmetic circuits. *International Journal on Approximate Reasoning*, 55(5):1207–1234, 2014.

64. Matthew A. Russell. *Mining the Social Web: Analyzing Data from Facebook, Twitter, LinkedIn, and Other Social Media Sites*. O'Reilly Media, Inc., 1st edition, 2011.

65. Johann Schumann, K. Y. Rozier, T. Reinbacher, Ole J. Mengshoel, T. Mbaya, and C. Ippolito. Real-time, on-board, hardware-supported sensor and software health management for unmanned aerial systems. In *Annual Conf. Prognostics and Health Mgmt. Soc.*, 2013.

66. Malte Schwarzkopf, Andy Konwinski, Michael Abd-El-Malek, and John Wilkes. Omega: Flexible, scalable schedulers for large compute clusters. In *EuroSys*, 2013.

67. Damián Serrano, Sara Bouchenak, Yousn Kouki, Thomas Ledoux, Jonathan Lejeune, et al. Towards QoS-oriented SLA guarantees for online cloud services. In *CCGrid*, 2013.

68. Damián Serrano, Sara Bouchenak, Yousri Kouki, Frederico Alvares de Oliveira Jr, Thomas Ledoux, et al. SLA guarantees for cloud services. *Future Generation Comp. Sys.*, 2015.

69. Siqi Shen, Kefeng Deng, Alexandru Iosup, and Dick H. J. Epema. Scheduling jobs in the cloud using on-demand and reserved instances. In *Euro-Par*, 2013.

70. Siqi Shen, Alexandru Iosup, Assaf Israel, Walfredo Cirne, Danny Raz, and Dick H. J. Epema. An availability-on-demand mechanism for datacenters. In *CCGRID*, 2015.

71. Siqi Shen, Vincent van Beek, and Alexandru Iosup. Statistical characterization of business-critical workloads hosted in cloud datacenters. In *CCGRID*, 2015.

72. Snir et al. Addressing failures in exascale computing. *IJHPCA*, 28(2):129–173, 2014.

73. Simon Spinner, Samuel Kounev, Xiaoyun Zhu, Lei Lu, Mustafa Uysal, Anne Holler, and Rean Griffith. Runtime vertical scaling of virtualized applications via online model estimation. In *SASO*, 2014.

74. Priya K. Sundararajan, Eugen Feller, Julien Forgeat, and Ole J. Mengshoel. A constrained genetic algorithm for rebalancing of services in cloud data centers. In *CLOUD*, 2015.

75. Vincent van Beek, Jesse Donkervliet, Tim Hegeman, Stefan Hugtenburg, and Alexandru Iosup. Mnemos: Self-expressive management of business-critical workloads in virtualized datacenters. *IEEE Computer*, 48(7):46–54, 2015.

76. Qiushi Wang and Katinka Wolter. Reducing task completion time in mobile offloading systems through online adaptive local restart. In *ICPE*, 2015.

77. Pengcheng Xiong, Calton Pu, Xiaoyun Zhu, and Rean Griffith. vPerfGuard: An automated model-driven framework for application performance diagnosis in consolidated cloud environments. In *ICPE*, 2013.

78. Yong Yang, Lu Su, Mohammad Khan, Michael Lemay, Tarek Abdelzaher, and Jiawei Han. Power-based diagnosis of node silence in remote high-end sensing systems. *ACM Trans. Sen. Netw.*, 11(2):33:1–33:33, 2014.

79. Nezih Yigitbasi, Matthieu Gallet, Derrick Kondo, Alexandru Iosup, and Dick H. J. Epema. Analysis and modeling of time-correlated failures in large-scale distributed systems. In *GRID*, 2010.

Chapter 21
Software Architectures for Self-protection in IaaS Clouds

K.R. Jayaram, Aleksandar Milenkoski and Samuel Kounev

Abstract In this chapter, we focus on software architectures for self-protection in IaaS clouds. IaaS clouds, especially hybrid clouds, are becoming increasingly popular because of the need for developers and enterprises to dynamically increase/decrease their use of computing resources to adapt quickly to market forces and customer demands, reduce costs, and increase fault tolerance. However, the adoption of public IaaS and hybrid clouds by enterprises is slower than expected because the current hybrid cloud infrastructures do not provide scalable and efficient mechanisms to prevent software tampering and configuration errors and ensure the trustworthiness and integrity of the software stack executing a hybrid application workload; or to enforce governmental privacy and audit regulations by ensuring that remote data and computation do not cross specified geographic boundaries. We discuss the recent research on integrating intrusion detection systems in IaaS infrastructures, as well as hardware-rooted integrity verification and geographic fencing to address the concerns outlined above.

21.1 Introduction

Enterprises have been adopting cloud computing in a variety of different abstraction levels, namely software-, platform-, and infrastructure-as-a-service systems, and in different deployment models (private, public, hybrid, and community). Security/protection issues/concerns associated with cloud computing differ according to the abstraction-level and deployment model but fall into two broad categories:

K.R. Jayaram (✉)
IBM Thomas J. Watson Research Center, New York City, NY, USA
e-mail: jayaramkr@us.ibm.com

A. Milenkoski · S. Kounev
University of Wurzburg, Würzburg, Germany
e-mail: aleksandar.milenkoski@uni-wuerzburg.de

S. Kounev
e-mail: samuel.kounev@uni-wuerzburg.de

© Springer International Publishing AG 2017
S. Kounev et al. (eds.), *Self-Aware Computing Systems*,
DOI 10.1007/978-3-319-47474-8_21

- security issues faced by cloud providers (organizations providing software-, platform-, or infrastructure-as-a-service via the cloud) and
- security issues faced by their customers (companies or organizations who host applications or store data on the cloud).

The responsibility for security and protection thus goes both ways; however, it is often the responsibility of the provider to:

- (as much as possible) ensure that their infrastructure is secure and that client data and applications are protected
- make it easy for the customer to take measures to fortify their application and encourage the use of strong passwords and authentication methods as general policy in their cloud

Before discussing system and software architectures for self-protection in cloud computing, let us address the main security threats faced by enterprise applications deployed in the cloud. We focus on threats that arise *due to the cloud*; i.e., they add to threats already faced by the application when it is deployed in a private data center in a customer-facing scenario. It is generally recommended that information security controls be selected and implemented according and in proportion to the risks, typically by assessing the threats, vulnerabilities, and impacts. While cloud security concerns can be grouped into any number of dimensions, some are outlined below:

- **Configuration and patching errors**. The extensive use of virtualization in cloud infrastructures brings unique security concerns for tenants of a public, private, and hybrid cloud services. Virtualization alters the relationships between applications and the underlying hardware, especially given the fact that even networking functions are virtualized in modern data center. The virtualization layers themselves have to be properly configured, managed, and secured. Specific concerns include compromises to the virtualization layer, especially the hypervisor. For example, a breach in the administrator workstation with the management software of the virtualization software can cause the whole data center to go down or be reconfigured to an attacker's liking. Typically, the cloud provider asks the customer to "trust" that the provider has performed all the necessary configurations, patching, etc., accurately. However, instead of blindly "trusting" the cloud provider, a better approach is to follow the classic "trust, but to verify" paradigm, where the cloud provider offers some visibility into the internal configuration and attests to its correctness and security compliance.
- **Software tampering**. When an organization elects to store data or host applications on the public cloud, it loses its ability to have physical access to the servers hosting its information. As a result, potentially business sensitive and confidential data are at risk from insider attacks. According to a recent Cloud Security Alliance report, insider attacks are the third biggest threat in cloud computing. Therefore, cloud service providers must ensure that thorough background checks are conducted for employees who have physical access to the servers in the data center. Additionally, data centers must be frequently monitored for suspicious

activity. But, such manual methods may not always be effective. We need automated integrity verification of the software stack executing applications in the cloud. A key hurdle to increased adoption of cloud computing infrastructures is a concern about the security of the software stack executing the workload. In a survey of large enterprises by Forrester, 46 % of respondents indicated that "Ensuring that the security policies on applications, operating systems, and workloads are the same in the public cloud as our data center" as a key hurdle for increased adoption of cloud computing infrastructures. There is a broad agreement that verbal or written assurances of cloud providers in advertisements and service-level agreements regarding security and compliance are not sufficient. Encryption of all data and homomorphic computations can assure data confidentiality only if the code performing encryptions does not maliciously do something else with the data. Certificates of computation based on probabilistically checkable proofs (PCPs) and trusted computing platforms based on said proofs are still not practical, requiring customization for each application and incurring high overheads.

- **Isolation and Security Management**. In order to conserve resources, cut costs, and maintain efficiency, cloud service providers often store more than one customer's data on the same server. As a result, there is a chance that one user's private data can be viewed by other users (possibly even competitors). To handle such sensitive situations, cloud service providers should ensure proper data isolation and logical storage segregation. A cloud self-protection architecture is effective only if the correct defensive implementations are in place. An efficient self-protection architecture should recognize the issues that will arise with security management. The security management addresses these issues with security controls. These controls are put in place to safeguard any weaknesses in the system and reduce the effect of an attack.
- **Identity management**: Every enterprise will have its own identity management system to control access to information and computing resources. Cloud providers either integrate the customer's identity management system (e.g., enterprise Kerberos) into their own infrastructure, using federation or SSO technology, or provide an identity management solution of their own (e.g., OpenStack KeyStone).
- **Physical security**: Cloud service providers physically secure the IT hardware (servers, routers, cables, etc.) against unauthorized access, interference, theft, fires, floods, etc., and ensure that essential supplies (such as electricity) are sufficiently robust to minimize the possibility of disruption. This is normally achieved by serving cloud applications from "world-class" (i.e., professionally specified, designed, constructed, managed, monitored, and maintained) data centers.
- **Application security**: Application security (short: AppSec) encompasses measures taken throughout the code's life cycle to prevent gaps in the security policy of an application or the underlying system (vulnerabilities) through flaws in the design, development, deployment, upgrade, or maintenance of the application. This includes measures against software tampering, where an attacker modifies an existing application's run-time behavior to perform unauthorized actions, exploited via binary patching, code substitution, or code extension. This also includes preventing unauthorized access to administration interfaces; unauthorized access to

configuration stores; retrieval of clear text configuration data; lack of individual accountability; and overprivileged process and service accounts

While there are many types of defense mechanisms behind a cloud self-protection architecture, they are broadly classified into:

- *Deterrent mechanisms*: These techniques are intended to reduce attacks on a cloud system. Much like a warning sign on a fence or a property, deterrent controls typically reduce the threat level by informing potential attackers that there will be adverse consequences for them if they proceed. (Some consider them a subset of preventive controls.)
- *Prevention mechanisms*: Preventive controls strengthen the system against incidents, generally by reducing if not actually eliminating vulnerabilities. Strong authentication of cloud users, for instance, makes it less likely that unauthorized users can access cloud systems and more likely that cloud users are positively identified.
- *Detection mechanisms*: Detection mechanisms are intended to detect and react appropriately to any incidents that occur. In the event of an attack, a detective control will signal the preventative or corrective controls to address the issue. System and network security monitoring, including intrusion detection and prevention arrangements, are typically employed to detect the attacks on cloud systems and the supporting communications infrastructure.
- *Corrective mechanisms*: Corrective controls reduce the consequences of an incident, normally by limiting the damage. They come into effect during or after an incident. Restoring system backups in order to rebuild a compromised system is an example of a corrective control.

In this chapter, we focus on software architectures for self-protection in IaaS clouds. IaaS clouds, especially hybrid clouds, are becoming increasingly popular because of the need for developers and enterprises to dynamically increase/decrease their use of computing resources to adapt quickly to market forces and customer demands, reduce costs, and increase fault tolerance. However, the adoption of hybrid clouds by enterprises is slower than expected because current hybrid cloud infrastructures do not provide scalable and efficient mechanisms to prevent software tampering and configuration errors and ensure the trustworthiness and integrity of the software stack executing a hybrid application workload; or to enforce governmental privacy and audit regulations by ensuring that remote data and computation do not cross specified geographic boundaries.

In traditional data centers, workloads and data were often static and had a hard binding to the physical systems on which they resided and executed. However, virtualization has made the migration of data and computing resources across physical hosts easy. Virtual machine (VM) migration is performed by data center and cloud management systems for a host of reasons including load balancing, consolidation, and maintenance. A private data center can employ sophisticated cluster management middleware and algorithms to reliably identify the location of physical servers on which the data and workloads reside during initial placement and migration and can put security policies in place to ensure that the management middleware is not compromised. But, this is infeasible in current IaaS cloud implementations, because it would require the cloud provider to expose its systems to a customer/developer who may be malicious.

Organizations considering hybrid clouds, however, need to produce audit trails of data and application movement, as well as carry out effective forensics when the occasion demands it. In particular, the workload location identification and attestation capability need to be verifiable and auditable by the customer and/or his designated third party and preferably anchored in hardware. These capabilities enable workload and data boundary control in hybrid clouds, effectively conferring users to control over where workloads and data are created, where they are run, and where they migrate to for performance, optimization, reliability, and high-availability purposes.

Given the enormous overheads involved in proof-carrying code and in PCP-based verifiable computation, in real-world deployments, ensuring trust in the public IaaS cloud's software stack (hypervisor, VM, and libraries) often involves *software integrity verification*—checking whether specific "known bug-free" or formally verified/model-checked versions of hypervisors, OS, and libraries are used by the IaaS provider, preventing injection of malicious code into the software stack and preventing low-level attacks on the hypervisor like those involving root kits. Hence, a self-protection architecture should provide:

- ability for developers to specify, at a high level, the integrity requirements of the software stack executing his applications/workloads,
- ensure compliance at run time by certifying the integrity of the software stack through certificates verifiable by the developer or a third party trusted by him,
- allow the specification of geographic locations and boundaries pertaining to computations in both IaaS and PaaS applications and ensure their compliance during placement of virtual machines (at the start of execution) and during VM life cycle events such as resizing, migration, and fault recovery, and
- perform all the available tasks at the scale of massive data centers and IaaS clouds, which contain hundreds of thousands of virtual machine instances.

21.2 Intrusion Detection Systems

An intrusion detection system (IDS) is a device or software application that monitors network or system activities for malicious activities or policy violations and produces reports to a management station. IDS comes in a variety of flavors and approaches the goal of detecting suspicious traffic in different ways. There are network-based (NIDS) and host-based (HIDS) intrusion detection systems. NIDS is a network security system focusing on the attacks that come from the inside of the network (authorized users). When we classify the design of the NIDS according to the system interactivity property, there are two types: online and off-line NIDS.

Online NIDS deals with the network in real time; it analyzes TCP/IP and UDP packets and applies some rules to decide whether there exists an attack or not. Off-line

NIDS deals with stored data and runs some analytics on the data to decide whether it is an attack or not. Some systems may attempt to stop an intrusion attempt, but this is neither required nor expected of a monitoring system. Intrusion detection and prevention systems (IDPSs) are primarily focused on identifying possible incidents, logging information about them, and reporting attempts. In addition, organizations use IDPSs for other purposes, such as identifying problems with security policies, documenting existing threats, and deterring individuals from violating security policies. IDPSs have become a necessary addition to the security infrastructure of nearly every organization using cloud computing systems.

IDPSs typically record information related to observed events, notify security administrators of important observed events, and produce reports. Many IDPSs can also respond to a detected threat by attempting to prevent it from succeeding. They use several response techniques, which involve the IDPS stopping the attack itself, changing the security environment (e.g., reconfiguring a firewall), or changing the attack's content

21.2.1 NIDS

Network intrusion detection systems (NIDSs) are placed at a strategic point or points within the network to monitor traffic to and from all devices on the network. An NIDS performs an analysis of passing traffic on the entire subnet and matches the traffic that is passed on the subnets to the library of known attacks. Once an attack is identified, or abnormal behavior is sensed, the alert can be sent to the administrator. An example of an NIDS would be installing it on the subnet where firewalls are located in order to see whether someone is trying to break into the firewall. Ideally, one would scan all inbound and outbound traffic; however, doing so might create a bottleneck that would impair the overall speed of the network. OPNET and NetSim are commonly used tools for simulation network intrusion detection systems. NID systems are also capable of comparing signatures for similar packets to link and drop harmful detected packets which have a signature matching the records in the NIDS. Providing NIDS systems is typically the responsibility of the IaaS cloud provider.

It is important to emphasize that the wide adoption of virtualization, a key enabling technology of cloud computing, has led to the emergence of the practice of deploying conventional NIDS as virtualized network functions (VNFs); that is, a network-based IDS may be deployed in a designated VM and configured to tap into the physical network interface card used by all VMs (see Chap. 22). Thus, the IDS can monitor the network activities of all VMs at the same time while being isolated from, and transparent to, their users.

21.2.2 HIDS

Host intrusion detection systems (HIDSs) run on individual hosts or devices on the network. A HIDS monitors the inbound and outbound packets from the device only and will alert the user or administrator if suspicious activity is detected. It takes a snapshot of existing system files and matches it to the previous snapshot. If the critical system files were modified or deleted, an alert is sent to the administrator to investigate.

In the case of IaaS clouds, HIDS should be deployed at both the hypervisor level and virtual machine level. In contrast to HIDS deployed at virtual machine level, providing HIDS at hypervisor level is a responsibility of the IaaS cloud provider.

Typical IaaS cloud IDS architectures have to provide good visibility into the state of the monitored host, while still providing strong isolation for the IDS, thus lending significant resistance to both evasion and attack. Typical hypervisor-based approaches leverage virtual machine monitor (VMM) technology. This mechanism enables the IDS to be placed external to the host it is monitoring, into a completely different hardware protection domain, providing a high-confidence barrier between the IDS and an attacker's malicious code. The VMM also provides the ability to directly inspect the hardware state of the virtual machine that a monitored host is running on. The VMM provides the ability to interpose at the architecture interface of the monitored host, yielding even better visibility than normal OS-level mechanisms by enabling monitoring of both hardware and software level events. This ability to interpose at the hardware interface also allows the IDS to mediate interactions between the hardware and the host software, allowing it to perform both intrusion detection and hardware access control.

An IDS running outside of a virtual machine only has access to hardware-level state (e.g., physical memory pages and registers) and events (e.g., interrupts and memory accesses), generally not the level of abstraction where we want to reason about IDS policies. Typical hypervisor-based IDSs leverage three properties of VMMs:

- Isolation: Software running in a virtual machine cannot access or modify the software running in the VMM or in a separate VM. Isolation ensures that even if an intruder has completely subverted the monitored host, he still cannot tamper with the IDS.
- Inspection: The VMM has access to all the state of a virtual machine: CPU state (e.g., registers), all memory, and all I/O device state such as the contents of storage devices and register state of I/O controllers. Being able to directly inspect the virtual machine makes it particularly difficult to evade a VMM IDS since there is no state in the monitored system that the IDS cannot see.
- Interposition: Fundamentally, VMMs need to interpose on certain virtual machine operations (e.g., executing privileged instructions). A VMM IDS can leverage this functionality for its own purposes. For example, with only minimal modification to the VMM, a VMM IDS can be notified if the code running in the VM attempts to modify a given register. VMMs offer other properties that are quite useful in a VMM IDS. For example, VMMs completely encapsulate the state of a virtual machine in software. This allows it to easily take a checkpoint of the virtual machine. Using this capability, we can compare the state of a VM under observation to a suspended VM in a known-good state, easily perform analysis off-line, or capture the entire state of a compromised machine for forensic purposes.

21.3 Trustworthy Geo-fenced IaaS and Hybrid Clouds

This section described the recent research on trustworthy geographically fenced hybrid clouds (TGHCs), a generic, scalable, and extensible middleware system to automatically bridge the gap between applications with their integrity and geo-fencing policies, and raw hardware infrastructure. It describes TGHCs modularly, by (a) outlining the challenges in certifying the trustworthiness of cloud computing infrastructures and in geo-fencing computation, including scalability limitations of existing solutions, (b) presenting scalable mechanisms to transform bare metal servers into trusted IaaS computing pools through integrity measurement, management, and monitoring that leverage open, off-the-shelf hardware technologies like Intel TPM, (c) introducing workload specification languages to specify integrity and geo-fencing policies on hybrid workloads, and (d) extending IaaS systems to ensure that workload bursting from private data centers to public clouds uses trusted computing pools and respects geographic boundaries during initial placement of virtual machines (VMs) and further migration. TGHCs are expected to be:

- *Generic*, targeted at a variety of distributed applications programmed in different languages and employing different software architectures, e.g., event-based and loosely coupled, service oriented, tightly coupled, and legacy softwares.
- *Fine-grained and Flexible,* offering developers the flexibility to chose between two granularities in their specification of integrity and "trustworthiness" policies, i.e., either using (1) application-level abstractions such as classes, components, and executables or (2) using IaaS abstractions such as VMs and VM pools/patterns.
- *Scalable,* enabling it to be applied to modern distributed applications and deployed to real-world clouds.
- *Easy to use,* requiring minimal effort from the developer, and requiring no more effort than the specification of integrity and geo-location policies in a high-level policy language/template and no more run-time configuration than state-of-the-art orchestration systems such as Puppet and Chef.

21.3.1 A Modular Hybrid IaaS Cloud

Figure 21.1 illustrates the architecture of TGHCs:

1. An IaaS infrastructure based on *open* standards, where the integrity and geographic location of each component—VM provisioning, migration, network provisioning, block and object storage, etc.,—is attested by certification authorities and can be trusted by developers and enterprises (modulo their trust in certification authorities).
2. Hybrid IaaS orchestration middleware, which leverages the infrastructure above to (a) enable the specification of integrity and geo-location policies at the level of IaaS cloud abstractions, i.e., using VM instances, virtual LANs, monitoring components and patterns and (b) ensure compliance with said policies at all stages

Fig. 21.1 A high-level overview of our trusted geo-fenced hybrid clouds vision

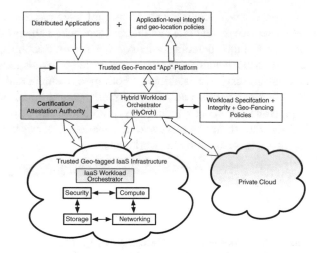

during the lifetime of the pattern by certifying bare metal compute infrastructure and the entire software stack executing on them—hypervisors, libraries, guest OS in VM instances, etc., along with the application binaries.

3. Ensure that the design and implementation of the components above is extensible and modular, enabling future design of trustworthy hybrid application platforms that use the trusted IaaS cloud. This paper, however, focusses on trusted hybrid IaaS and describes the research challenges in engineering hybrid geo-fenced application platforms.

21.3.2   Trusted Geo-Tagged IaaS Infrastructure

As illustrated in Fig. 21.1, a trusted geographically tagged IaaS infrastructure forms the basis of TGHCs. It consists of a trusted pool of servers running a trusted software stack, on which both customer workloads and management systems (i.e., those responsible for workload placement, migration, network provisioning, security, and storage) are executed. Each server in this trusted computing pool (TCP) runs a trusted software stack, i.e., the infrastructure ensures that neither the hypervisor, operating system, nor any of the packages on it have been maliciously modified and are "known-good" versions, as specified by the developer. Furthermore, the infrastructure measures the integrity of all additional patches, application code, and application middleware (e.g., Web servers and database servers) that are loaded at run time and attests their integrity to an attestation service run by a trusted third party.

The key challenge is to perform all these functions automatically. We propose using hardware-based security techniques to ensure the integrity of the software stack on the trusted IaaS. Specifically, Sect. 21.3.4 describes how we leverage off-the-shelf hardware chips (trusted platform modules or TPMs) to measure the integrity of hypervisors, operating systems, and software packages and interact with the attestation service to get these measurements checked against those supplied by the manufacturer of the operating system or hypervisor. Section 21.3.7 describes how TPMs can be further leveraged to securely store and transmit geographic location tags to the attestation service. Scalability of both measurement and attestation is key, because a trusted computing pool can potentially contain thousands of servers. Hardware-rooted attestation helps reduce trust placed in cloud providers, because the customer can use the attestation service to independently verify the integrity and geo-location of the servers executing his workloads.

21.3.3 IaaS Orchestration Middleware

The next component, as illustrated in Fig. 21.1, is the IaaS workload orchestrator, which interacts with the trusted geo-tagged compute pool, the third-party attestation service, and optionally, a workload specification from the developer. The IaaS cloud provider deploys the workload orchestrator on a trusted serverl; i.e., the cloud provider first uses the techniques mentioned above and detailed in Sect. 21.3.4 to boot a trusted operating system on a server and certify it to the attestation service. Then, it employs the techniques described in Sect. 21.3.4 to verify the integrity of the workload binares and deploys the workload on the trusted server connecting it to the attestation service. If the developer prefers to specify the public cloud portion of his hybrid cloud application as a pattern of virtual machines, e.g., using template languages such as OpenStack HOT, the IaaS workload orchestrator parses this specification and interacts with the attestation service to determine the subset of nodes in the IaaS provider's data center that are trusted in the geographic location specified by the developer. Then, orchestrator then deploys the VMs on trusted nodes while respecting geographic boundaries and instantiates the public cloud component of the application. Furthermore, all subsequent elastic scaling and VM migration only occur on trusted servers and respect geographic boundaries (geo-fencing).

21.3.4 Converting Raw Servers to Trusted Servers

The first step in engineering TGHCs is to create a pool of trusted servers that can be managed by the IaaS management software, especially the IaaS workload orchestrator. Converting raw servers to trusted servers involves leveraging and extends the best ideas from all existing system integrity verification techniques. A modular approach can be employed to create a trusted server, by starting from a small piece of trusted code stored securely in a crypto-processor to boot a trusted operating system and hypervisor, and then modularly use the trusted OS to validate all software packages on the server.

21.3.4.1   A Hardware Root of Trust

In current cloud computing systems, security (including malware prevention, detection, and remediation) is handled primarily by software—either at the operating system level or by the cloud management, authentication, and authorization systems. This requires customers to place higher levels of trust in cloud providers. A better approach is the creation of a root of trust at foundational layer of the system—hardware. Like other proposals [13], we use the trusted platform module (TPM) chip [11], a standard crypto-processor established by the trusted computing group (TCG) [10], to instantiate a root of trust at every server. Then, that root of trust grows upward, into and through the operating system, applications, and service layers. TPM provides many security functions including special registers, called platform configuration registers (PCRs) [11], which hold various measurements in a shielded location in a manner that prevents spoofing. Most laptops and desktops have been sold with a TPM module since 2006, and server motherboards are increasingly incorporating TPM chips.

21.3.4.2   OS + Hypervisor Boot Integrity

Most existing solutions for trustworthy clouds, including the EU TClouds [2] project the proposal by Intel [13], use trusted boot [9] based on trusted BIOS code—intel trusted execution technology (TXT) code [3, 13]. The TPM chip containing the TXT code is manually installed into servers in a data center. When OS booting starts, TXT measures (hashes) the initial boot code and commits the measurement to the TPM chip, which stores the measurement in PCRs. TXT measures the next piece of code to be executed and extends a platform configuration register (PCR) in the TPM based on the measurement in the PCR before the control is transferred to the next program loaded during the boot process. If each new code module loaded during the booting process in turn measures the next one before transferring control, there is a chain of trust established. If this measurement chain continues through the entire boot sequence, the resultant PCR values will reflect the measurement of all files used. TXT and TPM can attest (prove) this measurement to a third party by signing the measurement with a private key known only inside the TPM. The corresponding public key can be used by the third-party (attestation server) to verify the signature and thus the measurement of the boot code. To protect against the replay of measurements, the attestation protocol uses cryptographic nonces. The TPM is designed so that once a measurement is added to a PCR register, no operating system or user-level software can reset or remove the value; only a hardware reboot resets the chip and thus restarts the booting process, reinstantiating the root of trust. This *measurement before execution* model therefore leads to a chain of trust that is observable by the attestation service.

   In trusted boot, measurements can be of code, data structures, configuration, information, or anything that can be loaded into system memory. To further protect the integrity of the measurements, hash measurements are not written to PCRs, but rather a PCR is "extended" with a measurement. This means that the TPM takes the current value of the PCR and the measurement to be extended, hashes them together, and replaces the content of the PCR with that hash result. The effect is that the only way to arrive at a particular measurement in a PCR is to extend exactly the same measurements in exactly the same order. Therefore, if any module being measured has been modified, the resulting PCR measurement will be different, and thus, it is easy to detect whether any code, configuration, data, etc., that has been measured had been altered or corrupted. However, this mechanism has scalability issues when applied to a large ensemble of machines in a data center, which we address in the following sections. We explain two alternatives and then propose a mechanism for scalable verifiability.

21.3.4.3   Verifiability, but No Scalability with Native TXT

Trusted boot using Intel TXT and TPM, in their existing forms, can be used to prove the integrity of the operating system and hypervisor and all subsequent software packages that are installed on them to perform various functions (e.g., profiling, ssh, and Web server), as proposed by [2, 13]. If the chain of measurements during the boot process is kept by the attestation service in a software maintained list, it can be attested and verified, by the attestation service against the signed PCR value. If at any point, a piece of code is malicious, the model guarantees that the measurement of the malicious code is included in the list. Any attempt by malicious code to modify the measurement list would cause the validation to fail.

However, *this approach used by* [2, 13] *simply does not scale*. The attestation service, which has to check the measurements, should have not only a list of all possible "known-good" measurements for all versions of all operating systems and all versions of each trusted software package, but also all combinations of operating systems and subsets of software packages. This is because of the way trusted boot extends integrity measurements in PCRs—assuming that there are K operating systems and each operating system has at most P compatible packages, each server may chose to install an operating system and any subset of the P packages. So, the attestation server has to store $O(2^P)$ hash measurements for each OS, and they check the measurement reported by the TPM chip against these. The size of the *white list* is consequently $O(K \times 2^P)$. The attestation server has to perform this checking for thousands of machines in a data center and should accommodate multiple versions of packages to be of any real use.

To alleviate this, there have been proposals to modify TXT to record the sequence in which each code module is hashed and send the sequence to the attestation server. Then, the attestation server can compute expected integrity measurement by hashing the $p < P$ stored hash measurements corresponding to the p packages actually installed by the server containing TPM and TXT. Although this only requires the storage of $O(K \times P)$ hash measurements, it still has scalability limitations—we created a whitelist database for recent Fedora and RHEL distributions (Fedora 15–19, and RHEL 6). One such typical release has over 5000 available packages, with around 400,000 files. In addition, these packages are frequently updated within a release. The kernel packages are particularly large, each containing some 3,000 kernel modules, and each was updated on average 10–20 times. After a few months, the database grew to over 30 GB, growing progressively slower, and exceeding the partition allocated for it.

21.3.4.4   Scalability, but No Verifiability with Linux IMA

A popular integrity model is secure boot [12], which stores one or more public keys in the TPM chip. The keys can only be updated with physical presence. Secure boot assumes that all code is signed (which is reasonable for most modern software systems), and the public keys stored in the TPM are used to appraise (verify) signatures on the boot code, and if the signatures are not correct, the boot is terminated. Secure boot can also root a chain of trust, in which each stage verifies the signature on the next stage. The Linux integrity subsystem also supports digital signature appraisal with the IMA appraisal module [7], thus extending the secure boot chain of trust up into the Linux file systems. Digital signatures provide both integrity and authenticity, and they do so in a much more scalable way than simple measurements. However, this creates the problem of managing keys in the TPM module. Due to the fact that they can be updated only with physical presence, it is difficult to add or remove software vendors to a cloud application. One way to get around this is to sign all files with just the IaaS cloud provider's private key, but that defeats the whole purpose of reducing trust in the cloud provider. Also, secure boot model does not provide a hardware-rooted attestation to a third party, so a centralized management system cannot tell whether a system has been compromised.

21.3.4.5   Scalable Verifiability

A better approach is to use Intel's TXT technology to measure and attest the boot loader, kernel, and hypervisor code, along with the public keys of all trusted software and data vendors. If all the public keys are stored in one file, the attestation server should only store $O(K)$ measurements, assuming that there are K (bootloader + kernel + hypervisor) combinations. Further, integrity verification of the software packages can be accomplished by checking their digital signatures with the public keys of trusted software vendors through Linux's IMA appraisal module. This does not require developers to exclusively use software signed by the IaaS provider and also scales to a large number of software packages and versions by avoiding the storage of 2^P measurements. However, the TPM module is required in the physical compute host to certify the host's integrity to the attestation service, and verifying digital signatures through IMA does not accomplish this. Consequently, the IaaS provider and user should only trust hypervisors and operating systems with IMA code that verifies the digital signature of each executable before loading it during the boot process or before executing it in response to user needs. In other words, the way to ensure that the operating system/hypervisor on a server does not execute untrusted code is to (1) choose operating systems with kernels that check the signatures of all executables and do not have mechanisms to circumvent the digital signature verification process and (2) verify that the server has booted one of the *said kernels* at run time by measuring its integrity through TXT and attesting to the same through a trusted third-party attestation service. Once this is done, the booted kernel ensures that all subsequent software is digitally signed obviating the need to individually attest the hash of each package. Hardware-rooted attestation helps reduce trust placed in cloud providers, because the customer can use the attestation service to independently verify the integrity and geo-location of the servers executing his workloads. Furthermore, such techniques protect against and detect any attack on persistent data (files), regardless of whether it comes through the main processor's network interface or the management modules interface. Even a remote root is unable to forge a valid signature. This is because of the trusted BIOS code (TXT) which hashes each component during the boot process to boot a secure kernel, which subsequently does not allow any unsigned program to execute. Hence, attacks are impossible unless the attacker has the ability to break strong cryptographic primitives.

21.3.5   vTPMs and VM Launch Integrity

Through trusted hypervisor boot, we can ensure the integrity of prelaunch and launch components on a platform, from the BIOS to the operating system and hypervisor. However, no specific claims can be made about the virtual machines being launched, other than indicating that they are being launched on a measured and attested hypervisor platform. Although virtual machine monitors (VMMs) or hypervisors are naturally good at isolating workloads from each other because they mediate all access to physical resources by virtual machines, they cannot by themselves attest and assert the state of the virtual machine that is launched. Each virtual machine launched on a virtual machine manager and hypervisor platform can benefit from a hardware root of trust by storing its launch measurements in the TPM. However, this requires virtualizing the TPM, with a virtual TPM (vTPM) for each of the virtual machines. Each of these virtual TPM (vTPM) instances then emulates the functions of a hardware TPM.

One approach is to use the open-source IBM vTPM [1] system for TGHCs. It is to provide a TPM functionality to a virtual guest operating system. This allows programs to interact with a TPM in a virtual system the same way they interact with a TPM on the physical system. Each guest gets its own unique, emulated software TPM. However, each of the vTPM's secrets (Keys, NVRAM, etc.) is managed by a vTPM Manager domain, which seals the secrets to the physical TPM. If the process of creating each of these domains (manager, vTPM, and guest) is trusted, the vTPM subsystem extends the chain of trust rooted in the hardware TPM to virtual machines in the hypervisor. Each major component of vTPM is implemented as a separate domain, providing a secure separation guaranteed by the hypervisor.

Once vTPMs are instantiated, the launch of guest operating systems can be trusted and so can the packages installed on the guest operating systems. This is done using the scalable verifiability technique presented in Sect. 21.3.4.5.

21.3.6   Scalable Third-Party Attestation

The attestation server is typically managed by a trusted third party (TTP). Each server in a trusted infrastructure pool connects to the attestation server to provide TXT integrity measurement hash values, which are then checked by the attestation server against its database of integrity measurements. The most common attestation server is Intel's OpenAttestation server (OAT), which uses a `mysql` database to store hash values. The attestation server can be run either by a TTP or by the developer himself, if the IaaS cloud provider is willing to trust the developer with cryptographically secure hashes of its operating systems, software, and hypervisors. This is not uncommon, especially in aerospace, defense, and other sensitive workloads from governmental agencies. The main drawback of the existing OAT server and its implementation is that it still requires storage of hashes of all combinations of operating systems and software packages (2^P) as discussed above and that it is a stand-alone server which is neither highly available nor elastic. To scale to trusted IaaS pools, these mechanisms for scalable verifiability have been incorporated into Intel's OAT implementation, while additionally replacing the storage layer with a distributed three-way replicated key-value store (HyperDex), running on servers that have been manually verified to be trustworthy.

21.3.7   Trusted Geo-Location

The next step in engineering TGHCs is to identify the geographic location of each trusted server and to be able to certify its location to a trusted third party that also attests to the integrity of the software stack. In turn, cloud management software uses the trusted server location information to enforce constraints of sensitive applications with geo-fencing requirements. Geo-fencing ensures that the requirements on geographic boundaries are not violated and furthermore, if violations are detected, then appropriate remedial actions will be taken. In this section, we first outline an existing manual location provisioning technique and propose an RFID-based geo-location technique to reduce trust placed in a cloud provider. Manual location provisioning and the use of RFID tags described below are the only two solutions currently feasible using *off-the-shelf* hardware.

21.3.7.1 Manual Location Provisioning Using the Trusted Platform Module (TPM)

The IaaS cloud provider, administrator, or a trusted third party can securely provision the location (geo-tag) of the server motherboard (postal code, GPS coordinates, city/state/country) to the TPM chip on the motherboard when the server is installed in the cloud data center. There are no hardware changes required in this approach; the existing TPM takes care of secure storage for the geo-tags. Yeluri and Castro-Leon [13] provide an overview of this proposal—by reusing the PCR22 of the TPM. PCRs are *nonvolatile* RAM, and consequently, the location stored survives reboots unless PCR22 is manually erased and the TPM reprovisioned. The TCG specifications [9] allocate PCR22 in the TPM for OS/VMM use, and popular hypervisors such as VMWare ESX, Xen, and KVM do not use it for other purposes. The only drawback with manual provisioning is that it requires the developer to place some trust in the IaaS provider and its employees—to not physically remove the motherboard and ship it to another data center.

21.3.7.2 RFID Tags

A solution to slightly reduce the trust placed in an IaaS provider is to use radio-frequency identification (RFID) asset tags in servers in combination with a a specialized hardware tamperproof asset tracker. The asset tracker is installed by a trusted third party (TTP) in a data center and connects to the TTP's attestation service through a network connection separate from the IaaS provider's network, e.g., using a different wired ISP other than the IaaS provider or through high-speed wireless network (4G LTE) SIM cards or through satellite Internet. The tamperproof asset tracker consists of an RFID tracker, a GPS locator chip, and a trusted server that can read the GPS chip and RFID tracker to communicate with the TTP's attestation service. Each server in the data center is provisioned with an active secure RFID asset tag (costs about $30 per tag) that periodically transmits a tupple, consisting of the RFID tag's identifier and the server motherboard's universally unique identifier (UUID), encrypted by a shared key (shared between the active RFID tag and the tamperproof asset tracker) or through the asset tracker's public key. The asset tracker, in turn, hashes each of the elements of this tuple and sends them to the attestation service. TXT is also extended to hash the UUID of the motherboard which is securely stored in the TPM module and send this to the attestation service, which can then attest to the location of the server motherboard because it knows the location of the asset tracker.

21.3.8   Trusted Hybrid IaaS

The next step in engineering TGHCs is to transform a group of trusted servers to a trusted IaaS compute pool, which can be used by a hybrid cloud application. Engineering a trusted IaaS is challenging because of the complexity of the components of a modern IaaS cloud manager (e.g., OpenStack). We rely on our modular design approach to realize trustworthy hybrid IaaS clouds as shown in Fig. 21.2.

IaaS clouds consist of VMs, VM instances, and the IaaS management system. The main function of an IaaS cloud is to instantiate a virtual machine (VM) image or a pattern of VM images in response to authenticated user requests and network the instantiated VMs according to the user's specifications. Hence, the main components of an *IaaS management system*, with examples from the open-source IaaS platform OpenStack [5], are (1) authentication and identity management (Keystone), (2) compute provisioning, migration, and resource management (Nova), (3) network provisioning (Neutron), (4) VM image storage and management (Glance), (5) block and object storage, and (6) cloud orchestrator (Heat) and dashboard (Horizon). To realize a trusted IaaS cloud, each of these components must in turn be made trustworthy. In this section, we describe how to create a trusted IaaS using OpenStack

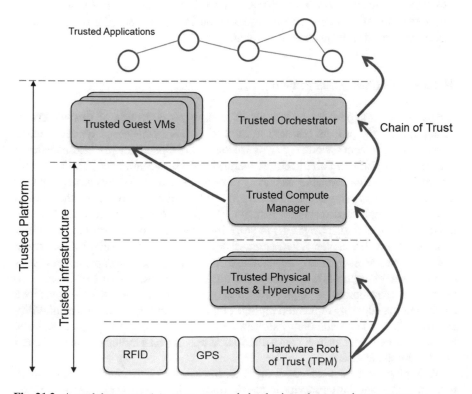

Fig. 21.2 A modular approach to create a trusted cloud using other trusted components

as an example and then detail how a trusted IaaS can be used by a hybrid cloud application.

21.3.8.1 IaaS Management System

For an IaaS cloud to be trusted, its management system should also be trusted. When the IaaS cloud is set up, trusted servers are set up using the techniques in Sect. 21.3.4. Then, various IaaS management packages are installed on some of these trusted servers and validated using the scalable attestation techniques described in Sect. 21.3.4. The customer, in turn, can verify from the attestation service that the management components of the IaaS cloud are running on trusted servers. In the case of OpenStack, Nova, Glance, Swift, Neutron, KeyStone, and Horizon are installed on trusted servers. The open-source nature of OpenStack, whose architecture and implementation have been vetted by an active community of developers, along with attestation of its installation through the third-party attestation service, ensures that the management layer performs as expected. Thus, the root of trust now extends to the IaaS management system, thus ensuring the integrity of the IaaS cloud software stack. A trusted IaaS cloud may contain both trusted and untrusted servers—the only requirements are that it contains a nonzero, nontrivial number of trusted servers and that it executes all its management functions on trusted servers. For this, the basic capability needed is resource management.

21.3.8.2 Resource Management

A trusted compute pool in an IaaS cloud is simply a collection of trusted servers obtained from the process outlined in Sect. 21.3.4. An IaaS cloud typically has a resource management system, e.g., Nova in the case of OpenStack [6]. These resource managers have different architectures (centralized vs. decentralized) and matching algorithms to match available resources to requests and reserve resources for user requests. In this paper, we describe how to implement a trusted computing pool in a centralized/replicated resource manager like Nova. Nova is centralized because it uses a single database (mySQL) to store information about all servers and other components in a data center. When a request (r) arrives at Nova for servers to schedule VM instances, Nova queries the database for available server capacity, retrieves matching server resources to allocate to the VM (e.g., 2 cores, 4 GB RAM on servers), reserves these resources for request r, and instantiates the requested VM on s. Nova can be replicated, using replicated mySQL, both for fault tolerance/high availability and to scale to a large number of servers and VM instantiation/migration requests. Resource allocation then becomes a distributed transaction handled by the replicated mySQL implementation.

To implement a trusted computing pool, the key idea is to connect the resource manager to the attestation service to check the veracity of a server's claims and then to use trustworthiness and geographic location as additional filters during placement and migration. We have extended Nova to communicate with the attestation service to verify whether a server that claims to be running a trusted hypervisor and our scalable attestation software (described in Sect. 21.3.4) is actually doing so. Our Nova implementation then stores information in its database about trusted servers in the computing pool that it manages. Additionally, our Nova also obtains the geographic location of the server and verifies it with the location reported by the attestation service. When a VM instantiation request requires a trusted server in a specific location, our extended Nova modifies its query accordingly to chose a server that has been attested and filters out untrusted servers. Similarly, during the migration of a VM, the new physical server should be attested as a trusted server, before Nova can move a VM to it. Similar techniques can also be used in other cloud resource managers, such as Omega [8] and Mesos [4], by connecting the resource manager to the attestation service, modifying its matching algorithm to distinguish between trusted and untrusted servers, and adding geo-location as a data attribute to each trusted server.

21.3.8.3   Authentication and Storage Management

The user authentication and identity management components do not need any changes to work with trusted hybrid IaaS; i.e., KeyStone in the case of OpenStack does not have to be changed. The image management system (Glance) requires minimal changes to ensure that images are stored on trusted geo-located servers, i.e., its API and functionality are extended to specify the location where an image has to be stored. The block store and object store should be extended to ensure that (1) storage requests from a trusted VM instance are handled by and the data stored on a trusted server and (2) the geo-fencing constraints on storage requests from a trusted VM remain the same as the constraints on the VM instance, i.e., if a VM is restricted to execute in the USA, then all its object and block storage reside in the USA.

21.3.8.4   A Trusted IaaS

Though resource management and server management are key components of every IaaS cloud, modern IaaS implementations provide several other functionalities, including but not limited to automatic elastic scaling at the level of virtual machine instances, floating IPs, security groups, virtual LANs, volume storage, and object storage. All such components of the IaaS implementation should be instantiated on trusted servers. Otherwise, malicious code in the other components of the IaaS system can circumvent the protections offered by the trusted compute pool.

In the case of the OpenStack IaaS platform, this includes all its management components, including the authentication and security subsystem (KeyStone), image management system (Glance), and network management (Neutron). In summary, we propose to modularly use TPM and our scalable attestation to convert raw servers into trusted servers attested by a trusted third party. Then, we instantiate OpenStack Nova on one or more trusted servers for resource management, which communicates with each of the servers and with the attestation service to determine whether they are a trusted software stack and their geo-location. We then use trusted Nova to instantiate the other components on trusted servers or trusted Linux VMs.

21.4   Conclusions and Future Research Directions

In this chapter, we have presented two key technologies for self-protection in IaaS clouds and describe their software architecture. This includes intrusion detection systems and hardware-rooted integrity verification of software stack executing applications in the cloud. We have illustrated how these technologies serve as preventive, detective, and deterrent controls for the various threats faced by applications executing in the cloud as outlined in Sect. 21.1.

References

1. Stefan Berger, Ramón Cáceres, Kenneth A. Goldman, Ronald Perez, Reiner Sailer, and Leendert van Doorn. vtpm: Virtualizing the trusted platform module. In *Proceedings of the 15th Conference on USENIX Security Symposium - Volume 15*, USENIX-SS'06, Berkeley, CA, USA, 2006. USENIX Association.
2. EU Framework 7 – TClouds Project. *Trustworthy Clouds Privacy and Resilience for Internet-scale Critical Infrastructure*, 2013. http://www.tclouds-project.eu/index.php/published-results/public-deliverables.
3. W. Futral and J. Greene. *Intel Trusted Execution Technology for Server Platforms*, 2014. http://www.intel.com/content/dam/www/public/us/en/documents/white-papers/trusted-execution-technology-security-paper.pdf.
4. Benjamin Hindman, Andy Konwinski, Matei Zaharia, Ali Ghodsi, Anthony D. Joseph, Randy Katz, Scott Shenker, and Ion Stoica. Mesos: A platform for fine-grained resource sharing in the data center. In *Proceedings of the 8th USENIX Conference on Networked Systems Design and Implementation*, NSDI'11, pages 295–308, Berkeley, CA, USA, 2011. USENIX Association.
5. OpenStack. *OpenStack Architecture*, 2014. http://docs.openstack.org/training-guides/content/module001-ch004-openstack-architecture.html.
6. OpenStack. *Nova Developer Documentation*, 2014. http://docs.openstack.org/developer/nova/.
7. Reiner Sailer, Xiaolan Zhang, Trent Jaeger, and Leendert van Doorn. Design and implementation of a tcg-based integrity measurement architecture. In *Proceedings of the 13th Conference on USENIX Security Symposium - Volume 13*, SSYM'04, pages 16–16, Berkeley, CA, USA, 2004. USENIX Association.
8. Malte Schwarzkopf, Andy Konwinski, Michael Abd-El-Malek, and John Wilkes. Omega: Flexible, scalable schedulers for large compute clusters. In *Proceedings of the 8th ACM European Conference on Computer Systems*, EuroSys '13, pages 351–364, New York, NY, USA, 2013. ACM.
9. Trusted Computing Group. *Trusted Boot*, 2014. http://www.trustedcomputinggroup.org/resources/trusted_boot.
10. Trusted Computing Group. *Trusted Computing Group Web Portal*, 2014. http://www.trustedcomputinggroup.org.

11. Trusted Computing Group. *Trusted Platform Module Specification*, 2014. http://www. trustedcomputinggroup.org/resources/tpm_main_specification.
12. R. Wilkins and B. Richardson. *UEFI Secure Boot in Modern Computer Security Solutions*, 2013. http://www.uefi.org/sites/default/files/resources/UEFI_Secure_Boot_in_ Modern_Computer_Security_Solutions_2013.pdf.
13. R. Yeluri and E. Castro-Leon. *Building the Infrastructure for Cloud Security A Solutions View*. Apress Inc., 2014.

Chapter 22
Benchmarking Intrusion Detection Systems with Adaptive Provisioning of Virtualized Resources

Aleksandar Milenkoski, K.R. Jayaram and Samuel Kounev

Abstract With the increasing popularity of virtualization, deploying intrusion detection systems (IDSes) in virtualized environments, for example, in virtual machines as virtualized network functions, has become an emerging practice. Modern virtualized environments feature on demand provisioning of virtualized processing and memory resources to virtual machines, dynamically adapting its intensity in order to meet resource demands. Such a provisioning may have a significant impact on many properties of an IDS deployed in a virtual machine, for example, on its attack detection accuracy. However, conventional metrics for quantifying IDS attack detection accuracy do not capture this impact, which may lead to inaccurate assessments of the IDS's accuracy at detecting attacks. In this chapter, we discuss in detail on the impact of on demand provisioning of virtualized resources on IDS attack detection accuracy. Further, we discuss on relevant issues related to the use of conventional metrics for quantifying IDS attack detection accuracy. Finally, we present a preliminary metric and measurement methodologies, which allow for the accurate assessment of IDS attack detection accuracy taking on-demand resource provisioning into account.

22.1 Introduction

In recent years, virtualization has received increasing interest, both from industry and academia, as a way to reduce costs through server consolidation and to enhance the flexibility of physical infrastructures. In a virtualized system, governed by a hypervisor, resources such as processor time, disk capacity, and network bandwidth,

A. Milenkoski (✉) · S. Kounev
University of Würzburg, Am Hubland, 97074 Würzburg, Germany
e-mail: milenkoski@acm.org

S. Kounev
e-mail: skounev@acm.org

K.R. Jayaram
Thomas J. Watson Research Center, Yorktown Heights, New York City, NY, USA
e-mail: jayaramkr@us.ibm.com

© Springer International Publishing AG 2017
S. Kounev et al. (eds.), *Self-Aware Computing Systems*,
DOI 10.1007/978-3-319-47474-8_22

are shared among virtual machines (VMs). Each VM accesses physical resources through the hypervisor and is entitled to a predefined fraction of capacity.

While server consolidation through virtualization provides many benefits, it also introduces some new challenges. For example, the increased dynamics and flexibility of virtualized systems increase the need for automated resource management mechanisms to guarantee system stability and adequate quality-of-service [7, 8]. Further, the introduction of a hypervisor and the allocation of multiple VMs on a single physical server are additional critical aspects introducing new potential threats and vulnerabilities [10, 16]. For instance, Gens et al. [3] report that security is a major concern for the users of modern virtualized service infrastructures, followed by availability and performance. Some critical security issues include data integrity, authentication, application security, and so on.

Intrusion detection is a common security mechanism for detecting malicious activities (attacks) in host and/or network environments. The accurate attack detection brings multiple benefits; for example, it allows for timely reaction in order to stop an ongoing attack. This is crucial for mission critical systems with high integrity and availability requirements, such as self-aware systems featuring self-protection (see Chap. 14).

The National Institute of Standards and Technology (NIST) defines intrusion detection as "*the process of monitoring the events occurring in a computer system or network and analyzing them for signs of possible incidents, which are violations or imminent threats of violation of computer security policies, acceptable use policies, or standard security practices*" [18]. Given this definition, under intrusion detection system (IDS), we understand the software that automates the intrusion detection process. The research and industrial communities have designed and developed many intrusion detection systems (IDSes), for example, the community-driven Snort [17] by Sourcefire and the commercial ISS (Internet security systems) by IBM,[1] which use a diverse set of intrusion detection techniques.

The wide adoption of virtualization technology has lead to the emergence of novel IDSes specifically designed to operate in virtualized environments, such as ACPS (Advanced Cloud Protection System) [9], Invincea,[2] Juniper Firefly Host,[3] and vShield Endpoint.[4] Many of these IDSes have components both inside the hypervisor and in a designated, secure VM (normally the host VM), which has several benefits. For instance, they can monitor the network and/or host activities of all collocated VMs and are isolated from malicious VMs' users since they do not operate inside the VMs, but leverage the functionalities of the underlying hypervisor.

The adoption of virtualization technology has also lead to the emergence of the practice of deploying conventional IDSes (e.g., hardware IDS appliances or common software-based IDSes) as virtualized network functions (VNFs). For instance, the

---

[1]http://www-935.ibm.com/services/in/en/it-services/intrusion-detection.html.

[2]http://www.invincea.com/.

[3]http://www.juniper.net/techpubs/en_US/firefly6.0/information-products/pathway-pages/security -virtual-host-product-family-index.html.

[4]https://www.vmware.com/de/products/vsphere/features/endpoint.

network-based IDS Snort [17] may be deployed in a designated VM and configured to tap into the physical network interface card used by all VMs. Thus, the IDS can monitor the network activities of all VMs at the same time while being isolated from, and transparent to, their users. Further, in comparison with deploying hardware IDS appliances, which are expensive and challenging to manage, deploying IDSes as VNFs is cost-effective and makes their management an easier task.

With the increasing complexity of IDSes, the development of methodologies, techniques, and tools for evaluating IDSes has become an important research topic. The benefits of IDS evaluation are manyfold. For instance, one may compare multiple IDSes in terms of their attack detection accuracy in order to deploy an IDS which operates optimally in a given environment, thus reducing the risks of a security breach. Further, one may tune already deployed IDS by varying its configuration parameters and investigating their influence through evaluation tests. This enables the comparison of the evaluation results with respect to the configuration space of the IDS, which can help to identify an optimal configuration. In Chap. 14, we discuss in detail on the importance of IDS evaluation in the context of self-aware systems that feature self-protection.

Any IDS evaluation experiment requires careful planning including the selection of (i) workloads, which are used for exercising the sensors of an IDS under test and (ii) metrics and measurement methodologies, which are used for quantifying IDS properties (e.g., attack detection accuracy). Workloads, metrics, and measurement methodologies are considered the standard components of any evaluation experiment.

A common aspect of all existing metrics for quantifying IDS attack detection accuracy (which we refer to as *IDS evaluation metrics*) is that they are defined with respect to a *fixed* set of hardware resources available to the IDS under test [5]. However, a virtualized environment may have *elastic* properties. Under elasticity, we understand on-demand provisioning (i.e., allocation or deallocation) of virtualized resources (i.e., CPU, memory, or network resources) to VMs, whose intensity dynamically adapts with respect to changes in the intensity of the workloads that the VMs process. For instance, the Xen and VMware VSphere hypervisors allow for on-demand hotplugging virtual CPUs and memory on VMs.[5]

On-demand provisioning of virtualized resources to VMs is also known as *vertical VM scaling*, a topic that has received a considerable amount of attention. Researchers, such as Spinner et al. [20], Xu et al. [22], and Dawoud et al. [1], have developed approaches for fine controlled provisioning of virtualized resources for the purpose of optimizing benefits gained, improving performance isolation between VMs, and so on.

Virtualized resources may be hotplugged on a VM where an IDS operates. This implies that resources can be provisioned and used by an IDS deployed in a virtualized environment during operation, which may have a significant impact on many properties of the IDS, including its attack detection accuracy. Thus, we argue that the use of existing IDS evaluation metrics, which do not take elasticity into account,

[5]See, for example, https://pubs.vmware.com/vsphere-60/index.jsp?topic=%2Fcom.vmware. vsphere.hostclient.doc%2FGUID-F102B9BD-1B92-4AC5-ADC0-BE4E90473C5F.html.

for evaluating IDSes deployed in virtualized environments may lead to inaccurate measurements.

In this chapter, we first systematize and review commonly used IDS evaluation metrics. We then discuss and show through case studies how elasticity of virtualized environments affects IDS attack detection accuracy. Further, we discuss the issues related to the use of conventional IDS evaluation metrics for evaluating IDSes deployed in elastic virtualized environments. Finally, we propose a preliminary metric and measurement methodologies, which take elasticity into account.

This chapter is organized as follows: In Sect. 22.2, we survey existing IDS evaluation metrics; in Sect. 22.3, we discuss and demonstrate through case studies relevant issues related to the use of these metrics; in Sect. 22.4, we present our preliminary ideas on a metric and measurement methodologies that take elasticity into account; in Sect. 22.5, we discuss future work and conclude this chapter.

22.2 An Overview of IDS Evaluation Metrics

In this section, we provide a compact overview of commonly used IDS evaluation metrics. In Chap. 14, we provide related contents focusing on IDS evaluation metrics relevant when it comes to evaluating IDSes employed as part of self-aware systems featuring self-protection.

We distinguish between two types of metrics: (i) performance-related metrics and (ii) security-related metrics (see Chap. 14). By performance-related metrics, we mean metrics that quantify non-functional properties of a tested IDS, such as capacity, performance overhead, resource consumption, and similar. The metrics that quantify these properties, such as processing throughput and CPU utilization, are typical for traditional performance evaluation suites. The practice in the area of IDS evaluation has shown that performance-related metrics are also applicable for evaluating IDSes. For instance, Meng et al. [13] measure workload processing throughput, Lombardi et al. [9] measure performance overhead, Mohammed et al. [15] measure power consumption of a distributed IDS, and Sinha et al. [19] measure memory consumption. We focus here on security-related metrics, not elaborating further on the performance-related ones.

22.2.1 Security-Related Metrics

By security-related metrics, we mean metrics that quantify security-relevant properties of an IDS under test. We focus here on metrics for quantifying the attack detection accuracy of an IDS, where attack detection is considered as having a binary output—attack/no attack—since this is the most typical case and common practice in IDS evaluation. When it comes to attack detection in general, an IDS may also be evaluated with respect to other features (e.g., evaluating provided additional information

Table 22.1 Metrics for quantifying IDS attack detection accuracy

Metric	Annotation/Formula
Basic metrics	
True positive rate	$1 - \beta = 1 - P(\neg A|I) = P(A|I)$
False positive rate	$\alpha = P(A|\neg I)$
Positive predictive value	$P(I|A) = \frac{P(I)P(A|I)}{P(I)P(A|I)+P(\neg I)P(A|\neg I)}$
Negative predictive value	$P(\neg I|\neg A) = \frac{P(\neg I)P(\neg A|\neg I)}{P(\neg I)P(\neg A|\neg I)+P(I)P(\neg A|I)}$
Composite metrics	
Expected cost	$C_{exp} = Min(C\beta B, (1 - \alpha)(1 - B)) + Min(C(1 - \beta)B, \alpha(1 - B))$
Intrusion detection capability	$C_{ID} = \frac{I(X;Y)}{H(X)}$
Notations of used symbols	
Symbol	Meaning
A	*Alert event*: An IDS generates an attack alert
I	*Intrusion event*: An attack is performed
C_α	Cost of an IDS generating an alert when an intrusion has not occurred
C_β	Cost of an IDS failing to detect an intrusion
C	*Cost ratio*: The ratio between the costs C_α and C_β
$B = P(I)$	*Base rate*: Prior probability that an intrusion event occurs
X	*IDS input*: Discrete random variable used to model input to an IDS such that $X = 0$ represents a benign activity and $X = 1$ represents a malicious activity (i.e., an intrusion)
Y	*IDS output*: Discrete random variable used to model the generation of alerts by an IDS such that $Y = 0$ represents no alert and $Y = 1$ represents an alert
$H(X)$	*Uncertainty of X: Entropy measure quantifying the uncertainty of the IDS input X*
$I(X;Y)$	*Mutual information*: The amount of information shared between the random variables X and Y, i.e., the amount of reduction in the uncertainty of the IDS input (X) after the IDS output (Y) is known

about the detected attack attempts). We refer the reader to the evaluation methodology specification of NSS Labs for further information on how other IDS attack detection features may be evaluated.[6]

We distinguish between basic and composite security-related metrics (see Chap. 14). We provide an overview of these metrics in Table 22.1. In Table 22.1, we also show the notation of used symbols (including variables).

---

[6]http://www.nsslabs.com/sites/default/files/import/assets/Methodologies/NSS_Labs_IPS%20Group%20Test%20Methodology%20v6.1.pdf.

22.2.1.1 Basic Metrics

The basic metrics are the most common and they quantify various individual attack detection properties. Although they are quantified individually, these properties need to be analyzed together in order to accurately characterize the attack detection efficiency of a given IDS. The true positive rate $1 - \beta = P(A|I)$ quantifies the probability that an alert generated by an IDS is really an intrusion. The false positive rate $\alpha = P(A|\neg I)$ quantifies the probability that an alert generated by an IDS is not an intrusion, but a regular benign activity. The respective complementary metrics, i.e., the true negative rate $1 - \alpha = P(\neg A|I)$ and the false negative rate $\beta = P(\neg A|\neg I)$, are also relevant. We do not list these metrics in Table 22.1 since they are simply arithmetically related to the true and false positive rates.

The positive predictive value (PPV) quantifies the probability that there is an intrusion when an IDS generates an alert, whereas the negative predictive value (NPV) quantifies the probability that there is no intrusion when an IDS does not generate an alert. These metrics are normally calculated once one has already calculated $P(A|I)$, $P(A|\neg I)$, $P(\neg A|\neg I)$, and $P(\neg A|I)$ by using the Bayesian theorem for calculating a conditional probability (see Table 22.1). Thus, PPV and NPV are also known as Bayesian positive detection rate and Bayesian negative detection rate, respectively.

The basic metrics listed in Table 22.1 originate from signal detection theory. Hancock and Wintz [6] describe the use of these metrics in the area of signal detection. In this paper, we denote these metrics as security-related only because we refer to them in the context of detecting attacks against computer systems and/or networks in particular.

22.2.1.2 Composite Metrics

IDS evaluators often combine the basic metrics in order to analyze relationships between them, for example, to discover an optimal IDS operating point—an IDS configuration which yields optimal values of both the true and false positive detection rates—or to compare multiple IDSes. It is a common practice to use a ROC (receiver operating characteristic) curve to investigate the relationship between the measured true positive and false positive detection rates of an IDS. A ROC curve plots true positive rate against the corresponding false positive rate [11]; that is, a ROC curve depicts multiple IDS operating points of an IDS under test and, as such, it is useful for identifying an optimal operating point or for comparing multiple IDSes.

Security researchers have proposed metrics that are more expressive than ROC curves. One of the most prominent metrics that belong to this category are the expected cost metric (C_{exp}) proposed by Gaffney et al. [2] and the intrusion detection capability metric (C_{ID}) proposed by Gu et al. [4]. We discuss in detail the expected-cost metric in Chap. 14. We focus here on the intrusion detection capability metric.

Intrusion Detection Capability

Gu et al. [4] propose a metric called intrusion detection capability (denoted by C_{ID}, see Table 22.1). They model the input to an IDS as a stream of a random variable X ($X = 1$ denotes an intrusion, $X = 0$ denotes benign activity), and the IDS output, respectively, as a stream of a random variable Y ($Y = 1$ denotes IDS alert, $Y = 0$ denotes no alert). It is assumed that both the input stream and the output stream have a certain degree of uncertainty reflected by the entropies $H(X)$ and $H(Y)$, respectively. Thus, Gu et al. [4] model the number of correct guesses of an IDS, i.e., $I(X; Y)$, as mutual shared information between the random variables X and Y— $I(X; Y) = H(X) - H(X|Y)$. An alternative interpretation is that the accuracy of an IDS is modeled as the reduction in the uncertainty of the IDS input, $H(X)$, after the IDS output Y is known. Finally, by normalizing the shared information $I(X; Y)$ with the entropy of the input variable $H(X)$, the intrusion detection capability metric C_{ID} is obtained. Note that C_{ID} incorporates the uncertainty of the input stream $H(X)$ (i.e., the distribution of intrusions in the IDS input) and the accuracy of an IDS under test $I(X; Y)$. Thus, one may conclude that C_{ID} incorporates the base rate B and many basic metrics, such as the true positive rate $(1 - \beta)$, the false positive rate (α), and similar. For the definition of the relationship between C_{ID}, on the one hand, and B, $1 - \beta$, and α, on the other hand, we refer the reader to [4]. Given this relationship, a value of C_{ID} may be assigned to any operating point of an IDS on the ROC curve. With this assignment, one obtains a new curve, i.e., a C_{ID} curve. A C_{ID} curve provides a straightforward identification of the optimal operating point of an IDS, i.e., the point that marks the highest C_{ID}.

22.2.2 Case Study

We now present a case study involving the de facto standard network-based IDS Snort [17] in order to demonstrate the use of the previously discussed metrics. We evaluate Snort 2.9.22 using a database of rules dated 11.07.2013. We deployed Snort in a host with a dual-core CPU, each core operating at the speed of 2 GHz, 3 GB of memory, and a Debian 7.0 OS. We use the DARPA (Defense Advanced Research Projects Agency) datasets as workloads, which have been recorded over several weeks in 1998. We note that at the time of writing, the accuracy of Snort in detecting the attacks recorded in the DARPA datasets is of no practical relevance since the attacks recorded in these datasets do not (or extremely rarely) occur in current real-world attack scenarios. However, the DARPA datasets are still the largest datasets that contain both malicious and benign activities. We replayed a trace file from the DARPA datasets that has been recorded on Monday of the first week of trace recording. In order to calculate metric values, we used the "ground truth" files provided by the Lincoln Laboratory at MIT.[7] They contain information useful for uniquely identifying each attack recorded in the trace file that we replayed, such as time of execution of the attack, IP addresses of the attacking and victim host, and the network protocol through which the attack has been carried out. To calculate the values of basic and composite security-related metrics, we compared the "ground truth" information with the alerts produced by Snort. As a result, we were able to calculate the number of detected and missed attacks as well as the number of false alerts, which information is required for calculating values of basic and composite security-related metrics.

With its default configuration enabled, Snort detected almost all replayed attacks. However, Snort also issued false alerts. More specifically, Snorts rule with ID 1417 led to mislabeling many benign SNMP (Simple Network Management Protocol) packets as malicious. To investigate whether Snort can be tuned such that the number of false alerts is reduced while the number of true alerts remains sufficiently high, we examined the influence of the configuration parameter *threshold* on the attack detection accuracy of Snort. The parameter *threshold* is used for reducing the number of false alerts generated by suppressing rules that often mislabel benign activities as malicious. A rule may be suppressed in a way such that it will not trigger the generation of an alert every time it labels an activity as malicious. Similarly, a suppressed rule may be configured to not trigger the generation of an alert for a specific number of times (specified with the keyword *count*) during a given time interval (specified with the keyword *seconds*).

The measurement of the attack detection accuracy of an IDS for different configurations of the IDS enables the identification of an optimal operating point (i.e., an IDS configuration that yields optimal values of both the true and false positive detection rates). We considered 6 operating points of Snort. We measured the attack detection accuracy of Snort for 5 different configurations where the rule with ID 1417 was suppressed by setting the value of *count* to 2, 3, 4, 5, and 6, while *seconds* was set to 12026. We also measured the attack detection accuracy of Snort when its default configuration was used, according to which the rule with ID 1417 is not suppressed.

In Table 22.2, we present the values of the basic security-related metrics true positive rate $(1 - \beta)$, false positive rate (α), positive predictive value (PPV), and negative predictive value (NPV). In Table 22.2, one can observe that the values of α and $1 - \beta$ decrease as the value of *count* increases. This is expected since the rule with ID 1477 is suppressed more often as the value of *count* is increased. Increasing the value of *count* leads to a decrease in the number of generated false alerts, which is manifested by the decreasing values of α presented in Table 22.2. However, increasing the value of *count* also leads to worsening of the true positive rate $1 - \beta$. This is a typical trade-off situation between the true and the false positive rates of an IDS.

---

[7]The trace file we used is available at http://www.ll.mit.edu/mission/communications/cyber/ CSTcorpora/ideval/data/1998/testing/week1/Monday/tcpdump.gz. The corresponding "ground truth" data is available at http://www.ll.mit.edu/mission/communications/cyber/CSTcorpora/ ideval/data/1998/Truth_Week_1.llist.tar.gz. To replay the trace file, we used tcpreplay [21]. We used this trace file for all experiments presented in this paper.

Table 22.2 Attack detection accuracy of Snort (seconds = 120)

Configuration	Metric values			
	α	$1 - \beta$	PPV	NPV
count = 6	0.0008	0.333	0.9788	0.9310
count = 5	0.0011	0.416	0.9768	0.9390
count = 4	0.0013	0.5	0.9771	0.9473
count = 3	0.0017	0.624	0.9761	0.9598
count = 2	0.0024	0.833	0.9747	0.9817
Default configuration	0.0026	0.958	0.9762	0.9953

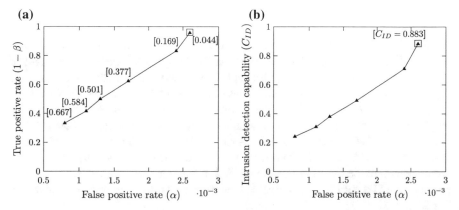

Fig. 22.1 Attack detection accuracy of Snort: **a** ROC curve and estimated costs associated with the depicted operating points, and **b** C_{ID} curve ($\square$ marks an optimal operating point)

Although the basic security-related metrics are quantified individually, they need to be analyzed together in order to accurately characterize the attack detection efficiency of a given IDS. To this end, we use composite security-related metrics.

In Fig. 22.1a, we depict a ROC curve that provides an overview of the previously mentioned trade-off between the true and false positive rates exhibited by Snort. In addition, in Fig. 22.1a, we annotate the depicted operating points with the associated estimated costs C_{exp}. The values of the estimated costs are values of the expected-cost metric proposed by Gaffney et al. [2], which we discuss in detail in Chap. 14. When calculating the values of the expected cost metric, we assumed a cost ratio C of 10 (i.e., the cost of not responding to an attack is 10 times higher than the cost of responding to a false alert). The base rate B is 0.10.

Once we calculated the cost associated with each operating point, we were able to identify an optimal operating point, i.e., the operating point that has the lowest C_{exp} associated with it compared to the other operating points (see Chap. 14). The optimal operating point is (0.0026, 0.958), which has an estimated cost of 0.044 associated with it. Based on our findings, we conclude that Snort operates optimally in terms of cost when configured with its default settings.

In Fig. 22.1b, we depict the values of the intrusion detection capability metric (C_{ID}) [4] for the different operating points of Snort. The C_{ID} curve depicted in Fig. 22.1b enables the identification of an optimal operating point of Snort in terms of intrusion detection capability (i.e., the point that marks the highest C_{ID}). The optimal operating point is (0.0026, 0.958), which marks a C_{ID} of 0.883. As a result, we conclude that Snort operates optimally in terms of intrusion detection capability when configured with its default settings.

22.3 Issues and Relevant Phenomena

In Sect. 22.1, we discussed the practice of deploying IDSes in virtualized environments; that is, we discussed IDSes specifically designed to operate in virtualized environments and conventional IDSes deployed as VNFs. In Fig. 22.2, we depict the deployment of a conventional network-based IDS as a VNF. The IDS, deployed in a designated VM (*IDS VM* in Fig. 22.2), taps into the physical network interface card (NIC) managed by the hypervisor in order to monitor incoming and outgoing traffic. Other VNFs (*VNF* in Fig. 22.2), such as routing or firewalling, may be deployed in co-located VMs (*Host VM, VM #n* in Fig. 22.2). In this section, we discuss relevant issues related to the use of conventional IDS evaluation metrics (see Sect. 22.2) for evaluating IDSes deployed in virtualized environments, for example, as depicted in Fig. 22.2.

In Sect. 22.1, we mentioned that a common aspect of current IDS evaluation metrics is that they are defined with respect to a *fixed* set of hardware resources available to a given IDS under test. This is contrary to what elasticity of modern virtualized environments enables — flexible, on-demand provisioning of resources to VMs where IDSes may be deployed (see Fig. 22.2 and Sect. 22.1). Mell et al. [12] and Hall et al. [5] confirm that conventional IDS evaluation metrics express the attack detection accuracy of an IDS only for a specific hardware environment in which the IDS is expected to reside during operation.

Based on the above, we argue that the use of conventional IDS evaluation metrics may lead to inaccurate measurements in cases where the elastic behavior of a given

Fig. 22.2 A network-based IDS deployed as a VNF

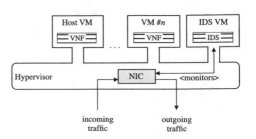

virtualized environment has a significant impact on the attack detection accuracy exhibited by an IDS deployed in the environment by impacting relevant transient behaviors of the IDS. Under relevant transient IDS behaviors, we understand IDS behaviors that are influenced by the amount of resources available to an IDS over time and may impact the attack detection accuracy exhibited by the IDS. For example, the attack detection accuracy exhibited by a network-based IDS may be correlated with the number of dropped packets by the IDS in the time intervals when attacks have been performed. Large amounts of dropped packets in such intervals due to lack of resources may manifest themselves as low IDS attack detection accuracy. Not quantifying the impact of the former on the latter may lead to incomplete, inaccurate observations about the accuracy of the IDS.

In a scenario where an IDS evaluator aims to understand the relation between a given transient behavior of an IDS and the attack detection accuracy the IDS exhibits, the use of conventional IDS evaluation metrics introduces the following inter-related issues:

- *Challenging metric value correlation*: The IDS evaluator would have to correlate the values of metrics belonging to two categories: (i) metrics that quantify attack detection accuracy (e.g., true and false positive rates) and (ii) metrics that quantify the considered transient IDS behavior (e.g., amount of dropped packets over time). However, given the lack of metrics and measurement methodologies specifically designed for that purpose, such a correlation would be approximative, which may lead to inaccurate observations;
- *Inaccurate comparisons of IDSes*: The approximative nature of the correlation mentioned above rules out accurate comparisons of the attack detection accuracy of multiple IDSes by taking elasticity into account. Note that IDS comparisons are a common goal of IDS evaluation studies [14]. Comparing IDSes requires precise measurement of considered metric values so that the comparisons are accurate and fair.

22.3.1   Transient IDS Behaviors and IDS Attack Detection Accuracy

In this section, we discuss and demonstrate the impact of relevant transient IDS behaviors on IDS attack detection accuracy. We consider the case of a network-based IDS deployed as a VNF (see Fig. 22.2). The transient IDS behavior of interest is amount of dropped packets over time (see Sect. 22.3).

There are many factors influencing the amount of packets dropped by an IDS over the duration of an evaluation experiment. These include the characteristics of processed workload (e.g., the speed the network traffic processed by the IDS), and the configuration and design of the IDS (e.g., use of multithreading for processing network packets in an efficient manner). If the IDS under test is deployed in a

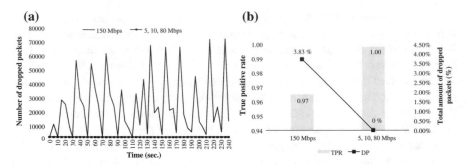

Fig. 22.3 Relevant transient behavior and attack detection accuracy of Snort: **a** number of dropped packets over time, and **b** measured true positive rate (TPR) in relation to the total amount of dropped packets (DP)

virtualized environment, an additional important factor is the hypervisor, which may provision on-demand resources to the VM where the IDS operates (see Sect. 22.3).

In this work, we focus on the hypervisor as a factor influencing transient IDS behaviors, which we discuss in detail in paragraph "the hypervisor." However, we note that having an overview of the other factors influencing a given transient IDS behavior of interest is beneficial when it comes to quantifying IDS attack detection accuracy by taking elasticity into account. This is because it allows for the precise measurement of the impact of the hypervisor on IDS attack detection accuracy by varying relevant configuration points between measurements (e.g., enforcing different resource provisioning policies), not changing characteristics of the other factors (e.g., the speed of the network traffic used as workload). Note that these factors may also have a significant impact on transient IDS behaviors and therefore on IDS attack detection accuracy. Next, we demonstrate how the speed of the network traffic processed by an IDS impacts the amount of packets dropped by the IDS over time, which, in turn, impacts the attack detection accuracy exhibited by the IDS.

We deployed Snort 2.9.7.0 in a paravirtualized VM with an Ubuntu 14.04 operating system running on top of a Xen 4.4.1 hypervisor. We allocated 2 CPUs of 2.6 GHz, 4GB of main memory, and a NIC with a maximal data transfer rate of 1 Gbit/s to the VM where Snort was deployed.[8] We replayed over 240 s a trace file from the 1998 DARPA datasets (see Footnote 7). We configured Snort to use a database of rules dated April 10, 2015. All other configuration options of Snort were set to their default values.

We performed four separate experiments such that we replayed network traffic at the speed of 5, 10, 80, and 150 Mbps. We repeatedly executed each experiment 30 times, and we averaged the results. In Fig. 22.3a, we depict the number of packets dropped by Snort over 240 s for each considered network traffic speed. In Fig. 22.3a, one can observe that Snort dropped a certain amount of packets when we replayed network traffic at the speed of 150 Mbps.

---

[8]We used this testbed environment for all experiments presented in this paper.

In Fig. 22.3b, we depict the true positive rate exhibited by Snort in relation to the total amount of dropped packets at the considered network traffic speeds. One can observe a decline of 0.03 of the measured true positive rate when network traffic is replayed at the speed of 150 Mbps. This can be attributed to the larger amount of packets dropped by Snort (i.e., 3.83 % of all replayed network packets), some of which are malicious.

The hypervisor We now discuss and demonstrate through case studies the impact that the hypervisor may have on relevant transient behaviors (i.e., number of dropped packets over time) of an IDS deployed in a virtualized environment (i.e., a network-based IDS deployed as a NVF). Modern hypervisors feature on-demand provisioning of CPU and memory resources, performed by hotplugging virtual CPU(s) and memory on running VMs (see Sect. 22.1). We investigate here the impact of two relevant characteristics of CPU and memory hotplugging on the number of packets dropped by an IDS over time and therefore on its attack detection accuracy: hotplugging *intensity* (i.e., amount of hotplugged resources) and hotplugging *speed* (i.e., the hypervisor's speed at provisioning resources with respect to resource demands).

Case Study #1: CPU hotplugging intensity We demonstrate through this case study the impact of CPU hotplugging intensity on IDS attack detection accuracy. We deployed the IDSes Snort 2.9.7.0 and Suricata 2.0.6 in our testbed environment. We allocated one virtual CPU to the VM where Snort and Suricata were deployed so that the VM is under CPU pressure when workloads are run. This enabled us to observe the impact of CPU hotplugging on IDS attack detection accuracy in scenarios where such a hotplugging is normally performed (i.e., in scenarios where a VM on which CPU is hotplugged is under CPU pressure). We replayed over 240 s, at the speed of 150 Mbps, a trace file from the 1998 DARPA datasets (see Footnote 7). All configuration options of Snort and Suricata were set to their default values.

By experimenting with both Snort and Suricata, we demonstrate how CPU hotplugging affects the number of packets dropped by IDSes with different designs. Therefore, besides the hypervisor, we also demonstrate the impact of IDS design as a factor influencing transient IDS behaviors (see Sect. 22.3). Note that Suricata features multi-threading and is therefore utilizing multiple CPUs more effectively than Snort.

We performed six separate experiments; that is, three experiments for each considered IDS such that we hotplugged one, two, and three additional virtual CPUs on the VM where Snort/Suricata was deployed, at the 120th second of each experiment. We repeated each experiment 30 times, and we averaged the results. In Fig. 22.4a, b, we depict the number of packets dropped by Snort and Suricata over 240 s for each considered CPU hotplugging scenario (1→2 CPUs, 1→3 CPUs, and 1→4 CPUs in Fig. 22.4). In Table 22.3, we present the attack detection accuracy of Snort and Suricata we measured for each hotplugging scenario, that is, exhibited true and false positive rates, in relation to the total amount of dropped packets (expressed in percentage in Table 22.3).

As expected, the true positive rates exhibited by Snort and Suricata increase as more CPUs are hotplugged on the VM where the IDSes are deployed. This is due to the decrease in the number of packets dropped by the IDSes after CPUs have

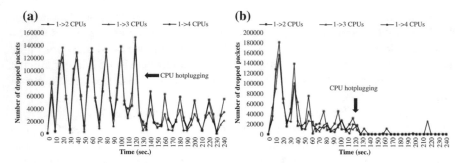

Fig. 22.4 Number of packets dropped over time: **a** by Snort and **b** by Suricata

Table 22.3 Attack detection accuracy of Snort and Suricata (TPR—true positive rate; FPR—false positive rate; DP—dropped packets)

CPU hotplugging scenario	Snort			Suricata		
	TPR	FPR	DP (%)	TPR	FPR	DP (%)
1 → 2 CPUs	0.924	0.0000034	8.26	0.967	0.0000098	3.37
1 → 3 CPUs	0.929	0.0000031	7.71	0.972	0.0000109	2.79
1 → 4 CPUs	0.932	0.0000032	7.48	0.975	0.0000108	2.73

been hotplugged (see Fig. 22.4a, b). The false positive rates exhibited by Snort and Suricata vary with respect to the accuracies of the IDSes as well as the particular packets dropped by the them (i.e., some of the dropped packets would have been falsely considered malicious if they had been processed by the IDSes). We do not elaborate further on the false positive rate.

In Fig. 22.4a, b, one can observe the impact of CPU hotplugging intensity on the number of packets dropped over time by IDSes with different designs; that is, in contrast to Snort, Suricata dropped significantly less packets (i.e., 3.37, 2.79 and 2.73 %, see Table 22.3) due to its ability to effectively utilize multiple CPUs. This results in Suricata exhibiting higher true positive rates than Suricata.

Case Study #2: *CPU hotplugging speed* We demonstrate through this case study the impact of CPU hotplugging speed on IDS attack detection accuracy. We deployed Suricata 2.0.6 in our testbed environment, and we allocated one virtual CPU to the VM where Suricata was deployed so that the VM is under CPU pressure when workloads are run. We replayed over 240 s, at the speed of 150 Mbps, a trace file from the 1998 DARPA datasets (see Footnote 7). All configuration options of Suricata were set to their default values. We performed four experiments such that we configured the hypervisor to hotplug three CPUs at the 20th, 30th, 40th, and the 80th second of the experiment. We repeated each experiment 30 times and we averaged the results.

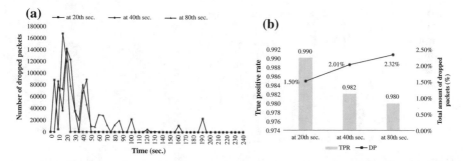

Fig. 22.5 Relevant transient behavior and attack detection accuracy of Suricata: **a** number of dropped packets over time, and **b** measured true positive rate (TPR) in relation to the total amount of dropped packets (DP)

In Fig. 22.5a, we depict the number of packets dropped by Suricata over 240 s for each considered hotplugging scenario (at 20th sec., at 40th sec., and at 80th sec. in Fig. 22.5a). In Fig. 22.5b, we depict the true positive rate exhibited by Suricata in relation to the total amount of dropped packets for each considered hotplugging scenario. As expected, one can observe in Fig. 22.5b that CPU hotplugging speed has significant impact on the attack detection accuracy exhibited by Suricata. For instance, there is a decrease of 0.01 of the true positive rate exhibited by Suricata when the hypervisor provisioned CPUs at the 80th instead of the 20th second of the experiment. This is due to the loss of additional 0.82 % of all replayed packets because of a delay in CPU provisioning of 60 s.

Case Study #3: *Memory hotplugging intensity* We demonstrate through this case study the impact of the memory hotplugging intensity on IDS attack detection accuracy. We deployed Snort 2.9.7.0 in our testbed environment and we allocated 1.5 GB of memory to the VM where Snort was deployed so that the VM is under memory pressure when workloads are run. This enabled us to observe the impact of memory hotplugging on the attack detection accuracy exhibited by Snort in scenarios where such a hotplugging is normally performed (i.e., in scenarios where a VM on which CPU is hotplugged is under memory pressure). We replayed over 240 s, at the speed of 150 Mbps, a trace file from the 1998 DARPA datasets (see Footnote 7). We set all configuration options of Snort to their default values. We performed three separate experiments such that we allocated additional 0.1, 0.3, and 2 GB of memory to the VM where Snort was deployed at the 120th second of the experiment. We repeated each experiment 30 times, and we averaged the results.

In Fig. 22.6a, we depict the number of packets dropped by Snort over 240 s for each considered hotplugging scenario (1.5→1.6 GB, 1.5→1.8 GB, and 1.5→3.5 GB in Fig. 22.6a). In Fig. 22.6b, we depict the true positive rate exhibited by Snort in relation to the total amount of dropped packets for each considered hotplugging scenario.

The results from this study show that on-demand resource provisioning may have diverse impacts on transient IDS behaviors and therefore on IDS attack

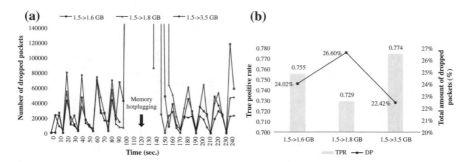

Fig. 22.6 Relevant transient behavior and attack detection accuracy of Snort: **a** number of dropped packets over time, and **b** measured true positive rate (TPR) in relation to the total amount of dropped packets (DP)

detection accuracy. This further emphasizes the need of novel metrics and measurement methods for quantifying these impacts (see Sect. 22.3). For instance, in Fig. 22.6a, one can observe a significant increase of packets dropped by Snort when memory is hotplugged. This is followed by a stable transient behavior of the IDS, which, as expected, is dropping less packets than before the memory hotplugging action. Depending on the amount of hotplugged memory, this normally leads to an improvement of the exhibited true positive rate to a certain extent (see in Fig. 22.6b the true positive rate exhibited by Snort when 0.1 and 2 GB are hotplugged). However, when 0.3 GB of memory is hotplugged, a significant amount of packets is dropped, which leads to the lowest true positive rate we measured (i.e., 0.729, see Fig. 22.6b). This is because of many factors involved, for example, the way in which the IDS under test and/or the operating system where the IDS is deployed have been designed to handle various amounts of newly allocated memory.

22.4 Metric and Measurement Methodology

In this section, we present our preliminary work on a novel metric and measurement methodologies that take elasticity of virtualized environments into account (see Sect. 22.1). The metric and methodologies we propose enable the measurement of the attack detection accuracy of an IDS deployed in a virtualized environment featuring on-demand resource provisioning; that is, they enable the evaluation of the attack detection accuracy of such an IDS with respect to the impact that on-demand resource provisioning performed by the underlying hypervisor has on the attack detection accuracy exhibited by the IDS (see for example Sect. 22.3.1, paragraph "the hypervisor"). The metric and measurement methodologies we propose aim to address the issues related to the use of conventional IDS evaluation metrics—possibility of inaccurate observations about the accuracy of an IDS, challenging metric value correlation, and inaccurate comparisons of IDSes (see Sect. 22.3).

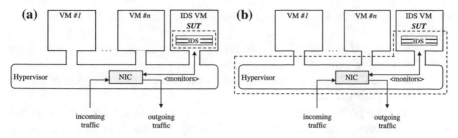

Fig. 22.7 Boundaries of: **a** the conventional SUT, and **b** novel SUT in the area of IDS evaluation

We stress that the metric and measurement methodologies we propose are meant to complement the conventional ones and are to be used only when it comes to evaluating IDSes deployed in virtualized environments featuring on-demand resource provisioning. We name the metric we propose *hypervisor factor (HF)*, since it quantifies the impact of the hypervisor as a factor impacting IDS attack detection accuracy (see Sect. 22.3.1).

Quantifying the impact of the hypervisor on IDS attack detection accuracy calls for a novel definition of the boundaries of a system-under-test (SUT) in the area of IDS evaluation. In the area of system evaluation, the precise definition of the boundaries of an SUT is critical for the accurate measurement of system performance and interpretation of evaluation results. In contrast to the conventional understanding in the area of IDS evaluation about what comprises an SUT (i.e., the IDS under test), we advocate a novel SUT with extended boundaries including the hypervisor as well, since it is an important factor impacting transient IDS behaviors, which, in turn, impact IDS attack detection accuracy. In Fig. 22.7, we depict the boundaries of the conventional SUT in the area of IDS evaluation and of the novel SUT we propose considering a network-based IDS deployed as a VNF (see Fig. 22.2).

22.4.1 Metric Design

We distinguish three states in which a given IDS, part of an SUT as we define it, may be over the duration of an IDS evaluation experiment: baseline, underprovisioned, and overprovisioned state. By baseline IDS state, we mean a state of the IDS in which it is provisioned by the hypervisor with the minimum amount of resources such that provisioning more resources does not have an impact on the attack detection accuracy of the IDS (e.g., it does not improve the positive rate exhibited by the IDS, see Sect. 22.3). Therefore, by overprovisioned, or underprovisioned, IDS state, we mean a state of the IDS in which it is provisioned by the hypervisor with more, or less, resources than the amount needed for the IDS to be considered in baseline state. Given these definitions of IDS states, we design the HF metric with respect to the following criteria, which are crucial for the accurate and practically useful IDS evaluation:

Criterion C_1: If configured accordingly, the HF metric penalizes resource over-provisioning with respect to the

(a) time the IDS has spent in overprovisioned state over the duration of an IDS evaluation experiment, and

(b) the false positive and false negative rates exhibited by the IDS under test when in overprovisioned state, since provisioning excess amount of resources has not contributed towards improving the accuracy of the IDS. We design the HF metric to penalize equally various extents of overprovisioning since we consider any extent of overprovisioning an equally negative phenomenon;

Criterion C_2: If configured accordingly, the HF metric penalizes resource under-provisioning with respect to the

(a) time the IDS has spent in underprovisioned state over the duration of an IDS evaluation experiment and

(b) the extent of the impact that the underprovisioning has had on the true positive rate exhibited by the IDS. We consider this impact a negative phenomenon since it causes the reduction in the number of true alerts issued by the IDS (see Sect. 22.3). The HF metric does not penalize resource underprovisioning that has had no impact on the true positive rate since we consider resource saving, which does not cause reduction in this rate, a positive phenomenon.

Criterion C_3: If configured accordingly, the HF metric rewards resource under-provisioning with respect to the

(a) time the IDS has spent in underprovisioned state over the duration of an IDS evaluation experiment and

(b) the extent of the impact that the underprovisioning has had on the false positive rate exhibited by the IDS. We consider this impact a positive phenomenon since it brings practical benefits—reduced number of issued false alerts and increased amount of saved resources. Underprovisioning may cause the reduction in the false positive rate exhibited by an IDS if a given amount of workload units (e.g., packets), which would have been falsely labeled as malicious by the IDS if processed by it, are not processed by the IDS due to lack of resources.

In summary, the HF metric favors the most an SUT configured in a way such that the hypervisor saves the most resources while impacting the true positive rate exhibited by the IDS to the least extent and the false positive rate exhibited by the IDS to the biggest extent.

Criterion C_4: The HF metric expresses the base rate. The attack detection perfor-mance of an IDS should be assessed with respect to a base rate measure in order for such an assessment to be accurate (see Sect. 22.2). Therefore, it is important that the HF metric expresses this rate.

Criterion C_5: The HF metric enables the straightforward identification of opti-mal operating points. In the context of IDS evaluation, an optimal operating point is an IDS configuration which yields values of both the true and false positive rates considered optimal with respect to a given measure (e.g., cost, see Sect. 22.2). In the context of this work, under optimal operating point, we understand a configuration of both the IDS under test *and* the underlying hypervisor, which yield values of metrics quantifying the performance of the hypervisor at provisioning resources and of metrics quantifying IDS attack detection accuracy (e.g., true and false positive rates) considered optimal with respect to the impact of the former on the latter (see criterion C_1, C_2, and C_3). This is because we consider a novel SUT with boundaries that include an IDS and a hypervisor provisioning the IDS with resources (see Fig. 22.7b).

We design the HF metric to enable a straightforward identification of optimal operating points; that is, for a given set of operating points, the optimal operating point yields an extreme value of HF. In Sect. 22.4.3, we discuss more on operating points and on identifying optimal operating points.

Criterion C_6: The HF metric enables the accurate comparison of multiple SUTs. This is feasible only if criterion C_5 is fulfilled, a topic that we discuss more in Sect. 22.4.3.

22.4.2   Metric Construction

We present here the main principles of construction for the HF metric. Similar to Gaffney et al. [2], we construct the HF metric using a construct from decision theory—a decision tree—as a basis. In Fig. 22.8, we depict the decision tree that we use for constructing the HF metric. The tree shows the sequence of uncertain events (circles) that describe:

- the *workload*, say $W[B]$, to which the IDS is subjected over the duration of a given IDS evaluation experiment, say T_{max}. We characterize W by the base rate (i.e., probability of an intrusion $B = P(I)$, see Sect. 22.2);
- the *operation* of the IDS processing workload $W[B]$. The operation of the IDS is characterized by the probabilities of the IDS issuing or not issuing an alert when an intrusion has or has not occurred (i.e., the probabilities $P(A|I)$, $P(\neg A|I)$, and so on, see Sect. 22.2);
- the *state* of the IDS (i.e., baseline, overprovisioned, or underprovisioned IDS state, see Sect. 22.4.1) when it issues or does not issue an alert. The IDS being in one of the considered states during operation primarily depends on the resource provisioning policy applied by the underlying hypervisor, say $H[T_o, T_b, T_u]$; that is, on its precision at meeting the demand for resources by the IDS over time T_{max}. We characterize H by the amount of time the IDS has spent in overprovisioned (T_o), baseline (T_b), and underprovisioned (T_u) states over time T_{max} (i.e., $T_{o/b/u} \in [0; T_{max}], T_o + Tb + Tu = T_{max}$).

Associated with each uncertain event is the probability of occurrence. There are six probabilities specified in the tree: $p_1 = P(I) = B$: the probability that an intrusion occurs; $p_2 = P(A|I) = 1 - \beta$: the probability that the IDS issues an alert when an intrusion occurs (i.e., the true positive rate); $p_3 = P(A|\neg I) = \alpha$: the probability that the IDS issues an alert when an intrusion does not occur (i.e., the false

Fig. 22.8 The decision tree used for constructing the HF metric

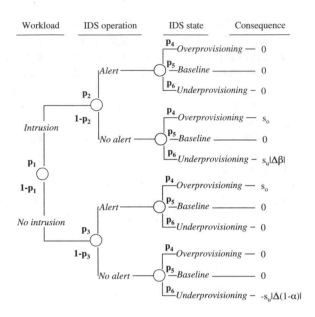

positive rate); $p_{4/5/6} = \frac{T_{o/b/u}}{T_{max}}$: the probability that the IDS under test is in overprovisioned/baseline/underprovisioned state when it issues or does not issue an alert (i.e., at any moment in the time interval $[0; T_{max}]$);

The attractiveness of each combination of events represented in the tree depicted in Fig. 22.8 is characterized by the *consequence* (i.e., the penalty or the reward score) associated with it. With respect to the metric design criteria C_1, C_2, and C_3 (see Sect. 22.4.1), the HF metric:

• penalizes the SUT for the IDS issuing false positive or false negative alerts when the IDS is in overprovisioned state. A user of the HF metric may disable or enable this penalization by setting the value of s_o, $s_o \in \{0, 1\}$ to 0 or 1, respectively;

• penalizes the SUT for the IDS (in underprovisioned state) not issuing an alert when an intrusion has occurred with the score $s_u|\Delta\beta|$, where $|\Delta\beta| = |\beta - \beta_b|$. A user of the HF metric may disable or enable this penalization by setting the value of s_u, $s_u \in \{0, 1\}$ to 0 or 1, respectively. β_b is the false negative rate exhibited by the IDS in a scenario where it has operated in baseline state over time T_{max} and subjected to workload $W[B]$. Therefore, the HF metric quantifies the impact of underprovisioning on the true positive rate $(1 - \beta)$ exhibited by the IDS—it penalizes the SUT for the IDS not issuing a true alert because of discarded workloads due to lack of resources;

• rewards the SUT for the IDS (in underprovisioned state) not issuing an alert when an intrusion has not occurred with the score $s_u|\Delta(1 - \alpha)|$, $|\Delta(1 - \alpha)| = |(1 - \alpha) - (1 - \alpha)_b|$. A user of the HF metric may disable or enable this rewarding by setting the value of s_u, $s_u \in \{0, 1\}$ to 0 or 1, respectively. $(1 - \alpha)_b$ is the true negative rate exhibited by the IDS in a scenario where it has operated in baseline state over time T_{max} and subjected to workload $W[B]$. Therefore, the HF metric quantifies the impact of underprovisioning on the false positive rate (α) exhibited by the IDS—it rewards the SUT for the IDS not issuing a false alert.

The formula of the HF metric can be obtained by "folding back" the decision tree depicted in Fig. 22.8; that is, from right to left, the penalty, or the reward, score at an event node is the sum of products of probabilities and scores for each branch:

$$HF = B[\beta(\frac{T_o}{T_{max}}s_o + \frac{T_u}{T_{max}}s_u|\Delta\beta|)] + (1-B)[\alpha\frac{T_o}{T_{max}}s_o - (1-\alpha)\frac{T_u}{T_{max}}s_u|\Delta(1-\alpha)|)]$$

$$= \frac{T_o}{T_{max}}s_o[B + (1-B)\alpha]\beta + \frac{T_u}{T_{max}}s_u[B\beta|\Delta\beta| - (1-B)(1-\alpha)|\Delta(1-\alpha)|] \quad (22.1)$$

If the values of s_o and s_u are set to 1, Eq. 22.1 can be alternatively represented as the sum of the two components of the HF metric, that is, HF_o and HF_u, where $HF_o = \frac{T_o}{T_{max}}[B\beta + (1-B)\alpha]$ is the penalty associated with overprovisioning and $HF_u = \frac{T_u}{T_{max}}[B\beta|\Delta\beta| - (1-B)(1-\alpha)|\Delta(1-\alpha)|]$ is the penalty, or reward, associated with underprovisioning. Distinguishing these components of the HF metric allows for separately observing the quantified consequences of the hypervisor over- and/or underprovisioning the IDS in relation to the attack detection accuracy exhibited by the IDS.

22.4.2.1 On Baseline IDS State

Calculating values of the HF metric requires calculating T_o, T_u, and T_b, and, in addition, β_b and $(1-\alpha)_b$ (see Eq. 22.1). This, in turn, may require extensive experimentation in order to: (i) identify the baseline state of the IDS that is part of the SUT; that is, to determine the minimum amount of resources, say R_b, such that provisioning more resources does not have an impact on the attack detection accuracy exhibited by the IDS (see Sect. 22.4.1); and (ii) compare this amount with the amount of resources provisioned by the hypervisor applying a given resource provisioning policy $H[T_o, T_b, T_u]$, say R_p.

The above activities may be practically challenging because they require the use of measurement approaches considering various resource unit and measurement granularities, and determining how R_b changes over time T_{max} with respect to the intensity of the workload to which the IDS is subjected. Therefore, we assume the following simplifications:

• R_b is constant over time T_{max}—we consider R_b the minimum amount of resources allocated to the VM where the IDS operates, such that the IDS does not discard workload when the workload is most intensive. This reflects a realistic scenario where resources are provisioned to an IDS considering the peak intensity of the workload that the IDS may process during operation;

• R_b and R_p differ with regard to a single measurement unit (e.g., MB of memory)—that is, we assume that the hypervisor allocates and/or deallocates a single type of resource over the duration of an IDS evaluation experiment. This allows for determining the difference between R_b and R_p over time T_{max} in a straightforward and accurate manner.

We plan to address the above simplifications as part of our future work.

22.4.3 Properties of the HF Metric

In this section, we show how the HF metric satisfies each of the design criteria we presented in Sect. 22.4.1:

Criterion C_1: For a given T_{max}, the value of the HF_o component of the HF metric (see Sect. 22.4.2) is positively correlated with T_o (i.e., the time the IDS has spent in overprovisioned state over time T_{max}), the false positive rate (α), and the false negative rate (β);

Criterion C_2 and C_3: For a given T_{max}, the value of the HF_u component of the HF metric (see Sect. 22.4.2):

- is positively correlated with T_u (i.e., the time the IDS has spent in underprovisioned state over time T_{max}) and $|\Delta\beta|$, which quantifies the extent of the impact that underprovisioning has had on the false negative rate, and therefore on the complementary true positive rate;
- is negatively correlated with T_u and $|\Delta(1 - \alpha)|$, which quantifies the extent of the impact that underprovisioning has had on the true negative rate, and therefore on the complementary false positive rate;

Criterion C_4: The HF metric expresses the base rate B (see Eq. 22.1);

Criterion C_5: In Definition 22.1, we define an operating point of an SUT (see Fig. 22.7b).

Definition 22.1 An operating point of an SUT consisting of an IDS and a hypervisor, say $O(I \rightarrow (\alpha_b, 1 - \beta_b); H[T_o, T_b, T_u]) \rightarrow (\alpha, 1 - \beta)$, is a configuration I of the IDS, which yields distinct values of α_b and $(1 - \beta)_b$, and a configuration of the hypervisor, that is, a configured resource provisioning policy $H[T_o, T_b, T_u]$. These configurations yield values of $1 - \beta$ and α (i.e., the true and false positive rates exhibited by the IDS with configuration I in a scenario where the hypervisor applies resource provisioning policy $H[T_o, T_b, T_u]$).

A single value of the HF metric may be associated with a specific configuration of the IDS and of the hypervisor comprising a given SUT (i.e., with each operating point of the SUT considered in a given evaluation study, see Eq. 22.1 and Definition 22.1). Given that the HF metric may penalize an SUT, a given operating point of the SUT is considered optimal if it has the lowest value of the HF metric associated with it. Theoretically, there may be more than one operating point having the same lowest value of the HF metric associated with them. In such a scenario, a given operating point may be considered optimal based on subjective criteria. For example, an IDS evaluator may consider optimal the operating point with the highest value of T_b (i.e., the operating point such that the IDS spends at most time in baseline state).

Measuring values of the HF metric and identifying the optimal operating point of an SUT, out of multiple operating points, is performed in practice by executing multiple experiments using a given workload, and varying the configuration of the IDS and/or of the hypervisor between experiments.

Criterion C_6: Multiple SUTs can be compared by comparing their optimal operating points—the SUT with the lowest value of the HF metric associated with its optimal operating point is considered best.

22.5 Conclusion

In this chapter, we elaborated on evaluating in an accurate manner attack detection accuracy of IDSes deployed in virtualized environments featuring on-demand resource provisioning. We demonstrated through case studies the impact of such a provisioning on IDS attack detection accuracy. We surveyed conventional metrics for quantifying IDS attack detection accuracy observing that they do not express this impact, which may lead to inaccurate assessments when using these metrics to evaluate an IDS deployed in a virtualized environment. We presented a novel metric—the *HF metric*—and a measurement methodology, which capture the impact of on-demand resource provisioning on IDS attack detection accuracy and therefore contribute towards addressing the previously mentioned issue.

We designed the HF metric with respect to several criteria, such as SUT penalizing and rewarding criteria, and expression of the base rate. We consider these criteria crucial for the credible assessment of the attack detection accuracy of an IDS deployed in a virtualized environment.

The metric and measurement methodologies we presented in this chapter are in their preliminary forms. This work can be continued in several directions. For instance, in-depth analysis of various properties of the HF metric is needed (e.g., analysis on how values of the HF metric relate to base rate measures). In addition, different SUT penalizing and rewarding criteria may be considered. Further, we plan to conduct realistic case studies involving the evaluation of single or multiple SUTs in order to demonstrate the practical usefulness of the HF metric.

We stress that rigorous metrics are essential not only for the accurate evaluation of IDSes, but also as a driver of innovation by enabling the identification of issues and the improvement of existing IDSes.

Acknowledgements This work was funded by the German Research Foundation (DFG) under grant No. KO 3445/16-1. This research has been supported by the Research Group of the Standard Performance Evaluation Corporation (SPEC, http://www.spec.org, http://research.spec.org). The authors would like to thank Alexander Leonhardt for providing experimental data.

References

1. Wesam Dawoud, Ibrahim Takouna, and Christoph Meinel. Elastic Virtual Machine for Fine-Grained Cloud Resource Provisioning. In P.Venkata Krishna, M.Rajasekhara Babu, and Ezendu Ariwa, editors, *Global Trends in Computing and Communication Systems*, volume 269 of *Communications in Computer and Information Science*, pages 11–25. Springer, 2012.
2. Jr. Gaffney, J.E. and J.W. Ulvila. Evaluation of intrusion detectors: a decision theory approach. In *Proceedings of the 2001 IEEE Symposium on Security and Privacy*, pages 50–61, 2001.
3. Frank Gens, Robert Mahowald, Richard L. Willards, David Bradshaw, and Chris Morris. Cloud computing 2010: An idc update, 2010.
4. Guofei Gu, Prahlad Fogla, David Dagon, Wenke Lee, and Boris Skorić. Measuring intrusion detection capability: an information-theoretic approach. In *Proceedings of the 2006 ACM Symposium on Information, computer and communications security (ASIACCS)*, pages 90–101, New York, NY, USA, 2006. ACM.
5. Mike Hall and Kevin Wiley. Capacity verification for high speed network intrusion detection systems. In *Proceedings of the 5th International Conference on Recent Advances in Intrusion Detection (RAID)*, pages 239–251, Berlin, Heidelberg, 2002. Springer-Verlag.
6. J. Hancock and P. Wintz. *Signal Detection Theory*. McGraw–Hill, New York, 1966.
7. Evangelos Kotsovinos. Virtualization: Blessing or curse? *Queue*, 8(11):40:40–40:46, November 2010.
8. Sajib Kundu, Raju Rangaswami, Ajay Gulati, Ming Zhao, and Kaushik Dutta. Modeling virtualized applications using machine learning techniques. In *Proceedings of the 8th ACM SIGPLAN/SIGOPS conference on Virtual Execution Environments*, VEE '12, pages 3–14, New York, NY, USA, 2012. ACM.
9. Flavio Lombardi and Roberto Di Pietro. Secure virtualization for cloud computing. *Journal of Network and Computer Applications*, 34(4):1113–1122, July 2011.
10. Neil MacDonald. Yes, Hypervisors are vulnerable. http://blogs.gartner.com/neil_macdonald/2011/01/26/yes-hypervisors-are-vulnerable/, 2011.
11. R. A. Maxion and R. R. Roberts. Proper Use of ROC Curves in Intrusion/Anomaly detection. Technical Report CS-TR-871, School of Computing Science, University of Newcastle upon Tyne, November 2004.
12. Peter Mell, Vincent Hu, Richard Lippmann, Josh Haines, and Marc Zissman. An Overview of Issues in Testing Intrusion Detection Systems, 2003.
13. Yuxin Meng and Wenjuan Li. Adaptive Character Frequency-Based Exclusive Signature Matching Scheme in Distributed Intrusion Detection Environment. In *IEEE 11th International Conference on Trust, Security and Privacy in Computing and Communications (TrustCom)*, pages 223–230, June 2012.
14. Aleksandar Milenkoski, Marco Vieira, Samuel Kounev, Alberto Avrtizer, and Bryan D. Payne. Evaluating Computer Intrusion Detection Systems: A Survey of Common Practices. *ACM Computing Surveys*, 2015. To appear.
15. N. Mohammed, H. Otrok, Lingyu Wang, M. Debbabi, and P. Bhattacharya. Mechanism Design-Based Secure Leader Election Model for Intrusion Detection in MANET. *IEEE Transactions on Dependable and Secure Computing*, 8(1):89–103, January-February 2011.
16. Diego Perez-Botero, Jakub Szefer, and Ruby B. Lee. Characterizing hypervisor vulnerabilities in cloud computing servers. In *Proceedings of the 2013 International Workshop on Security in Cloud Computing*, Cloud Computing '13, pages 3–10. ACM, 2013.
17. Martin Roesch. Snort - Lightweight Intrusion Detection for Networks. In *Proceedings of the 13th USENIX conference on System Administration (LISA)*, pages 229–238. USENIX Association, 1999.
18. Karen Scarfone and Peter Mell. Guide to Intrusion Detection and Prevention Systems (IDPS), 2007. NIST Special Publication 900-94.
19. Sushant Sinha, Farnam Jahanian, and Jignesh M. Patel. WIND: Workload-aware INtrusion Detection. In *Proceedings of the 9th International Conference on Recent Advances in Intrusion Detection (RAID)*, pages 290–310, Berlin, Heidelberg, 2006. Springer Verlag.

20. S. Spinner, S. Kounev, Xiaoyun Zhu, Lei Lu, M. Uysal, A. Holler, and R. Griffith. Runtime Vertical Scaling of Virtualized Applications via Online Model Estimation. In *IEEE Eighth International Conference on Self-Adaptive and Self-Organizing Systems (SASO)*, pages 157–166, 2014.
21. Tcpreplay.
22. Jing Xu, Ming Zhao, José Fortes, Robert Carpenter, and Mazin Yousif. Autonomic Resource Management in Virtualized Data Centers Using Fuzzy Logic-based Approaches. *Cluster Computing*, 11(3):213–227, 2008.

Chapter 23
Self-aware Networks: The Cognitive Packet Network and Its Performance

Erol Gelenbe

Abstract This article is a summary description of the cognitive packet network (CPN) which is an early example of a completely software-defined network (SDN) and of a fully implemented self-aware computer network (SAN). CPN has been completely implemented and is used in numerous experiments. CPN is able to observe its own internal performance as well as the interfaces of the external systems that it interacts with, in order to modify its behaviour so as to adaptively achieve objectives, such as discovering services for its users, improving their quality of service (QoS), reducing its own energy consumption, compensating for components that fail or malfunction, detecting and reacting to intrusions, and defending itself against attacks.

23.1 Introduction

The cognitive packet network (CPN) was largely implemented by the year 2004 [8] and is arguably the world's first software-defined network. It encapsulates IP packets into "dumb packets" (DPs) and also uses its own smart packets (SPs) and acknowledgement packets (ACKs). It routes its packets over a set of virtual nodes, or CPN nodes, so that one or more CPN nodes can be installed on computers or conventional network routers. CPN establishes awareness of its ongoing connectivity and quality of service using the SPs which constantly explore the network.

The measurements collected by the SPs are then returned by the ACKs to each of the nodes where traffic originates. CPN is an example both of a software-defined network (SDN) and of a self-aware computer network (SAN) [8, 13, 26], which uses concepts from autonomous search [14, 16, 22] to discover paths and observe its own internal performance as well as the interfaces of the external systems that it interacts with, in order to modify its behaviour so as to adaptively achieve certain objectives.

CPN's objectives or "goals" can include discovering services for its users, improving their quality of service (QoS) such as packet forwarding delay, packet loss and jitter, reducing its own energy consumption [10, 21], compensating for compo-

E. Gelenbe (✉)
Department of Electrical and Electronic Engineering, Imperial College, London SW7 2AZ, UK
e-mail: e.gelenbe@imperial.ac.uk

© Springer International Publishing AG 2017   659
S. Kounev et al. (eds.), *Self-Aware Computing Systems*,
DOI 10.1007/978-3-319-47474-8_23

nents that fail or malfunction, detecting and reacting to intrusions, and defending itself against external attacks [6, 19].

In addition to its strong link to software-defined networks (SDN), whose basic ideas go back to the earlier field of programmable networks [4], the study of networks such as CPN is also part of the field of autonomic communications [5] and of naturally based computation [15]. It also draws on a long experience in designing and implementing distributed systems that must occasionally synchronise across large topologies [23]. SDNs also relate to the need for network virtualisation [29] over different hardware/software architectures for packet networks.

CPN has been completely implemented in software [8] and can be ported to any infrastructure that supports Linux. The routing engine of CPN is installed in each of the virtual nodes and is used to select paths for SPs based on a numerically expressed "goal function"; it is based on reinforcement learning and uses a neural critic that is based on the random neural network [17, 25], which has also been used in many other applications [1, 7, 18, 24]. Such learning systems can also be modelled and analysed using probability models [2, 11, 12].

23.2   Self-Awareness

A commonly used term such as self-awareness can elicit different reactions in the layman and also among scientists and engineers from different disciplines. We all struggle with such concepts and may not have a clear understanding, or different understandings, about what such terms actually mean. Thus, we first review some relevant aspects of self-awareness and then discuss how these can be embodied in the context of computer networks.

According to the philosopher John Locke, the self "depends on consciousness, not on substance". Thus, we can identify our "self" by being conscious or aware of our past, present and future thoughts, and through the memory of actions and the planning of actions. Any concept is necessarily juxtaposed to other opposing concepts, so that "self" needs to be related to, or separated from, the "other".

The notion of self also includes an integrated view of our past sensory inputs over a period of time, as well as of current sensory inputs. Some form of "autobiographical memory" should be a part of self-awareness. Sensing should also include what engineers call "condition monitoring", are we in good health, do we feel well and are we performing our various tasks as expected.

Self-awareness allows the individual to select and then drive not only her/his actions but also thinking, by choosing (for instance) to turn to a past memory or to a future plan, rather than to musing over thoughts generated by current external stimuli.

When we turn our attention to ourselves, we can also compare our current and past behaviour to our own standards, and to the behaviour of other entities external to ourselves, so that we become critics or evaluators of ourselves.

This also leads to a notion of awareness of our location in different spaces: the physical space where we observe, feed, work, move, etc., but it may also be a space of actions, values, successes and so on. Different spatial dimensions can describe the attributes that we are interested in; the locations in attribute space are then different states that we may perceive that we (or others) are in, while the distances can represent the time and effort, or value, of moving from one set of values of the attributes to another.

This spatial paradigm [14], which we can consider to be a hippocampus-type internal representation, is present in most things we do and certainly in many of our planning activities: we are aware of "where we are", "where we would like to be" and "the distance between the two", including the time and effort needed to bridge the two. In many organisms (e.g. dogs), the notion of self is also accompanied by markers, e.g. smell, that the animal recognises and actually uses to mark its physical space, and to self-recognise its own presence and also to detect intrusion.

Thus, the sensory system, and the notion of self and space are intertwined. In much simpler organisms, much of the self may actually be contained in the immediate chemical or physical (heat, electromagnetic radiation and pressure) environment. At the other end, in complex living organisms such as mammals, self-awareness will use a neuronal system, so that the physical embodiment of "self-awareness" will include a network of interacting and self-adaptive components and sub-systems [13, 15, 23].

23.3 Desirable Properties

A self-aware network should offer a distributed internal representation of itself, coupled with the ability to discover actions that it can take, in the form of paths to destinations and services, and having a "motor" capability for forwarding streams of packets along selected paths. The internal representation of the past and present experience of the network, based on sensing and measurement, with proactive sensing as one of the concurrent activities undertaken by the SAN, would include performance monitoring to provide an internal evaluation of how well the network is "doing its job" and condition monitoring to evaluate the health of the network. The coupling of the internal representation with motor control is obviously necessary for the network to evaluate when its information is insufficient or obsolete and then sense its environment, such as other networks and network users, or to probe itself for condition monitoring or performance evaluation. A SAN should offer a distributed representation of potential future actions and plans, critical evaluations of past actions and behaviours, and potential courses of action. The internal representation should allow the system to locate its components and behaviour both in physical space and in different virtual spaces that are relevant to the network. Useful virtual spaces can include aspects such as security, energy consumption, delay, loss of packets and computational overhead. Network nodes placed in this geography could then be identified via these different attributes: e.g. those nodes that are secure, those that function properly and those that are parsimonious in energy usage.

Thus, such attributes could be used to distinguish between different parts (nodes and links) or sub-areas of the network. This distributed representation should be coupled to the computer network's distributed "sensor system" which probes and measures the network's behaviour, and its "motor control" which forwards streams of packets from node to node along paths in the network, to desired destinations. A SAN should be able to sense and evaluate threats, and detect intrusions and attacks.

The capability for threat evaluation [2, 3] should be coupled with distributed motor reactions concerning packet routing driven by self-preservation and the need to assure quasi-normal operation, even in the presence of transient or sustained attacks.

23.4 Practical Approach

Since routing and the conveying of packets reliably from some input or source point S to some other outpoint or destination D is a computer network's key function, we now focus on a practical scheme for implementing a self-aware network that offers many of the capabilities we describe, based on the cognitive packet network (CPN) [8] protocol.

Addressing one by one the requirements of the previous section, we first note that in CPN, each network node maintains an internal representation of its primary role as a forwarder of traffic through the network. Specifically, for any source and destination (S-D) pair, and relevant quality of service (QoS) characteristic:

(a) either a node does not know which of its neighbours is the best choice as the next hop for this S-D pair and the specified QoS; but it can discover this information using smart packets (SP), which are distinct from the payload packets which the network is forwarding as part of its "useful job", or
(b) it does have this information based on previous experience, and the information is stored in an oracle that is implemented in the form of a neural network.

This distributed representation is also coupled with the network's "motor" capability to forward packets. When a packet with a given S-D and QoS requirement arrives to the network, then in case (a), the packet is forwarded as prescribed, while in case (b), a stream of "smart packets" (SP) is forwarded by the node, starting with its immediate neighbours, in a search for the path that currently has the best QoS metric for reaching D. SPs that reach D will send back an acknowledgement (ACK) packet, whose information content is used to update the oracles using reinforcement learning (RL) concerning this S-D at all the intermediate nodes, and at S. The oracles can then be used to forward subsequent packets. When a packet that travels from S to D does reach D, an ACK containing the hop-by-hop QoS experienced by the packet returns to the source together with time stamps concerning the packet going forward and the ACK coming back. Thus, a record of the paths that was explored, the dates and the observed QoS create an "autobiographical memory" of the SAN's experience, which includes its past performance and the conditions that were prevalent at the times when this experience was collected. The most recent data in this

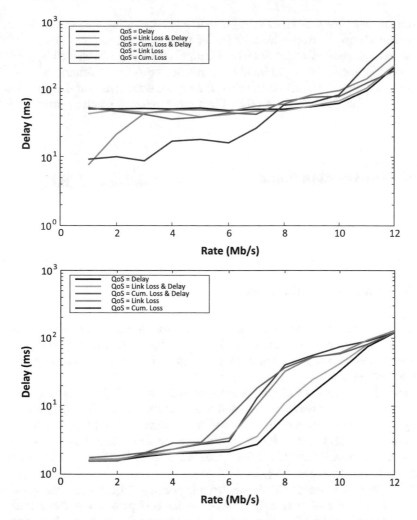

Fig. 23.1 The self-aware network observes its own performance and adapts itself to provide the users with the best possible QoS that the users have indicated. Thus, when the users specify "delay" as their desired QoS objective (*black*), the network achieves low delay (*top figure*) but is unable also to offer low loss rates (*bottom figure*). On the other hand, when low loss is desired (*red*), it is indeed achieved (*bottom*) but the delay may be higher (*top*)

autobiographical memory will be stored in the primary memory of the sources and nodes for rapid retrieval and for usage in decision making, while older elements may be moved to the secondary memory. SPs as well as payload packets that are sent out from a source and do not result in an ACK coming back also serve to estimate the packet loss rates and failures in the network (Fig. 23.1).

The QoS metrics used by the RL algorithm and by the SPs, and the information brought back by ACKs, can include different QoS characteristics that are either specified by network users as being relevant to themselves, or ingrained and relevant to the network's own performance criteria, such as delay, packet loss, jitter, security, energy consumption of nodes or links, or cumulative energy consumed by packets, or composite metrics that can be used to summarise several primary metrics. Essentially, any property that can be either directly measured (such as delay or energy consumption) or deduced from other direct measurements (such as jitter) may be used in CPN.

23.5   The Decision Engine

The decision engine or "oracle" in each of the CPN nodes is constituted by a random neural network [27, 28].

23.6   Avoiding Oscillations

When some node in a SAN makes a routing choice on the basis of its expectation that the outcome, e.g. in terms of QoS, will be favourable, it may not have the information concerning other nodes that might make the same choices based on similar information.

Thus, "best" decisions that are made independently at different entry nodes can then, some time after they are made and everyone tries to use the small number of initially best paths, become "bad" decisions when the quality of service perceived by subsequent users is themselves sensitive to the new traffic flows that use the previously identified "best" paths. This issue was also studied in terms of "sensitive" QoS metrics in previous work [12].

There are simple ways to avoid this from happening [13], such as randomisation over time, so that each user only switches to the best path in a manner which is random and hence less likely to synchronise across multiple users, or by the use of a performance threshold so that the user only makes path changes if it estimates that a significant performance improvement will occur.

Also, it is possible to introduce a random delay between the time that a decision is made and when it is actually applied, and furthermore, the node again senses the variables of interest to test whether the decision is sound. With time randomisation, the probability of a collision between different deciders [20] is negligible, similar to the way Ethernet operates using "carrier sensing" (Fig. 23.2).

Such schemes that exploit smart sensing and defer transmissions when interference, noise and other important channel characteristics can be handled in the best possible way, but also take the resulting delay, error and energy consumption into account, are also used to optimise various performance metrics in cognitive radio [9, 30].

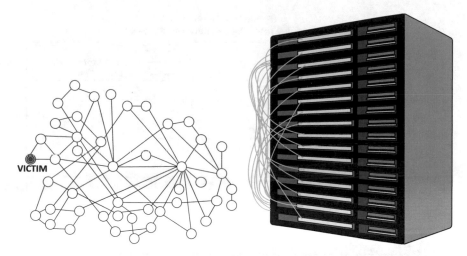

Fig. 23.2 Laboratory set-up for experiments on the self-aware network's defence capabilities to network attacks

23.7   Self-awareness and Network Attacks

Self-observation and coupled motor reaction carry over directly to the manner in which a SAN can detect attacks [6] and defend itself. These can be similar to attacks among living organisms: they are either very discrete, (1) trying to infiltrate "worms" or viruses which disable the network's useful activities, while letting through the attack itself which then delivers a "second" or "third" strike on the network's normal activities, or (2) they overwhelm the network's ability to handle traffic by an excessive number of requests that appear to be legitimate and may also in-filter into the network the attacking traffic of the first type (1).

Attacks of type (1) can require the SAN to conduct some form of eavesdropping or testing, which may or may not be allowed depending on the type of service the SAN has agreed to provide and the agreements with the users. Attacks of type (2) are usually detected without eavesdropping, using the observation of traffic characteristics. This reminds one of the local area networks [30], which react to changes in local network characterisics such as traffic in order to make decisions about whether to access the network, very similar to the way that a cognitive network operates (Fig. 23.3).

CPN offers the ability to monitor incoming traffic, to classify it into attack traffic, then counter-attack by destroying traffic that is identified as being part of an attack, and also storing it for offline analysis and comparison by deviating the attack traffic to a "honey pot". The honey pot may also be used to restore traffic which may have been mistakenly identified (i.e. a false alarm) as being part of an attack.

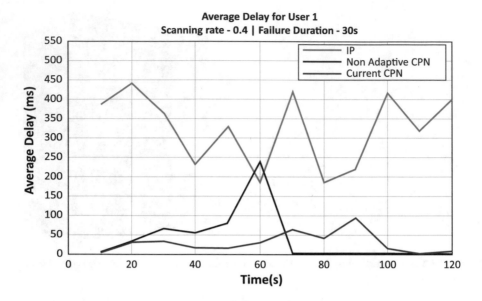

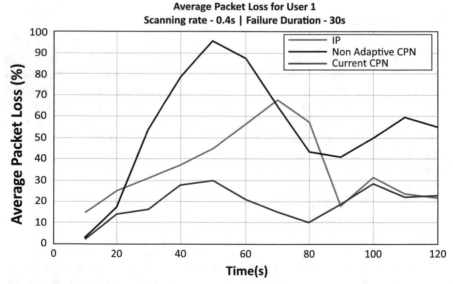

Fig. 23.3 Average packet delay (*top*) and average packet loss (*bottom*) experienced by one of the network users (the "victim") during a worm-based attack without (*blue* and *black*) and with (*red*) self-aware capabilities of the network

23.8   Conclusions

As packet networks become extremely large and diverse, a design based on a single view of how a network should operate becomes harder to justify [5]. Thus, each part of the network should be aware of its environment, its users, its resources, its performance and the threats that it is facing, and should use this awareness as an operational means to adapt its behaviour accordingly.

In addition, the possibility to adapt the network's algorithms and the software it uses, in response to changes in workload, updates in hardware infrastructure and network topology, should be incorporated into the network's core software. The software itself needs to be portable across different vendor hardware as well as various hardware generations. In addition to self-awareness and adaptivity, this creates a need for a software-defined network.

This paper summarises the work we have conducted over several years in an experimental setting for these ideas based on the cognitive packet network, which is a self-aware and completely implemented software-defined network, and reports on experiments with regard to specific choices and outcomes.

Acknowledgements   The author thanks Esin Seref, Drs Pu Su, Peixiang Liu, Ricardo Lent, Arturo Nunez, Mike Gellman, Jrmie Lain, Laurence Hey, George Loukas, Georgia Sakellari, Omer H. Abdelrahman, Gokce Gorbil, Christina Morfopoulou and Ms Lan Wang for their contributions to various aspects of this research.

References

1. Jose Aguilar and Erol Gelenbe. Task assignment and transaction clustering heuristics for distributed systems. *Information Sciences*, 97(12):199 – 219, 1997. Load balancing in distributed systems.
2. Avgoustinos Filippoupolitis and Erol Gelenbe. A distributed decision support system for building evacuation. In *Proceedings of the 2Nd Conference on Human System Interactions*, HSI'09, pages 320–327, Piscataway, NJ, USA, 2009. IEEE Press.
3. Avgoustinos Filippoupolitis, Laurence Hey, Georgios Loukas, Erol Gelenbe, and Stelios Timotheou. Emergency Response Simulation Using Wireless Sensor Networks. In *Proceedings of the 1st International Conference on Ambient Media and Systems*, Ambi-Sys '08, pages 21:1–21:7, ICST, Brussels, Belgium, 2008. ICST (Institute for Computer Sciences, Social-Informatics and Telecommunications Engineering).
4. Alex Galis, Celestin Brou, Spyros Denazis, and Cornel Klein. *Programmable Networks for IP Service Deployment*. Artech House, Norwood, 2004.
5. E. Gelenbe and D.G. Chair. Users and services in intelligent networks. In *Next Generation Internet Networks*, pages 211–218, April 2005.
6. E. Gelenbe, M. Gellman, and G. Loukas. An autonomic approach to denial of service defence. In *Sixth IEEE International Symposium on a World of Wireless Mobile and Multimedia Networks, 2005. WoWMoM 2005.*, pages 537–541, June 2005.
7. E. Gelenbe and T. Kocak. Area-based results for mine detection. *IEEE Transactions on Geoscience and Remote Sensing*, 38(1):12–24, Jan 2000.
8. E. Gelenbe, R. Lent, and A. Nunez. Self-aware networks and QoS. *Proceedings of the IEEE*, 92(9):1478–1489, Sept 2004.

9. E. Gelenbe and B. Oklander. Cognitive users with useful vacations. In *2013 IEEE International Conference on Communications Workshops (ICC)*, pages 370–374, June 2013.
10. E. Gelenbe and S. Silvestri. Reducing power consumption in wired networks. In *24th International Symposium on Computer and Information Sciences, 2009. ISCIS 2009.*, pages 292–297, Sept 2009.
11. Erol Gelenbe. Probabilistic models of computer systems. *Acta Informatica*, 12(4):285–303.
12. Erol Gelenbe. Sensible decisions based on qos. *Computational Management Science*, 1(1):1–14.
13. Erol Gelenbe. Steps Toward Self-aware Networks. *Commun. ACM*, 52(7):66–75, Jul 2009.
14. Erol Gelenbe. Search in unknown random environments. *Phys. Rev. E*, 82:061112, Dec 2010.
15. Erol Gelenbe. Natural computation. *Comput. J.*, 55(7):848–851, 2012.
16. Erol Gelenbe and Yonghuan Cao. Autonomous search for mines. *European Journal of Operational Research*, 108(2):319 – 333, 1998.
17. Erol Gelenbe and Jean-Michael Fourneau. Random Neural Networks with Multiple Classes of Signals. *Neural Comput.*, 11(4):953–963, May 1999.
18. Erol Gelenbe, Khaled Hussain, and Varol Kaptan. Simulating autonomous agents in augmented reality. *Journal of Systems and Software*, 74(3):255 – 268, 2005.
19. Erol Gelenbe and George Loukas. A Self-aware Approach to Denial of Service Defence. *Comput. Netw.*, 51(5):1299–1314, Apr 2007.
20. Erol Gelenbe and Isi Mitrani. Control Policies in CSMA Local Area Networks: Ethernet Controls. *SIGMETRICS Perform. Eval. Rev.*, 11(4):233–240, August 1982.
21. Erol Gelenbe and Christina Morfopoulou. A Framework for Energy-Aware Routing in Packet Networks. *Comput. J.*, 54(6):850–859, Jun 2011.
22. Erol Gelenbe, Nestor Schmajuk, John Staddon, and John Reif. Autonomous search by robots and animals: A survey. *Robotics and Autonomous Systems*, 22(1):23–34, 1997. Biologically Inspired Autonomous Systems.
23. Erol Gelenbe and K. Sevcik. Analysis of Update Synchronization for Multiple Copy Data Bases. *IEEE Transactions on Computers*, C-28(10):737–747, Oct 1979.
24. Erol Gelenbe, Mert Sungur, Christopher Cramer, and Pamir Gelenbe. Traffic and video quality with adaptive neural compression. *Multimedia Systems*, 4(6):357–369.
25. Erol Gelenbe and Stelios Timotheou. Random Neural Networks with Synchronized Interactions. *Neural Computation*, 20(9):2308–2324, 2008.
26. Gokce Gorbil and Erol Gelenbe. Opportunistic communications for emergency support systems. *Procedia Computer Science*, 5:39–47, 2011. The 2nd International Conference on Ambient Systems, Networks and Technologies (ANT-2011)/The 8th International Conference on Mobile Web Information Systems (MobiWIS 2011).
27. L.A. Hey, P.Y.K. Cheung, and M. Gellman. FPGA based router for cognitive packet networks. In *Field-Programmable Technology, 2005. Proceedings. 2005 IEEE International Conference on*, pages 331–332, Dec 2005.
28. Laurence A. Hey. Reduced complexity algorithms for cognitive packet network routers. *Computer Communications*, 31(16):3822–3830, 2008. Performance Evaluation of Communication Networks (SPECTS 2007).
29. Pedro Martinez-Julia, Antonio F. Skarmeta, and Alex Galis. *The Future Internet: Future Internet Assembly 2013: Validated Results and New Horizons*, chapter Towards a Secure Network Virtualization Architecture for the Future Internet, pages 141–152. Springer Berlin Heidelberg, 2013.
30. Boris Oklander and Erol Gelenbe. *Information Sciences and Systems 2013: Proceedings of the 28th International Symposium on Computer and Information Sciences*, chapter Optimal Behaviour of Smart Wireless Users, pages 87–95. Springer International Publishing, 2013.

Chapter 24
Leveraging Design and Runtime Architecture Models to Support Self-awareness

Philippe Lalanda, Stéphanie Chollet and Catherine Hamon

Abstract Self-aware computing systems possess knowledge about themselves and their environment in order to trigger the internal and external actions. Such ability is particularly interesting in new domains, such as IoT, where systems are often executed in fluctuating conditions and need frequent adaptations to meet their requirements. In this chapter, we show how such knowledge can be expressed as architectural models and how design and runtime architectures can be linked and remained synchronized. The approach is illustrated on a smart home health application called actimetrics, developed with Orange Labs.

24.1 Introduction

As defined in Chap. 1, self-aware computing systems are computing systems that possess some knowledge about themselves and their environment. This knowledge, which can evolve over time through reasoning or new information acquisition, is used to drive internal and external actions. Such ability is clearly interesting to increase the systems' ability to adapt their behaviour in dynamic, unpredictable environments.

This chapter, and indeed this book as a whole, is based on the idea that self-awareness relies on models. As explained in Chap. 1, the notion of the model is used in a general sense. It refers to any abstraction of the system and its environment that can be used for reasoning with respect to the system goals. This allows systems to act, internally or externally, to meet their goals in the dynamic situations.

P. Lalanda (✉)
Grenoble University LIG, 220 rue de la chimie, F-38041 Grenoble, France
e-mail: philippe.lalanda@imag.fr

S. Chollet
Grenoble University LCIS, 50 rue Barthélémy de Laffemas, F-26900 Valence, France
e-mail: stephanie.chollet@grenoble-inp.fr

C. Hamon
Orange Labs, 28 Chemin du Vieux Chêne, F-38243 Meylan, France
e-mail: catherine.hamon@orange.com

© Springer International Publishing AG 2017   669
S. Kounev et al. (eds.), *Self-Aware Computing Systems*,
DOI 10.1007/978-3-319-47474-8_24

Many different models can be built to meet the self-awareness. It includes models about internal structures, design goals and constraints, environmental characteristics, possible actions, and so on. Also, different techniques are used to build, update and reason about these models. This clearly raises the issues regarding the combined use of several models based on the different formalisms.

In this chapter, we focus on two major types of models used by self-aware systems: design models and runtime models. We seek to build a causal connection between abstract design models and more concrete runtime models. We are pursuing several objectives here. First, it is important to allow computing systems to be able to check the validity of their state regarding their design goals. This enables the computer systems to manage themselves and, as a consequence, to minimize the need for human inputs. This is of utter importance in new demanding fields such as Internet of Things [1].

Another major goal of this work is to allow designers to refine or update the design models while the system is under execution. Such modifications must be reflected automatically on the running systems, or rejected if it is not possible to implement it in the current running situation. The need to revise a design may appear when unexpected runtime situations are encountered and that no valid action is available to meet the new conditions.

The notion of knowledge, and associated models, is clearly central to our approach. An important challenge, however, is to figure out what should be explicitly represented. Of course, the more information is made explicit, the easier it is to implement and maintain the adaptation logic. The code is made leaner, more focused, easier to change and even reusable in certain cases. Unfortunately, capturing and modelling up-to-date information can be costly. Some compromise between completeness and cost is needed. Another challenge, of course, is to figure out how to express the information and how to allow the interoperability between different models.

In this chapter, we focus on the architectural models of the system. Unfortunately, the runtime architectures are often not traced back to design decisions, which often makes the adaptations hard to implement and test. The reason is that much knowledge has to be inserted in the adaptation algorithms and is not made explicit. Such an approach clearly does not favour code understanding and system evolution. In this chapter, we present an approach where explicit architecture models are built both at design time and runtime. A runtime architectural model describes the interconnections between components and connectors, and their mappings to implementation modules, as well as constraints on the different possible configurations. The mapping enables the changes specified in terms of the architectural model to effect corresponding changes in the implementation.

A limit of the existing approaches is related to the expressiveness of the target architectural model. Here, architectures are specified precisely through component, connectors and constraints to be maintained, and there are relatively few places for adaptation. That is, these architectures do not include much variability. Another shortcoming concerns the lack of tools managing the whole software life cycle. That is, there is a crucial for architectural tools helping the developers and administrators to model the architecture both at design time and at runtime. Most of the time, these artefacts are developed or modelled with different tools and kept separately.

The purpose of this work is to provide linked and up-to-date architectural models at runtime. These models are causal in the sense that their modifications are automatically propagated to the running software. Building such models is not straightforward. It requires to define a common formalism, to build and present causal artefacts, and to instrument running software to get relevant information during execution, without causing severe performance degradation.

24.2   Motivating Scenario and Used Technology

24.2.1   Actimetrics Use Case

Let us first introduce our motivating scenario, which is in the domain of smart homes as previously introduced in the book (see for instance Chap. 4).

The use case has been developed within a collaborative project called *Medical*.[1] It corresponds to situations commonly encountered in the health industry when it comes to home care. Precisely, the service we are working on is called *actimetrics* and is based on the measurement and analysis of the motor activities of a subject in his environment. Its purpose is to track and memorize the movement patterns of inhabitants in order to rapidly detect the abnormal changes. Indeed, for elderly or patients, behavioural changes at home can be a first sign of more serious underlying problems.

This service relies on localization information collected in homes from a network of heterogeneous and dynamic sensors. Any kind of sensors can be used to do so including presence detectors, pressure sensors and body localizers but also events emitted by any electronic devices such as a TV, an oven, a washing machine and a coffee machine. Collected data are regularly transferred in an appropriate format to a remote IT server that builds analysis matrices. Such matrices are then used to detect the behavioural deviances, which are presented to the treating doctors.

In technological terms, this use case heavily relies on the notion of software service [3], which is rather common today. Devices and applications are exposed as software services of different natures, including UPnP (www.upnp.org), web services (www.w3c.org), and DPWS (web services on devices). Implementing the use case requires integrating such services exposed on local or wide area networks.

Implementing the actimetrics use case in an open world, that is not limited to a fixed set of statically selected devices, turns out to be very challenging [4]. This is due to a number of reasons. First, the code needed to integrate the different sources

---

[1] The Medical project is funded by the OSEO and the French Ministry of industry. It brings together industrial and academic actors including Orange Labs, Grenoble University, ParisTech and Scalagent.

of information is complex and highly error-prone. In particular, the level of synchronization to be achieved brings significant difficulty. Also, it is difficult to effectively deal with the dynamicity and heterogeneity of devices. All situations cannot be anticipated at design time, and some intelligence is definitely needed at runtime to cope with the changing environments.

We believe that self-awareness abilities can be of high interest in such use case. Indeed, the main challenge of the system is to stay coherent and consistent with its goals in a very dynamic and unpredictable environment. As we will see in this chapter, building models and reasoning about them is an efficient way to do so.

24.2.2 Implementation with Cilia

To implement this use case, we use a service-oriented mediation framework [12]. This framework, called Cilia, is available in open source. Its purpose is to simplify the work of developers by offering a well-defined and limited set of abstractions to support design, deployment, and execution of data-oriented applications [10].

The Cilia framework takes the form of a domain-specific service-oriented component model, including a specification language and a flexible execution environment. A Cilia component is called a mediator. Its purpose is to apply a single mediation operation such as a data transformation, a security function and an aggregation. A mediator is characterized by a number of typed input and output ports. The input ports receive the data to be treated, whereas the output ports forward the results of the mediation processing. The ports are the means to connect mediators and, thus, form mediation chains. A mediator can also be characterized by a service dependency, resolved at runtime. Here, the dependency is expressed as a Java interface. This feature is convenient, for instance, to integrate dynamically available data sources exposed as services.

The content of the mediators is divided into three Java classes: a scheduler, a processor and a dispatcher. The purpose of the scheduler is to store the data received in the input ports and to apply a triggering condition. Simply put, the scheduler deals with all the synchronization issues. When the condition held by the scheduler becomes true, all the data retained by the scheduler are sent to the processor. The processor applies the mediation operation to the transmitted data. The result of this operation is sent to the dispatcher, whose purpose is to place the results in the output ports. The dispatcher handles the routing aspect in the mediation chains.

A composition of Cilia mediators is called a mediation chain. A mediation chain is formed by a set of connected adapters and mediators. Adapters feed the mediators (and the destination resources) with data in the appropriate format and with the appropriate timing. Mediators constitute the heart of the chain since they implement the effective mediation operations. Mediators (and adapters) are connected via bindings. A binding describes a connection between an output port and an input port. At execution time, a binding is realized by a communication protocol transferring data from a mediator (or adapter) to another mediator (or adapter). This protocol can be specified at deployment time, but also at development time. Cilia supports local and remote communication protocols.

The Cilia execution framework is built on top of OSGi and iPOJO, the Apache service-oriented component model (see Fig. 24.1). It also includes RoSe, an open source communication middleware that is able to dynamically import and export services (see https://github.com/AdeleResearchGroup/ROSE). A mediation chain is created in the following manner. A specification file is transmitted to the Cilia runtime. These specifications are transformed into a number of iPOJO component definitions. At least five iPOJO components are created for each mediator: one component for the scheduler, one component for the processor, one component for the dispatcher and two components for the in and out communication ports (more components are created if different protocols are used by different ports). The defined iPOJO components are then instantiated and executed. From this point, the mediation chain is operational (and the desired integration is achieved).

To sum up, Cilia is a recent service-oriented framework meeting the stringent requirements data mediation. It is well adapted to the implementation of commonly accepted integration patterns, which favours its acceptation by domain developers. The use of domain-specific concepts also simplifies the creation and understanding of the mediation chains. Cilia is currently used with the Orange Labs and Schneider Electric in order to implement the data integration in IoT applications.

Fig. 24.1 Cilia overview

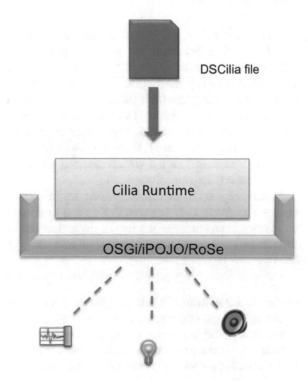

The use of service orientation is particularly effective to integrate dynamically available resources. It raises however important management issues. Indeed, the system changes its structure by itself. As a result, it is pretty difficult to follow and to check the availability of a given configuration.

Also, adapting Cilia chains to new runtime conditions or users' demands still depends on skilled administrators and generally requires some downtime. In many domains, administrators are not available or not skilled enough. Also, service interruption is not always allowed. Solutions must be developed in such cases in order to automate the administration or to provide the effective help to administrators.

The idea defended in this chapter is to rely on self-aware approach. That is, we seek to build knowledge about the system's goals, design constraints and runtime situation in order to allow the system to manage itself. Precisely, we want the system to be able to figure out if it is in a correct state (i.e. in conformance with its design constraints) and, if not, to determine the actions to be undergone. In the worst case, the system should be able to send an alert to human administrators. Then, specific management actions can be undergone or design constraints can be modified (and immediately considered by the system under execution).

As we will see now, knowledge in our approach is essentially based on the notion of software architecture.

24.3 Our Approach

As introduced earlier, our self-aware system is based on architectural knowledge. Based on such information, the system is able to adapt itself to changing conditions. An important advantage of this approach is that under the assumption that the architecture correctly mirrors the managed system, the architectural model can be used to verify that system integrity is preserved when applying an adaptation. This is because changes are planned and applied to the model first, which will show the resulting system state including any violations of constraints or requirements of the system present in the model. If the new state of the system is acceptable, the plan can then be executed on the actual managed system, thus ensuring that the model and implementation are consistent.

Specifically, we propose to formalize design, deployment and runtime architectures and maintain links between design and runtime decisions. Thus, architectural models are kept synchronized by the execution support. This simplifies reasoning since crucial information is presented and maintained by a separate module. This is illustrated by Fig. 24.2 here after.

Let us define more precisely the different types of architectures:

Design architectures.   These architectures are defined by domain architects and define the target structures of a system. They may include some variability, making room for the future runtime adaptation. Design architectures are said to be concrete when they include no variability. They are said to be abstract when some variability remains, for instance, regarding the component implementations to be used [8].

Fig. 24.2 Self-aware
architectures

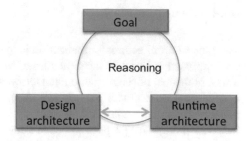

Deployment architectures.   These architectures are appropriately configured and
ready for the deployment at a target client site. They may also allow some variability for runtime adaptation. They are however more constrained than the design
architectures.

Runtime architectures.   These architectures are built from monitoring data and
formalize the architecture of a system under execution (at a given level of abstraction). They are still made of components and connectors, but the notions of variability and constraints are not present anymore.

All these architecture are based on the very same notions of components, connectors and constraints. However, they are defined and valued at different steps of the
software life cycle, from the design phase and to the execution time. For that reason,
they differ in terms of provided information regarding components, connectors and
constraints.

These architectures are derived from one another. That means that the deployment and runtime architectures meet all the constraints, structural and behavioural,
expressed by the design architecture. Since the design architectures may include
some variability, correct runtime architectures can be numerous.

Regarding design and deployment architectures, the key point is to express the
variability. Identifying and describing variability is a hard problem. Many different
approaches have actually been proposed to describe, and to resolve, the variability.
They can be based on the natural language, semi-formal languages, such as UML
or feature diagrams, or formal languages such as ADLs. Many approaches directly
focus on the notion of software architecture.

Design architectures have then to specify common and variable structures. Emerging tools have introduced the possibility to express the variations in architecture in
a systematic way. This has to be considered in two dimensions, space and time [7].
The locations in design artefacts, where a specific decision has been narrowed to
several options, are called variation points. Variability modelling comes down to the
identification and documentation of those variation points to facilitate the specific
configuration activity at runtime. However, the identification and explicit representation of variation points is a thorny problem. It requires not only to introduce the
variation points and their relative variants, but also to define the some dependencies
among variation points and to express the possible context-related restrictions.

24.4   Architectures

The goal of architectures formalization is to clearly identify the different concepts. Our approach is based on the principles of Model-Driven Engineering with the definition of meta-models. A meta-model allows to precisely specify without ambiguity a language used to model architectures. A meta-model defines a grammar and vocabulary to express the models. The resulting models are consistent and conformed to the meta-model. We propose to define a meta-model for each kind of architectures (design, deployment and runtime) and a global meta-model with the core concepts. The three meta-models inherit the global meta-model as illustrated by Fig. 24.3.

One of the major interests to keep the main concepts in a global meta-model is that the core concepts can be used and refined in the different sub-meta-model, which are simply specialized for each step of the life cycle. Thus, this solution guarantees the coherency of concepts, which is not the case with a unique meta-model. It also requires fewer rules definition, generally expressed with OCL (*Object Constraint Language*).

24.4.1   *Global Architecture Meta-Model*

Figure 24.4 describes the global architecture meta-model. It contains the core concepts used to depict the software architectures. An architecture is represented by the

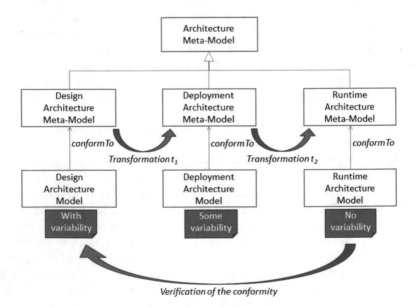

Fig. 24.3 Meta-model organization

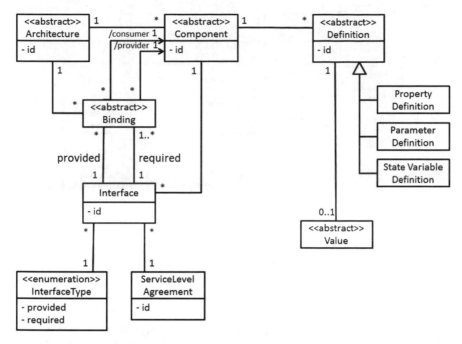

Fig. 24.4 Global architecture meta-model

abstract class *Architecture*. An architecture is composed by *components* and *bindings*. Each *component* and *binding* is a member of a unique architecture. A component has a set of *interfaces*. An *interface* is required or provided and described by a service-level agreement. *Bindings* are the links between two components with the same service-level agreement. The *definition* concept allows to express the variability in the different sub-meta-models. We propose three kinds of definition: *property*, *parameter* and *state variable*. In the following, we give examples of the variability.

It is to be noted that the core concepts are abstract. In each sub-meta-model, they are overloaded in compliance with the grammar and vocabulary defined in the global meta-model.

24.4.2   Design Architecture Meta-Model

The design meta-model defines the vocabulary and the grammar used at design time. It inherits from concepts of the global meta-model. We have introduced the elements required to express the design architectures. Figure 24.5 shows the design meta-model. A design architecture can be constrained. The components of the architecture are either specifications or implementations. An implementation may correspond to a specification. Bindings between components are expressed with cardinalities (minimum and maximum for provided and required components).

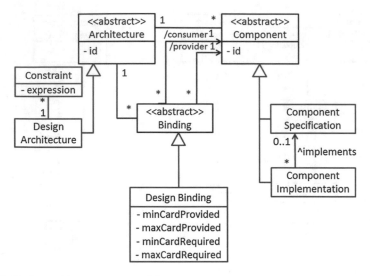

Fig. 24.5 Design architecture meta-model

This architecture contains variability constraints mainly expressed by the cardinalities for the bindings. Variability is a key point in design architectures. Design architectures have to specify common structures and, also, leave space to bring in specific characteristics at runtime, as expressed previously. Our design meta-model facilitates the variability definition at design time.

24.4.3 Deployment Architecture Meta-Model

The deployment architecture is the final refinement, if any, of the design architecture. This deployment architecture contains the structures, behaviours and constraints to be met by the application at hand, given the target platform and the quality-related goals. It is shown in Fig. 24.6.

24.4.4 Runtime Architecture Meta-Model

The runtime architecture, whose meta-model is shown in Fig. 24.7, stores the runtime information about the running software and the platform under operation. This architecture provides a model of runtime phenomena, with trends and past data [2, 13], and is intended for use by autonomic managers or by administrators [6, 9]. Using this knowledge module is a very convenient way for domain engineers to create autonomic managers.

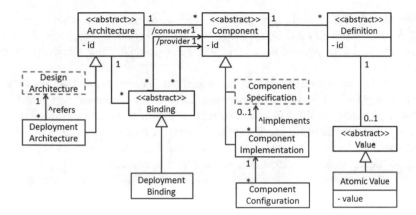

Fig. 24.6 Deployment architecture meta-model

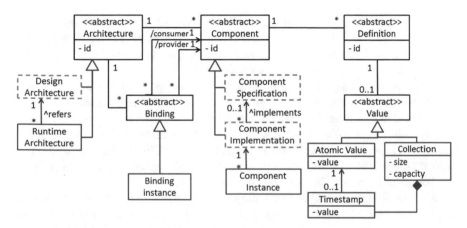

Fig. 24.7 Runtime architecture meta-model

Traceability links between design and runtime architectures are constantly maintained. To do so, we used and extended graph-based algorithms. Indeed, architectures can be formalized as graphs, where components (specification, implementation or under execution) are nodes and bindings between components (specification or real connections) are arcs.

24.5   Application to Cilia

We applied the proposed approach to Cilia and to the actimetrics use case (see Sect. 24.2). To do so, we had to realize the following developments:

- We extended Cilia with touch points, as defined in the third section, in order to dynamically monitor and adapt the mediation chains under execution and some aspects of the supporting execution platform (essentially the service discovery functions).
- We created an architecture-based tool dedicated to designers and administrators. This integrated development environment (IDE) allows the modelling of the design and deployment architectures, and the representation of the runtime architectures. Links between these different architectures are created and maintained. These artefacts can be used by the reasoning module of the self-aware system or possibly by an administrator to perform the maintenance operations.

24.5.1 Architectural Touch Points

The Cilia framework now provides a set of touch points to dynamically monitor and adapt the mediation chains under execution at the architectural level. Touch points can also be used to monitor some aspects of the execution platform such as the available services and the protocols used to do so.

Monitoring and adaptation features are flexible and configurable. Monitoring, in particular, can be controlled in a dynamic way. This means that Cilia monitoring can be activated or deactivated globally. It also means that the elements to be monitored, and the way they are monitored, can be configured without the interruption of services. This allows developers and administrators to use Cilia features in accordance with their needs and objectives. Expectations can obviously vary according to the runtime situation and to the problems that may arise.

We could envision the case where the system (and not its developers or administrators) could actually have sufficient resources and knowledge to choose new adaptation features as it is indicated in Chap. 9 on self-modelling capabilities in self-aware systems.

Specifically, the state variables attached to each mediator are as follows:

- Scheduler start time,
- Scheduler incoming data,
- Processor start time,
- Processor incoming data,
- Processor outgoing data,
- Processor end time,
- Value of a processor field annotated by the developer,
- Dispatcher start time,
- Dispatcher incoming data,
- Mediator execution time, and
- Number of messages sent out by a mediator.

It is possible in a self-aware approach for an autonomic manager to dynamically update the following architectural elements:

- A mediation chain can be dynamically added or removed;
- Configuration parameters of a mediation chain can be dynamically updated;
- A mediator can be dynamically removed from a running chain;
- A mediator can be dynamically added;
- A mediator can be dynamically replaced within a running chain (hot swapping);
- Configuration parameters of a mediator can be dynamically updated;
- Configuration parameters of the execution machine can be dynamically updated and
- An adapter can be dynamically replaced. Its configuration parameters can be changed.

24.5.2 Architecture-Focused Tool

We have developed an integrated development and administration environment in eclipse. This environment, specific to Cilia, is based on the approach presented in the fourth section. It allows the modelling of design mediation architectures, with variable aspects, and automatically builds runtime architectures in a configurable way.

A design mediation architecture is then a specification of a chain with some variability. As expressed in the meta-model, it is made of abstract and concrete mediators with service dependencies and bindings with possible cardinalities (adapters are not represented here for the sake of simplicity).

Three techniques can then be used to introduce variability in design mediation chains:

- Abstract mediators can be inserted in a chain. An abstract mediator is a high level description, independent of the implementation. This description specifies the mediation operation to be performed and may set some parameters values.
- Cardinality can be expressed in bindings. Cardinalities can be set to (1), (1..*) or (0..*). Thus, a branch of a mediation chain can be optional or multiple. That means that it can be absent or duplicated under various forms, depending on the runtime conditions.
- Service dependencies can be expressed for each mediator. A dependency is expressed with a Java interface and can be characterized by a cardinality and a ranking function. A ranking function can be seen as a utility function, as commonly developed in autonomic computing, used to classify the candidate services.

Depending on the target environment, more or less variability can be expressed in the design mediation chains. The more variability in a chain, the more there is a scope for runtime adaptation. But also the more challenging is the task of the administrator (or of the autonomic managers). On the contrary, with little variability in the design, there is not much contingency at runtime for controlled adaptations, which are anticipated at design time (even at a high level of abstraction).

Let us now return to the actimetrics use case introduced in Sect. 24.2. The purpose of the mediation chain is to collect as much information as possible regarding inhabitant's movements. This information can come from all devices placed in the house, albeit heterogeneous ones.

As illustrated by Fig. 24.8, the design mediation chain of the actimetrics use case is made of the following elements:

- A branch made of the mediators *push-button*, *button-enrich* and *button-translate*: This branch gets information from a special purpose button that can be pressed by the inhabitant, then enriches the captured information (timing or location information for instance) and translates it into a standard format.
- A branch made of the mediators *motion-sensor*, *motion-enrich* and *motion-translate*: This branch gets information from any kind of sensors able to detect a movement, then enriches the captured information and translates it into a standard format.

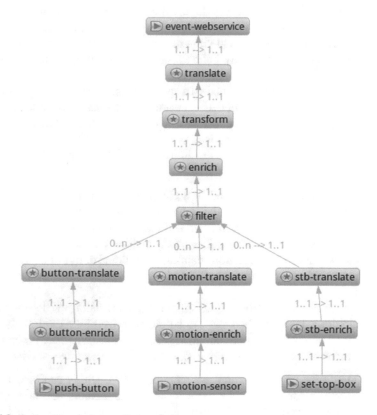

Fig. 24.8 Actimetrics design mediation chain

- A branch made of the mediators *set-top-box*, *stb-enrich* and *stb-translate*: This branch gets information from set-top-boxes (stb) when used by the inhabitant, then enriches the captured information and translates it into a standard format.
- A branch made of the mediators *filter, enrich, transform, translate* and *event-webservice*: The filter mediator receives data from different devices (from the corresponding branches), synchronizes them and eliminates the redundancy or dubious information. Then, data are enriched with information such as the house id, transformed, translated and sent to a web service (executed on remote server).

The first three branches (button, motion and set-top-box) are optional. They depend on the presence of devices that are not known at design time. The fourth branch is a base one, meaning that it is always instantiated, regardless of the environment and runtime conditions.

The runtime architecture stores runtime information about the mediation chains and the platform under operation. This architecture provides a model of runtime phenomena, with trends and past data, and is intended for use by autonomic managers or by administrators. This model is causal in the sense that modifications made on the runtime architecture are reflected on the Cilia runtime, and vice versa.

This approach facilitates the development of the reasoning part of a self-aware system. Indeed, reasoning can use high information provided by the knowledge module and trigger adaptations. Such approach does not demand to be familiar with the intricacies of Cilia; domain-specific mediation knowledge suffices to manage Cilia-based systems.

Let us get back to the actimetrics use case. An instance of runtime architecture is shown in Fig. 24.9. In the figure, state variables are not presented (they are in fact accessible in specific windows of the tool).

It appears that among the optional branches, two of them have been instantiated. These are similar branches that have been dynamically created to deal with buttons discovered in the environment. Here, branches are duplicated to separately integrate the two detected buttons. An alternative solution would have been to create a single mediation branch dealing with all the possible buttons detected in a house.

As shown by Fig. 24.10, the two branches dealing with concrete buttons in the runtime architecture are linked to the design mediation chain. Precisely, they are linked to the optional branch addressing the press buttons.

To illustrate this, let us get back to our actimetrics example. If, at runtime, a button is deficient and causes problems (for instance, the base branch waits too long for its inputs), then the administrator knows that he/she can suppress the branch without affecting the global mediation application. This is indeed expressed by the design mediation chain where the "button branches" are specified as optional. In spite of the system dynamicity due to services arrival and departure, the administrator is able to take a good decision in line with the designers' plans.

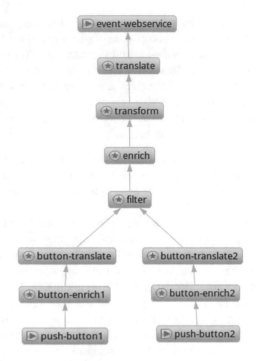

Fig. 24.9 Actimetrics runtime mediation chain

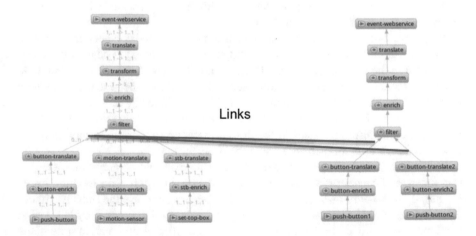

Fig. 24.10 Traceability links between design and runtime mediation chains

24.6 Conclusion

We believe that formalizing architectural models and maintaining links between them at runtime is an important step towards self-awareness. Indeed, self-awareness requires knowledge about one's objectives and design constraints and the way they are realized. Explicit links between design and realization allow a system to assess if the current situation answers the needs or if modifications are necessary.

In this chapter, we proposed to present a continuous, easily understandable, model of the design and runtime architectures and their links. Thus, when a decision has to be made, advanced architectural information is available for guidance. To do so, we had to precisely define the notions of design architecture, variability and runtime architectures. These notions are based on abstract components, concrete components, executed components, service dependencies and bindings with cardinality.

This proposal has been successfully implemented on a use case developed within the Orange Labs in the smart home health domain.

Several research directions can be envisaged. First, it is clear that we only deal with a limited number of architectural aspects. It would be interesting to apply our approach to other topics such as performance management. This would result in the definition of new models and associated meta-models. Another opportunity would be to allow autonomic adaptation of the design models. That would be a next step in self-awareness. That is, a system is able to modify its design rationales in order to face the unexpected runtime evolutions.

Also, it would be useful to investigate the different architectural styles. In particular, micro-services [11] are getting very popular in the service-oriented field. This approach can be compared to iPOJO but in a distributed form. This changes a lot of things regarding, for instance, communication delays or replication opportunities.

Finally, our approach can be related to the DevOps movement. Indeed, linking design and runtime models is a way to lower the separation between software development and system operations. In the same trend, our approach can be extended with continuous deployment as explored in [5].

References

1. Luigi Atzori, Antonio Iera, and Giacomo Morabito. The Internet of Things: A survey. *Computer Networks*, 54(15):2787–2805, 2010.
2. Gordon S. Blair, Nelly Bencomo, and Robert B. France. Models run.time. *IEEE Computer*, 42(10):22–27, 2009.
3. Stéphanie Chollet and Philippe Lalanda. Security Specification at Process Level. In *IEEE SCC*, pages 165–172. IEEE Computer Society, 2008.
4. Clément Escoffier, Stéphanie Chollet, and Philippe Lalanda. Lessons learned in building pervasive platforms. In *11th IEEE Consumer Communications and Networking Conference, CCNC 2014, Las Vegas, NV, USA, January 10-13, 2014*, pages 7–12. IEEE, 2014.
5. Ozan Günalp, Clément Escoffier, and Philippe Lalanda. Rondo: A Tool Suite for Continuous Deployment in Dynamic Environments. In *2015 IEEE International Conference on Services*

Computing, SCC 2015, New York City, NY, USA, June 27–July 2, 2015, pages 720–727. IEEE, 2015.

6. Jeffrey O Kephart and David M Chess. The vision of autonomic computing. *Computer*, 36(1):41–50, 2003.

7. Charles W. Krueger. Variation Management for Software Production Lines. In Gary J. Chastek, editor, *Software Product Lines, Second International Conference, SPLC 2, San Diego, CA, USA, August 19–22, 2002, Proceedings*, volume 2379 of *Lecture Notes in Computer Science*, pages 37–48. Springer, 2002.

8. Philippe Lalanda and Cristina Marin. A Domain-Configurable Development Environment for Service-Oriented Applications. *IEEE Software*, 24(6):31–38, 2007.

9. Philippe Lalanda, Julie A. McCann, and Ada Diaconescu. *Autonomic Computing - Principles, Design and Implementation*. Springer–Verlag, June 2013.

10. Denis Morand, Issac García, and Philippe Lalanda. Autonomic enterprise service bus. In Zoubir Mammeri, editor, *IEEE 16th Conference on Emerging Technologies & Factory Automation, ETFA 2011, Toulouse, France, September 5–9, 2011*, pages 1–8. IEEE, 2011.

11. Sam Newman. *Building Microservices: Designing Fine-Grained Systems*. O'Reilly Media, 1st edition, February 2015.

12. F.A. Schreiber, R. Camplani, M. Fortunato, M. Marelli, and G. Rota. PerLa: A Language and Middleware Architecture for Data Management and Integration in Pervasive Information Systems. *Software Engineering, IEEE Transactions on*, 38(2):478–496, 2012.

13. Michael Szvetits and Uwe Zdun. Systematic literature review of the objectives, techniques, kinds, and architectures of models at runtime. *Software and System Modeling*, 15(1):31–69, 2016.

Chapter 25
Spacecraft Autonomous Reaction Capabilities, Control Approaches, and Self-aware Computing

Klaus Schilling, Jürgen Walter and Samuel Kounev

Abstract Space exploration missions require very challenging autonomous reaction capabilities, as spacecraft have to react appropriately to the partially unknown environment in time-critical situations. Here, direct human interaction is often impossible due to significant signal propagation delays related to the huge distances. We discuss existing solution strategies for autonomy in space and exemplified by the missions CASSINI–HUYGEN (landing on the Saturnian moon) and ROSETTA (the accompanying and landing on a comet), and the NetSat project (low Earth orbit formations). Based on the state of the art, we outline how self-aware computing may improve autonomy in future space missions.

25.1 Introduction

In the last 60 years, exploration of our home planet's environment raised challenging technical tasks. While physics provided the basis for initial models, the specific parameters and relevant perturbations still had to be determined by experience with engineering such complex systems. Thus, today our Earth's environment is reasonably well known, while our knowledge about even the other bodies in our solar system is still very limited and therefore such bodies are the target of challenging space exploration tasks which are for their part subject to specific requirements. In this context, the on-board data handling systems have to act autonomously in order to adapt to unforeseen conditions. In this contribution, potential future approaches to improve autonomy by adding self-awareness capabilities are suggested. These capabilities are aimed at improving the spacecraft ability to continuously

K. Schilling (✉) · J. Walter · S. Kounev
Department of Computer Science, University of Würzburg, Am Hubland,
97074 Würzburg, Germany
e-mail: k_schi@t-online.de

J. Walter
e-mail: juergen.walter@uni-wuerzburg.de

S. Kounev
e-mail: samuel.kounev@uni-wuerzburg.de

© Springer International Publishing AG 2017   687
S. Kounev et al. (eds.), *Self-Aware Computing Systems*,
DOI 10.1007/978-3-319-47474-8_25

- characterize its status by its sensors as well as by the space environment status (self-reflective),
- assess from the known dynamics, what changes will occur in the near future (self-predictive), and
- react appropriately in time such that the operations necessary for the planned mission are initiated (self-adaptive).

The above three—already partially realized—properties (i.e., self-reflective, self-predictive, and self-adaptive) are in line with our notion of self-aware computing, defined in Chap. 1, which stresses model *learning* and *reasoning* as ongoing activities enabling "informed" actions in order to meet higher-level goals. Existing solutions in space missions are based on physical models and control theoretical solution approaches. This chapter summarizes them and discusses possible advances using self-aware methodologies.

The remainder of this chapter is organized as follows: Sect. 25.2 discusses the specific requirements in space, while Sect. 25.3 discusses self-awareness and other solution approaches. Section 25.4 depicts two classes of example missions. First, we emphasize two exemplary ESA missions to explore our solar system. These are HUYGENS (which landed in 2005 on the largest Saturnian moon Titan) and ROSETTA (which accompanied in 2015 the comet 67P/Churyumov-Gerasimenko during its closest approach to the sun, called perihel passage) [17]. Besides such traditional single multi-functional big spacecraft missions, there is a trend toward a distributed combination of multiple small spacecrafts. Therefore, secondly, Sect. 25.4 also addresses formations of cooperating satellites in low Earth orbits using the NetSat project as an example. Finally, Sect. 25.5 presents some concluding remarks.

25.2 Requirements in Space

Space system operations have to address the challenges such as higher levels of noise and huge distances causing significant signal propagation delays. Hence, unlike the often theoretical discussions of the benefits of autonomy for terrestrial robotic applications (e.g., in [4]), the autonomous reaction capabilities of space vehicles are needed to survive until the situation can be analyzed remotely by human tele-operators and ground control can intervene by appropriate reactions [9, 16]. A typical definition to characterize the required reaction capabilities for spacecraft is as follows:

Definition 25.1 *Autonomy* defines the capability of a vehicle

- to meet mission performance requirements for a specified period of time without external support and
- to optimize the mission science products, e.g., the scientific measurements, within the given constraints.

Here, in particular, interplanetary space probes encounter specific challenges due to:

- extreme working environments (radiation, temperature, pressure, and gravity),
- huge distances (leading to significant signal propagation delays, teleoperations autonomy needs, and no human interaction capabilities in time-critical situations), and
- major uncertainties (limited sensors to characterize the spacecraft's environment, poorly modeled working environments, and limited capabilities to verify and test).

Although there are well-known mathematical models of the physical environment, the crucial values for specific parameters are still to be determined on site. For example, the satellite dynamics are determined by gravity, where well-known generic mathematical models are available. Nevertheless, the mass distribution and inhomogeneities of a specific target planet still need to be determined and to be represented in the coefficients of the detailed power series expansion of the gravity field.

25.3 Solution Approaches

Compared to other contexts where autonomy is applied, space exploration missions have to survive in time-critical situations and learned aspects can only improve the next mission. Every experiment or exploration is unique. All these aspects are different compared to continuous service provisioning (e.g., in data centers). In space exploration, advanced classical control approaches are often applied in order to handle related uncertainties. In this section, solution approaches are reviewed and the potential for future use of model-driven algorithms and architectures from self-aware computing is outlined.

25.3.1 Model-Based Adaptive Control

The adaptive control approach has been applied in the context of highly reactive systems. One of the greatest challenges for modern aerospace applications is the ability to react in real time to changing environmental conditions and to adapt the related responses [3]. Thus, supersonic aircraft are often aerodynamically unstable and need continuously active control in order not to crash. Figure 25.1 depicts the basic adaptive control principle. While the design of a conventional feedback control system firstly targets the elimination of the effect of disturbances upon the controlled variables, the design of adaptive control systems firstly targets the elimination of the effect of parameter disturbances upon the performance of the control system [8].

Adaptive control addresses the update of parameters in models, but not adaptations of the whole solution strategy, like in self-aware computing. A new aspect of self-aware computing, compared to model-based control, is the use of semantic models. These can be transformed via model-to-model transformations that enable an easy swapping of solution strategies.

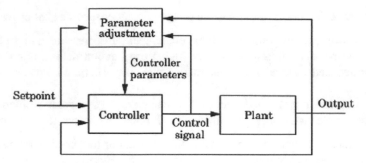

Fig. 25.1 Adaptive control principle

25.3.2 Supervisory Control

In contrast to automatic control, supervisory control considers a human in the control loop and provides a framework to assign tasks. While real-time reactions should be realized autonomously, the human operator contributes to higher level superimposed control loops (like at the planning level) with less stringent time constraints. An integrated human–machine control system can be described as a set of embedded control loops working at different time scales, as illustrated in Fig. 25.2 [22], with high frequency feedback in the center and more long-term "learning" schemes at the outer loop. The `plan` step includes attaining awareness of the environment situation and the system to control, as well as the setting of achievable goals or related intermediate steps. The `teach` step is about to decide the control actions. Sensor and model-based supervision of the current state of the spacecraft are done within `monitor` step. The `intervene` box depicts human intervention to modify the control algorithm. The `learn` step is about to record experience and updating models. The teach, monitor, and intervene functions are done iteratively and therefore are depicted within an inner and online loop [22]. The implementation challenges relate to avoiding conflicts between these nested control loops. While the real-time features are to be realized on-board the spacecraft, the planning levels are usually done by the tele-operators in the ground control centers.

We complete the description of supervisory control by discussing the relation to self-aware computing. Both try to reduce the dependency on human intervention by integrating the human at the highest levels of abstraction, while maintaining lower-level functions within the machine. However, self-aware systems may interact with each other and do not require human intervention. Regarding the differences, supervisory control sets the focus on interaction of human operator and machine. Instead, self-aware computing sets the focus on how the programs work internally (e.g., use of model-based approaches differing descriptive, prescriptive, and predictive models) and includes a concrete model-based solution strategy. Due to the different focus, we see a broad area of space applications where both paradigms form a good complement to each other.

Fig. 25.2 The five generic
supervisory control functions
with nested related control
loops

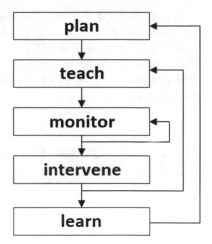

25.3.3   Distributed Networked Control

Distributed networked control addresses the control via communication links. In space applications, satellites form nodes that are connected and coordinated throughout a network. Linking technologies include dedicated space protocols, Internet Protocols (IP), delay tolerant networks (DTNs), and mobile ad-hoc networks (MANets) adapted to the space environment (e.g., high noise levels, link interruptions, interferences, radiation, and inaccuracies in pointing). The research on the distributed networked control [7] has a multidisciplinary nature, blending the areas of communication networks, computer science, and control. The properties of the telecommunication links together with the control characteristics are to be combined to an integrated system [5].

One application scenario that attained much attention in recent times is the provision of Internet via satellites (current projects are discussed in Sect. 25.4.3). For this purpose, existing approaches have to be extended and new strategies have to be found. In particular, the case of coordinating several spacecraft in a formation is challenging. In addition to the interaction between ground control and satellite, also the exchange of information between vehicles regarding their status and plans for future actions via inter-satellite links is to be analyzed. The challenge consists in a reliable coordination of the distributed computers and decision making resources in order to achieve the mission objectives in a consistent and robust way. Similar to the evolution in computing, where the traditional mainframe computers of the 1970s have been replaced by the Internet connected laptops or smart phones, also in spacecraft system design the established multi-functional large spacecraft are expected to become in specific application areas complemented or substituted by networked small satellites [14].

In contrast to the distributed networked control, self-aware computing describes a solution strategy using descriptive models that is independent of the problem domain. Due to the profile of the addressed problems in the distributed networked control, there is an interesting application potential for the future self-aware computing approaches. Self-aware computing can be applied to provide the distributed networked control.

25.3.4 System Health Management

Reliable spacecraft operations require system health management. Extreme radiation environments dramatically increase failure risks for all electric components. Radiation may cause a change of an electronic state due to one single ionizing particle (ions, electrons, photons...) striking a sensitive node in a micro-electronic device, such as in a microprocessor, semiconductor memory, or power transistors. The state change is a result of the free charge created by ionization in or close to an important node of a logic element (e.g., memory "bit").

Due to the high likelihood of errors, the system health has to be continuously monitored. In classical space engineering approaches, health management handles redundancy switching. Ideally, system health management should detect, resolve, and predict failures. NASA researchers promote statistical approaches of health management with Bayesian networks [20]. This solution approach is popular in the academic context but has not been applied in space missions so far. A major drawback is the computationally intensive reasoning algorithms [21]. Therefore, the use of special hardware, Field Programmable Gate Arrays (FPGAs), has been proposed in [21]. Bayesian networks are not the only solution to ensure system health. Furthermore, data mining techniques can be used for detection, diagnostics, and prognostics [23]. Advanced approaches to health monitoring often rely on model-based fault detection, isolation, and recovery (FDIR) methods. By this way, deviations from expected status are detected and corrected. Most often, this is realized by taking advantage of redundant systems.

Compared to self-aware computing, system health management describes the problem domain without specifying a concrete solution strategy beyond redundancy switching and disconnecting faulty components. Self-aware computing, instead, describes a solution strategy, using descriptive models, that is independent of the problem domain. According to Schuhmann et al. [21], the trend should go toward real-time, on-board, sensor and software health management. Our proposed realization is that aerial systems get self-awareness concerning their health status. For future applications, the concept of self-aware computing can help to incorporate different solution strategies such as Bayesian networks or data mining approaches into one combined view on system health management. This would enable a self-aware change of the system health insurance strategy that considers for example a trade-off between cost and accuracy of approaches.

25.3.5   Self-aware Computing

Compared to the previously presented approaches, the idea of self-aware computing, applied in the context of space applications, translates into combining model-based learning and reasoning as ongoing processes built into the spacecraft design to support autonomous reaction and control mechanisms. Space missions are becoming more and more complex and challenging. We see a need for further automation to reach new goals. We argue that inspiration from self-aware computing can help to advance the field. Despite sharing crucial aspects with classical adaptive control, self-aware computing introduces complementary new aspects:

- In addition to collecting observations and monitoring data during operation, self-aware computing emphasizes the learning of formal models capturing knowledge in an abstract and compact manner and supporting reasoning with respect to the system goals;
- Model learning processes are first-class entities in the system design that drive the spacecraft decisions; they integrate knowledge provided by the system designer with observations obtained during the operation;
- The learned models support complex reasoning and predictive analytics that go beyond applying simple rules or heuristics explicitly programmed at system design-time;
- Both the learning and reasoning processes are assumed to be running on an ongoing basis during operation; thus, models are expected to evolve as time progresses, leading to improved reasoning and more reliable decisions;
- Self-aware computing leverages models of different types in an integrated manner: (i) *descriptive models* describe selected aspects of the system and its environment in an abstract manner enabling formal analysis and reasoning, (ii) *prescriptive models* typically define behaviors to be applied in different situations, e.g., adaptation processes, and (iii) *predictive models* support more complex reasoning, e.g., predicting the system behavior under given conditions or predicting the impact of a considered possible adaptation action; and
- By leveraging model-to-model transformations, flexibility in trading-off between model accuracy and analysis overhead is provided. A suitable model combined with a tailored solution strategy can be selected depending on the specific reasoning scenario (urgency of the situation, criticality of the decision to be made, required accuracy, etc.).

25.4   Example Missions and Projects

The research on autonomy in space is driven by uncertainties of the space environment, where reliable reactions are required and will be evaluated in reality. In the following, we will describe several projects that faced challenging autonomous operation tasks. These are the landing on the Saturnian moon presented in Sect. 25.4.1, the accompanying and landing on a comet presented in Sect. 25.4.2, and the satellite formations in low Earth orbits presented in Sect. 25.4.3.

25.4.1 HUYGENS—Landing on the Saturnian Moon Titan

While NASA's VOYAGER 2 spacecraft approached, in November 1980, the largest Saturnian moon Titan at a close distance of 5000 km, the instruments could not penetrate the unexpectedly dense atmosphere. Nevertheless, during this flyby, hydrocarbon molecules were detected and justified a return for more detailed investigations of the exotic organic chemistry in this atmosphere. In the resulting joint mission, NASA contributed the CASSINI spacecraft for long-term remote sensing observations by orbiting the Saturnian system, while the European Space Agency (ESA) contributed the HUYGENS probe to descend to the surface of Titan. The CASSINI–HUYGENS-mission was launched on October 6, 1997, and arrived at the Saturnian system in June 2004 [9, 13]. The significant distance led to a signal propagation delay of 68 mins. Therefore, ground control interaction during the entry and descent, lasting 2.5 h, was not feasible, and autonomous adaptation and decision making on-board was unavoidable [10]. In the following, we will focus on the control approaches to pass through the poorly known Titan atmosphere by entry and parachute descent maneuvers in order to safely land on Titan's surface. The descent, illustrated in Fig. 25.3, had to meet the following requirements:

- minimum period for measurements in the different atmospheric layers,
- coordination of instrument activities for efficient energy consumption,
- monitored landing on the surface, and
- limited descent duration caused by the transmission geometry toward the CASSINI spacecraft, which acts as data relay toward Earth during its flyby.

A desirable control approach in that context would react adaptively to the incoming information from instrument measurements in order to update the atmospheric models and the predicted descent models. However, the means to realize such a control approach were rather limited and related to the timing of

- parachute deployment after significant deceleration in the atmospheric entry phase,
- separation from decelerator heat shield for mass reduction, thus increasing the descent duration, and
- change from the 8-m-diameter first parachute toward the smaller 3-m parachute, thus accelerating the descent duration.

The timing of the parachute deployment had to select the right moment:

- not too early; as otherwise, the high velocity would cause significant drag forces just destroying the parachute, and
- not too late; as otherwise, at lower velocities the atmospheric particles would not be able to inflate the parachute.

Fig. 25.3 The HUYGENS entry and descent scenario for exploration of Titans atmosphere and surface (image courtesy of ESA). Timing, speed adjustment, and the establishing and retaining of the communication link posed many challenges

Due to the high thermal flux at the time of parachute deployment (temperatures about 1000 °C at the outside of the heat shield), only inertial acceleration sensors could be used to determine the critical velocity to open the parachute. Another challenge in the Titan atmosphere was to cope with an uncertain atmospheric density model. The simulation results depicted in Fig. 25.4 exhibit the different potential atmospheric profiles for the velocity / acceleration evolution. Fortunately, the graphs of the atmospheric profiles `nominal`, `minimal`, and `maximal` converge at the planned deployment velocity of about Mach 1.5 (about 400 m/s). Thus, acceleration profiles could be used as timing criterion for the main parachutes deployment despite uncertainties in atmospheric density profiles.

During and after the decent, communication has to be ensured. Therefore, HUYGENS dropped an additional spacecraft named CASSINI to act as a relay link for transferring the measurement data to Earth. The descent of HUYGENS has to be coordinated with CASSINI without loose connection. HUYGENS had to respect the time constraints related to the flyby geometry of the CASSINI spacecraft. In case of delays on decent, CASSINI could have passed the horizon to keep the connection established. As a result, the interesting on-surface measurement could not have been transferred back to Earth when HUYGENS finally landed on the surface.

The decent was adaptively controlled, as depicted in Fig. 25.5. The height profile $h(t)$, including in particular the time for the surface impact, is predicted from the equations of motion depending on the gravity forces F_G of Titan (well known since

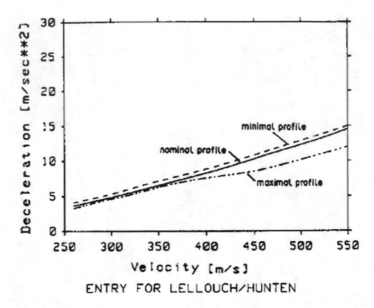

Fig. 25.4 The deceleration as a function of the velocity for different atmospheric models (according to Lellouch-Hunten). The three profiles converge at a velocity of about 400 m/s, which is the speed the parachute opening was triggered

$$m\ddot{x} = F_D + F_G$$

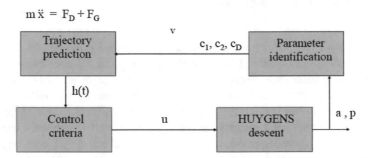

Fig. 25.5 Adaptive descent control scheme for HUYGENS landing on Titan. It includes many sources of uncertainty at the parameter identification that increase confidence intervals for decent time prediction. The parameters to be identified are the atmospheric density profile which introduced an uncertainty of ± 7.5 mins, and the HUYGENS drag coefficient which increased the confidence interval by ± 6.3 mins. Finally, the uncertainty concerning the Titan surface topography additionally added ± 7.2 mins

the flyby of VOYAGER 2) and the drag forces F_D (poorly known as the VOYAGER 2 instruments could only measure upper atmospheric layers). So in the beginning $h(t)$ will only be a rough estimate, but after parachute deployment, the atmospheric density ρ will be measured in addition to the deceleration a. The parameters inserted into the model of drag forces F_D are very poor during the initial period of the mission. However, over the mission progress, more measurements become available, which

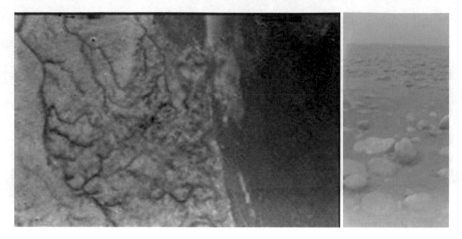

Fig. 25.6 Images from Titan: The picture on the *left shows* a swampy area with river features (*dark streams*) and the colorized image on the *right shows* the landing site in the dry bed of the lake (both images are original mission pictures and courtesy of ESA)

leads to continuous and significant improvements. On this basis, descent profile control has continuously been optimized during the descent and landing (Fig. 25.3).

On January 14, 2005, HUYGENS landed successfully on Titan in a dry riverbed (Fig. 25.6) with a deviation of less than 5 mins from the pre-planned values. Very impressive images and material composition data were acquired and transferred to Earth. More information on the mission can be found at http://sci.esa.int/cassini-huygens/ http://sci.esa.fnt/cassini-huygens/.

Until now, we described the HUYGENS mission in retrospect. Questions targeting prospective missions are "How could self-awareness be applied?" and "What are the benefits?" The HUYGENS mission was choreographed for a certain scenario and realized using a hard wiring of solution strategies. In contrast, an increased flexibility would be desirable for future missions. This could be achieved if future system creators are inspired by the self-awareness idea. Further, exchange and reuse of solution strategies would increase. The techniques applied in the CASSINI/HUYGENS mission enable to setup self-awareness. The mission design employed by example discrete models for payloads operations as well as thruster (trust on or off) and continuous models for physical phenomena. The data learned during operation for model parameterization was about position, temperature, and pressure. Complemented by a few rule-based approaches, the reasoning was dominated by measurement, control, and regulation technology. Besides HUYGENS specific aspects, typical mission constraints have to not only anticipate limited resources related to energy availability and consumption, but also fulfill objectives (e.g., to instrument pointing by attitude control). Mission objectives are to be compromised with resources available in time-critical situations. This is one example where self-aware computing incorporates easily: Predictive models support decision making, leading to a self-awareness concerning energy availability and consumption costs.

25.4.2 Rosetta—Accompanying and Landing on a Comet

The ESA-mission ROSETTA had the objective of a detailed comet exploration.
In 2014, a rendezvous maneuver injected the spacecraft into orbit around comet
67P/Churyumov-Gerasimenko, which enabled long-term observation during the evolution of the comets tail during perihel passage on August 13, 2015. On November
12, 2014, the PHILAE lander probe was deployed to the surface. Accidentally but
fortunately, all devices attaching it to the surface (one cold gas thruster, two harpoons, and three ice screws) failed. Thus, it finally settled after 3 times bouncing in
a scientifically more interesting riff. In the following, the intended adaptive drilling
in the poorly characterized soil will be described [11, 12]. Due to the unestablished
anchoring, drilling could not be applied; nevertheless, the challenge of dealing with
uncertain environments is of generic interest also for future missions. The distance
to Earth during the landing was about 500 million km, leading to a latency of 28 min.
Thus, the control commands arrive at the earliest after 56 mins after the input measurements occurred. So for almost one hour, all situations in this very uncertain
work environment had to be handled autonomously by the on-board data processing
system before any reactions from ground control could arrive. The core problem
was the coordination of the drilling device, the flight attitude control system, and the
anchoring system for a safe and energy efficient sample acquisition. For this purpose,
the targeted optimization goals (i) maximization of spacecraft attitude stability and
(ii) minimization of drilling duration provided the design requirements. For mission
design simulations, the following model components had to be taken into account:

- drilling equipment,
- cold gas thruster,
- mechanical soil properties of the comet surface,
- anchoring by harpoons,
- force and torque transfer in the structure of the probe, and
- force sensors, gyros, energy consumption monitoring.

The soil parameters to be identified during the drilling process included the following:
(i) Young's modulus and (ii) adhesive friction. These were expected to vary according
to drilling depth. Thus, while drilling progresses, the related parameters are identified
for the specific depth level based on encountered forces.

Figure 25.7 depicts the simulation tool for predicting the expected performance
properties. As self-aware computing was not introduced, the simulations were important to manually tailor the controller for the Rosetta mission. Figure 25.8 summarizes
the adaptive controller design to anticipate all potential situations for robust performance of drilling, considering multiple inherent uncertainties. Thus, the full control
chain, from sensor modeling, the data acquisition, and control reactions, to the impact
of the actuators on the spacecraft, is anticipated. The on-comet operations were considered high risk already during the initial mission planning phases in the early 1990s.
Malfunctions of single components and the appropriate reactions had been included
in the control strategy of the spacecraft. For example, the drilling assisted by the

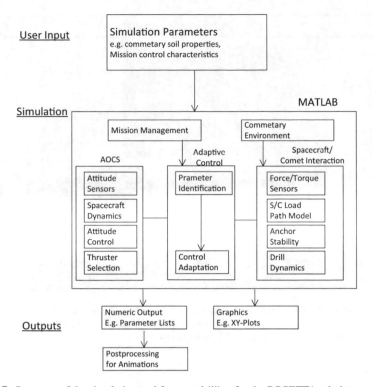

Fig. 25.7 Structure of the simulation tool for core drilling for the ROSETTA mission

thrusters was only planned in case harpoons and screws fail. Detailed variations of unknown soil parameters were assessed in simulations of typical mission scenarios in order to generate the most promising control strategy.

The obtained simulation results predicted significant performance improvements compared to an adaptive control scheme. The coordination of all capabilities on-board the spacecraft enabled a reduction of maximum forces and torques on the anchors of about 30 % (cf. Fig. 25.9). Despite the simulation strategy provided appropriate results, more flexible reactions, possibly enabled by self-aware approaches, would be desirable.

Surface science activities—except the drilling—had been performed by PHILAE with the energy provided from the batteries charged before launch, and the acquired data had been relied by ROSETTA to ground control. ROSETTA continues the journey as companion of the comet and just passed on the 13th of August 2015, the closest approach toward Sun with significant increase in material sublimation activities. Further details can be found at http://sci.esa.int/rosetta/.

The encountered surface operations well exceeded earlier anticipated situations, as all devices to attach the spacecraft to the cometary surface failed. Nevertheless, PHILAE was somehow fixed in gap, but modeling and assessment of this unforeseen situation were not possible. Self-aware computing offers a methodology to

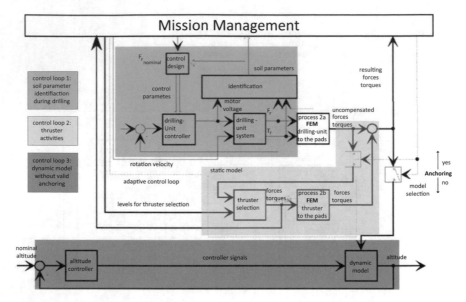

Fig. 25.8 Block diagram of the adaptive control strategy including three main control loops. These are focused on the adaptation to soil consistency (**control loop 1**), the controlling of thrusters (**control loop 2**), and the altitude control (**control loop 3**)

better cope with unforeseen situations. However, it is hard evaluate whether additional operations and measurements could have been performed using self-aware computing. In general, ROSETTA and HUYGENS had to face many challenges (summarized in Table 25.1) where the self-aware idea could have improved mission outcome (Fig. 25.10).

25.4.3   NetSat - A Satellite Formation in Low Earth Orbit

In Earth orbits, several multi-satellite systems have been established for applications in communications (e.g., IRIDIUM, Globalstar, TDRSS, and Orbcomm), in navigation (e.g., GPS, Glonass, Galileo, and BeiDou), in Earth observation (e.g., Rapid Eye and Dove), and in science (e.g., Cluster and Swarm). All these systems are realized as satellite *constellations*, where each satellite is individually controlled from the ground. Future—more advanced multi-satellite—systems are expected to be formations based on relative distances between spacecrafts. Appropriate topologies will be maintained using data exchange between the self-organizing spacecrafts. This is necessary, as for low Earth orbits (LEO), one ground station has less than 10 % of time access to the satellite. For several orbits, no contact at all occurs. In particular, currently planned mega-constellations in low Earth orbits are foreseen to provide a worldwide infrastructure for Internet access (e.g., OneWeb and SpaceX).

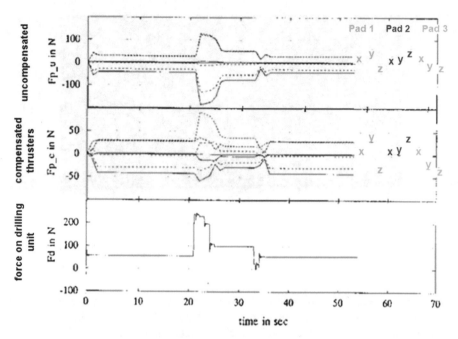

Fig. 25.9 The *first two rows* show the forces acting at the pads during the drilling process at a typical soil layer profile: F_p u = uncompensated, F_p c = compensated by cold gas thrusting. The graphs depict the force per direction (**x, y, z**) for each of the three pads (**pad1, pad2, pad3**). It can be seen that the thrusters reduced the forces on the pads. Beneath, in the *third row*, the reaction to the drill pushing force F_d is depicted

Table 25.1 Summary of challenges for autonomous reactions in the mission scenario for the interplanetary missions HUYGENS and ROSETTA

Mission	Huygens	Rosetta	
Phase	Atmospheric descent	Descent and landing on the comet	Soil sampling
Objectives	To achieve atmospheric descent profile suitable for scientific measurements	Safe landing near specified location	Safe acquisition of subsurface samples
Main environmental uncertainty	Atmospheric density profile	Dynamic/kinematic properties, topography of landing site	Mechanical soil properties for anchoring and drilling
Controlled states	Descent profile	Spacecraft attitude, orbit parameters	Flight attitude, drill pushing force, rotation rate
Available actuators	Timing of main parachute deployment	Hydrazine/cold gas thrusters	Drill motors, cold gas thrusters

Fig. 25.10 PHILAE finally landed on the comet: in front the Lander's leg is visible in front of the surprisingly hard cometary surface rocks (image courtesy of ESA, picture)

These constellations will require more advanced methods for efficient operations. Beyond these telecommunication applications, also in Earth observation and Space Weather characterization, commercial multi-satellite missions (e.g., by Planet Labs, Spire, PlanetIQ) have been recently placed in orbit and are expected to be further expanded [6]. These distributed networked multi-satellite systems provide data with high temporal and spatial resolution, and thus enable innovative environment monitoring. Huge additional numbers of satellite in such LEO orbits significantly increase the risks for collisions, especially in the regions near the poles. As satellite densities in the polar regions are expected to significantly increase due to orbit dynamics properties, range detection, and collision avoidance might become requirements for the future in order to avoid significant increase in space debris. There are significant similarities to networked automobiles as well as to networked industrial production methods. In this context, *formations* of multi-satellite systems have to be self-organizing, in order to provide appropriate position and orientation of the satellites for observations or for communication links. This requires an inter-satellite communication link to close the control loop in orbit. Cooperation and exchange of information will be based on relative distance and attitude measurements, as well as on telecommunication links [1, 2, 15] (Fig. 25.11).

At *U*niversity *W*ürzburg's *E*xperimental satellite (UWE) program, a long-term road map was established to realize the relevant technologies for formations at pico-satellite level (at a mass of just a few kilograms). The first German pico-satellite UWE-1 (launched in 2015 by a COSMOS-3M) addressed the scientific aspects of "internet in space" as basis for the inter-satellite network in orbit. While UWE-2 (launched 2009 by PSLV) had emphasis on attitude determination, the UWE-3 mission (launched 2013 by Dnepr) continued with attitude control. This technology base will be complemented by the currently prepared UWE-4 to demonstrate orbit control capabilities. On this basis, as next step the NetSat mission employing 4 satellites is

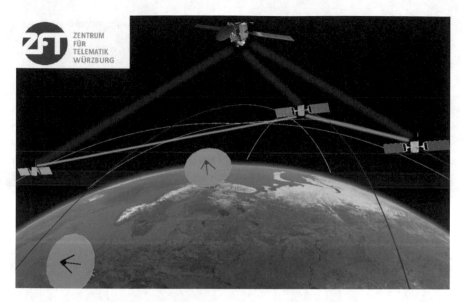

Fig. 25.11 NetSat: Networks of a ground stations and satellites formations promise potential for applications in future Earth observation and telecommunication services

implemented to analyze the control of 3-dimensional topologies in orbit (planned launch in 2018). This will enable innovative photogrammetric Earth observation approaches. Scientific challenges of NetSat address model-based orbit predictions and autonomous adaptive corrections of deviations with respect to telecommunication, data processing, and control [18, 19]. The objective of NetSat is the realization of a distributed, cooperating multi-satellite systems using autonomous formation control for optimization of observation periods. Relative distances at the beginning of mission will be between 50 and 10 km for safe operations. The first subgoal is to autonomously maintain the formation configuration. After having acquired sufficient experiences and derived appropriate models more risky, near proximity formations at distances between 20 and 40 m are foreseen. Technology challenges to be addressed by NetSat include:

- formation control
  - model reference-based adaptive control for attitude and orbit control by reaction wheels, magnetic torquers, and electric propulsion
  - relative attitude and position determination within the formation, based on data exchange and data fusion
- autonomous, networked satellite control
  - Reliable data exchange between the satellites by mobile DTNs and ad-hoc networks to adapt to changing communication topologies and interruptions

- Networked control of the satellite formation, combination of supervisory control from ground with autonomous reactions
- small satellite in-orbit demonstration
  - Implementation of a demonstrator mission based on 4 pico-satellites
  - navigation sensor system, in particular for relative distances and orientations

While the first phase of NetSat applies adaptive and supervisory control approaches in a conservative way, the NetSat mission offers the capabilities to upload new operational software. Thus, it could serve as a test bed for self-aware approaches the next phase. Candidate application fields might address health management at component and subsystem level. Other interesting features are collision avoidance and minimum fuel consumption detour maneuvers in a cluttered environment with space debris. With respect to planning, also suitable strategies for de-orbiting at the end of mission lifetime can be considered. Thus, direct comparisons of self-aware performance advantages with traditional techniques in orbit could be implemented.

25.5   Conclusions

Space missions raise challenging tasks for providing autonomous reaction capabilities in the context of interactions with poorly known environments being the target of explorations. Earth-based control for time-critical situations is often impossible due to significant signal propagation delay and link occultation periods. Additionally, we expect that more logic will move from the supervisor into the spacecraft. Space missions are becoming more and more complex and challenging. We see a need for further automation to reach new goals. We argue that inspiration from self-aware computing can help to advance the field.

In this chapter, we presented general solution approaches that have been applied for autonomy in space and explain their relation to self-aware computing. Further, we discussed the potential of self-aware computing for the application in space exemplified by two interplanetary missions HUYGENS and ROSETTA, and the satellite constellations of the NetSat project. Candidate application fields of self-aware computing might address health management, collision avoidance, minimum fuel consumption at detour maneuvers, and de-orbiting at the end of mission lifetime. Compared to the previously applied approaches, the idea of self-aware computing translates into combining model-based learning and reasoning as ongoing processes built into the spacecraft design to support autonomous reaction and control mechanisms. Despite sharing crucial aspects with classical adaptive control, self-aware computing introduces complementary new aspects. At self-aware computing, model learning processes are first-class entities. Formal models capture knowledge in an abstract and compact manner and support reasoning with respect to the system goals. Both the learning and reasoning processes are assumed to be running on an ongoing basis during operation; thus, models are expected to evolve as time progresses, leading to improved reasoning and more reliable decisions. The learned models support complex reasoning and predictive analytics that go beyond applying simple rules or heuristics explicitly programmed at system design-time. Self-aware computing leverages *descriptive*, *prescriptive*, and *predictive* in an integrated manner. Model-to-model transformations enable flexibility in trading-off between model accuracy and analysis overhead. A suitable model combined with a tailored solution strategy can be selected depending on the specific reasoning scenario. To move forward into unknown areas, these ideas of self-aware computing may support advanced autonomous behavior of spacecrafts and ground control in the future.

References

1. Kyle Alfriend, Srinivas Rao Vadali, Pini Gurfil, Jonathan How, and Louis Breger. *Space-craft Formation Flying: Dynamics, Control and Navigation*. Elsevier Astrodynamics Series. Elsevier, 2010.
2. F. Ankersen, editor. *3rd International Symposium on Formation Flying, Missions and Technologies*. ESA SP-654, 2008.
3. Karl Johan Astrom and Bjorn Wittenmark. *Adaptive Control*. Prentice Hall, 1994. [3] Astrom, K., B. Wittenmark, Adaptive Control, Addison-Wesley, 1989, 2d ed. 1994.
4. George A Bekey. *Autonomous robots: from biological inspiration to implementation and control*. MIT press, 2005.
5. Francesco Bullo, Jorge Cortés, and Sonia Martinez. *Distributed Control of Robotic Networks: A Mathematical Approach to Motion Coordination Algorithms: A Mathematical Approach to Motion Coordination Algorithms*. Princeton University Press, 2009.
6. Marco D'Errico. *Distributed Space Missions for Earth System Monitoring*, volume 31. Springer Science & Business Media, 2012.
7. Xiaohua Ge, Fuwen Yang, and Qing-Long Han. Distributed networked control systems: A brief overview. *Information Sciences*, pages –, 2015.
8. Ioan Doré Landau, Rogelio Lozano, Mohammed M'Saad, and Alireza Karimi. *Adaptive control*, volume 51. Springer Berlin, 1998.
9. K Schilling. Control aspects of interplanetary spacecrafts: An introduction to the CASSINI/HUYGENS mission. *Control Engineering Practice*, 3(11):1599–1601, 1995.
10. K Schilling and W Flury. Autonomy and on-board mission management aspects for the CASSINI Titan probe. *Acta Astronautica*, 21(1):55–68, 1990.
11. K Schilling, H Roth, and B Theobold. Autonomous on-comet operations aspects of the RoSETTA mission. *Control Engineering Practice*, 2(3):499–507, 1994.
12. Klaus Schilling. Simulation of ROSETTA on-comet operations. In *Annales Geophysicae*, volume 10, pages 141–144, 1992.
13. Klaus Schilling. The HUYGENS Mission to Explore the Saturnian Moon Titan. 2005.
14. Klaus Schilling. Networked control of cooperating distributed pico-satellites. In *19th International Federation of Automatic Control World Congress*, pages 7960–7964, 2014.
15. Klaus Schilling. Kleinstsatelliten - winzlinge im orbit. *Spektrum der Wissenschaft*, pages 48–51, May 2015.
16. Klaus Schilling, J De Lafontaine, and Hubert Roth. Autonomy capabilities of European deep space probes. *Autonomous Robots*, 3(1):19–30, 1996.
17. KLAUS Schilling and MICHAEL Eiden. Huygens und Rosetta. Die geplanten planetaren Missionen der Europäer. *Sterne und Weltraum*, 29:428–437, 1990.
18. Schmidt M. Schilling, K. Communication in distributed satellite systems. In *DErrico M. (ed.), Distributed Missions for Earth System Monitoring*. Springer, 2012.

19. Schmidt M. Busch S. Schilling, K. Crucial technologies for distributed systems of pico-satellites. In . IAC-12-D1.2.4, editor, *Proceedings 63rd International Astronautical Congress*, Naples, Italy, 2012.
20. J. Schumann, T. Mbaya, O. J. Mengshoel, K. Pipatsrisawat, A. Srivastava, A. Choi, and A. Darwiche. Software health management with bayesian networks. *Innov. Syst. Softw. Eng.*, 9(4):271–292, December 2013.
21. Johann Schumann, Kristin Y. Rozier, Thomas Reinbacher, Ole J. Mengshoel, Timmy Mbaya, and Corey Ippolito. Towards real-time, on-board, hardware-supported sensor and software health management for unmanned aerial systems. *International Journal of Prognostics and Health Management (IJPHM)*, 6(1):1–27, June 2015.
22. Thomas B Sheridan. *Telerobotics, automation, and human supervisory control*. MIT press, 1992.
23. A. Srivastava and J. Han, editors. *Data Mining in Systems Health Management: Detection, Diagnostics, and Prognostics*. Chapman and Hall/CRC Press, 2011.

Part V
Outlook

Chapter 26
Self-aware Computing Systems: Open Challenges and Future Research Directions

Robert Birke, Javier Cámara, Lydia Y. Chen, Lukas Esterle, Kurt Geihs, Erol Gelenbe, Holger Giese, Anders Robertsson and Xiaoyun Zhu

Abstract In this chapter, we discuss the open challenges in building self-aware computing systems that are still being faced by the research and development community. The challenges can be theoretical, technical, computational, or even sociological. First, we highlight the challenges associated with each of the earlier parts of the book and summarize on respective future research directions. We then offer concluding remarks and an outlook into the future in the last section.

R. Birke (✉) · L.Y. Chen
IBM Research Zurich, Zürich, Switzerland
e-mail: bir@zurich.ibm.com

L.Y. Chen
e-mail: YIC@zurich.ibm.com

J. Cámara
Carnegie Mellon University, Pittsburgh, PA, USA
e-mail: jcmoreno@cs.cmu.edu

L. Esterle
Vienna University of Technology, Vienna, Austria
e-mail: lukas.esterle@tuwien.ac.at

K. Geihs
University of Kassel, Kassel, Germany
e-mail: geihs@uni-kassel.de

E. Gelenbe
Imperial College London, London, UK
e-mail: e.gelenbe@imperial.ac.uk

H. Giese
Hasso Plattner Institute at the University of Potsdam, Potsdam, Germany
e-mail: holger.giese@hpi.de

A. Robertsson
Lund University, Lund, Sweden
e-mail: andersro@control.lth.se

X. Zhu
Futurewei Technologies, Santa Clara, CA, USA
e-mail: xiaoyun.zhu@huawei.com

© Springer International Publishing AG 2017
S. Kounev et al. (eds.), *Self-Aware Computing Systems*,
DOI 10.1007/978-3-319-47474-8_26

26.1 Introduction

Building self-aware computing systems entails tackling a set of theoretical, technical, or even sociological open challenges in different areas. Self-aware computing is an area that lies at the intersection of many others, some of which were discussed in Chap. 2, and in that sense, it inherits some of their respective major challenges. However, the idiosyncrasies of self-aware computing systems create the need to look at these challenges in areas such as architecting, analysis and verification, or modeling from a different perspective, and pose entirely new challenges that are exclusive to endowing systems with improved levels of self-awareness.

This chapter outlines major open challenges in some of the relevant areas discussed in this book and summarizes their respective future research directions.

In the remainder of this chapter, Sect. 26.2 discusses open challenges that concern the architecture of self-aware computing systems, including the handling of trade-offs at the architectural level between the level of self-awareness and the need for encapsulation and modularity. Next, Sect. 26.3 outlines challenges in analysis and verification, including those related to the scalability and timeliness of analysis techniques, as well as the handling of epistemic uncertainty. Section 26.4 discusses open challenges from the perspective of online models, including issues such as extraction, accuracy, or traceability. Open challenges from the perspective of self-adaptation and management are discussed in Sect. 26.5, making particular emphasis on decision-making. This leads to an outline in Sect. 26.6 of open challenges in assessing self-awareness, among which we can highlight the assessment of functionality that has not been considered at the design time and this issue is strongly related to the challenge concerning the run-time handling of epistemic logic as discussed in Sect. 26.6. Sections 26.7 and 26.8 discuss challenges in applications and in the socio-technical context, respectively, whereas Sect. 26.9 draws some conclusions.

26.2 Open Challenges in Architectures for Self-aware Computing Systems

For the architectures of self-aware computing systems as covered in Part 2, a number of open challenges have been identified in Chap. 8 organized jointly for the directions concerning the architectures of self-aware computing systems covering fundamental architectural concepts as discussed in Chap. 5, architectures for individual self-aware computing systems as covered in Chap. 6, architectures for collective self-aware computing systems as presented in Chap. 7, and general challenges for architectures for self-aware computing systems that apply to multiple of these directions. These challenges are summarized in the following.

The first group of challenges that apply to all studied architectural directions are related to the limitations of the proposed concepts for self-awareness and self-expression that do not adequately cover complex graphs resulting from the awareness and expression links and in particular loops in those that do not support more detailed aspects of self-awareness and self-expression links as discussed in Chap. 3, that do not consider static knowledge that may make the links and their run-time implications obsolete, and that do not cover uncertainty, which is a main driver for the activities linked to awareness.

Another group of challenges relates to the trade-off at the architectural level between powerful self-awareness and self-expression and the need for encapsulation and modularity. While encapsulation demands explicit and restrictive interfaces with strong encapsulation, powerful self-awareness and self-expression would require generic interfaces for computational reflection with nearly no encapsulation. Furthermore, concepts for reflection interfaces are required that are able to bridge the gap between the structure of the scope and the span of self-awareness and self-expression and also enable the long-term evolution of the architecture.

Besides the separation related to single awareness and expression links, the separation between multiple occurrences of self-awareness, how to separate them, and how to rule possible interference result in a number of challenges. While means for the separation of different self-awareness concerns such as self-healing or self-configuration are a general problem, for collectives, the specific challenges arise how collective self-awareness can emerge from individual self-awareness, how the impact of changes at the individual level can impact the collective level, and how concrete architectures for collective self-awareness best look like.

A challenge that applies to the individual as well as collective case is that at the architectural level a certain dynamics result from either external changes or adaptation of the system in response to change or to improve its behavior. A first challenge is that a notation to capture the dynamics is lacking. Furthermore, it is a major challenge that dynamics at the level of individual systems as well as dynamics at the level of collectives has to be ruled and that the adaptation has to be able to cope with it. In the case of collectives, in addition, the coherent behavior in case some subsystems of the collective evolve is a crucial challenge as no joint management can be assumed.

Finally, in the Part 2 outlined consideration are rather limited and generic as neither the challenge how to integrate legacy software nor how to support particular domains such as, for example, cyber-physical systems (CPS), sensor networks, Internet of Things (IoT), or enterprise application (EA) and their specific needs and constraints concerning self-awareness by domain-specific extensions have been yet sufficiently discussed.

26.3   Open Challenges in Analysis and Verification

Analysis and verification in the context of self-aware systems inextricably entail the tackling some of the open challenges in analysis and verification of self-adaptive systems, due to their shared characteristics, which include operating in dynamically changing environments and, potentially, their ability to adapt their structure and behavior to run-time changes.

In that arena, some of the most promising analysis and verification techniques, such as quantitative run-time verification and probabilistic model checking [18], are able to capture the probabilistic aspects inherent to the environments in which such systems have to operate, and potentially, their adversarial nature (e.g., model checking stochastic games, cf. Chap. 11). However, these techniques are affected by the well-known state explosion problem of model checking, which is of particular concern in the context of self-adaptive and self-aware computing systems, since verification of models updated at run-time has to be performed with acceptable overhead and in a timely fashion. Otherwise, longer computation times increase the risks associated with run-time changes that might invalidate results by the time analysis is completed. Although there are some techniques based on parametric [13], compositional/incremental [14], and distributed verification [3] that mitigate this issue, further research is required to improve the scalability of these analyses and verification techniques for their applicability to large-scale, rapidly changing complex systems.

As we move toward developing systems with higher degrees of self-awareness, there is another major open challenge that becomes apparent in their verification and analysis, which is related to the handling of epistemic uncertainty.

Uncertainty can be classified as *variable* or *epistemic* in nature. *Variable* (or *statistical*) uncertainty is related to the randomness or stochastic behavior of systems, which can be properly captured in models typically employed for quantitative and probabilistic verification (e.g., discrete-time Markov chains, Markov decision processes, probabilistic timed automata, stochastic multiplayer games). In fact, the probability distributions that govern certain transitions in the system and the environment encoded in such models (e.g., those related to operating conditions or human behavior) can often be learned from observations at run-time, even if they are unknown at the design time. In contrast, *epistemic* (or *systematic*) uncertainty is caused by a lack of knowledge. An example of epistemic uncertainty when calculating the speed of a falling object is given if, for instance, we employ models that do not account for factors that would affect the calculation such as air friction, should they be known. Epistemic uncertainty can be mitigated at the design time by carefully analyzing potential factors that might affect the relevant properties of the system that we want to analyze. Moreover, in systems with a low degree of self-awareness that are amenable to be taken offline for maintenance, epistemic uncertainty can be handled after system deployment by reworking models (and perhaps other system elements, such as the monitoring infrastructure) to capture new aspects relevant to the analysis that were not accounted for at design time. However, developing systems with a higher degree of self-awareness implies enabling them to dynamically handle epistemic uncertainty, for instance, when system goals change and new aspects of the organizational context of the system have to be taken into account to assess whether the new goals are being satisfied. How do we enable self-aware systems to automatically capture this new information in their models and incorporate it into their analysis and verification mechanisms? This remains an important open challenge, in which full automation of epistemic uncertainty handling associated with different sources (e.g., goals, human behavior, resource availability) still seems to be far-fetched, but intermediate steps can be taken toward partial automation by involving humans in the loop.

26.4   Open Challenges in Online Models

As discussed previously in the book, *online models* (aka. *run-time models*) are mathematical representations of a target system and its environment extracted during the system's operation. They have been employed to achieve multiple self-awareness properties in a variety of contexts. For example, run-time models may contain parameters that capture the time-varying characteristics and the complex resource requirements of user demands and can be very useful in a self-aware computing system for online performance and resource management in modern datacenters.

Many open problems remain with regard to using run-time models more effectively while building self-aware systems, including but not limited to the following:

- How to ensure that run-time models can be analyzed and solved in a computationally efficient and timely manner? This is particularly critical where the model represents a large-scale distributed system, or the model extraction relies on a large amount of online measurement data.
- How to properly assess the validity and accuracy of run-time models, especially given the dynamic nature of the environment a self-aware system faces. For example, equipping models with confidence intervals can provide hints on their validity. Efficient change-point detection algorithms are required to quickly identify when a model becomes outdated and therefore needs to be updated.
- In some cases, it is necessary to infer the model structure at run-time, which is a greater challenge than only estimating the parameter values online from a fixed model template. This is because extracting model structures imposes a higher computation cost and usually requires training data from a larger time window.
- How to ensure the robustness of a model-driven self-aware system with respect to the uncertainty in the real system that is not captured by the online model?
- Different types of models may be needed to capture different target metrics, such as performance, cost, reliability, security, and energy consumption. How to combine these different models in a self-aware system to automatically identify the most appropriate trade-off between multiple objectives?

There are further challenges specifically associated with online learning and extraction of run-time performance models:

- How to ensure the traceability between the performance models and the systems they represent? The solution may be to explicit store traceability information as part of the models.
- How to reduce the dependency of the overall solution on specific technology or software stacks?

- How to automatically identify an appropriate level of granularity for the performance models of different systems? The optimum granularity level is often determined by the specific self-aware use case the model is built for, as well as the dynamic characteristics of the target system.
- How to better leverage automatic extraction of parametric dependencies in call paths and resource demands to improve the accuracy of extracted models?
- Many run-time performance models are used to develop online adaptation strategies for performance assurance purposes. In some cases, the most suitable adaptation points (e.g., horizontal vs. vertical scaling of resources) need to be automatically or semiautomatically extracted online, which creates additional challenges for the overall solution.

26.5   Open Challenges in Self-adaptation and Management

In Chaps. 12 and 13, topics on self-adaptation for individual and collective self-aware computing systems, respectively, are considered. Problem formulations considered are both with respect to the different causes for adaptation, the used adaptation, and learning techniques, and to the awareness and representation of the system where explicit or implicit couplings in dynamics and objectives play a major role in analysis, adaptation, and achievable performance. In Chap. 10, several illustrative cases of different complexities are discussed together with reference to current state of the art, and we will here summarize and discuss some related open research challenges.

Also without the general concept of self-awareness, many classical learning adaptation-based schemes heavily rely on properties of assumed models such as known model structures, known interconnections, couplings between submodels, and high-frequency gain. These techniques thus comprise several of the challenges and issues already raised in the previous section on *Open Challenges in Online Models*.

Separation of concerns is a common design principle used to modularize both software and, in a more general setting, system functionality into well-defined subsystems by encapsulation and thereby provide a means to handle complex systems through design, implementation, analysis, and local optimization of (sub)system behavior as well as maintenance of the individual modules. To achieve similar separation among resource utilization and system objectives is by no means trivial, and systems are furthermore often designed to allow for extended functionality in an "open-world assumption" perspective, in which improved self-awareness plays a major role in self-adaptation and management.

In the quote—*"We used to think that if we knew one, we knew two, because one and one are two. We are finding that we must learn a great deal more about 'and'."*[1] by Arthur Eddington, the seemingly innocent connecting *"and"* could very well represent the sometimes significant amount of added complexity when different

---

[1] *A Dictionary of Scientific Quotations (1991) by Alan L. Mackay.*

subsystems come to interact by, for instance, shared resources and common, or even conflicting, objectives and goals.

Self-adaptation and decision-making are often categorized as fully "centralized," i.e., having one centralized point of decision with full system state overview, "distributed," where decision-making is shared across subsystems but possibly based on complete system knowledge, or "decentralized" among subsystems based on their local information only, each affecting the overall system behavior.

Whereas distributed and decentralized solutions may be preferable with respect to reduced communication, robustness through redundancy, and the ideas behind the separation of concerns to handle complexity, performance may degrade in many aspects. A large challenge is to formalize and quantify this in a general setting.

The case study of System of Autonomous Shuttles in Chap. 13 could in its most simple and decentralized form corresponds to the distance-keeping scenario of vehicle platoons in automated highway systems [25]. System performance may not scale well due to, for instance, delays, and by only looking at measured distance from the vehicle ahead, inherent problems of string instability will occur when the number of submodules/vehicles increases. This phenomenon is closely related to Forrester's "bullwhip effect" in supply chain systems and stability in networked systems [6, 20].

Using decentralized decision-making based on local criteria and system information only may cause a significant degradation in achievable performance in comparison with a centralized decision-making. This ratio of how efficient a certain Nash equilibrium is in comparison with an optimal centralized solution is referred to as the *price of anarchy*. Bounds on the degradation concerning "selfish routing" has been investigated in [22, 23]. Introducing the aspects of fairness of utilization in this context may be of significant importance but will also increase the complexity of optimization considerably.

As shown in Chap. 13, the couplings among subsystems may not only affect the performance but more importantly also introduce delays and unintended interaction loops that may endanger the overall system stability.

Depending on the degree of self-awareness, the self-adapting system may be more or less sensitive for interaction between subsystems, and the possibilities to identify, adapt, and manage. Corresponding model knowledge quantified in self-awareness could be compared with the concept of fault detection and fault correction, where fault detection is the easier task which consists in detecting and reporting an unspecified fault, whereas fault correction relies on the model knowledge to both detect, isolate, identify and finally adapt to changes.

Implicit interaction between subsystems could be very hard to predict, depending for instance on the granularity of modeling, and local adaptation with respect to decentralized objectives has been shown to introduce degrading oscillations or even instability through coupled systems. A related issue is to detect conflicting objectives among subsystems which may cause considerable problems on a systems level, either by wasting resources or by having consequences for the stability. Detection of undesired oscillations due to self-reinforced feedback loops on a systems level is therefore an important step in self-adaptation and case studies on this topic have been reported in both process industry and power management systems, see e.g., [15]. Robust fall-back solutions with lower efficiency have been reported for particular applications and systems, but major challenges remain to handle these issues in a general setting for complex systems.

A robust way to handle this during a design phase by distributing/decentralizing and splitting common objectives, utility functions, and constraints into coupled subsystems is another open challenge of large interest.

An inherent problem in techniques such as adaptive control and machine learning performed online (i.e., changing a running systems) is connected to excitation of signals and receiving information-rich data without degrading the system performance due to the adaptation. If training and self-adaptation are done online, timescales need to be separated to distinguish the origin of effects and related challenges are considered in the area of dual control.

A closely related challenge is to ensure system robustness in the presence of software errors. This challenge is especially relevant to systems where different requirements (and thus, different components) have different criticalities, as is common, for instance, in cyber-physical systems. Hence, different components may be validated to a different level of assurance. Errors may occur in less critical components but should not propagate and bring down the system. The most critical requirements in cyber-physical systems are the *safety* requirements.

A key adaptation challenge in this context becomes how to attain performance goals enforced by optimization algorithms that are less reliable (and hence may generate errors), while at the same time robustly guarantee meeting safety goals enforced by components that are intentionally simplified (and hence do not address performance). The answer lies in clever handover schemes between safety operation modes and performance modes (i.e., switching between different evaluation run-time models) depending on the current state. This adaptation allows the system to attain performance goals most of the time while ensuring overall robustness to unexpected failures, making sure that safety requirements are never violated.

Determining how a self-aware system might exploit models of itself and its environment to elicit additional goals and preferences that suffice to resolve detected conflicts is a worthy research challenge [16, 17].

A related key challenge associated with self-awareness in collective systems is that the learning which drives collective self-awareness occurs within individual components, based on the knowledge obtained from their own local perspectives. Hence, the knowledge on which to base the decisions which drive behavior, adaptation, explanation, etc. may be incomplete, out of date, or even contradictory. Therefore, the applicability of heterogeneous levels, domains, processes, and accuracy depends on their appropriateness for the corresponding entities in the collective.

26.6 Open Challenges in Assessing Self-awareness

Assessing self-aware systems is in very early stages of development as self-aware systems themselves are a completely new computing paradigm. However, we are able to build on well-known approaches employed in software and system testing, evaluation, and analysis.

When it comes to assessing self-aware systems, we discussed two main approaches in performing such an assessment in Chap. 15. On the one hand, we discussed run-time assessment where a human has to determine the capabilities of another machine. On the other hand, a future self-aware machine might be required to determine its own self-aware capabilities or the self-aware capabilities of another machine during run-time. We consider two approaches with fundamentally different assumptions where the assessor has knowledge about the inherent functionalities of the machine and where the machine can only be observed from the outside, and the assessor does not have any knowledge about the inherent functionalities of the assessed machine. This is important as approaches such as automated code inspection can be applied if the code base is available to the assessor [21].

However, there are still two important issues with run-time assessment. The first issue revolves around the problem of how to set the objective or goal functions autonomously. This needs to be performed during run-time for a specific system capability to be assessed by the assessing human or machine. In the case of black-box testing, we still lack test cases for the individual self-aware capabilities that can be performed at run-time even though Chap. 15 gives an initial idea on how to design such test cases. The second issue is even more severe when it comes to identifying and assessing functionality one has not considered at the design time of the system. This brings us to the second main approach on performing assessments of self-aware systems—design-time assessment.

In discussed design-time assessment, the designer has to carefully consider which components of the self-aware system may adapt during run-time and which components may not. The designer has to ensure that those systems show correct behavior not only in their normal functions but also in the behavior of the self-awareness mechanism. This requires to analyze the huge state space of such systems. This severe issue becomes more difficult when adding the state space introduced by the self-awareness mechanisms and all possible environments. Performing exhaustive tests or simulations for such systems is not possible. Hence, a clear definition of equivalence classes of behavior for such systems will be crucial. Furthermore, efficient methods are required to generate and/or identify representative test cases for sufficient test coverage. This will allow for model-based or real testing of such systems and hence reduce the risks of making inadequate design decisions. We considered an additional long-term evolutionary cycle in which the designer may adopt the system and hence perform a design-time evolution of the same. This additional evolutionary loop allows to adjust assessment capabilities for situations a designer may not have considered initially. However, it limits the assessment capabilities again until an full evolutionary cycle with additional human interaction has been performed.

26.7   Open Challenges in Applications
of Self-aware Computing

Though there are a great deal of ongoing efforts toward self-aware and self-managed systems from cloud and datacenter providers, there are still several open issues and challenges yet to be tackled. The immediately arising challenges are related to how to store and analyze the performance logs at scale, from the perspective of implementation as well as analysis.

To ensure the high dependability of datacenters, centralized performance monitoring systems are in place and collect information from highly distributed servers. The volume, velocity, and variety of logs flowing into the monitor systems can be extremely high and result in a big data problem itself. It is not straightforward to determine what data to store, for how long, and how to aggregate the data such that the maximum amount of information is retained using a minimum storage space. As such a data set eventually caters to a large number of users who try to mine the logs and identify performance optimization opportunities, the access patterns and network bandwidth requirements of these monitoring systems shall be carefully incorporated into the design. All in all, the overall requirements to store and analyze performance logs call for a distributed design of monitoring systems.

One of the key analyses carried out on performance logs is the time series analysis, e.g., predicting patterns of resource usage series, or detecting anomalies in workload demands. On the one hand, due to the storage requirements, performance logs are often aggregated in a rolling window fashion that results in coarse-grained information in the long run and fine-grained information in the near past. As the standard time series analysis requires uniform input from the history, i.e., with the same granularity, time series mining on existing logs is constrained by the coarse-grained information. On the other hand, there is a massive amount of time series of server usages, which could share similar patterns. Such a rich spatial information could offer opportunities to overcome the limitation from the problem of coarse-grained temporal data and the requirement of storing long-history data. Therefore, we argue that there is a need to develop a new type of methodology that can efficiently analyze large amounts of time series data of resource usages, addressing the issues of non-uniform granularity in the temporal data and taking advantages of rich spatial information.

Another obvious area of application for self-aware systems is the Internet itself [5, 10], where a large number of system components such as routers, Web servers, clouds, together with routing algorithms, and task allocation schemes must cooperate as an autonomic self-aware infrastructure. Network routing itself can be made into a self-aware subsystem of the Internet [9], which can benefit real-time applications such as Voice over IP [27], but a research challenge remains in handling possible oscillations [12], which can become useful if each decision change is preceded by a useful step of work that reduces future resource consumptions and if each change in decision actually improves future network performance.

At the edge of the network, and especially with the advent of the IoT (Internet of Things), there are increasing research challenges regarding smart sensing [11] that can benefit from a self-aware approach to prioritize the most timely or relevant information, for instance, in applications such as emergency communications [19] or communications for autonomous vehicles.

In applications such as e-commerce [8], the challenge of using self-awareness is to combine information about pricing and competition, together with technical characteristics of the network, to optimize the Internet's performance for the benefit of the different (and not necessarily cooperative) economic agents.

In core network routing, which today also supports the mobile devices including mobile telephony, "softwarization" and virtualization now constitute the leading edge of research; thus, a challenge is to demonstrate how self-awareness can be built into the SDN (software-defined network) controllers [7] that are increasingly used by the Internet service providers. As an alternative to making changes in the core routing, recent work [2] has shown that high-level overlays driven by self-aware methodologies can substantially improve the users' perceived quality of service in the long-haul intercontinental Internet. This is a promising direction of future research, especially when combined with SDN and smart allocation of tasks to the cloud that resides within our Internet infrastructure [26].

26.8 Socio-Technical Challenges for Self-aware Systems

Technical innovation can only be successful if it leads to avail and user acceptance. Thus, the success of technical innovations does depend not only on functional, but also critically on non-functional properties, in particular on properties that relate to the appropriate and careful embedding of technological advances into the users' personal, economical, and sociological environments. Self-aware computing systems will contribute substantially to the automation of processes and activities of our daily life. They will interweave information and communications technologies with our private, public, and business environments. It is a salient characteristic of self-aware computing systems that they might gather, store, process, and communicate personal information about the user's context—often transparently and imperceptibly for the user—in order to realize self-adaptivity. This leads inevitably to viewing these systems as socio-technical systems and corresponding non-functional design concerns that in some cases may create conflicting requirements. In the following, we will briefly discuss some examples for such concerns.

Many projects in the realm of autonomic self-adaptation in self-aware systems have aimed at "getting the user out of the loop," i.e., to achieve complete automation without any user interaction. In many real-life applications, this has turned out to be inappropriate. Human users should be able to intervene when the system does not know what to do, when it makes wrong decisions, or when adaptation is not wanted in a certain situation. Inappropriate automatic actions might distract or disrupt users from their current task, or in the worst case, they might prevent them from correctly carrying out their current task. Thus, the challenge is to find technical solutions for a reasonable compromise between automation and user control.

Self-aware systems require sensory input, i.e., context information, in order to be self-aware. In many application scenarios, such as smart home, e-health, and autonomous cars, this context information will contain highly sensitive personal data. Hence, security and privacy concerns have a crucial influence on the social acceptance of solutions in these scenarios. This is an extremely wide field where a lot of research is going on and where continuously more research is needed as technology progresses. Design paradigms such as "Security by Design" and "Privacy by Design" seem to take the right perspective on the problem space. However, we need to better understand the implications of such paradigms for the design and implementation of self-aware computing systems.

Automation in general raises questions of legal accountability and liability for any kind of wrong doing. Currently, these concerns are debated extensively and controversially for autonomous driving situations. These debates underline the inherent difficulties behind these legal issues. Self-aware systems cannot escape these difficulties. Law experts and software engineers need to collaborate in interdisciplinary design efforts to find appropriate solutions for different scenarios [24]. It seems like that in this area, the controversial debate will go on forever whether existing fundamental and constitutional laws already provide a satisfactory legal framework of whether completely new laws are required. An enormously difficult challenge is to find the right transformations that transform abstract normative statements into corresponding technical software artifacts.

Besides legal aspects, trust in the correctness and effectiveness of a complex technical system is a crucial determinant of user acceptance. Generating user trust with a self-aware system is a multifaceted problem which depends on many ingredients, such as perception of correctness, transparency, robustness, performance, and many more. While it is certainly difficult to keep all of these trust determinants in mind when designing a self-aware system, it is even more challenging to find suitable technical representations for them in the implementation.

Appropriate solutions for such socio-technical requirements need to be integrated into self-aware systems and thus need to be taken into account in the development process from the very beginning. Even if this fact is well known in practice, so far there is little discipline-overarching methodology available for the design and evaluation of socially embedded self-aware applications [4, 24]. Of course, there are methodological approaches to reflect non-functional requirements in software engineering processes and to specifically address the socio-technical embedding of technology in its organizational context [1]. However, a generalization of these approaches is needed. The real challenge in this respect lies in the mapping of normative requirements, e.g., given in the form of abstract legal or ethical regulations and norms, into technical artifacts of the self-aware software systems. Another challenge is to mediate between conflicting socio-technical requirements. We claim that self-awareness will only find widespread acceptance if the socio-technical concerns are taken seriously and appropriate interdisciplinary design methodologies are available that facilitate the development of such systems.

26.9   Conclusion

In this chapter, we have provided a brief survey of open challenges in the field of self-aware computing, based on the vision introduced in Chap. 1. These include challenges around necessary software architecture frameworks and elements, challenges in analysis and verification, especially as pertinent to self-adaptive systems, challenges in extracting, using, and updating online models as quantitative representations of self-aware systems, challenges in self-adaptation of both individual and collective self-aware systems, challenges in both design-time and run-time assessment of self-awareness, as well as challenges in applying self-awareness concepts and approaches to datacenters, clouds, and the Internet itself. Last but not least, there are fundamental socio-technical challenges associated with getting self-awareness fully accepted and appreciated by the whole user community.

The discussion of these open problems can hopefully inspire and enlighten the research and development community as they continue to seek new research directions. With a collective effort, we wish to advance the state of the art in self-aware computing systems to the next level.

References

1. G. Baxter and I. Sommerville. Socio-technical systems: From design methods to systems engineering. *Interacting with Computers*, 23(1):4–17, May 2010.
2. O. Brun, L. Wang, and E. Gelenbe. Data driven self-managing routing in intercontinental overlay networks. *IEEE Journal on Selected Areas in Communications*, 34:575–583, 2016.
3. Radu Calinescu, Simos Gerasimou, and Alec Banks. *Fundamental Approaches to Software Engineering: 18th International Conference, FASE 2015, Held as Part of the European Joint Conferences on Theory and Practice of Software, ETAPS 2015, London, UK, April 11–18, 2015, Proceedings*, chapter Self-adaptive Software with Decentralised Control Loops, pages 235–251. Springer Berlin Heidelberg, Berlin, Heidelberg, 2015.
4. K. David, K. Geihs, J.M. Leimeister, A. Rossnagel, L. Schmidt, G. Stumme, and A. Wacker. *Socio-Technical Design of Ubiquitous Computing Systems*. Springer, Berlin Heidelberg, 2014.
5. S. Dobson et al. A survey of autonomic communications. *ACM Transactions on Autonomous and Adaptive Systems*, 1(2):223–259, Dec 2006.
6. J. Forrester. *Industrial Dynamics*. MIT press, Cambridge MA, 1961.
7. F. Francois and E. Gelenbe. Towards a cognitive routing engine for software defined networks. In *Proceedings of the IEEE International Conference on Communications (ICC)*, May 2016.
8. E. Gelenbe. Analysis of single and networked auctions. *ACM Transactions on Internet Technology*, 9(2), May 2009.
9. E. Gelenbe. Steps toward self-aware networks. *Communications of the ACM*, 52(7):66–75, 2009.
10. E. Gelenbe. *McGraw-Hill Yearbook of Science & Technology 2011—Manuscript ID YB11-0175*, January 2011.
11. E. Gelenbe and E. Egai. Adaptive qos routing for significant events in wireless sensor networks. In *Proceedings of the 5th IEEE International Conference on Mobile Ad-Hoc and Sensor Systems (MASS)*, pages 410–415, September 2008.
12. E. Gelenbe and M. Gellman. Oscillations in a bio-inspired routing algorithm. In *Proceedings of the 4th IEEE International Conference on Mobile Ad-Hoc and Sensor Systems (MASS)*, pages 1–7, October 2007.

13. Ernst Moritz Hahn, Holger Hermanns, Björn Wachter, and Lijun Zhang. *Computer Aided Verification: 22nd International Conference, CAV 2010, Edinburgh, UK, July 15–19, 2010. Proceedings*, chapter PARAM: A Model Checker for Parametric Markov Models, pages 660–664. Springer Berlin Heidelberg, Berlin, Heidelberg, 2010.
14. Kenneth Johnson, Radu Calinescu, and Shinji Kikuchi. An incremental verification framework for component-based software systems. In *Proceedings of the 16th International ACM Sigsoft Symposium on Component-based Software Engineering*, CBSE'13, pages 33–42, New York, NY, USA, 2013. ACM.
15. Jeffrey O Kephart, Hoi Chan, Rajarshi Das, David W Levine, Gerald Tesauro, and Charles Lefurgy. Coordinating multiple autonomic managers to achieve specified power-performance tradeoffs. In *Proceedings of the Fourth International Conference on Autonomic Computing*. IEEE, 2007.
16. Jeffrey O Kephart and Jonathan Lenchner. A symbiotic cognitive computing perspective on autonomic computing. In *Proceedings of the 2015 IEEE International Conference on Autonomic Computing*. IEEE, 2015.
17. Jeffrey O Kephart and William E Walsh. An artificial intelligence perspective on autonomic computing policies. In *Policies for Distributed Systems and Networks, 2004. POLICY 2004. Proceedings. Fifth IEEE International Workshop on*, pages 3–12. IEEE, 2004.
18. Marta Kwiatkowska, Gethin Norman, and David Parker. *Formal Methods for Performance Evaluation: 7th International School on Formal Methods for the Design of Computer, Communication, and Software Systems, SFM 2007, Bertinoro, Italy, May 28-June 2, 2007, Advanced Lectures*, chapter Stochastic Model Checking, pages 220–270. Springer Berlin Heidelberg, Berlin, Heidelberg, 2007.
19. R. Lent, O.H. Abdelrahman, G. Gorbil, and E. Gelenbe. Fast message dissemination for emergency communications. In *Proceedings of PerCom Workshop on Pervasive Networks for Emergency Management (PerNEM)*, pages 370–375, April 2010.
20. R. Middleton and J.H. Braslavsky. String instability in classes of linear time invariant formation control with limited communication range. *IEEE Trans. on Automatic Control*, 55(7):1519–1530, 2010. doi:10.1109/TAC.2010.2042318.
21. Dudekula Mohammad Rafi, Katam Reddy Kiran Moses, Kai Petersen, and Mika V. Mäntylä. Benefits and limitations of automated software testing: Systematic literature review and practitioner survey. In *Proceedings of the 7th International Workshop on Automation of Software Test*, AST '12, pages 36–42, Piscataway, NJ, USA, 2012. IEEE Press.
22. T. Roughgarden. *Selfish Routing*. PhD thesis, Cornell University, 2002.
23. T. Roughgarden and E. Tardos. How bad is selfish routing? *Journal of the ACM*, 49(2):236–259, 2002.
24. Bradley Schmerl, Jesper Andersson, Thomas Vogel, Myra B. Cohen, Cecilia M. F. Rubira, Yuriy Brun, Alessandra Gorla, Franco Zambonelli, and Luciano Baresi. Challenges in composing and decomposing assurances for self-adaptive systems. *Software Engineering for Self-Adaptive Systems III: Assurances, Lecture Notes in Computer Science (LNCS)*, 2016.
25. D. Swaroop and J.K. Hedrick. String stability of interconnected systems,. *IEEE Trans. on Automatic Control*, 41(3):349–357, 1996. doi:10.1109/9.486636.
26. L. Wang and E. Gelenbe. Adaptive dispatching of tasks in the cloud. *IEEE Transactions on Cloud Computing*, 2015.
27. L. Wang and E. Gelenbe. Demonstrating voice over an autonomic network. In *Proceedings of IEEE 12th International Conference on Autonomic Computing (ICAC)*, July 2015.

Printed in the United States
By Bookmasters